W9-ARI-659

QK
D3
1849a

CLASSICA BOTANICA
AMERICANA

Edited by

JOSEPH EWAN
Professor of Biology
Tulane University

Supplement I:

WILLIAM DARLINGTON

Memorials of

JOHN BARTRAM and HUMPHRY MARSHALL

HAFNER PUBLISHING COMPANY
NEW YORK and LONDON
1967

QK
31
.B3
D3
1849c

Memorials
of
JOHN BARTRAM
and
HUMPHRY MARSHALL

by

WILLIAM DARLINGTON

(Facsimile of the edition of 1849)

Introduction by

JOSEPH EWAN

Tulane University

(Three Indices — of Persons,
Ship Captains, and Plant Names Appended.)

HAFNER PUBLISHING COMPANY

NEW YORK and LONDON

1967

KVCC WITHDRAWN ...EY COMMUNITY COLLEGE LIBRARY

36311

© 1967, Series title, introduction and indices
by HAFNER PUBLISHING COMPANY

Printed and Published by
HAFNER PUBLISHING COMPANY, INC.
31 East 10th Street
New York, N.Y. 10003

Library of Congress Catalog Card Number: 67-15310

Distributed in Europe by
VERLAG J. CRAMER
3301 Lehre, Germany
Postfach, 48

Printed in U.S.A. by
NOBLE OFFSET PRINTERS, INC.
NEW YORK 3, N. Y.

WITHDRAWN

Editor's Introduction

The *Memorials of John Bartram and Humphry Marshall,* published in Philadelphia 117 years ago, is probably the most frequently cited book today dealing with eighteenth-century botanical history in the American Colonies. Asa Gray, fellow botanist and close friend of the author wrote "Heartily do we acknowledge our obligations to Dr. Darlington for the unwearied editorial labors in rescuing these remains from oblivion and fast approaching decay." John Hendley Barnhart, American bibliographer, remarked that "Botany owes a great debt of gratitude to Dr. William Darlington for his volume." The historian Brooke Hindle lamented the "faulty editing," but it was E. G. Swem, Virginia historian and bibliographer, who made the most penetrating analysis of the book. Swem regretted the considerable editorial liberties that Darlington took with the original letters, insisting that today we would print everything legible, but he praises its usefulness and freely admits that the *Memorials* will remain "a chief reliance for the student of Collinson and Bartram, and for the history of botany in the United States."

William Darlington (1782-1863), native of Chester County, Pennsylvania, physician, botanist, friend of botanists, author, avid correspondent, and antiquarian, gathered historical facts on the progress of botanical science, which in the nineteenth century amounted to plant collecting, description, and writing of florulas, and left us a distillate in the form of short footnote sketches of the more important persons mentioned in the Bartram and Marshall correspondence. His notable library collected during his long and frugal life is kept intact at State Teachers College, West Chester, near Philadelphia. His extensive correspondence with colleagues here and abroad is preserved at West Chester and at the New York Historical Society's rooms in New York City.

A presentation copy of the *Memorials* was sent to "Prof. A. Gray, with the affectionate regards of his obliged friend, Wm. Darlington" accompanied by a note dated West Chester, Oct. 12, 1849, which read in part: "You will find the book rather ponderous, for a selection of old correspondence; but unfortunately, I did not make the discovery, myself, until it was too late to remedy the evil, completely. I, however, struck out about *half* of *Marshall's* correspondence." These unpublished letters are preserved in the

Historical Society of Pennsylvania. Darlington wittily noticed the role of 'presentation copies' to his friend:

> "That pleasant Humorist Charles Lamb, says 'A *Presentation Copy* is a copy of a book which does not sell, sent you by the author with his foolish autograph at the beginning of it; for which, if a stranger, he only demands your friendship; if a brother author, he expects from you a book of yours, which does sell, in return.". . . "I pray you accept this volume, as the last (literally, I apprehend, the *very last*) offering, of the kind, which it will ever be in my power to make."

The *Memorials* was not to be Darlington's "very last offering" for in his seventieth year he was to publish the third edition of *Flora Cestrica: an herborizing companion for the young botanists of Chester County, State of Pennsylvania* (1853). Unusual in any period for including mosses and lichens in one volume with higher plants, this manual will delight today for the 'observations' appended to most descriptions. "The bulbs of [Ornithogalum] are said to be much used for food, in the Levant; and Linnaeus imagined them to be the 'Dove's Dung', which was sold so dear at the siege of Samaria . . . Some of our Agriculturists could furnish almost any quantity,—and, I imagine, would gladly part with them at a very low price!"

The Memorials sold for $2.50 and Benjamin Silliman's copy, now in the Chase-Hitchcock Botanical Library, has the subscriber's receipt dated October 18, 1849, including the 50 cent "freight" charge but with a note from William H. Dillingham, agent, to the effect the copy is bound in ½ Turkey Morocco, "sent without additional charge over and above the subscription price," doubtless the apparel of one generous savant for another.

In addressing the Chester County Cabinet on December 5, 1835 on the "advantages of the study of natural science," Dillingham said: "His works speak for him and will continue to speak when we are in our graves. His name will live while the flowers of Chester bloom. A genuine votary of Nature, one of her true worshippers, it is by such that the lamp before her altars is kept forever trimmed and burning."

The three revised indices are reprinted here by the kindness of the Society for the Bibliography of Natural History in whose *Journal* they appeared in 1957. Identification of some of the incidental persons mentioned in the letters will involve search into local Pennsylvania, especially Quaker, records. The following references will prove useful in pursuing the biographies of the persons listed: (1) Norman G. Brett-James, *Life of Peter Collinson* (London, [1925])—especially useful for quick identification of Bartram's correspondents, though it harbors some annoying errors. (2) R. Hingston Fox, *Dr. John Fothergill and his friends* (London, 1919)—a carefully written account more to be deplored for its odd omissions than for errors committed. (3) E. G. Swem, Brothers of the Spade. Correspondence of Peter Collinson, of London, and of John Custis, of Williamsburg, Virginia, 1734-1746 (*Amer. Antiq. Soc. Proc.* 58: 17-190, 1948)—"virtually an introduction to the history and bibliography of botany in eighteenth century America" (Bell). The answer may be buried but the very digging is so worthwhile. (4) Samuel N. Baxter, Restoration of Plants in Bartram's Garden by the Fairmount Park Commission of Philadelphia (*Bartonia,* spec. suppl. to 12: 38-50, 1932)—useful for plant name problems. (5) S. Savage, *Calendar of the Ellis Manuscripts* (Linnean Society of London, 1948)—identifies many obscure eighteenth-century persons mentioned in those letters. (6) F. W. Pennell, Botanical Collectors of the Philadelphia local area (*Bartonia,* 21: 38-57, 64 and 22: 10-31, 66, 1942-43)—a documented account of particular use to herbarium workers. (7) John W. Harshberger, Additional Letters of Humphry Marshall, botanist and nurseryman (*Pennsylvania Mag. of Hist. & Biog.* 53: 269-282, 1929)—a generally overlooked supplement to Darlington's *Memorials* but which concerns commercial rather than botanical activities.

Forty-eight ship captains are mentioned in the *Memorials,* almost always by surname only. Botany and particularly horticulture owe a very large debt to these old salts for their solicitous care beyond the call of duty in safe delivery. A study of ship captains, their full identity, and an appreciation of their important contribution, long overdue, would be an excellent project for an amateur historian with botanical sympathies. Both the Essex Institute and the Peabody Museum, Salem, Massachusetts, boast superb collections of ships' logs.

JOHN BARTRAM
(1699-1777)

John Bartram was "perhaps the first Anglo-American who conceived the idea of establishing a botanic garden, for the reception and cultivation of the various vegetables, natives of the country, as well as of exotics, and of traveling for the discovery and acquisition of them." This was the verdict of his son William who "was the counterpart of his father in moral excellence, amiability, and love of natural history, and his superior in science." From their garden on the Schuylkill the influence of the Bartrams on natural history extended over a century, in Europe and the British Colonies in America, into the young Republic, and well beyond William's death in 1823.

A guide to Bartram literature by J. H. Barnhart appeared in the journal *Bartonia* in 1932. In 1958 Francis Harper published a richly annotated "Naturalist's Edition" of William Bartram's *Travels* (1791). An album of his drawings with my commentary and a chronology is to be published by the American Philosophical Society. The chronology which follows is only a working epitome because dates for John Bartram's excursions have not been fixed with certainty. Rodney H. True (1932) arrived at dates which differ from those cited by Harper (1942) who based his calendar on the letters in Darlington's *Memorials,* but even here discrepancies will be noticed.

CHRONOLOGY

1699
March 23 (o.s.). John Bartram born at Marple, near Darby, Pa.
1706
Jan. 17. Benjamin Franklin born in Boston, Mass.
1707
May 23. Carl von Linné born in parish of Roshult, Sweden.
1712
March 8. John Fothergill born at Wensleydale, Yorkshire, England.

1723
Jan. John Bartram married Mary Norris.

1727
Mary Norris died.

1728
Sept. 30. Bartram purchased property on the west side of the Schuylkill River, three miles from Philadelphia.

1729
Sept. John Bartram married Ann Mendenhall.

1730-1731
Bartram first came to the notice of Peter Collinson.

1735
Collinson first contracted with Bartram to collect seeds—"100 species in a box at five guineas each."

(1735? or) 1736
Fall (?) Journeyed to the sources of the Schuylkill River and Blue Mts., Pa.

1737
Spring (?) Journeyed through Lancaster Co., Pa.

Fall. Made a five weeks' trip through present Delaware and along Eastern Shore to present Northampton Co., Va., and return.

1738
Fall. Made a trip of 1100 miles via Fredericksburg; Dragon Swamp; Clayton's at Gloucester; Custis' at Williamsburg; probably to Westover to visit William Byrd II; to Randolph's at Dungeness; probably to the head of Rapidan; then across Blue Ridge and through the "Vale of Virginia"

1739
Feb. 9. William Bartram, third of five sons, born at Kingsessing.

Lord Petre gave Bartram Vol. 2 of Miller's *Gardener's Dictionary* (1735).

1740
Collinson wrote Bartram requesting mosses for Dillenius.

Bartram visited Peter Custis and John Clayton in Virginia.

1741?
Bartram wrote to Mark Catesby: "I have a great value for thy books; and esteem them as an excellent performance, and as an ornament for the finest library in the world."

1743

July 3. Bartram and cartographer Lewis Evans set out for Onondago, Oswego, and the shore of Lake Ontario, with Conrad Weiser.

Aug. 19. Arrived at Kingsessing on return from journey to the north.

1744

April 5. American Philosophical Society, founded the previous year, is organized with Bartram as one of the nine original members.

Fall. Cadwallader Colden visited Bartram.

1748

Sept. 15. Peter Kalm, aged 31, arrived in Philadelphia.

1749

Aug. 6. Kalm wrote Bartram from Quebec.

Nov. 30. Kalm visited Bartram's garden.

1750

June. Manuscript of Bartram's *Observations,* written, Collinson said, "to entertain mee," arrived in England.

1751

Observations published without Bartram's knowledge by Collinson who wrote: "I gave it to Whiston and Com. to Print who have done it scandelously."

Benjamin Franklin and D. Hall published an American edition of Dr. Thomas Short's *Medicina Britannica* with a preface by John Bartram.

(1751?) Bartram wrote Thomas François Dalibard, French botanist, inviting correspondence and sending a parcel of seeds.

1753

Sept. Journeyed with William, aged 15, up the Delaware River Valley to the vicinity of Milford or Port Jervis, then to Goshen, and the home of Cadwallader Colden west of Newburgh, enroute to the Catskills.

William began to draw birds.

1755

Fall. Journeyed with William to the home of Rev. Jared Eliot at present Clinton, Conn.

1756

Nov. 4. Bartram wrote to Philip Miller about hawthorns, the seeds of which he had gathered near the Connecticut River and "Blue Mts." [Catskills] "East Jersey."

1760

March. Stayed eighteen days with Alexander Garden in Charleston, S.C. Returned overland to Cape Fear River, thence by land (?) to Philadelphia.

Early summer. Visited Clayton in Gloucester.

Collinson terminated his engagement for Bartram's collecting seed for him.

1761

July 25. Mention of William Young first appeared in a letter from Alexander Garden to John Ellis.

William Bartram visited his Uncle William at "Ashwood" on Cape Fear River, N.C.

Fall. John Bartram visited Pittsburgh where he met Col. Henry Bouquet who presented him with plant "curiosities" from the Ohio River Valley.

1762

Fall. John Bartram visited southwestern Virginia including the Natural Bridge and upland North and South Carolina. He crossed the Blue Ridge at Roanoke Gap.

Collinson and Solander surveyed Bartram's collections recently received and thought "half a quire" were new genera.

William Bartram returned from his visit with his uncle on Cape Fear River, N.C.

1763

Summer? John Bartram made a trip to Great and Little Egg Harbor, N.J.

Disappointed at not being able to explore the Ohio and Mississippi rivers on projected trip with William.

1764

Aug. 19. John Bartram sent the journal of his Carolina and New River Journey to Collinson asking him to allow Solander to peruse it.

Sept. 23. He wrote to Collinson that he was sending a "little box" of plants to the King.

William Young appointed "Botanist to their Majestys."

1765

John Bartram sent dried specimens of *Dionaea* to Collinson.

Spring. Appointed Botanist to the King with an annual stipend of £50.

William Bartram engaged in a trading venture on Cape Fear River, N.C., near his uncle's plantation.

June 7. John Bartram wrote to William offering him the opportunity of accompanying him in an exploration of Florida.

July 1. John Bartram, aged 66, set out from Philadelphia to join William at Cape Fear for a journey through the Carolinas, Georgia, and Florida.

Sept. 28. John wrote to Collinson of his observations in Georgia.

Oct. 1. John and William Bartram discovered *Franklinia* near Fort Barrington, Ga.

1766

George Edwards sent John Bartram a copy of his *Gleanings of Natural History* which contains 23 Pennsylvania birds sent by William.

April 10. John Bartram sailed from Charleston for Philadelphia. William remained on St. John's River, Fla., to raise indigo and rice.

1767

The William Stork edition of John Bartram's *Account of East Florida* published in London.

1768

Summer. William Young took the first living *Dionaea* plants to England.

Aug. 11. Peter Collinson, aged 74, died.
Following Collinson's death Fothergill's garden at Upton, with many of Collinson's plants, became the center for American introductions.

Philip Miller published the eighth (and last edition during his lifetime) of *Gardener's Dictionary* which through several editions had made known Bartram's Pennsylvania plants.

1769

John Bartram's *A description of East Florida* published in London.

April 26. Elected to the Royal Academy of Sciences of Stockholm.

xii

1770

Fothergill sent John Bartram an account of *Dionaea* published by John Ellis.

1771

May 17. John Bartram wrote Fothergill asking if William Young's "halcyon days" had passed.

July 17. Franklin wrote Bartram from London assuring him that "Young is in no esteem here as far as I can learn."

Dec. 18. Philip Miller, aged 81, died.

1772

William stayed at his uncle's plantation on Cape Fear River.

John wrote to William urging him to return home.

Late Fall. William returned to Philadelphia.

Nov. 11. John Bartram wrote to Franklin about sowing rhubarb, etc.

Society of Gentlemen in Edinburgh, founded in 1764, awarded John Bartram a gold medal.

1773

Humphry Marshall established a botanic garden at Bradford, Chester Co., Pa., where he grew Bartram's discoveries.

Nils Collin sent the first shipment of plants, surely including Bartram's species, to Sweden (to P. J. Bergius?).

March 20. William Bartram, to begin his "Travels," sailed from Philadelphia for Charleston.

April. William revisited *Franklinia* colony near Fort Barrington.

1774

Sept. 8. Fothergill wrote John Bartram that about 100 dried plants had been received from William.

1775

April 19. Battle of Lexington.

Oct. 29. William Bartram at Point Coupee, La.—the westernmost point reached on his journey through se. U.S.

Nov. 16-27. William at Mobile on his eastbound return journey to Charleston.

1776

Jan. William crossed the Ocmulgee River, Georgia.

Oct. 15. John Ellis, aged 66, died.

William shipped from Charleston his last parcel of southern plants for Fothergill.

1777

Jan. William returned to Kingsessing.
Sept. 22. John Bartram, aged 78, died.
John Bartram Jr. became proprietor of the Bartram Garden.
Winter. Washington at Valley Forge.

REFERENCES

Barnhart, J. H. 1932. Bartram Bibliography. *Bartonia* 12 (Suppl.): 51-67. "1931."

Harper, F. 1942. Diary of a journey through the Carolinas, Georgia, and Florida from July 1, 1765 to April 10, 1766. John Bartram, *Trans Amer. Philos. Soc.* n.s. 33 (pt. 1): 1-124. 23 pls.

―――. 1958. *Travels of William Bartram,* Naturalist's Edition. New Haven: Yale University Press.

Swem, E. G. 1948. Brothers of the Spade. Correspondence of Peter Collinson, of London, and of John Custis, of Williamsburg, Virginia, 1734-1746. *Proc. Amer. Antiq. Soc.* 58: 17-190. Repr. Barre, Mass., Barre Gazette, 1957.

True, Rodney H. 1932. John Bartram's life and botanical explorations. *Bartonia* 12 (Suppl.): 7-19, "1931."

HUMPHRY MARSHALL

(1722-1801)

A sketch of Humphry Marshall's life prefaces the Hafner reprint edition of his *Arbustum Americanum* (1785). The chronology given here will mesh with our chronologies published on Bernard M'Mahon (1960), John Lyon (1963), William Bartram (in press), and John Bartram (included *ante* in this edition) toward a fuller understanding of the interrelationships during this colonial period. Abbreviations: *Corres* = Correspondence of Humphry Marshall in Historical Society of Pennsylvania, Philadelphia; D = Darlington, followed by page number(s) in his *Memorials;* HM = Humphry Marshall.

CHRONOLOGY

1722

Oct. 10. Born in the township of West Bradford, County of Chester, Penn., of Abraham and Mary, the eighth of nine children (D, 485), the cousin of John Bartram (D, 487, fn.).

1734 (aet. 12)

Last year of formal schooling (D, 486).

1748 (aet. 26)

Sept. 16. Married Sarah Pennock and assumed charge of his father's farm near the west branch of Brandywine River (D, 487). About this time began to acquire books and began collecting live plants (D, 487).

1753

Wrote his name in Cole's *Latin Dictionary;* Quincy's *Medical Lexicon;* and Gerard's *Herball* (D, 487).

1762

Appointed County Treasurer; served through 1766 (D, 487).

1764

Enlarged his parents' home, building what was doubtless the first conservatory in the County of Chester. Dug the clay, made the bricks, and built the building himself (D, 487).

1767

Inherited "a large portion of the patrimonial estate."

March 2. London: John Fothergill to HM: Thanks for the seeds, is planning to send a copy of Miller, *Gardener's Dictionary*. Requests reptiles, except rattlesnake of which he has one, insects, birds & animals. Requests further seeds and living shrubs or trees, particularly of a medical character (D, 495).

May 18. London: J. Fothergill to HM: Thanks for the seeds. Miller's work is out of print, and he is sending the abridged edition, but only as a token of acknowledgment (D, 496).

1768

Oct. 29. London: J. Fothergill to HM: Acknowledges "several parcels of curious seeds, birds, insects." Sends pocket-glass and ten guineas, and has ordered Anthony Purver's translation of the Bible. Requests more seeds, and suggests HM growing them, boxing and shipping. Would like "Calocassia" [Nelumbium luteum]. Asks for a replacement of the list of books desired by HM, a little live owl, and a mockingbird (D, 497).

1769

Jan. 25. London: J. Fothergill to HM: Received box of seed and box of live plants; has sent two magnifying glasses. Will always be glad to receive any new plants and always *Magnolias, Kalmias, Rhododendrons,* etc., and would like "Martagons" [*Lilium philadelphicum* and allies] of which he has a few, and "Lychnoides" [*Silene* and the like]; also always pines and acorns. He always keeps whatever soil is sent over, for sometimes there is a new and curious plant therein. Requests that HM send William Bartram any novelties to paint, especially tortoises (D, 499).

July 9. London: B. Franklin to HM (endorsed "B. Free Franklin"): Thanks for specimens of several colours for painting (D, 515).

1770

March 15. London: J. Fothergill to HM: Received seeds, plants, and cask of *Nelumbium*. Franklin will send "all the instruments thou requests. . . . Some of the books thou desires are, at present, out of print . . ." Is sending a special locked box for insects. "Continue to send me such new seeds or plants . . .

Ferns and *Polypodiums* . . . *Dionaea* . . . bulbous plants . . ."
(D, 501).

March 18. London: B. Franklin to HM: Finds one of the white earths sent over for Sevres, near Paris, good for its wares. Encourages boycott of British goods to force repeal of import duties. Has ordered a reflecting telescope for Marshall for which, with microscope and thermometer, Fothergill will pay. Thanks for the seeds with which he has obliged some "curious friends." (D, 516).

1771

Feb. 11. London: J. Fothergill to HM: Has received two letters dated 25 May and 19 Nov., 1770. Thanks for medicinal notes on sassafras bark and ipecacuanha. Plants and seeds delivered, but not yet opened because of cold. Box of insects arrived, but some were packed before dry, other insects infested, so please send duplicates and any new in the box returned with lock and key. Pack in camphor or powdered pepper. Now wants only *new* seeds and plants, or requested replacements. William Young packs successfully with moss around the roots, and tightly together. Suggests shipping seed with sphagnum. The mockingbird perished in the passage. (D, 503-504).

April 22. London: B. Franklin to HM: Encourages American production and manufacture. Is obliged for curious seeds—welcome gifts to some of his friends. Sends seed of the new barley lately introduced into England. (D, 517).

April 23. London: J. Fothergill to HM: Reports severe winter. Sends box for insects, roots of alpine strawberry. Sends a botanical dictionary and a translation of "some of Linnaeus' works." Still is not successful with "Calocassia" [Nelumbium]. Sends covers of some of his letters which he saves to wrap his seeds in so that Marshall may do likewise. (D, 505-506).

May 4. Philadelphia: Thomas Parke to HM: Offers to take anything to London for Marshall's friends (D, 523-524).

1772

March 20. London: Franklin to HM: Marshall's manuscript, "Observations [on the spots of the Sun]" appears to have been lost in shipment. Don't send things via Bristol, but by London (D, 518).

July 5. London: Thomas Parke to HM: Is unsuccessful in finding seedsmen in England who want American seeds (D, 525).

Sept. Country seat near Middlewich, Cheshire: Fothergill to HM: Plants came safe, & earth and moss saved for waif seeds. "There is not a richer bit of ground, in curious American plants, in Great Britain [than Fothergill's garden] and for many of the most curious" he is obliged to Marshall's diligence and care. Has received box of snakes. Hopes to send box of books when he returns to London. *Tetragonotheca* sent by John Bartram is lost in English gardens: would like some roots. William Young sent *Nymphaea* but it did not flourish; please send some roots, seed will not germinate. Young has glutted the market with common things. A seedsman has adulterated Young's seed to the detriment of his reputation. "I am sorry for him; have endeavoured to help him; but he is not discreet." (D, 506-510).

1773

Feb. 6. London: Fothergill to HM: Received box of insects in very good order, only a few had moulded. Repeats directions for drying box and insects, and for giving key to the captain for customs inspection. Wants bulbous roots, *Orchis,* and ferns. Is sending second part of Linnaeus, and will send other parts as published. Says of Marshall: "The laborer is worthy of his hire." Still wants *Nelumbium.* Thinks tea plants would thrive in Virginia and Maryland, and will send J. C. Lettsom's *Natural History of the Tea-Tree.* (D, 510-512).

Feb. 14. London: B. Franklin to HM: Manuscript, "Observations on the Spots of the Sun," and seeds have arrived. Franklin offers an explanation of sun-spots. Nurserymen are now so well supplied with American seed, few gardeners want the trouble of foreign correspondents. (D, 518-520).

Marshall began his residence adjoining present Marshallton, and began to develop a new garden (D, 488).

He is made Trustee of Pennsylvania State Loan Office (D, 489).

1774

He moved to his new residence.

June 26. London: B. Franklin to HM: Approves Marshall's attitude toward British taxation, etc. Royal Society received "Observations" well and manuscript will be published in

Philosophical Transactions. He is about to return home, and looks forward to seeing Marshall.

June 28. London: J. Fothergill to HM: Intended two glasses as compensation and shall "readily do what further thou may think needful, as an equivalent." Has sent "two more numbers of Miller's botanical work; and a treatise on *Coffee* [by John Ellis] . . . Nothing more of Linnaeus' is yet translated; when it is," he will send it. Wants especially another *Nymphaea* and ferns. Is considered to have best collection of American plants in the neighborhood, for which he is indebted to Marshall. (D, 512).

1775

Mar. 13. London: B. Franklin to HM: Has misplaced letter with Marshall's list of books desired. Will not buy set of *Philosophical Transactions* for him until advised. "If we are faithful to each other [in non-consumption of British goods] our adversaries are ruined." (D, 521).

May 23. Philadelphia: B. Franklin [unsigned] to HM: Thinks "non-importation & non-participation" will end controversy: "make yourselves sheep and the wolves will eat you" (D, 521).

Aug. 23. [Cheshire]: J. Fothergill to HM: New ferns in a box of plants received. Expects contacts between America and Britain will be cut off, so encourages Marshall to collect and grow all he can; gives advice on culturing plants. Only Kew (in five mile radius of London) can show either so large or so healthy a collection of American plants as Fothergill's. Deplores the "proud discontented people, who have been in office in America." Turtle came through alive though somewhat injured. Two owls arrived, but one appears to have killed and picked the brains of the other. Instruments sent Marshall by Franklin valued at £14 16s. 6d., also sent 10 guineas. (D, 513-515).

1778

Marshall resigned as did all trustees, from the Pennsylvania Land Office.

1779

Aug. 7. Philadelphia: Thomas Bond to HM: Wishes to introduce M. Conrad Gerard, French Minister, to arrange an exchange of foreign for American plants (D, 536).

Nov. 3. [Philadelphia?] T. Bond to HM: Received, and will pass on to Gerard, "a botanic collection" (D, 537).

Nov. 10. Philadelphia: Thomas Parke to HM: Gives advice on Moses Marshall's attending lectures at the Medical School (D, 527).

1780

Marshall began composing *Arbustum Americanum* (D, 489).

Oct. 18. Philadelphia: Thomas Bond to HM: Has not heard from Gerard of receipt of plant collection in Paris (D. 537).

Oct. 26. Philadelphia: T. Bond to HM: M. Marbois on behalf of Maréchal de Noailles of the Royal Gardens, Paris, desires seeds of trees in exchange (D, 538).

Nov. 20. Philadelphia: T. Bond to HM: Two letters and "botanic collection" arrived safely. Suggests Marshall come to Philadelphia to meet the Minister of France and M. Marbois, "their catalogue [of desiderata] being very large, and will give you much trouble to collect."

Dec. 2. Philadelphia: T. Bond to HM: Acknowledges box and letter and will let the Chevalier [Noailles] know of it. Collection, though small, is valuable and curious. Wishes to keep up a correspondence in Europe "on a small scale, and solely with a view of furnishing each country, reciprocally, with such things as may be useful." Since the request of the Minister of France and M. Marbois is "a very large affair, and will cost you much trouble, you ought to be well paid for it." (D, 539).

Dec. 26. John Fothergill died, aged 68.

1781

Undated. [London?]: J. C. Lettsom to HM: Consulted with Ann Fothergill for settlement with Marshall (D, 541-542).

March 16. Philadelphia: Thomas Bond to HM: "This covers a letter from M. Marbois." Has received friendly letter from M. Gerard who reciprocates with 2 boxes of seeds. King of France "examined every article of our collection, and was extremely pleased with it. This is a very respectful and may be a very useful correspondency. Let us support the patriotic spirit it deserves. I have prospect of adding to it greatly, via Pittsburg." (D, 539).

July 12. Philadelphia: T. Bond to HM: Dr. Gustav Hillman [or Keilman], "bred under Linnaeus," has arrived in Philadelphia after a series of misfortunes. Will Marshall take him into his home for a while? Dr. Hillman hopes to establish a practice nearby. (D, 540).

August 24. Philadelphia: T. Bond to HM: Finds his letter of July has not reached Marshall. Dr. Hillman is engaged at Pennsylvania Hospital. Opium Marshall sent is pure and of good quality. Most of the plants received from France have failed. Suggest they ask for more of these to be more carefully packed. "There is not the least prospect of peace." (D, 540).

1782

Sept. 5. Philadelphia: Thomas Parke to HM: Introduces William Hamilton of the "Woodlands" (D, 528).

1783

Aug. 26. Philadelphia: George Logan to HM: Encloses a letter from Felice Fontana, Director of the Museum of Physics and Natural History of the Grand Duke of Tuscany, friend of Franklin, requesting an exchange of natural productions from America for those of Italy, particularly *Dionaea muscipula*. Also a wish to establish correspondence between the Museum of the Grand Duke, Leopold, and the American Philosophical Society. (D, 550-552).

Marshall's seed list issued in 1783? Cf. letter, Parke to Humphry, 27 April, 1785.

1784

Jan. 16. Pisa: Felice Fontana to HM: Great pleasure in receiving 2 letters and 2 boxes of American plants: almost all the plants will live. He and the University will reciprocate. (D, 552-553).

Feb. 28. London: J. C. Lettsom to HM: Thanks for seeds. Any live plants will be welcome for his American section at Grove Hill. Has purchased Fothergill's stoves and greenhouse plants, but still wants American plants with advice on soil, cultivation, etc. (D, 542-543).

June 27. Bedford, Pa.: Moses Marshall to HM: Botanizing in "Pine Mountains" of w. Pennsylvania. Will bring seed of new plants. (D, 553).

Feb. 23. Philadelphia: Mary Norris to HM: Blind Doctor Henry Moyes is attracting crowds to his lectures on Philosophy of Chemistry and Natural History at the University (D, 535).

March 14. Philadelphia: Thomas Parke to HM: Philosophical Society is not interested in supporting Moses' trip to Kentucky; has little interest in Natural History (D, 528).

March 29. HM is elected an honorary member of the Philadelphia Society for Promoting Agriculture, and the Society invites his assistance (D, 489).

April 27. Philadelphia: T. Parke to HM: Received 2 small parcels from England, one from R. Barclay, one from Hamilton. Barclay requests seeds such as in Marshall's Seed List of of 1783 (D, 529).

April 28. Philadelphia: Joseph Crukshank to HM: Estimates will cost £70 or £80 to print 1000 copies of *Arbustum Americanum*. Will print announcements if HM sends copy. (D, 553; *Corres.* 1:18).

April 30. Philadelphia: Samuel Vaughan to HM: Society for Promoting Agriculture approved his *Arbustum,* but did not have money to publish it. Has left the manuscript with Crukshank who will print 1000 copies for £70, and Vaughan will make the index. Vaughan will subscribe for 50 or 60 copies. (D, 555-556).

May 14. Philadelphia: S. Vaughan to HM: Has sent an advertisement to the papers; sees poor sale for *Arbustum Americanum* in America; promises British aid, "but keep this to yourself." He wishes America to have the honor of publishing the work. Recommends Crukshank, but Cist knows botany and has newer type. (D, 555-557).

May 28. Philadelphia: S. Vaughan to HM: Requests suggestions for his continuing to plant the State House Square. Is solicitous for the *Arbustum* and still hopes Mr. Cist will revise and publish it. (D, 558).

Oct. 4. West Bradford, Pa.: HM to J. C. Lettsom: Appreciates repaired thermometer. Instead of Linnaeus' *Genera plantarum* translated into English by Colin Milne, Lettsom has sent the Lichfield publication which Barclay has already sent. Has sent 2 land turtles, a curious stone (crystal), Indian axes, etc. (D, 543-544).

Dec. 5. West Bradford: HM to B. Franklin: Proposes support by State of Pennsylvania, or other organization, for a westward trip by John and William Bartram. Will send Franklin a copy of his "Catalogue of the Forest Trees of our Thirteen United States." (D, 522-523).

[Dec. ?]: Crukshank published *Arbustum Americanum* (D, 489).

1786

Jan. 20. Humphry Marshall elected a member of the American Philosophical Society.

Feb. 7. Philadelphia: J. Crukshank to HM: At Marshall's request he has delivered a copy of *Arbustum* to Samuel Vaughan who will present it that evening to the Society for Promoting Agriculture, and will also present the Society with Humphry's paper, "Observations on the propriety of applying Botanical knowledge to agriculture, feeding cattle, etc." Twelve copies of *Arbustum* have been sent to James Gibbons. Not a dozen has been sold besides those to subscribers. Delivered Marshall's letter and a copy of *Arbustum* to the Philosophical Society some time ago. (D, 544).

Feb. 14. His paper, "Observations," read before the Society for Promoting Agriculture (D, 489).

Feb. 15. Philadelphia: Timothy Pickering to HM: Heard Vaughan read Marshall's paper last night. Requests a plan for reducing the idea to practice, and a calculation of the expense (D, 558-559).

April 5. Soho Square, London: Joseph Banks to HM: Wishes roots of Ginseng for experimentation. (D, 550-560).

May 22. Philadelphia: Samuel Vaughan to HM: Prof. Samuel Williams (1743-1817) of Harvard College, author of *Natural and Civil History of Vermont* (1794), wishes to ascertain the climate and flowering and fruiting times. Will Marshall please fill out the enclosed chart. (D, 558).

June 18. Philadelphia: Thomas Parke to HM: A young medical student [Benjamin Smith Barton?] departing for Edinburgh on June 23 wishes to take a box of the "most curious" flowering shrubs, seeds, etc., to the Professor of Botany [John Hope?]; wants *Franklinia* especially (D, 529-530; *Corres.* 1: f. 28).

July 27. Marshall's wife, Sarah, died (D, 490).

July 28. London: Charles Eddy to HM: Acknowledges letter of Dec. 24. with four boxes of seed and copies of *Arbustum*. Will send money when they are sold; none have been so far. (*Corres.* 1:30).

Aug. 14. London: J. C. Lettsom to B. Franklin: Mentions the possibility of support for Marshall's undertaking a "voyage of discovery" in America for natural history. Marshall would go for a year with expenses of three hundred pounds. Lettsom would willingly subscribe twenty guineas towards the trip for a share of seeds, plants, and ores collected. Lettsom now has a man in America, from Europe, for the purpose of collecting natural productions, especially vegetable. (Jared Sparks, *Works of Benjamin Franklin* 10: 267-268. 1840).

Sept. 4. Philadelphia: Thomas Parke to HM: Samuel Vaughan is intending to return to England; despite "some oddities" of character, he possesses many qualities useful to America. William Hamilton has returned pleased with his tour. Is glad Moses Marshall is endeavoring to please Banks. (D, 530).

Sept. 4. Philadelphia: Joseph Crukshank to HM: Samuel Vaughan is to remain in Philadelphia though he has sent his family to England. New York agent says *Arbustum* has sold only two copies and the sales appear over there. (D, 554).

Nov. 8. Philadelphia: Thomas Parke to HM: Has not been able to locate parcel sent by Lettsom, but shall continue inquiries (*Corres.* 1:34).

Nov. 14. West Bradford, Pa.: HM to Joseph Banks: Explains costliness of the one hundred pounds of ginseng collected by Moses Marshall and an assistant in western Pennsylvania (D, 560-561).

1787

Feb. 6. London: Grimwood, Hudson, and Barrit, Nurserymen, to HM: Request quotations for plants from Marshall's "Catalogue of American Plants" (*Corres.* 1:35).

Aug. 7. London: Grimwood, etc., to Humphry and Moses Marshall: Request that they send "as many as you can" of *Franklinia* (*Bartonia* 10:12. 1938).

July 14. London: J. C. Lettsom to HM: Parcels for Marshall, Parke, and Franklin sent, but lost. One tortoise died, would like two more. Royal Society is now admitting natural history to its *Transactions*. Linnean Society is being founded in London. (D, 544-545).

Oct. 21. Philadelphia: Caspar Wistar, Jr., to Humphry and Moses Marshall: Would like leaves of foxglove and a few seeds; sends on loan a treatise on its effects (D, 568-569).

1788

Jan. 10. Humphry Marshall married Margaret Minshall.

April 28: Weimar: Jean Reichert for the Duke of Weimar: Sends a long list of desiderata. Has had "several supplys" from New York. (*Corres.* 1:4).

May 7. West Bradford, Chester Co., Pa.: Moses Marshall to J. C. Lettsom: Sending three tortoises, *Sedum* and a "Portulaca" [*Talinum teretifolium*], also *Veronica* and a small evergreen [*Polygala pauciflora*] which he would like to name *Lettsomia* unless he has a chance to go west to the Mississippi River to find something new and more impressive (D, 545-548).

July 2. Nazareth, Pennsylvania: Rev. Samuel Kramsch to HM: Introduces himself as a Moravian teacher interested in botany. Admires *Arbustum* and encourages a Flora; desires to obtain copies of Walter's *Flora Caroliniana* and Kalm's *Travels*. (D, 571).

Aug. 10. London: J. C. Lettsom to HM: 3 turtles arrived safely. *Polygala pauciflora* is the name of the plant Moses proposed as "Lettsomia." Wishes more plants, expecially Ginseng. (D, 548).

Oct. 10. Philadelphia: Thomas Parke to HM: Received parcels for Marshall from Barclay and Lettsom. Had intended a copy of Walter's *Flora* for Marshall but finds Lettsom has already given him one. (D, 530).

Oct. 28. T. Parke to HM: Books (mentioned Oct. 10) now forwarded. Parcel delivered by Moses Marshall for Joseph Banks to be forwarded on the *Pigou*. (D, 530).

Nov. 4. HM to J. C. Lettsom: Several books came safely. Sending small box of plants including a rare azalea. Has sent some *Polygala pauciflora* to Banks. Believes "Plumed Andromeda" of Bartram is *Cyrilla,* and *Franklinia* is a *Gordonia.* Is pleased with Walter's *Flora*. (D, 548-549).

Feb. 2. London: J. C. Lettsom to HM: Plants mentioned Nov. 4 have arrived safely. Fraser has not answered expectation; his *Catalogue* is of his own merchandise, subscribers received very few plants indeed. (D, 549).

March 3. Londongrove, Chester Co., Pa.: John Jackson to HM: Sends a bush and wishes Geranium and Rosemary: "I hope the public peace will add fresh life and vigour to every useful science that may tend to adorn and enrich our country: the propagation of plants being one, and much to my delight." (D, 549-550).

May 6. Soho Square, London: Joseph Banks to HM: Box of plants arrived safely. *Franklinia* is a *Gordonia,* and refers to William Bartram's painting sent to Barclay. Encloses a list of desiderata for Aiton at Kew. (D, 562-563).

May 18. Philadelphia: Thomas Parke to HM: "R. Barclay writes me that he is much pleased with the plants he received, which, with W. Bartram's drawing of the *Franklinia,* arrived in good order. The botanists in England will not, however, allow it to be properly named." Barclay will want some plants in the fall, and wishes to know whether cranberry plants cannot be sent to England to be propagated. (D, 531).

June 3. London: Grimwood, Hudson, and Barrit, to HM: Requests thirty *Franklinia* plants for customers. (D, 531).

Jan. 18. Lancaster, Penn.: Henry Muhlenberg to HM: Letter, shrubs, and roots received. Has found *Spiraea hypericifolia;* thinks it better called *Hypericum kalmianum* or *prolificum.* *Arbustum* has been translated into German. Is sending Moses Marshall Linnaeus' *Materia medica.* Offers loan of his botanical books and would like to borrow Walter's *Flora.* Will send some seed from Germany. (D, 575-576).

Feb. 3. Washington: ——Baird to HM: Received request for seeds and roots "from this country." Has from time to time sent seeds to Philadelphia. Has enclosed a few beans received from New Orleans. Will send new items. (*Corres.* 2:5).

Feb. 20. Salem, N.C.: Samuel Kramsch to HM: Regrets illness has prevented his sending specimens; lost those he did collect. "Scarlet blowing Azalea" is sixty miles distant; will enquire about Physick nut. (D, 574-575).

April 3. Soho Square, London: Joseph Banks to HM: Plants received; Viola roots died; send larger. Enclosed *desiderata.* (D. 563).

April 17. Benjamin Franklin died, aged 84.

April 20. Philadelphia: Thomas Parke to HM: Could not procure all of plants requested for Humphry from John Bartram Jr. Did Marshall not promise some seeds for Lord Chesterfield? (D, 531).

Oct. 30. Philadelphia: Moses Marshall to Joseph Banks: Relates the itinerary of his journey to West Virginia and into North Carolina and Georgia, and his intention to go again to the area of *Franklinia.* Is sending box of plants ordered. (D, 563).

Nov. 22. "Woodlands" [near Philadelphia]: Wm. Hamilton to HM: Returning "draft" with thanks; invites him to come soon to see his botanical treasures (D, 577).

1791

Linnaeus, *Genera plantarum,* ed. Schreber, appears with *Marshallia* dedicated to HM and his nephew (D, 490 and 576).

March 2. Soho Square, London: Joseph Banks to HM: Box received in good order. Suggests three guineas value for each lot of plants the content at Marshall's discretion. Sends leaf unknown plant for which he would like a flowering specimen (D, 564).

June 21. Kensington, London: Grimwood, Hudson and Barrit, to Moses Marshall: List of plants desired (*Corres.* 2:16).

June 27. Aberdeen: John Gordon, Jr., to Moses Marshall: Desires plant list (*Corres.* 2:17).

Oct. 12. Brussels [?]: Frederick Eugene François, Baron de Beelen-Bertholff to Moses Marshall: Desires plant list (*Corres.* 2:20).

Oct. 29. Wilmington: John Dickinson to HM: Dr. Daniel Bancroft has a request from Europe for "some samples" described in *Arbustum* (D, 566-567).

Nov. 10. Moses Marshall to Joseph Banks: Has sent box of plants. Leaf is *Orphrys* but he has no flower to send. Does not have

Astragalus carolinensis; *Podophyllum diphyllum* grows 250 miles west; suggests he could travel in the coming summer. (D, 565).

1792

April 9. Lancaster: H. Muhlenberg to Moses Marshall: Linnaeus, *Genera,* new edition, Vol. 2, has arrived containing *"Marshallia."* Two volumes total 24s 4d. (D, 576-577).

May 27. [Philadelphia]: Caspar Wistar, Jr. to HM: American Philosophical Society has appointed a committee to study ravages of Hessian fly. European dealers are afraid to buy U.S. grain. Inquires whether Moses plans to travel west of the Mississippi. (D, 569).

June 20. [Philadelphia]: C. Wistar to Moses Marshall: Jefferson and he think they can raise 1000 guineas for Moses' trip up the Missouri (D, 570).

Dec. Philadelphia: Timothy Pickering to HM: Philadelphia Society for the Promotion of Agriculture intends to publish communications, and will appreciate contributions (D, 559).

1793

Dr. Wistar operated on Humphry Marshall's cataract, but with only partial success (D, 490).

Aug. 26. Kew: Baron L. A. F. von Itzenplitz to HM: Wishes to make an agreement for yearly shipment to Germany of seeds of trees and shrubs mentioned in "List A" (*Corres.* 2:28).

Aug. 28. Soho Square, London: Joseph Banks to HM: Introduces Baron von Itzenplitz who may introduce him to much business in Germany (D, 565).

Dec. 11. Moses Marshall to Grimwood, Hudson, and Barrit: One box of plants, one of seeds sent. Because of Yellow fever which carried off 4,000 Philadelphians, and 18 inches of snow, he has not gotten all requested. Other items are too far away: South Carolina for *Stewartia, Fothergilla, Magnolia* and *Sarracenia.* Will go to western Pennsylvania for *Pyrularia.* Stresses the great distances for small recompense received. (D, 580-582).

1795

March 20. Berlin [?]: Baron von Itzenplitz to Humphrey and Moses Marshall: Refers to box sent to Jean Reichert, gardener to Duke of Weimar (*Corres.* 2:33).

April 29. Philadelphia: Thomas Parke to Humphry Marshall: Sir John Menzies wishes to improve his grounds in Scotland, "by mixing" American forest trees with the pines (D, 531-532).

1796

Oct. 19. Philadelphia: Thomas Parke to Humphry and Moses Marshall: Robert Barclay wants box of plants for T. Kett of Norwich, Kalmias Azaleas, etc., and "everything new and curious," mixed with herbaceous (D, 532).

Nov. 1. Wilmington: John Dickinson to HM: Archibald Hamilton Rowan would like seeds to send his wife in Ireland with directions for planting (D, 567).

Nov. 23. Woodlands: William Hamilton to HM: Obliged for *Aesculus* and *Jeffersonia*. Wonders if Marshall could let him have by layering several plants seen in his garden and of seeds of native and Italian species (D, 578).

1797

July 13. Wilmington: John Dickinson to HM: Reminder of request for seeds for A. H. Rowan (D, 568).

1798

Dec. 12. Philadelphia: Thomas Parke to Moses Marshall: Sends his respects to HM (*Corres.* 2:49).

1799

Frederick Pursh visited HM who was then nearly blind from cataract (D, 492).

May 3. Woodlands: William Hamilton to HM: Sends "Tea Tree," etc., and seeds. Will share one if he has two of anything. Can Marshall give him "vulgar name" and nativity of *Menziesia ferruginea*—he will send his gardener, George Hilton, to Redstone for *Menziesia* and *Podophyllum*. Lost some things in severe winter, requests replacements. (D, 579-580).

Nov. 18. Berlin: Baron Itzenplitz to Moses Marshall: Hopes correspondence will not be further interrupted. No mention of Pursh. (*Corres.* 2:53).

1800

April 11. Philadelphia: Caspar Wistar, Jr. to HM: Cannot see him before mid-May; gives directions for preparation for eye operation (D, 570-571).

May 16. Philadelphia: C. Wistar Jr. to HM: Will come to operate in about a week. Expects Dr. Moses Marshall to assist in couching. (D, 571, and see D, 490).

1801

May 12. Strasbourg: F. S. Bammer to HM: Letter of respect for the author of *Arbustum americanum,* Adam Kuhn, bearer (*Corres.* 2:57).

Nov. 5. Humphry Marshall died of an attack of dysentery, age 79.

Index to Personal Names

Pages references for Darlington's biographical footnotes are cited although otherwise his notes are not indexed.

INDEX TO SHIP CAPTAINS

PLANT NAME INDEX

Names enclosed in square brackets appearing in their regular alphabetical position represent modern equivalents of the species, for example, "horse-chestnut" is indexed under "[Aesculus hippocastanum]." The attempt to list all vernacular names has been limited, but all important botanical names have been accounted for. Bracketed names which follow entries of the original text represent identifications of the species alluded to.

xlviii

l

MEMORIALS

OF

JOHN BARTRAM

AND

HUMPHRY MARSHALL.

RESIDENCE OF JOHN BARTRAM,

BUILT WITH HIS OWN HANDS, A. D. 1730.

MEMORIALS

OF

JOHN BARTRAM

AND

HUMPHRY MARSHALL.

WITH NOTICES OF

THEIR BOTANICAL CONTEMPORARIES.

BY

WILLIAM DARLINGTON, M.D., LL.D., ETC.

WITH ILLUSTRATIONS.

———

PHILADELPHIA:

LINDSAY & BLAKISTON.

1849.

Entered, according to Act of Congress, in the year 1849,

By LINDSAY & BLAKISTON,

In the Clerk's Office of the District Court of the Eastern District of Pennsylvania.

PHILADELPHIA:

C. SHERMAN, PRINTER.

TO THE

True Lovers of Botany,

ON EITHER SIDE OF THE ATLANTIC,

THESE MEMORIALS

OF THE MEN WHO,

THROUGH PERILS AND PRIVATIONS,

SO EARLY AND SO FAITHFULLY EXPLORED THE VEGETABLE TREASURES OF THIS
CONTINENT,

ARE RESPECTFULLY SUBMITTED BY

THE EDITOR.

ADVERTISEMENT.

IT may be well, perhaps, by a brief and simple statement here, to explain to the reader how it happened, that the compiler obtained access to the *materials* of this volume, and was permitted thus to use them.

More than thirty years ago, the late Doctor WILLIAM BALDWIN suggested to the Editor, the propriety of some tribute to the memory of HUMPHRY MARSHALL, to be prepared from his *Correspondence*, and other papers in the custody of his representatives. In that generous suggestion of his lamented friend, the Editor heartily concurred, and intimations of the purpose were accordingly made to the MARSHALL family; but the widow of HUMPHRY, who was then living, and had charge of the papers, seemed unwilling to let them pass out of her possession, in consequence of which, nothing further was done at that time.

Since the decease of Mrs. MARSHALL, the subject has been occasionally mentioned to the younger branches of the family, to whom the papers descended, and an urgent desire expressed, for the privilege of examining those interesting memorials. The request was politely assented to, as often as made; but, from the procrastination incident to such matters, it was only within a few months that Dr. MOSES MARSHALL, Junior, grand-nephew of HUMPHRY, actually placed the desired papers in the hands of the Editor, which, however, he did with the full permission and privilege of making such use of them as might be deemed appropriate. Dr. M. has also, in the most obliging manner, furnished a number of facts, dates, and traditionary anecdotes, connected with the history of his venerable kinsman.

The Editor found the correspondence so much to his own taste, that he imagined it might be gratifying to others, to peruse such evidences of devotion to Natural Science, in one of the primitive worthies of Chester County; and under that impression, he transcribed such portions as appeared to be illustrative of the character and labours of the man.

Scarcely was this pleasing task accomplished, when a voluminous mass of papers, consisting chiefly of the correspondence of JOHN BARTRAM, was also put into the hands of the Editor, and with a like permission as the preceding, by Colonel ROBERT CARR, proprietor of the Bartram Garden, who is married to a granddaughter of the distinguished Pennsylvania Botanist, and to whom those interesting records now belong. For this rare privilege, the Editor is primarily indebted to the partiality and kind intervention of his esteemed friends, THOMAS P. JAMES and DANIEL B. SMITH, of Philadelphia, whose anxiety for the preservation of such portions of the correspondence as are still extant (for much of it is irrecoverably lost), induced them to solicit the favour; but, it is due to the descendants of the Botanical Patriarch of our country, to add, that the privilege referred to, together with all the collateral information in their possession, was promptly and most obligingly granted.

Here, then, a new field of labour was unexpectedly presented, kindred in its nature, indeed, but of much greater extent than the preceding, and beset with more difficulties. Those ancient manuscripts were not only jumbled together in a chaotic mass, but were generally much injured by time, and many of them scarcely legible; so that it required no little care and patient perseverance, to decipher and arrange them. This was especially the case with the letters from JOHN BARTRAM to his friends, of which letters he seems to have been in the habit of retaining the original rough draughts. It is, in fact, too probable, that if the opportunity thus kindly afforded by Colonel CARR and his lady, had not been embraced, the portion of the Correspondence here preserved would, ere long, have been scattered among the various branches of the family, and the recovery of it rendered wholly impracticable.*

But the work is now performed. A large remnant of the epistolary corre-

---

* It is to be hoped, that the *originals* of these letters may yet pass into the safekeeping of the Pennsylvania Historical Society, and thus be handed down to a curious and grateful posterity.

spondence, between our two venerable *Pennsylvanians* and their distinguished contemporaries, is happily rescued from present oblivion : and, if the Editor is not utterly deceived by his own passion for such antiquities, he persuades himself that the lovers of nature, and the admirers of native worth amongst us, will regard with interest the illustrations of character, and of the times, which that correspondence exhibits.

In selecting from among the several *Biographical Notices* of JOHN BARTRAM. hitherto published, the preference has been given to one written by his son WILLIAM, which appeared in the first volume of Prof. BARTON's Medical and Physical Journal, in the year 1804. It is brief, and lacking in details ; yet probably in the main more reliable than the others. But even *that* is obscure, and somewhat inaccurate, in the account it gives of the elder portion of the family.

It is remarkable that none of the published biographies of JOHN BARTRAM mentions the name of his father ; nor could any of his descendants, inquired of by the Editor, furnish that name,—neither could they give the exact date of the Botanist's birth !

For these, and some other authentic particulars, the Editor is indebted to the kindness of a friend,—who obtained them from the ancient records of Darby Monthly Meeting ; to which Meeting the family originally belonged.

W. D.

West Chester, Pennsylvania,
April 28, 1849.

CONTENTS.

*

CONTENTS.

PROGRESS

OF

BOTANY IN NORTH AMERICA.

We have for some time indulged the idea, that it would not be unacceptable to those who may take an interest in Botany to find in this work a brief preliminary sketch of the progress of Botanical Science on this continent,—especially in that portion of it belonging to the United States. We have also thought it might be gratifying to such as have not made themselves familiar with the subject, to see a list of the works which have been expressly devoted to the Botany of this region,—together with a notice, however meagre, of the labours of those who have explored and illustrated the vegetable products of our country.

It would not be expedient, here—neither do the materials in possession of the writer warrant the attempt—to amplify the topic. He merely proposes to indicate, as far as known to him—and as nearly in chronological order as practicable—the titles and character of the several *Catalogues, Floras, Scientific Journals,* and other publications, illustrative of North American Plants,—with occasional notices of their authors, and of other lovers of nature, whose zeal and industry have made us acquainted with the floral beauties which decorate our valleys, and hill sides, and mountain tops—bespangling our prairies, imparting magnificence to our forests, and shedding a delicious fragrance over our land. It seemed to be germain to the object of the work, to afford a passing glance at what others have done, in the same field of science in which a BARTRAM and a MARSHALL were so early, so earnestly, and so successfully engaged.

One of the earliest productions, if not the very first, descriptive of North American plants, was a quarto volume, printed at Paris in the year 1635, entitled *Canadensium Plantarum aliarumque nondum editarum Historia ;* by a French botanist, named JAC. CORNUTUS. This author, it is believed, was never in America; but described the plants from specimens sent to him from Canada.

The person who next treated of the plants of this region, is believed to have been JOHN JOSSELYN,—an Englishman, who resided in Massachusetts for some years, (1633 to 1674,) and in 1672, published a work entitled *New England's Rarities,* discovered in birds, fishes, serpents, and plants of that country. This book is referred to in some of PETER COLLINSON'S letters to JOHN BARTRAM. The author seems to have been rather prone to the marvellous in his statements, and to have laboured under some of the old vulgar prejudices respecting the supposed transmutation of plants. He informs us that "some frogs, when they sit upon their breech, are a foot high;" and he furthermore alleges, that "*Barley* frequently degenerates into *Oats*"!*

The next botanist in the order of time, who noticed our plants, was the Rev. JOHN BANISTER, who, "in 1680, transmitted to Mr. RAY, a *Catalogue of Plants* observed by him in *Virginia.* He drew with his own hand figures of the rarer species. He fell a victim to his favourite pursuit; for in one of his botanical excursions, while clambering the rocks, he fell and was killed."†

About the year 1730, JOHN BARTRAM,—who, from his youth up, had been passionately fond of Natural History—and especially of Botany,—began to make collections of American plants and seeds, for his friend PETER COLLINSON, of London, and other correspondents. He probably detected more undescribed plants than any of his contemporaries in our country. "He was, perhaps, *the first Anglo-American* who conceived the idea of establishing a BOTANIC GARDEN for the reception and cultivation of the various vegetables, natives of the country, as well as exotics, and of travelling for the discovery and acquisition of them."‡

---

* This strange phantasy—once so prevalent among the unreflecting tillers of the soil—has been materially curtailed, or modified, in our own times; for, at the present day, the most credulous advocates of the doctrine only contend that *Wheat* is sometimes transformed into *Bromus,* or *Cheat.*

† BANISTER is called by Mr. RAY, in his *Historia Plantarum,* "eruditissimus Vir et consummatissimus Botanicus." Many of his descendants, it is said, are still living in Virginia. *See* BARTON'S *Med. and Phys. Journal,* vol. ii.

‡ The BARTRAM BOTANIC GARDEN, (established in or about the year 1730,) is most eligibly and beautifully situated, on the right bank of the river Schuylkill, a short distance below the city of Philadelphia. Being the oldest establishment

Doctor FOTHERGILL, in his memoir of PETER COLLINSON, A. D. 1769, says: "that eminent naturalist, JOHN BARTRAM, may almost be said to have been created such by my friend's [P. C.'s] assistance; he first recommended the collecting of seeds, and afterwards assisted in disposing of them in this country [England], and constantly excited him to persevere in investigating the plants of America, which he has executed with indefatigable labour through a long course of years, and with amazing success."

JOHN BARTRAM, also, at the request of some naturalists in Europe, instituted and satisfactorily conducted a series of experiments on the *Lychnis dioica*—illustrative of the doctrine of the sexes of plants, and corroborative of those previously made upon the Indian corn (*Zea Mays*), by JAMES LOGAN, the distinguished friend and secretary of the founder of our Commonwealth.

MARK CATESBY, in 1732, published the first volume of his *Natural History of Carolina, Florida and the Bahamas;* and the second volume appeared in 1743. The work was in large folio, with coloured plates,—and, for that day, was a magnificent performance, though its botanical merits were not quite equal to its pretensions.

In 1739, the publication of *the first systematic enumeration* of North American plants was commenced at Leyden, in Holland, under the title of *Flora Virginica.* It was edited by the learned Professor GRONOVIUS, from specimens and descriptions furnished by that excellent pioneer of American Botany, JOHN CLAYTON, of Virginia, who is entitled to more of the credit, due to that work, than has been generally awarded to him.*

About this time, that able and sagacious botanist, Doctor CAD-WALLADER COLDEN, of New York, began to pay attention to the Natural History of that province; and for a number of years, he continued to observe, collect, and describe the indigenous plants in the interesting region around his residence, at *Coldenham,* near

of the kind in this western world, and exceedingly interesting, from its history and associations,—one might almost hope, even in this utilitarian age, that, if no motive more commendable could avail, a feeling of *state* or *city pride*, would be sufficient to ensure its preservation, in its original character, and for the sake of its original objects. But, alas! there seems to be too much reason to apprehend that it will scarcely survive the immediate family of its noble-hearted founder, —and that even the present generation may live to see the accumulated treasures of a century laid waste—with all the once gay parterres and lovely borders converted into lumber-yards and coal-landings.

* PETER COLLINSON, in 1764, styles him "my friend JOHN CLAYTON, the great botanist of America."

Newburgh.* He corresponded much with the distinguished naturalists of Europe, and communicated to them his discoveries.

At that sylvan retreat, and in the delightful recreation afforded by botanical research—amid the cares of his public employments, Doctor COLDEN found a companion and assistant, worthy of special commemoration, in his accomplished daughter. Doctor GARDEN, writing to Doctor COLDEN, November 4, 1754, says: "I shall be glad to hear of Miss COLDEN'S improvements, which no doubt increase every day,—and may we again be surprised with more than a DACIER, even in America." In a letter to LINNÆUS, dated London, May 12, 1756, PETER COLLINSON says: "I but lately heard from Mr. COLDEN. He is well; but, what is marvellous, his daughter is perhaps the first lady that has so perfectly studied your system. She deserves to be celebrated." And in another, dated April 30, 1758, he says: "Last week, my friend, Mr. ELLIS, wrote you a letter, recommending a curious botanic dissertation, by Miss JANE COLDEN. As this accomplished lady is the only one of the fair sex that I have heard of, who is scientifically skilful in the Linnæan system, you no doubt will distinguish her merits, and recommend her example to the ladies of every country."

That eminent naturalist, JOHN ELLIS, in a letter to LINNÆUS (just referred to), dated London, April 25, 1758, says: "Mr. COLDEN of New York has sent Dr. FOTHERGILL a new plant, described by his daughter. It is called *Fibraurea*, Gold Thread" [*Helleborus trifolius, L. Coptis trifolia, Salisb.*]. "This young lady merits your esteem, and does honour to your system. She has drawn and described 400 plants in your method only : she uses English terms. Her father has a plant called after him, *Coldenia ;* suppose you should call this *Coldenella*, or any other name that might distinguish her among your genera."

LINNÆUS, however, referred the plant to his genus HELLEBORUS; and when it was subsequently ascertained to be distinct, SALISBURY, regardless alike of gallantry and justice—imposed upon it the name of *Coptis.*

* "The earliest treatise on the Botany of New York," says Dr. TORREY, in his preface to the *Flora* of that state, "that has come under my observation, is the ' *Plantæ Coldenhamiæ*' of Governor COLDEN, published in the Acts of the Royal Society of Upsal for the year 1744. It is an account of the plants growing spontaneously in the neighbourhood of Coldenham, in Orange County, and embraces only the first twelve classes of the Linnæan system. The second part was (I believe) never published."

In 1739, was published at Leyden, in Holland, an Essay in Latin, entitled "*Experimenta et Meletemata de Plantarum gene-ratione*," by the learned and ingenious JAMES LOGAN, of Pennsylvania. It was afterwards, viz., in 1747, republished in London, with an English translation by Dr. FOTHERGILL. The experiments and observations detailed in this Essay, were admirably illustrative of the Linnæan doctrine of the sexes of plants; and amply demonstrated the capacity of the author for successful philosophical research.*

Doctor JOHN MITCHELL—to whom the pretty little *Mitchella* is dedicated—came to Virginia early in the eighteenth century. He paid much attention to the plants of that province, collected extensively, and became a correspondent of LINNÆUS and others. About the year 1740, he sent to PETER COLLINSON "a paper in which thirty new genera of Virginia plants were proposed."

In the year 1748, PETER KALM, a Swedish naturalist, and pupil of LINNÆUS, visited Pennsylvania, and spent three years in exploring the botany of that and the adjacent provinces, and extended his researches into Canada. He was a vigilant observer, and an industrious collector, sending numerous nondescript plants to his great preceptor; and in 1753, published his *travels* in North America. He also contributed many articles on the natural history of this country, to the Memoirs of the Royal Swedish Academy of Sciences.

The accomplished Doctor ALEXANDER GARDEN, of Charleston, South Carolina, commenced his correspondence with LINNÆUS in 1755; and by his contributions of botanical information and specimens, to LINNÆUS, ELLIS, COLLINSON, and others, did much to promote a knowledge of American plants.

Doctor ADAM KUHN, of Philadelphia, was probably *the first Professor of botany* in this country (appointed *anno* 1768); yet,

---

* The writer of this had the satisfaction, in the summer of 1805, of repeating with complete success the Loganian experiments upon the *Indian corn.*

The observations of JAMES LOGAN upon the *Pollen grains*, their figure, function, &c., are very remarkable for that day. After stating that SAMUEL MORLAND, about the year 1696, had asserted that the *farina*, or minute pollen grains entered the ovary through the canal of the style, he adds:—"Ego quidem semel in medio unius ex supra memoratis stylis frumenti *Indici* granulum conspexi; nec dubitandum reor, quin exquisitiore adhibita diligentia, in iis delabentia facile deprehendantur." Which is thus rendered by Dr. FOTHERGILL:—"I once saw a small grain in the middle of this canal; nor is it to be doubted, but that stricter inquiries will discover more of them passing the same way."

although he had the advantage of studying under the illustrious SWEDE, and was said to have been a favourite pupil ("LINNÆO ex discipulis acceptissimus"),—it does not appear that he ever did much for the science.

In 1773, the *second botanical garden* within the British provinces of North America, was established by HUMPHRY MARSHALL, in the township of West Bradford, Chester County, Pennsylvania, at the site of the present village of *Marshallton*. HUMPHRY, however, had been previously indulging his taste, and employing his leisure time in collecting and cultivating useful and ornamental plants at his paternal residence, near the Brandywine.

The laudable example of HUMPHRY MARSHALL was not without its influence in the community where he resided. His friend and neighbour, the late estimable JOHN JACKSON, was endowed with a similar taste for the beauties of nature ; and, in the year 1777, commenced a highly interesting collection of plants, at his residence in Londongrove, which is still preserved in good condition, by his son, WILLIAM JACKSON, Esq. About the year 1800, also, the brothers JOSHUA and SAMUEL PEIRCE, of East Marlborough, began to adorn their premises by tasteful culture and planting ; and they have produced an *Arboretum* of evergreens, and other elegant forest trees, which is certainly unrivalled in Pennsylvania, and probably not surpassed in these United States.

Botanic gardens have likewise been instituted at Charleston, South Carolina, at New York, by the late Doctor DAVID HOSACK, and at Cambridge, near Boston.*

In 1781, a description of certain of our *forest trees*, under the title of *Beschreibung einiger Nord-Amerikanischen Holzarten*, was published at Göttingen, by JUL. AD. FRIED. VON WANGEN-HEIM, a German botanist, who, it is understood, had been a surgeon to the Hessian troops, employed by the British government, in the war of Independence.

In the first volume of the Memoirs of the *American Academy*—an institution established at Boston, in 1780—the Rev. MANASSEH CUTLER, LL.D., published the *first essay* towards a scientific de-

---

* The botanic garden at Charleston, S. C., was established about the year 1804; that by Dr. HOSACK, at New York, in 1801 ; and that at Cambridge, in or about the year 1805. The first two, it is believed, have wholly disappeared. The last-named, now under the skilful supervision of Professor A. GRAY, is in a flourishing condition ; and bids fair, if supported by an adequate endowment, to be a perennial monument of the liberality and love of science, of those who projected it.

scription of the *Plants of New England*. The volume is dated in 1785; but that *essay* was probably printed a year or two prior to the completion of the volume.

Doctor CUTLER was one of the valuable men of his day. He not only distinguished himself by his attainments in natural science, but was also one of that enterprising band who led the way into our western wilds, and became the founders of the great State of Ohio. He afterwards, however, returned to Massachusetts, where he died, on the 28th of July, 1823, aged 81 years.

In the latter end of the year 1785, HUMPHRY MARSHALL, of Chester County, Pennsylvania, published his *Arbustum Americanum*, a description of the forest trees and shrubs, natives of the American United States. This is believed to be *the first strictly American botanical work,*—that is to say, the *first* treatise on American plants, written by a native American, and printed in this country; and, under all the discouraging circumstances attending its production, it does much credit to the attainments and enterprise of the author.

In 1787, Dr. SCHOEPF, a German physician, who had passed several years in the United States, published, at Erlangen, an *American Materia Medica*, chiefly from the vegetable kingdom, which notices a considerable number of our plants, and their properties. Other interesting accounts of our *medicinal plants* have since been published: Professor B. S. BARTON, in 1798, and subsequently, published several tracts under the title of Collections for an Essay towards a Materia Medica of the United States; and a handsome work, entitled *American Medical Botany*, by JACOB BIGELOW, M.D., of Boston, appeared in 1817, and after.

The *Flora Caroliniana*, by THOMAS WALTER, was published in London, in the year 1788. It was a highly respectable and useful performance.

In 1791, WILLIAM BARTRAM'S *Travels* in the Carolinas, Georgia, and Florida, appeared, giving an interesting account of that region, and also of a number of new southern plants.

Some interesting papers on North American plants began now to be published in the *Transactions of the American Philosophical Society*, by Professor B. S. BARTON, Rev. Dr. MUHLENBERG, PALISOT DE BEAUVOIS, and others. In subsequent years, those *Transactions* were greatly enriched by botanical communications from THOMAS NUTTALL, Esq., and other investigators of American plants.

In 1801, ANDRE MICHAUX, a French botanist, published at Paris an interesting work on the *Oaks of North America* (*Histoire des Chênes de l'Amérique Septentrionale*); and in 1803, the *Flora Boreali-Americana* of the same author, ably edited by LOUIS CLAUDE RICHARD, was published in the same city. This *Flora*, though comprising but a portion of the plants of North America, is an excellent work, and remarkable for the accuracy and felicity of its descriptive phrases.

In the same year (1803), the first American *elementary* work on Botany was published, at Philadelphia, by the late Prof. B. S. BARTON. Though somewhat diffuse, it was an useful and respectable performance. Prof. BARTON, in those days, occasionally gave courses of *Lectures* on Natural History and Botany, to small classes in the University of Pennsylvania (one of which courses, in 1803–4, the writer had the privilege of attending): and there can be no doubt that he did more than any of his contemporaries, in diffusing a taste for the natural sciences, among the young men who then resorted to that school.

The expedition of Messrs. LEWIS and CLARK, across this continent to the Pacific Ocean, which was projected about this time, by President JEFFERSON, was a means of introducing to the knowledge of botanists, a number of plants which were previously unknown; though the principal collection made by those gentlemen was unfortunately lost. That region has been subsequently explored, and vast additions made to our *Flora*, by Messrs. NUTTALL, NICOLET, FREMONT, and others.

In 1807, Doctor SAMUEL L. MITCHILL published a *Catalogue* of the plants around his country-seat, at Plandome, New York. This catalogue, it is understood, was prepared by Dr. EDDY—a relative of Dr. MITCHILL.

In 1810, F. ANDRE MICHAUX, son of the above-mentioned A. MICHAUX, published at Paris, his splendid *History of the Forest Trees of North America* (*Histoire des Arbres Forestiers de l'Amérique Septentrionale*), with elegantly coloured plates. An English translation of this superb work was issued in 1817, under the title of *North American Sylva*.

In 1811, a *Catalogue of indigenous and naturalized plants,* growing spontaneously on the *island of New York*, was published in the *American Medical and Philosophical Register*, by that veteran botanist, Major JOHN LE CONTE. Many very valuable botanical contributions were subsequently made to our scientific journals, by the same distinguished naturalist.

An excellent *Catalogue of the hitherto known native and natu- ralized Plants of North America*, was published at Lancaster, Pennsylvania, in 1813, by the Rev. HENRY MUHLENBERG, of that city.*

In 1814, the valuable and comprehensive *Flora Americæ Sep- tentrionalis*, by FREDERICK PURSH, was published in London. In the same year, also, appeared the *Florula Bostoniensis*, by Dr. JACOB BIGELOW,—a charming specimen of a *local Flora*—of which a *second* edition was published in 1824; likewise, a neat little volume entitled a *Synopsis of the Genera of American Plants*, printed at Georgetown, D. C., and understood to be compiled by O. RICH, Esq.

Botanical works began now to multiply, in the United States,— and the students of "the amiable science" found helps in their delightful pursuit, which rendered it vastly more easy and satis- factory than it had been to their predecessors.

In 1816, STEPHEN ELLIOTT, Esq., commenced the publication of his *Sketch of the Botany of South Carolina and Georgia*,—a work of great value, and indispensable in the investigation of Southern plants. In preparing it, he was much indebted, for materials and information, to the industry and sagacity of that indefatigable botanist and most amiable man, the late Doctor WILLIAM BALDWIN.

In 1817, a pamphlet entitled *Florula Ludoviciana* was published, in New York, by C. S. RAFINESQUE. This eccentric and rambling naturalist—although he had, by long experience and observation, acquired considerable knowledge, and moreover issued several other botanical publications, in subsequent years,—yet, he made state- ments so little reliable, held such peculiar views, and withal was so addicted to extravagant innovations in nomenclature, that his pro-

---

* In 1815, the Abbe CORREA published, for the use of his class in Philadelphia, a reduction of the *genera* in MUHLENBERG's Catalogue to the *natural families* of JUSSIEU. This was appended to a *second edition* of the Catalogue, issued in 1818, by that amiable man and excellent botanist, the late SOLOMON W. CONRAD, and was probably the earliest attempt in the United States to group our plants in accordance with the natural method.

ductions, generally, were rather injurious than beneficial to the science.

In this year, also, appeared at Philadelphia, a posthumous work of the Rev. Dr. MUHLENBERG, upon the *Grasses and Cyperaceous Plants of North America.* It was written in Latin, and edited by his son. The detailed descriptions as far as they go, are generally accurate and satisfactory; but the work was left incomplete by the estimable author.

The *Philadelphia Academy of Natural Sciences* now began the publication of a *Journal* of their proceedings,—in which may be found a number of valuable papers on American plants.*

In 1818, a work of great merit, upon the *Genera of North American Plants*, with a catalogue of the species, and descriptions of such as were then new, or imperfectly known,—was published at Philadelphia, by THOMAS NUTTALL, Esq. This excellent performance gave a decided impulse to botanical studies in our country.

In the same year, appeared a compendium of a *Philadelphia Flora*, descriptive of plants found within ten miles round that city, by Dr. W. P. C. BARTON. Although apparently a hasty compilation, and marred by frequent inaccuracies, this was nevertheless a convenient and very useful companion to the herborizers of that district.

In 1819, Doctor JOHN TORREY and others, a committee of the *New York Lyceum of Natural History*, published a *Catalogue of Plants* growing within thirty miles of *the city of New York.*

In 1820, *A Compendium of Physiological and Systematic Botany*, with Plates, by GEORGE SUMNER, M.D., was published at Hartford, Connecticut.

In 1821, Dr. W. P. C. BARTON commenced the publication, at Philadelphia, of a *Flora of North America*, illustrated by coloured figures drawn from nature. This, though entirely without method, was tolerably well executed, and was extended to three volumes quarto, when it was discontinued.

In 1822, a *Monograph of the Genus Viola*, by the late amiable and Rev. LEWIS DAVID VON SCHWEINITZ, of Bethlehem, Pennsylvania, was published in SILLIMAN'S *American Journal of Science*, vol. v. This excellent *Journal*—which commenced in 1818, and is chiefly devoted to the natural sciences—contains many valu-

---

* The *Herbarium* of the Philadelphia Academy is also one of the richest and most valuable in the United States.

able communications upon American plants;—particularly the *Caricography* of Prof. DEWEY, commencing in the seventh, and continued through many subsequent volumes.

In 1824, Doctor JOHN TORREY, of New York, began the publication of a *Flora of the Northern and Middle Sections of the United States,* in accordance with the Linnæan arrangement. This was ably executed, as far as it extended, which was to the class *Icosandria,* inclusive; when it was discontinued.

In this year, also, the *New York Lyceum of Natural History* commenced the publication of their *Annals,* in which are many botanical articles of great value:—such as Dr. TORREY'S account of *Rocky Mountain Plants ;** SCHWEINITZ and TORREY'S *Monograph of North American Carices ;* LE CONTE'S *Observations on the North American Species of the Genus Viola,* &c. &c.

About this time, some of the *schools,* in the Northern States, began to make a profession of teaching *Botany ;* and thereupon arose a demand for suitable books for that purpose. Accordingly, a number, such as they were, soon appeared. Among the most successful, was a *Manual,* compiled by Prof. AMOS EATON, of Troy, N. Y., which has passed through several editions.† They were all useful, to some extent, in aiding to promote a taste for the study of plants; but few of them were exactly adapted to the wants of students, or calculated to make scientific botanists.

In 1826, Doctor TORREY published, at New York, a *compendium* of the Flora of the Northern and Middle States,—which was very convenient for herborizers. In the same year, a *Catalogue* of the Phænogamous Plants, native and naturalized, growing in the vicinity of West Chester, Penn., was published in that borough, by the writer of this, under the title of *Florula Cestrica.*

In this year also, Dr. LEWIS C. BECK commenced the publication, in SILLIMAN'S Journal, vol. x., of *Contributions towards the Botany of the States of Illinois and Missouri.* These made known a number of new plants,—and were otherwise highly interesting. The "Contributions" were arranged according to the *Linnæan Method,* and were continued in the 11th and 14th

---

* Prof. TORREY'S Memoir on the *Rocky Mountain Plants,* prepared in 1826, was the *first* specimen in our country, of a regular *Flora* arranged according to the *Natural System ;* and is, indeed, an admirable performance.

† The *first* edition of EATON'S *Manual of Botany* was published in 1818; the *eighth, and last,* which was much enlarged and improved, and was the joint labour of Messrs. EATON and WRIGHT, appeared in 1840.

volumes, extending as far as the class *Monadelphia*, inclusive. The residue does not appear to have been published.

In 1827, THOMAS NUTTALL, Esq., published at Cambridge, Mass., an *Introduction to Systematic and Physiological Botany*, which was well adapted to the wants of that day.

In 1829, Sir WILLIAM JACKSON HOOKER,—then Professor of Botany at Glasgow, Scotland, now Superintendent of the Royal Botanic Gardens at Kew, near London,—commenced the publication of his magnificent work, entitled *Flora Boreali-Americana*, or the Botany of the Northern parts of British America. It was published in *numbers* or portions, and was not completed until 1840; but it now stands, with its 238 quarto plates, a splendid monument of the scientific attainments, artistic skill, and untiring perseverance of its accomplished author. Sir WILLIAM has contributed largely to the knowledge of the plants of the *United States*, including *Texas*,* by the agency of his collectors, Messrs. DOUGLAS, DRUMMOND, and others,—who have very extensively explored the vegetation of this continent.

We have, moreover, been much indebted to the labours and researches of MENZIES, FRASER, LYON, BRADBURY, SCOULER, RICHARDSON, and other travelling investigators of North American Botany.

Our estimable countryman, Doctor F. BOOTT—now a resident of London—has also done much towards illustrating American Botany, by his researches and publications; and has rendered most important aid to the botanists of the United States, by his kind attentions and services, in comparing our plants with the authentic specimens contained in the *Herbaria* of the early collectors, in England.

In 1830, Dr. J. A. BRERETON, of Washington City, published a *catalogue* of the plants of that District, under the title of *Prodromus Floræ Columbianæ:* and soon afterwards, Prof. C. W. SHORT, of Kentucky, commenced the publication, in a Western

---

* As an evidence of the far-seeing sagacity with which that gentleman regarded our national career and tendencies, it may be permitted here to make an extract from a letter to the writer of this, which accompanied a large remittance of botanical specimens. The letter was dated as long ago as Dec. 28, 1835, and the passage referred to, is as follows:—" I had promised you some Southern plants of your vast Northern Continent, and I thought I could not do better than select from those of TEXAS, as affording a vegetation considerably different from that of the United States, *and which will probably form a part of your country.*"

journal, of the *Florula Lexingtoniensis*, or a description of plants growing around Lexington, Kentucky. He also published a *catalogue*, with several supplements, of the Phænogamous Plants and Ferns of Kentucky. That zealous and truly liberal botanist has probably done more towards bringing to light the vegetable treasures of the West, and in preparing beautiful specimens, than any other person in our country; and he has, certainly, in the way of exchanges and remittances, sent more western plants to his correspondents in the Atlantic States, and throughout the Old World, than all the rest of our American botanists put together.

In 1833, Doctor LEWIS C. BECK, of Albany, N. Y., published an excellent duodecimo volume, entitled *Botany of the Northern and Middle States*. This is arranged in conformity with the most approved *natural method*,—and is a very judicious, convenient, and useful work. A *second edition* has been recently issued.

In the *Transactions of the American Philosophical Society*, for 1834, was published an elaborate *Synopsis of North American Fungi*, by the late Rev. LEWIS D. VON SCHWEINITZ, of Bethlehem, Pennsylvania.

In the same year (1834), appeared a *Catalogue of Plants* in the vicinity of *Charleston, South Carolina*, by Prof. J. BACHMAN; *An Enumeration of Plants growing spontaneously around Wilmington, North Carolina*, by that careful observer and sagacious botanist, the Rev. M. A. CURTIS;* *A Monograph of North American Rhynchosporæ*, by Dr. A. GRAY; and two exceedingly interesting volumes of *Labelled Specimens* of American *Gramineæ* and *Cyperaceæ*, by the last-named gentleman.

In 1835, an excellent *Synopsis of the Flora of the Western States*, was published at *Cincinnati*, Ohio, by Prof. JOHN L. RIDDELL, of that city; and in the same year, appeared a *Catalogue of the Plants of Massachusetts*, by Prof. EDWARD HITCHCOCK.

In 1836, were published, at New York, *Elements of Botany*, by Dr. A. GRAY; and, in the Annals of the New York Lyceum, an excellent *Monograph of North American Cyperaceæ*, by Prof. JOHN TORREY.

In 1837, the following works appeared:—*A Catalogue of Plants*,

---

* This *Enumeration*, by the Rev. Mr. CURTIS, was published in the first volume of the *Boston Journal of Natural History*,—a valuable repository of papers and communications, which began to be published in 1834, by the Boston Society of Naturalists.

native and naturalized, in the vicinity of *Newbern, North Carolina,* by the lamented H. B. CROOM, Esq.;* *Flora Cestrica,* an attempt to enumerate and describe *the flowering and filicoid plants of Chester County, Pennsylvania,* by the writer of this sketch; *A Catalogue of Phœnogamous Plants and Ferns,* growing in the vicinity of *Baltimore, Maryland,* by W. E. A. AIKIN, M.D.; and *A Revision of the North American Melanthaceæ,* by Dr. A. GRAY.

In 1838 was commenced, at New York, the publication of a *Flora of North America,* according to the *natural system,* by those distinguished botanists, JOHN TORREY and ASA GRAY, a work which, unhappily, is at present in a state of suspense; but which, if duly completed, promises to excel all its predecessors, and will undoubtedly for a long period, be the *standard authority* among American botanists.

In this year, also, a *catalogue of plants* found in the vicinity of *Milwaukie, Wisconsin Territory,* was published by J. A. LAPHAM, Esq., of that young western city.

In 1840, appeared a *catalogue of native and naturalized plants,* growing near *Columbus, Ohio,* by W. S. SULLIVANT, Esq.

In 1841, Dr. A. GRAY published, in the 40th volume of SILLI-MAN'S *Journal of Science,* "Notices of *European Herbaria,* particularly those most interesting to the *North American botanist.*" This acceptable service he was enabled to perform, in consequence of having devoted a year to the inspection of those *herbaria,* examining the American specimens, and ascertaining exactly what plants were intended, by the published names. It was a glorious privilege for an accomplished botanist; and was the only mode by which a long-existing uncertainty, in regard to many species, could be satisfactorily cleared up. The task, moreover, could not have been entrusted to more competent hands; and the *Flora of North America,* whenever completed, will no doubt receive the full benefit of the knowledge thus obtained.

In 1842, a valuable *Monograph of the North American Cuscutineæ,* was published in SILLIMAN'S *Journal,* by that acute observer and able botanist, GEORGE ENGELMANN, M.D., of St. Louis, Missouri. In the same year, also, Professor A. GRAY, of Cam-

---

* This estimable gentleman—whose sad fate and premature loss the botanical world has so much reason to deplore—also prepared a valuable monograph of the *Sarracenias,* which is published in the third volume of the Annals of the New York Lyceum.

bridge, Mass., published an elementary treatise, under the title of the *Botanical Text Book*, of which a *second edition* appeared in 1845. This is unquestionably the best *introduction* to a scientific knowledge of the vegetable kingdom, which has yet appeared in our country, if not in our language.

In 1843, was published *A Flora of the State of New York*, in two ponderous quarto volumes, and embellished with one hundred and sixty-one coloured plates. This superb work was undertaken by Professor JOHN TORREY, in pursuance of an act for a geological survey of New York, passed in 1836, which made provision for a full account of the natural history of the state; and it is but justice to say, that it has been completed in a faithful and masterly manner.*

In the same year, the same distinguished botanist prepared a highly interesting *catalogue of plants*, collected during a journey across the *Rocky Mountains*, by that intelligent and enterprising traveller, Lieutenant (since Colonel) J. C. FREMONT.

Mr. EDWARD TUCKERMAN, Jr., then of Schenectady, New York, also published an ingenious *methodical enumeration* of our *Carices*.

In 1844, the *Botanical Society of Wilmington, Delaware*, published a *Catalogue of the Phœnogamous and Filicoid Plants of Newcastle County*, which was subsequently much enlarged.

In the same year a *Catalogue of Rhode Island Plants*, arranged by S. T. OLNEY, Esq., was published by the *Providence Franklin Society*, of that state, with additions the ensuing year.

In 1845, were published, *Contributions towards a Catalogue of Trees and Shrubs of Cumberland County, Pennsylvania*, by Professor SPENCER F. BAIRD, of Carlisle; a *Catalogue of Plants in Western New York*, by H. P. SARTWELL, M.D., of Penyan, Yates County; *A Catalogue of Plants of Lewis County, Ohio*, by FRANKLIN B. HOUGH, A.B.; *A List of Plants growing in the vicinity of Quincy, Florida*, by A. W. CHAPMAN, M.D., in the Western Journal of Medicine and Surgery; and in the Boston Journal of Natural History, *An Enumeration of F. Lindheimer's*

---

* The style in which "the Empire State" has illustrated *every department* of her natural history, is calculated to make a true *Pennsylvanian* blush for the contrast exhibited by the authorities of his own state; who, in the first place, meanly restricted the survey of her glorious domain to a *mere geological examination;* and now, when it is done, have not spirit enough to give to the public the benefit, even of *that!*

Collection of Texan Plants, by Dr. GEORGE ENGELMANN and Professor A. GRAY.

In this year, also, a "*Class Book of Botany*" was published by Mr. ALPHONSO WOOD, of New Hampshire; and two years afterwards, a second much improved edition appeared. The same gentleman has quite recently prepared an elementary work for young beginners, entitled, "*First Lessons in Botany.*" This has been adapted to the present state of the science; and seems well calculated, both to facilitate the first steps of juvenile students, and to impart correct views of the subject.

In 1846, Professor A. GRAY and W. S. SULLIVANT, Esq., published a beautiful little work on the *Mosses of the Alleghanies ;** Mr. SULLIVANT likewise commenced the publication of *Contributions to the Bryology and Hepaticology of North America;* and Professor GRAY also published *Illustrations of New, Rare, or otherwise interesting American Plants*, under the title of *Chloris Boreali-Americana.*

In the same year, appeared a *Report on the Trees and Shrubs growing naturally in the Forests of Massachusetts*, by GEORGE B. EMERSON, Esq., which is a model of its kind,—as well for accuracy of description, as for the amount of authentic information respecting the character, properties, and uses, of the objects described.

In 1847, a small volume treating of those plants which American agriculturists are more especially interested in knowing—a sort of *Practical Farmer's Flora*,—was compiled by the writer of this, and published under the title of *Agricultural Botany.*

In the present year (1848), we have been indebted to *Cambridge*, Mass., (which seems now to be the chosen seat of the science,) for *three* admirable botanical works, viz.:—1. *A Synopsis of the Lichenes of New England, the other Northern States, and British America*, by EDWARD TUCKERMAN, A.M.; which will be truly acceptable to those who study that remarkable family of plants. 2. Next, we have from Professor A. GRAY, a thick pocket volume, descriptive of the *Plants of the Northern and Middle States*, under the title of *Manual of Botany.*† This is the most complete

---

* Mr. SULLIVANT also, about this time, issued some fifty copies of *Sets of Mosses*, in two handsome quarto volumes. These were not intended for sale, but merely for presentation to the amateurs of *Muscology.* They contain specimens of 215 true *Mosses*, and 77 *Hepaticæ*, in all 292 ; and are beautifully prepared.

† The portion of the "*Manual*," describing the *Carices of the Northern United*

and authentic enumeration of the plants of those States which has yet appeared. The arrangement is according to the latest and most approved modification of the natural system, and, as a *vade mecum* for herborizers, the work is invaluable.

3. The same accomplished and indefatigable author has also issued, this year, an octavo volume, with one hundred plates, entitled *Genera Floræ Americæ Boreali-orientalis Illustrata.* It is the *first* of a contemplated series of *ten volumes,* designed to illustrate, by figures and analyses, the genera of the plants of the United States. This gigantic undertaking would be a desperate one, in any other hands; but if life and health be spared to him, the volume before us is a sufficient guarantee that the author will acquit himself of the task, in a manner as beneficial to botanical science, as it will be honourable to himself, and to the literature of his country. The illustrations in this work seem to leave nothing unexplained, in the generic characters of the plants treated of, which it is important to know.

It is as surprising as it is gratifying, to contemplate the aids and facilities now afforded to *the students of American Botany,* compared with the sorry helps and stinted means at command, when the writer of these desultory sketches first became a humble aspirant to that description of knowledge.

What, then, must have been the difficulties and discouragements attending the pursuit, when JOHN BARTRAM and HUMPHRY MARSHALL began to explore the vegetable treasures of this vast and varied continent! How kindly should we cherish the memory of the men who thus early and zealously toiled for our instruction and gratification! If the example of those venerable pioneers in the walks of natural science, as illustrated in this volume, shall exert a salutary influence upon their successors of the present, or of future times, the editor will be happy in the hope, that what with him has been a labour of love, has not also been a labour in vain.

W. D.

States, was contributed by JOHN CAREY, Esq., of which some copies were distributed separately, affording a convenient synopsis of that extensive genus. The value of Mr. CAREY's performance may be inferred from its position in the "Manual."

CORRESPONDENCE

OF

JOHN BARTRAM:

WITH

OCCASIONAL NOTES, AND BIOGRAPHICAL SKETCHES.

TO THE

𝔓𝔢𝔫𝔫𝔰𝔶𝔩𝔳𝔞𝔫𝔦𝔞 𝔥𝔬𝔯𝔱𝔦𝔠𝔲𝔩𝔱𝔲𝔯𝔞𝔩 𝔖𝔬𝔠𝔦𝔢𝔱𝔶,

THIS COMPILATION,

FROM THE CORRESPONDENCE OF THE

GREAT PIONEER IN

AMERICAN HORTICULTURE AND BOTANY,

IS RESPECTFULLY DEDICATED BY

THE EDITOR.

BIOGRAPHICAL SKETCH

OF

JOHN BARTRAM.

JOHN BARTRAM, the earliest native American Botanist, and the founder of the first Botanical Garden on this continent, was born near the village of Darby, in Delaware (then Chester) County, Pennsylvania, on the 23d day of March, 1699.

His great-grandfather, RICHARD BARTRAM, lived and died in Derbyshire, England. RICHARD had one son, named JOHN, who married in Derby (England), and, with his wife, was settled for some years in the town of Ashborn, where they had three sons and one daughter.

With this family, JOHN (following the fortunes of WILLIAM PENN) removed to Pennsylvania in 1682,—the year in which the city of Philadelphia was founded—and settled in what is now Delaware County, near Darby.* He died on the first of September, 1697.

The names of the three sons who accompanied him to this Western World, were JOHN, ISAAC, and WILLIAM. JOHN and ISAAC both died unmarried, the former on the 14th of June, 1692, and the latter on the 10th of January, 1708.

WILLIAM BARTRAM, the third son, was married to ELIZABETH,

---

* In PROUD's History of Pennsylvania (vol. i. p. 218), the following passage occurs in a note :—"In the year 1682 they had a religious meeting regularly fixed at *Darby*. Among the first and early settlers of the Society, at or near this place, are mentioned, John Blunston, Michael Blunston, George Wood, Joshua Kearn, Henry Gibbons, Samuel Sellers, Richard Bonsall, Edmund Cartledge, Thomas Hood, JOHN BARTRAM, Robert Naylor, and Adam Rhoads; who all came from *Derbyshire*, in England."

daughter of JAMES HUNT,* at Darby Meeting (the parties all belonging to the Society of *Friends*), on the 27th of March, 1696. The time of his death has not been ascertained. He had three sons, and a daughter who died young. The names of the sons were JOHN (the botanist), JAMES, and WILLIAM. Of these, WILLIAM went to North Carolina, and settled near Cape Fear ; JAMES, who remained in Pennsylvania, left no male descendants.

JOHN BARTRAM, eldest son of WILLIAM and ELIZABETH BAR-TRAM, and the subject of this brief memoir, inherited a farm near Darby, which was left to him by his uncle ISAAC.† "Being born in a newly-settled colony, of not more than fifty years' establish-ment, in a country where the sciences of the Old Continent were little known, it cannot be supposed that he could derive great ad-vantages or assistance from school-learning or literature. He had, however, all or most of the education that could at that time be acquired in country schools ; and whenever an opportunity offered, he studied such of the Latin and Greek grammars and classics, as his circumstances enabled him to purchase ; and he always sought the society of the most learned and virtuous men.

"He had a very early inclination to the study of physic and surgery. He even acquired so much knowledge in the practice of the latter science, as to be very useful : and, in many instances, he gave great relief to his poor neighbours, who were unable to apply for medicines and assistance to physicians of the city (Philadelphia). It is extremely probable that, as most of his medicines were derived from the vegetable kingdom, this circum-stance might point out to him the necessity of, and excite a desire for, the study of Botany.‡

* When the editor commenced his inquiries into the personal history of HUM-PHRY MARSHALL and JOHN BARTRAM, he had not the slightest suspicion that there was any kind of family connexion between them. In the progress of his researches, however, he ascertained not only that they were men of kindred minds and tastes, but that they were actually *cousins german*—the sons of two sisters ! JAMES HUNT, of Kingsessing, in the County of Philadelphia, had the happiness to call those ladies his daughters, and the rare privilege of enumerating two of the earliest and most distinguished botanists of Pennsylvania, among his grand-children.

† The portion of this sketch which here follows, and is designated by quota-tion marks, is taken from an account of JOHN BARTRAM, written by his son WIL-LIAM, and published in Professor BARTON's Medical and Physical Journal.

‡ His *penchant* for medical matters, no doubt, induced him to prepare the notes and appendix to the American edition of SHORT's *Medicina Britannica*, published in 1751, by B. FRANKLIN and D. HALL.

" He seemed to have been designed for the study and contemplation of nature, and the culture of philosophy. Although he was bred a farmer, or husbandman, as a means of procuring a subsistence, he pursued his avocations as a philosopher, being ever attentive to the works and operations of Nature. While engaged in ploughing his fields, and mowing his meadows, his inquisitive eye and mind were frequently exercised in the contemplation of vegetables; the beauty and harmony displayed in their mechanism; the admirable system of order which the great Author of the universe has established throughout their various tribes, and the equally wonderful powers of their generation, the progress of their growth, and the various stages of their maturity and perfection.

" He was, perhaps, the first Anglo-American who conceived the idea of establishing a BOTANIC GARDEN for the reception and cultivation of the various vegetables, natives of the country, as well as of exotics; and of travelling for the discovery and acquisition of them. He purchased a convenient piece of ground on the margin of the Schuylkill, at the distance of about three miles from Philadelphia; a happy situation, possessing every soil and exposure, adapted to the various nature of vegetables. Here he built, with his own hands, a large and comfortable house of hewn stone, and laid out a garden containing about five acres of ground.*

" He began his travels at his own expense. His various excursions rewarded his labours with the possession of a great variety of new, beautiful, and useful trees, shrubs, and herbaceous plants. His garden, at length, attracting the visits and notice of many virtuous and ingenious persons, he was encouraged to persist in his labours.

" Not yet content with having thus begun the establishment of this school of science and philosophy, in the blooming fields of FLORA, he sought farther means for its perfection and importance, by communicating his discoveries and collections to the curious in Europe, and elsewhere, for the benefit of science, commerce, and the useful arts.

" Having arranged his various collections and observations in natural history, one of his particular friends [JOSEPH BREINTNALL,

* The ground on which the Botanic Garden is laid out, was purchased at sheriff's sale. The deed poll—OWEN OWEN, Sheriff, to JOHN BARTRAM—bears date September 30th, 1728. The garden was probably commenced soon afterwards.

The year in which the dwelling-house was erected, may be gathered from an inscription on a stone in the wall, viz.,—" JOHN ✻ ANN BARTRAM, 1731."

an enterprising merchant of Philadelphia] undertook to convey them to the celebrated PETER COLLINSON, of London. This laid the foundation of that friendship and correspondence, which continued uninterrupted—and even increasing—for near fifty years of the lives of these two eminent men. COLLINSON, ever the disinterested friend, communicated from time to time to the learned in Europe, the discoveries and observations of BARTRAM. It was principally through the interest of COLLINSON that he became acquainted, and entered into a correspondence, with many of the most celebrated literary characters in Europe.

"He employed much of his time in travelling through the different provinces of North America, at that time subject to England. Neither dangers nor difficulties impeded or confined his researches after objects in natural history. The summits of our highest mountains were ascended and explored by him. The lakes Ontario, Iroquois, and George; the shores and sources of the rivers Hudson, Delaware, Schuylkill, Susquehanna, Alleghany, and San Juan, were visited by him at an early period,—when it was truly a perilous undertaking to travel in the territories, or even on the frontiers of the aborigines.*

"He travelled several thousand miles in Carolina and Florida. At the advanced age of near seventy years, embarking on board of a vessel at Philadelphia, he set sail for Charleston, in South Carolina. From thence he proceeded, by land, through part of Carolina and Georgia, to St. Augustine, in East Florida. When arrived at the last-mentioned place,—being then appointed botanist and

---

* As evidences of his talents and enthusiastic devotion to natural science, the following passages, from letters of his contemporaries, may not be inappropriate.

PETER COLLINSON, writing to Dr. COLDEN, March 7, 1741, says of JOHN BARTRAM—"I am persuaded you would have been pleased with him; you would have found a wonderful natural genius,—considering his education, and that he was never out of America, but is an husbandman. * * * * * His observations and accounts of all natural productions that happen in his way (and I believe few escape him) are much esteemed here for their accuracy." Dr. COLDEN, in a letter to P. COLLINSON, dated Nov. 13, 1744, says—"I had the pleasure of seeing Mr. BARTRAM at my house, this summer. It is really surprising what knowledge that man has attained merely by the force of industry and his own genius. He has a lively fancy, and a surprising memory and indefatigable disposition." Dr. GARDEN to Dr. COLDEN, writing from Philadelphia, Nov. 4, 1754, says—"One day he dragged me out of town, and entertained me so agreeably with some elevated botanical thoughts on oaks, ferns, rocks, &c., that I forgot I was hungry till we landed in his house, about four miles from town."

naturalist for the King of England,* for exploring the provinces,—
he received his orders to search for the sources of the great River
San Juan [or St. John's].

"Leaving St. Augustine, he travelled by land to the banks of
the river, and embarking in a boat at Picolata, ascended that
great and beautiful river (near 400 miles) to its sources—attending
carefully to its various branches, and the lakes connected with it.
Having ascended on one side of the river, he descended by the
other side to its confluence with the sea.

"In the course of this voyage or journey, he made an accurate
draft and survey of the various widths, depths, courses, and distances, both of the main stream, and of the lakes and branches.
He also noted the situation and quality of the soil, the vegetable
and animal productions, together with other interesting observations ; all of which were highly approved of by the Governor, and
sent to the Board of Trade and Plantations in England, by whose
direction they were ordered to be published, for the benefit of the
new colony.

"Mr. BARTRAM was a man of modest and gentle manners,
frank, cheerful, and of great good nature ; a lover of justice, truth,
and charity. He was himself an example of filial, conjugal, and
parental affection. His humanity, gentleness, and compassion were
manifested upon all occasions, and were even extended to the
animal creation. He was never known to have been at enmity
with any man. During the whole course of his life, there was not
a single instance of his engaging in a litigious contest with any
of his neighbours, or others. He zealously testified against
slavery ;† and, that his philanthropic precepts, on this subject,

In a letter to JOHN ELLIS, March 25, 1755, Dr. GARDEN says—"When we came
to Philadelphia, I met with JOHN BARTRAM, a plain Quaker, but a most accurate
observer of nature." Writing again to Mr. ELLIS, March 21, 1760, Dr. G. says—
"My worthy and kind friend JOHN BARTRAM came from Philadelphia here
[Charleston, S. C.] to see me, about eight days ago." And on March 25, adds—
"I have been lately in the woods for two hours with JOHN, and have shown him
most of our new things, with which he seems almost ravished of his senses, and
lost in astonishment."

* See PETER COLLINSON's Letters, from April 9 to November 13, 1765, in reference
to this *appointment ;* which seems to have been procured by the "repeated solicitations" of that faithful friend.

† Evidences of the zeal and earnestness of JOHN BARTRAM, in opposition to the
fearful curse of *slavery,* are still extant among his manuscript papers. He appears to have been among the earliest of our people in denouncing the abomi-
nation ; and, moreover, to have been in the habit of committing his sentiments
to paper, on that and all other subjects, with equal fervour and freedom.

might have their due weight and force, he gave liberty to a most valuable male slave, then in the prime of his life, who had been bred up in the family almost from his infancy.

" He was, through life, a striking example of temperance,— especially in the use of vinous and spirituous liquors; not from a passion of parsimony, but from a principle of morality. His common drink was pure water, small beer, or cider mixed with milk. Nevertheless, he always kept a good and plentiful table. Once a year—commonly on new year's day—he made a liberal entertainment for his relations and particular friends.

" His stature was rather above the middle size, and upright. His visage was long, and his countenance expressive of a degree of dignity, with a happy mixture of animation and sensibility.

" He was naturally industrious and active, both in body and mind; observing, that he never could find more time than he could employ to satisfaction and advantage, either in improving conversation, or in some healthy and useful bodily exercise: and he was astonished to hear men complaining, that they were weary of their time, and knew not what they should do.

" He was born and educated in the sect called Quakers. But his religious creed may, perhaps, be best collected from a pious distich, engraven by his own hand, in very conspicuous characters, upon a stone placed over the front window of the apartment which was destined for study and philosophical retirement.

> ' 'Tis God alone, Almighty Lord,
> The Holy One, by me adored.
> JOHN BARTRAM, 1770.'

" This may show the simplicity and sincerity of his heart, which never harboured, nor gave countenance to dissimulation.* His mind was frequently employed, and he enjoyed the highest pleasure, in the contemplation of nature, as exhibited in the great volume of creation. He generally concluded the narratives of his journeys

* " This distich, however," says Professor BARTON, " gave offence to many of Mr. BARTRAM's friends."

There is a tradition in the family that JOHN BARTRAM was excommunicated by the Monthly Meeting of Friends, at Darby, on account and in consequence of the above *inscription;* but it appears by the records, that his orthodoxy had been called in question a number of years prior to that date, and that the views which he entertained, had led to his exclusion from the Society, so early as the year 1758. The inscription of 1770, it seems, was made for the purpose of testifying that he still adhered to his former opinions.

with pious and philosophical reflections upon the majesty and power, the perfection and the beneficence, of the Creator.

"He had a high veneration for the moral and religious precepts of the Scriptures, both old and new. He read them often, particularly on the Sabbath day; and recommended to his children and family the following precept, as comprehending the great principles of moral duty in man : 'Do justice, love mercy, and walk humbly before God.'

"He never coveted old age, and often observed to his children and friends, that he sincerely desired that he might not live longer than he could afford assistance to himself; for he was unwilling to be a burden to his friends, or useless in society; and that when death came to perform his office, there might not be much delay. His wishes, in these respects, were gratified in a remarkable manner; for although he lived to be about eighty years of age, yet he was cheerful and active to almost the last hours. His illness was very short. About half an hour before he expired, he seemed, though but for a few moments, to be in considerable agony, and pronounced these words, ' *I want to die.*' "

JOHN BARTRAM was twice married. His *first* wife was MARY, daughter of RICHARD MARIS, of Chester Monthly Meeting. They were married in January, 1723, and had two sons, RICHARD and ISAAC; the former of whom died young. ISAAC died in 1801, aged about 76 years. MARY BARTRAM died in 1727.

His *second* wife was ANN MENDENHALL, of Concord Monthly Meeting, (then Chester, now) Delaware County. They were married in September, 1729, and had nine children.* ANN BARTRAM survived her husband upwards of six years, having died on the 29th of January, 1784, at the age of 87.

It appears, by the records of the *American Philosophical*

* The following statement is taken from a record which he caused to be printed, for the use of his children, in a convenient form, to be attached to their family Bibles:—

Children of JOHN and ANN BARTRAM.

JAMES BARTRAM,	.	.	.	born	June 25th, 1730.
MOSES BARTRAM,	.	.	.	"	June, 1732.
ELIZABETH BARTRAM	.	.	.	"	Aug. 27th, 1734 (died young).
MARY BARTRAM,	.	.	.	"	Sept. 21st, 1736.
WILLIAM and ELIZABETH BARTRAM, [twins]			"	Feb. 9th, 1739.
ANN BARTRAM,	.	.	.	"	June 24th, 1741.
JOHN BARTRAM,	.	.	.	"	October 24th, 1743.
BENJAMIN BARTRAM,	.	.	.	"	July 6th, 1748.

Society, of which JOHN BARTRAM was one of the *original members* (his name standing next to that of Dr. FRANKLIN, who headed the list), that he died on the 22d of September, 1777 ; and consequently, that he attained to the age of 78 years and 6 months.

One of the grand-daughters of the venerable botanist, who recollects him distinctly, says he was exceedingly annoyed and agitated (and she thinks his days were shortened), by the approach of the royal army, after the battle of Brandywine. As that army had been ravaging various portions of the revolted colonies, he was apprehensive it might also lay waste his darling *garden*, the cherished nursling of almost half a century.

The following epistle (of which a copy was politely furnished by Miss GIBSON, a descendant of JOHN BARTRAM,) is so admirably graphic, and exhibits, withal, such pleasant traits of truthful simplicity, that the editor cannot but regard it as an appropriate appendage to the preceding biographical sketch. It was published at London, in the year 1782, in an octavo volume, entitled, *Letters from an American Farmer*, by J. HECTOR ST. JOHN, *a Farmer in Pennsylvania.** It appears that Mr. ST. JOHN was a French gen-

* Mr. ST. JOHN afterwards returned to France, and was there induced to translate his own work into his native language. The *French edition*, somewhat modified and considerably enlarged, was published at Paris, in 1787 (in three vols. 12mo.), under the title of "*Lettres d'un Cultivateur Americain, adressées à* WM. S—ON, Esq., *depuis l'année* 1770 *jusqu'en* 1786. Par M. ST. JOHN DE CREVECŒUR. *Traduites de l'Anglais.*" It is a curious and entertaining performance ; containing also some affecting narratives, the perusal of which makes one desirous to know more of the man, and of his interesting family.

The editor has been favoured with the following notice of Mr. ST. JOHN, by the honourable and venerable SAMUEL BRECK, of Philadelphia, through the kindness of his friend, Dr. A. L. ELWYN, of the same city. "In the year 1787, (says Mr. BRECK,) I arrived at Paris, from the Royal and Military College of Soreze, in the then province of Languedoc, where I had spent more than four years. THOMAS JEFFERSON, who was our plenipotentiary at the court of LOUIS XVI., was travelling in Italy. A young Virginian, Mr. SHORT, received me in the Minister's name, being his secretary, and made me acquainted with a very amiable Frenchman, who had resided in the United States, and written there a work, entitled, 'Letters from an American Farmer,' flattering and favourable to our country. This gentleman was HECTOR SAINT JOHN DE CREVECŒUR. His work was exceedingly popular in France, and the fame acquired by it, was a passport to the highest circles. The romantic descriptions in which he had indulged, in reference to the manners and primitive habits of our countrymen, made some of the great lords and ladies of Paris desirous to see a native American ; among others, a Polish princess took a fancy to see me, upon ST. JOHN's report to her of his acquaintance with me, and invited me to dine with her. I went there, accompanied by Mons. CREVECŒUR.

tleman, a native of Normandy; that at the age of sixteen years he emigrated, first to England, and from thence to the North American colonies, where he resided nearly twenty-seven years (from 1754 to 1781), chiefly in the provinces of New York and Pennsylvania. It is understood that he died in 1813, aged about 82 years.

The annexed letter purports to be from a "Russian gentleman," named IWAN ALEXIOWITZ, and to be descriptive of a visit to the Pennsylvania botanist, in the year 1769. Of the writer of the letter, the editor has not been able to obtain any authentic information; but, by whomsoever written, the fidelity of the *portraiture* therein sketched, will not be questioned by any one having the slightest knowledge of the history, character, and pursuits of JOHN BARTRAM.

LETTER FROM MR. IW—N AL——TZ, A RUSSIAN GENTLEMAN; DESCRIBING THE VISIT HE PAID AT MY REQUEST TO MR. JOHN BERTRAM,* THE CELEBRATED PENNSYLVANIA BOTANIST.

Examine this flourishing province, in whatever light you will, the eyes as well as the mind of a European traveller are equally

" That gentleman took me, another day, to dine with Mons. DE BEAUMENOIR, at his apartments in the Hôtel des Invalides, of which he was governor, and who had a daughter about to embark for New York, in the same packet that Mr. DE CREVECŒUR and I had taken passage. She was coming out to America, under ST. JOHN's protection, to marry M. DE LA FOREST, who was then French consul at New York, and afterwards became a man of some note, as a diplomatist under Napoleon, who raised him to the dignity of a baron of his empire. ST. JOHN himself had been made consul-general by King LOUIS.

" That kind friend took me, one morning, to visit BRISSOT DE WARVILLE, who served PHILIPPE D'EGALITE (father of King LOUIS PHILIPPE) in some capacity, and had apartments at his residence, the Palais Royale. There we were received by BRISSOT. The Marquis de Valady, son-in-law of the Marquis de Vaudreuil, presented me with a copy of ST. JOHN's letters, which I still possess. ST. JOHN was by nature, by education, and by his writings, a philanthropist; a man of serene temper, and pure benevolence. The milk of human kindness circulated in every vein. Of manners unassuming; prompt to serve, slow to censure; intelligent, beloved, and highly worthy of the esteem and respect he everywhere received. His society on shipboard was a treasure.

" He had a daughter, whose early history was marked by some passages sufficiently curious and eventful, to make her the heroine of a novel. She married Mr. OTTO, a French gentleman, who was an attaché, I think, to the consular office; and who rose under the revolutionary government of France to considerable diplomatic rank, even to the embassy of England, for a short time."

* This is the orthography in the original; and it is that which prevails in

delighted; because a diffusive happiness appears in every part,—happiness which is established on the broadest basis. The wisdom of LYCURGUS and SOLON never conferred on man one-half of the blessings and uninterrupted prosperity which the Pennsylvanians now possess: the name of PENN, that simple but illustrious citizen, does more honour to the English nation than those of many of their kings.

In order to convince you that I have not bestowed undeserved praises in my former letters on this celebrated government, and that either nature or the climate seems to be more favourable here to the arts and sciences, than to any other American province,—let us together, agreeably to your desire, pay a visit to Mr. JOHN BERTRAM, the first botanist in this new hemisphere, become such by a native impulse of disposition. It is to this simple man that America is indebted for several discoveries, and the knowledge of many new plants. I had been greatly prepossessed in his favour by the extensive correspondence which I knew he held with the most eminent Scotch and French botanists: I knew also that he had been honoured with that of Queen ULRICA, of Sweden.

His house is small, but decent; there was something peculiar in its first appearance, which seemed to distinguish it from those of his neighbours: a small tower in the middle of it, not only helped to strengthen it, but afforded convenient room for a staircase. Every disposition of the fields, fences, and trees, seemed to bear the marks of perfect order and regularity,—which, in rural affairs, always indicate a prosperous industry.

I was received at the door by a woman dressed extremely neat and simple, who, without courtesying, or any other ceremonial, asked me, with an air of benignity, who I wanted? I answered, "I should be glad to see Mr. BERTRAM." "If thee wilt step in and take a chair, I will send for him." "No," I said, "I had rather have the pleasure of walking through his farm; I shall easily find him out, with your directions." After a little time I perceived the Schuylkill, winding through delightful meadows, and soon cast my eyes on a new-made bank, which seemed greatly to confine its stream. After having walked on its top a considerable way, I at last reached the place where ten men were at work. I asked if any of them could tell me where Mr. BERTRAM was? An elderly-looking man, with wide trousers and a large leather apron on, look-

the *Scottish* branch of the family. But the botanist himself, and his immediate connexions, always wrote the name BARTRAM.

ing at me, said,—"My name is BERTRAM—dost thee want me?" "Sir, I am come on purpose to converse with you, if you can be spared from your labour." "Very easily," he answered; "I direct and advise more than I work." We walked toward the house, where he made me take a chair while he went to put on clean clothes; after which he returned and sat down by me. "The fame of your knowledge," said I, "in American botany—and your well-known hospitality—have induced me to pay you a visit, which I hope you will not think troublesome. I should be glad to spend a few hours in your garden." "The greatest advantage," replied he, "which I receive from what thee callest my botanical fame, is the pleasure which it often procureth me in receiving the visits of friends and foreigners. But our jaunt into the garden must be postponed for the present, as the bell is ringing for dinner." We entered into a large hall, where there was a long table full of victuals; at the lowest part sat his negroes, his hired men were next, then the family and myself; and at the head, the venerable father and his wife presided. Each reclined his head and said his prayers, divested of the tedious cant of some, and of the ostentatious style of others. "After the luxuries of our cities," observed he, "this plain fare must appear to thee a severe fast." "By no means, Mr. BERTRAM; this honest country dinner convinces me that you receive me as a friend and an old acquaintance." "I am glad of it, for thee art heartily welcome. I never knew how to use ceremonies; they are insufficient proofs of sincerity; our Society, besides, are utterly strangers to what the world calleth polite expressions. We treat others as we treat ourselves. I received yesterday a letter from Philadelphia, by which I understand thee art a Russian: what motives can possibly have induced thee to quit thy native country, and to come so far in quest of knowledge or pleasure? Verily it is a great compliment thee payest to this our young province, to think that anything it exhibiteth may be worthy thy attention." "I have been most amply repaid for the trouble of the passage. I view the present Americans as the seed of future nations, which will replenish this boundless continent. The Russians may be in some respects compared to you; we, likewise, are a new people,— new, I mean, in knowledge, arts, and improvements. Who knows what revolutions Russia and America may one day bring about! We are, perhaps, nearer neighbours than we imagine. I view with peculiar attention, all your towns,—I examine their situation, and the police,—for which many are already famous. Though their foundations are now so recent, and so well remembered,—yet their origin will puzzle posterity as much as we are now puzzled to ascertain the beginning of those which time has in some measure destroyed. Your new buildings, your streets, put me in mind of those of the city of *Pompeii*—where I was a few years ago : I attentively examined everything there, particularly the footpath which runs along the houses. They appeared to have been considerably worn by the great number of people which had once travelled over them. But now, how distant! neither builders nor proprietors remain : nothing is known!"

"Why, thee hast been a great traveller, for a man of thy years." "Few years, sir, will enable anybody to journey over a great tract of country; but it requires a superior degree of knowledge to gather harvests as we go. Pray, Mr. BERTRAM, what banks are those which you are making; to what purpose is so much expense and so much labour bestowed?" "Friend IWAN, no branch of industry was ever more profitable to any country, as well as the proprietors. The Schuylkill, in its many windings, once covered a great extent of ground, though its waters were but shallow even in our highest tides; and though some parts were always dry, yet the whole of this great tract presented to the eye nothing but a putrid swampy soil, useless, either for the plough or for the scythe. The proprietors of these grounds are now incorporated ; we yearly pay to the treasurer of the company a certain sum, which makes an aggregate superior to the casualties that generally happen, either by inundations or the musksquash.* It is owing to this happy contrivance that so many thousand acres of meadow have been rescued from the Schuylkill [and Delaware], which now both enricheth and embellisheth so much of the neighbourhood of our city. Our brethren of Salem, in New Jersey, have carried the art of banking to a still higher degree of perfection." "It is really an admirable contrivance, which greatly redounds to the honour of the parties concerned, and shows a spirit of discernment and perseverance which is highly praiseworthy ; if the Virginians would imitate your example, the state of their husbandry would greatly improve ; I have not heard of

---

* *Musquash*, the Indian name of the *musk rat* (*Fiber zibethicus*, L.) ; an animal well known in the United States for its troublesome operations of *burrowing* in embankments along streams.

any such association in any other parts of the continent; Pennsylvania, hitherto, seems to reign the unrivalled queen of these fair provinces. Pray, sir, what expense are you at, ere these grounds be fit for the scythe?" " The expenses are very considerable, particularly when we have land, brooks, trees, and brush to clear away; but such is the excellence of these bottoms, and the goodness of the grass for fattening of cattle, that the produce of three years pays all advances." Happy the country where nature has bestowed such rich treasures! Treasures superior to mines; I said, "If all this fair province is thus cultivated, no wonder it has acquired such reputation for the prosperity and the industry of its inhabitants." By this time the working part of the family had finished their dinner, and had retired with a decency and silence which pleased me much. Soon after I heard, as I thought, a distant concert of instruments. " However simple and pastoral your fare was, Mr. BERTRAM, this is the dessert of a prince; pray, what is this I hear?" " Thee must not be alarmed; it is of a piece with the rest of thy treatment, friend IWAN." Anxious, I followed the sound, and, by ascending the staircase, found that it was the effect of the wind through the strings of an Æolian harp, an instrument which I had never before seen. After dinner we quaffed an honest bottle of Madeira wine, without the irksome labour of toasts, healths, or sentiments; and then retired into his study.

I was no sooner entered, than I observed a coat of arms, in a gilt frame, with the name of JOHN BERTRAM. The novelty of such a decoration, in such a place, struck me; I could not avoid asking, " Does the Society of Friends take any pride in those armorial bearings, which sometimes serve as marks of distinction between families, and much oftener as food for pride and ostentation? " Thee must know (said he) that my father was a Frenchman;* he brought this piece of painting over with him. I keep it as a piece of family furniture, and as a memorial of his removal hither."

From his study we went into the garden, which contained a

---

* This is evidently a misapprehension on the part of the "Russian gentleman." JOHN BARTRAM, no doubt, had reference to his *remote ancestor*, the *Norman* "Frenchman," who "came with WILLIAM the Conqueror," and "settled in the north of England." *See his letter to* ARCHIBALD BARTRAM, anno 1761.

great variety of curious plants and shrubs ; some grew in a green-house, over the door of which were written these lines :—

"Slave to no sect, who takes no private road,
But looks through nature, up to nature's God."

He informed me that he had often followed General BOUQUET to Pittsburg, with the view of herborizing; that he had made useful collections in Virginia; and that he had been employed by the King of England to visit the two Floridas.

Our walks and botanical observations engrossed so much of our time, that the sun was almost down ere I thought of returning to Philadelphia; I regretted that the day had been so short, as I had not spent so rational a one for a long time before. I wanted to stay, yet was doubtful whether it would not appear improper, being an utter stranger. Knowing, however, that I was visiting the least ceremonious people in the world, I bluntly informed him of the pleasure I had enjoyed, and with the desire I had of staying a few days with him. " Thee art as welcome as if I was thy father ; thee art no stranger; thy desire of knowledge, thy being a foreigner, besides, entitleth thee to consider my house as thine own, as long as thee pleaseth ; use thy time with the most perfect freedom; I, too, shall do so myself." I thankfully accepted the kind invitation.

We went to view his favourite bank ; he showed me the principles and method on which it was erected; and we walked over the grounds which had been already drained. The whole store of nature's kind luxuriance seemed to have been exhausted on these beautiful meadows ; he made me count the amazing number of cattle and horses now feeding on solid bottoms, which but a few years before had been covered with water. Thence we rambled through his fields, where the rightangular fences, the heaps of pitched stones, the flourishing clover, announced the best hus-bandry, as well as the most assiduous attention. His cows were then returning home, deep-bellied, short-legged, having udders ready to burst; seeking, with seeming toil, to be delivered from the great exuberance they contained. He next showed me his orchard, formerly planted on a barren, sandy soil, but long since converted into one of the richest spots in that vicinage. " This (said he) is altogether the fruit of my own contrivance. I pur-chased, some years ago, the privilege of a small spring, about a mile and a half from hence, which at a considerable expense I have brought to this reservoir; therein I throw old lime, ashes, horse-dung, &c., and twice a week I let it run, thus impregnated. I regularly spread on this ground, in the fall, old hay, straw, and whatever damaged fodder I have about my barn. By these simple means I mow, one year with another, fifty-three hundreds of excellent hay per acre, from a soil which scarcely produced *five fingers* [i. e., *Cinquefoil*, or *Potentilla Canadensis, L.*] some years before." "This is, sir, a miracle in husbandry; happy the country which is cultivated by a society of men whose application and taste lead them to prosecute and accomplish useful works." "I am not the only person who do these things (he said); wherever water can be had, it is always turned to that important use; wherever a farmer can water his meadows, the greatest crops of the best hay, and excellent after-grass, are the sure rewards of his labours. With the banks of my meadow ditches, I have greatly enriched my upland fields; those which I intend to rest for a few years, I constantly sow with red clover, which is the greatest meliorator of our lands. For three years after, they yield abundant pasture; when I want to break up my clover fields, I give them a good coat of mud, which hath been exposed to the severities of three or four of our winters. This is the reason that I commonly reap from twenty-eight to thirty-six bushels of wheat an acre; my flax, oats, and Indian corn I raise in the same proportion. Wouldst thee inform me whether the inhabitants of thy country follow the same methods of husbandry?" "No, sir; in the neighbourhood of our towns there are indeed some intelligent farmers who prosecute their rural schemes with attention; but we should be too numerous, too happy, too powerful a people, if it were possible for the whole Russian empire to be cultivated like the province of Pennsylvania. Our lands are so unequally divided, and so few of our farmers are possessors of the soil they till, that they cannot execute plans of husbandry with the same vigour as you do, who hold yours, as it were, from the master of nature, unincumbered and free. Oh, America!" exclaimed I, "thou knowest not, as yet, the whole extent of thy happiness; the foundation of thy civil polity must lead thee, in a few years, to a degree of population and power which Europe little thinks of!" "Long before this happens (answered the good man) we shall rest beneath the turf; it is vain for mortals to be presumptuous in their conjectures; our country is, no doubt, the cradle of an extensive future population; the old world is growing

weary of its inhabitants; they must come here to flee from the
tyranny of the great. But doth not thee imagine that the great
will, in the course of years, come over here also? for it is the
misfortune of all societies everywhere to hear of great men, great
rulers, and of great tyrants." "My dear sir," I replied, "tyranny
never can take a strong hold in this country, the land is too wisely
distributed; it is poverty in Europe that makes slaves." "Friend
IWAN, as I make no doubt thee understandest the Latin tongue,
read this kind epistle which the good Queen of Sweden, ULRICA,
sent me a few years ago. Good woman! that she should think, in
her palace at Stockholm, of poor JOHN BERTRAM on the banks of
the Schuylkill, appeareth to me very strange." "Not in the least,
dear sir; you are the first man whose name as a botanist hath done
honour to America; it is very natural at the same time to imagine
that so extensive a continent must contain many curious plants and
trees; is it then surprising to see a princess, fond of useful knowledge, descend sometimes from the throne, to walk in the gardens
of LINNÆUS?" "'Tis to the directions of that learned man (said
Mr. BERTRAM) that I am indebted for the method which has led
me to the knowledge I now possess; the science of botany is so
diffusive, that a proper thread is absolutely wanted to conduct the
beginner." "Pray, Mr. BERTRAM, when did you imbibe the first
wish to cultivate the science of botany? Was you regularly bred to
it in Philadelphia?" "I have never received any other education
than barely reading and writing; this small farm was all the patri-
mony my father left me; certain debts, and the want of meadows,
kept me rather low in the beginning of my life; my wife brought me
nothing in money, all her riches consisted in her good temper and
great knowledge of housewifery. I scarcely know how to trace my
steps in the botanical career; they appear to me, now, like unto a
dream; but thee mayest rely on what I shall relate, though I know
that some of our friends have laughed at it." "I am not one of
those people, Mr. BERTRAM, who aim at finding out the ridiculous,
in what is sincerely and honestly averred." "Well, then, I'll tell
thee. One day I was very busy in holding my plough (for thee
seest I am but a ploughman), and being weary, I ran under the
shade of a tree to repose myself. I cast my eyes on a *daisy*; I
plucked it mechanically, and viewed it with more curiosity than
common country farmers are wont to do, and observed therein very
many distinct parts, some perpendicular—some horizontal. *What*

a shame, said my mind, or something that inspired my mind, that thee shouldst have employed so many years in tilling the earth, and destroying so many flowers and plants, without being acquainted with their structures and their uses! This seeming inspiration suddenly awakened my curiosity, for these were not thoughts to which I had been accustomed. I returned to my team, but this new desire did not quit my mind; I mentioned it to my wife, who greatly discouraged me from prosecuting my new scheme, as she called it; I was not opulent enough, she said, to dedicate much of my time to studies and labours which might rob me of that portion of it which is the only wealth of the American farmer. However, her prudent caution did not discourage me; I thought about it continually,—at supper, in bed, and wherever I went. At last, I could not resist the impulse ; for on the fourth day of the following week, I hired a man to plough for me, and went to Philadelphia. Though I knew not what book to call for, I ingenuously told the bookseller my errand, who provided me with such as he thought best, and a Latin grammar beside. Next, I applied to a neighbouring schoolmaster, who, in three months, taught me Latin enough to understand LINNÆUS, which I purchased afterward. Then I began to botanize all over my farm. In a little time I became acquainted with every vegetable that grew in my neighbourhood; and next ventured into Maryland, living among the Friends. In proportion as I thought myself more learned, I proceeded farther, and by a steady application of several years, I have acquired a pretty general knowledge of every plant and tree to be found in our Continent. In process of time I was applied to from the old countries, whither I every year send many collections. Being now made easy in my circumstances, I have ceased to labour, and am never so happy as when I see and converse with my friends. If, among the many plants or shrubs I am acquainted with, there are any thee wantest to send to thy native country, I will cheerfully procure them ; and give thee, moreover, whatever directions thee mayest want."

Thus I passed several days, in ease, improvement, and pleasure. I observed, in all the operations of his farm—as well as in the mutual correspondence between the master and the inferior members of his family—the greatest ease and decorum : not a word like command seemed to exceed the tone of a simple wish. The very negroes, themselves, appeared to partake of such a decency of behaviour, and modesty of countenance, as I had never before observed. "By what means," said I, "Mr. BERTRAM, do you rule your slaves so well, that they seem to do their work with all the cheerfulness of white men?" "Though our erroneous prejudices and opinions once induced us to look upon them as fit only for slavery,—though ancient custom had very unfortunately taught us to keep them in bondage,—yet of late, in consequence of the remonstrances of several Friends, and of the good books they have published on that subject, our Society treats them very differently. With us they are now free. I give those whom thee didst see at my table, eighteen pounds a year, with victuals and clothes, and all other privileges which white men enjoy. Our Society treats them, now, as the companions of our labours; and by this management, as well as by means of the education we have given them, they are in general become a new set of beings. Those whom I admit to my table, I have found to be good, trusty, moral men: when they do not what we think they should do, we dismiss them, which is all the punishment we inflict. Other societies of Christians keep them still as slaves, without teaching them any kind of religious principles. What motive, beside fear, can they have to behave well? In the first settlement of this province, we employed them as slaves, I acknowledge; but when we found that good example, gentle admonition, and religious principles could lead them to subordination and sobriety, we relinquished a method so contrary to the profession of Christianity. We gave them freedom; and yet few have quitted their ancient masters. * * * * I taught mine to read and to write: they love God, and fear his judgments. The oldest person among them transacts my business in Philadelphia, with a punctuality from which he has never deviated. They constantly attend our meetings: they participate —in health and sickness, in infancy and old age—in the advantages our Society affords. Such are the means we have made use of, to relieve them from that bondage and ignorance in which they were kept before. Thee, perhaps, hast been surprised to see them at my table; but, by elevating them to the rank of freemen, they necessarily acquire that emulation, without which we ourselves should fall into debasement and profligate ways."

"Mr. BERTRAM, this is the most philosophical treatment of negroes that I have heard of. Happy would it be for America, would other denominations of Christians imbibe the same principles, and follow the same admirable rules. A great number of men would be relieved from those cruel shackles under which they now groan: and under this impression, I cannot endure to spend more time in the southern provinces. The method with which they are treated there,—the meanness of their food—the severity of their tasks,—are spectacles I have not patience to behold." "I am glad to see that thee hast so much compassion. Are there any slaves in thy country?" "Yes, unfortunately; but they are more properly civil than domestic slaves: they are attached to the soil on which they live; it is the remains of ancient barbarous customs, established in the days of the greatest ignorance and savageness of manners! and preserved, notwithstanding the repeated tears of humanity—the loud calls of policy—and the commands of religion. The pride of great men, with the avarice of landholders, makes them look on this class as necessary tools of husbandry; as if freemen could not cultivate the ground!" "And is it really so, friend Iwan? To be poor, to be wretched, to be a slave, is hard indeed: existence is not worth enjoying on those terms. I am afraid thy country can never flourish under such impolitic government." "I am very much of your opinion, Mr. Bertram, though I am in hopes that the present reign, illustrious by so many acts of the soundest policy, will not expire without this salutary—this necessary emancipation, which would fill the Russian Empire with tears of gratitude." "How long hast thee been in this country?" "Four years, sir." "Why, thee speakest English almost like a native. What a toil a traveller must undergo, to learn various languages— to divest himself of his native prejudices—and to accommodate himself to the customs of all those among whom he chooseth to reside."

Thus I spent my time with this enlightened botanist—this worthy citizen,—who united all the simplicity of rustic manners to the most useful learning. Various and extensive were the conversations that filled the measure of my visit. I accompanied him to his fields—to his barn—to his bank—to his garden—to his study—and at last to the meeting of the Society, on the Sunday following. It was at the town of Chester, whither the whole family went, in two wagons; Mr. Bertram and I on horseback. When I entered the house where the Friends were assembled,—who might be about two hundred, men and women,—the involuntary impulse of ancient custom made me pull off my hat; but soon recovering myself, I sat with it on, at the end of a bench. The meeting-house was a square building, devoid of any ornament whatever. The whiteness of the walls—the conveniency of seats —that of a large stove, which in cold weather keeps the whole house warm,—were the only essential things which I observed. Neither pulpit nor desk, fount nor altar, tabernacle nor organ, were there to be seen: it is merely a spacious room, in which these good people meet every Sunday. A profound silence ensued, which lasted about half an hour; every one had his head reclined, and seemed absorbed in profound meditation,—when a female Friend arose, and declared, with a most engaging modesty, that the Spirit moved her to entertain them on the subject she had chosen. She treated it with great propriety, as a moral, useful discourse, and delivered it without theological parade, or the ostentation of learn- ing. Either she must have been a great adept in public speaking, or had studiously prepared herself; a circumstance that cannot well be supposed, as it is a point, in their profession, to utter nothing but what arises from spontaneous impulse: or else the Great Spirit of the world—the patronage and influence of which they all came to invoke—must have inspired her with the soundest morality. Her discourse lasted three quarters of an hour. I did not observe one single face turned toward her: never before had I seen a con- gregation listening with so much attention to a public oration. I observed neither contortions of body, nor any kind of affectation in her face, style, or manner of utterance; everything was natural, and therefore pleasing, and, shall I tell you more? she was very handsome, although upward of forty. As soon as she had finished, every one seemed to return to their former meditation for about a quarter of an hour, when they rose up by common consent, and, after some general conversation, departed.

How simple their precepts,—how unadorned their religious system, how few the ceremonies through which they pass during the course of their lives! At their deaths they are interred by the fraternity, without pomp, without prayers,—thinking it then too late to alter the course of God's eternal decrees; and, as you well know, without either monument or tomb-stone. Thus, after having lived under the mildest government, after having been guided by the mildest doctrine, they die just as peaceably as those who, being educated in more pompous religions, pass through a variety of sacraments, subscribe to complicated creeds, and enjoy the benefits of a church establishment. These good people flatter themselves with following the doctrines of Jesus Christ, in that simplicity with which they were delivered. A happier system could not have been devised for the use of mankind. It appears to be entirely free from those ornaments and political additions which each country and each government hath fashioned after its own manners.

At the door of this meeting-house I had been invited to spend some days at the houses of some respectable farmers in the neighbourhood. The reception I met with everywhere, insensibly led me to spend two months among these good people; and I must say they were the golden days of my riper years. I never shall forget the gratitude I owe them for the innumerable kindnesses they heaped on me : it was to the letter you gave me, that I am indebted for the extensive acquaintance I now have throughout Pennsylvania. I must defer thanking you as I ought, until I see you again. Before that time comes, I may perhaps entertain you with more curious anecdotes than this letter affords. Farewell.

Iw——n Al————tz.

September y 17 1760

Dear Cousen

thee would oblige me much if thee would be so kind as to gather me a parcel of firing tree seeds & if it happens in thy way some black ash & a fair specimen of that plant so likey Madiola that I hardly know y difference (a) — I hope to come up in y fall to thy house & if thee comes up to town soon I hope thee will not go by without calling upon me. my garden now makes a glorious appearance with y Virginia & Carolina flowers —
My kind love to thy wife & to uncle & aunt we are all my fami-ly in good health. God Almighty be praised who alone is worthy of all Glory & honour to endless eternity

pray accept y respects & friendship of thy sincere Cousen
in hast

John Bartram

To Humphrey Marshal

(a) [Probably Bejaria verticillata, matt]

LETTERS

FROM PETER COLLINSON * TO JOHN BARTRAM.

London, Jan. 20, 1734–5.

MY GOOD FRIEND JOHN BARTRAM :
I now do myself a further pleasure to consider thy curious entertaining letters of November 6. I am only afraid, in doing me a

* PETER COLLINSON, F.R.S., and F.S.A., one of the earliest and most constant
correspondents of LINNÆUS, was highly distinguished in the circle of naturalists
and antiquaries in London, for nearly half a century. He belonged to the
Society of Quakers ; and his upright, benevolent, active character did honour to
his religious persuasion. He was born January 28, 1693–4, in a house opposite
to Church Alley, St. Clement's Lane, Lombard Street, London ; but he resided for
many years at the Red Lion, in Grace Church Street, as a wholesale woollen
draper, where he acquired an ample fortune. He married in 1724, MARY, the
daughter of MICHAEL RUSSELL, Esq., of Mill Hill, Hendon. This lady died in
1753, leaving him two children,—a son named MICHAEL, and a daughter MARY,
married to the late JOHN CATOR, Esq., of Beckenham, Kent. They are said to
have inherited much of the taste and amiable character of their father.

Mr. COLLINSON appears to have occupied, in the earlier part of his life, a
country-house and garden at Peckham, in Surrey (where his brother had also
a garden) ; from whence he removed in April, 1749, to Ridgeway House at Mill
Hill, and he was two years in transplanting his collection. The English gardens
are indebted to him for the introduction of many new and curious species, which
he acquired by means of an extensive correspondence, particularly from North
America. Among these was the *Collinsonia Canadensis*, so called by LINNÆUS,
who has given a beautiful engraving of this plant, in his *Hortus Cliffortianus*. It
was first imported (sent by JOHN BARTRAM), in 1735. He enjoyed throughout
a long life, the communications of most cultivators of science in general, for he
interested himself about every new or useful discovery, and was one of the first
who attended to the (then recent) wonders of electricity ; on which subject the
great FRANKLIN was obliged to him for the earliest European intelligence.

Nor was his personal friendship less valued by people of distinguished character
and abilities in various ranks, among which the names of DERHAM, SLOANE, ELLIS,
and FOTHERGILL stand pre-eminent ; as well as those of the accomplished ROBERT
Lord PETRE, who died in 1742, and the famous Earl of Bute.

Mr. COLLINSON became acquainted with LINNÆUS, when the latter visited
London in 1736. He died August 11, 1768, after a short illness, in the 75th year
of his age, in the full possession of all his faculties, and of all his enthusiasm

pleasure, so much time was lost which would turn to a more profitable account in thy own affairs.

Thee writes for some botanical books; and indeed I am at a loss which to recommend, for, as I have observed, a complete history of plants is not to be found in any author. For the present, I am persuaded the gentlemen of the Library Company, at my request, will indulge thee the liberty, when thee comes to town, to peruse their botanical books: there is MILLER's *Dictionary*, and some others.

Please to remember those Solomon's Seals, that escaped thee last year.

The great and small Hellebore are great rarities here, so pray send a root or two of each next year. Please to remember all your sorts of lilies, as they happen in thy way; and your spotted Martagons will be very acceptable.

The Devil's Bit, or Blazing Star, pray add a root or two, and any of the Lady's Slippers.

My dear friend, I only mention these plants; but I beg of thee not to neglect thy more material affairs to oblige me. A great many may be put in a box 20 inches or 2 feet square, and 15 or 16 inches high;—and a foot in earth is enough. This may be put under the captain's bed, or set in the cabin, if it is sent in October or November. Nail a few small narrow laths across it, to keep the cats from scratching it.

If thee could procure some layers of the woody vine, with variegated leaves, it would be acceptable: also, a root of the *Aristolochia* [by this is meant the *Saururus cernuus*, L., then called Aristolochia, by some], which is of such sovereign remedy for sore breasts, would be well worth having.

I hope thee had mine, per Captain DAVIS, with a box with seeds in sand, and two parcels of seeds per my good friend ISAAC NORRIS, Jr. One parcel I sent after him to the Downs; but whether he

for the beauties of Nature, attended by far more important consolations and supports.

The Philosophical Transactions and the *Archæologia* are enriched with several of Mr. COLLINSON's papers. Dr. FOTHERGILL published an account of his life.

The garden at Mill Hill, so assiduously cultivated by this gentleman and his son, and for many years abounding with rarities and beauties, fell afterwards into most barbarous and tasteless hands. After a transient restoration by an eminent botanist, it is now (1821), as far as we can learn, almost entirely stripped of its chief curiosities.—*See* BIOGRAPHICAL MEMOIR *in the first volume of the Correspondence of* LINNÆUS, *and other Naturalists; by Sir* JAMES EDWARD SMITH.

was sailed, or no, before it came to hand, I can't say : but by the list inclosed, thee will know if they are come to hand, or if he had them.

Pray what is your Sarsaparilla? The May-apple, a pretty plant, is what I have had for some years sent me per Doctor WITT. It flowers well with us ; but our summers are not hot enough to perfect its fruit.

The pretty humble beautiful plant, with a spike of yellow flowers, I take to be a species of *Orchis* or *Satyrion.* What sort of root it has thee hath not mentioned. If it is taken up with the earth about the roots, it will certainly flower the first, if not the second year. I wish thee'd send me two or three roots, if it is plenty.

The Ground Cypress is a singular pretty plant. If it bears berries or seeds, pray send some ; and if it bears flowers or seeds, pray send some specimens in both states.

Pray send me a good specimen or two of the shrub, 3 feet high, that grows by the water courses. The shrub that grows out of the sides of rocks, sometimes five or six feet high, bearing red berries hanging by the husks, is called *Euonymus,* or Spindle tree. We have the same plant, with a small difference ; grows plenty in England.

Your wild Senna, with yellow flowers, is a pretty plant. Send seeds of both this and Mountain Goat's Rue.

Thee need not collect any more of the White Thorn berries, that has prodigious long, sharp thorns. It is what we call the Cock-spur Thorn. I had a tree last year, that had at least a bushel of berries. But haws of any other sort of Thorns will be very acceptable.

Pray send me a root or two of cluster-bearing Solomon's Seal. It is in all appearance a very rare plant,—as is the *Panax.*

Pray send a root or two of JOSEPH BREINTNALL'S Snake-root.* Pray send a root of the grassy leaves, that bears pretty little blue flowers,—that's good against obstructions of the bowels, [probably *Sisyrinchium,* L.]

When it happens in thy way, send me a root or two of the little tuberous root called Devil's Bit, which produces one or two leaves yearly.

---

* In a subsequent communication, it appears that DILLENIUS pronounced "BREINTNALL'S Snake-root," to be " *Sanicula Canadensis,* amplissimo folio laciniato, of TOURNEFORT."—See P. COLLINSON'S Letter to JOSEPH BREINTNALL, 1738.

I only barely mention these plants; not that I expect thee to send them. I don't expect or desire them, but as they happen to be found accidentally : and what is not to be met with one year, may be another.

It happens that your late ships, in the autumn, come away before a great many of our seeds are ripe, and the spring I don't approve as the best season to send them; but as it rarely happens otherwise, I have taken a method to send some in paper, and some in sand. After thee has picked out the largest, which must be instantly set, for very probably they were chilled coming over. When it is my case, as it often happens, taking the following method, I have raised a great many pretty plants out of your earth. I lay out a bed 5 or 6 feet long by 3 feet wide ; then I pare off the earth an inch or two deep, then I loosen the bottom, and lay it very smooth again, and thereon, (if I may use the term,) I sow the sand and seed together as thin as I can, then I sift some good earth over it about half an inch thick. This bed ought to be in some place that it may not be disturbed, and kept very clear from weeds; for several seeds come not up till the second year. I have put some hard-shelled Almonds of my own growth, and some soft-shelled from Portugal : they are easily distinguished.

The almond makes a fine pie, taken whilst a pin can be run through them; for you eat husk, shell, and kernel, altogether. They must be first coddled over a gentle fire, and then put in crust. I query whether young peaches would be as good, before the shell is hard.

I have put in the sand some vine cuttings, and some of the great Neapolitan Medlar, which we always graft on white thorns, and so must you. As soon as these cuttings come to hand, soak them all over in water for twenty-four hours, and then plant the vines (the earth being well loosened) as deep as only the uppermost bud of the cutting may be level with the earth. Water them in dry weather. These seldom fail growing. The grafts, after soaking, may be laid in the earth, or in a moist place, till grafted, which should be soon.

I hope thee will take these two long rambling epistles in good part. They are writ, a bit now and then, as business will permit. Let me hear from thee at thy leisure, which will much oblige thy real friend,

P. COLLINSON.

Send a quantity of seed of the Birch or Black Beech; it seems to be new.   Send me a good root of the Swallow-wort, or *Apocinon*, with narrow leaves and orange-coloured flowers; and of the pretty shrub called Red Root, and of the Cotton-weed or Life-everlasting, and some more seed of the perannual Pea, that grows by rivers; this year, or next, or next after, as it happens. Pray send me a walking-cane, of the Cane-wood.

London, January 24th, 1735.

My good friend, John Bartram:—

I am very much obliged to thee for thy two choice cargoes of plants, which came very safe and in good condition, and are very curious and rare, and well worth my acceptance.   I am very sensible of the great pains, and many tiresome steps, to collect so many rare plants scattered at a distance.   I shall not forget it; but in some measure to show my gratitude, though not in proportion to thy trouble, I have sent thee a small token: a calico gown for thy wife, and some odd little things that may be of use amongst the children and family.   They come in a box of books to my worthy friend, Joseph Breintnall, with another parcel of waste paper, which will serve to wrap up seeds, &c.   But there is two quires of brown, and one of whited-brown paper, which I propose for this use and purpose, and will save thee a great deal of trouble in writing: that is, when thee observes a curious plant in flower, or when thee gathers seed of a plant thee has an intention to convey me a description of, on both these occasions, thee has nothing more to do than to gather branches or sprigs of the plants, then in flower, with their flowers on, and with their seed-vessels fully formed; for by these two characteristics, the genus is known that they belong to.   Then take these, and spread them between the sheets of brown paper, laying the stems straight and leaves smooth and regular; and when this is done, put a moderate weight on a board the size of the paper.   In two days remove the specimens into the other quire of brown paper, keeping the weight on; and then in a week or two, being pretty well dried, convey them thence into the quire of whited-brown paper.   Thus, when now and then thee observes a curious plant, thee may treat it in this manner, by which thee will convey a more lively idea than the best description; and when thee gathers seeds, mark the same number on the

seeds as thee marks in the sheet where the specimen is, only writing
under it the country name. So, once a year, return me the quire
of whited-brown paper, with the dried specimens tied fast between
two broad boards; and then I will send some more in their room.
When the sheet of paper will hold it, put one, two, or three specimens of the same plant in the same sheet, so they will but lie
smooth by each other.

Besides, what I have further to propose, per this method, is, thy
own improvement in the knowledge of plants; for thou shalt send
me another quire of duplicates of the same specimens; I will get
them named by our most knowing botanists, and then return them
again, which will improve thee more than books; for it is impossible for any one author to give a general history of plants. Let
the specimens be of the length of the paper.

Thee canst not think how well the little case of plants came,
being put under the captain's bed, and saw not the light till I went
for it; but then, Captain WRIGHT had a very quick passage; and
it was put on board in a right month, for when plants are down in
the ground, and in the winter months, they may be stowed anywhere; but it must not be attempted any time this side Christmas.

The warmth of the ship, and want of air, had occasioned the
Skunk-weed to put forth two fine blossoms, very beautiful; but it
is of the *Arum* genus. The *Sedum* is a very rare pretty plant,
the leaves finely veined; it came very fresh and green. Thy herb
Twopence was very acceptable. I have had it, formerly, but I lost
it. It is a pretty plant.

The Cane-wood is pretty common in our gardens. It goes,
here, by the name of the Virginian Guelder Rose [*Spiræa opuli-
folia, L.?*]. The two laurels were very fresh and lively; and the
shrub honeysuckles, which I have had formerly from South Carolina, flower very fine, but in two or three years went off. Neither
our soil nor climate agreed with it; but yours, perhaps, from the
northward, may do better. The laurel and shrub honeysuckle are
plants I much value.

I wish, at a proper season, thee would procure a strong box,
two feet square, and about fifteen or eighteen inches deep,—but a
foot deep in mould will be enough; then collect half a dozen
Laurels, and half a dozen shrub Honeysuckles, and plant in this box;
but be sure make the bottom of the box full of large holes, and
cover the holes with tiles, or oyster-shells, to let the water drain

better off. Then let this box stand in a proper place in thy
garden, for two or three years, till the plants have taken good
root, and made good shoots; but thee must be careful to water it
in dry weather.

I wish that thee would not fail to put three or four specimens of
the sprigs of the Laurel, with the flowers fully blown (for I long to
see it) in the paper, transferring them from one to another, as I
have directed. As my design is not to give thee more trouble, so
a few specimens will content me.

I have further to request thee to put up a little box of plants
(yearly) in earth, such as thou finds in the woods, that are odd and
uncommon.

What thee observes of the frost, to be sure, had the effect thee
describes. I once remember one like it in England; but the effects
were not so severe. I hope, next year, thee will be able to make
some selections that may make thee some returns.

The White Flowering Bay [*Magnolia glauca, L.*] is a plant
that grows in moist places; the leaves are long, of a bay shape,
and of a silver colour on the back of the leaves. It bears a fine
large white flower, like the Water Lily, of a fine perfumed smell,
which is succeeded with a seed-vessel of a cone-like figure. I have
a plant that flowers finely, in my garden. It is in abundance of
places, in Maryland; but whether it is found more northward, I
can't say. It is a fine plant to adorn thy own garden. But give
thyself no trouble about it: and, as the Fir and Cypress cones are
not found near thee, we will wait for some more favourable opportunity to collect them. Send first those seeds that are near thee.

The box of seeds came very safe, and in good order. Thy
remarks on them are very curious; but I think take up too much
of thy time and thought. I would not make my correspondence
burdensome; but must desire thee to continue the same collections
over again; and to prevent trouble, only number the papers, and
give the country name—or any name thee may know it by again;
then keep a list of them by thee, with the number to the names,
and when they come here, those that do not come up, we have only
to write to thee for the same seed to such a number, to send over
again. As I design to make a present of part of these seeds to
a very curious person [Lord PETRE,] I hope to procure thee some
present for thy trouble of collecting. I am thy very sincere friend,

P. COLLINSON.

London, Feb. 12, 1735.

DEAR FRIEND JOHN BARTRAM:

Though I am vastly hurried in business, and no leisure, yet the many instances of thy regard for us obliges me to steal time to say something farther to thy kind letters.

I am glad the roots, in a box per Captain WRIGHT, came to hand, and were acceptable. I received the box of berries, fresh and in good order. The Sassafras was a fine parcel, and the cherry-stones, and several others, are what we had not before. I sent them to our noble friend.

The leaves of that Golden Rod are finely scented. Pray, have we any of the seed? Now, dear friend, I have done with thine of the 9th of September. And now I shall only tell thee, I have received thine of November 18th, December 1st, and the 9th, and thine of the 10th, with the invoices. * * * * *

The box of specimens, with the seeds, came very dry, safe, and well. I think thee has discharged that affair very elegantly, and gives us great pleasure; and conveys to us stronger ideas of your plants than can be described, and saves a great deal of writing. I shall, at my first leisure, send thee their true botanical names, and I shall send thee more paper; but one quire a year will be sufficient.

The box of insects was very prettily and nicely put up, and described: but pray chain up that unruly creature, the Smith, that he may do us no more damage, next time. I shall have some fresh requests to make, as to insects; which, by enclosed instructions, thee may learn thy little boys to catch, and I will reward them.

Thee will hear at large from me, when I have opportunity to discourse with thy noble patron.

All the things thee wrote for, I shall send; the small things, by ISRAEL PEMBERTON, and the box of nails per Captain SAVAGE, or some other ship, which, I am not yet determined; but I shall acquaint thee with it.

But I almost forgot thy noble present of plants, which came very safe and well, to all appearance, and contains a many curious plants. This year, pray rest a little from thy labours. I shall only ask of thee one set of plants;—and that is, all the sorts of Ladies' Slippers thee happens to meet with, if not far to fetch, for I expect none from the Doctor [WITT]. He has, indeed, sent me a few seeds, but they are fine sorts—the large *Jacea,* or Blazing Star [*Liatris spicata, Willd.*], and two sorts of seeds of Martagons, and *Clinopodium,* a fine plant.

I have got a box of chestnuts, in sand, and some Spanish nuts, and some of our Katherine peach-stones. It is the last (and a large) peach that ripens with us in October, but will sooner with you. It is a hard, sound, well-flavoured peach—none better, and clings to the stone. In the little box that the insects came in, are some seeds. The China Aster is the noblest and finest plant thee ever saw, of that tribe. It was sent per the Jesuits from China to France; from thence to us: it is an annual. Sow it in rich mould, immediately, and when it has half a dozen leaves, transplant in the borders. It makes a glorious autumn flower. There is white and purple in the seeds.

The Lebanon cone, with a knife carefully pick out the seeds; sow in a box, but large holes in the bottom, and cover with shells, in sandy light mould. Let it only have the morning sun.

I sent two parcels of the Aster, for fear, by sowing late, it should not ripen seed. I have sent the Doctor some.

I am, my dear friend, with hearty acknowledgments for all thy pains and trouble, and thy many favours,

In haste, thine sincerely,

P. COLLINSON.

The Spanish chestnuts, &c., come in a little box, in sand, committed to the care of ISRAEL PEMBERTON.

We have been largely supplied with Chinquapins from Virginia, but I design thee shall have the credit and profit of them, for our noble friend knows nothing but that they come from thee. I can easily be supplied from that country; so give thyself no further trouble about them, for I know they grow not near you to the perfection they do in that country.

But one thing, dear JOHN, I must request of thee. Our curious botanists are sadly perplexed about the difference between the Red and White Cedars.* Pray be so kind to gather three or four specimens of each sort, of the size of the paper, branches with their leaves; and when dried, send by first opportunity, the size and height of each sort, and their uses, and a few berries of each sort

* The *red* Cedar is *Juniperus Virginiana,* L., and the *white* Cedar is *Cupressus thyoides,* L.

by way of sample; the Red we have, but want seeds of the White
Cedar. One of my curious friends is writing a book, and wants to
insert the cedars, red and white, and show their difference, which
is not particularly described by any author. So pray be exact,
and thee'll much oblige thine,

P. C.

London, February 20th, 1735.

Respected Friend J. Bartram :—

I have sent the goods, as under, which I hope will meet with
thy approbation; and as there was no direction, either to quality
or quantity, I have done the best of my judgment. When I have
settled with our noble friend, who takes all the cargo to his own
account, I will advise thee of the balance.

Young Israel Pemberton, to whom thou art much obliged, at
my request, has packed up thy goods with his. *   *   *

Whatever thou finds is not charged in thy bill of parcels, is
presents for thyself, wife, and children. Receive it in love, as it
was sent. I shall write thee fuller on all matters, the first leisure.

I have procured from my knowing friend, Philip Miller, gardener to the Physic Garden at Chelsea, belonging to the Company
of Apothecaries, sixty-nine sorts of curious seeds, and some others
of my own collecting. This, I hope, will convince thee I do what
I can; and if I lived, as thou does, always in the country, I should
do more; but in my situation it is impossible. Besides, most of the
plants thou writes for, are not to be found in gardens, but growing
spontaneously a many miles off, and a many miles from one another.
It is not to be expected I can do as thou does. My inclination's
good, but I have affairs of greater consequence to mind; and as I
have observed to thee before, affairs of this nature should not interfere with business, and I do request thee not to suffer anything
thee does for us to interfere with thine. Indeed, for the cargo
thou sent, there was some reason for thy making it thy business,
because thee will have some gratification; but in thy other curious
collections, which is done purely to oblige us, pray give thy business
the preference; but if, in the course of that, without neglecting it,
thou can pick up what thou thinks will be acceptable, we shall be
obliged to thee, and study some requital. So for the future, no
more censure me for not sending the one-sixth part thee wrote for,

for the reasons above ; but yet transmit me yearly what thou wants, and anything in my power, or my friend MILLER'S, will be always at thy service; and if I send thee the same thing two or three times over, thee must excuse it, and place it to the multiplicity of affairs that fill my thoughts, and not suspect my care ; and then thee will deal kindly, and friendly, and lovingly, by

P. COLLINSON.

All these seeds come in JOSEPH BREINTNALL'S packet.

London, March 1st, 1735.

KIND FRIEND JOHN BARTRAM :—

I am now just returned to town from paying a visit to a noble lord, my most valuable and intimate friend. One of my proposals, I sent thee last year, to collect the seeds of your forest trees, was for him, as he is a universal lover of plants. I presented him with a share of the seeds thou sent last year, which was very acceptable. As he is a man of a noble and generous spirit, he very rationally considered thy pains and trouble in collecting them, and desired to make thee some returns, and left it to me. I thought a good suit of clothes, for thy own wear, might be as acceptable as anything, so have sent thee one, with all appurtenances necessary for its making up, which I hope will meet with thy approbation, and help in some measure to compensate for thy loss of time.

My noble friend desires thee to continue the same collections. Send the same sorts over again, and what new ones happens in thy way, and sent at the same time o' year, and in the same manner, will do very well. Please to look in my other letter for my further remarks on this head.

All the seeds were in good order, except the Allspice seed, which was musty. Perhaps that was owing to the dampness of the roots put up for Sir HANS SLOANE. For the future, put up no moist thing with the seeds, but send them in a little box by themselves.

If thee can compass to send thirty or forty sorts of your herbaceous seeds every year, it will be sufficient. As to invoice of forest tree seeds, their quantity and price is fixed, so thee knows what thee does. Thee has had great luck, hitherto, in sending the seeds in good order ; I hope the like will attend thee in the forest tree seeds. I refer thee to my letters on that head, sent with the catalogues.

As our noble friend will be always grateful, I hope it will encourage thee to go on ; but yet I would have thee so proceed as not to interfere with thy private business. Indeed, the forest tree seeds I hope will bring money into thy pocket; so the time spent in making the collection cannot be said to be lost or misspent. * *

I hope thee hath mine per Captain RICHMOND ; with a parcel in the Library Company's trunk, and a box of seeds, in sand, per RICHMOND. I heartily wish thee and thine health and prosperity, and am   Thy real friend,

                                                    P. COLLINSON.

Pray give nobody a hint, how thee or thy wife came by the suit of clothes. There may be some, with you, may think they deserve something of that nature.

If thee observes any curious insects, beetles, butterflies, &c., they are easily preserved, being pinned through the body to the inside of a little box. When it is full, send it nailed up, and put nothing within it, and they will come very safe. Display the wings of the butterflies with pins, and rub off the down as little as possible. When thee goes abroad, put a little box in thy pocket, and as thee meets with them put them in, and then stick them in the other box when thee comes home. I want a *Terrapin* or two. Put them in a box with earth, and they will come safe. They will live a long while without food.

                                        London, August 16th, 1735.

KIND FRIEND JOHN BARTRAM :—

I had the pleasure of thine of June 13th, and am pleased the things was acceptable. I have sent the little box of seeds to our noble friend. What he raises, I have always share of. The large invoice that I sent thee was for him. I hope this will prove a good seed year, that thee may be able to send a cargo which will produce thee some money here.

The Water Beech, or Button-wood, is known here as the Western Plane, and is in great plenty here, and makes a noble tree. Thee need not send any, for it is raised plentifully by cuttings. But as for the Linden, or Lime tree, for aught I know, it may be a stranger, so pray send some seed.

There are two captains, RICHMOND and WRIGHT, whom I love and esteem, and will take care of anything for me.   If it is a suitable time, send what thee canst per them.   What is in casks, or boxes, tell them I will pay freight for ; but little matters they are so kind as to bring free.

I am mightily pleased with thy account of the Sugar tree. Pray send me a little sprig, with two or three leaves dried between a sheet of paper, and if thee canst, the blossom.   We imagine, here, it is a Poplar or Maple ; but when we see the flower, or seed-vessel, we shall soon determine.

*   *   *   *   *   *   *

My valuable friend, JOHN WHITE, who is curious in our way, carried over the best collection of Pears that I believe ever came from England.   If they come safe, and thrive, at my desire he will oblige thee with buds, or scions, at proper seasons.   Pray wait on him with my respects, and ask the favour.

As for Plums, Nectarines, and Apricots, I may send thee some grafts in the spring ; but it is my firm opinion, if they was budded or grafted on Peach or Almonds, which are stocks that produce the juices freer than any other, they would succeed much better. I should be glad thee'd try, that I may know the event.

If the frost has such an effect on your vines, which I could scarcely believe in so south a latitude to us, you must do as they do in Germany.   When the frosts set in, dig holes round the vines, and lay the last year's shoots in and cover them with earth, to preserve from the frosts ; and at spring take them up again, and then prune them for bearing.   I am glad to hear that the Medlar grows.   It is the large Neapolitan sort, which produces a large fruit.   Doctor WITT, at Germantown, wants it much.   I sent him some at the same time ; but whether he has any luck, I can't tell.

I shall be careful to send the seeds thee mentions, and what others I can collect.

My kind friend, I heartily wish thee and thy good wife health and prosperity.   I am thy real friend,

P. COLLINSON.

I have not seen my garden for near two months, having been a long journey into Cornwall and Devonshire ; so that what condition thy fine plants are in, I can't say.

London, March 12th, 1735-6.

DEAR FRIEND :—

On the other side thou will see thy account, drawn out with as much exactness as I could collect it from thy invoices. I have endeavoured to do justice between thee and thy noble employer. I have shown it to him, and he approves of it, and has ordered me to give thee credit for £18 13s. 3d. ; part of it has been sent to thy order, and for the balance, thou may draw a bill on me, or order it in goods, which suits thee best. His lordship paid freight and all charges on the seeds, being willing to give thee all the advantage for thy encouragement.

The things for thine and thy wife's wear, are a joint present from me and his lordship, for thy other seeds, and plants, and specimens, &c.

As Lord PETRE desired to see thy letters, they are all there. He admires thy plain natural way of writing, and thy observations and descriptions of several plants. For want of them, I shall only take notice of thy proposal, in one of them, for an annual allowance to encourage and enable thee to prosecute further discoveries. Lord PETRE is very willing to contribute very handsomely towards it. He will be ten guineas, and we are in hopes to raise ten more. This, we think, will enable thee to set apart a month, two, or three, to make an excursion on the banks of the Schuylkill, to trace it to its fountain. But as so great an undertaking may require two or three years, and as many journeys, to effect it, so we must leave that wholly to thee. But we do expect, that after harvest, and when the season is that all the seeds of trees and shrubs are ripe, thou will set out; and them that happen not to be ripe when thou goes, they may have attained to maturity when thou comes back. We shall send thee paper for specimens and writing, and a pocket compass,—expect thee'll keep a regular journal of what occurs every day ; and an exact observation of the course of the river, which, with a compass, thee may easily do.

It will, we apprehend, be necessary to take a servant with thee, and two horses for yourselves, and a spare one to carry linen, provisions, and all other necessaries. If the spare horse, and the man's horse, had two panniers or large baskets on each side, they will be very convenient to carry paper, to take specimens by the way, and to bring back the seeds ; thee may make a good many little, middling, and large paper bags to put the seeds in ; and be sure have some good covering of skins over the baskets, to keep

out the rain, &c.   Take some boxes for insects of all sorts, with the
nets; and on thy return, some particular plants, that thee most
fancies, may be brought in the baskets, if there is room.

Thee need not collect any more Tulip cones, Swamp Laurel
cones, Hickory, Black Walnut, Sassafras, nor Dogwood, Sweet
Gum, White Oak acorns, Swamp Spanish Oak, nor Red Cedar
berries; but all other sorts of acorns, Firs, Pines, Black Gum, or
Black Haw, Judas tree, Persimmon, Cherries, Plums, Services, Hop
tree, Benjamin, or Allspice; all the sorts of Ash, Sugar tree,
Wild Roses, Black Beech, or Hornbeam; all sorts of flowering and
berry-bearing shrubs, Honey Locust, Lime tree, Arrow-wood, a
particular Locust, Guelder Rose: not anything can come amiss to
thy friends, and in particular to thy true friend,

P. COLLINSON.

*   *   *   *   *   *   *

DEAR FRIEND,—As thee has given me many instances of thy
curious, speculative disposition, it has put me on enlarging thy
knowledge in natural inquiries, as the earth is filled with wonders,
and everywhere is to be seen the marks and effects of Almighty
power.   Most things were made for the use and pleasure of mankind; others, to raise our admiration and astonishment; as, in
particular, what are called *fossils*,—being stones, found all the
world over, that have either the impressions, or else the regular
form of shells, leaves, fishes, fungi, teeth, sea-eggs, and many other
productions.   That thee may better apprehend what I mean, I
have sent thee some specimens, in a packet of paper for specimens
of plants for Lord PETRE, with some seeds, and a pocket compass.
Captain SAVAGE has promised to take care of the parcel.   In the
course of thy travels, or in digging the earth, or in thy quarries,
possibly some sorts of figured stones may be found, mixed or compounded with earth, sand, or stone and chalk.   What use the
learned make of them, is, that they are evidences of the Deluge. *
* * I hope ISRAEL PEMBERTON is safe arrived, and the little box
with chestnuts, and all the other parcels, with my letters, and the
box of insects, are come safe.   Pray don't forget, as soon as possible, the specimens of Red and White Cedar, and a few white
cedar berries.

DEAR FRIEND,—I hope mine of the 12th instant, with the paper
parcels, with seeds and pocket compass enclosed, per Captain

SAVAGE, are come to hand, as well as the sundry parcels, and letters, per ISRAEL PEMBERTON. * * * * I further took notice of thine of November the 3d, in which thee modestly proposes to be allowed for thy pains and trouble in collecting seeds, and to enable thee to penetrate to the original of Schuylkill. His lordship is both ready and willing to encourage so laudable a design, and will endeavour to engage others to join with him. He proposes to be, himself, ten guineas, and to engage some others to be ten more. This, he is in hopes, will enable thee to set apart one, two, or three months, after harvest—or as near as thee guesses when all sorts of mast and seeds are ripe. Thee talks of the spring, which is no suitable time to set out on such an expedition, for the interest of the gentlemen concerned: for what they propose, is, that thou may be able to furnish them with sorts of seeds, &c., that they had not before, and so desire thou will make some essay this autumn, and make some progress on the Schuylkill; for such an expedition may require two or three journeys, to make the discoveries thou intends. Every uncommon thing thou finds, in any branch of Nature, will be acceptable. * * *

With the pocket compass, observe two or three times of the day the course of the river, and set it down in thy journal, in which, every day, write in short thy observations of that day. There is a dial to it, besides, which will be convenient to know the hour of the day. * * * *

Thy account of the effects of the Poison-stick, in thine of the 9th December, is very extraordinary. Pray send us a specimen of the plant, and make further inquiries about it. Give me a list, per first ship, what seeds thou wants. I have the gardener, at the Physic Garden at Oxford, will assist me.

Be mindful of insects of all kinds, and fossils; any bird's nest, that is uncommon in its structure or materials. I have two or three humming-birds already; however, if any more happens to fall in thy way, I'll not refuse them. I have heard say, your swallow's nest, and your bee's, wasp, or hornet's nest that hangs on the boughs of trees, is very curious.

My dear friend, I wish thee health and increase of thy store, and be assured that I am thy real loving friend. In haste,

P. COLLINSON.

London, March 20th, 1736.

London, April 21, 1736.
DEAR FRIEND J. BARTRAM :—

I have now the pleasure to tell thee that I have got subscribed twenty guineas, to encourage thee to undertake thy intended expedition ; and as our gentlemen find encouragement, it will be continued annually. This is a pretty sum in sterling money, which I hope will enable thee to supply thyself with necessaries from hence ; or, if more for thy profit, thou may draw for it when we have received thy cargoes. This, I believe thee will think reasonable,—that the gentlemen should first see what they have for their money. This I can assure thee,—that thee has to do with people that are not unreasonable in their expectations.   *   *   *

Pray remember two or three specimens of the white and red cedars, and, if possible, pray send the berries, or seed-vessel of each, in particular the *white cedar*, for the seeds of this I am a stranger to. Half a dozen, per way of specimen, will be sufficient ; for though you call it the white cedar, yet we are in doubt what class it belongs to, until we see its seed-vessels. Thy subscription keep to thyself. Remember the *Calceolus Marianus*, or Lady's slippers, and Gentians. I refer thee to my former letters, for I have nothing more to add, but my sincere wishes for thy health and safety, and am thy affectionate friend,

P. COLLINSON.

Specimens of the Sugar-tree blossom, and more seed. Remember all sorts of Fir and Pine cones, and more Spruce. I am informed that the Jerseys is noted for producing abundance of Firs and Pines. I wish thee could procure some specimens of the curious tree in the Jerseys,—either the leaves or the blossoms ;—or both together, would be better.

I am delighted with reading thine of the 3d November, with the pleasing account of thy expedition to the mountains, and the many valuable plants thee observed there. I hope thee will make an early expedition into those parts. The Thorn that thee tells me of must be very curious. It is a pity but it should be propagated. It will take easily, if grafted on other thorns in the spring ; which would be the most sure way, for seed does not always keep strictly to the mother plant.

I have sent the paper, so pray continue thy specimens of all rare plants.

One of the plants that is not named, that bears spikes of white flowers, and the leaves set on the joints like a star,—four at a joint,—is called *Veronica*, or Speedwell [doubtless *V. Virginica*, L.]

If thee can procure some terrapins for Lord PETRE, put them in a box of earth, and nail cross-bars on the top; and if thee knows what they feed on, put in some food. I know they eat apples, cut in slices.

London, June 1, 1736.

DEAR FRIEND JOHN BARTRAM :—

Captain RICHMOND being a friend of thine, could not let him sail without a line, though I have nothing to add to my former, but to inquire after thy welfare. For fear my formers, of March 12th and 20th, and April 21st, should any miscarry, I will now repeat what I then told thee,—that I have twenty guineas subscribed to encourage thy expedition : so I hope thou wilt proceed.

A great many of thy seeds are come up; but I am afraid the Tulip Tree cones was not well perfected, for none is yet come up. I indeed opened several, and found them imperfect, as well as the Sugar Tree. Must in particular desire thee to recruit these two sorts, next year. I am afraid the acorns will also fail :—so pray send a collection of all sorts, especially the narrow-leafed Oaks. The seeds of the Jersey Tree are come up. By present appearance, it seems to be a *Lotus*, or Nettle-leaved Tree,—which grows common in Italy, and Naples, and other parts of Europe. Per my next, I may give a more particular account of it.

The wetness of the mould, in the box of plants, rotted several things. I have but one Martagon, and I am afraid it is not the marsh one. Not one Lily. Pray be so kind to recruit thee with some of the fine large Slippers thou showed Doctor WITT; and pray send some more of that pretty plant thou calls the Rock Blood-wort. It was rotted by over wet. I take it to be a *Cistus*, by its flower. Devil's Bit, or Blazing Star, lost. If the pretty *Sedum* grows near thee, I would be glad of one trial more. All the white and red Shrub Honeysuckle failed. This is a ticklish plant. One of the Laurel stands.

Pray send a root or two of the White Minor Hellebore. I have two fine plants of the cluster-bearing Solomon's Seal; but the other sorts failed.

Pray make large holes in next box, and let it be light mould, and not clay, for that retains the wet.

Please to send over some good specimens, with the flowers to them, of the five humble evergreen plants that grow in the woods; for I despair to have them in the garden, they are so nice and difficult in their culture.

I am obliged to thee for the canes. I have put a neat head on one of them, and use it daily for thy sake.

Whatever seeds thou sends, for the future, send to me, and I shall divide them in proportion to my three contributors. Lord PETRE is ten guineas, the Duke of Richmond five, and PHILIP MILLER the other five.

I shall now conclude, referring thee to my other letters for what former requests and instruction I have made, and hope thee will excuse them, from thy loving friend.

P. COLLINSON.

Pray send root or seed of that sweet-scented Golden Rod, thou sent the leaves of.

Pray remember the White Cedar, to send two or three good specimens, and half a dozen of its cones, or seed-vessels: and pray send me, for a specimen, a little board, about two feet long, of each sort of Cedar, for a specimen. I have large trees of Cedars, raised from berries, in my garden, which I call Red Cedar; but I never was sure which was either white or red, and wherein the difference lay.

I have a tree of your Acacia, or Sweet White-flowering Locust, finely in blossom,—has an agreeable scent.

Friend JOHN, this is only a hint, by the way: Lord PETRE is a great admirer of your foreign wild water-fowl. If at any time an opportunity offers, send him some. Thou will lose nothing by it.

But this he desired me to tell thee, that he desires thy children will bring him up some Red Birds—cocks and hens—for he has an intention to naturalize them to our climate, and I doubt not of success.

These things I barely mention, for thy notice; and am thine,

P. C.

London, June 6, 1736.

FRIEND JOHN :

By the curious impressions sent per J. BREINTNALL, I find I have the Snake-root of PETER SONMANS, from Albany; being the same recommended per Dr. WITT, who sent me a plant two or three years agone. But I don't find, by another impression taken 18th August, 1734, that I have what my friend BREINTNALL calls thy Snake-root. As it is difficult keeping thy marks regular to the plant thee designs them, so I have some plants in thriving order that I can't tell what they are. To inform me, please to send a specimen of *Aristolochia*,* No. 3 ; a specimen of *Panax*, No. 5 ; *Ditto*, of BREINTNALL'S Snake-root,† No. 6, and a good specimen of the Minor Hellebore, in flower; *Ditto*, Cotton-weed, No. 17 ; Sarsaparilla, I don't see any, No. 20.

The Woody Vine has not yet shot. It is, by the berries, a *Euonymus*, or skewer-wood, used by the butchers, [doubtless *Celastrus scandens*, L.]

The *Apocinon*, or Swallow-wort, with orange flowers [*Asclepias tuberosa*, L.], thrives well. One of the Dwarf Laurel grows well.

The climbing *Apocinon* [*Gonolobus*, Mx.] that thee sent—the pods filled with silk—the seeds are come up. There is a great variety of plants, on the continent, that bear seed-vessels of the same figure and consistence; these are all *Apocinons*, and have particular distinctions, from the colour of the flower, shape of the leaf, or particular growth of the plant. One would conceive, from the great provision made (by our all-wise Creator) for the spreading this plant, it was designed for particular uses to mankind; for every seed has a silken *thrum* [or *coma*] fixed to it, sufficient to keep it floating in the air, and when the pod bursts, then the wind conveys the seed to all quarters.

If thee'll excuse my bits and scraps of letters, which I write as opportunity offers, thee'll oblige thine,

P. COLLINSON.

---

* Probably *Saururus cernuus*, L., the leaves of which somewhat resemble those of *Aristolochia Serpentaria*, L.

† *Sanicula Canadensis*, L.

June 7, 1736.

FRIEND JOHN:

I have now a very curious account before me, sent by PAUL DUDLEY, from his house in Roxbury, New England, October 24, 1735; who very ingeniously describes the Evergreens of New England, in two sheets of paper.

This is his catalogue:—

White Pine.	White Cedar.
Pitch Pine.	Red Cedar.
Saplin or Pople Pine.	Savin.
Apple Pine.	Juniper.
Hemlock, a small Fir.	Holly.
Balm of Gilead Fir.	Ivy, a shrub.
Spruce Tree, distinguished into white, black, and red, from the colour of the bark and leaf.	Box.

My kind friend, Dr. WITT, sent me, some years agone, several small plants that he called Spruce; but, by the very particular description of P. DUDLEY, they prove to be the Hemlock; for I have two fine plants, in my garden, which agree exactly with his description of the Hemlock; and, to confirm me that P. DUDLEY is right, I had this year, come from Newfoundland, two fine Spruce trees, which both grow, and prove very different plants from what the Doctor sent me; but agree exactly with P. DUDLEY's description of the Spruce. This I send by way of information, and to put thee on observing what you have, of these kinds, growing near you.

Very probably, in process of time, thy noble employers may send thee to visit New England, on one side, and Maryland and Virginia, on the other: but this by the by.

But be it how it may, thee may be assured of the friendship of thine,

P. COLLINSON.

If thee observes any sort of fresh-water or river shell-fish, pray send me two or three of each sort of shells, as specimens; or any sort of land-snails, &c. Send me two or three shells of a sort, for a specimen.   My inclination and fondness to natural productions of all kinds, is agreeable to the old proverb : *Like the parson's barn,—refuses nothing.*

London, August 28th, 1736.

DEAR FRIEND JOHN BARTRAM :—

I received thy entertaining letter,—the account of the expedition to the Rattlesnake Mountains, which his lordship now has ; so can't in particular answer it.

It was very well thought to put the small specimen of Cedar with the little cones in the letter.   My friend says it is a true Cypress,—having both the figure and properties of the common Cypress—but the cones exceedingly less.   The plant thee gathered last year, near the mountains, has the appearance, in leaves and flower, of Mallows ; but by the particular figure of the seed-vessels, it is called an *Abutilon.*   There is another species that much resembles Mallows, but the seed-vessel being like a pod, it's called *Ketmie.*

I did not send thy goods by this ship, because I am in hopes by the next, which sails in two or three weeks, to save the freight. Pray send some acorns of the narrow-leaved Oaks, cones of Tulip Tree, a specimen in flower of the Sugar Maple, and the seed, Flowering Bay cones, and whatever else thou thinks well of ; of timber trees and shrubs, &c.

I am thy real friend,

P. COLLINSON.

Send more Black Walnuts, Long Walnuts, and both sorts of Hickory, Acorns of all sorts, Sweet Gum, Dog-wood, Red Cedar berries, Allspice, Sassafras ; these will be acceptable to the Duke of Richmond ; and Lord PETRE will like some more.   Pack all the seed the same way as last year, for they succeed very well, a few excepted.   The Acorns and Sweet Gum, and indeed most of all the other seeds are finely come up.   The greatest deficiency is in the Poplar or Tulip cones, and the Sugar Tree.   Not one of the Sassafras, nor Cedar berries, appears, but I presume they lie two years.

Thy kind neighbour, JAMES LOGAN, is so good as to order me to buy thee PARKINSON'S *Herbal,* if I can have it for 25 shillings. He has shown a very tender regard for thee, in his letter to me.

It may look grateful, every now and then, to call and inquire after thy good friend LOGAN's welfare. He is a great man in every capacity, and for whom I have the highest value.

Dear friend, I thought when I began, to write but two or three lines; but I go on scribbling till the paper confines me.

Thine,

P. C.

London, Sept. 20th, 1736.

FRIEND JOHN :—

I writ thee per Captain PEARCE, and I have not much to add, but to acquaint thee that I have sent a case of glass, as per bill inclosed.   *   *   *   *   *   *   *

I have the pleasure to tell thee that the noble Marsh Martagon* flowered with me, which thou sent this spring. It is a delicate flower.

I have sent in a trunk to J. BREINTNALL, a paper parcel for thee, being Apricot, Nectarines, and some fine Peaches and Plum stones, of the best sorts. These fruits, I apprehend, will succeed better from seed than by grafting, unless on Peach stocks. Sow them in a proper place; if where they are always to stand, it may be better. But if they are removed, I apprehend if Apricots, Plums, and Nectarines were planted on the margin of a river, or on the side of a feeding spring, where they may be always supplied with moisture to their fibres, they would not be so apt to shrivel and drop their fruit, in the very hot weather.

I have further to request of thee, as thee on thy own affairs art obliged to traverse the woods, to take all opportunities to make observations on the rattlesnake, or, indeed, any other snake.

That birds, squirrels, &c., are found in their bellies, is notoriously known, but the question is, how they came there; whether the snake, lying *perdue*, on a sudden darts on her prey and bites it, and then lies on the spot expecting the effect of her poisonous bite will at last bring the little animal down dead to her devouring jaws. Sir HANS SLOANE, and a great many others, are of this

---

* This name, *Martagon*, it is believed, is applied to those *lilies* which have *revolute sepals*, to distinguish them from those with merely *campanulate* flowers. The "noble Marsh Martagon," here referred to, was probably the *Lilium superbum*, L., sometimes called *Turk's cap*.

opinion; and by an ingenious letter from a curious person in your city, their opinion is very much confirmed. But on the other side of the question, I have received from my ingenious friends, J. BREINTNALL and Doctor WITT, very particular accounts of the power it has over creatures, by *charming* them into its very jaws. Possibly some accidental discovery may be made, when it is least thought on. It will require a nice and exact observation to determine this matter. If thee knows anything of thy own knowledge, please to communicate it. The hearsay of others can't be depended on. The common and long-received opinion of *charming*, is so riveted in people's imagination, that unless they will divest themselves of it, they may not easily distinguish to the contrary.

Pray has thee heard, or observed, that a certain species of locust returns every fifteenth year? I have been informed of such a thing from New England.

I want very much to be satisfied about the Sugar Maple, as to its flowers, if they are white, as thee has informed me before. Please, in the spring, to gather some specimens when in flower, and send me, and be very particular in thy remarks on it.

We have raised a pretty many fine plants from the tree in the Jerseys. It is a real *Lotus* or Nettle tree [*Celtis occidentalis*, L.], and is a native of your part of the world; is found in Virginia and in other parts. PARKINSON knew only of one sort, which is the European, with black fruit; but we have in the gardens two sorts from your part of the world, distinguished by the colour of their fruit.   *   *   *   *

Dear friend John, I am thy real friend,

P. COLLINSON.

London, January 20th, 1736-7.

DEAR FRIEND JOHN:—

I can't enough admire thy industry and curiosity in descending to so many minute rarities that came in the box by SAVAGE; which are things very acceptable, but what commonly escape the observation of most, but such a prying eye as thine. They in an abundant manner deserve my thanks.

It is true, in doing this thou hast very much obliged me; but I suspect thee has entailed on thyself more trouble. The sight of those glorious large flies [meaning *butterflies*] thou sent, has not abated, but inflamed my curiosity to ask the same over again, or any others thou can add; for as some of these, notwithstanding thy care, are a little torn, I hope in time, with a little practice, we shall have them perfect in all their parts,—the horns, part of the wings, and bodies being deficient; for I must tell thee, I design to bestow some expense on them, and enshrine them between two plates of glass, that we may see both sides. I know they are ticklish ware to meddle with, and the very touch of one's fingers robs them of their beauty.

I will a little revive thy memory with our manner of catching them. We put sticks into the handle of the nets, two, three, or four feet long; for some flies are shyer than others, and will not suffer us to come near them. We always watch till they settle on a leaf, &c., then we apply both nets together, the one close under the leaf, and with agility clap the other over the fly. Thus she is caught between the nets. The next thing is to gently disengage the nets from the leaf, or twig, by gently drawing them; but be sure keep them close together, lest she escape in this action. Having disengaged the nets, we lay them on the next smooth ground, and whilst the fly is between the nets, we turn it on its wrong side, and give the body a pretty smart squeeze between the finger and thumb, till we hear the ribs crack. This prevents further struggling, or beating their wings, to rub off the fine down. Then, with a pin, run it through the body; and having a box large enough, we stick it in, with its right side to the box. When we come home, we display the wings with pins run through pieces of cork, which keep them regular and free from fluttering, as thee will find one in a box, for a pattern.

The two moths are very surprising, the greenish one especially. Our virtuosi cannot enough admire it, for the singularity of its shape, uncommon to moths. These, I know, are more difficult to find, being flies of the night. Our virtuosi either breed them from caterpillars, or else dig for their chrysalis in the ground, and keep them in earth till they change into flies, and then in an hour or two kill them with a hot knitting-needle run into their bodies (for they are much harder than flies to kill); and then they stick them up, as above mentioned. If thee has a fancy to breed them, let me know, and we will inform thee in a more particular manner. It is a most entertaining and surprising thing to observe their changing from the caterpillar to the chrysalis. Every fly has a different proceeding

Always walk with a box or two in thy pocket, and then thee art provided; for oftentimes, when one least expects, a curious thing is seen, but perhaps lost or broke for want of a proper conveniency to secure it.

February 1st, 1736–7.

FRIEND JOHN :—

I have a strong opinion that our misletoe may be propagated with you, in the manner I have often tried with success; and then, again, yours may be with us. I have sent some berries in a box.

My method is to choose the smoothest part of some branch of an apple tree, and thereon I bruise the berry, but not the seed. By virtue of the glutinous matter about it, it will stick to the bark. The north side of the branch is best. If it sticks but loosely at first, yet in a few days there is a mutual attraction on both sides, and the seed will be found closely stuck to the bark. It is very pretty to see the progress of vegetation, and how the seed pushes forth two roots, which insinuate themselves into the bark.

Its natural way of propagation is by a thrush, that is fond of the berries, and lives mostly on them whilst they last.

*   *   *   *   *

It is surprising to think the seed should preserve its vegetating quality through the heat of the intestines of the bird, and the glutinous part with it, that wherever it lights it sticks fast. But such is the order of Providence ; and an evidence of the great wisdom and power of the Creator, to whom all things are possible.

Pray send me some of your berries, for no doubt your misletoe differs from ours ; and please to send a specimen of what sorts you have. We have but one with us; but with this difference, —some are male, and some female that bear berries,—others none, but the farina to impregnate the female blossoms. I have a pretty deal on sundry trees in my garden ; for I try all sorts, by the method prescribed. Being an evergreen, it makes a pretty show in winter. As this is a secret, thee may make it so, for few believe it, but it is fact.   *   *   *   *   *

I am thine,
P. COLLINSON.

London, Feb. 3d, 1736–7.

DEAR FRIEND JOHN BARTRAM :—

I am vastly obliged to thee for thy many kind favours, which I shall answer in course. But if it is irregular, I can't help taking notice of thine of the 18th November, in which thee thinks I have neglected to take notice of thy favour by young ISRAEL PEMBER-TON, which thee certainly must misapprehend, or else my two letters (in answer to that), per Captain COX, August 16th, and per Captain GREEN, are not come to hand, for I keep a regular account of letters, and by whom answered, so can't mistake. Thee should not suspect thy friend, but suspend thy resentment till thee art certainly informed how things happened. Thee may assure thy-self, thee shall not fail of suitable and grateful returns from me. Perhaps I may be slow, but I am sure.

The box of seeds by ISRAEL, came safe, and was very acceptable to thy noble friend. The terrapins which I designed for him had bad luck. Some died, others the sailors stole : but ISRAEL made all the amends he could, and gave me one that he had. He is a very ingenious, kind, good-natured lad.

I was pleased to hear the few things proved worth your accept-ance. I hope this year to send thee something as a reward for thy trouble, which is more than I can imagine ; but thee may feli-citate thyself that the pains thee has taken is not for those who are insensible of it, and who will make suitable returns, though not equal to thy deserts.

Thee writes for scions of pears. If my good friend JOHN WHITE's collection came safe, he has the best we have in England. No doubt, for my sake, he will oblige thee with some scions.

I never heard it was insects that annoyed your Plums, Apricots, and Nectarines. If they are at the root, water that has tobacco leaves soaked in it will kill them, by making a basin round the tree, and watering it frequently with this water.

I am amazed to hear that the frost, in your latitude, kills the vines in the winter. You must use the German method. Dig a trench, or hole close to your vine, and therein lay the young shoots, and then cover them with earth, which protects them from the frosts, and when they are over, take them up again and prune them. Pray how fares it with your wild, country vines ? I am strongly of opinion they will be best to make a vineyard, because they are habituated to your seasons : but then it will much depend on the skill of the person that chooses the vines to propagate.

When they are ripe, a knowing person in grapes should ride the woods where they grow, and select out those that have good qualities,—as good bearers, best-flavoured fruit, large berries, close bunches, early ripeners,—and mark the trees, so as to know them again; and from these take cuttings for a vineyard. In all wild fruits, there is a remarkable difference. When these come to be cultivated (as all fruits were once wild, and have been improved by culture), who knows but you may make as pretty a wine—fit for your own drinking, and to serve your West India neighbours— as Madeira, or any other particular country wine?

I am pleased to hear the Medlar grows. It is the great sort, from Naples.

Please to remember, as I formerly desired, to get some strong plants, of your Ivy, or Bay [*Kalmia latifolia*, L.], that thee sent me some specimens of, and plant in a box, to stand a year, or two, or three, till it flowers in the box; and some of your shrub, white and red, Honeysuckles. These are ticklish plants to keep here.

I now come to answer thy kind letter of September 9th, per Budget. I am pleased to hear thee art acquainted with Dr. WITT,*

* For the following account of Dr. WITT, the editor is indebted to JOHN F. WATSON, Esq., author of the interesting "*Annals of Philadelphia.*" It was furnished in a letter, dated Germantown, May 8, 1848.

"Dr. CHRISTOPHER WITT was a *character* in his day; and, as such, has been duly noticed in my Annals of Philadelphia and Pennsylvania, vol. ii., pp. 22, 32, to wit:—He was born in England (Wiltshire) in 1675, came to this country in 1704, died in 1765, aged 90. He was a skillful physician, and a learned man; was reputed a *Magus* or diviner, or, in grosser terms, a conjurer; was a student and a believer in all the learned absurdities and marvellous pretensions of the *Rosicrucian* philosophy. The Germans of that day—and indeed many of the English—practised the casting of *nativities;* and, as this required mathematical and astronomical learning, it often followed, that such a competent scholar was called a 'fortune-teller.' Dr. WITT 'cast nativities,' and was called a conjurer; while CHRISTOPHER LEHMAN, who was a scholar, and a friend of WITT, and could cast nativities, and did it for all of his own nine children, but never for hire, was called a notary public, a surveyor, and a gentleman.

"Dr. WITT accumulated or owned considerable property in Germantown. He built the first *three* storied house ever erected in the place, and it was large in proportion. It is still standing; was the residence, for many years, of the Rev. Dr. BLAIR; is the same now owned by Colonel ALEXANDER, and called the 'Congress Hall,' and is just now to be opened by Mr. HOWELL, as a superior boarding-house. Dr. WITT left all his property to a family of the name of WARMER, he saying they had been kind to him, on his arrival, in bestowing him a hat in place of his, lost on shipboard.

"His remains now rest in a family ground, walled up by the WARMERS, and now situate on the premises of ANN W. MORRIS."

an old correspondent of mine, and has sent me many a valuable, curious plant. But I am afraid the old gentleman has been too cunning for thee. Those fine Lady's Slippers, which make my mouth water, have slipped beside it. The Doctor says he would have sent them me, but that he was afraid they were spoiled in bringing home, for want of proper care to wet the roots by the way.

This accident brings to my mind a very pretty method, by which plants will keep fresh three or four days on a journey. Take three or four largest ox bladders, cut off the neck high, and when a plant is found, take it up with little earth to the roots; put this into the bladder, then put water in the bladder, to cover the roots; then tie up the neck of the bladder close round the stalk of the plant, leaving the leaves, flowers, &c., without. Large plants won't do so well; but several small plants may be put in a bladder. When tied, hang it to the pummel, or skirts of the saddle, or any other convenient way thee may choose. If the water wastes, add more. Thus plants, with little trouble, may be kept a long while fresh. It is always best, if water can be had, to add it immediately at taking up the plants.

But these fine Lady's Slippers, don't let escape, for they are my favourite plants. I have your yellow one, that thrives well in my garden; but I much want the other sorts. Pray show the Doctor no more. But I find thee has taken the hint thyself. Don't say anything I have writ, neither shall I take any notice of thine.

It is with pleasure, when we read thy excursions (and wish to bear thee company); but then it is with concern that we reflect on the fatigue thee undergoes, the great risks of thy health in heats and colds; but above all, the danger of rattlesnakes. This would so curb my ardent desires to see vegetable curiosities, that I should be afraid to venture in your woods, unless on horseback, and so good a guide as thee art by my side.

Thy expedition for the curious tree, in the Jerseys, truly shows an indefatigable disposition in thee to oblige us here: I hope thee will not fail to find some gratitude in us. The seed is exceeding fresh, but such as I never saw before;—of a pleasant taste, something like Juniper berries. I wish thee had described the tree to us; but, what would have saved thee that pains, would have been, to send us two or three specimens of the leaves, or branches, of a size proper to enclose between a sheet of paper, and then to tell us whether it sheds its leaves, or is an evergreen, and what blossoms it has. Do not go on purpose; but whenever thee goes that way, pray procure some.

The leaves of the Sugar Tree are very informing, and are a great curiosity; but we wish thee had gathered little branches with the flowers on them, and some little branches with the keys on them. The seeds of this tree, (which, by the leaves and keys, is a real Maple,) I cracked a many of them, and not one has a kernel in them, which I am surprised at. Whether they were not fully ripe, thee canst best judge; but so it is. We must desire thee, next year, to make another attempt, and send us some specimens. Its bearing white blossoms is an elegance above any other of this tribe, that I know of; for we have two sorts in England— a major, which is commonly here called Sycamore, and the other is a minor, less every way; and both bear bunches of greenish blossoms, succeeded by keys, like those thee sent.

From thy assured friend,

P. COLLINSON.

London, February 17, 1737.

DEAR FRIEND:

 *   *   *   *   *   *

As thee designs for Virginia, in the fall, I have sent thee circular letters to all my friends; which letters come to J. LOGAN, to save thee postage. I think it would be better to proceed along the bay of the Western Shore of Maryland first, and so to Williamsburgh, and then up into the country, and so back, as thou proposed; and my reason is, little new, or curious, is to be met with along the Western Shore, or in the lower settlements of Virginia. The rare and valuable things are to be found above, in the unsettled places; and then thou will proceed directly home with what seeds thou has got: whereas, if thou goes the upper way first, thou will have to bring what thou has collected down Virginia, and over to Maryland, which will be very troublesome and fatiguing, and a long way about.

I have sent my letters open, that thou may make memorandums from some particular contents therein mentioned, and then seal them up. Of all my friends in Maryland, I know none that are curious in our branch of knowledge; so that, unless it is in the

course of thy travels, it is not worth thy while to go out of thy
way on purpose to see them. I would have thee go, if thee can,
to see ROBERT GOVER, to see the place where some surprisingly
fashioned angular stones are found. As to the rest, take them as
it suits thee. But in Virginia, there is Colonel CUSTIS, and Colonel
BYRD, are both curious men. Pray take down what I have remarked for thee to inquire after, the Umbrella Trees at the first,
and the Ginseng at the last.

Then when thee proceeds home, I know no person will make
thee more welcome than ISHAM RANDOLPH. He lives thirty or
forty miles above the falls of James River, in Goochland,—above
the other settlements. Now, I take his house to be a very suitable
place to make a settlement at,—for to take several days' excursions
all round, and to return to his house at night.   *   *   *   *   One
thing I must desire of thee, and do insist that thee oblige me
therein : that thou make up that drugget clothes, to go to Virginia
in, and not appear to disgrace thyself or me ; for though I should
not esteem thee the less, to come to me in what dress thou will,—
yet these Virginians are a very gentle, well-dressed people—and
look, perhaps, more at a man's outside than his inside. For these
and other reasons, pray go very clean, neat, and handsomely
dressed, to Virginia. Never mind thy clothes : I will send more
another year.

I a little wonder, that the eastern sea-shore, nor the island,
afforded no shells. That there was none, I am persuaded; for,
had they been there, they would not have escaped thee. Pray observe if there are no land or river shells, different from what thee
has sent me. I want a fair specimen of your oysters; an upper
and an under shell, both belonging to one another, will be acceptable ; but no more. Sassafras berries, the cones of the Swamp
Rose-bay, or Laurel, are much wanted, and acorns of Willow-leaved
Oak. Thy last cargo is a fine collection, and came in fine order.
Tulip Poplar and Sweet Gum are not wanting. I thank thee for
the Sweet Gum; but I want some of the Black Gum. Pig-nuts
will be acceptable : they are a very small species of hickory. Send
more acorns; and cones or seeds of all the evergreen tribe will be
acceptable ; and some more Allspice or Benjamin, and any other
forest trees.   *   *   *   *   *

I sent thee a case of boxes, which are very hard, and will save
the trouble of making. Thee may cut down the rims, and accommo-

date them to thy pocket. Pray take one or two, with the fly-nets, in a bag by thy side, and some pins. Perhaps thee may meet with something curious, and may want conveniency to catch and carry it. If the nets are torn, or worn out, send them back to be repaired.

My wishes are for thy health and safety.

I am truly thine,

P. COLLINSON.

The wasps, and nests, are all very curious and acceptable.

London, February 26th, 1736–7.

DEAR FRIEND JOHN :—

Thou omitted to tell us how many miles thou travelled from home. Pray, by the first ship, let me know to what part of the country thy inclination leads thee, next fall.

I believe it will be acceptable to all thy friends, to make a general collection of all the Pines, and Firs, your part affords. I am apt to think the Jerseys may afford all the Pines and Firs mentioned by DUDLEY, and save a further journey. We are very poorly furnished with this tribe. The few seeds, and specimen No. 113 of the White Pine, is a sort we very much want. The difference between Pines and Firs is, that all Pines have their leaves set by pairs [or fascicles]; and in all Firs, the leaves are set singly on the branches.

It is a noble collection of Spruce cones that thee has sent; but we are at a loss to know the plant it belongs to, for want of specimens. Pray send some by the first opportunity; for there are several sorts of Firs that bear small cones.

It is a fine parcel of White Cedar, that thee has sent. I wish we may be so fortunate to raise some. It is a plant that we have not in England. I wish thee would collect a few young seedlings, a foot or two high, and plant in thy garden till they have stood a year and taken root, and then send them; or what would be better is, to plant six or eight in a box, about two feet square, and if they grow, they may be sent without danger of removing: and pray send more seed next year.

What does thee make of those substances with the sprigs growing through them? I take them to be excrescences, though they have some small resemblance of the Cypress cone.

But of the great variety of new and curious plants, in the four quires of specimens, none strikes me so much as the Laurel No. 102. What class our botanists will rank it in, I can't say. Had we but the flowers, it could then be easily determined. But it has all the appearance of a noble plant, and will be, undoubtedly, a great ornament to our gardens. By all means, either send seeds or plants. I hope some may be discovered nearer home, than to go so far.

All those specimens that have neither flower nor seed-vessel, it will be difficult to determine what class they belong to.

This I must observe to thee : that I really think no pains have been wanting to oblige us with a prodigious variety, in every kind. As to thy particular regard to me, I am truly sensible of it : and that I may not be behindhand in gratitude, I have really taken a task on me, which takes up so much of my time, and is so much trouble, that for thy sake, only, I undertake it,—in hopes twenty guineas a year may be of some service : but thee art not sensible the time and trouble it takes up, to get these things from on board, and from the Custom-house ; and had I not good friends amongst the commissioners, I should have a great deal more, and pay a duty beside, and what is yet a greater difficulty on me, it happens * * * * As to thy objection, as to the size of your Cypress cone, it is none; for the same is to be observed in other seeds. There are very small acorns, and very large ones, and yet one as much an oak as the other. The cone of the Cypress that sheds the leaves, very much resembles the Italian, for size and figure. Of this we have raised abundance, from Virginia and Carolina. It is a fine tree, and thrives mightily with us.

London, March 14, 1736–7.

Friend John :—

I am just now returned from paying our noble friend a visit, where I have been viewing his plantations, and concerting measures for another progress, if thee thinks proper to undertake one. He thinks, with me, that to take a turn through your three lower counties, and then along the sea-coasts of the Eastern Shore to the capes, and then return round the bay home, leaving the Western Shore of Maryland and Virginia for another time ; and the going northward in search of Firs and Pines may be for the present deferred. Beside the sorts I mentioned before,—that a few of each would be sufficient for our two correspondents that did not share in the first cargo,—I have here added a list of what sorts will be acceptable to the general. But this I have to observe to thee; —if these seeds can be got nearer home, then there is no occasion to go far for them; for the time spent in journeying, may be spent nearer, in gathering: but this we shall leave to thee; being persuaded all thee does will be for the best. But, if thee should think fit to visit the Eastern Shore, I have some particular friends there, to whom I shall give thee letters, who, no doubt, will give thee hospitable entertainment.

March 20th.—Thy Columbine is in flower, which is earlier than any we have, by two months. It is a pretty plant, and more so for its earliness. We thought we should have had but a small crop of the wild cherries; for some came up the first year, and kept their leaves all winter like an evergreen; but, to our surprise, they are now coming up in abundance,—as well as the Red Cedar. The Sassafras does not stir yet. There are thousands of the Sweet Gum; some kept their green leaves all winter.

Inclosed are some berries of the Butcher's Broom and Juniper, which grows wild in his lordship's woods, and which he gathered with his own hands, March 10th; so must be full ripe, but will not appear till the second year. Where they are sown, be sure keep the bed clear from weeds.

Pray be so kind to mention if those nests are Wasp's, Bee's or Hornet's, and send me two or three of the creatures that build them. They are very curious: one I gave to Sir HANS SLOANE.

His lordship was mightily pleased with thy journal, but wants to know the length of the cave, and how far you went from home. He very much desires some seed of that fine Laurel thee discovered beyond the Blue Mountains, and some specimens of it when in flower, if this can be obtained without difficulty. There is another plant that we want seed and specimens of,—that is the Papaw. His lordship has one plant of it, but they tell us such stories of its fruit, that we would be glad to see it; which may be easily done, by gathering two or three bunches of its fruit, full ripe, and putting them into strong rum, in a jar or pot, and corking it up close, will keep very well here. Specimens of it in flower, will be acceptable.

Pray how long does thou think is the course of the Schuylkill?

Pray remember specimens of Sugar Maple, in flower. The Berry Tree in the Jerseys are come up freely; it is real *Lotus*.

I believe thee forgot to send the large specimens of White Cedar, with the cones on them. I take it, your Spruce is certainly DUDLEY's Hemlock Fir, which is called here the Yew-leafed Fir. I believe that tree in the Jerseys, by thy account of it, must be the Carolina Cypress. It is a noble, quick-growing tree, and thrives well here.

In thine of September 4th, thee gives a very particular account how your Plums are destroyed by an insect. Pray change the stock, and graft Plums and Nectarines on Peach stocks, which, being a vigorous, free stock, and not liable to these insects, may succeed better. Pray try; I have a great opinion of its succeeding.

What thou observes on the vines and their culture, ought not to discourage (nor will not,) the indefatigable man. Patience and perseverance overcome the hardest things. In time, no doubt but a vineyard may be raised, of the select sorts of your country grapes. From one vine the branches may be laid down on every side; and in a few years a large spot may be run over. One quarter of an acre, or half an acre, with us will yield five and ten hogsheads [?] per year, which is enough to make the experiment. But the great art, beside planting, is pruning. A person well skilled will never want fruit, if the seasons permit.

Some of the living creatures thou mentions—in particular the large squirrels,—to turn loose in his lordship's woods:—but this we must leave till we can find a captain that will take care of them. If our friend CHARLES REED's son CHARLES should have a ship, we might have some hopes: but to send red-birds or anything else, till we have a proper conveyance, is great time and trouble lost. But this, I think, may be easily done, to send terrapins; but put them into a cask, with earth at bottom, and holes all round; but this must be in the autumn, after they have had their summer's feed. And your water-turtles, no doubt, may be sent the same way, and at the same time of year,—being taken before they hide themselves in the ground; and then they will live without food, and have a chance of coming safe to us, for the last were all washed overboard.

Dear friend, thy entertaining letters of June 5th and 15th, I should have taken notice of sooner, but they have been out of my hands, at his lordship's.   Thy account of the White Cedar is very satisfactory.   It is a very odd whim, in your people, to think that the *Barberry* blasteth corn.*

Thy journey to the Blue Mountains shows thee art not to be daunted by faint-hearted fellows : but yet, where there is a mortal enemy near, it requires prudence and caution in every step that is taken.

If thee apprehends any of the specimens are not exactly named, it is but sending me the same over again, with thy remarks.   Thee forgot a specimen of the Leather-wood.   It seems to be bacciferous, or Berry-bearing.   Send more seed.   All the specimens are gone to Oxford.   When they are sent back, with their names, thee shall hear from me.

          *   *   *   *   *   *   *

Thy letter came too late for Briony seeds; but I will send some next year,—and some of those other seeds, thou mentions: but as they are plants that are but few of them cultivated in gardens, but grow wild up and down the country, that makes the difficulty to procure them.   *   *   *   *   *

Now, I shall take my leave of thee,—wishing thee and thy good woman and children, health and prosperity.

I am thy sincere friend,

P. COLLINSON.

London, March 22d, 1736–7.

DEAR FRIEND JOHN BARTRAM:—

At the receipt of this, go to Mr. SHIPPEN, who is partner with our worthy friend J. LOGAN, and ask for a parcel directed for thee. In it, thou wilt find a box with seeds, as per catalogue inclosed, with two letters for thee, and two more to gentlemen, my particular friends, on the Eastern Shore of Maryland.   Seal them, if they will be of any use to thee.   JAMES HOLLIDAY, Esq., lives on Chester River; and GEORGE ROBINS, Esq., on Choptank River. These directions, (being in a hurry,) I forgot to set down.   There is one for Doctor HILL, of London Town; but as that is on the Western Shore, lay it by till thou visits that quarter—where I

---

* This " odd whim," it is believed, was brought from the *mother country ;* but it is not as extensively entertained as some other notions from the same quarter : —such, for instance, as the *transmutation of plants*, and the *fascinating power of snakes.*

have many friends, and some of the first rank in Virginia.   If letters will be any service to thee, thou shall not want them.

Inclosed, is some seed of a noble annual,—grows six or seven
feet high, and makes a beautiful show with its long bunches of red
flowers: but I am afraid it will be too late to venture it, this year.
However, sow half, and keep the other till next year.   It is called
the great oriental *Persicaria*.

I am, with love, thy sincere friend,

P. COLLINSON.

Pray does the Marsh Trefoil, or Buck-bean, increase, that was
sent to our friend CHARLES REED?   It grows wonderfully, in very
moist, shallow, watery places.

I find I had none of the plants of the first cargo grow, as under.
If it happens in thy way to supply them, pray do.   *   *   *   *

Dittany, good against the bite of snakes, did not grow.

Devil's Bit, or Blazing Star, this failed.

Pray has thee happened to be that way, when the wild Lupin
was in seed?   It flowers in the spring, and grows in sand, as thee
observes.   The root is long and stringy; so must be raised from
seed,—being very difficult to transplant.

Pray have I that plant lately discovered, of such wonderful
efficacy to cure sore breasts?   A sort of Colt's-foot, by the Pala-
tines called *Aristolochia* [*Saururus cernuus*, L.].   Pray send the
method of cure, and some seed.

Pray what are the virtues of the plant sent me by the name of
the *Panax?*   It grows well, and is called by TOURNEFORT, *Aralia
Canadensis*.

Thee has twice sent me a catalogue of divers plants thou desires.
I have sent it to P. MILLER, and desired him to plant what he has
of them in a case, to be ready to be sent by the last ship in the
autumn.

London, May 20th, 1737.

FRIEND JOHN:—

I here inclose thee the names of the plants, or specimens, last
sent,—as I had them from Dr. DILLENIUS, Professor of Botany at
Oxford;* to whom I have yearly imparted of thy seeds.   He is

* The list of plants or specimens, here referred to, as named or remarked
upon, amounts to upwards of *two hundred*.   The authorities relied upon, seem to
be TOURNEFORT and PARKINSON.

willing to make thee some acknowledgment for the trouble of collecting. I could not think of anything I thought would be more
acceptable than P. MILLER'S Dictionary, as it contains the whole
system of Gardening and Botany. By the assistance of that book,
and PARKINSON'S, thou will be enabled, by their indexes, to find
out any plant with a Latin name, that may be mentioned in the
inclosed catalogue. As I have taken a pretty deal of pains in the
catalogue, I have the less to write here.

By what I can observe of the fine Laurels, No. 102 and 108, or
Chamœrhododendros, their seed seems to be light and chaffy, which
is the worst sort of seed to send over for keeping; that I don't expect we shall ever raise them here, but must depend on plants: so,
prithee, go at a proper season to the nearest place, and load a pair
of panniers or baskets, with young plants, and set some in thy
garden to take root, and send half a dozen at a time: for this
seems to me to be the most elegant tree that has been discovered
in your province.

Indeed, in South Carolina, there is the *Magnolia*, or great
Laurel-leafed Tulip Tree, which is an evergreen—grows sixty feet
high—its leaves are as large again as yours, and the flowers white,
of a rose or water-lily figure, but as large as the crown of one's
hat. There is one in England, that flowers every year finely; and
I have several plants in my garden.

Another particular thing I must request, that is, to get a handful or two of White Cedar cones, for PHILIP MILLER; for, in sepa-
rating the seeds, by accident he had none of the White Cedar
cones.

But what I admire is, that thou doth not tell me how thou
would have returns made for the twenty guineas. Thou loses time
in making money, and an opportunity to have sent goods freight
free, per Captain RICHMOND or Captain SAVAGE. It is surprising to
me thou did not send the order with the seeds, and leave it to my
discretion to send thy returns. Now, as soon as thou can, it will
be near a twelvemonth before thou will see anything for thy
trouble; and at last be obliged to pay freight, if a strange captain
—or else not send the goods; so that, be it as it will, thee art like
to be a sufferer by thy own neglect.

Another thing I would gently touch on, and that is, to be as
close and compact in the packing the seeds as possible; for the
freight and charges come to a great deal. The last cargo came to

2£. 12s. 6d.   Had thee a thought on this, thee would have packed
some things closer.   To give thee an idea of the charge, I shall
inclose a freight bill, in which the captain has charged primage to
every parcel, which is not customary; but that depends on an
agreement made in the bill of loading.   Next cargo, I shall beg
the assistance of our friend ISRAEL PEMBERTON, or JOSEPH BREINT-
NALL, to make the agreement in the bill of loading for thee.

If another time thee sends any growing plants, a great many
may be packed close together in a case two feet square, or two
feet wide, and three long.   As to thy care of the names, it does
not much signify; for when I see them grow, or flower, can soon
distinguish them.

I hope thee will take these friendly hints in good part, as it is
intended.   I am with much love,
                    Thy sincere friend,
                              P. COLLINSON.

*   *   *   The fine white Lady's Slippers have not
flowered.   We have had an unkindly spring, which has kept the
plants back; but most, if not all, seem alive, except the flowering
Shrub.   I must say, I never saw plants taken up with more judgment, and come better.   But great allowance must be made for
difference in climate, soil, and seasons.   We want a little more of
your heat, at this season of the year, for your country plants; and
yet some sorts grow and thrive as well as in their own country.
The Marsh Martagon is going to flower very strongly.   Pray look
out for two or three roots of yellow-flowering Lady's Slipper: mine
begins to decline.

I presume thee continues thy resolution for thy intended progress through the lower counties to the Capes, and then round the
Eastern Shore of Maryland home.   But if thee thinks thee can do
better nearer home, then save thyself that trouble.

Variety of acorns are wanting.   I refer thee to my other letters,
as to other particulars.

I hope thou have mine, and the things, by our friend ROBERT
GRACE, who has taken some pains to make himself master of flux-
ing metals.   He will be able to give our friend WOLLEY some
satisfaction as to the richness and quality of his ores.   I have
shown them to a knowing man, who has given me his opinion of

them, as far as he could guess, without smelting; which at my
leisure shall communicate.
    *   *   *   Dear JOHN, I shall only now acknowledge the
receipt of thine by Captain HEADMAN. It contains many curious
remarks and observations in nature, and very pertinently and well
expressed; needs no apology for thy natural way of expressing
thyself; is more acceptable, clear and intelligible than a fine set
of words and phrases. I take it very kind at thy hands. The
variety of matter it contains, affords a great pleasure to thy loving
friend,

                                            P. COLLINSON.

Our friend Captain RICHMOND often talks of thee, and of a fine
Ivy, or Bay, that grows on a bank going down to the river. Pray
send me a good specimen or two, in full flower.

                                    London, August 12, 1737.
DEAR FRIEND JOHN :—
    I am now to thank thee for thine, by LINDSAY, which contains
many curious things that deserve my notice and particular remarks; but at this time of year I am so unsettled between the
town and country, that I have not really time to consider thy last
two curious letters. For this reason, don't think I slight them,
because I am for the present silent about them. I assure thee,
thou canst not do me a greater pleasure than to entertain me with
any history of nature. But this I must tell thee, as a friend: I
am afraid thou takes up too much of thy time to oblige me. I am
so much thy friend, that I entreat thee not to let any of thy affairs
suffer on my account.
    Indeed, when thou art collecting, thou art paid for it. I hope
this year will prove kindly, that we may have a collection of Oaks.
Send but a few of the White Oak, and Swamp Spanish Oak. I
believe most thou sent are come up, and thrive finely. We have a
great quantity of the Cherry up: it is a fine plant. Red Cedar
comes up very strong; but I don't yet see the Sassafras. Tulip
Poplar in great abundance. This, with most other of your country
seeds, will some come up the first—but more the second year.
Send no more Tulip Poplar. Some of your Swamp Laurel, or Bay
[*Magnolia glauca*, L.], is come up, and thrives well; but we want

a great deal more of its cones.   It is a fine plant; and when the wind turns up the silver side of its leaves, it has a pretty effect. As to the Bay Laurel, called Ivy [*Kalmia*, L.], it is in vain to send any of its seed (unless soon as gathered sown in a box of mould); for it is so small and chaffy, it will not keep.   I have had a great deal from Virginia; but none grows.   There is no way so good as plants.   I have sufficient for myself; but Lord PETRE may want some.   But a year or two hence may do.   I am afraid a like fate will attend the seed of that noble Laurel thou discovered near the Blue Mountains.   A cargo of growing plants will be a rarity worth accepting.   Next time, thou must try what thou canst do.

First, get a strong cargo of young plants into thy garden.   Pray make it thy business this fall; and when they have stood a year, and drawn root, they may with more safety be sent, as opportunity offers.

I received very safe, thy two boxes by Captain LINDSAY.   The bulbous roots came all in very good order; seem singular odd plants.   I shall give thee Doctor DILLENIUS's opinion of them, when he has seen them.   I am much obliged to thee for them.

I have not yet had time to examine thy map up Schuylkill, and all the other curious things in that box; but I shall do it first opportunity.   Nothing that thou sends is lost or forgot with me.

But one thing I must tell thee, while I think on it: that I admire thou has not given me directions in what nature thou would have the twenty guineas remitted, for the last cargo.   Thou loses time.   Certainly the money, or money's worth, would be very useful to thee.   If to draw on me for it in money will be most advantageous to thee, do it; for it is entirely equal to me in what manner thee art paid.

As I have been up and down in the country, I could not forget my friend JOHN, but have collected a variety of seeds; possibly some will be acceptable.   They will have this use, to help thee to know our wild plants.   I would advise thee to sow them all, as soon as thou receives them.   Prepare a fresh bed of good mould; lay it out regular, and sow the seeds in rows, at a foot or ·more distant; mark each row with a number, and to that number in thy book, write the name.   Keep the bed nicely clean from weeds; for suffering them to grow is the reason that many small seeds are choked and lost; and observe never to disturb a bed till after the second spring; for some seeds lie two seasons.   I have sent thee two sorts of Pine, the Silesia Pine, and the Great Stone Pine, with the large cone. This grows on the Alps. The seeds are large and sweet, and much eaten in Italy. Sow these where they may not be dripped on by any trees, and where they may have only the rising or setting sun. The Stone Pine ought to be sown where it is to stand, for they are difficult to remove.

Pray does thou take a trip to the Eastern Shore in the fall? I am glad to hear CLAY is arrived. I hope thou has mine per RICHMOND. I sent thee a magnifying glass for thy pocket, and now send thee ELLIS'S book. I am, dear JOHN,

Thy sincere friend,

P. COLLINSON.

I hope the cargo by RICHMOND is come safe. Let me know what luck.

Pray remember to send me the blossom and fruit of the Papaw, in a little jar of rum. We never had yet a specimen of this tree in flower; and I want much to see the fruit, which will keep fresh in rum.   *   *   *   *

[Here follows a long list of European seeds sent.]

I hope this cargo and that per Captain RICHMOND will show thee I am no slothful, forgetful fellow.

Pray my love and respects to our friend, JOSEPH BREINTNALL.

Pray send or carry the enclosed letter to Dr. KEARSLEY.

I have given Lord PETRE the Humming-bird's nest and eggs, so pray look out for another.

London, Sept. 8th, 1737.

DEAR FRIEND JOHN :—

I can now only tell thee that I have sent a parcel of seeds, in a parcel to your proprietor, THOMAS PENN.

Dress thyself neatly in thy best habits, and wait on him for them; for I have in a particular manner recommended thee to him. I have desired him to show thee the Natural History of South Carolina, in eight books, finely coloured to the life; so forget not to ask that favour. First inquire his most leisure time, and then wait on him.

I hope the goods and box of seeds, per Captain LINDSAY, with these now sent, will let thee see I have not been idle this summer. Some may be acceptable. What thee does not like, throw away.

Pray think of the fine new Laurel. We sadly want a specimen of it in flower, with its description.

Pray remember, without fail if thou'll oblige me, to send the Papaw fruit, full ripe, sent in a bottle or little jar of rum, and two or three specimens of it in flower, with a description of the colour of the flower ; for I want to have it engraved and painted.

I am three letters in thy debt, but no leisure yet. I am just going out of town for some time, so must bid thee farewell.

P. Collinson.

Thee will see Doctor Dillenius's seeds, by his handwriting.

London, Dec. 10th, 1737.

Dear John :—

A little leisure invites me to peruse thy several entertaining letters. I shall proceed in order, and begin with thine of Feb. 27th.

Thy account of the locusts is very curious, and very entertaining to me and my friends, and shows that nothing escapes thy notice. Their surprising method of darting the sticks is admirable. Pray watch, as it happens in thy way, what shape they take as soon as they are hatched. Pray have they wings, when they creep out of the ground? Procure me one, if thee canst, in their first state of coming out of the ground ; and when the back opens, is it a real grasshopper? for I take it, all grasshoppers are locusts. Set me right if I am wrong.

Pin some of each sort in a box, with a number to each, for I have some doubts if they have not three or four different appearances. First, from the egg, they are a worm or caterpillar ; then they go into the ground, and change ; when they come out of the ground, their back opens, and produces a monstrous large fly ; then, I apprehend, they turn to a grasshopper or locust.

As to that caterpillar that comes in such numbers, we have something like it in England. They will eat the oaks and hedges bare, but never kill them, which I take to be owing that, as we have not the sun's heat so strong with us, so our vegetation is weaker, so the tree by degrees recovers its verdure again ; but with you, the heat so rarifies the sap or juices in trees, and puts it in such vigorous action, and for want of young shoots and leaves to divert it, by growth and perspiration, the vessels burst, or the circulation stops for want of vent, that the tree soon dies.

If thee was to observe, all these caterpillars that spin up like silkworms produce a large moth; and all chrysales that thee finds hang'ng naked, produce butterflies, or day-flies.

If thee was to take the cluster of eggs round the twigs, and keep them till time of hatching, and feed them with the leaves of the tree they were found on, thee might see the whole process; or, if I could have some sent time enough, with an account of what tree they were found on, we have people would think it well worth their while to hatch them. This would be a pretty amusement for thy children. They would soon learn, if a little instructed.

I have heard frequent accounts of the prodigious flocks of pigeons; but thy remarks on the wonderful provision made by our all-wise Creator, for the support of the creation, are well worth notice. The balance, kept between the vegetable and the animal productions, is really a fine thought, and what I never met with before. But it is more remarkable with you, than with us; for you have wild animals and mast, in greater plenty than we have.

I can't help but being of thy mind, with regard to the rattle-snake; for, if creatures were bit by him first, I can't imagine they could be able to run away. Pray compare notes with Dr. KEARS-LEY, who is of the contrary opinion, and supports it very inge-niously. I wish it may be thy lot, without harm, to meet with this creature, to observe his motions: but I am confirmed of his power over men, in the manner thou mentions, by a very curious friend of mine, and a great philosopher, Colonel BYRD, of Virginia,—who says, you must not think me fanciful, when I assure, I have ogled a Rattlesnake so long, till I have perceived a sickness at my sto-mach.

Now, dear JOHN, I have made some running remarks on thy curious letter, which contained so many fine remarks, that it de-served to be read before the Royal Society; and thee has their thanks for it, desiring thee to continue thy observations, and com-municate them. Pray make no apology. Thy style is much be-yond what one might expect from a man of thy education. The facts are well described, and very intelligible.

I am, with love, thy sincere friend,

P. COLLINSON.

London, December 14, 1737.

DEAR FRIEND:—

I now come to take notice of thine of the 26th of April. We are much obliged to thee for thy excursion to Conestogo; but it is a pity thee should have double trouble; for laying of pea-straw, litter, or ashes, or moss, or straw, thick about the roots of vegetables new planted, will very much secure them against the effects of the frosts.

The Gooseberry thou mentions, must be a curiosity.

Thy observations on the Locust are curious, (but the sticks are much more so.) It shows how indefatigable thee art after truth, and the processes of nature. It may be very providential, that they spread not over the country everywhere. This is undoubtedly to preserve the balance, that more is not produced than is necessary for food, and to propagate the species.

The book mentioned by SWITZERS, I have sent thee, which I hope is come to hand.

I have heard of thy house, and thy great art and industry in building it. It makes me long to see it, and the builder.

I believe I gave thee a hint that the Bays and the Cypress must be protected. But I will send more seed; and, if I can, a Cedar of Lebanon cone, which is very hardy, and grows in the midst of snow, so will endure your climate; but the cones are rare to get.

I commend thy caution, not to leave thy home but on the most necessary occasions, though it was a tempting expedition to go with Friend WOLLEY.

Thy caution, relating to the Doctor, is very good. As to what he may say of me, I mind it not. I can readily overlook his weaknesses, imputing them more to his natural disposition, which I take to be peevish and froward, than to his mind; for he has many good qualities.

I despair doing anything from the seed of the Laurel and Shrub Honeysuckles, the seed is so small and chaffy. If there is any likelihood of success, it must be from their being immediately, when ripe, sown in a box of mould, and so sent nailed up, only leaving some holes for circulation of air.

Thy thought of collecting the bulbous roots, was exceeding kind. They came in perfect order; so hope to see their appearance in the spring. There is one flower amongst the specimens, which is a very double white flower, with small leaves something like Columbine. This we call the small mountain *Ranunculus*, as it really is.* I had it formerly sent me, by Dr. WITT; but I should be glad of a few roots more. It is a pretty plant, and keeps a long while in flower. I hope to send the names of the rest.

Thy map of Schuylkill, is very prettily done, and very informing; for now I can read and travel at the same time. Lord PETRE has seen it, and is much pleased with that and thy journal; for one helps to illustrate the other. I intend to communicate it to a curious map-maker: it may be of use to him, in laying down that part of the River Schuylkill, undescribed.

Is there any account of the panthers? Do they attack men, or cattle? To see a live one, I presume, is not very common to Europeans. The other curiosities, I have made some remarks on in my general observations. I hope nothing has escaped me.

Thy next, in course, is July 6.

I shall first take notice of thy request to buy TOURNEFORT. I have inquired, and there are so many books, or parts, done, as come to fifty shillings. The first part may be got, perhaps, second-hand; but the others, are not yet to be expected. Now I shall be so friendly to tell thee, I think this is too much to lay out. Besides, now thee has got PARKINSON and MILLER, I would not have thee puzzle thyself with others; for they contain the ancient and modern knowledge of Botany. Remember SOLOMON'S advice; in reading (?) of books, there is no end.

Far be it from me, that I designed any reflection, or to find fault, when I required some information in certain particulars which escaped thee. I full well know thy many avocations, and hoped thee would not take it in that light, to draw an apology from thee, that I should overlook them, considering thy affairs. Yes, all this I could readily do, and would have done, if I thought thee had taken it in a sense I did not intend. So I hope, for the future, thee will never take anything in a lessening way, or, as if I expected more perfect matters than the nature of things will allow of. I only beg to be informed, and thee has done it; and I am obliged to thee for it.

Some Wild Crab seed will be very acceptable; but I believe it

---

* It is the *Anemone thalictroides*, L., or *Thalictrum anemonoides*, of MICHAUX. See P. COLLINSON's letter to JOSEPH BREINTNALL, 1738.

will keep better without the apple; for too much moisture may rot them.

The manner in which the hornets make their nests, is well worth knowing. Ours, in England, make a nest as large, but more beautifully coloured, and clouded with light and dark brown. They build in hollow trees, and hang them up to the upper corner of a barn, close to the ridge.

Dear friend, I am pleased to hear thee has been in the Jerseys, and Kent County,—and that thee has discovered the Pitch, or Red Pine; which is a sort we want. All sorts of Pines, and Firs, and White Cedar, and Spruce, are plants we want. Yet, as they live so remote from each other, content thyself with sending one sort a year,—unless any sort is near at hand. We expect no unreasonable and hard things, and will not have thee exert thyself out of reason to serve us. Thy accurate observation, and perfect knowledge in the times of gathering these sort of trees, must be thy director in these matters. But though thy excursions are attended with difficulties, and great fatigue,—yet, the secret pleasure that accrues—and the new discoveries—and the many observations, both informing and entertaining, which tend to enrich thy mind with natural knowledge, and fill it with exalted ideas of the wonderful Hand that made all these things,—must yield thee such a secret pleasure as will fully compensate for and counterbalance all the other.

I have some pretty young plants from the Spruce cones, which is certainly DUDLEY'S Hemlock.

I hope the Buck-bean is not entirely dead. Pray look next year again. The place it was planted in seems very suitable. It bears a curious, elegant flower, and has great virtues.

I shall endeavour to supply the Squills and G. Lilies. The frosts in your country are surprising. It requires, in a gardener, great care and diligence to secure and protect his plants against these injurious insults of the weather.

If thee will please to inquire of our worthy and learned friend, JAMES LOGAN, who is well versed in optics, he will tell thee, that there is no making a glass to magnify, to such a degree as thee wants, in such large dimensions as thee requires; for, the larger the magnifier the smaller the glass: that instead of taking objects altogether, they must be taken in parts. The greatest discoverers in nature have been obliged to this method.

My friend LOGAN tells me thee art very dexterous in detecting flowers; which requires, in some of them, both good eyes and good glasses to discover their very minute parts. This is a very curious study, and full of wonders,—but must take up a great deal of time to be exact; and is a pretty amusement for those that have it hang upon their hands. But, for thee and me, I think we can't allow it, without prejudice to our other weighty affairs. Yet I would not discourage thee, if thy circumstances will permit it.

Dear friend, thine of the 19th July is before me.   *   *   *   *

It is with great concern I see so many curious insects spoiled. Pray keep the Butterflies by themselves; and then no danger can happen. Some of the last are extravagantly fine. The white long-tailed Moth is amazing. Now and then, when a fine one happens in thy way, take him—being always provided with a box in thy pocket, when thee walks abroad; for these insects are seen accidentally. If thee was to go on purpose, it is a query if thee finds one. There are some new ones amongst these last, that I never saw before; and one that I think is, in all parts, exactly the same as here.

The curious Thorn, thee mentions, I wish thee was to see in flower; for I suspect the owner magnifies its beauties. Get it into thy own garden, and see for thyself; and then, if it proves what he says, it will be a present worth sending, and our accepting.

JOHN WHITE is now here, and gives thee great commendations. I am sorry so fine a collection of Pears is so little regarded.

I am heartily glad thee has so good a friend as JAMES LOGAN, being a man of great compassion and humanity. He writ to me, some time agone, in thy behalf,—fearing thee had no consideration for thy collections. This, I think, was an instance of his great regard for thee. No doubt but he considers thee, for any time taken up from thy own affairs, (if thee pursues the study of plants,) in order to satisfy his inquiries,—whose surprising genius has enabled him to write very skilful and knowing in this branch of natural history, as, I think I may safely say, in all others.

The *Systema Naturæ* is a curious performance, for a young man [LINNÆUS]; but his coining a set of new names for plants, tends but to embarrass and perplex the study of Botany. As to his system, on which they are founded, botanists are not agreed about it. Very few like it. Be that as it will, he is certainly a very ingenious man, and a great naturalist. As these were not in our mother tongue, was the only reason I did not send them to thee. I hope not to be forgetful for the future.

I am thy loving friend,

P. COLLINSON.

London, December 20, 1737.

DEAR FRIEND :—

I shall now consider the remaining part of thine of July 19.

The magic lantern is a contrivance to make sport with ignorant people. There is nothing extraordinary in it: so not worth thy further inquiry.

Thee art still desirous of a magnifier for flowers. Pray make this complaint to J. LOGAN, and try his thoughts. As thy inquiries seem in some measure to be owing to him, and as thee art his pupil, (which no man need be ashamed of,) no doubt but he will furnish thee with suitable instruments for that purpose, in order to render thy discoveries more perfect—so undoubtedly more to his satisfaction.

What I hinted, as to thy cargo coming when I am so much engaged, is not to have the season altered; but to show thee, that as thee strains a point to serve me, so I strain a point to serve thee. Pray pursue the same successful track and method thee has always done. But this I tell thee; what I do, I would do for none but thee: and yet, by the sequel of thy letter, thee thinks thyself not amply rewarded. Pray, friend JOHN, consider twenty-one pounds per annum sterling, returned in goods or money, is a hard case, if it will not make near, or quite, or more than forty pounds a year, your currency. This, I think, will pay for five or six weeks spent annually in thy collection, and hiring a man, and other expenses. Supposing thee art in expense, in this affair, ten pounds your currency per annum—which I don't think,—why, to have thirty pounds, your currency, in circulation in thy affairs, must certainly be a fine thing, and sufficient to content any reasonable person. I know thee art a man of more equity than to desire the subscribers' money for little matters; and on the other hand, thee art so honest to send the most thee can afford to procure for them;— more, they don't desire. Then what reason is there for thee to be uneasy? Pray let me hear no more of it. If thee canst not afford to go on with this business, tell us so, and it will be at an end.

Now, friend JOHN, I shall turn over [*i. e.*, the *leaf* on which he was writing], and never think of the last-mentioned matter, unless thee revives it.

I wonder thou should be sorry to see such a bundle of white and blue Lilacs. That wonder might have soon ceased, by throwing them away if you had them already. But as your neighbours of Virginia, in particular Colonel CUSTIS at Williamsburgh, who has undoubtedly the best collection in that country, desired some, I thought possibly you might want them, for I never was over to see. However, this shall be a caution, to send nothing but what you write for. But dost thee know that there is both blue and purple Lilacs? I like thy project of inarching the white and blue together. I have the five colours of the *Althea* inarched on one stock, which looks very pretty when in flower.

That you have Sloe trees enough, when JAMES LOGAN writ to me for some, is very surprising. I see I must venture to send nothing without orders, for fear you have it already.

That you have neither Horse nor Spanish Chestnuts, nor French Walnuts, is not I see, to be helped; for the last ships go before they are ripe, and the first in the spring, when they are rotten. I have kept them till near Christmas, and then put them in a box of sand, and yet they are lost by over wet or over drought. However, as thee art a great judge in these matters, prescribe a way, and I will endeavour to follow it.

I am glad the Junipers grow. Pray does the English broom grow? This may be hardier, and endure your climate better than the Spanish.

It is surprising that your winters kill Wood Sage, for it grows on our high hills, and never suffers. Plant it in cases, and house it, or else cover it well with pea straw at the approach of winter, removing it off in mild days, and covering at nights. I hope the seed will come this year acceptable, for I think I gathered it pretty ripe.

Dear friend JOHN, I have thine of August 12th, which gives me both pleasure and pain. I dreaded to go on board to see the disaster, and so much labour and pains thrown away by such a swarm of pestilent beetles. As we say by a fine old woman, "There's the ruins of a fine face," so I may say, "There's the ruins of fine flies," and such as I never saw before. Pray next time divide the precious from the vile; I will send thee boxes enough. Keep the butterflies, or day-flies, by themselves, the moths by themselves, and these devouring beetles by themselves, but drown them in rum, or heat them in a gentle oven will stop all their further progress. Moths are sometimes subject to breed insects which will eat up their bodies, but the heat of a very slack oven kills all. Butterflies are not liable to these accidents. But at the proper time of sending, they may be collected all in one box, and desire the captain to set it in any dry place in the cabin; for the last, being put in the Lazaretto, under the cabin, narrowly escaped all being spoilt by a bag or barrel of salt being put over them, which came through the box. Captain SAVAGE is a wonderful good-natured obliging man, and can't prevent the carelessness of his servants. As thee intends to repair that loss, which is very obliging, I only just give this hint, that I prefer butterflies and moths before beetles ; and reason good, for there is ten times the beauty and variety in one as the other.

I shall now tell thee something which very much pleased me, and will surprise thee. The box of turtle eggs (which was an ingenious thought of thine to send), on the day I brought it from on board ship, being the 20th of October, I took off the lid, having a mind to see the eggs, and on peeping about I saw a little head just above ground, and while I was looking, I saw the ground move in a place or two more. In short, in the space of three or four hours, eight tortoises were hatched. It was very well worth observing, how artfully they disengaged themselves from the shell, and then with their fore-feet scratched their eyes open. They have had many visiters, such a thing never happening, I dare say, in England before. They seem to be all one sort, but thee mentions two. I tried if they would eat, with Lettuce leaves, &c., or if they would drink, but they regarded neither. But after they had been crawling about three or four days, they buried themselves in the earth in the box, where they continue. Early in the spring I design to turn them out at Lord PETRE'S, who has large ponds, if they are water-turtles. I believe it was providential that this box was put in the Lazaretto, for the warmth of the ship supplied the sun's heat, and brought them to perfection. But the luckiness of the thing was their hatching the day they were brought home. I have specimens dried of four sorts of your American turtles, but these seem different from them all, by the length of their tail, and figure of their shell. As for their not eating, and burying themselves, in a state of sleep, the air supplies the vital flame; and as chickens are for some time supported by some part of the yolk in their stomachs, in order to sustain them while the remainder of the brood is hatching (for if the hen was to leave her charge to go and provide food for those first hatched, what must become of the remaining eggs?); so I conclude, as these are oviparous, or produced from eggs, something of the same provision is prepared to support them till next spring. If they were to be all the while in motion and action, it would not be sufficient, but as they soon enter into a dormant state, it may be sufficient to preserve life. I could be glad to see a larger one of this sort of land turtle dried, to compare with those I have by me.

All the other pretty curiosities were very acceptable. As for thy kind offer of squirrel skins, I would be far from rejecting it, if it would cost thee nothing; but to give anything, I am no ways free for thee to do it, for I presume it is more matter of curiosity, than really better than other skins. The shells, with the likeness of large snails, are peculiar to your part of the world, but the small scallop, found on East Jersey, are found at New and Old England. But the present is not the less esteemed, because it shows the produce of your shores.

I am persuaded not one of the red-bellied turtles is hatched. I should be glad to see one of these dry. The *Panax* is a choice plant.

I am thine,

P. COLLINSON.

January 27, 1737–8.

DEAR FRIEND:—

I had the pleasure of thine from Maryland. I am glad my friends were kind to thee, and that thee found fresh matter of entertainment. I can't enlarge now, but to tell thee that all the two boxes of seeds, two boxes of plants, one box specimens, one box wasp's nest, came all safe, and in perfect good order; which is very pleasing, and for which I shall make thee some returns, per Captain WRIGHT, with all the goods thee mentions—except the sewing silk, which is advanced to two shillings a pound. It is expected to be cheaper; and unless it is, neither thee nor I shall have any credit in sending it; so I would rather have the remainder of thy money ordered in other goods.

*   *   *   *   *   *   *

I hope to send thee letters to Maryland and Virginia. I have wrote, already, to several of my friends in Virginia.

I am, dear friend,
Thy sincere friend, in haste,
P. Collinson.

Lord Petre has ordered me to give thee two guineas, for thy extraordinary trouble about the specimens.

The Laurels are perfectly fine. That and the White Cedar are very acceptable. Thee shall not lose thy reward.

Dear friend, I must beg the favour of thee to remember what I have formerly requested, in behalf of a curious naturalist, who, to engage thy memory, sends thee a specimen of his performance. He neglected, when in Virginia, to draw the Papaw; and as this is a curious plant, in flower and fruit, and not figured by anybody, now there is no way to convey to us perfect ideas of this plant, but by gathering the blossoms and leaves, and drying them between paper; but as the colour and figure of the flower is liable to change, then he begs a short description of its colour; or else, to prevent further trouble, if some of the flowers growing on a small twig, were put into some rum, one small twig would be enough; but thee may put several loose flowers in the jar of spirits, and then a couple of fruit, full ripe; and if it was not too remote, a couple half ripe,—for I am informed they grow in couples.

It is observable, that spirits do very little alter the colour of fruits. If they do before thee sends it, pray give a little description of its colour. Now, by these helps, my ingenious friend will be able to delineate the plant and fruit: and if thee will further assist him in the height of its growth, and the size of its stem, and what soil and place is most natural to it,—we shall be all much obliged to thee. Pray fail not, and thee will oblige thine,

P. Collinson.

If it has any virtues, pray mention them.

[Not dated.*]

FRIEND JOHN:—

I now come to take notice of thy journal. I wish thee had been more particular; but possibly time did not admit. It was very

* The following extracts are from a letter of P. COLLINSON to JOSEPH BREINT-NALL, Merchant, Philadelphia; a copy of which was politely furnished to the editor, by EDWARD D. INGRAHAM, Esq. The date is not fully given in the original; but it is endorsed—"Received April 26, 1738."

London, January 31, [1738.]

RESPECTED FRIEND:—

I have several of thy obliging favours. * * * * *Thy Snake-root*—so called from thy first importing it, is a Sanicle [*Sanicula Canadensis*, L.], having all the characteristics belonging to that class: but I believe it is not mentioned in MILLER, because not known when he wrote that book. Thee has many thanks from the Royal Society, for thy account of the *Aurora Borealis*, as mentioned in thine of November 24.

It gives me great pleasure to hear of that generous proposal of your proprietor, to give you a lot for a Library House; who, in great gratitude, you should choose President of your Society, which may encourage him further. All thy observations and schemes relating to it, are an instance of thy zeal for promoting the good of mankind, and deserves the greatest commendation from all that are well-wishers to so noble and useful a design. Your worthy proprietor may be truly said to be a father to his people, when he has the public weal so much at heart. I hope ways and means will be found to carry on that laudable work: but, really, I cannot flatter thee with hopes of benefactions from hence. The love of money is too prevalent, and we have too few generous, public-spirited men, considering our numbers: however, I shall not fail to impart your design to some likely persons. If I have any success in my solicitations, the Company will be sure to hear from me.[a]

I am, with much respect, thy sincere friend,

P. COLLINSON.

P. S. I have here inclosed the Company's account, which I hope thee will find right.

The pretty white *Ranunculus* [*Anemone thalictroides*, L.], that Dr. WITT sent me, some time agone, is a neat, delicate, double flower; but I never knew before, it was a Snake-root. It is described by the celebrated PLUKENET, who has most of your country plants. He names it—"*Ranunculus nemorosus, Aquilegiæ foliis, Virginianus, Asphodeli radice.*"

Virginia Wood Ranunculus, with Columbine leaves, and an Asphodel or Kingspear Root.

    *   *   *   *   *   *   *   *   *

We had, last December 5th, a very remarkable and uncommon bloody *Aurora*

---

[a] P. COLLINSON not only rendered important aid in establishing the *Philadelphia Library*, but he was, for many years, the faithful agent of the Company, in making their purchases in London; and was at all times, a zealous friend and generous benefactor.

agreeable to me, to hear that my friends were kind to thee. I shall not fail to acknowledge it. But I should have been glad to have had thy particular observations on them and their families, and their dwellings, and their tastes in life; but this is exacting too much from a man of thy active genius, so pray think no more about it.

I am concerned ROBERT GOVER is dead; but I think his son or his family, are in being. I wish thee had gone and seen the cliff from whence the angular stones were taken, which are so curiously formed in squares, that far exceed the lapidary's art. No doubt but some belonging to him could have shown it thee: but as this is matter of curiosity, and only proposed for thy sake, another time may do as well.

I am sorry our brother CLAYTON was not at home. It was, no doubt, a great disappointment, that you could not open your budgets and compare notes.

I am informed my friend CUSTIS is a very curious man: pray what didst thee see new in his garden? But I am told Colonel BYRD has the best garden in Virginia, and a pretty green-house, well furnished with Orange trees. I knew him well when in England; and he was reckoned a very polite, ingenious man. As for my friend ISHAM, who I am also personally known to, I did not doubt his civility to thee. I only wish to have been there, and shared it with thee.

Thee does not mention any animals in this voyage; and yet I don't suppose the country destitute. Pray has thee observed two sorts of Fallow or small Deer,—whose principal distinction, I think, lies in their horns? There is, besides, the smaller Elk, or Stag; a pair of them I saw lately, with a pair of Buffaloes that was brought to England. But then there is the great Elk, or Moose, which I think frequents more to the northward.

Pray what height and bulk were those fine Pines, with three leaves, that thee discovered in the Great Vale? But, as to plants, I shall make my remarks when I return them named.

Thy map was very informing, and gave a pretty idea of thy

borealis, which was seen all over Europe. Pray does thee remember if it extended to your parts?

Inclosed in the Library books, &c., is a face-glass. I was at a loss what size would be most suitable. This is a middle size, and, I think, sufficient for the purpose thou mentions. It cost six shillings.

journey. Pray what inhabitants didst thee find in the Great Vale,
—whether Indians or English?

As this journey has proved very fatiguing and troublesome to
thee, I can't advise another, if it is possible to gratify thy correspondents without it.

It was very curious of thee, to collect the two noble chrysalises.
We wait with impatience their new birth. I wish the heat of our
climate may be able to perfect them; for the ring of eggs that thee
collected from the Apple trees, hatched the very next day I had
them from on board, it being very warm weather: but, in a day or
two, it changed to very cold, for the season; and I am afraid has
killed them all, notwithstanding they were kept in the house, and
fed with the young leaves and blossoms of Apple tree. If ever
thee meets with any more, I will keep the ring of eggs in a cold
place till May, and then I don't doubt but to raise them, and carry
them through their changes; which will be a great curiosity, and
is frequently done here, by those that would raise a quantity of
rare and scarce flies.

The two muscle shells are great curiosities, and what I never
saw before; but I apprehend, with you as well as with us, there is
a great variety of fresh-water and land shells—small and great.
But these require eyes like thine and mine to find them out. If
thee happens on such another wasp's nest, that the *Possum* destroyed in the bush, pray think of me.

*   *   *   *   *   *   *   *   *   *

I have inclosed, in my friend T. PENN's parcel, two cones, and
some seed of the Stone Pine. Please go to him for them.

I am, my good friend, thine, very truly,

P. COLLINSON.

One thing I forgot to mention before, and what very much surprises me, to find thee, who art a philosopher, prouder than I am.
My cap, it is true, had a small hole or two on the border; but the
lining was new. Instead of giving it away, I wish thee had sent
it me back again. It would have served me two or three years, to
have worn in the country, in rainy weather.

London, April 6, 1738

DEAR FRIEND JOHN :—

The first thing I have to desire of thee, is to send three or four or six specimens of the Sweet Gum, in blossom. This being a very extraordinary plant, some curious botanists in Holland beg this favour, in order to settle its botanical character. I desire specimens of these others—two or three of a sort;—Black Gum, and Black Haw,—these we desire in blossom, and in fruit and leaf, as it happens; Sugar Birch, Black Thorn, and sorts of White Thorn, in blossom and fruit. I have received three sorts of *Jaceas* from Doctor WITT. He distinguishes them by Early Jacea, Elegant Jacea, and Gigantic Jacea. I wish thee could find them out, to send specimens of them,—as they grow in your country.

Pray look out for a plant or two of White Cedar ; for I am afraid that last sent me will go off, though it has a clod of its own earth about it. The smell of the leaves, a little dried, smells like to cinnamon. It is a fine plant. If mine stands, it will be the only one in England ; though I have hopes to raise it from seed, this year. Set half a dozen young plants in a box, and let them stand a year or two, to strike root, before they are sent.

Renew thy collecting of acorns ; and if thee can, send specimens to each which is a great curiosity. Get what Sassafras berries thee can : and send as many Red Cedar berries, in a little box by themselves, as thee can afford for half a guinea,—being for a particular person ; and send some more, what thee can, for thy three correspondents. Send more Sugar Maple seed, and Rose Laurel cones : and send a specimen or two of the Upland Rose, and the Marsh Rose. Try what thee canst do to send us some cones of the Long-cone White Pine. It is a very remarkable Pine,—having five leaves in a sheath ; and the other, from Jersey, has but two leaves. I have great hopes most of the plants will grow. They promise well ; but I shall defer giving thee an account, till next opportunity.

The Terrapins came very safe and well : but I have lost all the young ones from the eggs, which were fifteen, which is a great loss. If I ever have any more, I will take another method with them. But the curiosity was great, and admired by many ; and it was very lucky that the first peeped its head out of the earth, the very day I brought the box from on board—which I think was the 21st

October. If I had sent them then directly into the country, I had saved them; but I thought keeping them in town, I could better secure them from the cold, and so I lost them all, which I was sorry for; being, I am persuaded, the first that ever hatched in England. But I take it, the warmth of the ship contributed much to it, and supplied the want of your sun's heat.

The Terrapins I gave to Lord PETRE; and he thanks thee for them.

Doctor DILLENIUS thanks thee for the seeds and specimens. Thy observation on your Pines is remarkable. The Stone Pine, and the Long-coned Pine, don't open like yours; but I think all the rest do.

Thee has obliged me much, with so fine a collection of Wasps, with their natural history, which is very entertaining and surprising: in particular the clay nests—their fabrication, and their provision for their young, with all the rest, are evidences of the unlimited power and wisdom of the Great Author of all things. But that these creatures—which are a common pest to mankind—should have such wonderful instincts bestowed on them, for securing themselves and their species, exceeds our comprehension, but raises our admiration. It may serve to abate our pride and conceit, when we see so much bestowed on these lower classes of being, which is not unworthy of our notice: and it is owing to thy indefatigable industry, that these things are brought to light. Great is thy pleasure, that at the same time thee art obliging thy friend, thee art improving thyself in the knowledge of nature.

Pray look out sharp, next year, and be beforehand with that saucy Raccoon,—that I may see that pretty nest, built in the bush; and send the Wasp, and a better specimen of the clay Wasp; for the last wanted its head. Such a variety of these creatures must be very troublesome. We have but one, and that is bad enough, that builds its nest in dry banks; two sorts of Bees—the Honey Bee, and a large Humming Bee that builds in dry banks; and one sort of Hornet; and three sorts of Ants. But I am like to introduce a fourth; for I found in the earth that the plants came in, the outer husk of a chestnut, and in it a colony of very small Ants. These I have carried into the country, to see how they will thrive in our climate.

Thee will continue thy observation on the Yellow Wasp. No. 1

and No. 2 may deserve thy notice; for I find their building, and increase, is unknown to thee.

If another insect, with those surprising long hairs, or horns, happens in thy way, pray secure it; for it is very extraordinary in its kind. The beautiful Sea Fly is a great beauty—could its wings be displayed. Pray never go without a box, and pins, in thy pocket.—The insect with what thee esteems a long horn, is no other than a proboscis, which he uses to suck out the sweets of flowers; for he has two small horns on each side.

I am glad thee met with such civil treatment in thy expedition through the Eastern Shore; and that thee found such variety of plants.

I am sorry thee missed some plants that thee observed. I wish thee had collected specimens of that *Periploca*, and that other with horned poppy leaves, and the *Hypericon*, and the Long-leafed Large-cone Pine, and a different Swamp Oak. Pray never fail getting *specimens*, if thee canst not get plants, or seeds. Provide two flat boards—the size of the paper thee intends for the specimens: between these, put thy paper, and specimens in it, and tie them fast. Thus, these may be carried any ways, as it suits thy convenience; and with safety, too.

I can't conceive what your Black Thorn is: pray send a specimen. We have but one sort,—which is the one that bears sloes; and but one sort of White Thorn. But I am surprised at their size, with you. I question if ever I saw one above the size of the small of a common-sized leg; and that but rare; for they are so useful in making fences, that they are rarely suffered to grow of any size.

The Great Laurel, or Chamærhododendron plants, promise well; which gives me great joy. I am extremely obliged to thee for them: and am, with love and respect,

Thy assured friend,
P. COLLINSON.

London, May 2, 1738.

DEAR FRIEND:—

I have sent thee, in a little jar, some of our *Dens Canis*. There are white and red flowers. This is in return for those with yellow flowers thee sent me, though they did not flower this year. If thee meets with any more, pray get them.

It is a great advantage, to send plants with a sod of earth about them; for, many times there comes up odd plants—as it has happened this year; for in the sods of Herb Twopence,* is come up two sorts of vegetables, the one I don't know, but one appears to be a sort of *Hepatica*, very like ours, but that the stalks of yours are very hoary, and not naked, as the footstalks of the leaves of ours are.

I also send thee one of our Humming Bees, from the sound it makes. These reside in dry banks; but whether they make combs, as others do, I doubt,—for this year I caught one in March, and whilst I looked on it, I perceived from round the neck a great many young ones creep out. Now, the combs I take to be repositories, both for food and to lay their eggs in; but, the way that these breed, and nurse their young up by the heat of their bodies, I take it there is no need of repositories for their young. Our Black Beetles, breed theirs the same way.

The jar I have tied in a parcel, with my letter, and one from Doctor Dillenius, and directed to our worthy friend James Logan, for thee.

Pray, next year, look out for the flower of the Sweet Gum, and the Papaw. Send a few in a little bottle or phial of spirits; and send some dried, in paper. Our friend Linnæus, wants them much, as thee will see by Doctor Gronovius's letter, that I have sent to J. Logan. Pray desire him to show it thee.

Pray my love to Joseph Breintnall.

I am thine,

P. Collinson.

Pray describe the colours of the flowers of the Papaw, and the Sweet Gum; for they may fade so in paper, and change so in spirits, that we may be at a loss to discern them; and send the seasons of their flowering—and send two or three of the fairest Gum burs thee can get. Pray forget not a specimen of the Black Gum, in flower and leaf; for we are at a loss to know what it is; and a specimen of Black Haw [*Viburnum prunifolium*, L.], in flower and leaf,—for this we know not.

* *Lysimachia.* "Herb Twopence," is one of the common English names of *L. Nummularia*, L.

JOHN BARTRAM TO P. COLLINSON.

May, 1738.

I am exceedingly pleased with thy long letters, as thee calls them; but I wish they had been as long again.   I shall make my observations on them, as follows:

December the 10*th*.—I am almost overjoyed in reading the contents of this letter,—wherein thee acknowledges thy satisfaction of my remarks on the Locusts, Caterpillars, Pigeons, and Snakes.   I am very thankful to thee, and the Royal Society, for taking so much notice of my poor performances.   It is a great encouragement for me to continue my observations of natural phenomena. If I see any Locusts this year, I shall be very particular in my remarks; as also the Papaw, to gratify thy curious friend, who, thee says, will send me a specimen of his performances; which will be very acceptable.

December the 14*th*.—I am glad my map of Schuylkill pleases thee and Lord PETRE.

The Panthers have not seized any of our people, that I have heard; but many have been sadly frightened with them.   They have pursued several men, both on horseback and foot.   Many have shot them down, and others have escaped by running away. But I believe, as a Panther doth not much fear a single man, so he hath no great desire to seize him; for if he had, running from him would be a poor means to escape such a nimble, strong creature,—which will leap above twenty feet at one leap.   *   *   *

*   I take thy advice about books very kindly,—although I love reading such dearly : and I believe, if SOLOMON had loved women less, and books more, he would have been a wiser and happier man than he was.

In thy letter of December the 20th, thee supposes me to spend five or six weeks in collections for you, and that ten pounds will defray all my annual expenses : but I assure thee, I spend more than twice that time, annually; and ten pounds will not, at a moderate expense, defray my charges abroad—beside my neglect of business at home, in fallowing, harvest, and seed time.

Indeed, I was more than two weeks' time in gathering the small acorns of the Willow-leafed Oak, which are very scarce, and falling with the leaves,—so that daily I had to rake up the leaves and shake the acorns out, before they were devoured by the squirrels and hogs; and I reckoned it good luck if I could gather twenty under one tree—and hardly one in twenty bore any. Yet I don't begrudge my labour; but would do anything reasonable to serve you. But by the sequel of thy letter, you are not sensible of the fourth part of the pains I take to oblige you.

Thee seems to be surprised that I should write that we have Sloe Trees enough—and JAMES LOGAN wrote to thee for some. But, my good friend, I assure thee, I assert nothing to thee but what is real fact. The first I observed of Sloe Trees, was at a plantation, whose owner came two years into this country before a house was built in Philadelphia. I brought some from there, when I settled on my plantation. I saw another tree, near Philadelphia, as thick as my thigh; and, last year, I showed JAMES LOGAN English Thorns, Bullaces, and Sloes, growing in a hedge which he rides close by, from his house to town, which I believe hath been planted twenty years: and many others grow in several distant places in the country, but are liable to be bit with the same insects as the rest of our stone fruits, except Peaches and Cherries; and are increased by plenty of suckers.

*   *   *   *   *   *   *

Now, my kind and generous friend, I shall return thee my hearty thanks for thy care and pains which thee hath taken, and the many good offices thee hath done for me; and further, if thee finds any expressions in my letter a little out of the way, thee will not take it in the wrong sense. I assure thee, I bear thee a great deal of good-will; or if thee thinks I am too short and imperfect in explaining any subject, which I give thee any account of, pray let me know, and I will satisfy thee according to the best of my knowledge; for I love plain dealing.

[December, 1738.]

DEAR FRIEND :—

I have performed my journey through Maryland and Virginia, as far as Williamsburgh, so up James River to the mountains, so over and between the mountains, in many very crooked turnings and windings, in which, according to the nearest computation I can make, betwixt my setting out and returning home, I travelled 1100 miles in five weeks' time; having rested but one day in all that time, and that was at Williamsburgh. I happened to go in the only time for gathering of seeds—the autumnal—both in Maryland and Virginia; and the exceeding mild fall favoured the opportunity upon and between the mountains, whereby I gathered abundance of kinds of seeds in perfection, which have not ripened for several years, because of the early frosts, which came a month or six weeks sooner than they did this year. Indeed, beyond the mountains in Virginia and Pennsylvania, there is a great variety, that I saw; and the inhabitants say, the ground is covered with delicate beautiful flowers in the spring, which are not to be found after hot weather comes on. When I first began to find many curious seeds, I wrapped them up in paper separately, and put them in my leather bags; but in riding, and shaking, they fretted the paper, and mixed together. So, afterwards, I gathered all together, as I found them,—which I send to you all mixed; and as they are most of them perennial, I suppose they will do well enough sown together.

I sent, by friend THOMAS BOND, a box of turtle eggs, and several roots packed up carefully; but the captain was so long before he sailed, after he talked of sailing within two or three days, that I am afraid they were damnified. I sent a box of insects, and a jar of Papaw flowers and fruit, which I hope are come safe to hand. This hath been but a scarce year for several kinds of forest seeds, so could not procure several which thee sent for; but I have made it up, in a great variety of seeds of curious plants which grow between and upon the mountains. Next year, there may be more plenty of several kinds which you want; so please to let me know what sort will be acceptable: and if you please to order me to New England, next fall, I am not much against it,—having health and prosperity also. I should be glad to have letters of recommendation to thy friends there.

I received thy letter of July the 10th, with the names of the plants I sent last year, with the seeds and Tulip roots; all which I am obliged to thee for. I wish there may be some, differing from what we have already; for we have a great variety obtained from the breeders, which we have had these many years. The Red Lily seldom produces above one flower upon a stalk. This year the Medlar bore, which thee sent me for the Neapolitan,—but I believe it is the English kind. However, one of our Persimmons is worth a dozen of them, for goodness in eating, and as big. But we have great variety of them; some are ripe in the middle of

September, others not till Christmas. They are extremely disagreeable to eat until they are thorough ripe and will fall with
shaking the tree : then their pulp is delicious. But their skin, which
is as thin as the finest paper, still retains an astringent bitterness :
yet many of our country people are so greedy of them, that they
swallow down skin, pulp, and seeds, all together. I admire they
are not cultivated with great care in Europe, instead of many other
kinds of fruit which are much inferior in goodness. They make
an excellent liquor, or wine, for pleasant drinking.

Our friend, ISHAM RANDOLPH, (a generous, good-natured gentleman, and well respected by most who are acquainted with him,)
hath agreed with me to have a correspondence together ; but can't
tell well which way to carry it on—whether back of the mountains, by the way of Shenandoah, or below the mountains, we can't
yet tell.

I think to be diligent in my observation on the flower of our
Sweet Gum, to gratify thee and thy curious friends. It seems
strange that some accurate botanist hath not already taken notice
of it ; but I suppose the difficulty of procuring the flowers, hath
been some reason of the neglect,—for the tree generally groweth
straight and tall, and seldom bears seed before the tree is forty or
fifty feet high.

When I was down in Virginia, my wife sent a box of Allspice
berries, which I had with some expense of time collected,—being
most of what I could find about where I live, and for twenty miles
distance.

I obtained a sight of the copy of Doctor GRONOVIUS's letter,
which thee sent to JAMES LOGAN, just before I sat out for Maryland,
which a gentleman had copied before LOGAN sent it back—which
was soon after he received it. If I can any ways, without much
loss of time, oblige LINNÆUS or GRONOVIUS, at thine or their request, I am willing to do it. I perceive they are curious and ingenious botanists.

I have put several Sweet Gum burs in the box of seeds.

July, 1739.

FRIEND PETER COLLINSON :—

I have received thy kind letters by WRIGHT, which were very
acceptable,—as also the cash, which came in the very nick of time,

when I wanted to pay the mortgage interest. It was help in time of need, and a demonstration of thy regard for my welfare, and readiness to oblige me, which lays me under an obligation to watch and improve all opportunities wherein I can gratify thee.

I could get nothing of what thee mentioned thee sent by Captain BREAM, but a letter by the post, and the print of the *Magnolia*, which JAMES LOGAN thought had been sent for him. I went to our proprietor, and to Captain BREAM, to inquire for the box of seeds thee mentioned, but they affirmed they knew nothing of such a box.

P. COLLINSON TO JOHN BARTRAM.

London, January 26, 1738–9.

FRIEND JOHN :—

I am much obliged to thy good wife, for her kind letter in thy absence; and next I must tell thee, I was pleased with thine,—to hear of thy safe return from thy Virginia expedition; but am very angry with that sorry man ASHTON, for not taking in thy cargo of seeds. He was under obligations to me. I did not treat him so; but trusted him five pounds' worth of goods, but was three or four years getting it; nay, had it not been for CHARLES READ, deceased, who got the money, I much question if he would have had honesty or honour enough to have paid it, to this day; for during the time he owed me the money, he came to England, and promised to pay me. I thought him to be a man of honour; but, in short, he slunk away and never paid me,—and after that, gave CHARLES READ much trouble to get it, and paid no interest; so I was a loser,—for I sold the goods for ready money, and because cash fell short, took his note; and thus he has served me for my civility. I shall remember him.

I am, at present, greatly hurried in business; so must be very short, and only tell that I have sent thee a box of seeds, under cover to THOMAS PENN, your proprietor, for I was willing to take the advantage of the first ship, because the season slips away for sowing.

There is a small packet for Doctor WITT. Pray, somehow or other, convey it to him. Some fine Melon seed for THOMAS PENN; some Burgundy Trefoil [*Medicago sativa*, L., or *Lucerne*], for J.

LOGAN; and pray, where there is sufficient, let him have a share of the other seeds.

The Scorpioides [*Scorpiurus vermiculata*, L.] is a surprising phenomenon in nature—that the seed, or fruit, or pod of a plant should be so like an animal: for, when these are green, and pretty near full grown, gather one and pin it artfully on thy neckcloth, and there is not one in a great many will distinguish it from a smooth green caterpillar. Beside this pretty curiosity, this class of plants are of great service in hot, dry countries, for green fodder for their milk cattle, in the summer months. Please to impart this to friend LOGAN, with some seed of each.

I have before said sufficient of the Burgundy Trefoil. But lest that sent in the autumn should not be perfectly ripe, I have sent some more. Doctor DILLENIUS is of a strong opinion that it will prove the best, most productive of herbage, and durable, of any grass. It requires some care, at first setting out: so let it be sown carefully in your gardens, in order to raise seed for greater crops abroad.

Please to ask friend LOGAN to let thee peruse the Philosophical Transactions, that I send him by Captain WRIGHT. In them, thee will find a Dissertation on the Deer and Moose of your Continent. We have but an imperfect idea of your male, or buck, of your Fallow Deer,—as thee will perceive by the print, or figures annexed. I could be glad to have the scalp of one of your bucks, with its horns, full grown, on it. Perhaps this may be attainable by thy own procurement, or some of thy friends: and if thee canst inform us further, or better, in relation to those animals—the Deer and Moose—thee will much oblige thy sincere friend,

P. COLLINSON.

Pray remember, for friend CATESBY, flowers of the Papaw. He will thank thee very kindly for the fruit; and come they either dry, or in spirits, they will lose their colour: so pray describe it as well as thee can, that he may be qualified to paint it; and what colour is the fruit, when ripe, and its time of flowering, and time when the fruit is ripe.

Possibly some of your Indian traders may procure a Deer, or Stag's scalp, with the horns on.

London, February 1, 1738-9.

DEAR FRIEND :—

I forgot in my former, to give thee some account of the success of the turtle eggs. Unlucky for thee and for me, the captain set the box in the forecastle of the ship, where it was cold and wet; and notwithstanding thy care in pitching part of it, some water got to it, and the earth being cold, chilled the eggs; and I am afraid the box was tumbled up and down, which might bruise the eggs; and I think the eggs were put in too large a quantity of heavy earth. I carried them in the mould, and set them in a warm bakehouse, where they bake constantly every day; but yet not one came to good. Now, before, they were packed in light dry mould, in a smaller box and less earth, and set under the cabin, which is a very close, warm place,—and by that genial heat, which penetrated easily through the earth, supplied the place of the sun, and carried them on to maturity.

But though our success was indifferent in one,—the good state of the plants that came in the mould, made ample amends. I take them very kindly at thy hands. I shall soon expect their appearance. I have little to wish, but for *Dens Canis* with the yellow flower. I hope those thou sent, will flower this year; though I suspect it, for I think they are not strong enough.

The box of insects came in perfect good order—are extremely fine, and a great variety, and nicely cured and displayed. I desire thy acceptance of a piece of Sagathy, in acknowledgment for them. It was very lucky to find the chrysalis of that noble fine Moth.

*   *   *   *   *   *   *   *   *   *

I am much in a hurry; so cannot but add, I am thy real friend,

P. COLLINSON.

I dare not look into thy letters, for I know there are many things that require my notice; but I can't yet do it.

I sent some Ginseng roots to China. If they sell well, a good profitable trade may be carried on. In the mean time, sow the seed, and raise a stock to furnish my friend, when he returns. I intend the benefit for thyself. Keep that a secret, and raise what thee canst; for I have an opinion it will turn to account, if my friend manages it rightly.

London, February 7, 1738–9.
DEAR FRIEND JOHN :—
Notwithstanding thy cargo of seeds is not arrived, yet, as I know thy probity, and the service a remittance may be to thee, and as such another opportunity may not offer this year, to send halfpence—because there is some difficulty attends it, unless the captain is in our interest ; for this reason, our right trusty and well-beloved Captain WRIGHT has procured for thee ten pounds' worth of halfpence : for which I this day took his receipt, and paid him the money for them. I wish them safe to thy hands, and am thy real friend,

P. COLLINSON.

London, February 7, 1738–9.
Captain EDWARD WRIGHT :—
Pray deliver to JOHN BARTRAM's own hand, ten pounds' worth of halfpence, for which I have your receipt ; and my friend JOHN's receipt shall be a sufficient discharge for so doing. I am your sincere friend,

P. COLLINSON.

Captain WRIGHT has also a brown paper parcel for thee.

Pray remember seed of the Red Cedar, for a friend of Lord PETRE, for which thou shall be paid thy price, separately—a bushel or two : and a large quantity small cones of Swamp Laurel, or White Tulip Tree [*Magnolia glauca*, L.].

I hope thy box of seeds, from your proprietor, has come safe to hand.

I long for next ship, to hear of thy Virginia expedition.

I fancy, now thee has made what discoveries thee for the present intends, thee will lie still, and let thy correspondent reap the benefit of them ; for I know, in rambling to and fro, not many seeds can be gathered, or at least, but a few sorts. But, when thee knows where to go for a particular plant, and the season of its ripening seed is a certainty, it is much securer than going on discoveries. However, thee will hear more by next ship.

Friend JOHN, pray call at J. LOGAN's. I have sent thee a print of the great *Magnolia;* and with it, thee will see a Catalogue of our American plants.

London, February 24, 1738-9.
Pensylvania Coffee-House.

FRIEND JOHN :—

To-morrow Captain WRIGHT sails: so that I have only time to acquaint thee that no ship is yet arrived, that makes me in pain for the cargo of seeds, for this year. He has been so good to procure for thy use, ten pounds' worth of halfpence. I paid him 4s. 6d. for procuring and carrying on board. He has also a piece of Sagathy, for thy own wear.

Captain BREAM is not yet got clear off the Channel. He has been stayed some weeks, so that WRIGHT may have a chance of getting as soon as him. I think I never remember the like. We have had southwest winds, with very short intervals of east-northeast, which was so variable, that no ship has got clear of the Channel since the 13th December. Some ships have had a terrible time on't, lying so long in the Downs. This wind has brought us exceeding temperate weather. Our Almond trees were in blossom by the latter end of January, and all vegetables in proportion. No frost since the 5th of January, and but very slight ones before.

I have writ by Captain BREAM, and sent a box of seeds under cover to THOMAS PENN ; and a parcel to J. LOGAN, per WRIGHT.

But the principal reason of my writing now is, to desire thee to procure what plants thee canst of Ginseng, and plant in thy garden, and raise what thee canst from seed. I am well assured it will prove a very profitable commodity to China, who value it above anything.

I have compared yours with the Chinese, and find them in all respects the same. Your proprietor was so kind to send me a considerable parcel, and I have trusted a particular friend with it, to carry to China, to see how they approve of it, and to find what price it bears ; but my friend is under promise not to discover that it is *American,* for if they know that, they are so fanciful, it may not be so good as their own.*

---

* "Fanciful" as the Chinese are, their prejudices on this head were not so firmly rooted as those of *John Bull.* "*American*" products, and especially the *Ginseng,* soon found a ready acceptance in the "Celestial Empire ;" whereas it

So get a stock by thee, as soon as thee can, and be sure conceal thy intention from every one. In twenty-four months my friend will be here again from China, and then shall give thee notice. Pray send me a root or two in mould, for my garden.

It is now very late, so must conclude.

Thy real frend,

P. COLLINSON.

London, April 12, 1739.

DEAR FRIEND : —

I hope thou has mine per Captain WRIGHT, with the ten pounds in halfpence, and a piece of Sagathy.

And now I shall take notice of thine of December 9th, which came very opportunely, and in pretty good season for the seeds ; for it was March the 9th I received thy letter, and in about a week's time I got the seeds from on board. All seemed in good order, but two parcels of acorns that had spired and were good for nothing—had been better left behind than sent. These I have distributed as formerly.

We think this year thee had better rest from thy labours, for I find travelling furnishes little but herbaceous seeds and specimens. What thy employers most want, are shrubs and trees ; and I find nothing new of these that thee has sent seeds of, but the fine Pine, which thou found in the Vale, which seems new to us ; and if thou could go at a proper season, and bring a horse-load of cones, it would be a very acceptable cargo. This sort, I observe, has three leaves in a sheath. The White Pine, of which thee sent a plant which thrives finely, is called here, as thee will find by MILLER'S Dictionary, Lord WEYMOUTH'S Pine. This sort is scarce and rare with us. Now a cargo of this will be very acceptable, and what thee must endeavour to collect ; and a quantity of the common Red or Jersey Pine, which has only two leaves in a sheath, more White and Red Cedar, Rose Laurel cones—this was the most valuable in the last cargo,—Papaw, Sugar Maple, Black Haw, or Indian Sweetmeat, Spruce cones, and all the sorts of Firs.

Perhaps thee'll say these are only or chiefly to be had in New

required ages—and a political revolution—to subdue the obstinate prepossessions cherished in the mother country against everything coming from or belonging to these colonies.

England, or Newfoundland. I should not be against going thither
for them at a proper time; but first let's get the seeds that are
nearer home, for by thy several expeditions thee art now fully
informed where there is the greatest quantity of the kinds we want
growing; and if thee should go to New England and bring home
but little, I think it hardly quits cost. In that country I know
nobody. After all that I have said, it must be left to thee; but I
think it had better be deferred, and only ransack the Jerseys, and
the country about, if it will afford the seeds we want. And to
encourage thee to proceed with spirit, I have got another person
who desires the value of ten pounds sterling of cones of all the
sorts of Pines thee can get. It is left to thee. Of the Jersey Pine
I take it there is no great difficulty to get sufficient, and what thou
can of the other sorts. Thee has not to do with unreasonable
people. The ten pound cargo put in a case by itself, for I will
have no more trouble of dividing; and it would save me a great
deal of trouble—as Lord PETRE has half—if his was put in a case
by itself. As to the other half, I may make a shift to divide that.

In my last I acquainted thee with the fate of the Turtle eggs.
Some of the roots are alive that came with them, in particular, the
Dwarf Double Mountain *Ranunculus;* and there is another with
Narcissus leaves, which seems to me what I have had by the name
of Atamasco Lilio-Narcissus, a pretty flower. None of the yellow
flowering *Dens Canis* flowered this year; perhaps the roots are not
of sufficient maturity. But the box of insects came safe and are
very fine, in particular that noble moth. The jar with the Papaws
came safe, and my friend CATESBY thanks thee very much.

Now, dear friend JOHN, I come to thank thee for thy curious
collection of living plants for myself. But oh! sad story for to
tell, not the least glimpse of one was to be seen. If the unworthy
captain had set that case only in his cabin, all had been safe; but
it was stowed on the deck above the hold, and covered all over
with pipe-staves. But all this might have been tolerable, if that
mischievous and unruly vermin, the rats, had not fell on board it;
for so it was, when I came to get it out of the ship, lo, behold, two
nests of young callow rats were kindled there; and I take it, what
with their trampling, &c., everything above ground was totally
destroyed; and I am afraid their excretions have affected the roots,
for only one appeared to have life. It grieved me to the heart to
see so many curious things, and so much labour and pains like to

be destroyed by these nasty creatures, and the neglect of the captain.

But for the future, I must desire thee to put the living things in a less case, which takes up so much room that, unless it is a large ship, there is not room for it : for all the sods of plants might have been packed in half the room, which would save a great deal of freight,—for thee knows the earth about them is only intended to keep them moist till they come here, and then they are soon transplanted; so that the sods may be thrust as close as possible to one another. Two inches of earth below, and covered two inches, may be sufficient to convey them hither. Be sure make the bottom full of large holes; and rather make two small cases, which are more manageable, and more convenient to be stowed, than such a large one as the last, which I believe weighed two or three hundred-weight, and as much as two men could carry.

I have very carefully planted all I could find of the roots, and please myself with hopes; for I have had a many pretty plants come out of the earth, beside those intended.

The White *Lychnis* I most regret; but pray don't part with it till thee has made sufficient increase. The Cluster Cherries thee formerly sent us, are grown fine plants; but what is admirable, they hold their leaves all winter, that P. MILLER takes them for an evergreen, and so do several of your shrubs.

The Mountain Laurels seem to bud strong this year; the Gooseberry and both the Shrub Honeysuckles grow finely, and most of that cargo,—also the White Cedar, and sundry others; which gives me great entertainment.

The *Spiræa*, with spikes of white flowers, holds its leaves all winter—is a pretty plant; and an *Opulus*, as it seems to be, grows strongly, and out of the mould is come your *Hepatica;* but what is surprising, your Herb Twopence [*Lysimachia ?*] scarcely shoots two new leaves a year,—and I have tried it various ways.

Most of the Ferns thee formerly sent me, grow finely. I have hopes of these in the sods. I shall conclude, with observing what seeds will be acceptable next spring; and am truly thine,

P. COLLINSON.

Doctor DILLENIUS, to whom I referred the naming of the two quires, has not been well,—which thee may perceive per the shortness of the names, and many wanting; but such as they are, I give thee, as under—but I hope the Doctor may review them again.

*   *   *   *   *

No. 5. *Obeliscotheca,* Hort. Eltham. or *Chrysanthemum.* This plant I have had long in my garden. I much admire it for its duration in flower. My friend GRACE can best tell if this is his *Corona,* or Tower flower. Pray ask him. [Probably the *Obeliscaria pinnata,* of CASSINI and DE CANDOLLE; or *Lepachys pinnata,* of RAFIN. and TORREY and GRAY.]   *   *   *

No. 6. The Yapon, of Virginia,—or Cassena, of Carolina [*Ilex Cassena,* Mx. and Ell.; *I. vomitoria,* Ait. & DC.]. The Indians drive a great trade with the berries (to make tea with) to the Gulf of Mexico. It is reckoned excellent for the miners. It grows nowhere to the northward of that island thee found it on,—which belongs to Colonel CUSTIS. I have it in my garden.   *   *

No. 12. It was very ingeniously done, to send the flowers of the great *Chamærhododendron,* which is a great satisfaction to our botanists, and anticipates the pleasure of seeing it in flower. Pray thank Mr. HAMILTON in my name for the favour, which did us a great pleasure, and saved thee much trouble.   *   *   *

No. 28. This white, long-coned Pine, we have had long in England, (but scarce,) called Lord WEYMOUTH'S Pine. (Send cones.)

No. 29. But what surprises me, that this, which is your common Pine, should not be described, or known to be in England, by all the search and inquiry that Dr. DILLENIUS or PHIL. MILLER, has been able yet to make. It is a fine plant.

*   *   *   *   *

No. 69. *Christophoriana (Baccis cœruleis,)* with blue berries. A good plant. We have it not. [*Leontice thalictroides,* L.].

*   *   *   *

London, July 10, 1739.
DEAR FRIEND:—

I am obliged to thee for thine per HEADMAN; and have the pleasure to tell thee, that most of the plants in the last cargo thrive

finely. I never had such luck before. That stately Martagon thee
sent, found on a bank near Schuylkill, is now near flowering. It
is five and a half feet high, and will, I believe, have fifteen flowers
—which is prodigious. It differs from the great Marsh Martagon,
for that will not flower till the middle of August, and another
sort, I had formerly from Doctor WITT; but that was a smaller
sort, and never has but four or five flowers on a stalk.

I had three of your Red Lilies, that flowered this year, that
came in the last cargo: they had but one flower on each root.
Pray, have they no more with you?

The Laurels all grow, or *Chamærhododendros;* the two Shrub
Honeysuckles; and a very pretty plant—a species of Hurtleberry,
a *Vitis idæa*—has been finely in blossom. The Gooseberry, from
Conestogo, grows well; and above all, the White Cedar thrives
finely,—and the Pine, which is what we call Lord WEYMOUTH'S;
and a many other pretty plants, which come out of the sods of
mould, taken up with the plants,—two or three sorts of Helleborine, as they seem to be;—which shows that your woods are sowed
thick with rare and odd plants.

There are several other odd plants, that I can't yet discover
what they are: for all these I am much obliged to thee, and hope
the things per Captain WRIGHT are come safe to hand,—and I
hope will make some part of amends for thy great care and
trouble.

I am much obliged to thee for thy kind offers of service. I
shall ask nothing that I have done sufficiently already. It's fit thee
should take breath a little.

As to the Society that thee hints at, had you a set of learned,
well-qualified members to set out with, it might draw your neighbours to correspond with you. Your Library Company I take to
be an essay towards such a Society. But to draw learned strangers
to you, to teach sciences, requires salaries and good encouragement;
and this will require public, as well as proprietary assistance,—
which can't be at present complied with—considering the infancy
of your colony.

I have sent a few double Tulips, to ornament thy garden, and
a few seeds; and some offsets of best breeding Tulips, which are
endowed with a wonderful faculty to diversify into variety of
colours. Consult MILLER, on their culture.

The *Ranunculuses* will not bear your severe frosts without great tendance, and covering: so I would advise them to be put into the ground when their severity is over.

The pretty *Spiræa*, that thee sent me a specimen of in the quire before last, that I doubted if it was of your natural growth, I have now a plant in flower, that Doctor WITT sent me, which shows that it is.

I have little more to add, but my love and respects.

I am thy sincere friend,

P. COLLINSON.

London, September 2, 1739.

DEAR FRIEND JOHN:—

In thine of last December, thee seems to doubt if the Medlar is the Neapolitan; but I do not doubt it. Perhaps the stock, or soil, does not suit it: for they grow here as large as the bottom of a common wine-glass. But thy dislike of the fruit may proceed from not knowing when they are ripe.　　*　　*　　*　　*

The Persimmon, that thee so much commends, is what I never met with from others. But there may be different sorts. That which is ripe in September is fittest for us who lie twelve degrees more to the north than you do. I have in my garden the tallest tree I ever yet saw, sent me some years agone by Doctor WITT. It thrives and grows vigorously, and bears blossoms, but no fruit. But I have seen fruit ripe in England; but it has but little reputation here,—perhaps for the same reason that I assigned for the Medlar. We have now plenty of this tree, in some gardens, which is much admired for its beautiful green leaves.

In thine of April 1st, thee observes what difficulty there is to raise the White Bryony,—which with us is a weed that we can't well get rid of. However, I intend to send more seed, for further trial. With us, it delights to grow on dry banks, that have stunted shrubs growing on them. These it covers, and makes a pretty show, when the berries are ripe.

I hope thee has better success with the Larch cones sent this year. I have some fine trees of this kind, sent me from Newfoundland.

I am surprised the Gorse should be killed with your cold, when they grow in the north of England, where the weather is much more severe than in the south. If this was sown on some dry banks, in your woods, I can't but think it would succeed better; for thick woods, and the falling leaves, keep off the severe cold. I conceive it would be a good protection to any woody plant, if heaps of dry leaves were heaped up about it, in sharp weather. It would keep the cold from penetrating from above and below;—as for instance, if the Tree Sage was protected in this manner. As for the Wood Sage, that goes down every year. I am glad that thee has the Archangel and *Galeopsis;* they will endure.

I do not wonder that neither Rose nor Sweetbriar comes double, like their original. Thee hadst a chance for it. But if thee considers, no full double flowers are apt to produce seed—some few excepted; but seed is generally produced from what we call semi-double flowers, and these are the more liable to go to single.

*   *   *   *

I have this day received a letter from Petersburgh; and am assured, per Doctor AMMANN, Professor of Botany there, that the Siberian Rhubarb is the true sort. I wish a quantity was produced with you, to try the experiment. Both this and the Rhapontic make excellent tarts, before most other fruits fit for that purpose are ripe. All you have to do, is to take the stalks from the root, and from the leaves; peel off the rind, and cut them in two or three pieces, and put them in crust with sugar and a little cinnamon; then bake the pie, or tart: eats best cold. It is much admired here, and has none of the effects that the roots have. It eats most like gooseberry pie.

Our friend CATESBY gives thee many thanks for thy remembrance of him, and for the Papaw blossoms and fruit.

An acceptable present to Lady PETRE, I believe, would be a Humming-bird's nest, with eggs.

I am obliged to thee for thy care of the Sugar Birch (pray send me a good specimen of it), and for the Laurustinus thee intends me. Pray let it be well grown, and a flowering plant: I am not in haste. The root of the Oak shows what a rich depth of soil you have.

*   *   *   *

If I write the same things over again, thee must excuse it; for multitude of affairs divert my memory, and my letters are not worth copying,—being mostly writ behind the counter.

I have procured the other things mentioned in thy order, which I have committed to the care of LAWRENCE WILLIAMS. They are all in a box, marked I. B. No. 1, and thy name in length on the side.—At the bottom of the box, is a specimen of what our botanists have dubbed *Collinsonia*, but I think it should rather be *Bartramia;* for I had it in the very first seeds thee sent me. MILLER is mistaken in making it come from Maryland. Pray fail not, next year, to send me some seed for it, for it flowers so late it will not ripen here.

$$*　　　*　　　*　　　*　　　*$$

Lord PETRE has sent thee a present of PHILIP MILLER'S second part of his Dictionary, in return for the specimens sent him. Thou will see a cut in P. M.'s Dictionary, of a *Polygala*, which is a reputed specific for a pleurisy [doubtless the *P. Senega*, L.].

London, June 10, 1740.

DEAR FRIEND :—

On the other sides are a miscellany of matters, as they come into my noddle.

I find in the cargo of Martagons, had from thee and others, that there is apparently two sorts; and two sorts of your Lilies with single flowers. I have one opened this day, that may be called literally the Fiery Lily. It is the deepest flame-colour I ever saw. It is really a fine flower, and, I think, of thy sending. The other Lilies will not flower this month.　　　*　　　*　　　*

Thee sent me what we call the Atamasco Lily, from its shape. It has a blush of purple before the flower opens ; is white within. It is properly a *Lilio-Narciss:* the leaves of the last, and flower of the first. If, in thy rambles, thee happens on this flower, pray send a root or two. And please to remember a lump of Sweet Gum ; Sour Gum ; Allspice Gum, if it bears any. Does the Red or White Cedar produce any? This last thrives finely. The leaves have a fine spicy smell.

$$*　　　*　　　*　　　*　　　*$$

I shall conclude with my best wishes for thy prosperity; and am thy real friend,

P. COLLINSON.

$$*　　　*　　　*　　　*　　　*$$

Pray see what further Mosses thee canst collect for Doctor DILLENIUS. He defers completing his work, till he sees what comes from thee, CLAYTON, and Doctor MITCHELL.

The *Calceolus*, in the last cargo, proves at last a fine red one—a very curious flower, indeed. M. CATESBY has painted it.

Amongst the last things, there is a very pretty *Lychnis*, with pale blue flowers, and sweet smell; but a many of the lumps of mould don't yet appear. I wish the beasts of rats han't killed them. The little box, by SEYMOUR, han't fared much better; for they made a nest in that.   *   *   *

London, July 22d, 1740.

DEAR FRIEND :—

I had the pleasure of thine, of April 29th, 1740. Thy experiment of the usefulness of the *Farina*, is very curious and entertaining.* Where plants of a class are growing near together, they will mix and produce a mingled species. An instance we have in our gardens, raised by the late THOMAS FAIRCHILD, who had a plant from seed, that was compounded of the Carnation and Sweet William. It has the leaves of the first, and its flowers double like the Carnation—the size of a Pink,—but in clusters like the Sweet William. It is named a *Mule*,—per analogy to the mule produced from the Horse and Ass.

Writing on these matters, brings to mind the Papaw—an Indian fruit,—which in our stoves is produced in great plenty. On this tree, is very remarkably distinct, male, female, and hermaphrodite blossoms, which are very extraordinary to see : but whether the last is an assistant in generation, or is a sport in nature, is not yet agreed.

Thy journey to the mountains must be very delightful, and affords a double gratification, to please both thyself and friends.

It is something particular, in your Yew's taking root as it trails on the ground. I never observed ours to do so.   *   *   *

Of all the American people I ever talked with about your Mulberries (which we have in our gardens), that one of ours, for largeness and flavour, is worth a many of yours : but how it happens that Doctor KEARSLEY thinks the contrary, I can't say.

*   *   *   *   *

Doctor WITT'S hollow-leafed Lavender, is, no doubt, the Side-

---

* This, doubtless, refers to the experiments by JOHN BARTRAM on the *Lychnis dioica*, in corroboration of those upon Indian Corn, then recently made by JAMES LOGAN.

saddle flower; but what relation it has to *Lavender*, I must leave to him. The plant with tricolor leaves, I am well assured, is your fine *Clinopodium*. Our late severe winter has carried all mine off; so pray send me some more seed,—and of the *Lychnis* with Crosswort leaves.

The Doctor did not carefully distinguish, or observe, the fruit he mentions, which I take to be no more than an excrescence raised by insects, like Galls and Oak-apples; which have a pulpy substance in them of a beautiful complexion—sufficient to set a breeding woman a longing,—and yet are raised only as a proper nidus, and vehicle, to contain and nourish the infant insect till it is fit to take wing, and provide for itself. It is certainly so, by the small white worm which he mentions, which grows brown— which is then in chrysalis as the fruit grows riper.　　　＊　　　＊

London, October 20, 1740.

DEAR FRIEND :—

Inclosed is the Mate's receipt for a box of bulbs, directed for thee. Make much of them; for they are such a collection as is rarely to be met with, all at once: for, all the sorts of bulbous roots being taken up this year, there is some of every sort. There is above twenty sorts of *Crocus*—as many of *Narcissus*—all our sorts of Martagons and Lilies—with *Gladiolus*, *Ornithogalums*, Moleys and *Irises*, with many others I don't now remember, which time will show thee. It is likely some sorts thee may have; but I believe there is more that you have not; so pray take great care of them. Give them a good soil, and keep them clear from weeds, which are a great prejudice to these flowers in the spring.

I have several very curious flowers out of the mixed Virginia seeds; in particular a new *Jacea*, with hoary rough leaves; a very pretty dwarf Gentian, with a large blue flower, the extremity of the flower-leaves, all notched or jagged. The whole plant is not above three or four inches high; I am afraid it is an annual.＊ But there is a great variety, besides: a very pretty *Gratiola*, and a *Dracocephalon*,—it has a labiated flower like Snap Dragon,

---

＊ This, apparently, refers to our *Gentiana crinita*, though it is seldom so dwarf- ish with us. Authors, generally, speak of it as a *biennial:* and when I hinted a suspicion (in *Flora Cestrica*) that it might be an *annual*, I was not aware that PETER COLLINSON had the same suspicion, nearly a century before.

and is very near akin to it. Lord PETRE has had the greatest
luck, having the largest quantity of seed. He has two or three
sorts of fine *Chrysanthemums*, or Sun-flowers: *Asters*, I have a
fine new sort. Your thickets must make a beautiful show in the
autumn, with these plants; for I see they must be in great plenty,
—for almost every sod has an *Aster* growing with the curious
plant that thee sent.   *   *   *   *   *

I hope I shall now see JOSSELYN's Daffodil, or your *Dens Canis*,
with a yellow flower, in perfection.

I am much obliged to thee for the account of Dr. WITT's rarities. Thee has unravelled the whole mystery.

Pray tell me, is the plant thee calls a *Valerian*, with blue
flowers, which came in the last cargo, a native of your country?
for it has been long in our gardens. We call it Greek Valerian
[*Polemonium.*].

Every day I expect thy last specimens from Holland. They
have been long delayed by many accidents, but I can't help myself; for Doctor GRONOVIUS is so kind to fix them neatly on fine
white paper, that they look as beautiful as so many pictures, and
names them into the bargain. Neither my skill nor time would
permit me to do this; so I am glad to comply with his own time:
but this will prevent me giving names to the last two quires, till
next year. I can tell thee in the next edition of Virginia plants,
thee will see *Bartramia*.   *   *   *   *

I am thy true and sincere friend,

P. COLLINSON.

London, December 20, 1740.

FRIEND JOHN :—

It is to be hoped that thy patience will be rewarded with some
knowledge, as the other part of the sheet will inform thee.*

There are many names not to be met with in old botanists.
The discoveries of such numbers of plants in your world, has obliged
our moderns, being new genuses—to give them new names.

* "The other part of the sheet" contains a *numbered list*, as named by GRO-
NOVIUS—of the specimens which had been sent by JOHN BARTRAM to P. COLLIN-
SON. In that list, one of the specimens is thus noticed:

"CORTUSÆ *sive* VERBASCI. *Fl. Virg.* pp. 74, 75. *This, being a new genus, may
be called* BARTRAMIA."

If thee hast any complaint, Doctor GRONOVIUS is answerable.
I am, my good friend, much thine, in haste,

P. COLLINSON.

We are much in fear, lest the rascally Spaniards should fall foul
on our vegetable cargoes.   *   *   *
As thee has the *Flora Virginica*, thee will find most if not all
the plants mentioned there. I have sent thee a correct preface,
in our worthy friend J. LOGAN'S parcel.

London, February 25, 1740–1.

DEAR FRIEND:

I now come to answer thine of November 7th, 1740, and give
thee some account of thy cargoes.

The three long boxes of seeds came all safe and in very good
order, and gave content. The two boxes of plants in earth, were
of a right size, and came in excellent order; everything appearing
as fresh and lively as if that minute taken out of the woods.

I wish we had been so lucky to have thought of this method before: thy pains, and so many fine plants had not been lost.

One box I gave to Lord PETRE, and the other to M. CATESBY,
and reserved only for myself the Lady's Slipper and Ipecacuanha;
the others I had before; and the little box of insects was in fine
order.   *   *   *   *
The box of specimens, with seeds and nests, came very well. The
mechanism of the last will afford much contemplation. One I
shall give Lord PETRE, and the other keep myself. The Indian
curiosity and piece of pot, I shall speak more particularly to, at
more leisure, for now is our greatest hurry.

In return for so many rare things, I desire thy acceptance of
four volumes of Natural History, which I don't doubt will give thee
great entertainment. Thee will find the account of the Sea Muscle
will explain what thee has formerly observed, and writ to me about;
which I had intended to have answered, but that I intended to send
thee these books, which are much esteemed here.

I can't enough commend thy diligence in procuring such a noble
collection of herbaceous seeds. Lord PETRE, P. MILLER, and Dr.
DILLENIUS, have principally shared in them. Then I pick and
choose what plants I like. A few favourites I sow myself; but as

theirs are botanic gardens, all sorts are greatly acceptable to them. I love all fine, showy, specious plants.

I am extremely obliged to thee for the chrysalises. It is wonderful, as thee observes, to see the surprising instinct and contrivance of the creature, to preserve itself from being lost and trodden under foot, by the strong web, that both secures it and the stalk of the leaf to the twig.   *   *   *

The shell thee sent is very curious. I shall remember thee for it. The petrifactions are as extraordinary : shall at proper time further consider them. But pray what distance is the mountain from the sea ?

The cavern thee was so hardy to ramble through—every creek and corner—is a strange phenomenon in nature ; and what can be the original cause and intention, or real use of these cavities in the earth, is best known to the Great Architect of them. We know of little else, than to raise our admiration. They have, indeed, sometimes served for a retreat and place of hiding, but they are not habitable ; though some creature thought fit to use one of its isles for its magazine.

This puts me in mind to ask thee a question,—if thee ever met with a harmless land animal, about the size of the large gray Fox-Squirrel, called a *Monack*. It has a long brown fur, and seems to have much of the squirrel and rat in its composition. It has lived several years, running about house like a cat, eats green roots and fruits ; was sent me from Maryland, where it is also called One of the Seven Sleepers,—for it buries itself in the cellar in September or October, as the season happens warmer or colder, and comes out again in March or April. I never met with any one mention this creature but LAWSON, in his History of Carolina.*

But now I come to take notice of the main article, and tell thee that I have procured twenty pounds, ten shillings, in halfpence, which I have put up in a strong cask. Thy name is writ on the head at length, and I have ordered D. BARCLAY to put up two pieces cloth in I. PEMBERTON, Jr.'s goods for thee.   *   *   *

I could not omit sending thee the above-mentioned £20. 10s. by Captain WRIGHT, who is a most obliging man, and he knows thee, and perhaps may give the carriage, though I shall not receive the money this twelvemonth, nay, I have now some standing two years;

* The reference here, is to the Marmot, or Maryland Woodchuck ; called Ground-hog in Pennsylvania (*Arctomys Monax*, Harlan).

for it is very hard getting money of great people, though I give them my labour and pains into the bargain. They are glad of the cargo, but are apt to forget all the rest. They give good words, but that will not always do; but for thy sake, and if it will but contribute to keep thee in thy circumstances, I gladly will do all, and much more, if it will but be of service to thee, and encourage thy ingenuity.   *   *   *   *   *

It is very entertaining to survey the great variety of Mosses that there is with you, as well as with us. I have sent mine down to the Doctor, who admires at thy diligence. He observes paper is scanty, so has desired me to send thee half a ream of writing paper, which comes in a parcel per Captain WRIGHT, with some paper for specimens. The books, TOURNEFORT, are a present from Lord PETRE, which I hope will make thee easy.

I sent all thou desired to Doctor LAWSON; doubt not but thee will hear from him and CATESBY. The last has a mind to figure the Laurel, or Chamærhododendron, and by the fine specimens thee hast sent, is pretty able to do it; but we are at a loss for the exact figure and shape of the flowers. Thee says it is of a pale red, or blush colour; but in thy last letter thee says they are studded with green spots. Now here we are at a loss again, so if thee can help us, pray do. Thee tells me that thee has a mind to draw or paint it, pray try. One single flower is sufficient, and some marks where the spots are; we can easily add the rest. Leaves and seed-vessels we have, and also growing plants.

Colonel CUSTIS and I. RANDOLPH kindly remember thee.

The draft of the cavern, and map of thy journal, make each very conceivable and intelligible; but pray what does WHITFIELD pretend to do with the five thousand acres of land?

*   *   *   *   *

Wheat is now seven shillings per bushel, but is expected lower. I am, dear JOHN, thy sincere friend,

P. COLLINSON.

Inclosed is a seed-vessel of a plant that may deserve some observations. It proves to be a species of Chamærhododendros. It was sent me, with more seed and a specimen, from Russia. It abounds in the woods that are found in the neighbourhood of the lake of Baikal, in lat. 55°, which lies in Eastern Tartary, but now in the possession of Russia. Another species of this fine plant is found

in the country near the Euxine Sea, in Turkey; and that found
with you being nearly in the same latitude, it shows the unlimited
power and goodness of the Creator, that such fine plants, so nearly
related, should be dispersed in places so remote from each other,
to gratify and please mankind. It flowers beginning of May; the
inside of the flower white, the outside of a faint red or blush
colour. The green leaves are exactly like yours, and the flowers
come in clusters, like yours.

M. CATESBY has sent thee his first part as a present. *   *

Inclosed is a letter to Doctor COLDEN, surveyor-general of New
York. He may be of great service to thee, to inform thee where
is the likeliest place to find the Firs. He is a very ingenious man,
and has writ a very entertaining and informing history of the Six
Indian Nations, which he has been so kind to send me. Pray go
soon, and look out sharp for the Balm of Gilead Firs, and Black,
Red, and White Spruce, as Mr. DUDLEY calls them. I hope thee
will meet with more of the White Pine, for our people are insatiable
after them.

London, June 6, 1741.

DEAR FRIEND :—

I was glad to see thine of December 4th, and March 22d: and
am sorry for the fate of the two boxes, which are all spoilt. I
shall answer thine fully by next ship.

We all hope thee has taken, or will take, a progress to Hudson's River, to find the Balm of Gilead Fir. Pray call on Doctor
COLDEN, at Albany, who may inform thee where these trees grow.
*   *   *   I saw to-day, at Sir HANS SLOANE'S, a
great curiosity,—a Porcupine, brought from Hudson's Bay. It
was two feet nine inches from head to tail, and a foot high, with a
young one. It was wonderful to observe how this animal, which
is found in the very hot countries, was so contrived to endure and
subsist in the coldest; for it is provided with a very thick fur coat,
covered with hairs, and in this its quills are secreted; so that, unless the hair is turned up, they are not discovered: but no doubt
the creature can erect them for defence. It is a wonderful animal
—of a dark brown; but its little one was of a shining sleek black,
and had no quills, but there was some appearance of their coming.
The Porcupines from the South, are covered all over with quills,

without any other mixture of hair, or down, and their quills four
times as long.

M. CATESBY is wonderfully pleased with his letter.

I am thine,

P. COLLINSON.

London, July 21, 1741.

DEAR FRIEND J. BARTRAM :—

*   *   The *Calceolus* thrives finely, that thee sent me
this year; but did not flower, which I believe is owing to a *Corona
Solis* that unluckily grows out of the midst of it, which robs it of
its nourishment, which I did not know when I planted it—and now
I can't remove it without danger to both. Sure your woods and
thickets are all flowers. The *Mitella* has flowered strongly : it is
a pretty, odd thing. Consult MILLER on it.   *   *

*   In answer to thine of December 4, 1740 ; and March
22d ult. The specimens of Sweet and Sour Gum I received, and
prove to satisfaction ; but I want the *Gum* of each sort, and the
Gum of Arbor Benzoin, or your Allspice Tree. And pray send
me a Wasp or two, of that sort that builds their nests with clay;
for that I had, happened to be broke. Your *Valerian* [*Polemonium*] is pretty, and different from ours.

We see the particular effects of resentment and antipathy, in thy
contempt of the Opossum. I have both seen them and handled
them, and put my hand in her pouch, and thought her a pretty
creature, without any offensive smell, or anything disagreeable. *

*   *   *   I have filled the little box with mould
that all came with Currant vines from the island of Zante, in the
Archipelago. In it I have sown seeds of *Cyclamens*, and TOURNE-
FORT's fine Armenian perennial Poppy.   *   *   *

*   *   *   My friend CHARLES READ acquainted
me thou intended to set out for Albany, May 22d ; a delightful
month to travel in, when Nature is in all her beauty ; but I conclude that was purely for discoveries against the fall. I hope this
will find thee safe returned, and everything answering to thy
wishes. The last seeds came up very well. The Pine seeds, and
Oaks, came up as thick as grass.

Doctor DILLENIUS gives his service, and has sent three or four
reams of the largest size paper, being sheets of his *Hortus Eltha-*

mensis; which will make noble books for specimens. But as freight is dear, and captains strangers, I shall defer sending them till I have an opportunity by our worthy generous friend, Captain WRIGHT, to whom pray my hearty respects.

Doctor LAWSON is likely to go physician to the next supply of land forces that are soon intended for Jamaica, to recruit Admiral VERNON. Whatever is sent for him, must be directed to me.

Pray has thee ever seen the *Monack*, or Seven Sleeper—the Moose, Martin, and Black Fox? Something of this I have hinted in my former letters. Should be glad, at thy leisure, of some observations on them.   *   *   *

We have had, since the 7th of May, the most delightful summer I ever knew. Before that memorable day, there seemed a prospect of dearth and famine to all grass-feeding animals; for we had had no rain for months past,—that there was no more appearance of grass, or herbage, than in winter. But then it pleased God, in his great compassion to the work of his hands, which was perishing in numbers, to open the windows of heaven, and give us plenty of rain, which soon filled up the gaping crannies of the thirsty ground, and an abundant plenty of grass ensued, and such a crop of corn, of all kinds, was scarcely ever known in England, and the finest harvest to get it in.

Now, dear JOHN, with a cheerful heart, I can bid thee farewell; and am thy sincere friend,

P. COLLINSON.

The Armenian Poppy is called, by TOURNEFORT, "*Papaver orientale hirsutissimum flore magno.*"

London, September 1, 1741.

FRIEND JOHN :—

I have little to add to former accounts. I fully expected thy last quire of specimens from Holland, in time to send thee their names, but they are not yet arrived; but perhaps they may before this ship sails,—which I think will be the last from this port this year.

I shall now wait with some impatience to hear from thee, and how thou fared in thy expedition to Hudson's River; what discoveries thou has made, to tempt thy subscribers to continue their subscriptions.

The trees and shrubs raised from thy first seeds, are grown to great maturity. Last year Lord PETRE planted out about ten thousand Americans, which, being at the same time mixed with about twenty thousand Europeans, and some Asians, make a very beautiful appearance;—great art and skill being shown in consulting every one's particular growth, and the well blending the variety of greens. Dark green being a great foil to lighter ones, and bluish green to yellow ones, and those trees that have their bark and back of their leaves of white, or silver, make a beautiful contrast with the others.

The whole is planted in thickets and clumps, and with these mixtures are perfectly picturesque, and have a delightful effect. This will just give thee a faint idea of the method Lord PETRE plants in, which has not been so happily executed by any: and, indeed, they want the materials, whilst his lordship has them in plenty.

His nursery being fully stocked with flowering shrubs, of all sorts that can be procured,—with these, he borders the outskirts of all his plantations: and he continues, annually, raising from seed, and layering, budding, grafting—that twenty thousand trees are hardly to be missed out of his nurseries.

When I walk amongst them, one cannot well help thinking he is in North American thickets, there are such quantities. But, to be at his table, one would think South America was really there,—to see a servant come in every day, with ten or a dozen Pine Apples—as much as he can carry. I am lately come from thence, quite cloyed with them.

Thee will not think I talk figuratively, when I tell thee that his Pine Apple stove is sixty feet long, twenty feet wide, and height proportionable; and if I further tell thee, that his Guavas, Papaws, Ginger and Limes, are in such plenty, that yearly he makes abundance of wet sweetmeats, of his own growth, that serves his table and makes presents to his friends. Finer I never saw or tasted from Barbadoes, nor better cured; but these trees grow in beds of earth, in houses, some twenty, some thirty feet high. It is really wonderful, to see how nature is helped and imitated by art: but besides, his collection of the West and East India plants is beyond thy imagination.

Here I must end; because it is endless to mention the great

variety of contrivances in his gardens, to produce all fruits and plants in the greatest perfection.

So, dear JOHN, farewell,

P. COLLINSON.

I have collected a parcel of mostly Nectarine stones, being a fruit most wanted with you. Perhaps they may thrive best on their own stocks. The Plum stones are mostly Green Gage,— which is the best Plum that grows. I apprehend they will all come up the first year; though I am told some will not till the second.

London, Sept. 16th, 1741.

FRIEND JOHN :—

There came up amongst the new sort of Poplar seed, sent in last cargo, a pretty many plants that were formerly in our gardens, called the Jesuit's Bark Tree. It's a pithy plant, like Elder; but the leaves are longer, and of a deep green. Dost thou know any-thing of it? [*Iva frutescens*, L.?].

Pray send some Ginseng seed; but roots will be better. · I had great expectation I had this rare plant, but don't find it proves so. The young leaves of the *Prenanthes*, or Doctor WITT'S Snake-root, I took for it.

These are stones of the Katherine Peach; which is the best late peach we have.

I have sent some Horse Chestnuts, which are ripe earlier than usual: hope they will come fit for planting.

Thine,

P. COLLINSON.

I am glad I can send you Doctor GRONOVIUS's List of your plants, collected *anno* 1740.

Some Observations on Specimens, 1741.

No. 1. Sweet Fern. This seems to me a shrub; but whether Ever-green or no, can't tell. [*Comptonia asplenifolia*, Ait.]. Should be glad of a root or two.

No. 15. Pray send me one or two growing plants of the Ginseng,— for I mightily want it. Every one expects I have it.

No. 62. Sea Plum, is a curiosity,—especially the large one—as big as a Nectarine [*Prunus Americana*, Marshall ?].

Your Holly, I am pleased to see : have often heard of it.

Remember seed of *Collinsonia;* for I want it much, for several correspondents.

The downy specimen, 69 of Lord PETRE, that thou gathered near Cape May, is a plant that we have long had in our gardens, by the name of *Senecio arborescens*, or Groundsel Tree [*Baccharis halimifolia*, L.]; but ours never seen in this beautiful downy state, for which reason we think it the male. If thee happens where this shrub grows, again, pray make some observation about it,—if there is male and female plants. These in haste : I wish thou may guess at my meaning.

Send specimen of Black Gum, in flower. Hast thee observed the mechanism of the seed-vessel, when it chips or sprouts ? It thrusts off a valve, to let the gemma come forth, which is so hard at first, as not to be opened without breaking. The power of vegetation is great.

I shall soon send thy specimens to Holland, to Doctor GRONO-VIUS, from whom thou may expect a good account : but only one must stay some time for it.

London, Feb. 3d, 1741–2.

DEAR FRIEND JOHN :—

All thy cargoes came safe and well, by Captain WRIGHT : so shall defer saying more, till I come to answer thy other letters in particular.

I have thine before me of March 22d, which, if I remember right, I have fully answered per Captain BREAM, in mine of September 16th.

I must also inform thee, that the box of seeds per Captain BROWN, and thy letter, are come safe. We have been very fortunate, to escape the Spaniards in all our cargoes, on both sides.

In answer to thine of July 22d :

I am delighted with thy account of your Muscle, and with the specimen thee has sent, which confirms all that thee has said on this head : and being on this subject, I will send thee a rough sketch of a muscle that I discovered by accident in one of our markets. It is wonderful to think that anything new is to be discovered on our coasts; but so it is. We have not been able to find this described in any book, or author of Natural History. In its nature it seems to agree near with our and your *Solen*—by some called Razor-shell, by others, Finger-shell, and what thou reckons a sort of clams, which I delivered to Sir HANS per thy order.

I observe that thou takes no notice of any natural history relating to the *Monac*, or ground-hog. As the creature will be as tame as a cat (for I gave one to Sir HANS SLOANE, who was much delighted with it—and became a domestic animal, ran up and down, like dog or cat, for years),—it would be pretty to keep one, and observe the provision he makes for his winter's abode, for six or seven months—sleeping, or living all that time without food.

I find thee has seen some of the fruit, or nuts, I mentioned; but I don't find the butter-nut—which is plenty in New England, as a gentleman tells me—has yet come under thy notice, with the Medlar and Sagamore's head.

I have much ado to read thy letter; for some mischievous insect has eaten thy letter in large holes, in four places. To prevent this, wrap them up in dry tobacco leaves.

I shall endeavour to look about the Sweet and Sour Gum. Is this last called Black Gum? Or are they different plants? I hope thou has Doctor GRONOVIUS'S names to thy cargo, 1741. What notice he takes of these plants, I can't well remember; but will look, at my leisure.

That some variegations may be occasioned by insects, is certain; but then these are only annual, and cease with the year. But those variegations that are permanent, in our Hollies and *Phillyreas*, proceed from a distemper in the juices (like jaundice, in men and women). Take a bud from a variegated Jessamine, and insert it into a plain Jessamine; not only the bud will continue its variegation, but will also infect and impregnate the circulating juices, that the branches and leaves, above and below the bud, will appear variegated.

This is a plain demonstration of the circulation of the sap, and is a vegetable inoculation, which is very analogous to that practised on the human species—which I hear is very successfully operated with you—but obtains little with us; for we are fearful of bringing on a distemper, which oft proves mortal on persons that never might have had it in a natural way. I have two children, but dare not venture on the experiment, for fear of the consequences.

I am now about entering upon thy journey to Albany; but must first stop to tell thee that the History that thou so much admired at our good friend Governor MORRIS'S, thou may soon have the pleasure to call thy own; for, with what thou sent, and I have added, Sir HANS was so pleased, that he said, " What shall I send Mr. BARTRAM?" I proposed his History. He paused. I said how acceptable such a thing would be. In short, without entering into a detail of a little contrivance, he has sent it thee as a present, and it will come by WRIGHT.

The mole I sent him he was much pleased with, because it was new and different from ours, but the insects had made sad havoc with it. A better specimen will please better. The bole and blue stone I sent him, and others. If thee hast a specimen of petrifaction gathered on a hill betwixt the Highlands and Shongo Mountains, that I sent to Sir HANS,—I should like such another.

The Wasps' nests, of both sorts, were new, and pleased much. He desires—and so do I—specimens of the Wasps, that are the builders,—particularly distinguished.

I am extremely obliged to Governor MORRIS, and his son, for their kind assistance. Pray, did thee find no sort of shells on the verge of those lakes, on the mountains?

I am not a little concerned, that thou missed seeing Doctor COLDEN: he is a very ingenious, intelligent man. And also for thy disaster, in passing the river. Pray, be very careful for the future, and look before thou leaps.

Of the seeds thou sent, the Rose Laurel are some come up, and are very thriving; Red Cedar, by thousands; White Cedar, a few; Black Haws, none—must send a young tree—two, three, or four; White Pine, some; Sassafras, a few; Sugar Maple, a few; All-spice, a few; Witch Hazel, one,—what they belong to, I can't say. Make these queries to Doctor DILLENIUS. Has thee consulted MILLER? The last being new, he may know nothing of.

Rose Laurel, White Cedar, White Pine, and Sassafras, thou cannot send too much,—for we can never have enough of them.

I was out in the country when specimen 105 flowered; but, by making no seed, fancy it is male.

I heartily wish a subscription may go on for thy encouragement; for thy subscribers may soon be furnished, and then will withdraw their subscriptions. Some talk of doing it.

So much, I think, for thine of July 22d.—But, before we part,

I must thank thee for thy dissertation on WHITFIELD. It has afforded some entertainment. He has, for some time, made no noise here; which I presume is on the account of a rich wife, he has lately got,—which may spoil his spiritual exercises.   *   *

It's now late; and it is with much difficulty I have stole this time, to assure thee that I am thy sincere friend,

P. COLLINSON.

London, March 3, 1741–2.

DEAR FRIEND JOHN :—

By our good friend Captain WRIGHT, I have sent Sir HANS's kind present, of his Natural History of Jamaica, in two volumes. These I have put in a box, I had made on purpose for them, and directed it on two places for thee; and with it, I sent on board, in a canvass wrapper, a large bundle of paper, a present from Doctor DILLENIUS; which, I think, will furnish thee with paper for specimens, and for seeds, for thy lifetime. It is fine Dutch paper, and very fit for such purposes, because it will bear ink. It is the printing [paper] of his *Hortus Elthamensis*, a very curious work, when the cuts are with it.

I thank thee for the Pellitory of Spain seed; the name Girondella was by mistake applied to it. I had only one root survived the hard winter of 1739–40. The root is esteemed excellent for the toothache, if from a cold humor : a little slice laid to the tooth, will draw out the cold rheum.

Amongst the many curious herbaceous seeds, there is the *Collinsonia* omitted, which I am solicited for, both at home and abroad, and can't oblige my friends with ; for, though mine grows strong, and flowers finely, yet our summers are not sufficient to bring its seed to perfection.—For this reason, thee must send all sorts of herbaceous seeds over again, as they happen ripe in thy way : for unless such plants as increase from the root, most others go off in a year or two ; especially those beautiful small yellow-flowering Sunflowers, *Obeliscothecas*, or *Chrysanthemums* (all names nearly synonymous), which are biennials, and flower, and then die ;—and by slipping, or laying, or any other art, I have not been able to perannuate them : whereas the low, dwarf sort, with a size larger flower, continues many years in the ground, and makes a fine show all summer, with its yellow flowers with purplish brown bottoms.

This, M. CATESBY brought first from Virginia.   I think thou found it there also.

I am much obliged to thee for the noble Skunk-root.   I divided it into three parts; so that I hope I shall now be so furnished as not to want again.   All the other things were in order: so that I now begin to long to see them peep,—there being so many fine things amongst them.   The Chamærhododendrons move very slow. They seem to like Lord PETRE's soil better.   They seem to die daily, with me; and I have tried them in different methods.

I was much delighted with the birds' nests—in particular with the hanging nests, which are most wonderfully fabricated, and seem to be of two sorts.   As M. CATESBY intends to send thee his History of American Birds, both he as well as myself desire to know the birds that belong to them, for he does not remember to have seen them; and also that bird thou calls a Marsh Wren.   These thou may send over to his name, for I have the same by me: and so, when any eggs come, pray tie a label with the bird's name, according to his catalogue.   I desire the little man's acceptance of the picture-books, that sent them me.—The Swallow's nest is exactly the same as ours, and built in the same manner, with the same materials.   But what I greatly want, is the Swallow or Marten's nest, that builds in chimneys.   These nests are of a different, curious make, being a sort of basket-work—very pretty, and different from any nest I ever saw.   M. CATESBY had one sent him from Virginia.   And the eggs are different in shape from others. This is so nicely constructed, that it requires a very steady hand to take it without breaking.

The two Humming-bird's nests are neatly built; but it would be an addition to their curiosity, to cut off the twig that they are built on, with the nest on it.   Pray, from what do they gather that woolly or downy composition, that is inside of their nests? for it is much finer and softer than sheep's wool.   Lady PETRE wants a nest and eggs, and an old dead Humming-bird—cock and hen.

I observe in the shells of your Muscles, there are rudiments of pearl,—that is pearl-like protuberances.   Is there none ever found in them?   I have some, taken out of your oysters; but those from your Muscle are of a better complexion, for they generally partake of the complexion of the shell.   I think I observe three different sorts of Muscles, found with you.

Pray, from which species of Fir, or Pine, were those bladders gathered? Our Balm of Gilead Fir sweats out tears of balsam from the buds, in the summer months.

I thank thee for the Sweet Gum, or Liquid Ambar, as we call it,—and for the White Cedar Gum. I never saw any before. It is odd to call a plant sour *Gum*, or black *Gum*, and it not produce any. But when thou observes any trees gum, that we have not, pray think of me; and to send me two or three roots of growing Ginseng, and *Polygala* or Seneka Snakeroot, if they happen to be seen in thy route. I want them in my garden—and *Serpentaria*, of the shops.

I have taken care to put the clay Wasps' nests in boxes, to see their produce. They are exceeding curious,—especially the last flat ones, which are prettily marked with ribs, &c. Pray, are these a new discovery?

Thy account of the *Tumble Bug* (Beetle) is very curious and entertaining: but M. CATESBY says they have another sort that they call so, in Virginia. Pray send two or three more specimens; for I presume they are not scarce. One or two for Sir HANS, with thy account, will wonderfully please him.

I thank thee for thy curious present of thy map, and thy draught of the fall of the river Owegos [?]. I was really both delighted and surprised to see it so naturally done,—and at thy ingenuity in the performance. Upon my word, friend JOHN, I can't help admiring thy abilities, in so many instances. I shall be sparing to say what more I think. A man of thy prudence will place this to a right account, to encourage thee to proceed gently in these curious things, which belong to a man of leisure, and not to a man of business. The main chance must be minded. Many an ingenious man has lost himself for want of this regard,—by devoting too much of his time to these matters. A hint thee will take in friendship: thy obliging, grateful disposition, may carry thee too far. I am glad, and delight much in all these things—none more: but then I would not purchase them at the expense of my friend's precious time—to the detriment of his interest, and business (now, dear JOHN, take me right).—I showed them to Sir HANS. He was much pleased. Lord PETRE deservedly much admires them; and, indeed, does every one that sees them, when they are told who was the performer.

All this is writ by rote, or from memory, for I dare not, nay, I cannot look into thy letters; for I have no time to add more, but to tell thee—in the trunk of the Library Company, thee'll find a suit of clothes for thyself. This may serve to protect thy outward man,—being a drugget coat, black waistcoat, and shagg breeches. And now, that thou may see that I am not thoughtless of thy better part, I send thee R. BARCLAY'S *Apology*, to replenish thy inward man. So farewell. Success attend thee in all thy expeditions. The first leisure, will consider all thy letters. They are all carefully laid up. The chrysalises are all in fine order. I am in hopes of some new beauties. I can now add no more, but that I am thine.

P. COLLINSON.

As these are very precarious, uncertain times, I have insured to the value of ten pounds,—that all may not be lost.

Inclosed, is the mate's receipt for Sir HANS SLOANE'S books, and Doctor DILLENIUS'S paper. There is a map, and another parcel or two, beside, for thee,—and CATESBY'S books ; and Doctor DILLENIUS will send thee his History of Mosses.

April 25, 1742.

DEAR FRIEND :—

I have the pleasure of thine, inclosed in friend BLAND'S letter of March the 7th. I think I have answered all the articles per my sundry letters; however, I will again take notice of them. * *

* * There were some fine insects in the box, and very beautiful; but the major part was sadly eaten, or lacerated, by some mischievous insect. It is a thousand pities it can't be prevented. If there was tobacco dust, or leaves, spread over the bottom, and the insects pinned on that, it might be a means to prevent it for the future.

The first leisure, I shall show those relating to the animals, to our friend CATESBY.

The *Monac* I know well—proved a pretty domestic animal—lived with Sir HANS SLOANE many years, and ran about house like a cat,—is one of the Sleepers—for he made a nest in the cellar, and went into it in September, and came out in March or April. We were in hopes thee might have known something more particular of it,—being so remarkable in its nature. * *

* The box of berries, and map, per Captain BOUND, came

safe and well. I much admire thy performance. It really conveys a good idea of that wonderful natural cascade.

To-day, I breakfasted with Sir HANS. He always inquires after thee. I hope his books, per WRIGHT, will come safe to hand. *

Doctor LAWSON gives his humble service to thee, and our friend WOOLLEY. I wish I could have a specimen of that large piece of polished iron ore, sent him, last parcel.   *   *   *

M. CATESBY desires a dried bird of a night-bird, who has a note that sounds like *whippewill*, which he chants all night long.

Pray look after the elk-horns. Perhaps a broad hint may procure a gift of those from Governor MORRIS.

My first leisure, I shall read over all thy letters, again ; and then will take further notice of them. I have sent thy orders for next year's collection, by this ship, and by way of New York per Captain GILL. So hope there will be no occasion to say more, but that I am thy sincere friend,

P. COLLINSON.

London, May 16th, 1742.

DEAR JOHN:—

Having a little leisure, it gives me great pleasure to review thy entertaining letters. Possibly the following hints may have been made before ; but that I rely on thy candour to excuse,—for I keep no copies.

September 25th, 1740, and September 7th, ditto, are the first that comes to hand. I take them in order.

In thy journey to Minnesink, thou saw the three-leaved and long-coned Pine, and a swamp of Spruce, or Fir, like the Newfoundland sort. Query, if this is not a proper place to collect cones, being the sorts we want ?

Pray send half a dozen yellow wasps, to place with their nests.

I observe thou mentions three sorts of three-leaved Pines, and they are thus distinguished : *First*, the Great three-leafed Pine [*P. palustris*, L.?] ; *Second*, the three-leafed Pine whose cones keep shut for one, two, or three years [*P. rigida*, Mill.?] ; *Third*, the Bastard three-leafed Pine [*P. variabilis*, Lamb.?]. As our knowledge of these noble trees is very slender, Lord PETRE, as well as myself, desires, when opportunity offers, that thou wilt gather fair specimens of each sort, with their ripe cones on them,—each distinguished by its name.　Thou may also send two specimens of the long-coned or five-leafed Pine, with the cones hanging on.

It is now a rainy day; and, being at Peckham, I and my wife were agreeably entertained by reviewing thy journey, and thy map to Minnesink.

Pray, how far from the sea is that mountain where thou found the figured stones?

When the *Larix* was discovered, were there no old trees that yielded turpentine?　For the finest and best sort is made by the Venetians from this tree; whence it has the name of Venice Turpentine.

Pray, have we had that new Maple with red stalks, and leaves rough?　The large red-flowering Raspberry thou found, is a fine showy plant—has been long in our gardens; but I never saw it bear any fruit, with us.*　The Conestogo Gooseberry, also, annually flowers,—but the fruit does not set.

I am much pleased with thy account of Doctor WITT.　It is confirmed to me, in many instances, in his letters.　I believe he is very credulous, and deals much in the marvellous.　It's plain he was mistaken in the Golden Rod; for no doubt, the pod he mentions that plant bore—as thou well observes—was but an excrescence.　The like I have often observed here, in several plants. His Daisy, or double mountain *Ranunculus* [*Anemone thalictroides*, L.], is a pretty thing.　*　*　*　*　I received the specimens of Sweet and Sour Gum.　They are plants peculiar to themselves, and each a distinct genus.　Consult the *Flora Virginica*.

Canst thee assign any reasonable conjecture why your House Wasps don't sting, in October?

Your Greek Valerian thrives well with me.　I like it, because it comes before ours, and grows lower.

Thy account of the Muskrat is very just and natural.　Few can give any reasonable account for antipathies.　Some, we suck in with our nurse's milk.　They often instil into our minds dislikes for things they dislike; and this we rarely get over, but retain as long as we live.　What parents are frightened at, by their example children conceive the same.　Perhaps this may be thy case, in relation to the *Opossum*—a prejudice arising from some of these causes; or else, really, I can see no reason for it; for I have had

---

* *Rubus odoratus*, L.　It rarely, if ever, perfects its fruit in the *gardens* here; and is often abortive in its native localities.

the opportunity of seeing, and handling, and playing with a female, that had three young nearly as large as herself; and by frequent use, were as docile as cats—and in colour, not much unlike.

This contemptible creature—in thy eyes—has been remarkably distinguished from other animals, in the wonderful provision contrived for the preservation of its young, (as if a creature of great consequence); and another wonder attending it, is, how the young comes so very small to the teat. This, none has yet been able to ascertain, but by conjecture; and it has puzzled all our anatomists to find the apparatus requisite to carry on this delicate operation. Doctor MITCHELL, at Urbana, in Virginia, has employed some of his leisure time in examining the internal structure of this wonderful creature; and I doubt not, but in time, will clear up the doubtful points.*   *   *   *

London, June 16, 1742.

DEAR JOHN:—

Not any of the wasps belonging to the clay nests, are yet come out, nor any of the chrysalises,—which we much wonder at; but we are not yet without hopes.

And, hitherto, as bad luck attends the growing plants. Several curious things in the clods of earth don't appear—especially those Iris-like flowers, from Cape May, which we both so much admire; which may be owing to our long, cold, dry spring. One Gentian, with small narrow leaves, appears; and I think, two of the Witch Hazel; one Snake-root; the Skunk-weed thrives well; one *Lychnis;* but I have a *Lychnis*, from Doctor WITT, different from any yet that I have seen. It seems to be the king of that tribe. Its stalk is near as thick as my little finger (which is but small, for a man). It is now about two feet high, and yet no flowers appear. The stalk is most finely spotted,—which is very distinguishing from all the rest that I have seen.

One or two of the Sassafras sprout; but I can't depend on them,—for they will often go off after that.

The ground-hog, I presume, may be the *Monac*, of LAWSON. Does it partake nothing of our badger—which GESNER mentions?

* For an interesting paper on this subject, see *Proceedings of the Academy of Natural Sciences of Philadelphia, for April*, 1848.

Perhaps our learned friend, J. LOGAN, can show thee its description.

Pray remember some growing roots of Ginseng, and TENNANT'S Snake-root.

What thou calls a black scink, we should be glad to know. Send a skin, or draw his picture,—whether it belongs to rabbit, or squirrel, fox, or what.

I am delighted to hear that thou has a prospect of a subscription. I wish it may operate. It will be a fine opportunity for us both.   *   *   *

Health and success attend thee. Farewell.

P. COLLINSON.

London, July 3d, 1742.

OH! FRIEND JOHN:

I can't express the concern of mind that I am under, on so many accounts. I have lost my friend—my brother. The man I loved, and was dearer to me than all men—is no more. I could fill this sheet, and many more: but oh! my anxiety of mind is so great, that I can hardly write; and yet I must tell thee, that on Friday, July 2d, our dear friend, Lord PETRE, was carried off by the small-pox, in the thirtieth year of his age. Hard, hard, cruel hard, be taken from his friends—his family—his country—in the prime of life; when he had so many thousand things locked up in his breast, for the benefit of them all, are now lost in embryo.

I can go no further, but to assure thee that I am thy friend,

P. COLLINSON.

All our schemes are broke.

Send no seeds for him, nor the Duke of Norfolk; for now, he that gave motion, is motionless,—all is at an end.

As I know that this will be a great disappointment to thee, if thee hast a mind to send the seeds, as was ordered for Lord P. and Duke of Norfolk, on thy own account and risk,—I will do what I can, to dispose of them. The Duke of Norfolk shall have the preference; but there is no obliging him to take them,—as I had not the order from him, but from Lord PETRE.

Send those for the Duke of Richmond, and P. MILLER.

Lord PETRE was a fine, tall, comely personage,—handsome—

had the presence of a prince; yet was so happily mixed, that love
and awe were begot at the same time. The affability and sweet-
ness of his temper were beyond expression, without the least mixture of pride, or haughtiness. With an engaging smile he always
met his friends. But oh! the endowments of his mind are not to
be described. Few or none could excel him, in the knowledge of
the liberal arts and sciences. He was a great mechanic, as well
as a great mathematician; ready at figures and calculations—and
elegant in his tastes.

In his religious way,* an example of great piety; his morals of
great temperance and sobriety; no loose word, or *double entendre*,
did I ever hear (this is something of the man). For his virtues,
and his excellencies, and his endowments, I loved him, and he me,
more like a brother than a friend.

JOHN BARTRAM TO PETER COLLINSON.

July the 6th, 1742.

A few hours past, I received thy letters of March the 3d, and
20th, and April the 25th, 1742.

Yesterday the ship arrived, which our dear friend Captain
WRIGHT sailed in from London, but alas! hath left her captain
asleep in Neptune's bosom: and now, such a mortal sickness is on
board, that she is ordered to ride quarantine below the town. No
goods can be got off.

I heartily thank Sir HANS SLOANE for his kind remembrance of
me. I long to see his History; and particularly M. CATESBY's
books, to see what birds he hath figured, before I set out next week
for a journey along our sea-coast, where I believe there are many
birds which he omitted to draw—which I shall be very particular
to observe their dimensions, shape and colours, if I can compel
them, by the charms of sulphur and nitre and lead, to let me dispose of them as I think most suitable.

I shall endeavour to procure Lady PETRE a humming-bird's nest,
and eggs, as soon as possible. I have not heard of any being found
this year. They commonly build their nest upright upon a limb
of a tree, and a little shake with the fall of the tree separates them.
The fine, downy composition, is gathered from the stalks of our

* Lord PETRE belonged to the Roman Catholic Church.

Fern. The bladders of balm, which I sent thee, I gathered on the Balm of Gilead Tree, on the Katskill Mountain,—a delicate, fragrant liquor, as clear as water.

I design, next month, to go myself and gather some seed for you, which I hope will be as much pleasure to you, as fatigue and charge to me to get them. There is no more trust in our Americans, than curiosity. Colonel SALISBURY, who lives near them, sent me last winter, a very loving letter, affirming he did what he could to procure them, leaving orders, when he went to York, to gather them; but at his return, there is none gathered. He sent a man on purpose to the mountains, to gather them; but he said the birds had picked all the seed out, being very fond of them.

I am glad my map and draught were acceptable, although clumsily done,—having neither proper instruments nor convenient time; being, most of them, in part of a first day, or by candle-light,—having no whole original but nature, nor time to take a copy,—being hurried in gathering or packing of seeds.

I am greatly obliged to thee for thy necessary present of a suit of clothes, which just came in the right time; and BARCLAY's *Apology*, I shall take care of, for thy sake. It answers thy advice, much better than if thee had sent me one of Natural History, or Botany, which I should have spent ten times the hours in reading of, while I might have laboured for the maintenance of my family. Indeed, I have little respect to *apologies* and disputes about the ceremonial parts of religion, which often introduce animosities, confusion, and disorders in the mind—and sometimes body too: but, dear PETER, let us worship the one Almighty Power, in sincerity of heart, with resignation to His divine will,—doing to others as we would have them do to us, if we were in their circumstances. Living in love and innocency, we may die in hope.

*   *   *   *   *

July 24, 1742.

I am just returned from Amboy, and Shrewsbury; having waited on Governor MORRIS, and discoursed with him about those great horns, which I was informed he kept as a curiosity. He told me he had sent them to England, several years ago. The beast was killed near Albany; and was supposed to be above fifteen hundred pounds weight; and was excellent good eating. The horns differed much, in shape, from those figured in the Transactions of the Society, for the moose deer.

I design, as soon as I have gathered the cones of Rose Laurel, and White Pine, and Sassafras berries, to go to the Katskill to gather the Balm seed; and, as soon as returned, to gather what seed is ripe nearer home; then, directly to the Five Nations of Indians, up the branches of Susquehanna,—having engaged our chief interpreter to go with me, the beginning of September; from whence, when I have returned home, I hope to give you a good account of my journey.

Yesterday and to-day, I have been at Philadelphia, looking after the goods and presents thee and our friends sent me. I have found all that thee mentions, in thy letters which I received. The goods answer as well as can be expected, here—being such abundance of all sorts, in our stores, that they stick on our hands.

Thy presents of clothes are fine, and very acceptable; as also the curious presents from M. CATESBY and Sir HANS. Pray give my hearty thanks to them. I hope, by next opportunity, to write largely to them; which I hope will be accompanied with some curiosities. I should have sent you some, now; but the ship sails sooner than I expected,—and I, as aforesaid, just returned home.

By reason that there is no vessel, that I know of, to sail this fall from here, directly to Bristol; but yet, notwithstanding, to alleviate thy disappointment, I have sent about fifty different sorts of seeds of our finest wild flowers, gathered in their best state of ripeness, and well dried, and sent with Doctor DILLENIUS's parcel, and directed for thee; and if our winter should prove moderate, and any vessel should go from hence to Bristol, before spring, I shall endeavour to send a box of roots.

This comes, with sincere respect and good will, from thy friend,

J. B.

September 5th, 1742.

DEAR PETER :—

I am lately returned from the Katskill Mountains,—having gathered a fine parcel of the Balm cones, just at the time of their full ripeness; with many other curious seeds, and other fine curiosities. This hath been a happy journey: and I met with our friend, Doctor COLDEN, who received and entertained me with all the

demonstrations of civility and respect that were convenient.   He
is one of the most facetious, agreeable gentlemen, I ever met with;
and his capacity thee may judge of, by the last account he gave
thee of the economy of the Five Nations, and some other subjects
which he may soon acquaint thee with.   I hope to give thee a
fuller account of him this fall, when I delineate the particularities
of my journey.

I received thy kind letter of June the 16th, and the seeds and
book of Doctor DILLENIUS, last night.   I take it to be the com-
pletest of that kind that ever was wrote; for we don't read that
SOLOMON wrote of any plants of humbler growth than the Hyssop:
so I conclude he knew as little of Mosses, as he did of the plants
that grew beyond Mount Lebanon, or in America.

I am just setting out towards Susquehanna, to gather seeds; but
I question whether I shall go to the Five Nations.   Our interpreter
was obliged to go with a gentleman from Maryland, to treat with
them, while I was on my journey from Hudson's River; which baffled
our conclusions.

December 18th, 1742.

DEAR PETER :—

We are daily expecting Captain STEPHENS from London,—and
many are almost out of hopes, and afraid the Spaniards have
catched him.

I hope my cargo, sent in the Constantine, will come safe to thy
hands.   I sent three boxes of shrubs; but could not conveniently
dig up, or find, several plants which I thought to have sent, by
reason of the great snow that fell on the first day of November,
and the frost and several other snows that followed within two
weeks after: and I had a grievous bad time to gather the Pine
cones, near Egg Harbour, for the Duke of Norfolk.   I climbed the
trees in the rain, in a desert, and lopped off the boughs; then must
stand up to the knees in snow, to pluck off the cones.   But now,
and for three weeks past, we have had fine weather; and yesterday, the frogs made a noise—the birds sang—and the bees flew
about, as in spring; and I doubt it will be worse in next March,
if not in April.—We, in Pennsylvania, have had a fine plentiful
harvest this year.

I have been with our ingenious friend, COLDEN, who treated me very civilly,—as I have related in two letters to thee. He advised me to travel into the Mohawk's country, and to Oswego, and the lakes,—and he would recommend me to the inhabitants there. He believes there is a great variety of plants and other curiosities there. But I suppose the death of our dear friend, Lord PETRE, will discourage such distant travels; and our Americans have not zeal enough to encourage any discoveries of this kind, at their expense.

Captain DAVIS, by whom I sent the box of Red Cedar berries, and Maple keys, last summer, complains that thee took no care of it, but let it stay on board until he was loaded again. Such delays will discourage the captains from taking things of that kind, unless I pay here.

May 27th, 1743.

DEAR FRIEND PETER :—

This day, Captain RUTHERFORD, accompanied with several gentlemen of distinction from Philadelphia, bestowed upon me the honour of a visit. The captain very generously offered to take care of any letter I should send to thee; which opportunity I will make use of, notwithstanding a vessel is to sail from Philadelphia in about two weeks. I have received all the goods, sent for last fall, in good order, and excellent good. The thickset I have a suit made of, which pleaseth me exceedingly. I am heartily thankful to thee for it. It's a fine present. The silk is very good.

By thy good offices, our Library Company hath made me a present (with an unanimous consent) of a share during life. Dear friend, by these demonstrations of thy particular regard for my interest and satisfaction, thee engages to thyself my grateful service and remembrance, for such favours. But to proceed with thy letter of February the 15th.

I am sorry thee overlooked several roots of Ginseng, which I put in thy box, and observed when I put them in, just before the vessel sailed, a lively bud to each root.

We have expected Captain BUDDEN in so long, that now his employer gives him over for lost,—by whom I expected to have had more particular orders.

The Arbor Vitæ, which I gathered on Hudson's River, I take to be the same kind with that I gathered on James River,—I think

upon Captain ISHAM RANDOLPH'S land, or very near it. He went
with and showed it to me,—supposing it to be a Juniper. Within a
few yards, grew the Leather-bark, or Mezereon ; both which I
believe he would send thee the seed of, if thee writes to him for it.
He is a man of great humanity, whom my heart opens to receive,
when I think of him, which is very often.   *   *   *
My wife is well pleased with the silk thee chose for her. She
is much obliged to thee for thy care. I am very thankful to my
good friend, Sir HANS SLOANE, for his fine present of five guineas.
Being he hath so generously bestowed it upon me, I desire thee
would send me a silver can, or cup, as big and good as thee can
get for that sum, which I or mine may keep to entertain our
friends withal, in remembrance of my noble benefactor.*

June 11th, 1743.

FRIEND PETER :—
I have lately been to visit our friend Doctor WITT, where I
spent four or five hours very agreeably—sometimes in his garden,—
where I viewed every kind of plant, I believe, that grew therein ;
which afforded me a convenient opportunity of asking him whether
he ever observed any kind of Wild Roses, in this country, that was
double. He said he could not remember that ever he did. So
being satisfied with this amusement, we went into his study, which
was furnished with books containing different kinds of learning ;—
as Philosophy, Natural Magic, Divinity, nay, even Mystic Divinity;
all of which were the subjects of our discourse, within doors,—
which alternately gave way to Botany, every time we walked in the
garden. I could have wished thee the enjoyment of so much
diversion, as to have heard our discourse, provided thee had been
well swathed from hips to arm-pits. But it happened, a little of
our spiritual discourse was interrupted by a material object within
doors ; for the Doctor had lately purchased, of a great traveller in
Spain and Italy, a sample of what was imposed upon him for Snake
Stones,—which took me up a little time—beside laughing at him—
to convince the Doctor that they were nothing but calcined old
horse bones.

* This seems to be the origin of the *Silver Cup*, presented by Sir HANS, in lieu
of the "five guineas." See JOHN BARTRAM's letter to Sir HANS SLOANE, dated
November 16, 1743.

Indeed, to give the Doctor his due, he is very pleasant, facetious and pliant; and will exchange as many freedoms as most men of his years, with those he respects. His understanding and judgment, thee art not unacquainted with,—having had so long and frequent intercourse with him by letters.

When we are upon the topic of astrology, magic, and mystic divinity, I am apt to be a little troublesome, by inquiring into the foundation and reasonableness of these notions—which, thee knows, will not bear to be searched and examined into: though I handle these fancies with more tenderness with him, than I should with many others that are so superstitiously inclined, because I respect the man. He hath a considerable share of good in him.

The Doctor's famous *Lychnis*, which thee has dignified so highly, is, I think, unworthy of that character. Our swamps and low grounds are full of them. I had so contemptible an opinion of it, as not to think it worth sending, nor afford it room in my garden; but I suppose, by thy account, your climate agreeth so well, that it is much improved. The other, which I brought from Virginia, grows with me about five feet high, bearing large spikes of different coloured flowers, for three or four months in the year, exceeding beautiful. I have another wild one, finely speckled, and striped with red upon a white ground, and a red eye in the middle —the only one I ever saw.

Now I will conclude this botanical discourse; having answered thy queries in a letter via Bristol. I believe my subscription our proprietor inquired after, is wholly dropped. Some people lay the blame upon JAMES LOGAN, and not without cause.

Our worthy friend, Doctor COLDEN, wrote to me that he had received a new edition of LINNÆUS's *Characteres Plantarum*, lately printed. He advised me to desire GRONOVIUS to send it to me. I should be very glad to see it. The first I saw, was at the Doctor's; and chiefly by it he hath attained to the greatest knowledge in Botany, of any I have discoursed with.

June the 21st, 1743.

DEAR PETER :—

    *   *   *   *   *   *   *

If ever I can come to pay you a visit, I would bring abundance of trees and shrubs with me, which is very difficult if not impossible for you ever to have growing, without one that understands them comes with them, and takes particular care of them in their passage. But I don't know how to leave my family. I have many small children, and none yet grown up to take care of business; and servants, in this country, strive to do as little work, and spend as much time as they can in cárelessness. * * * I am obliged to thee for recommending me to our proprietor. If he would please to be so honourable as allow me an annual salary, worth while to furnish his walks with all the natural productions of trees, shrubs, and plants, which grow in our four governments, I would undertake to do it.

It pleaseth me, that what I sent to Sir HANS and M. CATESBY proved acceptable. I think that Hanging-bird's nest, belongs to the Baltimore bird. The *Aralia spinosa* I brought from Virginia. It grows well, with me. * * * The fossil shells are found at the distance of a hundred or a hundred and fifty miles from the sea,—most of the way, by places, from Hudson's River to Susquehanna. The Katskill Mountains, are in York government.

I am apt to imagine our chimney swallows might build in hollow trees, before Europeans built chimneys. My Rose is now producing its second crop, out of the centre of its old flowers,—which many do.

*   *   *   *   *   *   *

In the township of Darby, several have joined together and signed articles of agreement, pretty much like the Library Company at Philadelphia. They advised with me how the books should be procured. I told them, I thought thee could send them better than any that I knew—if thee would favour such a design; that thee had abundance of business other ways; and that if thee condescended to oblige them so much, it must be more for the love and inclination thee bore to the promotion of learning, and thy generous disposition to assist those that were thereto inclined, than the benefit of what might be thought a reasonable satisfaction for thy trouble, in buying and shipping them. However, they being very desirous of having the books, assumed the freedom of addressing thee by letter, with a catalogue of the books they want, and a bill of exchange,—which I put in the box directed to thee. If thee pleases to comply with their request, pray pack them up with the goods I sent for.

JOHN BARTRAM.

London, January 16, 1743–4.

My dear Friend John:—

I was mightily pleased to see the specimens of both sorts *Arbor Vitæ*. That of poor Isham's is much the finest; but the good man is gone to his long home, and I doubt not but is happy. I have at this juncture writ to his wife, to send some of her people to gather and send me some seed. We all esteem it, here, to be an American plant, and brought by the French from Canada; for, by all the Herbals that I have examined, they all make it a native of America. I never knew it grew in Germany, till thou informed me of it.

The specimens of Crabs were sufficient to see the species. I had not the sort before,—but I have seen them described. If they had been perfect, they would have been a greater curiosity; but their make is so delicate, it is scarcely to be expected whole. If such a thing should happen, doubt not of thy care to send it me. There is a very great variety of this species. Every part of the world, bounded by the sea, furnishes new kinds.

The eggs thou hast sent, are very pretty, and curious to see such a variety. But what affords M. Catesby and me great matter of speculation, is to see so many sorts of Turtle,—which, if we may judge by the eggs, are specifically different. But this is like to bring some trouble on thee; for we naturalists are impatient, and never easy until we are satisfied; so, what we have to request of thee is, that when any of these kinds happen in thy excursions, thou will send us a shell or two to each of these kinds, viz.:

The flatter back, red-bellied water turtle—smaller long eggs.

The common land turtle—the next larger and long eggs.

The round-back, stinking turtle—the smallest, pretty long, shining eggs.

The great black turtle—with round eggs.

The great red-bellied turtle—with largest sized eggs of all.

M. Catesby admires so many of these sorts escaped him; but it is next to impossible that he could, as a sojourner, make such discoveries as a curious man, that is a native. It is really true, what my friend SAM CHEW said (who recommended thee to me,) that nothing can well escape thee.

The small nest has this singularity, that it seems all tied, twisted, and wove together, with flaxen or hempen threads: nay, some white thread-like substance has assisted, with the others, to tie the branch and nest together. As these seem to be all the refuse of the thread-spinners, which may be thrown out and picked up by the birds, for their use, pray how may we conjecture these pretty artists were supplied with materials, before the Europeans came? And then, how must we account for another observation—that birds never alter the original order of their materials for nests, but the same instinct, in the choice of them prevails through the whole species? I should further be glad to know the name of the cunning fabricator; for, I take it, I had a piece or two of his operations before, which we much admired.

The logs thou sent me, perforated by the species of bees, produced six bees in May and June—very lively and brisk; but the clay wasp-nests, that thou sent me from time to time, none ever produced any more than one wasp; the reason I cannot account for.

I am now, by thine and Colonel CUSTIS's obliging disposition, well furnished with chimney swallow's nests, which are deservedly to be admired; but now I want some eggs, to furnish my nests; and some humming-bird's eggs,—for I have many nests of this pretty creature. But they are so cunning in their contrivance, that it is merely by chance when they are found. But if old or young ones can be caught, pray send them.

The substance thou sends me to guess, is, I conceive, belonging to a *Fungus.*   *   *   *   *

I am, in haste,

Very much thine,

P. COLLINSON.

London, February 3d, 1743–4.

I wrote, my dear JOHN, by the King of Prussia, under cover to our friend FRANKLIN.

Now I shall give thee some account of the cargo. The old proverb is, that there is no fence against a flail; so there is no securing

them from the teeth of rats; for, at the corner of each box, they
had made a proper hole for access,—and in each box was a warm
nest, of straw and the leaves and stalks of the shrubs. It grieved
me to see how they had stripped the great *Rhododendron* and
lesser *Kalmias*.   *   *   *

The deciduous shrubs were in good order, and all the sods of
curious roots, and the Martagons were not hurt. *Warneria*, or
Yellow root [*Hydrastis Canadensis*, L.], is so remarkable, that if
it had been in the last cargo, I could not help seeing it. It is impossible to account for its absence. Loblolly was eat by the rats;
but I hope will shoot from the root. It is one of the charming
evergreens. Does it stand your winters? Your Skunk-root is now
in full flower.   *   *   *   Pray tell me, how many species of Solomon's Seal hath thee observed in all thy travels?   *   *

I find I have three distinct species of *Epigœa*. This last sent,
differs from the others. .

The striped *Pyrola* is a pretty plant, and my favourite. I fancy
it is very scarce, or else there had been another sod. Gentians are
also my favourites.

Thy fine collection of specimens is under Doctor SOLANDER's
examination. Your autumn flowers I pretty well know; but pray
tell me, what are your spring flowers, beside the Puccoon or *Sanguinaria*, the little white *Ranunculus* [*Anemone*], and *Meadia*,
and *Orchis*,—pray, what are the other species with which your
woods, thickets, swamps, fields, and meadows, are adorned in the
spring months of March, April, and May?

I wish, for my satisfaction, thy good son JAMES would put up a
quire of specimens of all your flowers, for only those three months,
—I mean only herbaceous or bulbous flowers—no trees nor shrubs;
for though I have been so many years conversant with your vegetables, yet I think myself entirely ignorant (except the above mentioned) of Flora's beauties, in your spring months.

Our fields so abound with flowers in those months, that they are
a flowery carpet. The Primroses, Daisies, and Pilewort [*Ranunculus*], are now beginning—will be succeeded by the two or three
species of Crow-foot, called Butter-flowers. Dandelion makes a
great show; then the fields are rich with Cowslips, Lady-smocks,
Caltha palustris, or Marsh Marygolds; then they are covered with
blue Hyacinths, Daffodils, Saxifrage, Stitchwort, blue and white
Violets, and a great variety of *Orchis*,—our woods covered with

Anemones, and Periwinkle, and Woodroff [*Asperula*], with its white flowers.

Now I want to know what you abound with—instead of our flowers; for I presume you have not one of them, that are natural to your country: but have a progressive set of flowers, for every spring month, that differs from ours, and is peculiar to your soil and climate.

I can't add more, but that I am thy sincere friend,

P. COLLINSON.

JOHN BARTRAM TO P. COLLINSON.

[Date obliterated, but some time in 1743–4.]

DEAR PETER :—

I am now returned from my long journey, from the country of the Five Nations of Indians, and the Fort of Oswego, on the Ontario Lake,—having had a very prosperous journey. I also found several curious plants, shrubs, and trees, particularly a great mountain *Magnolia* [*M. acuminata*, L.], three feet in diameter, and above an hundred feet high—very straight, and very fine wood; specimens of which I hope to send by next ship, with a particular account of my journey, and the Indians' manner of living, and order of their councils; having been at their chief town, and the meeting of the deputies, and the treaty of peace between the Virginians and them.

I visited the Salt Springs, and boiled the water thereof into salt. I observed the fossil shells all over the country—even on the top of the mountain that separates the waters of Susquehanna and St. Lawrence, in the Vale of Onondago, and on the banks of the Lake Frontenac [Ontario]. I designed, when I went from home, to have returned by the way of Albany,—then to travel from Hudson's River, and climb the Katskill Mountains, to gather the Balm of Gilead cones, and Fir cones, on my way to Delaware: but I found it impracticable to ride between Onondago and the Mohawk's River, and I missed of them, this year; for there is none to be found where we travelled, which was too far westward for them and the Paper Birch; for I find more difference in the kinds of plants, in the same distance of longitude, than latitude. If I am employed next year, to gather seeds—especially of the Fir kinds—I design to travel to the Katskill Mountains, and thence back of New England, northeastward; where I believe I could find many curious evergreens that are not yet known,—for I can't learn that any botanist was ever there, yet.

I received thine of May the 11th, writ in Sir HANS SLOANE's letter; by which I perceive that freedom and openness is exercised, in our correspondency, which I love.

Doctor GRONOVIUS hath sent me his *Index Lapideœ*, and LINNÆUS, the second edition of his *Characteres Plantarum*,—with a very loving letter desiring my correspondence, to furnish him with some natural curiosities of our country. I hope by next ship to send him some.

In the mean time, if thee hath an opportunity, pray return my thanks to him, for that fine present.

I am providing to set out, to-morrow, to travel up Delaware, to gather some Ginseng roots, to send to thee by next ship. So, in great haste, farewell.

J. B.

PETER COLLINSON TO JOHN BARTRAM.

London, March 10, 1743–4.

FRIEND JOHN:—

*   * The prices of microscopes are advanced to a guinea; so have only sent thee one for thyself,—and desire thy acceptance of it, with a book.   *   *   *   *   *

* At present, can give thee no assurance of any new contributors: only the Duke of Richmond and P. MILLER continue—who love new things; but whether so small a subscription will countervail thy going among the saints, in New England, I must submit to thy consideration.

I am looking for new subscribers; am persuaded that many would be glad of the opportunity, if they knew where to apply: but if the worst comes to the worst, if thou sends over three or four five-guinea cases, prettily sorted with something of everything—but in particular, Pine, Fir, and Cedar, and Walnut Hickory, I fancy I shall find means to dispose of them amongst our seedsmen. But thou must be very particular, and send me an exact list of every individual sort of seed in each of them,—and the number of the large seeds, and the quantity of smaller sorts.

    *   *   *   *   *   *   *

I sent all the things to Sir HANS SLOANE,—and writ him a letter to remind him that a ship was going—if he had anything to send thee.

Doctor DILLENIUS has writ thee a letter;—is greatly delighted with the last seeds, they are so good; says that thou art the only man that ever did things to the purpose.

The curiosities for Doctor GRONOVIUS are gone for Holland, with the specimens. I have writ, both to him and LINNÆUS, not to forget the pains and travel of indefatigable JOHN BARTRAM,— but stick a feather in his cap, who is as deserving as the rest.

Doctor COLDEN, our worthy, ingenious friend, is quite a profi- cient. I was surprised with his proficiency in the Linnæan system.

I am in haste : farewell.

P. COLLINSON.

Oh! dear JOHN, I long to see thy Journal, and sentiments and observations of thy expedition to the Five Nations. It was a lucky opportunity.

I was glad to see cones of the fine *Magnolia*. The wood must be beautiful. I had specimens, before I saw thine, from Doctor MITCHELL, of Urbana, in Virginia, two or three years agone,— where there is a stately tree on the plantation of NICHOLAS SMITH, in Essex County, on the head of Piscataway, Rappahannock River, in his pasture. It is well known by all, and visited by all tra- vellers.

I now come to take a little notice of thine of the 2d December. I was pleased to see the digitated-leafed plant prove a Mallow. I know it will be acceptable to Doctor GRONOVIUS.

Thee need not trouble thyself to send nests of the swallows and martens,—but the eggs. The chimney one beats them all, for curiosity; but thou and Colonel CUSTIS have well supplied me. I only want some whole eggs.

To be sure, a shell of each sort of your turtles, dried, will be acceptable,—and if anything remarkable in their head and feet. They may be easily cured in a slack oven, after the bread is out.

Pray, how does Doctor WITT do? I have not heard from him this year.   *   *   *   *
        *   *   Now, dear JOHN, farewell.

P. COLLINSON.

JOHN BARTRAM TO P. COLLINSON.

July 24, 1744.

DEAR PETER:—

I sent, last spring, by Captain REEVES, my Journal to the Five Nations, and the Lake Ontario,* containing a particular account of the soil, productions, mountains, and lakes, which I observed in our journey thither; also the daily proceedings of the Indian chiefs, in their assembly, while we were there; but I have lately heard that REEVES is taken by the French. I conclude, that which I took so much pains about will never come to thy hands; nor the letter I sent in the same ship, which I have not time to write over again, to send by this vessel. I am glad the specimens of Crabs were new to thee. I never could yet see any more perfect than those I sent thee. If I find any, I shall endeavour to send them.

I endeavoured to send the Turtle shells by this ship; but unfortunately have lost several that I had prepared.

The bird's nest thee mentions, with flax or hempen threads, is mostly peeled off our *Apocinums*. We call it a yellow bird,—though it hath a little greenish cast.

That substance which I sent thee to guess at, was a kind of scum on the water of a mill pond, which had been drawn off, and the scum settling on the bottom, and being bleached by the rain, dew and sun, appears in that form.   *   *   *

The names of the specimens were very welcome. I hope my great *Magnolia* [*M. acuminata*, L.] may be different from any thee hath yet seen. You are sometimes mistaken in specimens. Our friend Doctor WITT is as well as usual.   *   *

It is very kind in thee to recommend me to LINNÆUS and GRONOVIUS.   *   *   *   *

* This *Journal* was afterwards printed in London: a copy of which is in the Philadelphia Library.

December, 1744.

DEAR PETER :—

I have received thy kind letters of April the 9th, 19th, and 24th, with all the books mentioned in those letters, very safe and in good order.

The *Sesamum* seed, which I intend to try to propagate, and give thee an account of my success, I am afraid our summers will be full short.   *   *   *   Our friend Doctor COLDEN hath been this fall at my house, whom I received with much satisfaction. Also Doctor MITCHELL, who stayed at Philadelphia near three weeks, and made me several visits.   He is a man of good parts, but his constitution is miserably broken.   I correspond very freely with him and CLAYTON.   *   *   *

*   *   I have put two or three handsful of the seeds of a climbing species of *Euonymus* [*Celastrus scandens*, L.], which MITCHELL said thee wanted very much.   Its berries make a fine appearance, in the fall.   It twists about the trees, or poles, like hops.   *   *   *   *

December 10th, 1745.

FRIEND PETER :—

I have put on board Captain MESNARD, one long cedar box containing a Hornet's nest, and a variety of seeds, for thee ; and a box of curiosities and Musk-rat skin for GRONOVIUS, which I hope thee will take care to send him, as soon and safe as possible. *   *
*   *   *   I have sent, by the two last ships to London, five boxes in each ship ; three in each of forest seeds, for those gentlemen thee sent me orders from ; and a box with roots in earth for thee in one ship—in the other a long cedar box with a variety of seeds for thyself, and some curiosities for Sir HANS SLOANE and for thee.   I have sent, also, two quarters of Hickory, and a square box of plants in earth, viz., one root of my great Mountain *Magnolia*—several roots of Papaw, one fine root of our Laurel, full of flower buds, one sod of sweet Persian *Iris*, one sod of the fine creeping spring *Lychnis*, and a sod of what you call *Dracocephalum*. Pray give CATESBY one root of Papaw.   I sent several in our last ship.

I have received the nails, calico, Russia linen, and the clothes for my boys: all which are very good and well chosen, and give great satisfaction. The only thing that gives me any uneasiness, is, that thee hath sent more than what is my due.

Now, though oracles be ceased, and thee hath not the spirit of divination,—yet, according to our friend Doctor WITT, we friends that love one another sincerely, may, by an extraordinary spirit of sympathy, not only know each other's desires, but may have a spiritual conversation at great distances one from another. Now, if this be truly so,—if I love thee sincerely—and thy love and friendship be so to me—thee must have a spiritual feeling and sense of what particular sorts of things will give satisfaction; and doth not thy actions make it manifest? for, what I send to thee for, thee hath chosen of just such sorts and colours as I wanted. Nay, as my wife and I are one, so she is initiated into this spiritual union; for thee has sent her a piece of calico so directly to her mind, that she saith that if she had been there herself, she could not have pleased her fancy better.   *   *   *   *

In opening those fine cones of Cluster Pine, I observed how close the scales adhered, which is contrary to all our Pines and Firs (except one species of the three-leaved Pine); which, before they are well dried, spring open and shed all the seed out, which makes them the difficultest to gather. One may, in the beginning of the week, see the cones green—and before the latter end, all the seed that is good will be shed out, especially the five-leaved, which you are so fond of—and which it is not possible for me to gather any great quantities thereof, as I wrote to thee, last year. I design to get what I can, yearly; but, as I can't be in three or four hundred distant places in three or four days' time, I can't procure great quantities; and if I depend upon others' assistance, I am sure of being deceived.

As our friend MILLER seems to question my account of our Pines, I now tell thee I generally take care to speak truth—even to those that I think will bestow no more pains of examination, than to tell me it is not so,—to whom silence suits better than arguments—as ignorance doth to their capacity; but, as I have a great opinion of MILLER's learning and judgment, I am engaged in duty and friendship to inform him the best I can, at present.

All our Pine cones are two summers and one winter, from their first appearance to their perfecting and casting their seed, but this one species,—which open not till the second or third year after they seem perfectly ripe.   I have been much surprised at observing these trees have upon one branch all the cones of three, four, or five years' growth, at once.

*   *   *   *   *   *   *

April 12, 1746.

DEAR PETER :—

I have now but little to write, having received no letter from thee since last fall.   I sent a cargo of forest seeds for my correspondents, and garden seeds for thee—with many curiosities, as presents, for several of our friends, in three ships ; but can hear nothing, whether they be arrived at London or not.   We hear there are great troubles in England, and dread the consequences.

Our friend JOSEPH BREINTNALL, departed this life, the middle of last month ; so that now, what letters thee sends for me, let them be directed to me, or to the care of I. PEMBERTON, Jun.; for every merchant of note in town knows me.

I am mightily pleased with thy letter from Petersburgh, giving an account of the Russians' discovery of America.   Pray, doth thee hear any more of it ?   I love to hear of any new discovery of any kind.

April the 16th.

This day I received thy kind letters of October the 12th, 1745, and January the 24th, 1745–6,—and Sir HANS SLOANE'S of October the 16th, with all the seeds mentioned in those letters, except the Strawberry and Sloe,—the last of which we have had in the country these fifty years.   I plant them about my hedges, where it grows to a large size.   The blossoms are prodigious full, but never one ripe fruit.   They are bit with the insect, as all our stone fruit is, but the Peaches, and some kinds of Cherries overgrow them.

I have some hopes of the Horse-chestnuts, though most of them were blue moulded, yet some seemed to be pretty sound.   But alas ! the four fine large roots of Madder, had no more appearance of life than if they had been drying in the house a year.

*   *   *   *   *   *   *

My pretty plant is just in flower, that thee saith DILLENIUS calls a Borage,—which I think hath no affinity with it, or likeness to it, save only barely in the shape of a single flower; and I believe is as much a new genus as any plant that ever was sent out of America; and not the only one that adorns that spacious vale of six hundred miles in length, S. W. by West, in which I have gathered the finest of my autumnal flowers; and where, by report of the inhabitants, it is like as if *Flora* sported in solitary retirement, as *Sylva* doth on the Katskill Mountains,—where there is the greatest variety of uncommon trees and shrubs, that I ever saw in such a compass of ground.

I am glad the white-berried *Christophoriana* [*Actœa alba*, Bigel.] grows with thee: but thee should have that with great blue berries [*Leontice*], which is much the finest plant. There is abundance of it growing by Rappahannock, in Virginia; so made no question but our friend MITCHELL, or CLAYTON, had sent it to thee long ago. It grows nowhere less than fifty miles of me, that I remember.*

April the 23d, 1746.
DEAR PETER:—

I have packed up in a box directed to thee, four of our turtles, dried after their bowels were taken out, and well washed, having preserved their shell, head, feet and tail, entire; by which you may observe the difference of them almost as well as if they had been alive. I cannot get any other kinds; it's too soon in the year. These females had the yolks of eggs in them, almost at their full bigness, but no whites nor shell to them. It is near a month to their time of laying.

I design, this summer, to collect all our kinds of turtles, with the eggs belonging to them—with insects and fishes—and send some or other by every ship that sails from here to London; so that, if some are taken, others may escape. We had extraordinary luck, last year. I doubt there will but few sail from here, this year. I have expected, by every ship since HARGRAVE came in, last summer, those books GRONOVIUS sent me. Pray what is become of them? All the ships that sailed from London, last year, for Philadelphia, arrived safe; yet I have no account of them.

* J. B. was not then aware that this plant grew, abundantly, much nearer to his residence;—viz., on the banks of the Brandywine and Susquehanna.

How doth our friend CATESBY do? He won't speak a word to me, now-a-days. He hath had several opportunities, within these two years, of writing to me, and I have sent some curiosities to him every year.

The account of REAUMUR, about bees and wasps, was very entertaining. I love Natural History dearly.

J. BARTRAM.

PETER COLLINSON TO JOHN BARTRAM.

Now, friend JOHN, I come to consider further of some of thy observations, by thine of the 10th of December. I am glad to find that thee art so well recovered, and that all the goods are come safe to hand, and please; which is more than I expected, and ought not to excuse thee from being more particular and exact in thy orders next time.

Though thou canst not see, yet I have told thee what inoculating on a Peach stock may do. If I am not out in my conjecture—as it is a free stock, and sends up its sap plentifully, it may assist the Nectarine and Apricot, at a season when supplies are wanting. As thou hast tried the north side of buildings, and sides of water-courses, &c., to no purpose, with Plums, pray give the other fruits as fair a chance.

To prevent the depredations of the Beetle, I confess, is not so easy as some other bad effects: yet, as we know the duration of this insect is but short, if, while he is so noxious, some contrivance could be found out, to disturb or destroy him, you then might hope to taste a Nectarine,—one of the most delicious fruits in the universe, and much exceeds a Peach, in a rich vinous-flavoured juice. And an Apricot is also one of the fine fruits. Last year, our standards were overloaded, which are allowed to excel the wall fruit.

Suppose, as soon as this Beetle is discovered, if the trees were to be smoked, with burning straw under them, or at some distance, so as to fumigate their branches at a time the beetles are most liable to attack the fruit; or, if the trees were to be squirted on by a hand engine, with water in which Tobacco leaves were soaked; either of these two methods, I should think, if they did not totally prevent, yet, at least, would secure so much of these fine fruits as would be worth the labour of people of circumstances, who are curious to taste these delicious fruits in perfection.

I take it, the reason the Plum succeeds so well, is the frequent shaking the trees, by being planted in a frequented place. The beetles are tumbled off, or else are disturbed, and frightened from settling on the trees: and the ground being trod so much, may be a great help, by keeping in the moisture, which is so conducive to bring the fruit to maturity.

This brings to my mind a contrivance I was told, a few days agone. An Englishman went and settled at Naples, about your latitude, and writ over to P. MILLER, that Apricots throve very well, but all the fruit dropped off: which he was surprised at; for he expected the finest fruits in that fine climate. But he was mistaken; for the natural fruits of that country are Figs, Pomegranates, Olives, Grapes, Oranges, and Lemons. My friend MILLER writ him word, to lay a great deal of muck (rotten dung and straw mixed), or a great quantity of Fern leaves, or any compost that would keep the ground moist, and prevent the sun's action, which is very penetrating in that country, as well as with you.

This had the desired effect; and the gentleman writes him word, that since he has practised it, he has never failed of fruit in plenty, and in the greatest perfection.

Now, friend JOHN, improve this hint; and if your Apricots are too forward, plant them under all disadvantages possible; that is, in the most exposed places, and in all the coldest, shadiest aspects that can be found. Perhaps, when mountains come to be settled, the north sides may succeed with this fruit and others, and may not be so much frequented by the Beetles. I apprehend, if your Gooseberries were littered, it would prevent their dropping off; and if this litter was now and then watered, both under the Apricot, &c., it would be of service.

Friend JOHN, I have writ more fully by Captain MESNARD; but this will hint to thee thy good fortune of all thy cargoes coming safe, which is great luck, these very perilous times.

Notwithstanding all my endeavours, I can only raise thee one new subscriber, * * who desires a little of everything, and the Duke of Richmond and P. MILLER are continued. Send them any sort of Pine but Jersey Pine; some acorns, a few of a sort; Sassafras; Sweet Gum; Sweet flowering Bay, or small *Magnolia*, or Laurel; and any new tree or shrub; and some of all sorts of wild flowers.

I thank thee for the fine cones of small *Magnolia*, and the great sort [*M. acuminata*, L.]. They are so fresh, I hope to raise some. Is there no more Chinquapin to be had? Why does thou not raise a plantation in thy own garden of Chinquapin trees, to serve thy correspondents? From the first, we wanted them; and if they had been then sown, by this time thou would have had plenty to serve us; for it is a tree that is not to be had here for money.

The *Larix* and Evergreen seeds, that our friend JOHN MILLER has collected for thee, I have divided; and sent half by this conveyance, and half by MESNARD.

Now farewell.
P. COLLINSON.

London, April 26, 1746.

JOHN BARTRAM TO P. COLLINSON.

July 20th, 1747.

DEAR PETER :—

I have received six of thy letters, and two of GRONOVIUS, and some seeds which I sowed directly; and though a very warm, wet season, not one of them is come up. Two of thy letters by the way of Boston, and one by the way of York, I received by the hands of our friend BENJAMIN FRANKLIN, and several of the others. He was so kind as to tell me to acquaint thee that any letter thee pleases to send to me, if thee hath an opportunity by either Boston or York, if thee incloseth it in a letter directed to him, he will deliver it to me post free; which is very kind, indeed; and I hope to prevail with him to inclose one in his, when he sends to thee by the way of York, by which means I hope we may hear often from one another.

This is like to be a plentiful year for forest seeds. I hope to gather a fine parcel; but how I shall have an opportunity of sending them, I know not. Thee adviseth me to send them by two vessels; which would do very well, if two vessels should sail from here to London. At present, we know of none but MESNARD,— and he is too soon to send by.   *   *   *

*   *   The cylindrical columns are certainly in New England. BENJAMIN FRANKLIN saw them at three miles distance; but being very cold, did not care to turn out of his way.

Our proprietor is almost as crafty as covetous. He won't sell land, because the people being necessitated for land to live upon, raiseth its price prodigiously, so that, in a few years, he may get five times as much as he could now—or may set it at an extortionate ground rent.

I design to go to the sea-coast this fall, to fetch from thence curiosities of what kind soever I can find. I have wrote to my friend to gather what he can for me.

January the 30th, 1747–8.

DEAR PETER :—

I have put on board the ship Beulah, three boxes of forest seeds: No. 1 for the Duke of Argyle ; No. 2 for Squire HAMILTON ; and No. 3 is for thyself. I sent, in a vessel that sailed last November, four boxes: No. 1 for SMITHSON ;* No. 2 for WILLIAMSON ; No. 3 for Lord Deskford ; No. 4 for Lord Hopetoun. I have sent none for the Dukes of Richmond, and Bedford, this year ; for I had nothing new to send them, but what I had sent them several times before. I sent them a fine parcel of the White Pine, last spring, by SEYMOUR. I have not been at the Cedar Swamps, myself. I sent several, to gather the Cedar seeds, but they found but few ; so I could send but a little seed to each correspondent that wanted : and it was not safe going beyond our mountains,—for fear of the French Indians.

I have not received one letter from thee, this long time. The last was dated June the 6th. We are surprised that we have no news from London these many months.

We expect a visit from the French, early in the spring ; and numbers of our people are daily exercising and learning the martial discipline, in order to oppose them, if they should attempt to land,—and are making preparations for forts and batteries, to stop any vessels that come in a hostile manner.

*   *   *   *   *   *   *

* Perhaps an ancestor of him who endowed the noble SMITHSONIAN INSTITUTION, at the city of Washington, *"for the increase and diffusion of knowledge among men."*

PETER COLLINSON TO JOHN BARTRAM.

London, February 22d, 1750.

FRIEND JOHN :—

I have paid thy bill, and sent the two quarto Bibles, val. 14*s.* each—£1. 8*s.* 0*d.*

Remember when thou draws, next year, do it in £25 bills; and let each bill be a month after the other;—as for instance, one at thirty days, one at sixty days, and at ninety days after sight; for these great people are dilatory in paying,—and when thy bills come, I have a pretext to press hard for thy money—which I choose not to mix with my other cash. As thine is a particular and separate account, I keep it by itself.

I am now deeply engaged in business ; so must excuse entering into particulars.

   *　　*　　*　　*　　*　　*　　*

The plant thou mentions, of our ingenious friend KALM's finding, I know full well. It is called the *Faba Ægyptiaca* [*Nelumbium,* Juss.]* It grows in Carolina ; but I did not think it grew so far to the northward. The seed-vessel is very curious. I always thought the *Colocasia* was a species of *Arum.* It is so esteemed by the moderns. Pray, if thou visits the place, send me a good specimen of the leaves, &c. What blossom it has, I cannot guess.

If thee hast any young Chinquapins, pray put in two or three plants, next cargo.

But I had almost forgot a material article ; that is, to send me

---

* There is a tradition, in the BARTRAM family, that the Great Water Lily (*Nelumbium luteum,* Willd.) was brought by JOHN BARTRAM from Georgia, or South Carolina, and planted in the waters near Philadelphia:—viz., in "BROGDEN'S *ditch,*" a short distance below the city—and in "*Old Man's Creek,*" Salem County, New Jersey; in which places, Colonel CARR informs me, it may yet be seen,—and in the last-named place, abundant.

It would seem, however, from this letter of P. COLLINSON, that KALM had the credit—even with JOHN BARTRAM—of "finding" the plant, in that vicinity,—or, at least, of bringing it into notice; and moreover, it is believed that JOHN BARTRAM had not, at that date (1750), been so far south as Carolina. Whether the *Nelumbium* really is, or is not *indigenous* in the *Delaware,* or its tributaries,—and if *not, when,* and *by whom, introduced*—are questions not easily solved to satisfaction, at the present day. The letters in which JOHN BARTRAM speaks of it, are, unfortunately, missing. See, further, P. COLLINSON's letter of February 2, 1760; which is calculated to throw additional doubt on the subject.

some terrapins; for I have two gardens walled in, that I can secure them from running away. They will come in the box of plants, or by themselves, as thee thinks best. The proprietor's gardener sent two sorts. The yellow and black I know well; but there was a black flat-shell sort, with most beautifully painted shell round the edges, that is very nimble to the other. Pray, let thy lads look out sharp for some for me.

*   *   *   *   *

London, January 20, 1751.

I am very much obliged to my good friend J. BARTRAM, for so fine a collection of growing plants. If they had all come to my hand, I should have troubled thee no further; but, to my great loss, some prying, knowing people, looked into the cases, and out of that No. 2, took the three roots of Chamærhododendron, Red Honeysuckle, Laurel, root of Silver-leafed Arum, and the *Spiræa alni folio* [*Clethra alnifolia*, L.]. These were the most valuable part, and what I most wanted. It is very vexatious. Whether taken out, on board—or coming up from the ship, I can't say; but this is certain, they were gone. I wish Lord Northumberland had not the same bad luck; for, as I peeped in, I could see but very little. But, as I have had no complaints, I hope it was otherwise.

I fancy some of the sailors, having relatives gardeners, seeing these plants so carefully boxed up, took them for rarities; so were tempted to steal them, to give to their friends.   *   *   *

This day, I gathered the finest nosegay, to carry to town,—being plenty of Violets, Crocus, Snow-drops, Polyanthos, Single Anemone, double and single Stocks, and Wall-flowers, very sweet.

I conceive the three-leafed Pines growing in a different form, is entirely owing to the soil they grow in, and exposure to the sea-winds.   *   *   *   *

Did the berries of the evergreen *Rhamnus*, that was found in the Great Plains in the Desert—growing five or six inches high, amongst the Dwarf Pines, come up, in thy garden? None did with me. It was a very rare and curious plant.   *   *

Thy journal is in the press; hope to send it by next ship.

I am thy sincere friend,

P. COLLINSON.

March 5, 1750–1.

MY GOOD FRIEND JOHN :—

Pray what is the reason I have no acorns from that particular species of Oak that Doctor MITCHELL found in thy meadow [*Quercus heterophylla*, Mx.?]? And I observe, in thy specimens, two other narrow-leafed Oaks. As I have now ground enough, I wish for a dozen good acorns of each. A few Sugar Maple keys, unless thou could send me a young plant. The particular sort of Hazelnut grows, that was sent me two years agone; but, in removing my garden, I lost the early sweet Iris, and the curious species of *Arum*. Pray repair these losses; besides a sweet *Spiræa alni folio*, named *Clethra*, by LINNÆUS, which I much admire; but that must come in a plant or two; and a plant or two of Ivy, or your Laurel [*Kalmia*, L.].　　*　　　*　　　*

London, March 22d, 1751.

I hope my good friend JOHN BARTRAM has mine by BUDDEN. I am so engaged always, at this time o' year, that I always write in a hurry; and write perhaps the same thing over and over again, —for my memory is burdened with a thousand things.　　*

I observe four species of Hickory. Send me half a score of each, for my own sowing.

I am much obliged to thee for the cargo in the little box; it was well stuffed. All came in fine order.　　*　　　*

I believe I told thee of the great loss of the Duke of Richmond, my intimate and familiar friend. Next to Lord PETRE, none so ardently encouraged gardening and plants, and every laudable design—both in public and private life.

Pray remember the terrapins—and early ripe Indian corn—and Squash seed.　　　　　　Thine,

P. COLLINSON.

London, April 24, 1751.

TO MY ESTEEMED FRIEND JOHN BARTRAM :—

Lest my letters, by other vessels, should miscarry, I here renew my orders for seeds, with additions.　　*　　　*　　　*

It is very extraordinary, what thou writes of the Larch. It grows very fast here, on all soils.

Pray remember the *Faba Ægyptiaca*, that our friend KALM found in West Jersey: specimens of leaf, flower and fruit.

He and his wife arrived safe here. We have had many conferences. He desires his service; commends thee in most things, but much blames thee for not enriching thy journal [of the expedition to Lake Ontario] with a many curious articles which he has collected from thy mouth, and which, had he come time enough, he would have added.   *   *   *

*   *   The death of our late excellent Prince of Wales has cast a great damp over all the nation. Gardening and planting have lost their best friend and encourager; for the prince had delighted in that rational amusement, a long while: but lately, he had a laudable and princely ambition to excel all others. But the good thing will not die with him: for there is such a spirit and love of it, amongst the nobility and gentry, and the pleasure and profit that attends it, will render it a lasting delight.

I admire in thine and KALM's travels, that you got no intelligence of the great Moose Deer, so celebrated by the first settlers. This great formidable animal cannot be extinct. I wish only to see a pair of its horns, to compare with the great fossil horns found in Ireland, which is certainly extinct in that kingdom.

Now, my dear JOHN, it's time to conclude, with my sincere wishes for thine and family's preservation.

Thy real friend,

P. COLLINSON.

[Date omitted: probably in the summer of 1751.]

I was delighted to see the son* of my old friend JOHN BARTRAM. The honesty and good disposition of the youth pleases me, as well as his industrious disposition.

The ship being sold, the poor lad is adrift; and no passage to be had back, without paying for it. He thinks it a hard case, and I think so too: for at this time there are very few ships going, until about Christmas, which is too long to stay, and then will only have the chance to go to Maryland, or Virginia, or West Indies,

* MOSES BARTRAM, third son of JOHN BARTRAM, born June, 1732.

which he has been very industrious to find out. He would willingly give his labour for his passage; but neither to your port, nor to New York, will they take him, on those terms. As to his hiring himself to the West Indies, I can no ways agree to it, though he is very desirous of it. But I shall persuade him off of it; for it will be exposing his virtue to too severe trials; for he must associate with our London common sailors, who are a most profligate crew, and, if possible, will never be easy until they make him like themselves. And then our wages are very low; the best sailor has but 25s. a month. The only method I can advise, is to get him in a settled employ in some of your own ships—either trading here or to the West Indies; that he may return and pass the winter (if from London) under thy inspection.

As he was very bare of clothes, and those he had in a ragged condition, I have, according to thy order, fitted him up in the most frugal manner I could. I must say for him, that he was even contented in his rags, and thought I did too much; and yet, in his poor equipment, I could not see how I could do less.　　*　　*

I must acknowledge, my good friend has taken great pains to oblige me, with so many entertaining letters. Thy observations on the *Faba Ægyptiaca* [*Nelumbium luteum*, Willd.], are well worthy our notice. Doctor Gronovius will be delighted with it. I have had specimens from South Carolina, but never imagined it grew so far to the northward. The specimens are fine. I will send one to Holland the first opportunity. Next year, if it is not too remote, get more of leaves, fruit, and the flower *in its full size*, which will make the whole complete; and I have some curious botanical friends to oblige with specimens.

It must certainly be some other sharp, strong-pointed production, that could annoy the scaly sides of the Crocodile; its belly, indeed, is easier penetrated. The *Tribulus aquaticus* [*Trapa natans*, L.] is much harder and sharper.

It is possible this rare plant may have been eradicated from Egypt, &c., by the great increase of people, animals, and traffic: but in China it subsists, with a variety of rare species,—as I have seen, and showed Moses, from a Chinese Herbal containing near a thousand vegetables—all most curiously drawn and painted in their natural colours. There are delineated three species, with large white, yellow, and purple flowers. These have their seed-vessels

represented upright : that yours should hang down, is very singular.

All aquatic leaves have the property thou mentions, I presume,
from their downy surfaces, though not perceptible to our eyes without a glass ; as all web-footed fowls shoot off the water from the
oily downiness that is on the surface.

Thy expedition up the creek, shows with what energy thou pursues nature. The hidden deeps cannot secure her treasure. She
rewards thy labours with her spoils.

There is great reason to believe, from the beds of petrified shells
that are found all over the level country below the mountains, and
confined by the ocean, that its waves once washed the feet of those
hills,—but, on some great revolution, retreated, and left those
memorials behind it. Indeed, we refer all such phenomena to the
effects of the Deluge; but it is believed, and also known, that there
have been great alterations on the face of nature, from earthquakes, &c. That Belemnites are found with sea-shells, I think is
a confirmation that they are marine productions ; which many
doubt, but think them stones, after their own kind, which, for
many reasons, I can by no means agree to. It may seem wonderful to thee, that new shells are found, not known before : but who
can tell what lies concealed in the fathomless depths of the ocean ?
The Belemnites may lie concealed there ; their weight may prevent
their being washed on the shores. We have a cliff in England,
near Lymington, that abounds with such variety of shells. I have
at least twenty different species, large and small, all unknown on
our coasts, being from the East and West Indies. What a *ren-
versement* must this have been ! The productions of the South,
East, and West, thrown so far to the North !

I observe well, in thine of the 26th June, thy account of the
original building of the Swallows. I think it very feasible ; but
it is pretty singular none should continue their original institution.   *   *   *   *

What thee calls Water Swallows, we call Sand Martins,—from
their building in sandy precipices, near rivers, and in inland places
remote from them. They are, with us, of a different colour from
our chimney Martins or house Swallows.

As to thy desire of an assistant, it would, to be sure, be of great
service, to relieve and assist thee ; but such as thou'd like is not

to be had : for none care to leave their native land, but those that, from their bad principles and morals, cannot live in it.   *   *

By thine of July 19th, both thy son and myself were glad to find some degree of health restored to thy family.

As CATESBY only resided in Virginia and Carolina, it was impossible he could describe more than the animals of those provinces, —and not all them, neither.

I shall be pleased to see both your Pheasant and Heath Cock. As it may not be possible to procure both cock and hen of each species, pray be careful to examine their internal parts, that we may be sure ; for in birds, as the cock and hen vary so much, for want of certainly knowing which, has made confusion, and multiplied species.

Their thumping is a very extraordinary action, and MOSES confirms thy account.   Possibly it is a piece of gallantry the cock uses, to recommend himself to the hen.   I admire I never heard of it before.

When the skin is stuffed, gentle drying in an oven, after the bread is out, will preserve them, packed in dry Tobacco leaves, or dust.   *Vale.*

P. COLLINSON.

Mill Hill, September 20 [1751 ?].

MY DEAR FRIEND:—

I have now thine of the 18th June before me, and MOSES by my side ; so I cannot fail of many intelligences.   He has surveyed my garden, and finds many things wanting.   As the weather has proved very fine, I believe he will think his trip hither no ways disagreeable.

Our good friend, B. FRANKLIN, has some papers on husbandry, from a curious friend of mine,—from which it's likely thou may borrow some useful hints ; but great allowances must be made for the difference of our soil and climate with yours.   I have also desired him to let Mr. ELIOT, of Connecticut, see them ; for they may tend to the improvement of that colony.

As thy son's inclination is bent to the sea, and he is very desirous to qualify himself for that business, it would be much to his advantage to be settled in some regular, certain employ.   Then his industry and diligence will be taken notice of, and will be a means for his advancement; whereas, if he is from time to time changing his masters, and his ships, he will be lost amongst the vulgar. At first, it might be well enough to go abroad and see the world; but when his curiosity has been sufficiently gratified, a settled employ is to be preferred. He will inform how he employed his time here. He was not idle.

*   *   *   *   *   *

I have often with thankfulness observed, how good Providence has checked the devouring caterpillars, by a course of natural causes, and preserved a balance of his creatures, in the creation. Each species has its natural check,—which arises from accidents we cannot foresee, or prevent.

If it raises thy wonder, to see how the caterpillar lies in the egg, what will it do, if thou was to see the Oak existing in the acorn?

I am glad the snakes did not come. There is a sort of natural aversion in human nature against this creature.

But any of the species of turtle, or terrapins, would be innocent, and pretty, in my garden; and are easily sent in the fall, in a box of leaves, &c., when they have done eating.

Poor MOSES is sadly concerned about paying his passage; and yet there is no remedy. It may be of service to him, in future life, to take care and make a sure bargain, and not trust to any man's promises; but have it under their handwriting. Now, friend JOHN, farewell; and remember that I am thy friend,

P. COLLINSON.

MOSES can give thee an account of my plants and garden.

January 11th, 1753.

I have only just time now to thank my good friend J. BARTRAM for his three kind letters. The seven boxes are come safe, and all the others. But Dr. MITCHELL is displeased that he has no letter, neither the seeds which he says he gave thee orders for.

Pray thank MOSES for his letter; and pray look out, this year, for land Terrapins, for my son is very desirous of them.   *

*   *   Doctor KEARSLEY is very much mistaken, to take the *Mechoacan* for the True Scammony; for I have seen it growing several times, raised from true seed, sent from Aleppo. I will not deny but it may be a species, as they are both *Convolvuluses*.

*   *   *   *   *   *

Is that charming autumn Blue Gentian [*G. crinita*, L.], an annual, or biennial, or perennial?

I shall acquaint Doctor MITCHELL with thy reasons for not sending his order.   *   *   *   *

*   *   I want to know if the Laurel and the Horse-chestnut,
that MOSES carried, grow, and suit your climate.

The difference is very remarkable between our country and
yours; for I have heard thunder but once this year—and that at a
distance; whilst you have had it so terrible all over your continent,
—as our friend CLAYTON writes me from Virginia; and we have
scarcely had sufficient to make our ingenious friend FRANKLIN'S
experiment.   Our summer was wet; but our harvest good, and our
autumn long and fine.   I gathered such a nosegay, on Christmas
day, would have delighted thee to have seen it.   *   *

In England vegetation may be said never to cease; for the
spring flowers tread so on the heels of the autumn flowers, that the
ring is carried on without intermission.

I am, in haste, thine,

P. COLLINSON.

February 13, 1753.

From my country cottage, called *Ridgeway House*.   Under that title it is to be
found in our old maps; so I conclude it little less than 200 years standing; but
yet is a tolerable dwelling.

DEAR JOHN:—

Being retreated here from the hurries of the town, while snow
covers the ground in this Alpine situation (the country, near the
town, being clear of it), I retired to my study, with a good fire, and
found great serenity and pleasure of mind in conversing with my
distant friends.

Thy sundry packets lay before me.   As often as I peruse them,
I still find entertainment, and much matter for speculation and reflection.

The first that I laid my hands on, was the well-wrote dissertation on your Oaks and Hickories.   *   *   Thy descriptions
are so exact and natural, that I am always delighted with reading
them; but, my good friend, I must impart to thee my doubts.   I
am afraid the species are so multiplied, that it will be a difficult
task to distinguish them here.

The difference between the Lowland White Oak [*Quercus bicolor,* Willd. ?] and the Mountain White Oak [*Q. obtusiloba,* Mx. ?], is purely owing to their situation,*—and that cannot be determined but by experiments. Take the acorns of each, and plant in thy garden; a few years' observation will put that matter out of doubt. And the like may be, in the Swamp, and Mountain Chestnut Oak [*Q. Prinus,* L. ? and *Q. montana,* Willd. ?], a difference owing to soil and situation—not sufficient to constitute two distinct species; and so of the Spanish, and Swamp Spanish Oak [*Q. falcata,* and *Q. palustris,* of Mx. ?] I know this tribe of trees sport so, in their leaves, that it is easy for thee to collect specimens that shall have a great appearance of a distinct species; but the question is, will this hold through the forest? In England, we have but two species of Oak; and yet, in the course of my observation, I could extend them to variety of species,—from the different figure of their leaves, and the shape and size of their acorns.

As an account of your forest trees is a very desirable piece of knowledge here, with their properties and uses,—since the humour of cultivating them is so much indulged: yet, when the Lowland and Mountain Oaks grow up here together—and no very remarkable difference,—then our ingenious friend, JOHN BARTRAM, will be arraigned with want of judgment to distinguish things aright. To prevent such an impeachment of his skill, I much wish he would revise his account again, and confirm his opinion with fair specimens and acorns, *impartially collected;* for I have a great desire to have them engraved, and published. Our friend CATESBY has, indeed, exhibited variety; but then his work is so expensive, few can afford to buy it.   *   *   *   *

Ridgeway House, February 13, 1753.

I now come next to examine thine of June 7th, perhaps over again.   *   *   *   *

Thy expedition to the mountains must be an agreeable jaunt to one of thy taste, and mine. In these expeditions, forget not

* Friend COLLINSON manifests a laudable desire to avoid the unnecessary multiplication of species; but the modern botanists, generally, have sustained the views of JOHN BARTRAM, in reference to the specific differences of the Oaks here mentioned.

to collect any insects, or observations on them, that I have not had before; for some frequent the hills—others the dales. I don't remember thou ever sent me any of your land-snails,—of which there must be different species in different places. It delights me, to see the boundless variety that fills every corner of the earth and the sea.

* * What thou names the Sea-beach Cherry, by its leaves seems rather a *Plum* [*Prunus maritima*, Wang. ?]. If we are right in the plant, pray send a specimen of the Beach Cherry, —which will set us right.

I commend thy method of sowing Parsley, &c., with the Fir seed. In the northern province of Germany, where it is sandy and barren, and will produce little but Firs and Pines,—to prevent the seedlings being burnt up, they sow Oats with their seed, to screen it in the summer, and its dry straw protects it in the winter; for they do not reap the oats; and one reason may be, in such a barren soil, they are not worth it. * * *

Doctor COLDEN has lately confirmed to me the success of the *Phytolacca*, in cancers. As it is to be applied outwardly, the danger is the less. * * *

The White Cedar expedition must be pleasant. But it would spoil trade to tell how easily the White Cedar is propagated from cuttings. Not one will miss. I have two dozen of the finest, straight, upright plants from cuttings thou ever saw; but this, GORDON and I keep a great secret.

* * * * *

I presume, before this, thou has received Dr. BUTTNER's remarks on thy *Appendix* to the MEDICINA BRITANNICA.* I thank thee for it; and will take care to send the other to LINNÆUS.

---

* This was a sort of vegetable *Materia Medica*, reduced to popular apprehension, by THO. SHORT, of *Sheffield*, M.D.[a]

The American edition was reprinted in Philadelphia, 1751, by B. FRANKLIN, and D. HALL, at the Post-office, in Market Street; "with a PREFACE by Mr. JOHN

---

[a] This author was, probably, the medical personage referred to, in the first volume of MACAULAY's History of England, where, speaking of the sudden illness of CHARLES II., (Feb., 1685,) it is stated, that "all the medical men of note in London, were summoned. So high did political animosities run, that the presence of some Whig physicians was regarded as an extraordinary circumstance. One Roman Catholic, whose skill was then widely renowned, Doctor THOMAS SHORT, was in attendance. Several of the prescriptions have been preserved. One of them is signed by fourteen doctors. The patient was bled largely. Hot iron was applied to his head. A loathsome volatile salt, extracted from human skulls, was forced into his mouth."

I can't imagine at the long silence of Doctor GRONOVIUS;—whether it is his employ in the government, or whether his taste for Natural History abates, I can't say; but this our friend CLAYTON tells me,—that he writ him a letter complaining of the expense that attended the conveyance of his specimens to Holland, and as good as forbid his sending more; so that, it seems to me, the last vice that attacks human nature has laid hold on him—that is, covetousness. I wish it may not be so; but it is more than probable. Postage becomes chargeable, and so he is silent. He is two letters in my debt, and used to be the most punctual correspondent.

Many are asking me, why the name of *Hemlock* is given to the smallest coned Fir, which we call Yew-leafed Fir [*Pinus Canadensis*, L.].

    *   *   *   *   *   *

London, July 19, 1753.

If my friend JOHN BARTRAM knew better my affairs, my situation in life, my public business, my many engagements and incumbrances,—instead of being in a pet, that I answer not the letter he sends by one ship by the next that sails—he would wonder I do so well as I do, though he thinks it so ill. * *   He should never suspect his friend, until he has better foundation for so doing. To serve him, I often neglect my own business. His surmises are well meant; yet they arise from want of experience, and not knowing me, and the share I have in the busy world, so well as I could wish; then he would not think me so bad a correspondent. And I dare venture, now I have given him these friendly hints, he will not think me so again; but continue his friendly and informing, as well as his entertaining correspondence.

 * * I thought he had known me better, than to think anything he sends me either lost or neglected.   *   *

BARTRAM, Botanist of *Pennsylvania*, and his NOTES throughout the work, showing the places where many of the described PLANTS are to be found in these parts of *America*, their differences in name, appearance, and virtue, from those of the same kind in *Europe;* and an APPENDIX, containing a description of a number of PLANTS peculiar to *America*, their uses, virtues, &c."

The original work is surcharged with all that sort of nonsensical credulity and trumpery which disgraced the profession in former times; but the brief *Appendix* by JOHN BARTRAM, (noticing some twenty of our indigenous vegetables,) is more reputable, and possesses some degree of interest. The book is now exceedingly rare. For an opportunity to examine the only copy I have seen, I am indebted to the kindness of my valued friend, DANIEL B. SMITH, of Philadelphia.

The Cranberry thrives wonderfully, and is in blossom; every way agreeing with ours, but much larger.   *   *

Pray give my thanks to MOSES, for his two letters. In the box, with the other things, I have sent two fine Cedar of Lebanon cones, just come from thence.   *   *   *   *

There is a little token, in a box, for BILLY,* whose pretty performances please me much.

Thy account of the frogs is very humorous; but would it not be more so, to import a cargo of them? And had I a park, or place inclosed, I would wish it. But as it is, strolling people and boys would destroy them. A bull-frog would surprise the whole village; but then it would be certainly killed.

Dear JOHN, farewell.

P. COLLINSON.

JOHN BARTRAM TO P. COLLINSON.

August the 20th, 1753.

DEAR PETER:—

I am now very intent upon examining the true distinguishing characters of our forest trees, finding it a very difficult task—as I can have no help from either ancient or modern authors, they having taken no particular observation worth notice. I expect, by our worthy friend BENJAMIN, specimens of the evergreens of New England,—which I intend to compare with ours, and those of York government; so that I may give a particular account of the evergreens natural to our northern parts, which I hope to send thee, this fall or next spring—with a fuller account of our Oaks and Hickories; and for thy present amusement, I here send thee, as a specimen of my method of proceeding, a near perfect description of the characters of our Hop Hornbeam.

*   *   *   *   *   *   *

I am preparing for a journey to Doctor COLDEN's, and the mountains. I design to set out with my little botanist ["BILLY"], the first of September, which is ten days sooner than usual; hoping to gather the Balm of Gilead and Larix seed—which was generally

* "BILLY," the fourth son of JOHN BARTRAM, discovered an early talent for drawing. He was, at this date, in his fifteenth year.

fallen before I got there. Neither do I design to be in such a hurry as I have been.

TO PETER COLLINSON, ON THE DEATH OF HIS WIFE.

[1753.]

DEAR AFFLICTED FRIEND:—

As I have been once near, in some respects, in the same gloomy, disconsolate circumstance with thine, I believe I am in some measure qualified to sympathize with one of my dearest friends, in his close and tender affliction. It seems hard to have one's dearest consort, a loving spouse—an affectionate wife—an object that we love above all terrestrial enjoyments—taken from our arms. How grievous is it, for one that is thus agreeable, to be torn from our hearts! Her dear sweet bosom is cold; her tender heart—the centre of mutual love—is motionless; her dear arms are no more extended to embrace her beloved; the partner of his cares, and sharer of his pleasures must no more sit down with her husband at his table. Oh! my dear friend,—let us resign all to God Almighty; His will be done! He knows what is best for our ultimate good. * * * *

A JOURNEY TO THE KATSKILL MOUNTAINS, WITH BILLY, 1753.

After two weeks' sickness, being pretty well recovered, but still a lurking fever hanging on me. * * * We set out the 1st of September, and travelled forty miles; the next day we travelled near fifty; and the next day crossed the South Chains, being three ridges of our Blue Mountain, on Jersey side, where we stayed about noon, to rest ourselves, and observe the vegetables that grew thereon; which were, Mountain Chestnut Oak, Mountain or Champagne Red Oak, and some Spanish Oak, Sassafras, Chestnut, and Maple—Ash, black and white,—Wild Cherry, Persimmon, and three-leaved Pine. Shrubs, Sweet Fern, and, in swampy places, *Prinos;* and very good Fox grapes. * * * *
* * * * We continued our travelling till eleven o'clock, near the river; and then turned on our right hand along a road that crossed the Blue Mountain again, being the road the

people take to Goshen. I took this road, to show my son the broken, mountainous, desolate part of the country;—where we took
the first particular notice of the Alder with a silver colour on the
under side of the leaf [*Alnus incana*, Willd.], which is plentiful in
this part of the country. On the branches of the North River, I
saw it plentifully in my first journey; but took no particular notice
of it, but its largeness. It grows fifteen or twenty feet high, and
four inches diameter; whereas ours grows about two. As we came
down the mountain, on a sunny, rich bank, I found many roots of
this Wild Lovage, and brought seed to sow in my garden, after
despairing fifteen years of ever seeing it again. At last we came
to a little cottage, one hour by sun, and ordered our horses to pasture. Our host said there was the strangest plants growed on his
land, that growed anywhere in the country. We went directly;
but they all proved to be but common plants to me, though,
indeed, there were such as did not grow amongst the inhabitants.

At night, we lodged seven or eight of us (they being two families) in the hut, hardly big enough for a hen-roost—I and BILLY
on the ground—after a piece of a musty supper. Slept but little
in this lousy hut, which we left, as soon as we could well see our
path, in the morning, having paid him half a crown, which he
charged, and reached Dr. COLDEN's by noon. Got our dinner,
and set out to gather seeds, and did not get back till two hours
within night; then looked over some of the Doctor's daughter's
botanical, curious observations. Next morning, as soon as I could
see, we hunted plants till breakfast: then the Doctor's son went
with me to Doctor JONES's, where we observed the Pines, on a
high hill near the Doctor's. After dinner, we went to the river to
gather *Arbor Vitæ* seeds; then returned to Dr. COLDEN's by two
hours within night. In the morning, gathered seeds till breakfast. These two days I could have refreshed myself finely, if the
Doctor had been at home, or durst have eaten freely of what was
set before me; for they all were very kind.   *   *

July, 1754.
DEAR PETER :—
    *   * I have examined HILL, now, pretty well, and am very
well pleased that I have got him, although it be very far from
being exact, true, or fully intelligible: on the contrary, he hath

not gone half way through with it. There are many great omissions, and errors, I suppose for want of opportunity to examine the subjects himself; and doubtless there are also neglects, by being concerned in other business, which diverted him from taking so much notice of the minute particulars, as he might otherwise have done: yet, notwithstanding these deficiencies, there are many curious observations, and certain truths, contained in it.

I am much pleased with Dr. PARSONS' *Analogy.* I look upon it to be an introduction to a very extensive field of observations. I should be glad to correspond with him; and if he lives near thee, or comes to thy house, I wish thee would show him my description of our forest trees: but don't hinder thy own affairs about them.

I have just now received thy letter of May the 2d, 1754. I am glad of your remarks on my deficiencies, which I hope you will favourably excuse, and consider that my descriptions were done, and specimens placed, in the greatest hurry; most of them by candlelight, or First days, being hurried in travelling, and gathering, drying and sorting seeds, or labour about my farm.   *   *

                                        November 3, 1754.
DEAR PETER :—
    I received thy kind letter of July the 30th. Good grammar and good spelling, may please those that are more taken with a fine superficial flourish than real truth; but my chief aim was to inform my readers of the true, real, distinguishing characters of each genus, and where, and how, each species differed from one another, of the same genus: and if you find that my descriptions are not agreeable with the specimens, pray let me know where the disagreement is, and send my descriptions back again that I may correct them,—or if they prove deficient, that I may add farther observations; for I have no copy, and you have the original. So, by all means, send my descriptions back again by the first opportunity; for I have forgot what I wrote.

    The microscope I like very well: it is prettily adapted to the observation of plants.   *   *   *   *
*   *   *   The great Water Turtle of New England, I take to be our great Mud Turtle, which is much hunted for, to feast our gentry withal; and is reckoned to be as delicious a morsel as those brought from the Summer Islands.   *   *   *   They

are very large—of a dark muddy colour—large round tail, and
feet with claws,—the old ones mossy on the back, and often several horse leeches sucking the superfluous blood ; a large head,
sharp nose, and mouth wide enough to cram one's fist in,—very
sharp gums, or lips, which you will,—with which they will catch
hold of a stick, offered to them—or, if you had rather, your finger
—which they will hold so fast that you may lift the turtle by it as
high as your head, if you have strength or courage enough to lift
them up so high by it. But as for their barking, I believe thy
relator *barked*, instead of the turtle. They creep all over, in the
mud, where they lie *perdu;* and when a duck, or fish, swims near
them, they dart out their head as quick as light, and snap him up.
Their eggs are round as a bullet, and choice eating.

As for the Opossums, I can't endure to touch them,—or hardly
look at them, without sickness at stomach ; and I question whether
any beast of prey is so fond of them as to kill them for food : and
as they make but little resistance, but by their loathsome scent,
few creatures will kill them for sport, except dogs. But if Wolves
or Panthers should chase them, they can creep into less holes—in
a hollow tree, or between rocks, than their pursuers can : or if
suddenly surprised, there is a tree or bush mostly at hand, where
they can be secure ; for they can run to the extremity of a horizontal branch, and lap their tail-end round a slender twig, by which
they will hang, pendulous, out of the reach of larger animals.

*   *   *   *   *

December 16, 1754.

And now I have shipped on the Myrtilla, BUDDEN, * * and
for thyself, one box of plants in moss, and a box of a great variety
of seeds, and a quire of specimens of our Oaks, with their acorns
on in perfection, according to thy desire ; besides, my son WILLIAM
hath drawn most of our real species of Oaks, and all our real species of Birches, with an exact description of their particular characters, not according to grammar rules, or science, but nature.

*   *   *   *   *

March, 1755.

DEAR PETER :—
I have received thy kind letters of October the 8th and 24th,
1754 ; am well pleased with the description of the agreeable situa-

tion of thy country-seat; and more so, that thy heart flows with gratitude to our heavenly Father and great benefactor.

It gives me much satisfaction that BILLY'S drawing is so well received; and that thee hath so much regard for my son MOSES and his welfare.   *   *   *   *   *

I wholly purposed, last fall, to go to the Virginia and Carolina mountains; but now, being certainly informed of the great danger of travelling near those delightful situations, I must forbear, at present. But I am sadly afraid your ministry will be fooled by the French, who, no doubt, will pretend they will not act in a hostile manner, in order that you may forbid us to drive them back,— that they may, in the mean time, not only encroach upon us, but also fortify themselves strongly in their encroachments.   *   *

April 27th, 1755.

DEAR PETER :—

I have received thy kind letters of January the 5th, February the 1st, 12th, and 19th.   *   *   *   *

I design to set BILLY to draw all our turtles, with remarks, as he has time, which is only on Seventh days, in the afternoon, and First day mornings; for he is constantly kept to school, to learn Latin and French. We intend to take notice of the frogs and lizards, as they come in our way, or we know where to find them. I have often sent thee the seed of our great *Aster;* next expect a root.   *   *   *   *   *

I am well pleased that thee let PHILIP MILLER see my specimens of Oaks and Evergreens. It's pity but he had wrote to me many years ago. Time is now far spent with us both.

I hope Dr. FOTHERGILL won't condemn me without giving me liberty to plead my own cause. I have abundance of undigested thoughts to communicate, if I could explain my sentiments so as you could understand my meaning.

Dr. MITCHELL sent a letter to FRANKLIN, I believe by HARGRAVE, in which he desired me to send him several boxes of seeds. I wish he would write to me more particular, before it is too late.

Thee writes to me to draw fifty pounds; but if there should be a war with France, I had rather have it in thy hands,—if it could be secured to my children, if thee or I should die—as we are all mortal.

Our Philadelphia people seem at ease, and dissolved in luxury. I think two twenty-gun ships could take the town, in two hours' time.   *   *   *   *   *

Thee art very much mistaken in the striped Maple [*Acer Pennsylvanicum*, L.] being a seminal *variety*, or an accidental one either. It is a very particular, distinct species, both in its manner and place of growth. It hath the most constant appearance of any species I know; and place of growth being particular to the northern ridges of our Blue Mountains, from the North River to Susquehanna. I never observed one naturally to grow on the three southern ridges, or between them and the sea. KALM looked for them on the Katskill.

I hope to send seeds of the *Bartsia*, and Christophoriana with white seeds.   *   *   *   *   *

My son WILLIAM is just turned of sixteen. It is now time to propose some way for him to get his living by. I don't want him to be what is commonly called a gentleman. I want to put him to some business by which he may, with care and industry, get a temperate, reasonable living. I am afraid that botany and drawing will not afford him one, and hard labour don't agree with him. I have designed, several years, to put him to a doctor, to learn physic and surgery; but that will take him from his drawing, which he takes particular delight in. Pray, my dear PETER, let me have thy opinion about it.

I am glad my friend Dr. FOTHERGILL hath the perusal of my notion of the antediluvian impressions of marine shells, in our mountainous rocks, or any other of my rambling observations. I hope, if I can stand the test with his trial, I shall come out like gold well purified. I had rather undergo, now, a thorough purging —a long fusion, than to have any dross left behind.

Dear friend, if thee proposes to me any questions of philosophy, pray let me have as many as thee pleases, in the fall. It will be fine winter diversion. And questions in botany, in spring, that I may have the summer to make proper observations of vegetables in.

If there should be a war with France, how shall I send my descriptions of trees, or BILLY's drawings, without falling into ignorant people's hands, that will not take any notice of them—or may be, throw them away? Suppose I should direct them (under the cover) to Mr. DALIBARD, BUFFON, or JUSSIEU, or Dr. GRONOVIUS. If the French should take them, and see them directed to such noted men, they might take care to send them to them.

Last war, they took care to send my letters, and part of the curiosities, to GRONOVIUS, as directed; the rest, JUSSIEU kept himself. Pray direct me how to act for the best; for I suppose little can be sent in merchant ships, without a convoy, but what will fall into the enemy's hands; and I had rather that the descriptions and drawings should fall into learned, than ignorant hands. *   *

September the 28th, 1755.

DEAR PETER:—

I have received thy kind letters of March 25, April 23, June 17, and July 3d, sent in by Captain BUDDEN; also one by N. E., and one by New York.

I have been at Killingsworth, with our friend ELIOT, who is a good sort of a man, and endeavours for the general good of mankind. His time is fully employed in visiting the sick, looking after his farm, supplication and thanksgiving in his family, praying and preaching in the pulpit; and very agreeable in his conversation with his friends.

In my return home, I travelled more back in the country, and crossed the North River below the Highlands, and went with my BILLY to observe the falls of Second River, which are very remarkable for such a body of water to precipitate about sixty feet perpendicular into a narrow gulf, between two rocks about ten feet distance.   *   *   *   *   *

I am well pleased that BILLY gives you such satisfaction in his drawing. I wish he could get a handsome livelihood by it. Botany and drawing are his darling delight; am afraid he can't settle to any business else. Indeed, surveying may afford an opportunity to exercise his botany; but we have five times more surveyors already than can get half employ. If he could get a surveyor-general's office, for life, it might do.

The specimen of your Oak comes near our White Oak; yet differs pretty much in its acorn-cups: seems to be of the summer kind.   *   *   *   *

*   *   I doubt Dr. COLDEN can't find that stone, composed of sand and cockle-shells. I found it on the south side of the

drowned lands, near the mountain, on much higher ground than it is where the Doctor lives,—where most of the stones are composed of a coarse, sandy limestone, and scallop shells of a large size and particular form, peculiar to this vale. I find, in our present bays, or sea, the scallops lie much deeper than the cockle, which lie in the sandy shores. If I should travel to the Doctor's again, I design to search the south side, and try to find that stone: but there is now great alteration since I was there; and very like, the woods in which I found it may now be corn-fields, and it will be like searching a needle in a bundle of hay.

P. COLLINSON TO JOHN BARTRAM.

January 20, 1756.

I have the pleasure to tell my dear friend, that his boxes of plants came in fine order, by BUDDEN.   *   *

My son and I were both surprised at the sight of the great Mud Turtle. It is really a formidable animal. He bit very fierce at a stick. He had near bit my finger. Thy former description is very good, excepting his sharp hook at the point of its bill, and his shell being very jagged, or notched, near his tail. It made an uncouth noise, I can't say barking; but what a full-grown one might do, I can't say. It is really a curiosity, and we are obliged to thee for sending it; for we had no notion of such an animal, for writers, in general, content themselves by saying there's terrapins, or land and water turtles, &c.

I wish BILLY could get one of this size, and draw it, in its natural dress: but pray let the shell be well washed, that the sutures of the shell may be well expressed. What eye it has, we can't well say, for they seemed closed up, as if asleep.

All the species of turtles, drawn as they come in your way, with some account of them, would prove a new piece of natural history, well worth knowing.

The pretty Frog came safe and well, and very brisk: more of these innocent creatures would not be amiss. But pray send no more Mud Turtle. One is enough. The other Water Turtle is a pretty species; came very well.

      *   *   *   *

*   *   I am pleased to hear thy daughter is like to be disposed of to thy mind. Poor MOSES has been tumbling and tossing about the world. Inclosed is his letter from Gibraltar. Indeed, by what we can learn, the whole globe has been shaken terribly in some places, as I find it has reached your continent, also, which thou takes no notice of; so I presume could not be very remarkable. The terrible lot of Lisbon, being totally ruined, and other places, too long even to touch upon, thou'll see in the Magazines, or your public newspapers.   *   *   *   *

*   *   *   BILLY's drawing and painting of the Tupelo, is fine, and is deservedly admired by every one. There is a delightful natural freedom through the whole, and no minute particular omitted—the insects on the leaves, &c. It's a pity he had not kept it, to add the flowers; and to have dissected a flower—showing the style, and stamina, &c., each part distinct by itself, after LINNÆUS's method, which seems to be the prevailing taste.

Our friend COLDEN's daughter has, in a scientific manner, sent over several sheets of plants, very curiously anatomized after his method. I believe she is the first lady that has attempted anything of this nature. They are to be sent to Dr. GRONOVIUS; and he, poor man! I believe is in a bad state of health; for I cannot get a line from him (who used to be very punctual), if he has received BILLY's fine drawings of Oaks, and thy system. Though I have writ several letters, I shall this day send another.   *   *

*   *   I am really concerned there are no acorns. I am afraid we shall be outdone by that ALEXANDER. I must not print thy list, this year, for that reason.

By the common Laurel, does thou mean the small *Magnolia?* If thou does, thou should say so; for the name *Magnolia* will sell a box of seeds. If this is wanting, we shall be undone.

By all means make BILLY a printer. It is a pretty, ingenious employ. Never let him reproach thee, and say, " Father, if thou had put me to some business by which I might get my bread, I should have by my industry lived in life as well as other people." Let the fault be his, not thine, if he does not.

So for this time, dear JOHN, farewell.

P. COLLINSON.

London, February 10, 1756.

MY DEAR FRIEND JOHN'S

Next letter is May 17th, which I answered July 8th.　　*　　*

*　　　　*　　　　*　　　　*　　　　*

It is true; I have been in the hot bath; and just over the spring, it is really as hot as one well can bear it. But what is that to some hot springs, in other parts of the world, that the natives boil their eggs, and dress their victuals, with the hot water? It would be exceeding my time, and the extent of this paper, to retail the various opinions about this wonderful operation. So, my dear JOHN, content thyself. This is one of the many things that's concealed from us.

I before hinted my opinion with relation to BILLY. He is now come to years of understanding; and therefore it is time for him to consider how he must live in the world, and give up his darling amusements, in some degree, that he may attain a knowledge in some art, or business, by which he may, with care and industry, support himself in life: and as printing is an ingenious art, drawing and engraving may with advantage be applied to it. I would fain have thee embrace our kind friend B. FRANKLIN's obliging offer: but, unless BILLY will determine to settle close, and apply himself, it will never answer the good purpose intended.

In case of a war, I approve thy plan of directing all to Mr. BUFFON's, at the Royal Garden, Paris;—and then, underneath, direct for me. Then I should have it, one time or other. But our affairs are so surprisingly situated, that none knows, yet, whether it will be war or peace. We continue taking the French ships,— but they take none of ours. So reconcile this piece of French policy, if thou can, and foretell its consequences.　　*　　*

I thought thine and our friend CLAYTON's observations so material, on Dr. ALSTON's system, that I put them in the Gentleman's Magazine.　　　*　　　　*　　　　*　　　　*

My dear JOHN, what shall I say to the Great Vale, but admire thy account of it, and think how happy will those in future times be whose lot it is to cultivate so rich and fertile a tract?　　*　　*

Thy observation on the Birches, and other trees, is peculiarly thy own : pray how does it agree with the sentiments of our great botanist, PHIL. MILLER ?

*   *   *   *

No one doubts but that the marble of Tadmor was hewn out of the neighbouring mountains : but thy notion of its formation by a mixture of slime, or mud, with what thee calls nitrous or marine salts, enters not into my comprehension. So thou hath it all to thyself.

But I am thy friend,
P. COLLINSON.

February 18, 1756.

My first letter to my worthy friend, was of January 20th; which was a sort of general letter, writ in haste, to send by first opportunity.

Now I come to consider thine in course.

*   *   *   I commend putting off thy expedition to the western provinces.   *   *   *

*   *   We think our weather very inconstant; but yours is much more so.   *   *   *

Thy soliloquy is very pathetic. No part of God's works but raise rapturous ideas in a well-disposed mind. *   *

It is said—how true I don't know—that your vast flocks of pigeons, once a year, return from your inland parts, to regale themselves on the sea-shore. This I know, that our pigeons are great lovers of salts : for our columbarians make salt cakes, to engage them to stay at home.   *   *   *

*   *   My dear JOHN says truly, his hypothesis is composed of broken links, for I cannot unite them; but yet there are many ingenious conjectures. But suppositions are endless, and we are still in the dark, relating to the many wonderful phenomena in nature. The great Author of our being has set bounds to our reasoning faculty, that we may be sensible of our imperfections; yet has permitted us mental excursions,—and those the best connected—and to us most probable—may be nearest the mark.

*   *   *   *

I am greatly obliged for the last box of seeds thee sent,—in particular the *Galega*, which we never could raise, though we have had seed so often; so pray send two or three roots more, next year : but, my dear JOHN, how canst thou imagine I could remember a specimen, sent so many years agone ? But BILLY'S fine painting has given me a complete idea of its beauty ; and that fine Red Helleborine [*Calopogon*, R. Br. ?], which I have long wanted. The female *Cornus* is exquisitely done. It resembles ours ; and yet there is a difference.

I am very sensible of the great pains BILLY has taken, about the turtles. I can't reward him equal to his merit. I send him a small token, and some fine drawing-paper—all in the Library Company's box, to B. FRANKLIN, with sundry parcels for thee. The Marsh Hawk is admirable. I don't see that either EDWARDS, or EHRET, can much excel it : but I wish he would paint the Pond Turtle over again. It is the most indifferently performed ; the shell is made almost white,—whereas it is black. But then, again, I must do him justice. Nothing can be finer executed than the Horned Turtle. Such ingenuity brings truth to light. Time won't permit what I could say, on this strange creature. What can be the use of its horns ? To strike its prey ?—I have another request to BILLY : that is, to draw the wrong side of the Spotted Turtle, he has sent with fine Red Helleborine. So paint all the belly-side of all the turtles ; for there is always something remarkable there. *   *   But, as I hope BILLY will go into the printing business, I desire he will apply himself diligently, and not think on me, or his favourite amusement.

But yesterday, I had a letter from Dr. GRONOVIUS. He admires much the drawings of the Oaks ; but he can get nobody to engrave and print them : so will return them to me. Our friend EHRET will do them, he tells me ; but I can't say when. Those original drawings of plants were our ingenious friend CATESBY'S.

I am, my dear friend, thine in great sincerity,

P. COLLINSON.

JOHN BARTRAM TO P. COLLINSON.

February 21, 1756.

DEAR PETER : —

We are now in a grievous distressed condition: the barbarous, inhuman, ungrateful natives weekly murdering our back inhabitants ; and those few Indians that profess some friendship to us, are mostly watching for an opportunity to ruin us. And we that are near the city are under apprehensions, too, from the neutral French, which are sent amongst us full of resentment and revenge, although they yet appear tolerably civil, when we feed them with the best we can afford. They are very fond of their brethren— the Irish and Dutch Romans, which are very numerous amongst us; many of which openly declare their wishes, that the French and Indians would destroy us all, and others of them privately rejoice at our calamities. O deplorable condition! that we suspect our friend of treachery while he is willing to assist us,—and can't discover our enemy till it is too late!

By what we can understand, by the reports of our back inhabitants, most of the Indians which are so cruel, are such as were almost daily familiars at their houses, ate, drank, cursed and swore together—were even intimate playmates; and now, without any provocation, destroy all before them with fire, ball, and tomahawk. They commonly, now, shoot with rifles, with which they will, at a great distance, from behind a tree, fence, ditch, or rock, or under the covert of leaves, take such sure aim as seldom misseth their mark. If they attack a house that is pretty well manned, they creep behind some fence, or hedge, or tree, and shoot red-hot iron slugs, or punk, into the roof, and fire the house over their heads; and if they run out, they are sure to be shot at, and most or all of them killed. If they come to a house where the most of the family are women and children, they break into it, kill them all, plunder the house, and burn it with the dead in it; or if any escape out, they pursue and kill them. If the cattle are in the stable, they fire it, and burn the cattle: if they are out, they are shot, and the barn burnt.

If our captains pursue them, in the level woods, they skip from tree to tree like monkeys; if in the mountains, like wild goats, they leap from rock to rock, or hide themselves, and attack us in flank and rear, when, but the minute before, we pursued their track, and thought they were all before us. They are like the Angel of Death—give us the mortal stroke, when we think ourselves secure from danger.

O Pennsylvania! thou that was the most flourishing and peaceable province in North America, art now scourged by the most barbarous creatures in the universe. All ages, sexes, and stations, have no mercy extended to them.   *   *   *

*   *   *   We have had a fine moderate winter, hitherto. The 1st of February, my *Crocus* was out, and the Aconite the week before. The red-flowered, and silver-leaved Maples—the Hazel, Filbert and Alder—much about the same time. The double Snowdrop, *Claytonia* and *Paronychia*, have been out about two weeks. The seeds of Mustard, Orach and Lettuce are come up: but now, I suppose they will be nipped. Last night, a snow fell ten inches deep; and now the northwest wind blows very cold.   *   *

May the 30th, 1756.

DEAR PETER :—

I have received thy kind letters of January 20th, and February 28th, by MESNARD, and since, some seeds, and two books of Natural History; all which are very acceptable. I am well pleased with thy choice of the magazines. I expected greater matters of philosophy, and new discovery in Natural History, in MARTIN'S, than I found. BILLY is much obliged to thee for his drawing-paper. He has drawn many rare birds, in order to send to thee; and dried the birds to send to his friend EDWARDS, to whom he is much obliged for those two curious books. He spent his time, this spring, in shooting and drawing the rare birds of quick passage, which stayed with us but a few days, to rest, and fill their bellies, on their flight northward, where they breed; as he observed, by the hens having immature eggs in them, which their quick passage through our country before, rendered them unobserved. We propose to send them by Captain MESNARD, by whom we intend to write largely.

Last night, I was with our friend BENJAMIN [FRANKLIN], and desired his farther advice about BILLY; and reasoned with him about the difficulty of falling into good business; that, as he well knew, he was the only printer that did ever make a good livelihood by it, in this place, though many had set up, both before and since he did, and that was by his extraordinary and superior abilities, and close application; and merchandizing was very precarious; and extreme difficult to make remittances to Europe. He sate and paused awhile, then said that there was a profitable business which he thought was now upon the increase; that there was a very ingenious man in town, who had more business than he could well manage himself, and that was *engraving;* and which he thought would suit BILLY well.   *   *   *

We had a small shock of an earthquake. It awakened me; but many were not sensible of it.   *   *   *

By the common Laurel, I mean what you sometimes call Ivy [*Kalmia*].   *   *   *   *

PETER COLLINSON TO JOHN BARTRAM.

London, June 8, 1756.

I am obliged to my kind friend, for his letter of the 21st of February.

We here are greatly affected at the ravages and cruelties exercised by your ungrateful perfidious Indians. We hope proper measures will be taken to prevent their depredations for the future.

*   *   *   *   *

Why may not a murrain fall upon dogs, as well as amongst our bulls and cows? which has now been many years in several parts of this nation. At first, the distemper made great havoc; but it grows less and less, and we hope is now gone off.

Great and many are the calamities of war, and the expenses that attend it. It is new to you, the yoke sits very uneasy; but we have felt it in every sense. We all wish for peace. The ways of Providence are unsearchable; it may be nearer than we imagine.

I am concerned that I hear nothing from MOSES, since the letter from him, that I sent thee. How does my friend BILLY go on? I shall be glad to hear that he is with our friend FRANKLIN.

Our friend COLDEN has writ me how he was obliged to leave his habitation. I truly sympathize with him, under such severe calamities. Oh! the delights of peace, when every man can sit under his own vine and fig tree, and none make him afraid. He has sent me the curious stone, thou mentions, that is impressed with a species of bivalve shells that I don't remember to have seen.

About a week ago, I dined with your new governor [WILLIAM DENNY]. If I may judge by his countenance, he seems a mild, moderate man. He assured me he went over determined, if possible, to heal all differences. I heartily wish he may be so happy.

Our last winter was very mild. The Aconite was in flower about the middle of December. Many of your American deciduous trees, never lost their leaves.   *   *

* * I wish, if without much trouble, thou could procure for me half a dozen plants of the small *Magnolia*, or Sweet-flowering Bay, or Swamp Laurel. I wish they could be plants of about two feet high, with sods to them. I saw some most delightful fine young plants, of that size, sent by J. ALEXANDER. And if a young Papaw or two of that size, I should like it well, and a sod or two of thy Dittany, and Snakeroot. But, if these things must be sought for where skulking Indians molest, never think more on them.   *   *   *

I have many of thy letters lays behind, which I shall take notice of at my leisure. So for this time, my dear JOHN, farewell.

P. COLLINSON.

The Governor will want seeds, &c., to send home. I have recommended him to thee for them.

As thou art an admirer of Doctor HILL's performances, I persuade myself his History of Plants will not be unacceptable to thee; and, to do him justice, I think he has handled the subject skilfully, and treated our friend LINNÆUS decently, as ingenious men should always do one another, when they differ in judgment. There are only eighteen numbers yet published. These are sent with Dr. RUSSEL's History of Aleppo, for the Library Company.   *

JOHN BARTRAM TO P. COLLINSON.

June 12th, 1756.

DEAR PETER :—

I wrote lately, and answered thy letters and presents, and sent it by SAMUEL FOTHERGILL, by the way of Ireland; and now since, by REEVES, I have received thine of February 10th and April 3d. Thee mentions the Bath water being warm, and several springs, in other parts of the world, being exceeding hot, of which we have frequent accounts. But, to render the phenomenon more surprising, and the works of Eternal Wisdom more wonderful, there is, as I have read, a very cold spring within a few yards of the hot one. Nay, even in Iceland, near the base of Mount Hecla, there is a very hot spring and a cold one, near one another. What different sources these rise from, or what alteration they undergo, in their passage to the surface, God Almighty knows.

I can't imagine how, or after what manner, or with what, JAMES ALEXANDER fills so many boxes; but this I know, he frequents the market, and discourses with all the people he can get any intelligence of, where any trees grow that he wants, and offers them money for any quantity they can gather of the seeds, if they will bring them to town. So that, when I go to gather seeds, where I used to find them, the people near where they grow will not let me have them; but tell me they will gather them all to send to London. But where he gets so much Bog Moss to pack up his trees with, unless he fetcheth it from Jersey, I know not, nor what variety he puts in his boxes. We always speak friendly together, and visit one another; but do not communicate the affairs of our correspondents.

My dear worthy friend, thee can't bang me out of the notion that limestone and marble were originally mud, impregnated by a marine salt, which I take to be the original of all our terrestrial soils.

PETER COLLINSON TO JOHN BARTRAM.

London, July 20, 1756.

DEAR JOHN :—

I have been just perusing Dr. DOUGLASS's Summary. Pray tell me, what are those Pines he calls American Pitch Pine, with leaves about three inches long, with a prominent longitudinal rib instead of a sulcus?

In New England, there is another distinct Pitch Pine, called the Yellow Pine. If these are peculiar to this country, perhaps our friend ELIOT, or some of his friends, may inform us. He was mightily pleased with thy visit.

This day I received thy letter of May 30th. It gives me pleasure to hear my old friend is well. I hope he will not expose himself to Indian cruelties; and yet I want a dozen boxes of seeds.

I am glad the trifles came safe; and that BILLY has a business offers, that may suit his genius. By all means don't delay it; for I think engraving a curious art,—and if he succeeds in it, will not want encouragement. We want one very much here, skilful in engraving birds, plants, &c. EDWARDS has, in a manner, left off. We have engravers enough—I may call them scratchers; but a fine hand is much wanted. See ELLIS's book of Corallines, at the

Library Company. It was with great difficulty, and a long time, to do it as well as it is, which is reckoned well done, in comparison with others.

*   *   *   *

I have a great opinion of your new Governor.* He assured me, he went over with a heart full of good-will, and that he would spare no pains to reconcile all parties; and hoped our friends would decline a majority, *for the present*, in the next assembly, and choose moderate churchmen; and then he doubted not but to put the province in such a posture of defence, as to be able to repel your enemies; and JOHN HUNT and CHRISTOPHER WILSON, are sailed from Bristol, as deputies from the Society, who come over in a spirit of brotherly love, without fee or reward, to restore it amongst you. We rely on good Providence to operate with them, in the restoring love and unity.

I am thy sincere friend,
P. COLLINSON.

JOHN BARTRAM TO PETER COLLINSON.

January 22d, 1757.

DEAR PETER:—

I have shipped on the Carolina, Captain DUNCAN, and consigned to thee, twenty-six boxes; the first ten, marked on the sides, are for our Governor.   *   *

Many birds, in their migrations, are observed to go in flocks,—as the geese, brants, pigeons, and blackbirds; others flutter and hop about from tree to tree, or upon the ground, feeding backwards and forwards, interspersed so that their progressive movement is not commonly observed. Our blue, or rather ash-coloured, great herons, and the white ones, do not observe a direct progression, but follow the banks of rivers—sometimes flying from one side to the other, sometimes a little backwards, but generally northward, until all places be supplied sufficiently where there is conveniency of food; for when some arrive at a particular place, and find as many there before them as can readily find food, some of them

---

* P. COLLINSON was under the disagreeable necessity of changing this "opinion" at a subsequent period. See his letter, dated April 6, 1759.

move forward, and some stay behind.   For all these wild creatures, of one species, generally seem of one community; and rather than quarrel, will move still a farther distance, where there is more plenty of food—like ABRAHAM and LOT; but most of our domestic animals are more like their masters: every one contends for his own dunghill, and is for driving all off that come to encroach upon them.

It is very probable that many kinds of birds, in their migrations, fly out of our sight, so high as to be unobserved,—as for instance, our Hooping Cranes, in their passage from Florida to Hudson's Bay. They fly in flocks of about half a score, so exceeding high as scarcely to be observed, but by the particular noise of their loud hooping.   We then can but just see them, though so particularly directed where to look for them.   *   *   *

I want the rest of HILL's English Herbal, that I may have them bound up all together.   I have received twenty-one numbers.   It seems odd, that in his History of Plants he kept so close to LIN-NÆUS,—and now, in this, he pulls him all to pieces, and seemingly with good reason, too.   Poor LINNÆUS!   He is an industrious   *   *   * [*hiatus in MS.*]; but I always thought he crowded too many species into one genus.

PETER COLLINSON TO JOHN BARTRAM.

February, 1757.

I wish my good friend J. BARTRAM, would peruse a little tract, called *New England's Rarities*, by JOHN JOSSELYN, and see his account of the *White Mountain*, and *Sugar-loaf Mountain*, which is very extraordinary.   If it was peaceable times, who knows how thou might be tempted to make them a visit?

What was his bird, Pilhannaw? a monstrous great bird.

He must have a fine palate, and a good digestion, to say a turkey-buzzard was good meat.   The porcupine shooting his quills, is a vulgar error.

Pray see his account of the Moose Deer.   They were plenty in his time [1633—1674], in that remote part where his brother lived; unless he reckons the deer holding up his head with a full-grown pair of horns on, it could not be twelve feet high, by the method of measuring a horse.   The width of their horns, and their being palmated, agrees nearly with the Irish fossil-horns—perhaps the same animal.   *   *   *

I don't know how to distinguish between his Raccoon and his Jackal. Are they all one ? or is there with you, the two distinct animals, as in other countries of the world ?

I presume they must have mistook a panther for a lion, especially a she lion. But lions are never found in such cold climates.

*   *   *   *

The Tyrian Dye was collected from a vein found in a species of * * * ; and I know some other fish beside his scarlet muscle, that has the red vein, that will stain linen effectually; but being so long gathering a quantity to dye a cloak or mantle, made it of such value as only to array princes. But the discovery of cochineal reduced the price so, that every common person can wear scarlet.

Does he not exaggerate in his article of frogs a foot high ? His rattlesnake vapour shows him to be a vapourer.

*   *   *   *

He seems enamoured with the young Indian nymphs. What sayeth thee to these originals in their native dress ? Have they ever been able to charm an Englishman, as they do the French, who are not so delicate ?

As thou loves curiosities and novelties, I herewith send thee a book will let thee see the notions of a virtuoso, about one hundred years agone.

*   *   *   *

I was so extremely pleased with thy letter to Phil. Miller, that I had it copied. My observations on it are lost.

I have lately had a letter from Doctor Linnæus ; and he gives his service, and desired me not to forget to tell thee with what respect Dr. P. Kalm mentions thee in his books of travels in your country and Canada. There are only two books published.

*   *   *   *

Our friend Neve carefully delivered Billy's drawings, which are very elegant, and much admired. I am glad he has found out that he may be in a way to rise in the world. Probably there may be, at times, some leisure hours in which he may divert himself in his favourite amusement; so have sent him the best books we have extant, by which he may improve himself.   *   *

It is now the 10th of February, and no seeds are yet arrived.

* * * *

If you knew our distress for wheat, we should have your merchants run all risks, the profit is so great, and insurance, with you, on the prime cost, would be inconsiderable. Wheat is now, and has been for some time, from eight shillings to 8*s.* 6*d.* a bushel, sterling. This makes it very hard for the poor; and if it should please God that the present crop on the ground should by accidents prove bad, a famine must ensue, unless relieved by you. * * * Thou seest we are not without our calamities, no more than you. So, dear JOHN, let's be resigned. Trust in Providence; and hope and do all we can for the best.

I am thy real friend,
P. COLLINSON.

London, March 18, 1757.

DEAR JOHN :—

I was glad at my heart that the ship is come, that brings the seeds. Where she delivered her letters, I cannot say; but hope she will come safe into our river. There is a fine cargo of seeds, &c., indeed. * * *

I am extremely pleased with thy account of the migration of birds. I shall add each to its bird, in CATESBY's History; which will help much to their natural history. By friend CARMALT comes, with other parcels, a large brown paper bundle from P. MILLER. I presume that may prove the books thou wants; and there is more of HILL's Herbal. I know some were taken, on the Lydia.

Such accidents will happen, these perilous times. I think there are three New York ships taken.

* * * *

My friend EDWARDS has a fifth book published. When complete and delivered, I think he intends to send it to BILLY. I have sent him a fine drawing-book, which I hope will come safe,—for I know it will please him.

I have just scrawled this, as it will be long before any other goes.

So, dear JOHN, farewell.
P. COLLINSON.

The Skunk-weed (*Arum Betæ folio*) began to show its flowers, 7th of February, though we have had a very severe winter.

*　　　　*　　　　*　　　　*

I shall be heartily glad your treaty with the Indians may produce a settled peace, that bloodshed may cease. 　　*　　　*

JOHN BARTRAM TO P. COLLINSON.

September the 25th, 1757.

DEAR PETER :—

I have received thy kind letter of June the 16th, 1757. I am glad that my cargo came safe to your hands, and was in some degree acceptable; yet must reckon myself in several cases unfortunate,—and in particular in this, that when I have endeavoured to give the greatest satisfaction, my labours have been the least valued. Last year, thee wrote to me to send thee a variety of seeds of forest trees, shrubs, and plants, to give to thy friends, for that they expected thee was able to supply them with a variety; and, according to thy earnest request, I did what I could to oblige both thee and thy friends, and freely sent a variety, which came safe to thy hand. But when I read these lines in thy letter, " *What didst mean, to send me so large a box of seeds ?　It made much trouble, and time, to part it,*" this answer quite astonished me ;—to think it a trouble to part a few seeds, sent ready to hand to one's intimate friends.

I reflected upon myself what pains I had taken to collect those seeds, in several hundred miles' travel, drying, packing, boxing and shipping, and all to put my friend to trouble !

Indeed, my good friend, if thee was not a widower, I should be inclined to tell thee that old age advanced as fast upon thee as upon myself! And perhaps these lines may give offence ; for, as times go now, we must not complain of either private or public disappointment, no, not to one's particular friends. 　　*　　　*

*　　*　　* My family is generally pretty well, at present; but it is, I believe, the most grievous time for general sickness, in the provinces, that has ever been since their settlement. 　*　　*

My BILLY comes on finely with Captain CHILD, who is very kind to him, and keeps him very close to his business. He hath sent thee a letter, and acknowledged thy kind present of the draw-ing-book.

We want to know how poor MOSES fares, and where he is. We were glad to see his letter to thee, and that he showed so much respect to his worthy friend.

PETER COLLINSON TO JOHN BARTRAM.

[February, 1759.]

I now come to thank my good friend JOHN BARTRAM for his cargo of plants, and congratulate him on the success that has attended all his cargoes of seeds, during this war. All the plants seemed in good order; but why was I tantalized about the dwarf Oaks? My son examined everything with great attention, but could find nothing we ´could liken to them, except two or three sticks with knobs at their end; but neither the least root, nor fibre, we could discern. We therefore conclude they were by accident left behind; for we are persuaded our ingenious, knowing friend, knew better than to send such rootless sticks to produce growing plants.

We have great hopes, as Fort Duquesne is in our hands, and if Crown Point is as happily surrendered, all the nations of Indians will see it their interest to join us, and establish peace in all our borders.

Then thou will be able to sally forth again on new discoveries; and I think with safety thou may venture to Fort Duquesne,—as there will be continual traffic thither, both from your country and from Virginia.

As there is a fine straight road now made, it will be very easy of access. Inquire in time what parties of trading people, or troops, are going thither, and then join thyself with them. From the fort, little excursions may be made every day, and come and lie there at night.

That fine country has been unsearched. So rich a soil will be productive of new and rare vegetables, that we are strangers to: but as thou art a better judge how safe and practicable such an expedition may be, I submit to thee. But, for certain, it must be a pleasant one; and what may be discovered would recompense the length of such a journey.

We have had, hitherto, one of the mildest winters that can possibly happen in this country—all January, south winds, warm and
mild—only two frosty days: and now, this 25th February, the
Itea, Sweet Bay, Dogwood, &c., have as green leaves on them, as
in summer.   *   *   *   *

We were sadly disappointed,—being in hopes of seeing some
grafts of the true Newtown Pippin; but there was none. Pray
remember, another year; for what comes from you are delicious
fruit—if our sun will ripen them to such perfection. Our friend
BENJAMIN had a fine parcel of the apples came over, this year,—
in which I shared.

I received BILLY's letter. I am pleased to see him improved in
his writing. I wish I could say as much in his spelling,—which
will be easily attained with application. I send him a book to
assist him.

I wish it could be any way contrived for him to give us a draught
of your great Mud Turtle. Our friend EDWARDS wants to see it.
I thought I had lost that thou sent me; but last year, I saw it
several times on the water, but there is no catching it: and then I
would wish to have a larger painted.

                *   *   *   *
We are of various opinions about Swallows. Some assert that
they take their winter abode under water; others say they resort
in great numbers into caves or caverns, and sleep all winter. But
the prevailing opinion is, that when food grows scarce, they retire
to other countries, to the southward, and return in our spring.
Many want to know if your Swallows are the same as ours. We
agree on the number of the four species. So, if it can be conveniently done, send a cock and hen of those that can be caught. I
have writ in my former letters, but by thy answers I know some
have miscarried these precarious times.

I have lately been reading HENNEPIN's *Travels*—who first discovered the great River Mississippi. He often mentions they
were sustained by killing *goats*. Now, I don't remember ever
reading of any in the country about the lakes, nor with you. They
must be aborigines, because met with in countries very remote, and
where no Europeans had been before.

The present situation of our public affairs makes it very difficult
how to advise laying out money. Our stocks fall every day. I

have some thousands lying by me—and have done for some time; and I don't know how to lay it out.   *   *

I am thy old friend,

P. COLLINSON.

London, April 6th, 1759.

DEAR JOHN:—

I have writ largely by Captain HAMMET, in the Dragon, and another ship, in answer to all thine.   *   *   *

In the Library Company's trunk, by this ship, is the Magazine for last year, and another parcel with books, and some prints for thy study.

I am in haste, thy old friend,

P. COLLINSON.

*   *   Pray send a sod or two more of thy pretty *Pyrola* with variegated leaves [*P. maculata*, L.]. It flowered finely last year; but I see no young shoots, which makes me think it will go off after flowering.   *   *   *

BILLY sent me a delightful drawing of what is called, with you, the Yellow Root. Pray look out and send me a plant or two; for it seems a new genus [*Hydrastis Canadensis*, L.].   *   *

We are all much entertained with thy draught of thy house and garden. The situation is delightful; and that for our plants, is well chosen. I shall endeavour to furnish it.   *   *

Pray give my kind love to my worthy old friend, Doctor WITT. I am concerned for the loss of his outward sight. May his inward receive a flow of Divine illumination.   *   *   *

*   *   I am glad thou hast got the money of the Governor. He is an unworthy man, to oblige me to dun him in his government.*

London, May 29th, 1759.

I have now only leisure to thank my good friend JOHN, for his entertaining letter of January 28th, of two sheets of paper, which

---

* I am afraid this was the *same Governor*, of whom Friend PETER formed so favourable an opinion at the dinner table, while he was "new." *See his letter of June* 8, 1756. In a subsequent letter, (dated July 20, 1759,) I find an account, in which JOHN BARTRAM is charged with the "*Bill on Gov. Denny, £6. 2s. 6d.*"

I shall take more notice of in process of time : and I have since received thine of February 28th, March 15th, and April 6th.

* * The grafts were such poor slender weak things, I am afraid they will come to nothing ; besides, there were so few of them, our chance was the less.

I am glad your Governor has paid his bill. I desire to have no more to do with so unworthy a person.

What I have writ before, I will repeat again. If thou will im-power by a proper writing, signed, and attested under your city seal, in which I may be indemnified if any loss should happen on thy money laid out in bank stock, or annuities, I will readily do it. I have not the least suspicion of thee, my dear friend, but I don't think it reasonable to be called to account by thy executors for what I did as an act of kindness, having only my labour for my pains.   *   *   *

If any Land or Water Terrapins happen in thy way, save them and send them ; but not the great Mud Turtle. I only want his shell ; and if BILLY would paint his curious figure, it would be better. If any *Orchis, Calceolus Maria,* Martagons, Lilies, or any other curious plant—think on thy old friend,

P. COLLINSON.

In JARED ELIOT'S letter, I perceive thou has a method of splitting rocks with water. Pray tell me how that is performed ; and give me thy answer to his five queries about that operation.
        *   *   *   *

London, July 20th, 1759.

I answered my dear JOHN'S letter of the 28th January, and February 8th, per Captain SIMPSON, April 9th.
        *   *   *   *

I am greatly pleased with thy account of our English wild plants. So early as JOSSELYN, he makes an article, or list, of our plants growing in New England, in his time, which came in grass seeds, or by strange accidents : as the willow and the Scotch Thistle, which I think a fine plant. I had it once in my garden.

See what climate and soil do. The Yellow *Linaria* is no pest with us. I keep it in my garden; and it is very orderly, for the sake of its fine spike of orange and yellow flowers.

The *Hypericum* keeps always on the borders of our fields ; but the *Leucanthemum*, or Ox-eye Daisy, overruns some fields. But then it makes a fine show.* For that reason I give it a proper place in my garden,—as I love all flowers.

*   *   *   *

I am concerned to hear poor Dr. WITT, my old friend, is blind. A well-spent life, I doubt not, will give him consolation, and illuminate his darkness. I must conclude, my dear JOHN, against my inclination.

Thy sincere friend,
P. COLLINSON.

London, October 10, 1759.

I received my dear JOHN's letter of the 16th June. His hodge-podge digests very well with me. I may give him as good as he sends.   *   *   *

I shall be pleased if the White *Campanella* is come up. It is a stately, fine plant; but I have lost it, by some accident, though it is perennial : so send me seed again.

Ah! JOHN, I thought thou had been too cunning to be deceived by a DEBORAH.

*   *   *   *

I am much obliged to thee for grafting the Newtown Pippins. What fruit comes from you is excellent. I wish our sun may bring it to the like perfection. We will give them a fair trial in different situations.

I think thy query needless (if the punch-bowl in the blue rock, was that filled by Governor KEITH). Doth not thy own memory confirm it ? It is really a very remarkable instance of the growth of stone, in thy own memory of fifteen years, to be grown up within three inches of its surface.

It was very curious to observe those stone basins, and the method of their formation.

At my leisure I may consider more particularly. All thy remarks deserve my attention : for these wonders in nature would be lost, if it was not for thy happy genius and turn of mind for these discoveries.

---

* This Ox-eye Daisy makes rather more of " a fine show" in Eastern Pennsylvania than is agreeable to the farmers of the present day (1848). It is one of the most troublesome intruders in our upland meadows and pastures.

I hope the boxes of seeds will come in time. If this is not too late, I can dispose of two or three more. People come at all seasons—" Pray, sir, let me have a box or two of seeds;" just as if I could write into the country for them ; never thinking, they must come near four thousand miles. So very thoughtless are the generality of mankind. * * * Now, my dear JOHN, farewell.

In haste,

P. COLLINSON.

London, November 3, 1759.

* * * I am pleased to find thee in such high spirits. Now I am convinced more than ever that thou art a deep-rooted botanist ; for a little enthusiastic turn, probably the effect of your hot weather, has set thy ideas a rambling in the wide fields of nature. She is not so docile as thou imagines, and will be put very little out of her course by all thy inventions. However, by the trials thou proposes to make, thou will be convinced of the weakness of thy efforts, to produce any settled or remarkable change in her laws. Pray, let me know the success of thy experiments.

It is frequent with us, after long summer droughts, rains the beginning of August, and warm, dry weather ensuing, many trees will blossom, too many to enumerate. But then, this is the effect of a particular season, and does not happen every year. This year, I saw a cherry tree in blossom in August ; but that tree may never do so again. It is accidental, and not to be brought into practice by art, in the common course of nature.

It is frequent in curious gardens, whose owners are men of fortune, to plant fruit trees and vines in warm stoves, to bring them very early into blossom, to have early fruit. But this so exhausts the trees, that new trees must be planted every year.   *
* * Thou frequently talks of having sent specimens to me and Lord PETRE, of this, that, and the other species, as if it was but a year or two agone; when, alas! he has been dead fourteen or fifteen years. All such items are but wasting paper and ink.

*   *   *   *

It must be a surprising fine sight to see the White Calceolus [*Cypripedium spectabile*, Sw. ?] near three feet high ; but your warmth and soil greatly promote vegetation. My plant flattered

me with two strong stems, but no flower.   Perhaps next year may
bring it.   *   *   *

I am, my dear JOHN,

Thy sincere friend,

P. COLLINSON.

* * * Prithee, friend JOHN, when thou goes to the Library,
ask for JOSSELYN'S Two Voyages, a little book of the size of his
New England Rarities, and a book well worth thy perusal.   In
page 61, he mentions an admirable creature that the Indians call
a Tree Buck.   Pray tell me what thou canst make of it, which he
says he often found.

*   *   *   *

I am concerned for poor MOSES.   Now he has eat his brown
bread, his white will come next.   I wish he would write a little
Journal in his own way and style, from his first going to sea to
this present time.   *Short hints will do.*   I question if it is to be
paralleled.   We don't know what human nature will bear until it
is tried.   *   *   *

London, February 2d, 1760.

By Captain HAMMET, I wrote my dear JOHN, of his good success; for both cargoes of seeds arrived safe, in proper time and
without damage.   * * *   I apprehend my letter miscarried,
that I wrote on receiving the two large tortoise-shells.   Thine
and BILLY'S account of the Snapping Turtle, with his fine drawing, would make a curious piece of Natural History; but our
authors of the Magazine are so careless on these affairs, that I
don't know how to trust them, and yet it is with regret I cannot
find a better way to communicate them to the public.

*   *   *   *

This reminds me of the elegant species of the Water Lily [*Nelumbium luteum*, Willd.], that is in the Jerseys.   Does it occupy
such a depth of water that the roots can't be come at?   Thou art
ambitious of plants from us: but here is the most charming plant
of Asia including China, and Egypt, in thy neighbourhood; and
yet so little is thy curiosity, or industry, that thou canst not avail
thyself of so great a curiosity.   Thou that hast springs in thy

garden to make a pond for its reception; or a river so close by, if more proper for its culture. Prithee, JOHN, never more let me reproach thy want of taste and curiosity in this article. I wish thou could employ some person to gather the seeds when ripe, and put in a bottle of water, with a little sand or earth in its bottom. I conceive, thus preserved, they would come in a growing state to us. This I have mentioned often before; but *roots* well packed in a great deal of wet moss, in a box, would do better.

If I was in thy place, I should spare no pains or expense to be possessed of a curiosity, that none in the province could boast of beside thyself; which thou art ambitious of in other plants in no comparison so charming when in flower.   *   *

Dear JOHN, farewell.

P. COLLINSON.

London, June 6, 1760.

I hope this will find my good friend arrived safe at his own dwelling, from his Carolina expedition. Thine from thence came safe to my hands; and I thank thy good wife for hers. I have writ largely by BUDDEN; but, for fear of miscarriage, I write this by way of New York, to inform thee what seeds will be wanting next fall.

And am thy old friend,

P. COLLINSON.

I am charmed, nay, in ecstasy, to see the White *Calceolus* thee sent me in flower; — with Mountain Laurel, Red Acacia, and Fringetree, and Allspice of Carolina, all in flower together. Remember me to BILLY, MOSES, and JOHNNY.

JOHN BARTRAM TO PETER COLLINSON.

June 24th, 1760.

DEAR PETER : —

I have now my dear worthy PETER'S letter before me, of February 10th. I am very sorry that the seeds were damaged by the rotten squash. It seemed, when I put it in the box, to be ripe enough, and I thought to oblige my dear friend with the best sort

I ever ate ; but, I believe misfortune will pursue me to the grave,
let my intention and care be ever so good.

The seeds that I collected on the South Mountains, on the
branches of James River, were excellent good. Those that I
sowed, are come up as close as they can grow, except the Mountain *Angelica ;* which CLAYTON tells me will never come up : but
I hope yet to find him mistaken, though he is a worthy, ingenious
man. I took such care to gather the seed in several degrees of
ripeness.

* * * * *

Dear friend, I am going to build a green-house. Stone is got;
and hope as soon as harvest is over to begin to build it,—to put
some pretty flowering winter shrubs, and plants for winter's diversion ;—not to be crowded with orange trees, or those natural to
the Torrid Zone, but such as will do, being protected from frost.

PETER COLLINSON TO JOHN BARTRAM.

London, September 15, 1760.

I am highly pleased with my friend JOHN'S expedition to Carolina ; because I know how he would be delighted with the striking
beauties of that fine climate. One of the principal, the great
Laurel-leaved *Magnolia,* complimented me this morning with a
glorious large white flower ; which I raised from seed about twenty
years agone. It is now about sixteen feet high. This fine tree is
grown pretty common, and flowers in several places ; but will
never arrive to the height they do in their native country ; for
they go much into flowering, and that checks the growth.

The Atamasco Lily has flowered often with me ; but thou sees
how plants that are most common, are neglected by those that see
them every day. They are like our wild Daffodils in our fields—no
one regards them; but a person of thy curiosity, who never saw them
before, would admire them. But thou must not accuse CATESBY,
for he has figured the Atamasco Lily.   *   *

By the success thou hast had with the seeds from the South
Mountains, thou sees plainly how they are impaired by transportation ; for very few come up with us.   *   *

I am pleased thou will build a green-house. I will send thee
seeds of Geraniums to furnish it. They have a charming variety,

and make a pretty show in a green-house ; but contrive and make
a stove in it, to give heat in severe weather.

No marvel that the Scotch have sent thee some heath, as it
grows at their doors; but we must send many miles for it.

I am, my dear JOHN, thy sincere friend,

P. COLLINSON.

London, October 2d, 1760.

By Captain BOLETHO, I answered my dear JOHN's letter of
June 16. Before that, I wrote two letters, and for fear of miscarriage, inclosed it to my friend COLDEN, Postmaster of New York,
in his packet to forward to thee. And yet thou art always complaining for want of letters, making no allowance for miscarriages.
Thine of March 21, I answered September 15th, and yet the good
man is never easy. If all my correspondents were of thy restless
turn of mind, I would never set pen to paper.   *   *

Now I come to thank my kind friend for his letter of the 28th
July. I am delighted with his operations on the Larkspur. The
product is wonderful. If these charming flowers can be continued
by seed, they will be the greatest ornament to the garden in their
season of blowing.

This purple-stalked Martagon is the glory of that tribe. In my
soil and climate, I had it grow above eight and a half feet high,
and had twenty-eight flowers on the spike. By all means sow the
seed directly, for it deserves all our care; but it never produces
seed in our climate. * * The yellow-spotted Martagon, thou
formerly sent me. CATESBY figured his from my plant. After
some years it went off.   *   *

It has been long my sentiments, that plants and animals as they
advance northward, decline in their size. For instance, the croco-
diles of Carolina, which is the highest latitude they are found in,
are diminutives to those found in countries between the Tropics.
So this *Pancratium*, which I have had from my friend LAMBOLL,
as it comes farther north may grow less. Yet it is a very different
species from that which grows in the Bahama Islands, which I
have seen flower often.

*   *   *   *

The specimens for MILLER, I received safe, and thy letter by
thy kind neighbour the Swede; but I happened to be out of town

every time he called ; so did not see him, or else I should have
paid him due respect. He is gone to Sweden. Pray, when may
I hope to see thy Journal to Carolina ?

The British Chronicle is inclosed, for the sake of WILLIAM
PENN's Letter. How customs and manners in the Indians are
altered since that time, thou canst best tell or be informed. So,
at thy leisure, thy remarks will be acceptable to thy friend,

P. COLLINSON.

B. FRANKLIN and son are well ; are gone a tour into Wales ;
may expect them in the spring ships.

London, May 7th, 1761.

It is a long while since I heard from my good friend JOHN
BARTRAM. I hope no illness has prevented him giving me that
pleasure. Not for want of materials, for those are always ready
to a speculative genius like his. For my part, I have been so
engaged, I had little room for speculations.

As I have left off transacting the Library Company's business,
I miss the opportunity of sending thy last year's Magazine ; however, I hope to do it by our friend FRANKLIN, who is very well
and his son. I have the pleasure to see them often.

The seeds came admirably well, and gave satisfaction. I heard
quite otherwise of ALEXANDER's.

My son says, "Father, what is the matter ? friend JOHN has
quite forgot you, who take so much pains to dispose of his seeds,
&c. What ! no plants this year ? Sure, he might have sent them,
having two opportunities, by the two ships in which he sent the
seeds." Indeed, friend JOHN, I leave thee to settle this account
with my son, who is an enthusiast after *Orchis*, Lady's Slippers,
Hellebores, Lilies, and all new things.

The Yellow Slipper is now in glorious flower ; five shoots from
a root, and two flowers on a stalk ; and the white one just now
peeping out of ground, not half an inch high. What singular difference in plants of the same tribe.   *   *

Thy old friend,

P. COLLINSON.

Remember me to BILLY and MOSES and JOHNNY.

JOHN BARTRAM TO P. COLLINSON.

May the 22d, 1761.

* * * Thee very unjustly reproacheth me for want of curiosity in the article of the Colocasia [*Nelumbium luteum*, Willd.]. I have made three trials of it at different times. Twice it miscarried ; and the last it grows so slow as scarcely to be seen. It will be very difficult to send the roots ; they are almost as brittle as glass, and run two or three feet deep in the mud. I hope to send the seed next fall, and perhaps a root. Doctor WITT and ALEXANDER went on purpose and fetched seeds and roots ; but both miscarried. Spring-water kills them, and the marsh weeds choke them.* BILLY received the fine present of EDWARDS, and promised me to send a letter of thanks, or else I should have done it. * * I sent GORDON a fine parcel of Holly berries, the getting of which had like to broke my bones. I was on the top of the tree, when the top that I had hold of and the branch I stood on, broke—and I fell to the ground. My little son, BENJAMIN, was not able to help me up ; my pain was grievous ; afterwards very sick ; then in a wet sweat, in a dark thicket, no house near, and a very cold, sharp wind, and above twenty miles to ride home. Thee may judge what a poor circumstance I was in ; and my arm is yet so weak that sometimes I can hardly pull off my clothes : Yet I have a great mind to go next fall to Pittsburg, in hopes to find some curious plants there.

P. COLLINSON TO JOHN BARTRAM.

London, June 12, 1761.

I have no letters from my dear friend JOHN since December 6, and November 8th, that came with the seeds. I don't think I am forgotten, as my friend JOHN is often apt to imagine. If no letter comes, I always make allowance for accidents ; of ships being taken or cast away, as I am persuaded is now the case. As the

---

* The culture of this plant was better understood afterwards, for I have seen it flourishing finely in several Botanic Gardens, and, among others, in a pond in the old BARTRAM Garden itself.

New York packet is more safe and convenient, I write by that, as
ALEXANDER COLDEN, the postmaster, is my particular friend.

Pray, what is the Double Wild *Crocus?* I thought you had
none of this species in your country. If thou .canst not send a
root send a specimen of it, that I may see this marvellous fine
thing.   *   *   *

The Ivy, Laurel, or Broad-leaved *Kalmia,* is now in flower. Certainly it is one of the finest evergreen shrubs that is in the world.
The *stamina* are elegantly disposed in the angles of the flowers;
and what a pretty blush, its bullated flower-buds! But, in a few
days will the glorious Mountain Laurel, or great Chamærhododendron, appear with its charming clusters of flowers. Prithee,
friend JOHN, look out sharp for some more of these two fine plants;
for one can never have too many.

          *   *   *   *

I have a sprig (in flower) of the *Kalmia* in water, and it stares
me in the face all the while I am writing; saying, or seeming to
say, "As you are so fond of me, tell my friend, JOHN BARTRAM,
who sent me, to send more to keep me company; for they will
be sure to be well nursed and well treated."

          *   *   *   *

There has been much talk of a peace; and we have a Frenchman here, that is said to come about it, and yet it seems a great
way off. What millions of men are slaughtered to gratify the
wicked, cruel ambition of princes! O, dear JOHN, I am much
affected to see and hear the annual sacrifice of our brave countrymen. But the necessity of our affairs was such, from French per-
fidy and treachery, that it was not to be avoided. May the God
of peace send peace again on the earth, is the earnest prayer of
thy friend,

                                        P. COLLINSON.

JOHN BARTRAM TO P. COLLINSON.

                                        July the 19th, 1761.
DEAR PETER:—

     *   *   *   I now send my Journal to Carolina, and some speci-
mens which my friend Dr. CHANCELLOR hath promised to deliver
safe to thy hands. The specimens are, most of them, from the

seed I gathered from the South Mountains of Virginia, most of which came up last year, the rest this spring. They grow prodigiously. So do my North and South Carolina plants.　*　* This extraordinary success with our American plants, hath set me all in a flame to go to Pittsburg, and down the Ohio, as far as I can get a safe escort. I design to set out the beginning of September.

I have now a glorious appearance of Carnations from thy seed— the brightest colours that ever eyes beheld. Now, what with thine, Dr. WITT's and others, I can challenge any garden in America for variety. Poor old man! he was lately in my garden, but could not distinguish a leaf from a flower.

* * * My son WILLIAM is safely arrived at Cape Fear, and met with a kind reception from Governor DOBBS, and his uncle.

PETER COLLINSON TO JOHN BARTRAM.

London, August 1, 1761.

MY DEAR JOHN

Is always in the same strain,—grumbling and complaining— makes no allowance for accidents, although I have often admonished so to do. I writ him a long letter soon after I received the Tortoise Shells, with my observations on them. But right or wrong, he upbraids me with not doing it in two years. This frequent censorious temper is not becoming our friendship. The very same positive assertion goes on (" No list or letter with the plants from GORDON"); whereas, I inclosed GORDON's list, and advice of the plants.

But if letters miscarry, as both these certainly did, is it friendly to censure us so severely with neglect? Pray, let me never more find occasion to remonstrate on this head, for it is disagreeable to me,—and much more to read what thou writes, after GORDON had taken so much pains, and sent two such valuable cargoes, to find no thankfulness, no acknowledgments: for who can help long passages and accidents at sea? I saw the plants growing in the box and basket, in the finest order imaginable. Well, GORDON is so good-natured, he forgives all thy complaints, and will try another cargo this fall.

As times are so perilous, pray don't send thy Journal until a peace, which we are in hopes of; for though I long to see it, it would grieve me to the heart to hear of its being taken, as I do for the cargo of plants. And then, again, I consolate myself to think how many have escaped this war. Indeed, my good friend, thou hast much reason to be thankful, since all thy cargoes of seeds have come safe. The loss of thy box of plants for my near neighbour, PONTHIEU, was the more bearable, as they had so fine a cargo of ALEXANDER. The great Chamærhododendron and *Kalmia* Laurel were the largest and finest I ever saw, and so fresh, I can't imagine where he gets them.   *   *   But there are great complaints of ALEXANDER'S seeds. Thine bear the bell: but his do well enough for the Scots.

Thou sees, my dear JOHN, how necessary it is to persevere, and mind no complaints; for if I had, thou hadst never had the Meadow Sweet, and *Polyanthos*, which I have been sending at times off and on for thirty years past. How often has Doctor WITT upbraided me (for he was an everlasting grumbler), that the seeds were musty and bad; sometimes came too soon, then too late, so that I believe little or none was raised; and yet thou finds I hit the lucky time at last. Make much of it, for I dare say none in your province can show the like.   *   *   Really, friend JOHN, complain on. I am now so used to that, I shall not mind it for the future.   *   *   But, as thou canst write diverting and curious observations, in this manner I expect to be entertained for the future; which will always give pleasure to thy old friend,

P. COLLINSON.

I am greatly concerned to hear of thy dangerous fall. Reflect on thy many narrow escapes, and be thankful it was no worse. But let me advise thee to be very careful for the future.

I plainly see thou knowest how to fascinate the longing widow, by so close a correspondence.* When the women enter into these

---

* This refers to a passage in JOHN BARTRAM's letter of May 22, 1761, where he is speaking of some fine species of Carolina Holly; "which," says he, "I hope to have by the favour of an elderly widow lady [Mrs. MARTHA LOGAN, of Charleston], who spares no pains nor cost to oblige me. Her garden is her delight. I was with her about five minutes, in much company, yet we contracted such a mutual correspondence, that one silk bag hath passed and repassed full of seeds three times since last fall. I desired her last March to send me some seeds of the Horse Sugar or Yellow Leaf. She directly sent me a box with three fine growing plants, mixed with several other sorts that she thought would

amusements, I ever found them the best assistants. Now, I shall not wonder if thy garden abounds with all the rarities of Carolina.

Governor DOBBS and his Secretary sent me a box with Swamp Pines, and two or three of the great *Sarracenia*, which grows admirably, and has shot leaves of a surprising length. I planted your sort in the same bog, that the difference in the species may be an agreeable sight.   *   *

I have often taken notice to thee, how very few of the bulbous tribe are found through all the colony countries. But who knows what stores of wonderful productions may be discovered about the lakes ? If thou art able to make an expedition to Pittsburg, thy penetrating eye will bring hidden things to light, and come home fraught with vegetable treasures.   *   *

*   *   A day or two agone I was fishing in one of my ponds. I caught a perch ; the hook was swallowed so deep, I cut the perch in halves to get it out ; but instead of doing it, I threw in my line with the half perch on the hook to try what would take it, and let it lay in all night. So when I came to pull it out, up comes the great Mud Turtle, that I had not seen for a year and a half, much grown. By this experiment, I know how to catch the devourer. My fish have much decreased ; and now I know the poacher. I believe I must transport him.   *   *   My son-in-law has built him a large fine house, and has everything to plant. Prithee, send a box of your more rare trees ; for I have none to spare, of Rhododendrons, Kalmias, Azaleas, Small Magnolia, and Sassafras. I can help him with all others. Of the Mountain Magnolia, I have fine plants from layers.

I presume BILLY will return laden with curiosities.

JOHN BARTRAM TO P. COLLINSON.

August the 14th, 1761.

DEAR PETER :—

I have just now received two letters that came by the packet.   *   *   My Yellow Slipper improves well; but the White declines. " *Send double boxes for* PINE *and* POWEL *and* WILLIAM-

please, and paid freight, with promises to send any vegetable in her power to procure : and they thrive finely."

son." Who is this PINE? "POWEL and EDDY desire but half the quantity of walnuts." Who is this EDDY? "But all desire new things; they are tired of old ones." Do they think I can make new ones? I have sent them seeds of almost every tree and shrub from Nova Scotia to Carolina; very few are wanting: and from the sea across the continent to the lakes. It's very likely ignorant people may give strange names to tickle your ears withal; but, as I have travelled through most of these provinces, and have specimens sent by the best hands, I know well what grows there. Indeed, I have not yet been at the Ohio, but have many specimens from there. But in about two weeks I hope to set out to search myself, if the barbarous Indians don't hinder me (and if I die a martyr to Botany, God's will be done ;—His will be done in all things). They domineer, threaten, and steal most of the best horses they can. None could have worse luck than I with your roots sent last fall and this spring.   *   *   *

The Double Wild *Crocus* was a mistake. I suppose I meant the *Ranunculus*.   *   *   *

November, 1761.
DEAR PETER :—

In the little box, No. IX., I have packed up these plants :—four roots of Mountain *Kalmia*, a sod of evergreen *Andromeda*, of *Sarracenia*, of low Calceolus [*Cypripedium acaule*, Ait. ?], of a lovely evergreen grassy plant—perhaps an Asphodel [probably *Xerophyllum asphodeloides*, Nutt.]. * * I have just received two fine cargoes of fresh plants from South Carolina, from two different correspondents. But Dr. GARDEN hath sent me nothing this fall, but thanks in a letter to my son, for a large parcel of bulbous roots I sent him. He is so hurried in his practice, that he can hardly go out of town. But I am packing up a chest of apples for him, which I hope will make him speak by next spring. But I can't yet get one plant from BILLY. He sent me some in the summer, but they were washed overboard by a storm. * *

* * My correspondents near London write to me as freely for the Carolina plants, as if they thought I could get them as easily as they do the plants in the European gardens; that is, to walk at their leisure along the alleys and dig what they please out of the beds, without the danger of life or limb. * *

P. COLLINSON TO JOHN BARTRAM.

London, April 1, 1762.

I had my dear JOHN'S letter of December 12th, which is always acceptable. But what have I to do with PONTHIEU, that I must be charged double postage; 20s. for his bill of loading? Why had I the trouble of it? And then, what is very singular, thou mentions no price for either his box of plants, or for that to POWEL and EDDY. But if thou art so generous to give both, all that is at once settled.

I really believe my honest JOHN is a *great wag*, and has sent seven hard, stony seeds, something shaped like an acorn, to puzzle us; for there is no name to them. I have a vast collection of seeds, but none like them. I do laugh at GORDON, for he guesses them to be a species of Hickory.* Perhaps I may be laughed at in turn, for I think they may be, what I wish, seeds of the Bon-duc Tree [*Gymnocladus Canadensis*, Lam.], which thou picked up in thy rambles on the Ohio. For thou must know there are trees of this rare species that grow in the French settlements in Canada; but whether it grows near Quebec, Montreal, or near the lakes, I cannot learn. We have three in our English gardens, that thrive finely, and if the war had not broke out, mine would have been the fourth. A few days agone, I had a letter from Paris, informing me they keep two trees for me, when it shall please God to send a peace. This elegant tree has large leaves, divided into many portions, very much resembling the Angelica Tree. It bears its fruit in pods, like the West India Bonduc, or Nickar Tree; but what blossom, I could never learn. This is the only fine tree in which the French rival us. But now we have got possession, we shall rival them. * * I am always careful of your earth; for I have raised many odd plants out of it, that thou never would think to send seeds of. * * *

* GORDON made decidedly the best *guess*, for those "stony seeds" were no doubt the nuts of the *Pecan* or Illinois Hickory [*Carya olivæformis*, Nutt.]. In reply to PETER's remarks, JOHN BARTRAM says, "The hard nuts I sent were given me at Pittsburg by Col. BOUQUET. He called them Hickory nuts. He had them from the country of the Illinois. Their kernel was very sweet. I am afraid they won't sprout, as being a year old."

Thy hypothetical systems on the phenomena in nature, show a fertile conception and a fruitful genius; but as I have neither leisure nor inclination to oppose thy sentiments, I subscribe to them. And if I had, it would be fruitless; for when we had both said our say out, it would be all conjecture at last. What I desire to see is thy Diary; which consists of facts that cannot fail to give sensible pleasure, by instilling some knowledge into the mind, and enlarging my ideas of the inconceivable power and wisdom of the great Creator.

The dearest of friends must part. I regret to lose so valuable a member of society. I see our friend FRANKLIN preparing to depart. By him I send the Magazine, and two books which will give entertainment to thy speculative genius.

Thou must take this letter as an instance of great friendship; for I am so hurried in business that I write a bit and a scrap, now and then, to show thee how much thou hast the esteem of thy real

Friend,
P. COLLINSON.

My love to thy wife.

When thou writes by the packet, always inclose it to my friend ALEXANDER COLDEN, Esq., Postmaster at New York; and then it costs me nothing.

I have heard nothing, a long time, from MOSES, BILLY, or JOHNNY. *I don't want them to write me letters;* but for thee to tell me how they go on and how they do.

JOHN BARTRAM TO P. COLLINSON.

May the 10th, 1762.

DEAR PETER :—

I have received thy kind letter of December 31, 1761.

I am glad my Journal to Carolina is acceptable. I wish my remarks on the Ohio may be so too. I have roughly wrote my Journal to Pittsburg; but I should write it over again before I send it. But when I can get time to do it, I can't say, nor how to send it safe. It is larger than that to Carolina.

As thee hath made little mention of insects these many years, I thought thee had lost thy taste for them long ago; and the nets

being broke, I bent my mind to the search of minerals, and especially vegetables. As for the animals and insects, it is very few
that I touch of choice, and most with uneasiness. Neither can I
behold any of them, that have not done me a manifest injury, in
their agonizing, mortal pains, without pity. I also am of opinion
that the creatures commonly called brutes, possess higher qualifi-
cations, and more exalted ideas, than our traditional mystery-
mongers are willing to allow them.

The back parts of the country, where I chiefly travel, do not
abound with such a great variety of insects as nearer the sea-coast.
That seems to be, in most countries, the first and main situation or
resort for most animals.

   *   *   *   *   *

Now I hope to be stocked with *Padus*, as I have received a
lovely parcel this spring, from Mrs. LOGAN, my fascinated widow.
I saw the lovely tree growing in Governor GLENN's garden. She also
sent me a young tree from there, but the rats almost demolished it.
I have also fascinated two men's wives, although one I never saw;
that is, Mrs. LAMBOLL, who hath sent me two noble cargoes; one
last fall, the other this spring. The other hath sent me, I think,
a great curiosity. She calls it a Golden Lily. I thought, when I
planted it, to be the Atamasco, but the bud seems different.

I am apt to think I have not yet got the true Loblolly Bay,
though several say they have sent it; but I believe they are a
species of Sweet Bay. Though I have walked and rode by
thousands of them, yet I could not find a good root. The Sorrel
Tree, and three or four more that I am very fond of, I can't yet
procure, though I believe my correspondents strive which can
oblige me most.

PETER COLLINSON TO JOHN BARTRAM.

London, May 22d, 1762.

Whilst my dear JOHN is in melancholy mood for the loss of PITT,
I keep myself in equal poise; put the successes *in one scale*, and
his two rash French expeditions, on their coasts, *in the other*, in
which he wantonly sacrificed so many brave Englishmen, to answer
no purpose but his vain-glory. Had they been sent *then* to Mar-
tinico, some millions had been the difference to England. If we

consider the number of our ships taken, and their rich cargoes, the men useless, and the vast produce of that island kept from us, so all things put together (for this is a short sketch), I don't find any cause to lament his abdication. We go on full as well without him. So prithee, my dear JOHN, revive and don't sink, and be lost in doleful dumps under so terrible an event, which portends no harm that I can see; for we have a brave King, and good men at the helm. Never fear; we shall keep Canada, and have a good peace; and PITT is as well pleased with his mercenary pension of £3000 per annum, and a title in reversion; and has cleverly slipped his neck out of the collar, when it most became him to keep in, to serve his country, but he preferred serving himself before it.

From one melancholy story we come to another;—the loss of so many fine plants, which affects me more than the loss of PITT.

It is a fair probation, how far the principles of vegetation may be maintained when removed from a warmer latitude to a colder. Art will assist nature. There are many fine plants that grow on this side the Tropics, if we will bestow a south wall on them, will thrive and flower well in our northern climate.

   *   *   *   *

I cannot advise, for I am fearful thy grand expedition to the Lakes will be too much to undertake without suitable companions, for accidents may happen in so long a journey. But if it was thy resolution, my advice will come too late.

So, my dear JOHN, farewell.

            P. COLLINSON.

Doctor SOLANDER wrote by a Swedish parson, on the last specimens. * * *

It may be twenty years agone since I gave the White Broom to our friend LAMBOLL, which was sent me from Portugal.

Doctor GRONOVIUS has sent thee a present of a new edition of his *Flora Virginica*, which I have got bound, and given our friend FRANKLIN to convey to thy hands with two other tracts.

           London, June 11, 1762.

Notwithstanding I have wrote so lately by Doctor SHIPPEN,

(May 22,) in answer to thine of the 17th January, and February 5, yet I can't let the packet sail without a few lines.

I forgot in my last to tell thee my deciduous Mountain *Magnolia*, I raised from seed about twenty years agone, flowered for the first time with me ; and I presume is the first of that species that ever flowered in England, and the largest and tallest. The flowers come early ; soon after the leaves are formed. The great Laurel Magnolia and Umbrella, both fine trees in my garden, showed their flower-buds the first of June. My Red flowering Acacia is now in full flower, and makes a glorious show, as well as the White. But above all, is the great Mountain Laurel, or *Rhododendron*, in all its glory. What a ravishing sight must the mountains appear when clad with this rich embroidery ! How glorious are thy works, O Lord ! They inspire me with adoration and praise.

In the sod with thy *Sarracenia*, is come up a seeming species of *Orchis*, a very singular flower. It would be worth while importing sods from wild, boggy, swampy places, where so many odd and rare plants grow, for the sake of the uncommon variety they produce.   *   *   *

My dear JOHN, if thou knewest the pleasure thou so often gives to thy old friend, by perusing thy Journals ! The time taken in digesting them cannot be said to be thrown away, as they afford an endless fund of entertainment and reflection from the various incidents and objects that diversify every page.

By thy description, *Pittsburg* must be a delightful situation, both for health, convenience, and trade. No doubt but our people will avail themselves of these advantages. When the country grows populous and the wood scarce and dear, coal may be of infinite service to supply that deficiency.

What shall we say to the strata abounding with fossil sea-shells, petrifactions, &c. ? Very probably, as thou conceives, the sea flowed higher, or once overflowed all. All our conjectures may be beside the mark, as we know not the true causes of these phenomena.

The want of fish in the Ohio, may be as thou observes, from its great distance from the sea; but this cannot be the absolute cause : for it is well known that inland lakes, in many parts of the world abound with fish.

The new species of turtle I should like to see. But there is another four-footed amphibious creature, that is peculiar to the River Ohio, that may deserve thy farther inquiry. I printed an account of it, and the figure, the best I could procure, in the Gentleman's Magazine, two or three years agone.

A skin of this rare creature would be a great curiosity, as well as an addition to Natural History. And some more particular observations on the Great Buffalo. Their bones or skeletons are now standing in a licking-place, not far from the Ohio, of which I have two of their teeth.

One GREENWOOD, an Indian trader, and my friend GEORGE CROGHAN, both saw them, and gave me relation of them : but they omitted to take notice what hoofs they had, and what horns. These two material articles known, would help to determine their genus, or species. Prithee, inquire after them, for they are won-derful beyond description, if what is related of them may be depended on. I heartily wish thou had been properly informed of them, and the place they were to be found in ; then we should have had some certainty.

Thus, dear JOHN, I scrawl on : but now I must conclude.

Thy real friend,

P. COLLINSON.

The last packet from New York was taken : so I am afraid I have lost one of thy letters.

London, July 25, 1762.

I cannot let our dear FRANKLIN pass over without a line to my dear JOHN. In my last of July 9th, by packet, I acknowledged the receipt of thine, 10th of May.

I know thy many avocations ; therefore, will patiently wait thy own time for thy Journal to Pittsburg.

There is no end of the wonders in nature. The more I see the more I covet to see ; not to gratify a trifling curiosity, but to raise my mind in sublime contemplation on the unlimited power and wisdom of the Great Creator of all things.

I am glad to hear my two pretty friends, JOHN and BENJAMIN,

are not so squeamish as their father.* How is my friend WILLIAM
—and MOSES? I expect some discoveries from WILLIAM, who has
curiosity and ingenuity. I much wish he could give a sketch of
the Sensitive Leaf. If he is with his uncle, it may then be no
difficult thing to procure. I wish I could hear it was once in thy
own garden, and that I had good specimens. I then could form
some idea of this waggish plant,—as waggishly described.

Birds and insects have their certain periods. At the time thou
was on the Ohio, most of the first were absent, and the last in
their chrysalis state. It requires a year's sojournment to have a
tolerable knowledge of the animals of a country.

       *   *   *   *

The *Basteria* [*Calycanthus floridus*, L.] my good friend LAM-
BOLL sent me many years agone. It is a fine bush, and flowers
plentifully every year. Its fragrance is smelt at a great distance ;
is very hardy : as its wood is very aromatic, certainly has eminent
virtues. Is it noways applied as a medicine ?

My great *Magnolia* is full of flowers this year, in which we have
had the least rain, and longest warm, sultry weather, I ever remember. I have had much to do, with all our watering, to keep
many of your plants alive.

    *   * The Grassy Plant [*Xerophyllum ?*] sent last, stands at a
stay. Send me more, and give me a hint how to manage this in-
tractable vegetable. * * I have two new *Asters* come up out
of the sods, the one perfoliated, which I never saw before. Sure
your country is inexhaustible in Asters, Virga Aureas, and Corona
Solis.

I forget if I ever mentioned two monstrous teeth I had sent me
by the Governor of Virginia. One tooth weighs 3¾ pounds, 18
inches round. The other weighs 1¾ pound, 13½ inches round.
One other has Dr. FOTHERGILL, and T. PENN another.

One GREENWOOD, well known to B. FRANKLIN, an Indian
trader, knocked some of the teeth out of their jaws ; and GEORGE
CROGHAN has been at the licking-place, near the Ohio, where the
skeletons of six monstrous animals were standing, as they will inform thee.

* This refers to JOHN's remark on his repugnance to handling and inflicting
pain on insects and other animals, in his letter of May 10, where he adds—"but
my sons, JOHN and BENJAMIN, are not so squeamish. They can handle, and kill
them too, without any emotion."

CROGHAN is well known to B. FRANKLIN. To him I have wrote a long letter, which I have desired B. FRANKLIN to show thee, before he sends it to CROGHAN. * * I briefly mention these wonders of wonders that, in thy next excursion to the heads of the rivers, if thou art within an hundred miles of them, they deserve a visit to see, what nobody knows is to be seen in the world beside.

The Indian tradition is, that the monstrous Buffaloes (so called by the Indians) were all struck dead with lightning at this licking-place. But is it likely to think all the race were here collected, and extinguished at one stroke ?

P. COLLINSON.

JOHN BARTRAM TO P. COLLINSON.

August 15th, 1762.

DEAR PETER :—

I wrote by BUDDEN last, by whom I sent my Journal to Pitts-burg, having a fine opportunity by my friend TAYLOR, who pro-mised to deliver it to thee with his own hands. * * Our extreme hot, dry weather still continueth, although we have once in two or three weeks a shower that wets the ground two or three inches deep ; but yet the ground is one foot deep as dry as dust. Yet some plants that grow naturally in or near water, bear the dry weather as well as any I have.   *   *

I am obliged to SOLANDER for the names of the specimens of my last collection. The names of most are very just, and show the great learning and ingenuity of the Doctor ; but as dried specimens are not to be depended upon, like the growing plant, so he hath mistaken several. I shall begin with remarking a very odd, new genus, 54. The Doctor calls it *Asclepias linifolia*. I found one with broad leaves, near the coast of North Carolina. The leaves are milky, and I thought it had been an *Asclepias* at first, but observing the leaves growing alternately, the flowers and seeds being so very different from that, or any other known genus, I concluded it was new. It is surprising how it casts its long, rough, misshapen seeds, like bits of rotten wood, out of the top of its long, upright pods. I take it, the lower part of the pod contracts as it dries, and, by slow degrees, squeezeth the seed out of the top of the pod, which openeth by its contraction below.   *   *

PETER COLLINSON TO JOHN BARTRAM.

London, October 5, 1762.

My DEAR JOHN :—

What good luck attends thy Journals ! For thy last was carefully delivered by Mr. TAYLOR, in a very obliging manner.

There is an everlasting fund of entertainment and information,
which will be subjects of consideration at more leisure. But I remark how few or none of your wild animals came under thy notice,
except snakes. I expected often to hear the panther had sprung
out of a thicket, or a bear wakened from his den, or a beaver-dam
broke up, to observe its structure and artful contrivance, &c.

Your weather has remarkable vicissitudes. Ours has been more
certain, for all our summer has been a constant hot, dry season,—
all burnt up longer than ever I knew. Plants languishing and
perishing for want of rain, and many totally killed. But my
greatest loss has been from a villain who came and robbed me of
twenty-two different species of my most rare and beautiful plants ;
took all my fine tall Marsh Martagons, and that thee sent me last
year, which was different in colour from any I have had before ;
all my fine yellow Lady's Slippers that I have had so long, and
flowered so finely every year. These I regret most, for they are
not to be had again, but by thy assistance ; and though I doubt
not of thy inclination, yet, as I apprehend, they are found accidentally, so it may not be in thy power to assist me.   *   *
*   *   I have what is called the Evergreen Padus, of South Carolina, but I doubt if it will hold when it grows older, and in our
climate. I have observed many young, vigorous plants will keep
their leaves for two or three years, and then become deciduous.   *
*   *   *   *   I am impatient to see a specimen of the leaves and
flower of thy *Tipitiwitchet* [*Schrankia uncinata*, Willd. ?]. Pray,
good JOHN, never let a letter pass without a specimen, as it advances. Is it possible for BILLY to paint it ? I am much concerned
that his affairs are encumbered. Pray take care of this singular
plant, and protect the root carefully against your severe weather.
    *   *   *   *   *   *
I wish thou could get more of the hard nuts of Colonel BOU-
QUET. If they are Hickories, they are very different from what

thou has sent, or what I have ever seen. I flattered myself they
were the *Bonduc*, a most elegant-leafed tree, found by the French
somewhere in Canada—is in all the rare gardens of France, and in
some gardens in England. If the war had not broke out, I should
have had it sent me from thence; and now I shall have it with a
peace, which I hope is not far off.   *   *   *

How early your harvest is, to ours! which shows your fertile
soil, and warm climate. And although we are so much advanced
to the north, yet there are many concurring circumstances that
give us plentiful crops and a successful harvest.   *   *

Gout-wort, or what is called *Podagraria*, is a notorious running
weed in a garden, for which reason we rarely save the seed of it.
It is only a native of Europe. You do not abound in umbelliferous
plants, which are plentiful, and in variety, with us. Our fields and
banks are overrun with them. But your tribe of *Asters* exceed
them. Almost every sod brings over a new one.   *   *

*   *   By Doctor SHIPPEN I sent thy account, who I
shall be glad to hear is arrived; and now at thy request I send it
again, which I doubt not but will prove right ; and the old proverb
says, " Right reckonings make long friends." Let those that
inquire my age know that I am thy senior some months [rather
more than five years].   *   *   *   *

Dear JOHN, thou must guess at my meaning in many places.   I
write a piece now and then, having variety of affairs on my hands:
but I am thy sincere friend,

P. COLLINSON.

JOHN BARTRAM TO PETER COLLINSON.

December 3d, 1762.

DEAR PETER :—

In answer to thine of May the 22d, brought me by Doctor
SHIPPEN :—I should be glad of an honourable peace, but if
Louisiana be not delivered to us, we, on the continent, can hardly
call it a peace, for the French will, directly, by encouraging and
supplying the Indians, set them against us, and also encroach
themselves, which will soon cause, first quarrelling, and next a war.

I can't find, in our country, that south walls are much protection
against our cold, for if we cover so close as to keep out the frost,

they are suffocated. I observed at the distance of one hundred and twenty miles from Charleston, all the Fig trees are yearly killed down to the ground, that are exposed to the south or west, but those in the same garden that faced the north, and were shaded from the sun, did well. The hot sun in the day, and the sharp frosts in the night, kill them.   *   *   *   *   *

I am obliged to thee for the books and prints thee sent me. The print of the Bastard Pheasant, and Cinnamon, I had not before. That fine piece of STILLINGFLEET's, I had two years ago. The miscellanies no way suited my taste, except the Calendar of Flora. My head runs all upon the works of God, in nature. It is through that telescope I see God in his glory.   *   *   *   As for those monstrous skeletons on the Ohio, I have wrote to thee largely, just before I set out for Carolina, and since my return. But by thy letter thee seems to think the skeletons stand in the posture the beasts stood in when alive, which is impossible. The ligaments would rot, and the bones fall out of joint, and tumble confusedly on the ground. But it's a great pity, and shame to the learned curiosos, that have great estates, that they don't send some person that will take pains to measure every bone exactly, before they are broken and carried away, which they will soon be, by ignorant, careless people, for gain.   *   *   *

My thanks to GRONOVIUS for his new edition of the *Flora Virginica*. It's pity the plants beyond the South Mountain, and the draft of that fine country, had not been in it.

PETER COLLINSON TO JOHN BARTRAM.

Mill Hill, December 10th, 1762.

I am here all alone, and yet I have the company of my friends with me. This will be no paradox, when I tell thee, on the table lie their speaking letters, in that silent language which conveys their most intimate thoughts to my mind. In course, thine, my dear JOHN, comes first. I thank thee for thine of the 15th August. I have, in my former letters, acknowledged the receipt of thy Journal, which is a lasting fund of entertainment to me and my son, these long evenings.   *   *   *   Whilst the Frenchman was ready to burst with laughing, I am ready to burst with desire

for root, seed, or specimen of the waggish *Tipitiwitchet* Sensitive.*
I wish BILLY, when he was with thee, had taken but the least
sketch of it, to save my longing. But if I have not a specimen in
thy next letter, never write me more, for it is cruel to tantalize me
with relations, and not to send me a little specimen in thine of the
15th of August, nor in thine of the 29th. It shows thou hast no
sympathy nor compassion for a virtuoso. I wish it was in my
power to mortify thee as much.

Don't use the Pomegranate inhospitably, a stranger that has
come so far to pay his respects to thee. Don't turn him adrift in
the wide world; but plant it against the south side of thy house,
nail it close to the wall. In this manner it thrives wonderfully
with us, and flowers beautifully and bears fruit this hot year. I
have twenty-four on one tree, and some well ripened. Doctor
FOTHERGILL says, of all trees this is the most salutiferous to
mankind.   *   *   *   *   *   *

I was much comforted with thy good wife's postscript, that thou
wast got to the Congaree in health, September 14th. I trust that a
good Providence will be with thee, in so laudable an undertaking
as to explore and discover the wonders of his creative power, and
bring thee home in safety, to the joy of thy wife and family; and
in particular of thy affectionate friend,

P. COLLINSON.

Now, my dear JOHN, look on the map, and see by this glorious
peace, what an immense country is added to our long, narrow slip
of colonies, from the banks of the Mississippi to Terra Labrador
and Newfoundland, &c. See what a complete empire we have
now got within ourselves; what a grand figure it will now make in
the map of North America.   *   *   *

JOHN BARTRAM TO PETER COLLINSON.

January the 6th, 1763.

DEAR PETER:—

I received thy kind letter of October the 5th, 1762. I am glad
thee received my rough Journal by Mr. TAYLOR. He was always
ready to do me all the kindness he could.

* Probably the *Schrankia uncinata*, Willd., sometimes called *Bashful Brier*.

I did not see any wild animals in all that journey, except two or three deer; only one tame bear at the Fort; nor so much as a wolf or fox, to be seen or heard, although I lay six nights in the woods, on the banks of the Ohio and Monongahela, and was two nights very late on the Alleghany Mountains.

I am much astonished in reading the histories of Europe and Asia, those old, settled, clear countries, that they should abound so much with wild beasts of prey, and others for food, as travellers give relation of, as also much wild water-fowl, and plenty of fish; all which we had in great plenty sixty years ago, but now very few are to be seen. All our small creeks used to abound with trouts, but I have not seen one catched these three or four years, though travelled more than ever. I did not see one fish catched in all my last journey, but at the Wateree, so many great rivers as I crossed, nor one wild goose, a very few ducks, and but three or four small flocks of turkeys.

It's very provoking to have so many of thy curious roots stole. That rogue was too greedy to take all; however, my dear friend, I shall endeavour to furnish thee again, though they are now very scarce with us, as most of the land is cleared where they used to grow, quite to the mountains. What our people will do for fencing and firewood fifty years hence, I can't imagine.*   *   *

*   *   By my friend FISHER, by whom I wrote largely, I sent the leaves and flower of my pretty *Tipitiwitchet.*

I every day expect Colonel BOUQUET at my house, when I intend to mention the Hickory nuts from Illinois.

By the Indians' description, I am apt to think the Bonduc [*Gymnocladus Canadensis,* Lam.] grows down the Ohio, towards the Shawnee town.

I believe the Striped Rose is not a native of Carolina. It is pretty double, and smells like the garden roses.

The long-leaved *Sarracenia* is a charming plant—grows near two feet high; but I found one of that kind on the Wateree that grew six inches high—was delicately striped with red and green. I dug up several roots and planted them in a box, with many other

---

* The apprehensions felt by JOHN BARTRAM of an approaching scarcity of timber, for fuel and fencing, were extensively prevalent in Pennsylvania, within my recollection; but although more than *eighty years* have elapsed since the date of this letter, there is nothing like a scarcity of wood yet felt. As it regards *fuel*, the discovery of our vast *coal fields,* has for ever dissipated all fear of that want.

curious plants that I could not find in seed, to be sent down to Charleston, for Philadelphia; but I can't hear anything of them. I doubt they are lost, or spoiled.   *   *

As thee observes, we have very few Umbelliferous plants. I did not see one new in all the last journey. Perhaps, next fall, I may send thee specimens of all the kinds we have.   *   *

*   * Evergreen *Prinos* [in JAMES ALEXANDER'S list of plants sent to England] is what I call Evergreen Privet, or Ink-berries [*Prinos glaber*, L.], in Jersey.   *   *

*   * I can't find thy amphibious creature, that thee published in the Magazine. My BILLY has stole two from me to carry to his uncle at Cape Fear; perhaps it was in one of them. Those in the Ohio are very odd creatures.

Amber of a very curious sort is found in West Jersey lately, in detached masses, near the surface of the ground, and not far from the River Delaware. It is inflammable, nearly transparent, and almost as tough as horn, and will turn very smooth for cane heads, of a yellowish colour, waved or checkered with a lighter colour. I think it was ploughed up in a field, but I can't yet learn, certainly, where it was found—but I intend to make more inquiry about it.

PETER COLLINSON TO JOHN BARTRAM.

London, February 23d, 1763.

I am greatly rejoiced to read in thine of the 31st of October, of thy safe return from thy delightful journey from the terrestrial Paradise, for such it must be, that could raise such ecstasies of joy at viewing those charming scenes, enriched with such elegant productions. I long to see a sketch of thy Journal.

The Pyramid of Eden must be a glorious sight in full flower. LINNÆUS makes it a *Swertia*—is the next genus to the Gentians; and differs from them by having beautiful *nectariums*, consisting of little tufts of small hairs in the hollow of each petal. Doctor GARDEN calls it the glory of the Blue Mountains. I hope we shall have seed of it, that GORDON may raise it.   *   *

*   * I delivered thy letter into Doctor SHIPPEN'S own hands. I admire he should delay giving it to thee. It is very unpolite to keep a letter two or three months by him. It is not using thee as

he would be used himself.   He seems a gentleman, but this is not gentleman-like to treat thee in this manner.   My letter was dated May the 12th.   December 10th wrote a long letter by packet.

I inclose Doctor WITT's letter, which may be some entertainment, as thou knows the man.

I am thy sincere friend,
P. COLLINSON.

I thank thy wife for her kind intelligence of our friend FRANKLIN'S arrival.   *   *   Give my love to him and that of our family.

If the small Alligator caught at Pittsburg has a remarkable flat proboscis, then it is the animal I published in the Magazine.

A complete skin of that animal would be a great and a new curiosity to all naturalists.   Look back to the Magazine, and thou will find what I say about it, I fancy about three years agone.

London, March 11, 1763.

Being much engaged, I missed the last packet; but by the Sally, Captain PATRICK, of Philadelphia, I thanked my dear JOHN for the acceptable letter that gave me advice of his safe return from the Garden of Eden.

Since that, I have suffered much concern for the Carolina, Captain FRIEND, being taken by the Spaniards and carried into Bilboa; but as she was taken eleven or twelve days after the treaty was signed, she has been claimed, and I hear, this day, she will be delivered.   I presume all our seed boxes are on board, but, as is customary, all letters were thrown overboard, so shall be at a great loss to find things.   So pray write by very first, and send to our friend ALEX. COLDEN, postmaster at New York, to go by first mail from thence, which sails every month.

I am, in a hurry of business, thine,
P. COLLINSON.

London, April 7th, 1763.

I am exceedingly engaged in business for your world, yet, as I know, it must be very satisfactory to hear that thy boxes arrived, and delivered the 6th; though late, it's better than never, and that all Louisiana is yielded to us by an honourable peace. I hope my dear JOHN will recover his spirits and be no longer in melancholy mood. He sees a good peace can be made without his worthy PITT, who deserted the helm to become a pensioner, with £3000 per annum, and his wife made a lady. So he is now known by the name of the Grand Pensioner,—a blast on his reputation that will last for ever.

Now, my dear JOHN, does not the ardour of curiosity burn in thy mind to explore the wonders of Louisiana ?

I joyfully received thine of December 3d, by the hands of Friend FISHER, but I have not yet got the turtle, &c., and the seeds. I hope there is some of the Pyramids of Eden.   *   *
    *   *   Last warm summer ripened our pears. I never had such good seed before. They are of the most delicious sorts ; so either thee or thine may hope for choice fruits. They come late, but soak them a night in water, that will plump them, and they'll soon vegetate.

Pray my love to B. FRANKLIN. I received his kind letter, but cannot write more than that I am thine,

P. COLLINSON.

JOHN BARTRAM TO P. COLLINSON.

May the 1st, 1763.

A few days past, with great joy, I received thy agreeable letter of December 10th, 1762, and soon after, another dated February 23d, 1763. I was really afraid my dear friend was dead; but thought surely his son would have let me known it, before now.

My Loblolly Bay, though grown prodigiously in the summer, is entirely killed last winter, though in a warm place. It is in vain for us to expect to have the broad-leaved evergreens of Carolina to flourish with us in the winter, unless in a green-house.   *   *   *

I have but one root of the *Tipitiwitchet*. It bears our winter— is strong this spring. I sent thee twice of its leaves. Last fall, by FISHER, I sent both flower and leaf, with a noble collection of Carolina specimens.   *   *   *   *   That they call an alligator [at the Ohio], I take to be as much a water lizard ; but I believe a new genus,—very odd mouth, like a cat-fish, and tail like a musk-rat, with a fin round it,—nails like a man, with a membrane on each side, reaching from the fore to the hind foot, like a flying squirrel.

I take our wild cat to be a lynx, in every respect like a cat, but a short tail. KALM told me it is like theirs.   *   *   *

*   *   We have many accounts from the different parts of Europe, of the severe cold of last winter,—nay, even from Rome ; and yet my dear PETER mentions not a syllable how it fared with his garden.   *   *

PETER COLLINSON TO JOHN BARTRAM.

London, May 10, 1763.

I have pleasure upon pleasure beyond measure, with perusing my dear JOHN's letters, of October 31st, with the rare plants in Eden, which I answered 23d of February. Then I have to thank thee for thine, December 3d,.and January 6th. My last to thee was April 7th, by packet, giving an account of the arrival of the seeds, after a visit to Spain.   *   *

It is really very wonderful that, as thy ramble was amongst the wastes, wilds, and unfrequented countries, no more wild animals were seen. From whence, then, comes that vast quantity and great variety of skins of animals that I have this year seen in our public sales ? What does thou think of two or three thousand raccoon skins ? Where do they hide themselves, that thou didst not see one ?   *   *

*   *   I can only now acknowledge thy piece of natural history of the countries thou passed through ; and the map annexed is both entertaining and informing.

Yesterday I saw at my neighbour PONTHIEU's, the *Warneria* [*Hydrastis Canadensis*, L.], or Yellow Root, in flower. It is singular to have no petals.   *   *   *

Think, my dear JOHN, with what amazement and delight I, with Doctor SOLANDER, surveyed the quire of specimens. He thinks near half are new genera. This will enrich the fountain of knowledge. The Doctor is very busy examining them. I hope soon to send thee a list of them.   *   *   *   But what surprises us most, is the *Tipitiwitchet* Sensitive. It is quite a new species, a new genus. It was impossible to comprehend it from any description, which made me so very impatient to see it. I wish we had good seed ; I doubt not but GORDON would raise it. But so many seeds lose their vegetation coming over, that few are raised (notwithstanding all his skill), when we consider the infinite quantity of seeds that we have received from thee, in thirty years past.

*   *   *   *   *   *   *

But I will try thy patience no longer, than to assure thee I am thy sincere friend,

P. Collinson.

London, June 8th, 1763.

My dear John:—

I am in high delight.   My two Mountain Magnolias are pyramids of flowers,—almost the extremity of every branch is a flower. My short and long-leafed *Sarracenia*, growing close together, are both in flower, and make a charming contrast,—the one red—the other a golden hue.   Well mightest thou say, how fine they looked to see a number together.

I received thy acceptable letters of April 24th and May 1st. My good John makes no allowance for one or two packets that were taken—thinks enemies, wind, and tide should obey his wishes.   I never had thy letter with the leaves of *Tipitiwitchet*, yet I never complain, and think my dear friend dead and buried. Bad news comes fast enough, and therefore I always think the best.   *   *   *   I cannot get Solander, who has thy list, to settle the names of the last specimens.   I want to send them to thee.

Gordon has raised the fine *Periploca*, from the Ohio.   It is growing in my garden.

Pray look, *where grows nearest*, some *Azaleas*, *Kalmias*, and *Rhododendrons*, for my son-in-law, who has lately bought a fine estate, and built a noble house, and made extensive plantations, and is quite cracked after plants,—has plundered my garden all he can, and looks with such a longing eye on what remains, that unless thou sends me a box of those plants to keep all quiet—for my own son is so ardent to keep what I have—that I shall have something to do to manage my two sons.   They are so fond of plants, and take such care in planting in proper soil and situation, it gives me entertainment to see their ingenuity and emulation.

But my son Cator deserves encouragement; for when he married my daughter, about ten years agone, he scarcely knew an apple tree from an oak; but by seeing often my garden, and conversing with me and his brother, is now resolved, if he can, to rival us. In his new, fresh soil, plants thrive finely.

I wish thou may pick out what I mean: being much engaged, can add no more, but that I am thy sincere friend,

P. COLLINSON.

London, June 30th, 1763.

I am glad, my dear JOHN, I can send our friend SOLANDER's catalogue of thy last curious collection of specimens. There are wonderful things amongst them, especially the Sensitive, *Empetrum*, &c.   *   *   *   *   *   *
They enrich our knowledge, and anticipate our pleasures, and give us a good idea of the riches in store, to gratify the botanists of after ages. O, Botany! delightfulest of all sciences! There is no end of thy gratifications. All botanists will join with me in thanking my dear JOHN for his unwearied pains to gratify every inquisitive genius. I have sent LINNÆUS a specimen, and one leaf of *Tipitiwitchet* Sensitive; only to him would I spare such a jewel. Pray send more specimens. I am afraid we can never raise it. LINNÆUS will be in raptures at the sight of it. How happens it, in thy Journal, that thou did not give a sketch, or map, of the rivers *Wateree* and *Congaree?*—names I never heard of. What rivers do they join before they come to the sea?   *   *

Thine,

P. COLLINSON.

London, August 4th, 1763.

I had the pleasure of my dear JOHN's letter of May 30th, which was sensibly abated by the severe disorder thou hast to encounter with. I shall be glad to hear thou hast got the victory. At the same time it raises in my mind thankfulness for a long series of health, without any such calamities, or indeed any other.

My garden, like thine, makes a glorious appearance; with fine long-spiked purple *Ononis;* with the Allspice of Carolina [*Calycanthus floridus*, L.], abundantly in flower, spreading its perfumes abroad; the delectable red-flowering *Acacia;* my laurel-leafed *Magnolia*, with its noble blossoms, which will continue for two months or more. The great *Rhododendron* has been glorious beyond expression ; and before, I told thee of the Mountain *Magnolia,* and the surprising flowers of the red and yellow *Sarracenia.* Thus, my dear JOHN, thou sees I am not much behind thee in a fine show. But when thy Eden plants flower, I shall not be able to bear the report of them.

But what delights me is, to hear that our Horse Chestnut has flowered. I think it much excels the Virginia, if the spikes of flowers are as large with you as with us. To see a long avenue of them at Hampton Court,—of trees fifty feet high—being perfect pyramids of flowers from top to bottom, for all the spikes of flowers are at the extremities,—is one of the grandest and most charming sights in the world.   *   *   *   My dear JOHN, what art thou talking of ? Wait two years for the double white Daffodil ! Think, man ! and know how to value so great a rarity ; for I waited almost all my lifetime, to get this rare flower. I read of it, and saw it figured in books, but despaired of ever possessing it. But about seven years agone, happening in a tour, forty miles from London, my botanic genius carried me into a garden where I expected to find nothing ; on a sudden my eyes were ravished with the sight of this flower, and my heart leaped for joy, that I should find it at last ; and never saw it since in any garden but my own. And I tell thee for thy comfort, if thou had not been JOHN BAR-TRAM, thou hadst not possessed such a rarity. But as thou grudgest the time, and so little esteems it, I shall be careful where I cast my pearls another time.   *   *   *

Consider, my dear JOHN, what a pleasure I feel, now I can give thee an order for a ten guinea box, for young Lord PETRE. Little did I think, when I gave thee the first like order for his valuable father, in the year 1735 or 1736, that I should live to give the like for his son. It may be truly said the spirit of ELIJAH rests on ELISHA, for he began this year with a box of thy seeds.

I am delighted with thy dissertation on the good old Doctor [WITT]. It is very much the idea I had formed of him, from the numerous letters of a long correspondence, which has given me much entertainment, when he tells of the fascinating power of some women over men, and of the effects and fatal consequences of the penetrating look of an evil eye from some women. But as thou hast summed up his character, upon the whole I believe he meant well, did what good he could, and lived up to the convictions of his own mind ; so I hope will meet with a suitable reward.

May we persevere in the path of verity and uprightness, that our end may be happy, is the sincere desire of thy real friend,

P. COLLINSON.

I received my dear JOHN's letter of July 3d. Assure him his complaint is not founded on my neglect, for I have writ long letters by every packet, and by the Carolina I sent him books, &c.

I am concerned for the fatal effects of the rising of the Indians, but the instructions that are gone over, I hope, will bring them again into friendship.

But, my dear JOHN, I am sorry to say thou art of that unhappy cast of mind there is no pleasing.

Look into PITT's peace, and see what a pitiful figure we should have made, when he adopted MONTCALM's boundary for our colonies. As PITT did it, and accepted it, and made it the foundation of his peace—*it was glorious!* Pray look back and see what slaughter and destruction the Cherokees made (when PITT's British glory was lost in Germany) on the back settlements of Carolina; but everything the *turn-coat* did, was glorious with my dear JOHN! He heard all their cruelties, but did not then open his lips to complain. Whilst PITT was sacrificing thousands of the best British heroes to his projects on the coast of France, to gratify his vanity —all was glorious!

My dear JOHN, take heart and don't be carried away with reports. Revive thy drooping spirits, and look forward and hope for the best.

I have thy charming blue *Campanella* in flower,—six feet high, branched on every side. Pray where was the identical spot it was found? And the red or purple *Ulmaria* has flowered, a sweet, pretty thing, and quite new.   *   *   *   Pray how is the ulcer?—that affects me with true sympathy. I hope it is better, as no mention is made of it. *Glorious* PITT so presides in my dear JOHN's mind, he is insensible to complaints, except on the *sorry peace* that hath given so *great an empire* to Britain!

I am cordially thine,

P. COLLINSON.

London, August 23d, 1763.

I have a respect for Mr. PITT; and he has his merits, but everything he did was not glorious, though my friend JOHN thinks so.

We had a long, dry spring, which is succeeded by a long, wet summer. I am in pain for our harvest, a great plenty, if the weather favours to get it in.

JOHN BARTRAM TO P. COLLINSON.

September 30th, 1763.

DEAR PETER :—

* * I have now travelled near thirty years through our provinces, and in some, twenty times in the same provinces, and yet never, as I remember, once found one single species in all after times, that I did not observe in my first journey through the same province. But many times I found that plant the first, which neither I nor any person could find after, which plants, I suppose, were destroyed by the cattle. * * The first time I crossed the Shenandoah, I saw one or two plants, or rather stalk and seed, of the *Meadia*, on its bank. I jumped off, got the seed and brought it home, sent part to thee, and part I sowed myself; both which succeeded, and if I had not gone to that spot, perhaps it had been wholly lost to the world. JOHN CLAYTON asked me where I found it. I described the very spot to him, but neither he nor any person from him could find it after. O! what a noble discovery I could have made on the banks of the Ohio and Mississippi, if I had gone down, and the Indians had been peaceably inclined, as I knew many plants that grew on its northeast branches. But we are at present all disappointed. My son WILLIAM wanted to go as draughtsman.

I read lately, in our newspaper, of a noble and absolutely necessary scheme that was proposed in England, if it was practicable ; that was, to search all the country of Canada and Louisiana for all natural productions, convenient situations for manufactories, and different soils, minerals, and vegetables. The last of which, I dare take upon myself, as I know more of the North American plants than any others. But this would alarm the Indians to the highest degree. All the discoverers would be exposed to the greatest savage cruelty, the gun, tomahawk, torture, or revengeful devouring jaws. Before this scheme can be executed, the Indians must be subdued or drove above a thousand miles back. No treaty will make discovery safe. Many years past, in our most peaceable times, far beyond our mountains, as I was walking in a path with an Indian guide, hired for two dollars, an Indian man met me and pulled off my hat in a great passion, and chawed it all round—I suppose to show me that they would eat me if I came in that country again.

I admire thee should not know the Congaree and Wateree, seeing they are in all the late maps of South Carolina ; both being branches of the great Santee River.

October the 23d, 1763.

DEAR PETER :—

Last night I received thy kind letter of August the 4th, 1763. The ulcer in my right leg is finely healed up, but I have a much worse one in my left, occasioned by a cut to, or into, my shin bone, which is now much exasperated by travelling two journeys, one to Little Egg Harbour, the other to Great, with my JOHN, to show him the very spot where grew a pretty *Ornithogalum*, I saw growing three years past ; but now not one is to be found.   *   *

I have been the subject of many misfortunes all my lifetime, but as many have had worse, and many better than I, so I praise our God in leading me about the middle way.   *   *

If I had known the White double Daffodil had been such a rarity with thee, I could have sent thee large quantities thirty years ago. Our first settlers brought them with them, and they multiply so that thousands are thrown away.

*   *   I am heartily glad that young Lord PETRE is possessed of the botanical taste of his father. I wish he may resemble him in virtue. I have intended to inquire after him and his mother in every late letter. The Pear raised from her seed hath borne a number of the finest relished fruit. I think a better is not in the world.*

*   *   The most probable and only method to establish a lasting peace with the barbarous Indians, is to bang them stoutly, and make them sensible that we are men, whom they for many years despised as women. Until then, it is only throwing away men, blood and treasure, to make peace with them. They will not

---

* This tree, known as "Lady PETRE's Pear tree," is still (1848) flourishing at the BARTRAM *Garden*, standing close by the house.

keep to any treaty of peace. They all are, with their fathers, the French, resolved to drive the English out of North America. And although some tribes pretend to be neutral friends, it is only with a design to supply the rest with ammunition to murder us. Perhaps now, and only now, is the critical time offered to Britain to secure not only her old possessions, but her so much boasted new acquisitions, by sending us sufficient supplies to repel effectually those barbarous savages.

November 11th, 1763.

DEAR WORTHY PETER :—

I have received my dear friend's letter of August 23d, 1763.

I think most of our people here look upon all our boasted acquisitions in North America to be titular, and that only of short duration, as the French still claim all one side of the Mississippi, and part of our side. They will draw the chief of their fur trade near them, and will always be setting the Indians against us, suppose we do keep possession of the Lakes. But unless we bang the Indians stoutly, and make them fear us, they will never love us, nor keep peace long with us. They are now got so cunning, they will not sell their land, and stand so to their bargain as to let the people live quietly upon it. But when they want goods, it is but rob the traders, steal horses, plunder and insult the back inhabitants, and instead of us calling them to account for their mischief, we sue to them for peace, and give them great presents to kill no more white people for three or four years. By such proceedings, they have us in the greatest contempt, believing they may do us all the mischief they please, and we are ready at any time to buy a peace with them for a few years, under great insults.   *   *

The variety of plants and flowers in our southwestern continent, is beyond expression. Is it not, dear PETER, the very palace garden of old Madam *Flora?* Oh! if I could but spend six months on the Ohio, Mississippi, and Florida, in health, I believe I could find more curiosities than the English, French and Spaniards have done in six score of years. But the Indians, instigated by the French, will not let us look at so much as a plant, or tree, in this great British empire.

PETER COLLINSON TO JOHN BARTRAM.

Ridgeway House, December 6, 1763.

I am here retired, all alone, from the bustle and hurry of the town, meditating on the comforts I enjoy; and whilst the old log is burning, the fire of friendship is blazing—warms my imagination with reflecting on the variety of incidents that hath attended our long and agreeable correspondence.   *   *   *

My dear JOHN, thou does not consider the law of right, and doing to others as we would be done unto.

We, every manner of way, trick, cheat, and abuse these Indians with impunity. They were notoriously jockeyed and cheated out of their land in your province, by a man's walking a tract of ground in one day, that was to be purchased of them.

Your Governor promised the Indians if they would not join the French, that when the war was over, our troops should withdraw from Pittsburg. They sent to claim his promise, but were shuffled off. They resented it, as that fortress was situated on their hunting country.

I could fill this letter with our arbitrary proceedings, all the colonies through; with our arbitrary, illegal taking their lands from them, making them drunk, and cheating them of their property. As their merciless, barbarous methods of revenge and resentment are so well known, our people should be more careful how they provoke them.

Let a person of power come and take five or ten acres of my friend JOHN's land from him, and give him half price, or no price for it, how easy and resigned he would be, and tamely submit to such usage ! But if an *Indian* resents it in his way, instead of doing him justice, and making peace with him, nothing but fire and faggot will do with my friend JOHN ! He does not search into the bottom of these insurrections. They are smothered up, because we are the aggressors. But see my two *proposals*, in the October Gentleman's Magazine, for a peace with the Indians.

My dear JOHN, I am glad thou art so happily recovered from that cruel complaint; and that our good Colonel escaped those terrible fellows. I hope such prudent measures will be taken as will put a stop to their ravages, and establish a lasting peace.

The peace that thou art so merry with, in your mock mourning, is only glorious by comparison; I mean by comparing it with that peace that PITT would have made (but thanks to our enemies could not). Then you must have been thankful to him and the French, that they would allow you to keep your own narrow strip of land; but now your bounds are so extensively enlarged, how ungrateful! how unthankful you are! for ever grumbling, never pleased. I refer thee to the preliminary of PITT's peace, and BUTE's. Facts speak louder than faction. We all know here what PITT's peace would have been, and what BUTE's is.

So much for a touch at politics. Now we change the scene to something that pleases us both.

I can tell thee, GORDON has raised the fine, stately, broad-leafed *Silphium*, but thou mentions three fine species from New Virginia, by the Ohio, and from Pedee River, but which of them ours is, I don't know; but thy specimens will set us right.

I often reflect with what a numerous train of yellow flowers, your continent abounds. Seeds of the two fine red-petaled *Rudbeckias* will be very acceptable. I have one many years in my garden, but then it never ripened seed.

What a glorious scene is opened in that rich country about Pensacola—if that despised country is worthy thy visitation. But because PITT did not get it, thou canst not venture there on any pretence! All beyond the Carolinas is forbidden ground. They are none of thy darling PITT's acquisition!

But thy son JOHN may go with a good grace. I am glad to find the spirit of ELIJAH rests upon him.

Thou cheers my heart and flatters my hopes with thy kind and friendly donations. But we are under all the disadvantages to show our gratitude. A run of cross accidents always attends our cargo, and I never could contrive any ways to prevent it, unless a person skilled in those matters could attend upon them and make it his delight to nurse them daily.

I lament with thee the disappointment of so promising an expedition on the Ohio. Take heart; other doors may open to gratify thy inquisitive genius.

I was delighted to see the *Tipitiwitchet* Sensitive. I instantly sent it to GORDON, for his skill exceeds all others in raising seeds. Pray, where is poor WILLIAM and MOSES? As for JOHN, I find

he is our right hand man.   How happy is it to have children of so
agreeable a cast !   I speak it feelingly by my own son.

I hope what I have writ will be read with candour.   Our long
friendship will allow us to rally one another, and crack a joke
without offence, as none was intended by

Thy sincere friend,
P. COLLINSON.

Doctor SOLANDER gives his service ; is obliged to thee for remembering him.

*   *   *   The first paragraph in my Proposals [for a peace with
the Indians] is shamefully printed,—by omissions is made unintelli-
gible.   No remedy but patience; though it vexes me to the heart to
have it read as my genuine copy : for it is impossible for me to tell
the printer's carelessness.   *   *   *

London, January 1, 1763 [4].

I am very thankful to the great Author of my being that I enter
the new year in perfect good health and spirits.   I heartily wish
the like comfortable situation may attend my dear friend, and his
family.

It was a pleasure to me to receive thine of the 30th September ;
but that joy was allayed by the sad accident, which I hope will not
prove of bad consequence.

I don't wonder your autumn gardens are so delightful, as your
country more abounds with stately fine flowers than in the spring,
and we, through thine and other friends' benevolence, have many
of these beauties in great perfection, which makes our gardens gay
to the depth of winter, and if mild, the autumn flowers join the
spring as they do now.

GORDON has been fortunate enough to raise one of the fine, tall
Silphiums, with scaly heads, and we hope some others that have
not yet flowered.

The broad-leafed *Commelyna*, I take to be what was formerly
called JOHN TRADESCANT'S Spider-wort [?].   We have three
species.

Thy quick discernment of plants is a knack peculiar to thyself,
and is attained by the long exercise of thy faculties in that amuse-

ment, and is like the hare-finders with us. Some can't discover
them if close under their feet; others see them at a great distance.

Indeed, my dear JOHN, I must congratulate thee on that happy
discovery of my favourite *Meadia*. It is really remarkable none
should be found since.

I hear nothing more of that proposal thou mentions; but if there
was any real intention of carrying it into execution, no one pro-
perer than thyself for Natural History and Botany.

That the Indians would be alarmed at our sounding or measuring,—I don't wonder they should be jealous of the invasion of their
property. Every man is tenacious of his native rights, and if you
invade their rights, you must take the consequences.

Let those be well banged—I may say, well hanged—that by
their unjust proceedings provoked the Indians to hostilities, knowing, beforehand, their cruel resentments.

I am greatly pleased the long-expected Horse Chestnut has
gratified thee with its beautiful flowers. I think it exceeds a Hya-
cinth. But to see a pyramid fifty feet high, and every extreme
bud a blossom, is beyond thy imagination, but is one of the finest
sights in the world. But pray tell me if your curious people have
not had these fine trees long before, in your province. Is none at
your proprietor's?

I perceive what thou calls the Double Sweet Daffodil, we call the
Sweet White *Narcissus*. That, indeed, may be common, but yet,
how could I know it? Remove and part the roots, every other
year, and they will blow strong and fine; but let them grow in
great numbers together, the roots are weakened, and rarely bring
their flowers to perfection.

It has been thy patience to wait, but my pleasure to hear of the
delicious pear, raised from Lady PETRE's seed; but she, dear good
woman, is gone to rest.

What I am persuaded will prevent its dropping its fruit, if some
quinces were planted in the lower part of thy garden, near the
spring, and graft them with the pear—it meliorates the fruit. By
long experience, all our pears are grafted on quince stocks, and
succeed better than on pear stocks with us.   *   *

*   *   JOHN, thou needest not be glad the £100 bill is
paid, for I am not running away. Any bill thou draws will be
always paid. If there is any gladness in the case, it is I that am
to be glad to do it.   *   *   *

It is with concern I hear of the insurrection at Pittsburg.   In such a hurry, I don't wonder the curious things suffered.   The loss of the alligator is most to be regretted, if it is an alligator, which I much doubt, as these animals have never been found in such cold latitudes; but few in North Carolina, and none ever heard of in Virginia.   *   *   *

I must defer answering thy kind letter of November 11th, being much engaged packing goods for your country—I mean Virginia and Maryland,—and am thy sincere friend,

P. COLLINSON.

Pray hast thou got trees in thy garden of that odd kind of Hazel nut, that was found in the forks of Schuylkill, beyond the Blue Mountains, of which there was plenty?   It seems a different species from the Cuckold's nut, which I take to be your common sort [?]; but the Schuylkill nut is very different.   *   *

JOHN BARTRAM TO P. COLLINSON.

March 4th, 1764.
DEAR PETER:—

*   *   *   *   My true correspondent, Mrs. LOGAN, hath lately sent me two bulbous roots, of what she calls a white *Iris*, which she had from Georgia, which I hope will be a fine curiosity, with several other seeds and roots.   *   *   My JOHN is a worthy, sober, industrious son, and delights in plants; but I doubt WILL will be ruined in Carolina.   Everything goes wrong with him there.

Pray give my respects to the worthy Dr. SOLANDER.   I hope you have examined the specimens I sent by Captain BUDDEN.

*   *   I think our Indians received a full value for that cheating walk, and pretended to be fully satisfied with what they received above the first agreement; and as for Pittsburg, they let the French settle and build there; then why may not the English, after they had drove the French out, keep possession of it?   And as the Indians have committed such barbarous destruction on our people, we have more reason to destroy them and possess their land than you have to keep Canada.   And must all our provinces suffer a prodigious yearly expense, and have thousands of our inno-cent people barbarously murdered, because some of our traders made them drunk, to get a skin cheap,—or an Irishman settles on

a bit of their land, which they will never make use of? And if we must not settle any more land, or any of the branches of the Mississippi, pray say no more about our great British empire, while we must not be a farthing the better for it.

I should be exceedingly pleased if I could afford it, to make a thorough search, not only at Pensacola, but the coast of Florida, Alabama, Georgia, and the banks of the Mississippi. I make no difference *who got it*, if I could but travel safely in it. * * *

* * * My dear friend, I am so far from taking offence at thy familiar way of writing, that it gives me much pleasure.

P. COLLINSON TO JOHN BARTRAM.

London, March 7th, 1764.

MY DEAR JOHN :—

Disaffected, ignorant people, are always supposing improbabilities, and putting worst constructions on the best-intended schemes; so do not deserve further notice.

In thine of August 6th, there was a query why some animals saw clear in the night, others not. Inclosed is my friend Doctor PARSONS' answer, and I have added something.

Is it reasonable to think the Indians will love us, after such a cruel, unprovoked slaughter, at Lancaster, &c.? I hope the authors will be made examples of justice.

I congratulate thee on so elegant a present, as the charming autumn Gentian. The specimen is fine.

I was in hopes to send the names of the last specimens, but I cannot get them from SOLANDER, but I hope to do it by next conveyance.

My dear JOHN, Providence orders all things for the best. Have patience, and see how things will turn. I don't despair of thy treading paradisiacal ground, and returning loaded with spoils. Nothing concerns me, but that unlucky stroke on thy leg. * *

I am thine sincerely,

P. COLLINSON.

*   * Pray how goes on MOSES? WILLIAM was a very ingenious lad, but I am afraid made some mistakes, that I hear nothing of him.

JOHNNY seems now to be our sheet anchor.   I hope he will inherit his father's virtues, and at leisure and suitable opportunities, make nature his study.   *   *   *

JOHN BARTRAM TO P. COLLINSON.

May 1st, 1764.

DEAR PETER :—

I have received my worthy friend's letter of January 1st, 1763, I suppose it should be '64.   *   *   *

The broad-leaved Carolina *Commelyna*, and our narrow-leaved, is a late fall flower, and very different from the spring TRADE-SCANT'S Spider wort.

I had always, since ten years old, a great inclination to plants, and knew all that I once observed by sight, though not their proper names, having no person, nor books, to instruct me.   *   *

My dear friend is much mistaken to think what we call the Cuckold nut to be the common sort.   With us, one may travel a thousand miles and not see one of them ; whereas, formerly, in that distance, we might not travel half an hour without being surrounded with them.   They covered the surface of most of the best ground, for which reason they are already almost eradicated among the inhabitants, except in fence-rows, and very rocky ground ; but the others grow on the steep precipices of rocky mountains, though sometimes on declining ground.   I observed the Hazel plant in the forks of the Schuylkill, thirty years ago ; and since, in York government, and Virginia, in several places.   The fire burns them down to the ground every few years, and the old roots send up shoots some two to four feet high, which in a year or two bear nuts ; but where they grow in rich low land, they commonly grow six or eight feet high, bearing nuts four or six in a bunch.   I thought you had this sort long ago in plenty.   *   *

*   *   I have not yet consulted the Doctor's letter about snakes.   I never had an opportunity of examining the affair myself, and I can't believe reports, like him.   I intend to consider it better.

London, June 1st, 1764.

I thank my dear friend for his obliging letter of the 4th March. It gives me comfort to hear thy leg is healed. As wounds are fatal things to some constitutions, take great care for the future.

Your season in March is something like ours, for then the sharp cutting winds do our plants more damage than all the winter before.

I ought not to envy my friend's happiness, but I should like such a mistress as thou hast got, who is always treating thee with dainties. A new yellow Lily, and white *Iris*, will be fine things.

Before this comes to hand I hope thou will have received Dr. SOLANDER'S names of the specimens, sent by last packet. * *
* * * I want to go to GORDON'S, to see if he has any luck with the *Tipitiwitchet*, and the Tree of Life of Eden.

I wish we had some wealthy, public-spirited people, who would encourage a search of those fine countries,—our new acquisitions. No one so well accomplished for that work as thyself; but court politics so engross the attention of the great men, they have no room to think of anything else. It is by no means advisable to undertake it at thy own expense. Besides, unless a settled peace with Indians, who would venture ? * * *

I have from China a tree of surprising growth, that much resembles a Sumach [probably *Ailanthus glandulosa*, Desf., introduced into the United States some fifty or sixty years after the date of this letter], which is the admiration of all that see it. Perhaps thine may be the same. It endures all our winters. Thou says thine came from the East, but mentions not what country. We call ours the Varnish Tree.

I am really concerned at the present situation of your province, under the arbitrary proceedings of the Presbyterians, and the ill-concerted plan of opposition in the Governor and his party. I hope good Providence will open a way to settle these commotions.

I have read the able, spirited resolutions of your Assembly, and commend their zeal for equity and justice—hope it will have a good effect.

I am pleased with the account of thy family, and am glad JOHN inherits the spirit of his father. He will find his advantage in it.

But I am concerned that BILLY—so ingenious a lad—is, as it were, lost in indolence and obscurity.

I am pleased to hear poor MOSES, after so many imminent dangers, is got into a safe harbour, where I hope he will do well.

Spare not to draw on me, when thou can do it to advantage.

I am thy sincere friend,

P. COLLINSON.

JOHN BARTRAM TO P. COLLINSON.

August the 19th, 1764.

DEAR PETER :—

I received thine of March the 7th, 1764, with Dr. PARSONS' letter, both which are very acceptable ; and since, I received Dr. SOLANDER'S names to thé specimens I sent last fall, for which I paid half a crown postage from New York. Pray send in the merchant ships, or under cover to our friend BENJAMIN, and then I shall have them directly,—as I had thine of June the first. * *

*   *   I sent by Captain FRIEND, my Journal to Carolina and New River. Pray, let our worthy mutual friend SOLANDER peruse it. He sent several letters under cover to me, from Swede-land, which this day I delivered to Dr. WRANGEL, who is, I believe, the most indefatigable and zealous minister that ever crossed the seas, of any sect whatever. This day, as usual, he preached in our township, then came to my house, dined, read the letters I gave him, walked in the garden, discoursed a few hours, then forced to part to visit the sick in the neighbourhood, and then, though a very rainy, stormy day, he must go to town. It is surprising what pains he takes to reform the people, by tender preaching, innocent persuasion, and pious practice, that he gains the love of all socie-ties.   *   *   *   It's strange how the pretty *Empetrum* is procured. Since I brought it to Justice WYLIE'S, and told him where I got it, he has sent it several times to Charleston, but none grows ; only LAMBOLL has raised one from seed. I suppose Go-vernor DOBBS got his seed from the Justice's, as they are both Irish ; and they and the Scots will hang together like bees. * *

September 23d, 1764.

DEAR PETER :—

I received thy kind letter of June the 30th, with the Strawberry seed. The *Commelyna* I wrote to thee about many years past, presently after I found it.   *   *   *   My neighbour YOUNG'S sudden preferment has astonished great part of our inhabitants. They are daily talking to me about him, that he has got more honour by a few miles' travelling to pick up a few common plants, than I have by near thirty years' travel, with great danger and peril. It is shocking, the plants you have had, many of them known a hundred years, and most twenty or thirty, should be esteemed at court as new discoveries. Several of my friends put me upon sending my new discovered specimens to the King, to try my success. Accordingly I have put up a little box of such specimens as I am sure he never found, and I believe never came to England, before I sent them. The box I sent to thy care, with a letter to the king, under cover to thee, which pray deliver to his Majesty ; or if thee hath not freedom to do it, pray deliver it to Dr. PRINGLE, whom BENJAMIN FRANKLIN promises to acquaint with the whole affair.   *   *   *   *

If I should be appointed, by authority or private subscription, to travel through Florida or the Illinois, I am too old to go alone, and I think my son WILLIAM will be a fit person to accompany me, as he by this time, I believe, can draw well.

There is a subscription set on foot at Edinburgh, to enable a person to send them plants and seeds for their new Public Garden. They wrote to BENJAMIN to see if I would undertake it, which I did ; but how it goes on, I can't say. But I can't expect to be able many years to perform such a journey. I should spend a whole year there, to make full discoveries. Hitherto, I have travelled at my own expense, except to Onondago ; so was obliged to make haste home.

October the 15th, 1764.

DEAR PETER :—

I received thy kind letter of July the 30th, 1764, with the seeds, which were very acceptable ; since which, Captain FALCONER is arrived, by whom I have received no letters. I sent by Captain BUDDEN, by my neighbour YOUNG, my spring specimens, and a vial of Chinquapins, to try how they will do that way.

Various are the opinions of YOUNG'S success. Some think he will make such an awkward appearance at court that he will soon come back again. Others, that the Queen will take care of the German gentleman. I think that if he is put under Doctor HILL'S care, he will make a botanist, as he is very industrious and hath a good share of ingenuity.

I hope thee will find some way to forward the box I sent to thee, for the King; not that I depend on having any such preferment as YOUNG had, but chiefly as a curiosity, to see what difference will be made betwixt such rare plants as never grew in Europe or Asia, and such as have been growing in the English gardens between twenty and one hundred years past; for such, I believe, were most that YOUNG sent. But I and several others would be greatly pleased with a list of what he sent, if it could readily be obtained.

My good old friend, I am well assured that thee is well acquainted with many of the nobility, some of whom, no doubt, are men of curiosity. Could not they be prevailed upon to enable me to travel a year or two through our King's new acquisitions, to make a thorough natural and vegetable search, either by public authority, or private subscription? And I must insist upon two articles: first, that I have one to accompany me; second, to have an allowance sufficient to make full discovery, and not be hurried for time to make remarks, and carriage to transport what I discover. But I can't expect to be able to perform such a task many years hence.* I must yield to the infirmities of age, or death.

November the 22d, 1764.

DEAR PETER:—

I wrote lately by our dear worthy friend, BENJAMIN FRANKLIN, who was sent off here with the greatest demonstration of respect—in accompanying him to the ship—far beyond any that ever sailed from America. I being no party man, but wishing for the general good of the province, stayed at home, being extremely hurried

---

* He was then in his *sixty-sixth* year.

in packing, praying for the desired success; and that he may at his return home be received with as much or more applause, and triumph over his enemies.

I have sent thee and GORDON, each, a box of plants and shrubs; and now I send twenty-two boxes, consigned to thee. * * I have also sent a little box, with thy name at large, containing above one hundred different kinds of seeds, for thee and GORDON. There is a parcel of Chinquapins and Willow-Oak Acorns, that was missed in the last packed sixteen boxes, by the extreme hurry we were in for above two weeks, day and night—*First-day* not excepted. The Captain positively affirmed he would sail by such a day, and leave them if they were not brought before, and now he stays for sailors. If I had known he would have stayed so long, I might have sent every article in order.

PETER COLLINSON TO JOHN BARTRAM.

London, April 9th, 1765.

I have the pleasure to inform my good friend, that my repeated solicitations have not been in vain; for this day I received certain intelligence from our gracious King, that he had appointed thee his botanist, with a salary of fifty pounds a year; and in pursuance thereof, I received thy first half-year's payment of thy salary, being twenty-five pounds to Lady day last, which I have carried to thy account.

Now, dear JOHN, thy wishes are in some degree accomplished, to range over Georgia and the Floridas. As this is a great work, and must be accomplished by degrees, it must be left to thy own judgment how to proceed.

I hope by this packet or by next, to procure letters of recommendation to the Governors of East and West Florida; because either from them or by the aid of our friend LAMBOLL, seeds and specimens may be sent directly to me for the King.

It is a great work, but thou must contract it; and not hurry, but take time to make observations on the soil, the country, or to gather specimens of Plants, Fossils, Ores, &c., where they can conveniently be done, and not too remote for conveyance, either to Charleston, St. Augustine, or Pensacola.

Thou will do well to provide large paper, for the reception of specimens, and to get a leather cover the size of the paper to secure the specimens from wet; and leather bags for to secure the seeds from the rain.

As for living plants, it will be impossible, unless they grow not far from the sea-port.

Now, as thou knows my love for Natural History, I desire thou will provide thyself with little flat boxes fit for the pocket, and with pins, that if thou sees any species of insects, to have some contrivance to catch them, such as all sorts of Beetles, Bees, Wasps, Locusts (that is Grasshoppers, for the Cicadas, that you call Locusts, I have enough). Butterflies and Moths are too difficult to manage. Pray, look out for all sorts of Land Snails, and River Shells, one, two, or three of a sort, is enough, and any other production, that I may see the wonderful creatures of this new world. Many of these may be stuck thick together in a little box.

*   *   Whether it will not be better to go by sea to Carolina, taking thy son or a servant with thee, and there hire horses for the expedition, than taking so long a journey by land, over and over again, without meeting with anything new, this must be submitted to thy better judgment and experience to determine.

For thy health and preservation, thou hast the best wishes of thy sincere friend,

P. COLLINSON.

About a month agone, I advised my friend JOHN of the King's intention, by a Pennsylvania ship and a New York ship.

At the same time that thou art collecting seeds for the King, where thou finds plenty, thou may think on me and thy other correspondents.

London, May [1765].

I wrote, my dear JOHN, by the packet of April 12th, by way of New York, informing of him that he was appointed the King's botanist, at £50 per annum, and that I have received the first payment of £25, which is carried to account.

JOHN, thou knows nothing what it is to solicit at court any favour; nay, though it is for their own interest, they are so taken up with public affairs, little things slip through their fingers. For all I can do, I cannot get thee letters of recommendation to any of the Governors.

All I can at present do, is, our good friend ELLIS, who is appointed to an office in the Floridas, has writ to the Governors in thy favour. I send one here inclosed, and will send the other by next ship.   *   *   *   So thou must make the best of it, and do what seems most agreeable to thy own inclination. Thou may think the appointment not enough. I did not expect anything. So thou may use it, or refuse it, as thou likes best, or search as far as the salary will go to support it. In this case, I cannot advise thee.

As thou grows in years, thou will do well to consider if thy present constitution and habit of body can undergo the fatigue of such expeditions.   *   *   *

As the Colocasia seed falls into the water, and finds nourishment and protection, until it shoots forth in the spring, so if the seeds had been put immediately in a bottle of water, there would have been a probability of their growing. I put them, as soon as they came to hand, in water and mud, but none makes an offer to shoot. Pray tell me, what colour is the flower?

I have not seen YOUNG for some time. I conclude he is prosecuting his botanic studies.

I sent the fine seed-vessel of *Faba Egyptiaca* to the Queen, but heard nothing more of it.

What were the methods observed by the Indians to procure fire, before the Europeans came amongst them?

*   *   *   If BILLY goes the expedition, he may take slight sketches of such odd things, and finish afterwards. A single flower coloured, is sufficient to carry the idea.   *   *   What is become of the Bull Grape? what is its colour, and is it short jointed?

I am thine sincerely,

P. COLLINSON.

I lament the loss of my oldest correspondent, Doctor WITT. What was his age? [90 years. *See Mr.* WATSON's *Letter*, p. 86.]

Our good friend B. FRANKLIN, grows fat and jolly. There is hope of accommodation.   *   *

London, 19th September, 1765.

It was highly acceptable to me to hear of my dear JOHN's safe arrival in Carolina, and to find his botanic genius began to exert itself in new discoveries.   I wish thou may temper thy zeal with prudence, but I do not think it an instance of it, when thou and Mrs. LAMBOLL rambled in the intense heat of a midday sun. Perhaps it was to procure thee a seasoning.

A horse is a necessary article for a King's botanist.   But dost thou know who thou art to thank for that title ?   Between our-selves, *an old friend*, who knew thou deserved it; but under what character the King is pleased to rank thee, I do not know.   Only this I know, he allows thee £50 per annum.   Forty pounds [for a horse] sink deep [into the fifty], if it was sterling; but I presume that may be about ten pounds sterling.   I should think horses cheaper where they breed wild, and are had for catching.   How-ever, when thou hast done with him, the horse will be worth some-thing.

Keep an exact account of all thy expenses. I know thy economy and moderation.   But want for nothing that nature requires, if it is to be had.

I wish thou may get thy son WILLIAM to go with thee, who is a very ingenious young man, and I believe has a general knowledge in natural things, and will be very assistant in procuring them.

We have such revolutions at court, and so unsettled, I have not delivered thy specimens, until more settled times, to take due care and notice of them.

Thy brother's making so free with the King is ridiculous, and giving me a great deal of trouble at the custom-house, and himself to the expense of 6s. 6d., which I have charged to thy account, or else I must dispose of the ores to pay it.   You don't know the difficulty, trouble, and attendance, to get things to the King. Though I undertook it for thee, I shall not for anybody else.

We have had a long, hot, dry summer.   FAHRENHEIT'S ther-mometer, in my parlour, was often at 95°; and in the open air, in the shade, at 84° and 85°.   I have had little comfort this summer, for I cannot endure hot weather.   *   *   *

Doctor SOLANDER is a strange, idle man.   I cannot get thy spring specimens from him, is the reason thou hears nothing from me, about them.

It is wonderful to see the fertility of your country, in *Phlox* and *Viburnums*.   There are many things in the King's specimens that set me a longing, which I hinted to thy son JOHN, of this date.

Thine of May 29th and June 16th I answered, directed to

General Bouquet, in Florida. Pray remember me respectfully to him. The like to my most worthy friend, Mr. Lamboll, not forgetting my ingenious friend, Doctor Garden.

Now, my dear John, farewell. Thou hast the best wishes of thy old friend,

P. Collinson.

P. COLLINSON TO JOHN BARTRAM, Jr.

London, 19th September, 1765.

Friend John:—

Thy good father sends over so many fine specimens for the King, that sets our minds a longing for the plants, as under:—

*   *   *   *   *   *   *

I had the pleasure of receiving a letter from thy father—was glad to hear of his safe arrival in Carolina. I hope he may have his health, that he may be able to gratify his botanic genius, and bring the rarities of the new world to light. I wish he may get his son William to go with him, or some other companion, for it is not fit he should go alone.

I presume the boxes of seeds that I have ordered will come, as usual, by the first ships. I am thy well-wishing friend,

P. Collinson.

Thy uncle's making so free with the King to send him ores, is ridiculous,* and putting me to a great deal of trouble at the custom-house, and himself to the expense of 6s. 6d., which I have charged to thy father's account, or I must sell the ores to pay it. He don't know the difficulty and trouble to get any things to the King. Though I undertook it for thy father, I shall not for anybody else.

P. COLLINSON TO JOHN BARTRAM.

London, November 13, 1765.

I received my dear John's letter of the 28th August on the 13th November. I delayed not a minute to return this answer.

_____

* If the worthy Peter had lived to witness the manner in which *kings* have been *made free with* since his time, and especially at the present day (1848), he would probably conclude that there were *some* rather more "ridiculous" incidents about courts, than sending a few mineral specimens to Majesty.

I am concerned for thy disorder; but more, to think a wise man should have so little prudence to ramble about with Mrs. LAMBOLL in your midday sun, with such a distemper on him.   *What cannot be cured must be endured*, for I see no remedy.

We are now again on a change of the Ministry.   Whilst the members of the helm are thus fluctuating, no application can be made, for those by whom thou wast appointed have been out some time, and the set that is come in their room is expected to be changed every day.   So pray, make no more remonstrances on that head, for I am tired with a repetition of them in every letter.

Thou knows the length of the chain of fifty links; go as far as that goes, and when that's at an end cease to go any farther.

I have received two half-year's salary of £50, and shall receive £25 more in March, and so on, and if we live to Michaelmas there will be 25 more.   This will, in the whole, be £100.   Keep within this compass, and be not a loser; nay, if the King lives and thou gives him credit, thou mayst be no loser, perhaps a gainer, if you both live long enough.

I allow all thou says.   The premium is not equal to the risk; but in these precarious, unsettled times, there is no hope for an alteration.

I beg of thee, don't expose thy health; but return home and wait until thy allowance amounts to a sum in hand, and then begin again.

I am glad BILLY is with thee to take care of thee.   Pray, give my kind respects to him.

I doubt not of our good friend Mr. LAMBOLL'S care of the box. My kind respects to him.

I am, my dear JOHN, thy sincere friend,

P. COLLINSON.

Our friend Mr. ELLIS writ a letter recommending thee to Governor GRANT, which I hope he hath received.   He also wrote to the Governor of Pensacola, to the same purpose.

London, December 28, 1765.

DEAR JOHN :—

I don't know what to add to mine of November 13th, by ship Minerva, but to inform thee of my welfare and my hope for thine.

We hear with concern with what riotous mobs the public tran-
quillity is disturbed. I hope when our Parliament meets some
happy medium will be found to allay such unjustifiable proceedings
and prevent them for the future.

I condole with thee on the great loss of that worthy man,
General BOUQUET. I am sensible how it afflicts thee to be be-
reaved of so generous and kind a friend, especially in a country
where his notice and regard gave such a reputation to thy undertaking. However, I hope good Providence will raise thee up some
other friend to assist thee.

I have had a letter from thy son, informing me he was preparing
the seeds, but was fearful they would fall short to supply all my
orders, which will be a great disappointment to some.

I lately saw a quire of specimens sent by Doctor GARDEN to
Doctor RUSSELL ; amongst them are some curious new species.
When thine comes to hand, which I conclude I may hourly expect,
what high spirits will attend our friends SOLANDER and ELLIS, on
the survey of such rare and new productions !

I hope by that time this comes to hand the fine temperate
season will be near concluding. Be sure make a retreat in time,
before the great heats come on, and sit down under thy own vine,
and enjoy thy family, contemplating on the wonders thou hast seen,
and when the evenings grow long, give thy old friend a taste of
these dainties, who, thou knowest, will relish them as they deserve,
and treasure them up with the rest of thy curious and ingenious
observations.

As there are few pleasures in this life but what are subject to
alloys and disappointments, this I have lately experienced to my
no small mortification, having been again robbed of my most curious
plants. What I most regret was thy kind present of Loblolly
Bays, which throve finely ; thy sod of *Orchis* in full flower, and a
too long list to mention here. But amongst others, I regret the
loss of the long-leafed *Sarracenia*. As it is a plant of the south
countries where thou art, or may meet with it in thy passage home,
pray, contrive to get three or four plants and send me. Thou
knowest, packed up all over in moss, and tied up with moss round
each plant, is the way to send them securely.

My last was by the Minerva, November 13, which I hope is
come to hand. I therein hinted our change of Ministry, so no
hopes of additional salary. I therein advised to retire with what

discoveries and collections thou hast made, and wait until thou art re-imbursed all thy charges, and until thou hast got stock in hand, and then, if in health and strength, may make another expedition; for I don't see there is any reason, neither is it required, that a man should wear himself out to serve others, on so slender an encouragement. But I was willing to get that, with pretty good hopes of doubling it, if that Ministry had continued.

I am impatient to hear from thee, for I am fearful of the climate, and that thy ardency will push thee beyond thy strength, and I shall be glad to hear thou art got safe home ; and yet I believe it must be delightful passing an autumn, a winter, and a spring in so fine a climate.   *   *

*   *   Captain OREYS was so obliging as to deliver the quire of specimens, but times are so unsettled I keep them by me until there is a probability of more leisure to examine them. In the mean time, Doctor SOLANDER will settle them after the Linnæan system.   *   *   *

Pray, remember me sincerely and heartily to dear friend, Mr. LAMBOLL. I feel for him and sympathize with him, for the great loss that he has sustained in his son.

I hear with concern, the great commotions in the provinces, but I hope our new Ministry will set all to rights. My dear JOHN, farewell, take care of thyself.

P. COLLINSON.

My love to BILLY.

P. COLLINSON TO JOHN BARTRAM, JR.

London, March 20, 1766.

I received my friend JOHN's letter of the 7th December, and have the pleasure to tell him that all the boxes came safe and in good order, and the seeds well packed.

I am much obliged to thee for the box of plants, in particular for the pretty thyme-leaved *Kalmia*, which LINNÆUS now makes an   . It came in fine order ; as did the Sensitive Briar [*Schrankia uncinata*, Willd.], which is growing, and it was kind to add Loblolly Bay ; for the rogues came twelve miles to rob my garden about two months agone, and stole two fine Loblolly Bays, all I had, and many other curious American plants, too long to mention. But we are now getting an act of Parliament to punish them, by transporting them to you, which you will not thank us for.

The last letter I received from thy father was from Savannah town, September 28th, and it came to my hands January 15th. * * * I shall be glad to hear he is safe come home. From thy friend,

P. COLLINSON.

P. COLLINSON TO JOHN BARTRAM.

London, March 26th, 1766.

I received my dear JOHN's letter of September 28th,—highly delighted with the rich cargo that the letter promised, but, (sad story to tell!) when I came to see Captain ARBUCKLE, he said no such box directed for me was put on board him. But he promised to search everywhere; and next time I saw him could find nothing, and was sure that there was no such box put on board him. Think, my dear friend, what disappointment and vexation I was under at this great loss. The only way to have prevented it lay at thy door; and that by having a receipt of the captain for the box, and inclosing it in thy letter to me. Then I should have demanded the box with authority, and made him pay damages if it was lost; but now I had only thy letter to show, and that he did not regard, and said thou might intend to put the box on board, but never did it.

The boxes of seeds came all safe and well, and thy son had packed them very careful. I was pleased to find he was so capable to supply thy place. * * * One trouble seldom comes alone, for it gives me much concern to hear of your troublesome, dangerous journey, from Georgia to St. Augustine. It was a great pity you attempted it at so unseasonable a time.

Thou vexes thyself and me with perpetual complaints, thinking it is in my power to redress them; but really it lays too much at thy own door, in being so hasty for the expedition. Thou should have staid and got two or three hundred pounds beforehand, and then set out. But, as I told thee before, if thou lives, and the King lives, thou will be no loser, so pray do not tire me any more with repetition of complaints, but return home as soon as thou can, and sit down and gather strength, and receive thy income.

It is very fortunate to have so good an opportunity to go to the Congress at Picolata.

Your work for the Duke of Cumberland is fruitless, for the British hero is no more.

The odd scene that an old Spanish town must make to an Englishman, must afford him entertainment, to see the different modes of the two nations, in their buildings, &c., and I apprehend the rural prospects must be fine, and afford a variety of rare plants, &c.

In this happy climate, turn where one will, new beauties rise. Little did I think some months agone, nature's virgin charms were reserved to be rifled by an enterprising BARTRAM ; but pray, take care that we are not deprived of these precious spoils. The loss of the last hangs heavily on the mind of thy old friend,

P. COLLINSON.

Pray, remember me to BILLY. I am much concerned for the disasters that befel him.

March 27th.—My dear JOHN, I have good news to tell thee. The box that thou intended by Captain ARBUCKLE, is safe arrived by Captain BALL, at Dover ; advised of it by a very civil letter from Mr. GRAHAM, inclosing the captain's receipt for it.

P. COLLINSON TO JOHN BARTRAM, Jr.

London, May 5th, 1766.

I had the satisfaction of my kind friend JOHN BARTRAM's, Jr., letter, March 1st ; and Captain SPARKS was so very obliging to bring me the box of fossils, which contains many curious articles, which, I am sensible, there must be some trouble in getting toge-ther. But one cannot tell what judgment to form from these rude masses, because every *stratum* varies, as there may be many on the side of the cliff. So no conclusions can be drawn, but on the spot. Those fossils that contain shells, are most acceptable to me, as something that's probable may be drawn from them.   *   *   *   In fossil wood it is wonderful to see how the lapidescent juices have entered into all the pores of the wood, &c.   I have some large pieces of Hickory, two or three feet long, so very completely saturated with petrifying matter, that it is become real stone.

It is a very fine discovery, the finding that species of stone, for the mills, for we are obliged to have all our stones that grind wheat from France.　*　*　*　*

Amongst the millions [of fossil remains] that thou observes, are all over the country, I dare say they are found of different shapes and sizes, which may determine the species. These are undoubted evidences that the sea once covered the level country, to near the foot of the first hills; and in retreating, left these marine animals behind.　*　*　*　When this great event happened, or from what cause, is locked up amongst the arcana of Providence, beyond human penetration.　*　*　* I long to hear of thy father's return, and to know how it fares with him. It is now a long time since I had any letter. But it was very lucky I got the box from Georgia, with thy father's Journal, which I value more than all the rest, and some of BILLY's fine drawings. I am glad to see that he has not lost that curious art, which so few attain. I wish it could any way turn to his profit.

I am no stranger to the native Bread of Carolina and Virginia. It's a *Tuber terræ*, or Earth Fungus. I have it sent me, near as big as my head. In time of want it is of great importance to the Indians. They call it *Tuckahoe*.　*　*　*

Now, friend JOHN, farewell.

P. COLLINSON.

P. COLLINSON TO JOHN BARTRAM.

Mill Hill, May 28th, 1766.

I received my dear JOHN's, from Carolina, and accepted thy bill for £150. 5s. 8d.

I think thou hast done prudently, to settle thy son WILLIAM: for he is an ingenious young man, and I hope his ingenuity will prompt him to industry, to improve the talent, that, in thy paternal goodness, thou hast bestowed on him. I wish I could tell how to write to him, without any expense to him, to give him my friendly advice, as I have a great respect for him. But one thing is not to be omitted, and that is, to get him a virtuous, industrious wife, such as knows how to share the toils, as well as the comforts of a marriage state. He will not settle rightly to business until this is done; for then home will be always agreeable to him. If this is not done, he'll fall into the snares of a loose, unlawful way of life, from whence no good can come, but much evil and inconvenience.

I have read thy Journal over and over, with much entertainment; but observe, by the specimens, that nature seems to have exhausted her stores in the Carolinas, in the variety of the *Magnolias*, Loblolly Bays, Allspice, *Stuartias*, Red Acacias, *Halesias*, &c. I think Georgia affords no new plants equal to any of these. There are, indeed, some pretty things, but they are not striking flowering trees, like the above.

My dear JOHN, I wonder thou should trouble thyself about the Queen, as she has YOUNG, and everything will be shown him. It cannot be expected he will favour any one's interest but his own. He is now so new modelled, and grown so fine and fashionable, with his hair curled and tied in a black bag, that my people, who have seen him often, did not know him. I happened not to be at home, so could not inquire what scheme he is upon.

I shall be glad to hear that thou art safely returned home, and in such good health and spirits as will permit thee to sit down calmly to reflect with thankfulness on the pleasures and dangers past.

I have sent the three quires of specimens to the King, with the seeds. It was a great disadvantage to the specimens that they had suffered by wet. However, Doctor SOLANDER could discover many new, undescribed articles, amongst them, as well as those from Georgia and Florida.

Thy short account of St. Augustine was very acceptable, to see the buildings of the Spaniards, and other of their contrivances. Pray, tell me what sort of improvements they have made in the country, for the support of themselves and their cattle; what sort of fabric was their church, no doubt all the ornaments they carried away; and further tell me, if there are any true genuine Spaniards, tempted by their possessions to remain there. I think its situation is pleasant. If no Spaniards are left, it must be a great advantage to the English new settlers to enter on their premises, and possess their improvements, which I suspect, from their native sloth and laziness, are inconsiderable; for a Spaniard is content with a very little, provided he can but indulge himself with sitting in the sun and doing next to nothing.

In all thy expeditions, didst thee fall in with any Indians? What nation? and how did they behave? Is there a disposition in them to continue in peace and friendship? There is much talk of civilizing them. A good, sensible man, named HAMMERER, a foreigner, who was long in London, could not be easy without going to reside among the Cherokees, in order to try to bring them to a sense of moral duties.

I have heard that the *Opuntia*, or Indian Fig, grows in such abundance at Augustine, that the fruit was a great food of the inhabitants. Is it a different species from those at New York? I conclude the Palmetto arrives to a greater size than those in Carolina.

*   *   *   *

BILLY'S elegant drawings are admired by all that see them. When he comes to be settled I must get him to look out for insects of any kind, for in his warm, southern situation,* these creatures increase in size and beauty, with many new species that you have not. When thou writes to him, pray give my respects and thanks for his curious presents.

I don't forget my honest friend MOSES, who sent me a very sensible, respectful letter; and remember me to our young botanist, thy son JOHNNY.

People begin to be tired with the same seeds over and over again. Could no plan be formed for BILLY to send seeds from Georgia, to make a little new variety in your cargoes?   *   *

So now, dear JOHN, farewell.

P. COLLINSON.

Mr. EHRET, our famous flower painter, was with me, and I showed him BILLY'S paintings. He admired, as we do all, his fine Red Centaury; a most elegant plant, if we can but get it in our gardens. His butterflies are nature itself. His yellow fly is admirable.

I am pleased to see that he has got so pretty a way of drying fish. By it, we may have a *Hortus siccus*, or rather, *Oceanus*

---

* About this time, "BILLY" took a notion to settle on a plantation, on the River St. John, in Florida, where he soon found himself in a very forlorn "situation." *See the letter* of HENRY LAURENS to JOHN BARTRAM, August 9, 1766.

siccus of fish !   When I see SOLANDER, he will tell me the species, and if it is new will inform thee.   *   *   *

JOHN BARTRAM TO P. COLLINSON.

Schuylkill, at my own house, June, 1766.

DEAR PETER :—

I am now returned to my family ; all of whom I found in good health.   God almighty be praised for his favours.   I am at present tolerable well,.but can hardly get over the dreadful sea-sickness and the southward fever.

I have left my son BILLY in Florida.   Nothing will do with him now, but he will be a planter upon St. John's River, about twenty-four miles from Augustine, and six from the Fort of Picolata. This frolic of his, and our maintenance, hath drove me to great straits ; so that I was forced to draw upon thee, at Augustine, and twice at Charleston.   *   *   *

I have brought home with me, a fine collection of strange Florida Plants ; which, perhaps, I may send sometime this summer, some for the King and some for thyself.   But I want to know how those I sent from Charleston and Georgia are accepted, or those I sent last spring to the King, from home.   I hope what specimens I sent for thyself will give thee great pleasure, as many of them are entirely new ; the collecting of which hath cost thy friend many score pounds, pains, and sickness, which held me constantly near or quite two months; in Florida, the fever and jaundice ; and a looseness through North and South Carolina, and Georgia ; yet, some how or other, I lost not an hour's time of travelling through those provinces ; and when at Augustine, with the fever and jaundice, I travelled both by water and land all round the town for many miles, and to Picolata, to the Congress, although so weak as hard set to get up to bed ; and during the meeting of the Governor and Indians, in the Pavilion, I was forced to sit or lie down upon the ground, close by its side, that I might observe what passed.

PETER COLLINSON TO JOHN BARTRAM.

London, August 21, 1766.

I received my dear JOHN's letter of June 30th.   *   *

The Florida Seeds and Fossils came safe, and were delivered to the King, who is pleased with them.

I am much concerned for thy ulcer. Doctor FOTHERGILL is gone out of town for two months, else would have sent thee his advice. But you have, I should think, skilful people at Philadelphia, though a good old woman's nostrum has carried the prize from them 'all. Pray, consult some Indians: they have done wonders in obstinate cases by their simples.

I believe our friend WILLIAM LOGAN's correspondent is GORDON. No one packs better, although thou had bad luck.   *   *

*   *   *   *

My friend JOHN makes no allowance for letters miscarrying, when seeds don't come that he writ for. Repeat them every letter. Remember, the widow in the Gospel succeeded at last by her importunity.

The *Stuartia* flowered for the first time in the Princess of Wales' Garden, at Kew, which is the Paradise of our world, where all plants are found, that money or interest can procure. When I am there, I am transported with the novelty and variety; and don't know which to admire first or most.

I am ruined with two great robberies; so I cannot stand in any competition. Once, I bore the bell; but now, I very humbly condescend to be on an equal footing with my neighbours. We have got an Act passed this session to transport the rogues; but we must first catch them, and that's not easily done, as they come by night.   *   *   *   *

Now, my dear JOHN, farewell.

P. COLLINSON.

We have had a tedious, uncommon wet summer, which threatened distress and famine; but more than two weeks past good Providence has sent us fine, seasonable, warm, dry weather, for our harvest, and our crops are reported to be plentiful. I dare say thou wonders at my ignorance in this matter, but thy wonder will cease when I tell thee I go every week twelve miles, and don't see a cornfield. Nay, I may go two or three miles further, and not see it; for our country is an evergreen country,—all grass for hay, but no dairies. Our fields feed cattle for the slaughter, and afford pasturage for sheep that suckle lambs. All the winter—at Christmas—I see the lambkins play in the open fields all around me, and hear their tender bleatings, which is pastoral and rural.

JOHN BARTRAM TO P. COLLINSON.

August 26th, 1766.

DEAR PETER :—

I wrote to thee last week by the brig Elizabeth, Captain GOLLEY; the day after which I received thy kind letter, the last date of which was June the 6th. Am glad to hear thy acceptance of my bill for £150. 5s. 8d., and that from Augustine ; and shall be pleased with the acceptance of another from Augustine and Charleston, and to know how our accounts stand. But I am afraid all will be thrown away upon him [WILLIAM]. He is so whimsical, and so unhappy, as not to take any of his friends' advice. Mr. DE BR—— wanted him to go with him to draw draughts for him, in his survey of Florida ; but BILLY would not, though by that journey he would have had the finest opportunity of seeing the country and its productions.

I have forgot what part of my journal I sent thee from Augustine, except the Thermometrical observations. I allow that these flowering trees thee mentions, in Carolina, are very fine, most of which grow in Georgia and Florida; but then there grow, in both these last places, many more curious evergreen trees and shrubs, which, if not so beautiful in flowers, come fully up with those, and perhaps surpass them in beauty of fruit, and sweet scent, as may be observed by my specimens gathered on the banks of St. John's River.

I am obliged to thee for sending the specimens to the King, and also thy advice about the Queen. I sent, last spring, the seeds I collected in East Florida.

Augustine, now, is in a very ruinous condition to what it was when the Spaniards lived there. The soldiers have pulled down above half the town, for the sake of the timber, to burn. Most of the best houses stand yet, several of which are much altered by the English, who drive the chimney through the tops of the house roofs, and the sun begins to shine through glass, where before its light was admitted between the bannisters; and where the well-cultivated gardens were, it is now grown over with weeds, and is the common pasture for cattle. Many of the Orange trees and Figs, near or quite a foot in diameter, cut down or grubbed up for firewood; for the English don't make such use of the sour Oranges as the Spaniards. Lemons, Limes, and Guavas, are chiefly taken care of; but the two latter are most of them killed (especially the branches) last winter. So were the Bananas. As for the Figs, and Pomegranates, the English are not very fond of them.

I saw two of the *Opuntias*, as thick as my middle, and six feet high, much branched. They seemed to be nearly the same kind with ours; but I am apt to think the fruit the Spaniards ate so much of, was the species of Huica [*Yucca ?*], with terrible sharp spines at the ends of their leaves, which some call Adam's Needles, others, Palmetto Royal, and some Bananas, from their fruit, which is sweet, with a little bitterness, and is the chief fencing about Augustine, both against man and beast, and is frequently planted on their sandy ditch-banks.*

As for the Spanish improvements, I suppose formerly they had made some, both considerable and extensive, there being the vestiges of large roads to several distant parts of St. John's River, and many miles beyond it.† But since the Creek Indians, by the help of the English, turned their arms against the Spaniards, they have been cooped up within their own fortifications, and could not till any ground out of the reach of their cannon balls, neither could they keep any cattle out of sight, or cut a stick without a guard. The Indians in both these provinces profess a strict friendship, and perhaps will keep to it, if the English don't give them just occasion to break out. There are but very few Spaniards at Augustine, I think but one of any account. There were four churches

* There is some uncertainty as to the precise plant here intended, but the reference seems to be to the *Yucca gloriosa*, L. Mr. ELLIOT describes the fruit as a " *capsule*, oblong, glabrous, *pulpy*," yet I was not aware that any of the species yielded an esculent pericarp.

† For an interesting sketch and comparative view of the condition and appearance of this region, *half a century subsequent* to the date of this letter, see the correspondence of Dr. WILLIAM BALDWIN, who visited St. Augustine in the spring of 1817.

belonging to the town, two in it, and the others very near. One was the Dutch church, with a steeple, and stone cupola. They are built of hewn stone. The more particular description of them, see in my Journal.   *   *   *   *

                                           December the 5th, 1766.
DEAR FRIEND PETER :—
    I have packed up, and shipped, and consigned these following boxes to thy care.   *   *   *   P. C. No. 11, on the top are plants in earth, for the King.   *   *   *   P. C. No. 17, plants in earth, a present to thee. If it is disagreeable to thee to have so many boxes consigned to thee, of other people's, pray let me know, and I shall forbear.   *   *   *   I have packed up a great variety of curious seeds, for thee and GORDON ; and a little parcel of very curious fresh Florida seeds, for our friend ELLIS, in remembrance of his kind recommendation to the Governor of Florida. They were sent to me by Mrs. LAMBOLL, with whom I left a share, which she sowed immediately, and some of them produced good seed, of which I send thee a share ; as also a few to our gracious King, which pray send to him, with the box No. 11, of plants.
    I am surprised that YOUNG is come back so soon. He cuts the greatest figure in town, struts along the streets, whistling, with his sword and gold lace, &c. He hath been three times to visit me —pretends a great respect for me. He is just going to winter in the Carolinas ; saith there is three hundred pounds sterling annually settled upon him.
    But Captain CHANCELOR tells odd stories of him : that he was put in prison, from whence he was taken by two officers, and put on board ship ; but his friends utterly deny it. It's pity but the truth was known, and the lying party snubbed.
    *   *   *   *December* 10th, 1766.—This day I met Captain FALCONER in the street. He spoke very civilly to me, and told me he had been with thee, and seemed to be wonderfully pleased with thy agreeable company and entertainment. He told me he intended to sail for London early next spring. This, I hope, will be a 'fine opportunity of sending thee my true and general Journal, and the plants I found up St. John's River.   *   *

PETER COLLINSON TO JOHN BARTRAM.

London, February 10th, 1767.

On the 4th February, I received my friend JOHN's letters of December 6th and 10th, which came very seasonable to relieve all our fears : for the seeds, the people were impatient, and, indeed, I was very uneasy for thy welfare, under such terrible disorders. It gives me comfort to find thou art perfectly restored ; as I know the value of health, and partake of it in a degree beyond most men ; therefore, I feel the more for my friends who are deprived of that blessing of blessings.

I am glad thou hast sent some plants and seeds to our gracious King, as thy annuity is regularly paid. I dare say any of thy Journals would be very acceptable to him ; could they be copied fair ?   Send him every year one ; for he must not be cloyed by too much at once. Begin with the first after thou received the salary. This would keep thee in his memory.

I presume, Doctor HOPE, Professor of Botany, hath wrote to thee of the boxes being detained at Chester, and had them not until this winter, by which he thinks the seeds are spoiled. *   *

I am glad the Colocasia is put in water. Now there is hope of success in my ponds. I long for a good painting of the flower ; but am much concerned for WILLIAM's unsteady conduct. Nothing but marrying will settle him. With a prudent, discreet woman, he may return to Florida, and amend his conduct.   *   *

I had rather all the plants had been left than the *Agave*, which I have longed to see all my life ; writ to CLAYTON and others, but never could get it ; did not think it grew so far to the northward, as with you. Pray, send a good specimen of it in full flower. Pray, what is the seed-vessel ?   *   *   *

It is late, so, my dear JOHN, adieu.

P. COLLINSON.

I believe there is too much truth in what the Captain says about YOUNG. He may live to repent his folly and extravagance. Such an opportunity lost is never to be regained, unless he has better fortune than he deserves. As a friend, I advised him often to economy and industry, and not sacrifice everything to his pleasures ;

for I foresaw, by his way of going on, how it must end; for I
knew his salary could by no means support his expensive way of
living.

Mill Hill, April 10, 1767.

I wrote my old friend largely of February 10th, so have not a
great deal to add; but, lest that should miscarry, this will inform
thee all the boxes came safe and in good order. That for Doctor
HOPE, I forwarded to Edinburgh.   *   *

Think, my dear JOHN, by length of time your country productions are most, if not all naturalized in our gardens; but some few
delicate things will be always acceptable, as thyme-leaved *Kalmia*.

I have a sweet plant thy son JOHN sent me last year, which
thrives finely and flowered as beautiful, and is now set thick with
flower-buds.   *   *   *

The plants and seeds for the King were carefully delivered, and
no doubt but were acceptable. The honour of giving is sufficient;
but there is no notice taken of the freight and other charges; so I
believe must be carried to thy account; but then, consider, thy
salary is regularly paid.   *   *   Our friend ELLIS thanks thee for
his present of seeds.

JOHNNY sent me what thou calls a Deciduous Bay, which thrives
well; but pray, tell me how it comes by that name.

The *Sarracenia* promises well. I was pleased to see it come,
for the rogues stole our fine old plants.   *   *

Doctor FOTHERGILL tells me he has ordered some roots of *Colocasia* to be dragged up for him, and sent over in a cask of water
[See his letters to HUMPHRY MARSHALL]; so I hope, by one way or
another, we shall see this beautiful plant. But I have had no
description of the flower from any one that has seen it. I want
much a particular description, but much more a drawing from
BILLY's inimitable pencil. But if he is with you, I am afraid he
is under such dejection from his late disappointments, that he has
not spirits to undertake such a business.

I have often thought what a pity it is that his ingenuity could
not be of service to him. I have, for years past, been looking out
for him, but no opening has offered. The difficulties to introduce
an entire stranger, are insurmountable; for whilst he is attempting
to make himself known, he may be starving, which has been the

case of some ingenious people in his way (that I have known) that have been foreigners. If my advice may have any weight with him, it is, to get him a good, notable wife,—a farmer's daughter, and return to his estate, and set his shoulders heartily to work to improve it. A moderate industry goes a great way, too, (in so fine a climate,) to supply the belly, as little is wanting for the back.

The *Spigelia* I have in great prosperity; but I lament the loss of the *Agave*. For more than thirty years past, I have wished for it. If all the plants had been left, and that sent, I should not have regretted so much. I see the heart must not be set on anything. I dare say it never was in England. A drawing of it in flower would be quite new. I suppose it is so succulent there is no curing a specimen.   *   *   *

*   *   * Puccoon [*Sanguinaria*] and *Claytonia*, in flower, April 5th.

Don't it make thee smile? I set out to say little, and now I scrawl on; for I know thou loves long stories. It's past ten o'clock: so good night.

P. COLLINSON.

Pray, send specimen of BEE's flower.

PETER COLLINSON TO WILLIAM BARTRAM.*

Mill Hill, July 28, 1767.

I am extremely obliged to my very ingenious friend, WILLIAM BARTRAM, for so many instances of his respect and regard for his

---

* WILLIAM BARTRAM, the fourth son of JOHN BARTRAM, and twin brother of ELIZABETH BARTRAM, was born on the 9th of February, in the year 1739, at the Botanic Garden, Kingsessing, near Philadelphia. He was educated at the old College, in Philadelphia, under the care of CHARLES THOMSON, afterwards the well-known Secretary of the Revolutionary Congress. Early in life he manifested a considerable talent for drawing, especially in delineating objects of Natural History, and this predilection occasioned some delay and difficulty in deciding upon a profession. At one time he inclined to be a printer; next, an engraver; but he was finally, at the age of eighteen years, placed with a respectable merchant of Philadelphia, where he continued about four years; after which he went to North Carolina, with a view of doing business there as a merchant; but being ardently attached to the study of Botany he soon relinquished his mercantile pursuits (in which he was rather unsuccessful), and accompanied his father in a journey into East Florida, to explore the natural productions of that

good father's old friend. I am glad to see amongst so many disappointments, which give me concern, the spirit of ingenuity is not

country ; after which, he settled on the River St. Johns, in that region, and commenced the cultivation of indigo, but soon abandoned this business in consequence of bad health, and returned about the year 1767 to his father's residence. In 1772, at the request of Doctor FOTHERGILL, of London, he embarked for Charleston, South Carolina, in order to examine the natural productions of the Floridas, and the western parts of Carolina and Georgia, chiefly in the vegetable kingdom. In this employment he was engaged nearly five years, and made numerous contributions to the Natural History of the country through which he travelled. His collections and drawings were forwarded to Doctor FOTHERGILL, who defrayed the expenses of the expedition ; and in the year 1791, he published an account of his travels and discoveries, in one volume, small 8vo, with an account of the manners and customs of the Creeks, Seminoles, and other tribes of Indians. This work, though shockingly disfigured by typographical errors, soon acquired extensive popularity, and is still frequently consulted.

After his return from his travels, WILLIAM BARTRAM devoted himself to Science ; and in 1782, was elected Professor of Botany in the University of Pennsylvania, which post he declined, in consequence of the state of his health. In 1786, he was elected a member of the American Philosophical Society ; and he was also a member of several other learned Societies in Europe and America. We are indebted to him for the knowledge of many curious and beautiful plants peculiar to North America, and for the most complete and correct list of American Birds, prior to the work of WILSON, who was greatly assisted (and, in fact, was induced to undertake that splendid production, the *American Ornithology*), by the co-operation and encouragement afforded by WILLIAM BARTRAM.

The Botanic Garden, established by his father, was inherited by his brother JOHN, and has descended to JOHN's only surviving child, ANNE, the wife of Colonel ROBERT CARR ; but WILLIAM BARTRAM was taken into partnership by his brother JOHN for many years, and subsequently volunteered his assistance until the death of JOHN, in 1812. After that, he resided at the garden, in the family of Colonel CARR. Although so often exhorted to matrimony by his venerable and judicious friend, PETER COLLINSON, WILLIAM BARTRAM was never married. He was a very ingenious mechanic, and fond of using tools ; but his greatest delight was in drawing and painting. In this employment, he laboured much for others. The late Professor BARTON in the preface to his *Elements of Botany* (published in 1803), speaks of services rendered as follows :—" The greater number of the plates by which the work is illustrated, have been engraven from the original drawings of Mr. WILLIAM BARTRAM, of Kingsessing, in the vicinity of Philadelphia. While I thus publicly return my thanks to this ingenious naturalist, for his kind liberality in enriching my work, I sincerely rejoice to, have an opportunity of declaring, how much of my happiness in the study of Natural History has been owing to my acquaintance with him ; how often I have availed myself of his knowledge in the investigation of the natural productions of our native country ; how sincerely I have loved him for the happiest union of moral integrity with original genius, and unaspiring science, for which he is eminently distinguished. ' *Sero in cœlum redeat.*' "

In his latter years, WILLIAM BARTRAM found a pleasing intellectual resource in the contemplation of the vegetable beauties around him, and was particularly

quite sunk and lost. It would give me and thyself pleasure, if it was productive of real advantage, and brought grist to the mill. Time, industry, and application, bring things to pass that were not expected. I can truly say, I have never had thee long from my mind, and watched for any opening that might prove advantageous ; but fortune has not thrown any in my way ; and to come over on speculation and uncertainty will never do.

I have shown thy performances to many, who deservedly admire and commend them, in hopes to find encouragement, but none as yet has offered. Yet, as we all have our diversions and amusements, perhaps there is not any one, in which the artist exhibits superior talents, than in drawing and painting, which must highly gratify an ingenious mind.

When art is arrived to such perfection to copy close after nature, who can describe the pleasure, but them that feel it, to see the moving pencil display a sort of paper creation, which may endure for ages, and transfer a name with applause to posterity ! I have now before me those elegant masterly drawings, inclosed in thy good father's Journal. It's with concern and regret, that I see so much skill lavished away on such vile paper, that deserves the finest vellum. But I suppose necessity had no law,—no other was to be had. Poorly set off as they are, they have been much admired by the best judges. I am preparing to secure them, by fixing them on the best paper, that so many delicate touches, and the many-laboured strokes, may not be exposed to accidents.

The numbers and figures on the drawings, I apprehend, refer to some description, but I can find none, which is mortifying ; for though the representation is to the life, yet some particular information will make the Natural History complete. Pray send it by the very first opportunity. I was in hopes the numbers and figures referred to, were to be found in thy father's Journal, but they do not correspond.   *   *   *

The Aromatic Evergreen is a new and very curious shrub. I hope I shall find some account of it in the quire of specimens.

gratified by the visits of botanical friends. He wrote an article on the natural history of a plant, a few minutes before his death, which happened suddenly, by the rupture of a blood-vessel in the lungs, July 22, 1823, in the 85th year of his age.—*See Encyclopædia Americana.*

But its seed-vessel is very like what we have from the East Indies, by the name of the *Anisum stellatum*.

Thy sincere friend,

P. COLLINSON.

PETER COLLINSON TO JOHN BARTRAM.

Mill Hill, July 31st, 1767.

My dear JOHN hath at last gratified my longing wishes with the sight and perusal of his laborious, entertaining Journal, full of fine discoveries, useful reflections, and pertinent observations.

I can take a squib from JOHN BARTRAM, without the least resentment. Friends may be allowed to rally one another, when it is not done in anger, or sharp resentment, which I never intended, however my words may be taken.

If I can be thought too quick, my dear JOHN, thou wast too slow, and so we will let the matter go.

The King's specimens came safe, and are delivered; and that's all I ever know about them. I am much obliged for those directed to me; there are many new, curious plants among them. If I have time, I will give thee Dr. SOLANDER'S observations on them, who is a very acute botanist, little inferior to LINNÆUS; and not only in Botany, but in all branches of Natural History. Think how happy I am, at this present writing, to have the two Doctors, FRANKLIN and SOLANDER, my guests for a few days, to enjoy the delights of Mill Hill.　　*　　*　　*　　*

The *Agave* I have long known, but never imagined it was to be found so far northeast as with you, was the reason I never mentioned it; and what I wonder, thou hast never sent me a specimen of so singular and so rare a plant, in all thy collections.

The *Spigelia* is a pretty plant, and a curious flower. I have three roots, by the generosity of our common friend LAMBOLL. It is just now going to flower. I had it many years agone, but, in dividing the root, lost it; as I once did the evergreen *Veratrum*, and Skunk Weed; so I shall never try the experiment again.

*　　　*　　　*　　　*　　　*

I dare say the *Guilandina* will be the Bonduc, that I and others have in our gardens. I conclude some Indian traders brought the nuts to Quebec, from thence to France, and so the French believe

 KALAMAZOO VALLEY COMMUNITY COLLEGE LIBRARY

it grows in Canada, but they never could tell where. I always believed it a southern tree, yet it endures all our winters. How could my dear JOHN forget to send me some nuts, one at least? It would have helpt to guess what it is. My tree shoots strongly. I think its pinnated leaves are something akin to the Angelica tree.

The Wild Lime [*Nyssa candicans*, Mx.] is a singular plant. Dr. SOLANDER wishes for its fructifications. At that season the flowers could not be expected; but probably the fruit lay under the trees,—and yet none sent—is a disappointment; because the like opportunity may not offer again. Some of these nuts should have been carefully sent to the King, for the Kew Garden, where are all conveniences for raising and protection.

It is well known the New England people brought over Bees, and they may have spread to the Blue Mountains; but they never could have reached to the wilds of Florida; and it is well known the Spaniards have no curiosity, and but little industry. I take the Florida Bees to be Aborigines.   *   *   *

* * I was a long time in hopes of the *Faba Egyptiaca*, but now I doubt. The nuts have been kept constantly in water, and are yet very fresh, but they do not germinate. I was in hopes the colour was like the Chinese, of a fine red shade. If BILLY comes, I wish a drawing could be made, as there is no drying the flower so as to give any good idea of it, being so rare a plant. Suppose a drawing of the *Faba* was made, and sent to the King,—of the leaf, flower, and seed-vessel, in a picturesque figure as growing in the water; but it must be on a contracted scale, for no sized paper will take in the leaves, &c.

I have BILLY'S seven charming drawings before me,—have been just now pasting them on paper to secure them.   *   *

*   *   *   *   *   *   *

I have read thy Journal once over, and am beginning again, to make my remarks as I go along, and shall communicate as opportunity offers.

So, my dear JOHN, wishing thee health, which I am much concerned to hear is so precarious. Cupping used to relieve much my brother, for dizziness in his head. Doctor FOTHERGILL is gone out of town for two months. However, I shall write to him for advice. Am, in the interim, thy sincere friend, in perfect health,

                                                  P. COLLINSON.

I don't remember thy finding the Red Acacia. It has been so loaded with flowers, I am obliged to prop up the branches. It is the glory of our gardens, and flowers twice a year. I think it one of the finest trees of America.   *   *   *

I have sent thy case to Doctor FOTHERGILL, who resides in Cheshire for two months, to get rid of too much practice. If it comes time enough, will send it by this ship. I wish it may, for thou art in a bad way.

Mill Hill, September 19th, 1767.

I cannot let this ship sail without inquiring after my dear JOHN and family's welfare, and acquainting him with mine. I am, thank God, in perfect health, no complaints of any sort attending me; I wish my old friend could say the like.

I hope thou hast mine, with Doctor FOTHERGILL's advice, by, I think, Captain FALCONER, with a box of Tulips and Hyacinths, a present from JAMES GORDON, Jr., an ingenious young man who deserves thy encouragement, for he has a garden of his own.

This day thy countryman, Doctor KUHN, and Doctor SOLANDER, dined with me here. He will tell thee of the prosperity of my garden, and how all thy kind presents flourish, being now arrived to some magnitude and perfection. Unless something new and rare, don't trouble thyself in my behalf.

*   *   *   *

Thou canst scarcely think, my dear JOHN, what I have been for some time employed about: then I will tell thee. After perusing thy entertaining Journal, two or three times, I found so many curious articles blended together, in the length of seventy-nine pages, that it was impossible to find them out, after a tedious search. If there had been a large margin left on the sheets, then note of the principal matters would have led to the principal subjects on that page. But as there was no room left for this, I then determined to compose three *indexes*. In the *first* I selected all thy botanic discoveries; in the first column the page of thy Journal, next the particular place, then enumerating the plants there found. This is contained in two sheets of paper, which I can presently run over, and see the produce of each place in each province. The *second* contained all thy remarks and observations, abridged, on the petrified rocks and bluffs. This comprehends a sheet, and from this view it is wonderful to think what was the original state of all the lower country, throughout all our colonies, once, undoubtedly covered by the sea ; but what great revolution in nature brought about this extensive retreat of the ocean, who can pretend to say ?

The *third* index contains all the remarkable things not comprehended under the other two. All have the pages annexed ; so that for a further explanation, I can immediately have recourse to the article itself.

Now, any curious friend can be entertained, that hath not leisure to peruse seventy-nine pages ; yet, what I have done can only serve for private amusement. It is too short an abstract for publication ; and the original wants more pains and leisure than I am master of, to dress it fit for the public, which gives me no little concern, that so many useful discoveries should lie concealed.

What fills us with admiration is the wonderful fossil presents, of elephant's teeth, &c., sent over to Lord SHELBURNE, and our friend BENJAMIN FRANKLIN, by GEORGE CROGHAN. Elephants were never known in America; and yet the great fossil teeth of elephants, found under a high bank on the sides of the great lick, near the River Ohio, would force one to believe, by their vast remains, that they once existed there. Some of these great tusks, or teeth, were entire, near seven feet long, and of the thickness of common Elephant's teeth, of that length. But what increases the wonder and surprise is, that with these long teeth (which are fine ivory), is found great numbers of grinding teeth ; but the marvel is, they are not the grinding teeth of Elephants, as we have recent Elephant grinders to compare them with. So that this phenomenon must be resolved into this conclusion ;—that these remains that GEORGE CROGHAN says are at least of thirty animals, are some vast creatures, with the long teeth or tusks of Elephants, but with great grinders belonging to some animal not yet known. This affords room for endless reflection and admiration,   *   *

*   *   *   *

We have had a continual dripping summer ; but yet some intervals to get in the harvest, which is plentiful, that I hope will soon reduce the high price of bread.

Now, dear JOHN, farewell,

P. COLLINSON.

Mill Hill, 25th December, 1767.

I had the pleasure of my dear JOHN's letter of the 14th September, which is full of many entertaining articles. It is with you
as it is with us. It was a long while before some of your plants
could be reconciled to our culture ; but since we have found that
planting them in our bog earth, and making artificial bogs, I don't
remember any plant of yours, now, but what takes a liking to our
country. It may be the same with you, when you have found a
proper soil, and management.   *   *   *

My dear JOHN, don't be astonished at anything. We remember
and forget, forget and remember. Some years agone I wanted the
Agave ; being disappointed, I thought no more of it ; but looking
over the *Flora Virginica*, it revived again ; and so we go on, until
we forget ourselves, and are soon forgot.

We have no luck with the *Colocasia*, so give it over ; BILLY's
fine drawing will supply that defect.

About the latitude 40° is generally allowed to be the finest
climate for habitation. Rome, Constantinople, and Madrid, and
others under it, are celebrated by travellers for their temperature,
and choice vegetable productions. To find so remarkable a difference with you, is very incomprehensible with me. The severities
of your last winter exceed any I have known here about twelve
degrees to the northward. I never knew a Privet killed by our
cold ; pray, was it our Privet, or some native plant of yours like
it ? Is it possible the cold could kill our friend LAMBOLL's vine
to the ground, in South Carolina ? Of how penetrating a nature
must your cold be ! for I never knew an instance here of a Vine
killed by it.

These surprising extremes will never tempt me to change climates ; for every fruit seems degenerating, that comes from
Europe, but cherries. Is it not possible these defects can be prevented by art ? For, as you increase, luxury will increase—riches
will increase ; then rewards will encourage ingenious artists to
find ways and means to produce our fruits in perfection. This is
now something the case in England ; Cucumbers at Christmas,
Green Peas and Beans in February, March, and April,—ripe
Grapes in plenty in May. I have myself seen, more than once,
some hundred bunches of the finest ripe grapes, in May ; cherries
ripe in March or April, at a guinea or two a pound. This golden
gain stimulates every artist to be first at market.

It grieves me much to hear of poor BILLY'S adversity; but I hope his virtuous mind will support him under it. Amongst thy numerous acquaintance, it will be very hard if he cannot be got into some business above the servile drudgery of *a day labourer*. But that should operate in his favour, as an instance of his industry and humility, which I hope will be rewarded, at last, with something more suitable to his abilities.

Thy account of Augustine was very pleasing; but the walling is so complicate, I cannot form a tolerable idea of the place. Pray, at thy leisure, with BILLY'S assistance, just draw me the outlines on paper, marking each place with its name, and the rivers that surround it on the one side and the other. This, I hope, will not give much trouble, as it is only composed of lines. If the situations of the Forts, Churches, Governor's House, and other public buildings, are added, and numbered with the figures, they will make it more complete.   *   *   *

PETER COLLINSON TO WILLIAM BARTRAM.

Mill Hill, February 16, 1768.

I and my son opened my ingenious friend WILLIAM'S inimitable picture of the *Colocasia* [*Nelumbium*]. So great was the deception, it being candle-light, that we disputed for some time whether it was an engraving, or a drawing. It is really a noble piece of pencil-work; and the skill of the artist is shown in following nature in her progressive operations: I will not say more in its commendation, because I shall say too little where so much is due.

I wish the King had any taste in flowers or plants; but as he has none, there are no hopes of encouragement from him, for his talent is architecture. But I shall show it, with thy other curious performances, to Lord BUTE, who is the only great man that encourages ingenious men in painting botanic rarities.

*   *   *   *   *

The Wild Lime [*Nyssa candicans*, Mx.] would make an elegant green-house plant, from its being an Evergreen [?]. It's a little odd, no tolerably good specimen is sent of it. I wish some nuts could be procured. There is no doubt of raising it.

The crimson *Hibiscus* is a charming flower. I could have no perfect idea of it, but from thy elegant painting. Pray desire father to spare no pains to get us seed from Charleston, where I dare say it ripens seed.   *   *   *   *

The Scarlet Sage is excessively pretty. It grieves me it is an annual, for it will never ripen seed in our climate. So thy painting must supply that defect.

The *Lycium* is a new species. We have two or three sorts that bear purple berries. If berries could be had, it would make a variety.

I wish I had two or three of those olive-coloured snails, found at the bottom of St. John's River. Thy good father knows my love for these things.

That rich aromatic Evergreen, *Amisum stellatum* [*Illicium Floridanum?* Ellis], is a rich production, which, as the country fills, we may hope to be in possession of.

These short hints receive in earnest of my regard to many other curious articles in thy History of Florida, that time will not allow. I am sensible of the pains taken in it, and the neatness and accuracy of the performance. But I must not forget to tell thee how much I am delighted to see thy progress in the Linnæan system.

I am sensible some expense hath attended in procuring paper, paints, &c., for so many rare articles sent me. Pray accept of a small token, of a guinea, for I can never retaliate them, than by assuring thee I wish it may be ever in my power to serve thee as I wish.

P. COLLINSON,
In haste.

I have writ something in a hurry, that my ingenious friend should not think I paid him the respect he deserved. He has amply gratified my wishes to see the *Colocasia*, and I desire no more.

As both letter and guinea may be lost, I have desired thy father to pay it to thee, and I will make myself debtor to him for it.

I desire he will be very sparing of his time for the future, in employing it to oblige me, as there is not the least obligation ; and it will make me uneasy to receive further marks of his friendship, as I cannot make grateful returns. My love to father.

P. COLLINSON TO JOHN BARTRAM.

Mill Hill, 17th February, [1768].

MY DEAR JOHN :—

I have received thy ingenious son BILLY'S wonderful perform-ances; but, what surpasses all, is the *Colocasia*. Now I am amply gratified, and wish for no more.

I am sensible there has been much paper, paint, &c., expended on my account. I request that thou will pay to thy son WILLIAM the value of a guinea, sterling, in your currency. I intended to have put it in a letter, but I recollected I had formerly lost the letter, for the sake of the money, and that to boot; for the low officers, that have the handling and sorting the letters, can easily feel, and cannot resist pocketing a weighty letter. For that reason I ask the favour, and I will make myself debtor in thy account. What pleasure it must give thee to have such ingenious sons. WILLIAM, and MOSES in his way, has obliged me with his curious observations; and JOHNNY in his way for plants and insects;—are all very grateful to me, their father's old friend.   *   *   My love to them all.

I saw the box of plants opened for the King. They are in good order, and a fine collection—as is mine; but there is some formality to deliver a King's box, which will go to Kew garden, where all vegetables are treated with the utmost care, and all that art can do, to bring them to perfection in our climate.   *   *

It's late, so adieu.

P. COLLINSON.

Mill Hill, May 17th, 1768.

I had the pleasure of my dear JOHN's two letters of December 20th and January 24th. These I received April 15th.

My *Colocasia* nuts don't appear. I despair of them. They are in a pot, in a pond, always covered with water. If any fresh nuts offer again, put them instantly in a bottle of water, and so send them over. Though BILLY's lively drawing gives a clear idea of it, yet, to be sure, the real thing is to be preferred to the most perfect work of art.   *   *   *   *

I had some doubts, so carefully examined the Ohio Elephant's long teeth, with a great number (at a warehouse) from
Asia and from Africa, and found them agree in every circumstance; and they agree with what is called the *Mammot's* Teeth,
from Siberia, of which I have many fine specimens, sent me from
thence.

It is all a wonder how they came to America; and yet a greater
is, that no Elephant's grinding-teeth are found with them, but very
larged forked, or pronged teeth, that have no relation to elephants.
I have one, weighs near four pounds, with as fine an enamel on it
as if a recent tooth just taken out of the head of the animal. This
puzzles beyond measure; from whence no other conclusion can be
drawn, but that they may belong to a new species of Elephant, that
has long teeth, with these pronged or forked grinders; or else they
belong to some vast animal that have these forked grinders, different from any other animal yet known. But how they came mixt
with the Elephant's, is incomprehensible.

As to the Fossil Horns, digged up in Ireland, that long contested
point is now settled; for last year, my friend, the Duke of Richmond, had a large pair of your country Moose-deer horns sent him
from Quebec. At the first sight they have not any affinity with
the Irish Fossil Horns, but come very near to the European Elk.

So here are two animals, the creature to which the Irish horns
belong, and the creature to which the great forked or pronged
teeth belong. Whether they exist, God Almighty knows,—for no
man knows: whether antediluvians, or if in being since the flood.
But it is contrary to the common course of Providence to suffer
any of his creatures to be annihilated.   *   *   *

It is wonderful the snakes should forget their mutual animosity,
for the means of keeping one another warm.

Thy suggestions on the decrease of your animals are very likely
to be the cause that so few are now found.

I have the pleasure to tell thee, that the *Agave* prospers wonderfully. I shall have SOLANDER here to-morrow,—will show it him
as a great rarity, being, I believe, the first that has been seen
here. But I am not so great a favourite with the ladies as my
friend JOHN, for Mrs. BEE, notwithstanding all my care and
indulgence, remains quite inactive, yet I live in hopes.   *   *   *

If the Pennsylvania first settlers naturalized Bees, in your
province, then I have no doubt of their extending themselves in so

fine a climate ; but I thought it too far to come from New England.
As the Indians have no name for a Bee, that is a plain proof they
were foreigners.

*   *   *   *

Thy annuity is regularly paid. I am, my dear friend, thine
whilst I am

P. COLLINSON.

Mill Hill, July 6, 1768.

This day I was delighted with the sight of my dear JOHN's
letter of the 15th of May.

The two prospects of St. Augustine give me and my son great
satisfaction ; for now thy accurate descriptions are perfectly intelligible.   It is conveniently situate for trade, and a safe harbour,
if the bar could admit vessels of greater burden.   The island
must have a pretty effect from the town.   I am much obliged for
BILLY'S assistance in drawing the plan.

The Duchess of Portland dined here, this day.   She is a great
virtuoso, in shells and all marine productions.   I took the opportunity to show her BILLY's drawings.   She admired them as they
deserve.   She desires to bestow twenty guineas on his performances, *for a trial.*   She would wish to have the *Faba Egyptiaca* drawn of the size of that he sent ; and drawings of all Land,
River, and your Sea Shells, *from the very least to the greatest.*

*   *   *   I have further views for Billy if I can bring them to
bear.

Thou hast told me a very pleasing story of your Mocking-Bird ;
which I have often seen and heard sing, and some of my lady
friends have kept them seven, eight, and ten years ; but require
to be delicately and nicely fed every day, with fresh provisions.
Yet his song, they thought, amply rewarded them for their pains
and care about them.   *   *   *

From thy real friend,

P. COLLINSON.

PETER COLLINSON TO WILLIAM BARTRAM.

Mill Hill, July 18, 1768.

This morning, Doctor FOTHERGILL came and breakfasted here.
As I am always thoughtful how to make BILLY's ingenuity turn

to some advantage, I bethought of showing the Doctor his last
elegant performances. He deservedly admired them, and thinks
so fine a pencil is worthy of encouragement; and BILLY may
value himself on having such a patron, who is eminent for his
generosity, and his noble spirit to promote every branch in Natural
History. He desires BILLY would employ some of his time in
drawing all the Land, River, and Sea Shells, from the very smallest to the largest; when very small, eight or six in a half sheet,
as they grow larger, six or four, then two or one, without any
shade, which oftentimes confounds the shape of the shell. Note
the place where found, and add if anything peculiar to them
besides.

He is not in haste, and desires nothing may be done in a hurry.
When two or three shells are done, send them when there is convenient opportunity.

I further proposed to him, as you have such a variety of Water
and Land Terrapins, or Turtles, that BILLY would take a fit opportunity to draw them all, good, full-grown subjects, as may for
size, be contained in a half sheet of paper; and if there is any difference between male and female, to give both; and also be sure
to give the *under and upper shells*, and all from live subjects;
and give their Natural History, as far as can be collected. I
doubt not but thy father, &c. will assist thee. As these animals,
of a proper size and growth, are to be met with casually, so it will
be a work of time. So send now and then one or two, as it happens. And in time, lay out to procure good subjects of those
three new species, found in West Florida, the Soft Shell, Shovel
Nose, &c., and that other species of Soft Shell, found in the River
Ohio.

Set all thy wits and ingenuity to work, to gratify so deserving a
patron.

A few weeks agone, I gave my friend BILLY orders to send a
drawing of the *Faba Egyptiaca*, like that sent me; and as many
Land, River, and Sea Shells, as he can afford for twenty guineas,
for the Duchess of Portland. Don't crowd the shells; a few in a
sheet shows better; and *be sure no shade*. This she does by way
of specimen. If she likes thy performance, she will give orders to
keep drawing on, until all the shells are drawn. Send all to me,
rolled on a roller, and put in a little box, for fear of getting wet.

I am thy sincere friend,

P. COLLINSON.

I doubt not but thy brother MOSES, as he walks the fields, and woods, and river sides, will assist; and brother JOHNNY also, will look for Land Shells, Snails, &c. when he goes abroad to collect seeds. My respects to thy good father. I wrote him a long letter July 7th, in answer to his of 15th May.

[The preceding is probably the *last* letter from P. COLLINSON to the BARTRAMS, as his death took place on the 11th of August, just twenty-four days after the date of this to WILLIAM.]

JOHN BARTRAM TO SIR HANS SLOANE.*

July the 22d, 1741.

DESIRED FRIEND,

Sir HANS SLOANE : my good, faithful friend PETER COLLINSON, in his last letter to me, that I received, acquainted me that thee desired I would send thee some petrified representations of Sea Shells. Accordingly, I have sent thee a few, which I gathered toward the northward, the latter end of last May, which was before I received the before-mentioned letter. I hope these may find acceptance; so as to introduce a further correspondence. However, I design to send thee another collection by Captain WRIGHT (who talks of sailing by the latter end of August); when I hope to give thee a fuller demonstration that I am thy vigilant and industrious friend.

SIR HANS SLOANE TO JOHN BARTRAM.

SIR :—

I am very much obliged to you for several Natural Curiosities,

* Sir HANS SLOANE, an eminent physician and naturalist, was born in 1660, at Killileagh, in Ireland; took his degree at Montpellier; settled in London, in 1684; and became a fellow of the College, and a member of the Royal Society. In 1687, he went to Jamaica, as physician to the Duke of Albemarle; and during the fifteen months that he remained there, he made a valuable collection of objects of Natural History. After his return to London, he acquired great reputation, and an ample fortune. He was Secretary, and, on the decease of NEWTON, President of the Royal Society; President of the College of Physicians; Physician-General to the Army; Physician to GEORGE II.; and was created a baronet. He died in 1752, aged ninety-two years. Sir HANS bequeathed the whole of his immense collection of Natural Curiosities, Medals, and books, to the public, on payment of a comparatively trifling sum; and it constitutes the basis of the British Museum. His chief work is a *Natural History of Jamaica*, in two ponderous folio volumes.—BLAKE's *Biographical Dictionary*.

Shells and Petrifactions, which my very good friend, Mr. PETER COLLINSON, hath delivered to me with great care ; and for which I reckon myself very much obliged to you ; especially on account of the remarks that you had sent along with them, in your letter to me.

The triangular arrow-head is of white chrystal, or spar ; the like of which, in green jasper, I have had from Tierra del Fuego, on the south side of the Straits of Magellan, used by the inhabitants of that country. The Indian instrument you sent, was the head of a hatchet, made of a sort of jasper. This, fitted to a handle, was made use of by the Indians of Jamaica, and several parts of the West Indies, for making their canoes, before they were taught the use of iron and steel. I have one of them fitted up for use by them. It's believed they could not make canoes, and large periaguas, with these hatchets, before they had first with fire made the part of the log, to be hollowed, into coal, to be friable, and brought out by the hatchets.

I have, with the approbation of Mr. COLLINSON, sent you my Natural History of Jamaica, together with the catalogue of the plants I found there, referred to in that History ; whereby, you may find what has been said by any authors I have seen, that write of them. I should be glad to have some seeds, or samples of your plants, for my collections of dried herbs, fruits, &c.

I should be extremely pleased to know wherein I can be useful to you, and retaliate the obligations you have laid upon

Your most humble servant,
HANS SLOANE.

January 16, 1741-2.

JOHN BARTRAM TO SIR HANS SLOANE.

November the 14th, 1742.

RESPECTED FRIEND,

SIR HANS SLOANE:—I have received thy kind letter, and curious books of thy history of Jamaica, which are very acceptable to me (as are all such fine instructions, for I exceedingly delight in reading books of Natural History or Botany). This noble present engageth not only my grateful acknowledgment, but also my endeavours to oblige thee with any curiosity my small capacity and circumstance will conveniently afford ; and in compliance with thy modest request, I have *first*, sent a quire of paper filled with dry specimens of plants, numbered, so that if thee wants any more of any sort there, or any more particular remarks on any of them, please to mention it to each number.   *Secondly*, I have sent thee a box of insects, numbered, and a paper with my remarks to each number.   *Thirdly*, I have sent thee a collection of curious stones, figured with Sea Shells, and some other curiosities, which, if they should many of them prove new and acceptable, I shall be well pleased.   But when I read in thy second volume of thy extraordinary collection of curiosities, I thought it would be difficult to send thee any thing of that nature that would be new.

I have procured an Indian Tobacco Pipe of stone, entire. It was dug by chance out of an old Indian grave ; the figure and dimensions as in the margin. This I esteem as a great curiosity, and if I knew that thee had none of this kind, I should endeavour to give thee an opportunity of calling it thy own.

September the 23d, 1743.

RESPECTED FRIEND,

SIR HANS SLOANE:—I received thy kind letter of April the 4th, 1743. I am glad what I sent last fall was acceptable. I have filled the two quires of specimens of plants, in their perfect bloom, and am collecting a fine variety of Mosses to send with them, which I design to send with our dear friend PETER'S specimens.

I have been a long journey this summer—unexpected, till a few days before I set out ; but having such an opportunity as very likely never to have such another, I embraced it, so could not gather insects as I designed.

I am much obliged to thee for thy kindness in desiring me to send thee a catalogue of my botanical books. Indeed it is soon done, I have so few of them on Natural History, which I love dearly to read.

The first authors I read, were SALMON, CULPEPER, and TURNER. These JAMES LOGAN gave me. * * * Doctor DILLENIUS sent me MILLER'S Dictionary, and his own book of Mosses. Lord PETRE sent me MILLER'S Second Part, and the second book of TURNER'S complete Herbal ; and thee kindly obliged me with thy History of Jamaica. Our friend PETER sent me them fine books of Nature Delineated. CATESBY sent me his books of Birds, and some books of Physic and Surgery, which was my chief study in my youthful years. I have heard of PETIVER's fine collections of Plants and Animals, which thee published; nay, I am well acquainted with his nephew, Captain GLENTWORTH, who lived with his Uncle PETIVER. He tells me he used to change, spread, and dry his uncle's specimens, and carried many curiosities between thee and his uncle.

November the 16th, 1743.

FRIEND SIR HANS SLOANE :—

I have received thy kind present of a silver cup, and am well pleased that thy name is engraved upon it at large, so that when my friends drink out of it, they may see who was my benefactor.*

I received thy kind letter, and have endeavoured to answer thy desires. I have sent thee two quires of specimens, gathered in their full bloom—as many as I could, but several that I found amongst the Indians, could not be found with their proper

* The cup, of which the above is a correct representation, is now the property of ISAAC BARTRAM, grandson of the Botanist by his first marriage.

characteristics. So pray accept them as I found them, rather than none of that species. I have collected several kinds of seeds belonging to the specimens, numbered as the specimens are to which they belong. I have also wrapped up, in separate papers, several of our North American Mosses, and packed them up with the seeds. If thee wants more another year, of Mosses, Seeds, or Specimens, pray let me know particularly by a letter, and I hope to endeavour to procure them for thee.

I have put in the box of specimens one of our yellow Wasp's nests, that was built in my ditch bank. We have another sort like these, that build a hanging nest on the twigs of bushes, or trees, like our Hornets.

I have wrapped up in paper some of our Humblebee breeding cells, or combs, and have procured a large Hornet's nest, to send. Dear Sir HANS, if these few curiosities are acceptable to thee, it will not only encourage me to strive to oblige thee more, but will exceedingly please thy sincere and obliged friend.

December the 8th, 1745.

FRIEND HANS SLOANE :—

By our last ship to London, I sent thee a Hornet's nest, and a bag of our Mosses, with some other odd things. I wish they may come safe to thy hands; but if they should miscarry, I have sent another this time, which I shall order PETER to let thee have, if the other failed,—if not, to keep it himself. He wrote to me, last spring, to send a quire or two of specimens, but it came to my hands this fall too late to send any this year. I desire thee would please to send to me what thee would in particular have me to send thee, and I will use all reasonable endeavours to oblige thee with any curiosity that is in my power to procure.

However, in the mean time, thee hath fully engaged—by thy many favours and kindnesses—the respect, with the hearty love and good will of thy sincere friend,

JOHN BARTRAM.

JAMES LOGAN* TO JOHN BARTRAM.

FRIEND J. BARTRAM :—

Last night, in the twilight, I received the inclosed, and opened it by mistake. Last year PETER sent me some tables, which I never examined till since I last saw thee. They are six very large sheets, in which the author [LINNÆUS] digests all the productions of Nature in classes. Two of them he bestows on the inanimate, as Stones, Minerals, Earths; two more on Vegetables, and the other two on Animals. His method in the Vegetables is altogether new, for he takes all his distinctions from the *stamina* and the *styles*, the first of which he calls husbands, and the other wives. He ranges them, therefore, under those of 1 husband, 2, 3, 4, 5, 6, 7, 8, 9, 10, 12, 20, and then of many husbands. He further distinguishes by the styles, and has many heads, under which he reduces all known plants.

The performance is very curious, and at this time worth thy notice. I would send it to thee, but being in Latin, it will want some explanation, which, after I have given thee, thou wilt, I believe, be fully able to deal with it thyself, since thou generally knows the plants' names. If thou wilt step to town to-morrow, thou wilt find me there with them, at E. SHIPPEN'S, or J. PEMBER-

* JAMES LOGAN, one of the primitive fathers of Pennsylvania, and greatly distinguished for his learning and worth, was born in England, in the year 1674. He came to America in company with WILLIAM PENN, in 1699. In 1701, he was appointed Secretary of the Province of Pennsylvania, and Clerk of the Council. He afterwards held the offices of Commissioner of Property, Chief Justice, and President of the Council. Upon the death of Governor GORDON, in October, 1736, the government of course devolved upon him, as president of the council, and during his administration of two years, the utmost harmony prevailed throughout the province.

Several years previous to his death, he retired from public affairs, and spent the latter part of his life among his books, and in corresponding with learned men in different parts of Europe. He died in 1751, aged seventy-seven years. The well-known *Loganian Library* was bequeathed by him to the citizens of Philadelphia. In 1735 he published his experiments upon Maize, in support of the Linnæan doctrine of the sexes of plants. The work was afterwards published in Latin, at Leyden, 1739, and at London, by Dr. FOTHERGILL, in Latin and English, 1747. In 1739 he published another Latin tract, at Leyden; and a translation of CICERO's treatise, *De Senectute*, at Philadelphia, in 1744.—BLAKE'S *Biog. Dict.*

TON'S, from 12 to 3.   I want also to say something further to thee, on microscopical observations.

Thy real friend,

J. LOGAN.

Stenton, 19th of June, 1736.

JOHN BARTRAM TO J. J. DILLENIUS.*

August the 1st, 1738.

RESPECTED FRIEND DOCTOR DILLENIUS :—

I am very thankful to thee for thy kind letter, and if thee thinks me worthy of thy friendship, and that I can oblige thee, pray write often to me, and let me know wherein I can serve thee.   *   *

*   * I never saw our great Laurel [*Rhododendron*] grow any where but near Schuylkill, though I have been told it grows beyond the mountains.   Up Delaware river it grows near the water, upon the steep bank side, on poor dry soil, sometimes on the flats, high up the river, where it is dry, poor, and sandy.   There it grows ten feet high, but will bear flowers at five feet high, in great white bunches.

Thee mentions the Cornelian Cherry, with a Bay leaf, growing in Virginia, mentioned by Doctor PLUKENET.   I do not, at present, know what tree he means, nor how he describes it, never yet having an opportunity of reading that valuable author, though often desired it.   I believe it neither is, nor was ever in Pennsylva-

* JOHN JAMES DILLENIUS, M.D., whose name is familiar to every student of Cryptogamic Botany, and whose *Historia Muscorum*, published in 1741, still remains unrivalled in that department, with regard to botanical learning and criticism, as well as specific discrimination, was born at Darmstadt, in Germany, in 1684 or 1685. He was educated as a physician at Giessen, and while resident there, published several botanical essays, of considerable acuteness. Being brought to England by the distinguished WILLIAM SHERARD, the greatest botanist of his day, who had been English consul at Smyrna, DILLENIUS remained here from August, 1721, till his death.   He was closely attached to consul SHERARD, and his brother JAMES, an opulent apothecary, who had a garden at *Eltham ;* of the rare plants of which DILLENIUS published, in 1732, a splendid history, in two folio volumes, under the title of *Hortus Elthamensis*, the plates, like those of all his other publications, being drawn and engraved with his own hand. They excel in characteristic fidelity.

Consul SHERARD, in founding his botanical professorship at Oxford, appointed DILLENIUS the first professor, which place he held, fulfilling its duties, with respect to the garden at least, very assiduously, till he died there of an apoplexy, April 2d, 1747, in the sixty-third year of his age.—SMITH's *Linnæan Correspondence*.

nia; although I have observed five or six species of the *Cornus* with us. The Yapon [*Ilex vomitoria*, Ait.] grows no nearer us than about the Capes of Virginia.   *   *   *

The White Pine is a very poor bearer; I never saw any ripe seed on this side the Blue Mountains.   On the other side I felled a tree about ten inches diameter, and sixty feet high, for the seed, and found three or four perfect seeds; but most of them were dropt out.   *   *   *   *

I am thy real friend,

J. B.

JOHN JAMES DILLENIUS TO JOHN BARTRAM.

*   *   *   *

I have sent you with this a few seeds, most of which are handsome garden plants.   You will find three sorts of snails or *Medica*, in one paper, which are annuals, and which you may try whether they will serve for cattle.   You will likewise find a paper named *Medica legitima* CLUSII, or Burgundy Trefoil [*Medicago sativa*, L., now known as *Lucerne*,] which is still a better sort; for it is perennial, will stand six or more years, runs much in herb, and our cattle are greedy of it.   This may prove a great improvement, not only to yourself, but the whole country, which I have often heard wants pasture.

I am your obliged friend,

J. J. DILLENIUS.

Oxford, September 11, 1738.

P. S. Sow the Burgundy Trefoil very thin, for it spreads much.

GOOD MR. BARTRAM:—

Herewith, I send you some seeds of officinal plants, and a plate of Mosses.   The sort marked (*) groweth on trees, hath larger dishes than any other known sort, and was formerly observed in Maryland, by VERNON.   I don't doubt you will find it in your country; and shall be obliged if you will send me some specimens of this, as well as other sorts.

Your last parcel of Mosses, and letter from April 20, is safe come to hands, by the care of P. COLLINSON. I return you thanks for them, and remain your obliged friend

And humble servant,

J. J. DILLENIUS.

Oxford, October 15, 1740.

Oxford, June 22, 1741.

DEAR FRIEND MR. BARTRAM :—

I received your letter of December 16, 1740, per post; and that of March 24, was sent to me by SAMUEL WHYTING ; so that I had it, together with the Mosses, without any trouble. After two days looking over and comparing them with my own, and those I had formerly from you, I found but five or six new sorts. There might be some more, but as they were in an imperfect state, I could make nothing of them. However, I thank you for them, but desire, for the future, to send me nothing but what hath heads.

You complain, you never received any paper on my account. When I was in London, last Whitsunday, I paid to our friend, Mr. COLLINSON, amongst other things I had of him, for half a ream of writing paper, which he had bought for you, November 10, 1740 ; and I hope you have received that since. But, finding that you are wanting, and sparing paper in wrapping up Mosses, I have sent this day se'en night, by our carrier to Mr. COLLINSON, a large bundle of waste *Hortus Elthamensis* paper, upwards of ½ C, to be forwarded to you; which I hope you will receive in its time. When you have an opportunity, I shall be glad to have one of your Muskrat Skins.

The inclosed Moss, you said grew in a moist shady swamp. I should be glad to see it with his heads,—which I guess it bears in summer—as all swamp Mosses commonly do.

I remain your obliged friend and servant.

J. J. DILLENIUS.

JOHN BARTRAM TO J. J. DILLENIUS.

The 14th of the 9th month, 1742.

RESPECTED FRIEND DOCTOR DILLENIUS :—

I received thy kind letter, accompanied with thy kind present of thy book of Mosses, which is very acceptable; as also a great parcel of paper for specimens and seed. This summer, I have not gathered any Mosses, because I thought thee wanted no more, after thy book was published; and this fall, I have been long sick, since I received thy letter.

When I was upon the Katskill Mountains, last August, I found a comical species of *Lycopodium*, which I gathered—but lost it upon the mount, in coming down: but if I should ever go there again, I intend to search the mounts on purpose, having engaged a hearty young fellow to go with me, and concluded to stay on them a good share of a week, day and night. But since I have heard of the death of my good friend, Lord PETRE, I know not whether I shall be employed again,—and so my journeys may terminate. But if I receive orders to travel again, I shall endeavour to serve thee. I have collected a large parcel of seeds for thee, and sent in a box, directed to P. COLLINSON. There is the seed of the variegated *Clinopodium*, and Virginia *Yucca*. This, and the spining *Yucca*, are all the *Yuccas* I know. I found a plant at the falls of James River, which I planted in my garden,—and the second year, shot up a stalk four feet high, producing a long spike of flowers, exceeding sweet smelling, like spice; but it had the exact characteristics of an *Aloe*. It hath not flowered these two years.

November the 29th, 1743.

RESPECTED FRIEND,

Doctor DILLENIUS:—I have sent thee two or three sorts of Mosses, that I gathered in the country of the Five Nations, which I think are a little different from any that thee has figured. Also, I have sent thee a large collection of seeds of our country plants, gathered in their proper season, and carefully dried, which I hope many of them will grow with thee.

In looking over thy curious book of Mosses, I can't find any figure of the Old Man's Beard Moss,* which I saw grow in Virginia, on the trees. It groweth six or seven feet long, and is fine food

---

* JOHN does not seem to have been aware at that time, that the "Old Man's Beard Moss" is no *moss* at all, but a regular *flowering* plant (viz., the *Tillandsia usneoides*, L.); and is referred to the same *natural family* with the delicious *Pineapple*.

for horses and deer. Pray, my good friend, write to me, and let
me know wherein I can do thee any farther service ; which will
oblige thy sincere friend,

J. B.

JOHN BARTRAM TO COLONEL CUSTIS.

The 19th of November, 1738.

DEAR FRIEND COLONEL CUSTIS :—

I am safely returned home to my family, which I found in good
health, as I have been ever since I left thee ; for which I am
thankful to Divine Providence, whose powerful regard is to all his
creation.

Now, dear friend, I can't forget thy kind entertainment ; and it
is with a great satisfaction and pleasure that I think upon the
agreeable hours I spent in thy conversation, as well as thy kind
expressions at parting, which hath engaged my respect after a particular manner.

I had a successful journey up to, upon, and beyond the Blue
Mountains, where I collected a fine variety of curious plants.

There grows on the other side of James River, a little above
ISHAM RANDOLPH'S, a tree, the kind of which is known in Europe
by the name of *Thuja*, or Arbor Vitæ, which, if thee could procure some seed thereof, if it growed, would be a curious ornament
in thy garden. I doubt not, if thee was to write or speak to
ISHAM, he would procure thee some. He was very kind to me,
during the time I stayed with him, and sent his man with me to
the mountains, which was kind indeed. If it lieth in thy way,
pray, give my love to him. There is the Umbrella-tree cones
near thee, and the ripe berries of Yapon, and the acorns of the
Live Oak, growing near Captain CASWELL'S, would be very acceptable to me ; but I know not how to get them to Philadelphia.

     *   *   *   *

COLONEL W. BYRD* TO JOHN BARTRAM.

Virginia, the 30th of November, 1738.

SIR :—

No sooner than yesterday did I receive your kind letter, which

* Colonel WILLIAM BYRD, a distinguished citizen of Virginia, was a member of
the Council about the year 1682. When, in 1699, about three hundred of the

was twice as long in travelling from Philadelphia as the writer was, when he favoured us with his company here. I am glad you met with so many curiosities, as to recompense the fatigue of a long journey ; and it is with particular satisfaction that I hear of your having got safe home to your family, and that you found them in perfect health. It is always a pleasure to look back upon labour past, especially when it procured an improvement of knowledge that continues to the end of the chapter.

I am surprised to understand that M. S. turns out a knave, because he had the appearance of a plain, honest man. But no faith is to be given to outward appearances, since we are told that the Devil himself puts on the clothing of an Angel of Light. However, I have learnt, by long experience, to be upon my guard against all strangers not well recommended, so that they can cheat me of nothing but my civilities, to which all mankind are welcome.

I expect every day the arrival of a little ship, with Switzers and Germans, to settle upon part of my land at Roanoke. But they have been now thirteen weeks at sea, so that I am under great apprehensions for them. They have purchased thirty-three thousand acres only, in one body ; so that there are seventy-two thousand still remaining, to which your friend, GASPER WISTER, is very welcome, if he, or any of his countrymen, are so inclined. I am greatly obliged to you for your good character, and by the grace of God shall endeavour never to forfeit it upon any temptation of advantage. The land is really very good, for so large a quantity ; the climate moderate and wholesome ; the river navigable to the great Falls ; and the road to James River very dry and level. Besides, I have now a bill depending before our Assembly, to make all foreigners that shall seat upon our frontiers, free from taxes for seven years, which I have reason to believe will pass.

If these, and many other advantages, which I have not room to mention, will tempt any of your Germans to remove hither, I shall be very glad—upon the easy terms mentioned in my paper ; and if

persecuted French Protestants arrived in the Colony, he received them with the affection of a father, and gave them the most liberal assistance. His generous charity to the poor foreigners is particularly described by BEVERLY. He had received a liberal education in England, and was distinguished for his literary taste, and his patronage of science. He had one of the largest Libraries on the continent. In 1723, he was one of the commissioners for establishing the line between North Carolina and Virginia. He died about 1743, at an advanced age. —BLAKE'S *Biographical Dictionary*.

you will be so good as employ your interest and kind offices with them, for that purpose, it will be an obligation ever to be acknowledged by him who wishes everything that is good to you and your household, and is, without guile,

Sir, your hearty friend and humble servant,

W. BYRD.

Westover, the 23d of March, 1738-9.

SIR :—

I sent an answer to your kind letter by the post, several months ago, and congratulated your safe return to your family. This kisses your hand by my friend, Dr. TSCHIFFELY, a Swiss gentleman, who is bound to Philadelphia, to try if he can prevail with any of his countrymen to come and settle upon my land at Roanoke ; and if you will be so kind as to lend a helping hand towards it, I shall ever acknowledge the obligation. The land is exceedingly good, with a fine river running through the whole length of it, more than a quarter of a mile wide ; full of wild fowl in winter, and alive with fish all the year. Very many rivulets and creeks run into it on both sides, which help to fertilize the soil, and will afford all manner of convenience for mills of every kind. The situation is high, and the air very wholesome—free from those aguish vapours which infect the lower part of the country : and as the land lies forty miles on this side the mountains, the Indians have no manner of claim or pretence to it, by the last peace we made with them. The price I sell this land for, you know, is very easy, being no more than £3 of our currency for every hundred acres. The quit-rent is but two shillings a year, and since I saw you, I have prevailed with our Assembly to make all foreign Protestants free from taxes for ten years, that shall come and inhabit that part of the country. These, I think, are such temptations and encouragements, as are not to be met with elsewhere. Nor will the distance exceed seventy miles to a ship landing, and the road will be very good, and very level all the way, when we have cleared the ridge that we intend ; so that there will be little difficulty in bringing the fruits of their industry to market. We have had the misfortune, lately, to lose a ship, either by the villany or stupidity of the master, which had 250 Switzers and Germans on board, with effects to a considerable value. These were to seat on part of

my land, under the conduct of several gentlemen of fortune, who
came along with them.   But these gentlemen perished, and most
of the people, and very little of their effects is saved.   Some few
of these unhappy wretches are gone upon my land to make a
beginning, and will soon be followed by more.

The bearer is a man of skill in his profession ; has been a great
traveller, and has great knowledge in Chemistry and Surgery.
Thus, as a virtuoso, I recommend him to you, and likewise as a
friend of   Sir, your most humble servant,

W. BYRD.

Mrs. BYRD joins her best wishes with mine, for the happiness of
yourself and your family.

JOHN BARTRAM TO COLONEL W. BYRD.

[1739.]

DEAR FRIEND COLONEL BYRD:—
I received thy kind letter by the post last winter, and another
dated March the 23d, which I received by the hand of thy friend,
Doctor TSCHIFFELY, whom I received very kindly, and made as
welcome as my present circumstances would afford, for thy sake—
having no other acquaintance than thine and another recommendation.

I have this spring made several microscopical observations upon
the male and female parts in vegetables, to oblige some ingenious
botanists in Leyden, who requested that favour of me, which I
hope I have performed to their satisfaction, and as a mechanical
demonstration of the certainty of this hypothesis, of the different
sex, in all plants that have come under my notice.   *   *

* * I have made several successful experiments, of joining several species of the same genus, whereby I have obtained curious
mixed colours in flowers, never known before ; but this requires an
accurate observation and judgment, to know the precise time.   * *

I hope by these practical observations to open a gate into a very
large field of experimental knowledge, which, if judiciously improved, may be a considerable addition to the beauty of the florist's
garden.

DR. THOMAS BOND* TO JOHN BARTRAM.

Paris, February 20, 1738-9.
MY GOOD FRIEND :—

As I am writing to my American friends, I cannot forget my good friend BARTRAM, and send you my best respects, and hearty desire for your and family's health and happiness, than which nothing is more my wish.

I expected to have given you more pleasure in this letter than I find I shall ; for by the assistance of that good man, our friend COLLINSON, I have a particular acquaintance with Monsieur JUSSIEU, Professor of Botany at the King's Garden, who is supposed to be one of the greatest men in that way in Europe. He promised to inform me what were the species of those plants you called Incognita, and in others where he thought you were mistaken.

I gave him all the dry specimens ; five of which were new, and pleased him exceedingly, particularly the Seneka Root, which he then took to be a *Polygala*. But I could not meet him anywhere this week ; for which reason, I must put it off to the next opportunity. He told me the Virginia Seneka Root was sent him with a recommendation and method of use in pleurisies, and repeatedly tried with surprising success, and is in the highest esteem with him, and many other physicians ; but that another here, of the same species, was tried for the want of it, with equal advantage.

The Ginseng is now here common, but in no esteem. It was brought from Canada, and is exactly the same with what you discovered.

I have now spent three months in Paris, the most diligently I ever did any in my life, and, I fear, to the prejudice of my tender constitution ; but if I was almost sure 'twould kill me, I could not avoid tending the curious courses of Anatomy, Surgery, Phy-

* "THOMAS BOND, a distinguished physician and surgeon, was born in Maryland, in 1712. After studying with Dr. HAMILTON, he spent a considerable time in Paris. In 1734 [?] he commenced practice at Philadelphia. The first clinical lectures in the Pennsylvania Hospital were delivered by him. He assisted in founding the college and academy. Of a literary society, composed of FRANKLIN, BARTRAM, GODFREY, and others, he was a member; and an officer of the Philosophical Society, from its establishment. The annual address before the society was delivered by him, in 1782, on The Rank of Man in the Scale of Being. He died in 1784, aged 72."—BLAKE's *Biog. Dictionary*.

siology, &c.   And, in short, 'tis impossible there can be better, if so good schools in the world.

My friend JUSSIEU tells me, that I shall believe myself at home, by being amongst so many of my native plants, as brought from America by himself; in quest whereof, he was sent by the King.

If I am not otherways too busy, I propose by his assistance, to improve myself in that science, at the King's Garden, which is a most beautiful place.

Pray do me the favour to recommend my best respects to your good spouse, and assure yourself I am with great esteem,

Your real friend,

TH. BOND.

ISHAM RANDOLPH TO JOHN BARTRAM.

Virginia, May 24, 1739.

DEAR SIR :—

According to the method we proposed to correspond, this is the first opportunity that has offered since I had the pleasure of seeing you : it is by my friend and acquaintance, Doctor TSCHIFFELY, who I believe to be a proficient in the art of Chemistry.   I take him to be a very honest gentleman.   He hath a mind to see Philadelphia, out of curiosity ; and therefore, I recommend him to your friendship.

I am to acknowledge the letter you wrote by my man CORNELIUS, which is all that I have received.   I have lately had a letter from my friend P. COLLINSON.   He makes no mention of my letter, via Philadelphia ; so I conclude you did not save the opportunity by your latter ships to Great Britain.

I wish I could entertain you with an account of some new discovery, since your progress here : but, for the want of a penetrating genius, in the curious beauties of nature, I must make it good in assuring you, that I am with great sincerity of heart,

Your affectionate friend

And humble servant,

ISHAM RANDOLPH.

If you see any of my acquaintance, make me acceptable to 'em.

My wife and family join in their best respects to you and Mrs.
BARTRAM.

ALEXANDER COLHOUN* TO JOHN BARTRAM.

New York, August 18th, 1739.

SIR : —

I was favoured with yours of the 27th of last month. I assure
you, was sorry I had not the pleasure of visiting you a second
time, being obliged to set out for this place. I am heartily glad
to hear you intend next month to be in the Jerseys, and from
thence to proceed to this town ; where I shall be very glad to see
you. There are a great variety of plants, &c., upon this island.

As you express a desire to know the distance between New York
and Albany, how far this Province is peopled backwards, &c. We
are distant from Albany 150 miles. It is situate on the west side
of Hudson's River. I went there by water, with our late Governor ; and from thence travelled beyond the farthest Palatine Settlement, belonging to this Province, northwest from Albany, about
150 or 160 miles, near half-way to our Garrison of Oswego, on the
great Lake of Cataraqui.

Several people travel from hence to Albany by land, (and I
believe it is much the same distance as by water.) From what I
hear, there is good accommodation on the road.

Two of our officers went up in a sledge last winter, as several
people do from hence ; as well as on horseback, in the summer
time. But more of this, &c., at meeting.

From, sir, your sincere friend,

And humble servant,

ALEXANDER COLHOUN.

P. S. I shall esteem myself very much obliged if you can procure for me some *Ginseng* Root.

* Mr. COLHOUN, as appears by a memorandum in the BARTRAM Papers, was
"Surgeon to the Garrison, in New York."

MARK CATESBY* TO JOHN BARTRAM.

London, May 20, 1740.

Mr. Bartram :—

Your kind remembrance of me, in the three plants you sent me with those of Mr. COLLINSON, encourages me to give you further trouble, though not without an intention of retaliation.

As I have the pleasure of reading your letters, I see your time is well employed; therefore, in what I propose, I shall be cautious of desiring anything that may much obstruct your other affairs. But, as you send yearly to our good friend Mr. P. COLLINSON, the same conveyance may supply me; which I shall confine to as narrow a compass as may be, for I find my taste is agreeable with yours, which is, that I regard most, those plants that are specious in their appearance, or use in physic, or otherwise. The return that I propose to make you, is my book; but it will be first necessary to give you some account of it. The whole book, when finished, will be in two folio volumes, each volume consisting of an hundred plates of Animals and Vegetables.

This laborious work has been some years in agitation; and as the whole, when finished, amounts to twenty guineas, a sum too great, probably, to dispose of many, I chose to publish it in parts: viz., twenty plates with their descriptions, at a time, at two guineas. By this easy method, I disposed of many more than I otherwise should. Though I shall set a due value on your labours, the whole book would be too considerable to send you at once;

* MARK CATESBY, an English naturalist, born about the latter end of the year 1679. He visited Virginia in 1712, where he remained seven years, collecting the various productions of the country, and occasionally transmitting seeds and specimens of plants to his correspondents in England, and particularly to Doctor WILLIAM SHERARD. On his return to England in 1719, he was encouraged by Sir HANS SLOANE, Doctor SHERARD, and others, to return to America, with the professed design of describing, delineating, and painting, the more curious objects of nature. He arrived in Carolina, which was selected as the place of his residence, in 1722. Having spent nearly three years on the Continent, he visited the Bahama Islands, residing in the Isle of Providence, until he returned to England, in 1726. His *Natural History of Carolina, Florida, and the Bahama Islands*, was completed in 1748, in 2 vols., folio, with coloured plates. It was republished in 1754, and 1771. He died in London, in 1749, at the age of seventy.—REES's *Cyclopædia*.

Therefore, I propose to send you, annually, *a Part* (i. e. twenty plates with their descriptions), for what you send me.

I, having already told you what plants I most affect, shall, in the general leave it to you what plants to send me, though the specimens you send Mr. COLLINSON will somewhat direct me.

My method has been to set down a greater number of things than I could expect to be complied with, to be sent at one time ; because, as all things are not at all times to be had, others may offer. Thus far, is a duplicate of my first letter to you.

February 25, 1740–1.

MR. BARTRAM :—

I have received from you a box of plants, containing a tree of the Sugar Birch, with others I could not tell, because I have no letter, or account of them. I conclude you had not received my letter, at your sending away the box of plants, otherwise I might have expected the favour of an answer.

The plants seem to be in good condition, and I heartily thank you for them ; and in return, desire you'll accept the first part of my book ; and for fear of Spanish depredations, I send, as above, a duplicate of my first letter.   *   *   *

In the box you sent, I find there are two plants of *Chamærho-dodendron*, which seem not to agree with our climate ; therefore, please to send no more, till better encouragement.

Your beautiful Rock Cistus, which for many years I have received from Carolina, but could never make it blossom, last July we were favoured with a sight of its elegant flowers ; the first, I dare say, that ever flowered in Europe. It was from a plant you sent Mr. COLLINSON ;—the climate from which it came being nearer ours, than from whence those came that I was unsuccessful in. This plant is again set to blossom, though it increases not at all.

Wishing you all happiness, I conclude, sir,

Your obliged friend and servant,

M. CATESBY.

P. S. I must inform you that the part of my book I send you is in a more contracted manner, and smaller paper, than that you have seen of Mr. PENN'S, but in other respects the same.

JOHN BARTRAM TO MARK CATESBY.

[Without date.]

FRIEND MARK CATESBY :—

I received thy kind letter of the 29th of November, but thee not having inserted when or where it was writ, I am at a loss to know where to direct my answer, otherwise than to thee, and to the care of our well-beloved and trusty friend, PETER COLLINSON, who merits the esteem and friendship of most of the curious. The reading of thy acceptable letter incited in me the different passions of joy, in receiving a letter of friendship and request from one so much esteemed, and sorrow in considering what time we have lost, when we might have obliged each other. It's a pity thee had not wrote to me ten years ago. I should by this time have furnished thee with many different species of plants, and, perhaps some animals; but the time past can't be recalled, therefore, pray, write often to me, and inform me in every particular what thee wishes of me, and wherein I can oblige thee; for when I am travelling on the mountains, or in the valleys, the most desolate, craggy, dismal places I can find, where no mortal ever trod, I chiefly search out. Not that I naturally delight in such solitudes, but entirely to observe the wonderful productions in nature.

*　　　　*　　　　*　　　　*

Before Doctor DILLENIUS gave me a hint of it, I took no particular notice of Mosses, but looked upon them as a cow looks at a pair of new barn doors; yet now he is pleased to say, I have made a good progress in that branch of Botany, which really is a very curious part of vegetation.

I am exceedingly pleased with thy proposals, and shall do what I can, conveniently, to comply with them. I have a great value for thy books, and esteem them as an excellent performance, and an ornament for the finest library in the world.

MARK CATESBY TO JOHN BARTRAM.

London [year obliterated].

DEAR FRIEND :—

I am much obliged to you for two kind letters, one of them dated the 20th of July, 1741, the other the 15th of October following. The first contained a very accurate account and dissection of the *Chamærhododendron*, which gives me so good an idea of its form and colours, that are an assistance of the specimens you sent, when occasion requires, I shall be enabled to give a tolerable figure of it ; which will be so much the more necessary, as there being little probability of ever seeing it in blossom here. Those plants you have already sent us, plainly show the aversion they have to our soil and climate, by their slow progress and stunted appearance.

In answer to your conjecture, of their growing here as well as with you, in the like moist land, I say, that plants, which, in America, grow in moist land, are generally killed when planted in such like here. It is, by experience, found, that a dry, warm soil, is most agreeable to American plants—even aquatics. This, I conceive, is not from our too great cold in winter, more than with you ; but from a deficiency of heat in our summers ; wherefore, a situation by being warmer, may compensate for that difference of heat in a wet situation.   *   *   *   *

Mr. CLAYTON mentions a plant in the remote parts of Virginia, called Leather-wood. It is a *Thymelœa*, or Spurge Laurel, perhaps the same as your Leather-wood.

Among the Shell animals of New England, one is called the *Signœ* [?]. Its eyes are placed under a covert of thick shells ; but so ordered that the part above the eyes is transparent, that the creature can see its way, though otherwise it is blinded. These are somewhat like the eyes of a Mole, which are covered with a thin skin, to fit it for working under ground.

In New England is also the Monk-fish, having a hood like a friar's cowl. In BAKER'S Cave, in New England, are scarlet muscles, yielding a juice of a purple colour, that gives so deep a dye that no water can wash out.

I am told of an animal in Pennsylvania, called a *Monax*, and by some, a Ground-hog. It lives and burrows under ground, and sleeps much ; is about the size of a rabbit. I shall be glad of what you know concerning it.

Have you observed any other of the Deer kind, beside the Moose, Elk, and common Deer ? Do you think that the Black Fox, common in North America, is a different species, or only varying in colour from the common Gray Fox ?

There is a bird in Virginia and Carolina, and I suppose in Pennsylvania, that at night calls *Whipper Will*, and sometimes,

Whip Will's widow, by which names it is called (as the bird clinketh, the fool thinketh). I have omitted to describe it, and therefore should be glad of it. I believe it is a kind of cuckoo.

Your House Swallow is different from ours, and singular in its tail, and nest, which is artfully made with small sticks, and cemented together with a kind of glue. The bird with the nest, would be acceptable.

With what I now send of my book, you have all the American small birds that I have figured, except seven or eight, by which you may guess what other birds your country affords. But such observations may be too troublesome, without a strong inclination. New animals of any kind are always acceptable. Birds are best preserved (if not too large) by drying them gradually in an oven : and when sent, cover them in tobacco dust. There is no other way in preserving fish, and reptiles, than in spirits or rum, which method will also do for birds.

I present you now, the second and third parts of my book, in retaliation of your kindness.

* * * I am, Mr. BARTRAM, with all sincerity,

Your obliged friend and servant,

M. CATESBY.

DEAR FRIEND :—

I own myself your debtor, not from design or inclination, but I have really been discouraged by my ill fortune, of losing not only what I sent to America, but also the two last years' cargoes you intended me ; which loss the deprivation of time doubles. Yet, nevertheless, your kind intentions equally oblige me as if attended with success, and require a retaliation which I shall endeavour, the first opportunity, to acquit myself of. In the mean time, accept of this book of birds.

As Mr. COLLINSON gives me the pleasure of reading your entertaining letters, I find you have sent me a plant of your *Anona*, some seeds of your tall *Magnolia*, &c., for which I heartily thank you.

In a letter to you, in April, 1744, I have mentioned in general what will be acceptable ; which I mention, because I don't remember any of your succeeding letters take any notice of your receiving it.   In it was an account of the *Sesamum*, &c.

I am sincerely

Your obliged friend and servant,

M. CATESBY.

April 15, 1746.

JOHN BARTRAM TO ALEXANDER CATCOT.

May 26, 1742.

RESPECTED FRIEND :—

I have now before me thy two kind letters of February the 2d, and March the 13th.   I am well pleased those seeds I collected for thee were acceptable.

I find by thy letter, thee supposes I was born in England; but I assure thee I was born in Pennsylvania, and never have been out of sight of land since; and I believe have taken more pains after the study of Botany, and the operations of nature, than any other that was born in English America, notwithstanding my low fortune in the world, which laid me under a necessity of very hard labour for the support of my family; having now a wife and seven small children, whose subsistence depends on the produce that is raised on my farm, which is situate on a navigable river, near Philadelphia.   But I have had, ever since I was twelve years of age, a great inclination to Botany and Natural History; but could not make much improvement therein, for want of books, or other instructions, until I entered into correspondence with my good friend PETER COLLINSON, who engaged, first, Lord PETRE, then, PHILIP MILLER, and the Dukes of Richmond and Norfolk, to sub-scribe thirty guineas, in order to enable me to travel into Maryland, Virginia, New Jersey, and York Government, to search for forest seeds, roots, and plants, to adorn their gardens, and other apartments where they thought proper to dispose of them.   They have also sent me varieties of roots and seeds for my garden, and several books for my instruction.

To my friends, Doctor DILLENIUS and M. CATESBY, I sent my observations on such things as will be proper materials to assist them in composing their fine histories, for which they promised me one of their books.

Sir HANS SLOANE desired I would send him some curiosities,

which I did last fall; for which, I hear he hath sent me his two books of the History of Jamaica,—which I expect every day.

We have great variety of Martagons. I have sent my friend COLLINSON many, which flowered finely in his garden. Thee may expect a curious collection of them, and other fine flowers, from me by the first opportunity.

Merchant WILLING expresses a mighty respect for thee, and saith he will do anything in assisting me to oblige thee.

What plant PLUKENET names a *Cyclamen*, that is a native of our colony, I can't imagine.* Indeed, we have several plants whose leaves somewhat resemble it, but they belong to other tribes; and I saw a plant near the mountains of Virginia, whose leaves had the appearance of a *Cyclamen*, in the shape and marks of its leaves, but really was a species of the *Asarum*. If I knew how PLUKENET described his *Cyclamen*, I could judge better; but I could never yet have the happiness to read any of that valuable author's books, though much desired. I believe there is not one of them in our parts. Our Americans have very little taste for these amusements. I can't find one that will bear the fatigue to accompany me in my peregrinations. Therefore, consequently, thee may suppose I am often exposed to solitary and difficult travelling, beyond our inhabitants, and often under dangerous circumstances, in passing over rivers, climbing over mountains and precipices, amongst the rattlesnakes, and often obliged to follow the track, or path, of wild beasts for my guide through these desolate and gloomy thickets.   *   *   *   *

November 24, 1743.

RESPECTED FRIEND CATCOT :—

I received thy kind present of three books. GREW and BRADLEY

* The Editor is indebted to his friend, DANIEL B. SMITH, for the subjoined note :—

"The plant here spoken of, as *Cyclamen*, is no doubt the *Dodecatheon Meadia*, L. Of JOHN BARTRAM's finding this plant, I have heard THOMAS STEWARDSON relate the following story. A person visiting the BARTRAM Garden, noticed the *Cyclamen*, and told J. B. he had seen such a plant in a certain place, which he described, and which was then far in the wilderness. Some months after, J. B. met him in the street, and said, 'Well, I have got the plant.' Not recollecting the circumstance, he asked, 'What plant?' J. B. reminded him of the conversation at his Garden, and told him he had travelled on foot to the place he described, and obtained the plant!—This letter accounts for the great interest he took in it, as confirming the accuracy of PLUKENET."

I had read before ; but now, by thy favour, I have them my own ; before, I borrowed them. As for LOBEL, I had his long ago. There is little in him, but collections from others ; but I am obliged to thee for thy good will, in sending them. But I had rather thee had sent TOURNEFORT'S third book of his Complete Herbal, or Botanical Institutions, in English, which I very much want ; having never seen it, nor know not where to borrow it.

I have now sent thee, by friend WILLING, a box of curious flowering plants, in earth. One root of *Yucca*, I slipped off one of my old roots, in the spring, and planted it for thee,—which I now send. It grows eight feet high, with near a hundred flowers upon one stalk. Thee will also receive a fine collection of seeds, of our best flowering wild plants, with my remarks upon each particular.

JOHN BARTRAM TO DOCTOR COLDEN.*

January 16th, 1742–3.

RESPECTED FRIEND :—

If I had not had some acquaintance with thy person and thy disposition, I should be apt to think thee could hardly believe the

* CADWALLADER COLDEN was born in Scotland, February 17, 1688. Having received a liberal education, he next applied himself particularly to Medicine and Mathematics, and was distinguished for his proficiency in both. Allured by the fame of WILLIAM PENN's Colony of Pennsylvania, and also by some expectations from an aunt residing in Philadelphia, he came over to this Province in the year 1710, where he practised physic for some years with considerable reputation, and then returned to England, which he found greatly distracted in consequence of the troubles of 1715. After a short residence there, he married a young lady of a respectable Scotch family, by the name of CHRISTIE, with whom he returned to America, in 1716. Governor HUNTER, of New York, conceived so favourable an opinion of Doctor COLDEN, after a short acquaintance, that he became his warm friend, and offered his patronage if he would remove to New York. In 1718, he therefore settled in that city. He was the first who filled the office of Surveyor-General in the Colonies. He received also the appointment of Master in Chancery. In 1722, he was honoured with a seat in the King's Council of the Province, to the head of which Board he afterwards rose by survivorship; and in that station succeeded to the administration of the government, in 1760. Previous to this, Doctor COLDEN had obtained a patent for a tract of land, in the then county of Ulster (now Orange), about nine miles from Newburgh ; and to this place, which in his patent is called *Coldengham*, he retired with his family about the year 1739. There he undertook to clear and cultivate a small part of the tract, as a farm ; and where his attention was divided between agricultural and philosophi-

pleasure I received, in reading thy agreeable letter of December 22d, which I received yesterday. It put me in mind of what our friend COLLINSON wrote to me, last fall, and desired me to call and see, for that I should find thee a man after my own heart. I had before sent thee three letters, and had no answer, which almost discouraged me from writing, yet resolved to write once more.

I am now as well in health as I have been for several years; and since my recovery, have been along our sea-coast, as I gave thee an account of in my last letter, sent with the walnuts, which I am glad are under thy son's care; but am sorry that thee had not received them directly, soon after their arrival at York, for I had taken care to keep them in moderate moist vegetative condition until the day the sloop sailed with them; and if they dry or

cal pursuits, and the duties of his office of Surveyor-General. The spot which he had selected for his retirement is entirely inland, and has nothing remarkably pleasant in it. At the time he chose it for a residence, it was solitary, uncultivated, and the country around it absolutely a wilderness. It was, besides, a frontier to the Indians, who were often in a state of hostility, and committed frequent barbarities.

In 1761, Dr. COLDEN was appointed Lieutenant-Governor of New York; which commission he held till near the time of his death; which took place at his country seat, on Long Island, on the 28th of September, 1776, in the 89th year of his age.

Notwithstanding his numerous and important public duties, Doctor COLDEN was zealously devoted to the pursuits of Literature and Science; and while he maintained an extensive correspondence with the learned of the old world, he was ever delighted to receive his scientific friends beneath his own hospitable roof. In a letter from Doctor GARDEN to LINNÆUS, dated Charleston, South Carolina, March 15, 1755, that gentleman says, " When I came to New York, I immediately inquired for *Coldenhamia*, the seat of that most eminent botanist, Mr. COLDEN. Here, by good fortune, I first met with JOHN BARTRAM, returning from the Blue Mountains, as they are called. How grateful was such a meeting to me! And how unusual in this part of the world! What congratulations and salutations passed between us! How happy should I be to pass my life with men so distinguished by genius, acuteness and liberality, as well as by eminent botanical learning and experience! Men, in whom the greatest knowledge and skill are united to the most amiable candour—

> ——— *Animæ, quales neque candidiores*
> *Terra tulit.*

" Whilst I was passing my time most delightfully with these gentlemen, they were both so obliging as to show me your letters to them; which has induced me, sir, to take the liberty of writing to you, in order to begin a correspondence, for which I have long wished, but never before found the means of beginning."— REES's *Cyclopædia; and the Linnæan Correspondence.*

mould in the box, I doubt the vegetative life will be destroyed before they are planted, which I would have performed in this manner ; after a spot of ground is dug, or ploughed, then hoe or plough a furrow two inches deep ; then drop the nuts therein about six inches asunder, and cover them with earth. Next summer, they may grow six, eight, or ten inches high ; then, the spring following they may be taken up, and planted in a row for a hedge, about five feet distance ; and when they are grown as thick as one's arm, they may be plashed in the beginning of March, just before the sap interposes between the bark and the wood. Pray, is your river frozen so as to hinder boats to pass to and fro ? Our rivers are very open this winter ; and, in my garden, the Mezereon, Groundsel, Black Hellebore, Henbit, *Esula*, and *Veronica*, are in flower, and many others in bud ; but we had a sharp time the beginning of November.   *   *   *   *

June the 26th, 1743.

FRIEND COLDEN :—

I have lately received orders from London to travel, to gather the seeds of the Balm of Gilead, and other species of evergreens. The Duke of Norfolk hath subscribed twenty guineas, the Duke of Richmond and two other gentlemen fifteen more ; besides, our proprietor hath sent me orders to procure some curiosities for him.

I am now providing for a journey up Susquehanna, with our interpreter, in order to introduce a peaceable understanding between the Virginians and the Five Nations. We suppose the meeting will be in the Onondaga's country, not far from your Fort Oswego. We are to set out in a week or two. If thee would please to be so kind as to write to the Captain of your Fort, or the Minister in the Mohawk's country, in my favour, it might do me a kindness in a strange land, if I should return home that way, and through Albany, which I can't yet know.

Neither do I know whether we shall ride any farther up Susquehanna, than the great Western Branch (which runs towards Alleghany), where one of their chiefs lives, whom we are to take with us to the treaty ; and according to his advice we are to proceed, either on horseback, or by water, up the river as far as navigable ; thence by land to the Onondaga's River. This journey, I hope, if we have good success, may afford us a fine opportunity of many curious observations.

DOCTOR COLDEN TO JOHN BARTRAM.

Coldengham, November 7th,'1745.

DEAR MR. BARTRAM :—

I am much obliged to you for the information in yours of the 4th of October, which did not come to my hands till the 3d of this month. Mr. COLLINSON wrote to me that he had forwarded my packet to Doctor GRONOVIUS; and mentioned the curious instructions Doctor GRONOVIUS had sent you, and wished I could see them. Perhaps LEWIS EVANS may take the trouble to copy them for me.

The experiments Doctor FOTHERGILL would set you upon, and has enabled you to make, may certainly be very useful, if carefully executed.

We have very few Mineral Springs in this Province.* All that I have heard of, is a stream on the south side of Anthony's Nose, a mountain in the Highlands, between my house and New York. It runs down a precipice into Hudson's River. Sloop men, who use the river, say that they have always found it purgative; and lately I heard that a sloop, being in want of water, took in some from that stream. They had many passengers, men and women. The water proved purgative to all of them.   *   *   *   *

*   *   *   As there is no anchorage on that side of the river, near that stream, I never had any opportunity to observe it; and I doubted of the truth of the accounts I had casually received of it. But now, if I have any opportunity, I shall take some more notice of it.

There is a good deal of ore found in that hill—a mixture of iron and copper; and they being mixed, has made the ore of no use. I am not sufficiently acquainted with the methods of trying mineral waters. I have never thought on that subject; but I find that *Sal Ammoniac* will give a blue tincture to anything impregnated with copper, and galls give a black to the tinctures from iron. If

---

* The waters of *Saratoga*, now so celebrated, and so much resorted to by the fashionable world, were then unknown.

my memory do not fail me, I shall try this with galls, and *Sal Ammoniac.*

My son tells me, that upon a survey in the Mohawk's River, they met with a spring which let fall considerable quantities of sulphur; and that the Indians who were with him filled their kegs with the water of this spring, to carry home for the use of some that were sick. It is not a hot spring. I have never heard of any hot springs in this country. Colonel MORRIS, I remember, several years since told me of a very good chalybeate spring, in Monmouth County, in East Jersey: and this is all the information I can give you, on this subject. I forgot to mention the spring in the Onondaga country, which, perhaps, you saw when you were there, which throws up a kind of Naphtha, or Petroleum, or Barbadoes Tar.

Mr. COLLINSON wrote to me, that he had directed my brother's letter to your care, and from thence I concluded that it was put up among your papers. I have received a letter from my brother since the date of that, which makes the loss of it of no consequence. I thank you for the piece of news, of the Russian Expedition to America, which is well worth the notice of Great Britain; as likewise for the seeds of *Saururus,* and Stargrass.

I inclose a few seeds of the *Arbor vitæ.* When at my son's, in the end of September, I found the seed ripe, and gathered a little; but being obliged to return home speedily, I resolved to send my son JOHN to gather more, who was then with me. Something made me delay it for five or six days; and when he came, the seed were everywhere fallen. I little suspected its being so soon gone, otherwise I should have taken care to have got you enough to send to your correspondents.

As to your Philosophical Society, I can say nothing but that, as it is certain that some have been too lazy, so others may have been too officious; which makes the more prudent afraid of them.

Doctor MITCHELL writes to me, that he has sent you some account of the Virginia Pines. I should be glad to see anything that comes from that curious and learned gentleman.

I heartily wish you and yours all health and prosperity; and am your affectionate friend and servant,

CADWALLADER COLDEN.

Since I wrote this, I received by way of London, Doctor GRO-

NOVIUS'S packet, with LINNÆUS'S *Fundamenta Botanica, Critica Botanica*, and GRONOVII *Flor. Virg.*, 1st and 2d parts, and his *Index suppellect.* I have likewise sent away my letters for him and Mr. COLLINSON ; therefore, when you write to Doctor GRO-NOVIUS, tell him that I received, the 8th of November, those books, and his letters dated the 6th of August, and 3d of October, 1743, after I had wrote to him.

Coldengham, May 9th, 1746.

DEAR MR. BARTRAM :—

You must excuse my not answering your kind letter of the 25th of January sooner. It was above two months in coming to my hand ; and since that time, I have had my head so much set on a certain affair, that I could not think of anything else.

I return inclosed to you Doctor GRONOVIUS'S letter to you, and am obliged to you for the perusal of it. That part of learning of which it treats, I am so little acquainted with, that if I were to translate what he writes, it is probable I may make nothing but a series of blunders ; but for your satisfaction, I shall turn the first sentence the best I can, as it is to show the manner in which he intends to publish what you send him ; viz.

" We must now pass to such stones as have a resemblance of some animal, or of its shell or covering, and which authors commonly call petrifactions, and which they make no doubt in producing them as proofs of the ancient deluge. This excellent man [JOHN BARTRAM] observed these, variously situated on the ground; some on the surface of the earth, others sunk deep ; for what he found in the *southern* parts of Pennsylvania, towards the great Lakes of Canada [is not this a mistake ?], lay on the surface of the ground ; and in a journey which he made of some hundreds of miles, he found them scattered everywhere."*

Your account of the Indian grave, is so far from requiring any excuse for writing it, that I am much pleased with your account, as it discovers how long bread and corn may be preserved, when kept in dry sand from the air; and shows that the Indians did not get their Indian corn from the Europeans.

* For the *original* of this paragraph, see the letter of GRONOVIUS to JOHN BAR-TRAM, dated *Leyden*, 25th of July, 1744. The query in brackets is Doctor COL-DEN'S. *Southern* is evidently a mistake for northern.

You may expect to see more from me, when I can obtain anything that I can think will be entertaining to you; and which may better serve to show how much I value your correspondence, than anything I can write at present.

I am, very affectionately,

Your humble servant,

CADWALLADER COLDEN.

Coldengham, January 27th, 1746-7.

DEAR MR. BARTRAM:—

It is so long that I have lost the pleasure of my wonted correspondence with you, that I am afraid of my having fallen under your censure; and which would give me more concern, than the censure of some great men in the world. But if you knew the true reason of my discontinuing to write, as usual, you would be so far from blaming me, that you would pity me.

I was unexpectedly engaged in the public business, and when I entered upon it, I expected it would only have been for one single piece of service; but one drew on another, and I was kept more months from my family, than I expected to have been weeks from them.

But at last I have got to my country retirement, and to those amusements in which I place my delight; but not to enjoy them so fully as formerly, by reason of interruptions which unexpectedly break in upon me.

The distempers which you mention to have been epidemical with you, seem, by what you wrote to me, of the same nature with the malignant fever that was at Albany while I was there, and carried off many. It was of the remittent kind, accompanied with profuse sweating and prostration of appetite. Madeira wine proved the most effectual specific; which most people were surprised at, when I advised it; but I had so old an authority as HIPPOCRATES for the use of wine in some kind of fevers. This was attended with so much success, that the use of it became common.

It gives me much pleasure to think that your name and mine may continue together, in remembrance of our friendship. I do not know the plant, of which you send me the description from GRONOVIUS. It is none of them I described to him; and therefore I suppose you have sent it to him, and that he has honoured it with your name.

It was not possible for me to comply with your desire, of sending you a plant of the *Arbor vitæ*, for it was the 14th of December before I returned home from New York.

All my botanical pleasures have been stopped this summer, while I was at Albany. We durst not go without the fortifications without a guard, for fear of having our scalps taken; and while I was at New York, I was perpetually in company, or upon business, so that I shall be a very dull correspondent. However, I designed to have sent you something of our transactions, by Mr. FRANKLIN, at his return from Boston; but he stayed so long, that I left New York before he returned; and I was at last exceedingly hurried, in leaving that place. If I had stayed one day longer, the river had become impassable.

Now, dear Mr. BARTRAM, take pity on me, and let me have some share of that pleasure which you receive from your correspondents. I have not a line from any, but a short one from Mr. COLLINSON, of the 3d of August. I expected to have heard from GRONOVIUS, by a ship expected from Amsterdam, and by which I wrote to him; but I do not hear that she is arrived. I sowed some of the seed of the *Arbor vitæ*, but it failed as yours did. Perhaps they may germinate next year.

Can you give me no hopes of seeing you, in your rambles next summer, in search of new knowledge of things? Pray, make my compliments to the good woman, your spouse, and be assured,

That I am your affectionate, humble servant,

CADWALLADER COLDEN.

DOCTOR FOTHERGILL* TO JOHN BARTRAM.

London, 22d twelfth month, 1743–4.

ESTEEMED FRIEND JOHN BARTRAM :—

I think myself highly obliged, in the first place to my friend

---

* JOHN FOTHERGILL, an eminent physician and philanthropist, was born at Carr-end, Yorkshire, England, on the 8th March, 1712, of respectable parents, who were members of the Society of Friends. He was educated at Sedberg School, Yorkshire, where he obtained a competent knowledge of the Latin language, and some acquaintance with the Greek. About the year 1728, he was apprenticed to an apothecary, at Bradford. After the completion of his appren-

Doctor BOND, for his favourable description of me, and in the next, to thyself, for thy acceptable present, which came safe ; and yet more, for thy generous offers of assisting me, in procuring such

ticeship, he removed to Edinburgh, where he pursued his studies with diligence, and graduated on the 13th of August, 1736. He then entered himself a physician's pupil, at St. Thomas's Hospital, in London, the practice of which he attended for two years. After a short excursion to the Continent with a few friends, in the spring of 1740, he returned to London, and took up his residence in White Hart Court, Grace Church Street, where he continued during the greater part of his life ; and where he acquired and established both his fame and his fortune. In 1754, Doctor FOTHERGILL was elected a fellow of the College of Physicians, at Edinburgh ; and in 1763, a similar honour was conferred upon him by the Royal Society of London. These were not the only academical honours which his great merits procured for him. He was one of the earliest members of the American Philosophical Society ; and in 1776, when a Royal Medical Society was instituted at Paris, Doctor FOTHERGILL was one of a select number of foreign physicians, whom the Society thought proper to rank among their associates.

Doctor FOTHERGILL had very early acquired a taste for *Botany*, which he indulged in proportion as the profits of his practice increased. For this purpose, he purchased an estate at Upton, in Essex, containing, beside other lands, between five and six acres of garden-ground. In this place, at an expense seldom undertaken by an individual, and with an ardour that was visible in the whole of his conduct, he procured from all parts of the world a great number of the rarest plants, and protected them in the most ample buildings, which England or any other country, had then seen. In compliment to his zeal and abilities, the younger LINNÆUS distinguished a plant, of the class Polyandria Digynia [a North American shrub, somewhat resembling the *Alder*, in habit, and referred to the natural order of HAMAMELACEÆ], by the name of *Fothergilla*. But the exertions of Doctor FOTHERGILL were not confined to Botany ; he studied the other departments of Natural History, and patronised its ingenious cultivators. The great botanical work by MILLER [*The Gardener's Dictionary*], was begun and finished under the patronage of Doctor FOTHERGILL, to whom it was with great propriety inscribed ; but the dedication was afterwards cancelled, at his express solicitation ; for, although he took pleasure in encouraging ingenuity, he disliked to be told of it ; and, indeed, he was averse to dedications in general, considering them as a species of literary pageantry, more productive of envy to the patron than of advantage to the author.

Doctor FOTHERGILL was not content with exerting his talents for the benefit of science, and of his profession ; his benevolence prompted him to many other labours. But the institution of the *Seminary at Ackworth*, in Yorkshire, of which he was the projector in 1778, and to which he was a liberal benefactor, both during his lifetime and by his will, was one of the most important plans which his zeal to promote the welfare of society led him to undertake. Of his kindness and bounty to individuals, there may be mentioned an instance, in the case of his worthy but unfortunate friend, Doctor GOWIN KNIGHT, who applied to Doctor FOTHERGILL in a moment of pecuniary distress, and returned with a heart set at ease, by the noble benefaction of *a thousand guineas*. He also assisted SYDNEY PARKINSON in his account of his South Sea voyage ; and, at the expense of *two*

natural productions as your country affords. I must own it was what I had long wanted, and must have intruded myself into the number of thy correspondents, had not my friend P. COLLINSON frequently communicated whatever he could spare me.

I always admire thy industry and exactness, as well as the surprising progress thou hast made in the knowledge of plants,—a branch of my profession, which I have just applied myself to, so as to be able to know the principal *officinals* of our own country, and to collect the best accounts I could meet with, of their genuine effects. I retain this acquaintance with them, by now and then taking a walk to Peckham, or Chelsea; but cannot prevail upon myself to launch far into a study, which would rob me of more time, to cultivate with success, than my present situation will admit of.

The fossil productions have always suited my inclinations most; but I have made but little progress. I don't so much collect with a view to have a great number of odd things together, as to have so many productions of different kinds, natures, compositions, figures, &c., as, when laid together, may assist me in forming some general idea of the production of several of these kinds of substances, more consistent with the nature of things, than I have yet met with, from others. This is the entertainment of leisure hours; and is a structure which can only be erected from a multitude of materials, which time, perhaps, may supply me with, and the kindness of my friends.

The *Amianthus*, or Cotton Stone, was very acceptable. E.

thousand pounds, printed a translation of the Bible from the Hebrew and Greek originals, by ANTHONY PURVER, the Quaker, in 2 vols. folio, 1764, and in 1780, published PERCY's Key to the New Testament, for the use of his cherished seminary at Ackworth.

Finding his pleasant retreat at Upton too remote to be often visited while engaged in his profession, and yet too much within the sphere of action to be a refuge from care and importunity, Doctor FOTHERGILL procured a lease of Lea Hall, near Middlewich, in Cheshire, in the summer of 1765, to which secluded spot he afterwards made an annual retreat [with his maiden sister, himself, moreover, being a bachelor], as long as he lived; commonly leaving London in the month of July, and returning in the beginning of October,

On the 12th of December, 1780, he was attacked by a painful disease, which, notwithstanding every effort of the experienced physicians and surgeon, who attended him, terminated his life on the 26th day of the same month. His remains were deposited in the Quaker's burial ground, at Winchmore Hill, about twelve miles from London. — *See* REES's *Cyclopædia, and* BLAKE's *Biographical Dictionary.*

BLAND had sent me a very little bit, which was the only specimen
I had, till thine came to hand.

The fossil shells were likewise very acceptable. Whatever of this
kind comes to hand, will always be welcome. ELIAS likewise sent
me a little bit or two of bolar earth. I should be glad to know
whether you have it in plenty, and to have a pound weight or two
sent, for experiment. He sent me, likewise, a small, square, black
Pyrites. Have you these in plenty? If you have, please to send
a few of them. Crystals, spars, ores, sulphureous matters,—as
liquid or solid bitumen, if you have any Marcasites, very singular
earths, stones, and fossil shells, will be agreeable.

But there is another affair of more consequence than these, in
which I should be, glad of thy assistance. 'Tis possible I may now
and then have occasion to prescribe for persons in your country.
I should be glad to be informed of what helps I might expect,
which are peculiar to your country. In the first class of which, I
must mention mineral waters. Have you any of considerable note?
and near the inhabited part? Hot, or cold? Chalybeate, sulphureous, or not manifestly either, but salt and purgative? Tincture of galls, oak bark, or green tea leaves made in water, will
discover the first. If sulphureous, the smell will discover it, and
its changing silver black; if salt, the taste will manifest it. After
I am informed of these circumstances, I can easily give the directions how to acquire a still more accurate knowledge of their
nature and effects.

The next thing I should be glad to be informed about, is, what
simples of considerable efficacy, peculiar to your clime, at least indigenous, are in use among your practitioners; or even celebrated
among the vulgar. I should be glad of some specimens of such,
whether roots, leaves, fruits, or what else; not barely as specimens
to know the plants by, but a handful or two of each, carefully
dried, for experiments, with the names they are commonly known
by.

I am told that the Sassafras tree, when in bloom, casts a most
delightful fragrance around it. Pray, has ever ány trial been
made to procure a distilled water from the flowers? I fancy they
would afford a grateful and efficacious one, unless the odoriferous
particles are extremely fugitive indeed. I think, if the experiment has not been made, it would be worth while to have some
gathered at the proper season, and distilled; some with water

alone, some with the addition of a third part of rum, molasses spirit, or some other spirit, if you have any clean and cheaper. I should be glad to have a few dried flowers sent over, and some put into a quart bottle when fresh gathered, and some molasses spirit or rum, poured upon them, and then close corked.

Thus thou sees, my good friend, that thy generous offer is like to be followed with not a little trouble, and some expense ; but whatever of this kind happens, shall be thankfully repaid, and thy trouble acknowledged in the best manner I can.

I am thy obliged friend,

JOHN FOTHERGILL, JR.

P. S.   *   *   *   It just now occurs to my thoughts, and which I shall endeavour to think on again, that a collection of the several natural productions of your colony, would be a fine addition to your Public Library. No one is fitter for the undertaking than J. BARTRAM ; and some means ought to be considered, to make it worth his while. This hint may at least be so far useful, as to induce thee to keep a part by thee, of everything curious, lest thou should be called upon for that purpose.

Farewell,

J. F.

JOHN BARTRAM TO DOCTOR FOTHERGILL.

July the 24th, 1744.

RESPECTED FRIEND DOCTOR FOTHERGILL :—

I have now before me, thy kind letter of the 22d of 12th month, 1743–4. I am glad those things I sent thee prove acceptable. Perhaps I may send some few curiosities next fall ; but as times are so precarious, and my subscriptions this year, are small, I shall hardly travel above one hundred miles from home, in each direction, and consequently can't find many.

The Sassafras flowers were all fallen before I received thy letter. There is a very penetrating oil extracted from the berries, by frying them in a pan, like as you do coffee. We have abundance of medicinal roots, herbs, and barks, used with success amongst the common people, which are extolled for wonderful specifics, in many infirmities, upon the first discovery made by the

Indians on most of them. But when our people take them, not
considering age, constitution, season, nor the particular progress,
or crisis, of the distemper, but expect an immediate cure upon the
first or second dose, they are sometimes disappointed. Then it
is directly discarded and thrown out of use (especially if the
patient grows worse after taking it), and another famous specific
gains applause for awhile, then is subject to the other's fate, and
another taken into favour.

We have several springs in our province, on which many people
have bestowed a large income ; but many of them being impregnated with iron, and not agreeing with all constitutions, so as to
perfect a cure, they are of late neglected. One of them, I believe,
might be of great use to mankind under proper regulations. It is
a large spring, almost big enough to turn a mill, very cold, clear
where it springs up, but where it runs away there is a great quantity of reddish, or orange-coloured curdled matter, mixed with the
current. We have other springs partaking of vitriol, and, amongst
the mountains, some of alum ; and some places, black, fœtid, sulphureous springs.

December the 7th, 1745.

DEAR FRIEND DOCTOR FOTHERGILL :—

I received thy letter, and a box of vials, and book of L—— Spa,
which I am obliged to thee for. I sent to thee by Captain LISLE,
a box of Sassafras flowers, and other odd things, which I hope
PETER COLLINSON will give thee, if they come safe to his hands.

Doctor WITT tells me he got a good quantity of the expressed
oil of the berries, drawn at the common oil-mill, and that it makes
the best *minium* plaster of all.   *   *   *   *   *

I have not yet made much observation on our mineral waters,
for want of time to examine them, being hurried in the fall, to
procure forest seeds for my correspondents ; and indeed, if I
should make diligent and proper observations on all our mineral
waters, it would take up most of my time, or, I am sure, more than
I can spare, beside serving my benefactors in Europe, and my
plantation at home ; and still worse, because most of the trials
must be made at great distances from home.   *   *   *   I
like very well to serve my country, but as I have nine children

alive, most of which are not able to help themselves, it is my duty to provide for them.

I have lately heard of many mineral waters; one up the Mohawk River, that lets fall a quantity of sulphur. The Indians fetch the water away in kegs, for the sick to drink. One on the Highlands by the North River. Several men and women, passengers that were going up the river, drank at this spring to quench their thirst, which purged them stoutly.   *   *   *   One chalybeate spring in East Jersey; and Doctor SHAW, a brewer in Burlington, affirmed to me, that a Spa water broke into his well, which he brewed beer with, which affected the beer so much, that it purged those who drank it so much, that they thought he put a trick upon them. So he was forced to throw away fifty pounds' worth of beer, and make use of other water to brew with. Another Doctor told me of a spring near him, that if any that had the ague should drink of it, they would vomit, and cure them. And one that I was lately at, had a vitriolic taste, like copperas water.

DOCTOR FOTHERGILL TO JOHN BARTRAM.

London, 5th mo. 1st, 1769.

ESTEEMED FRIEND :—

I received thy acceptable letter on the 17th of last month; and in a short time after, I also received the box of plants in pretty good condition. Most of them will live, and divers of them are new to me. One of the Ginseng plants is coming up vigorously. I am much obliged to thee for this valuable present, and shall be glad to make returns for it, as well as I can. If a copy of PURVER'S Translation of the Bible will be acceptable, please to call upon THOMAS FISHER, in Philadelphia, and desire him to deliver one bound, and place it to my account. The author of this great undertaking, like thyself, is self-taught and instructed.*

* ANTHONY PURVER was a learned shoemaker,—a member of the *Society of Friends*, who, by his own exertions, acquired such a knowledge of the Hebrew and Greek languages, that, in 1764, he completed a literal translation of the Old and New Testament, with critical notes, a most laborious performance, the fruit of thirty years' application. This he was enabled to publish in two folio volumes, by the generosity of his friend, Doctor FOTHERGILL, who, "made him a present of £1000 for the copy, and took upon himself the expense of printing the work." A. PURVER was also highly respected as a public minister among *Friends*. He died at Andover, in 1777, aged seventy five years.

Almost without any assistance, but from books, he has acquired the knowledge of many languages; and the best judges allow that this translation is the most faithful one of the original Scripture, that ever was made in the English tongue. Let me know if there is anything here, in which I can make thee proper satisfaction, and I will do it cheerfully. I don't want my friends should make brick without straw.

There will be a considerable demand for American seeds to various parts of Germany, and were there any in town, I know they might be disposed of. I have a nephew by marriage, who lives in our deceased friend P. COLLINSON's house, and carries on the business of a mercer. If MICHAEL COLLINSON does not choose to engage in the business of disposing of the seeds, I know I can readily prevail upon him to undertake it. He has no skill in these matters; but he would take care to render a faithful account of the sales, and make due remittances. I am afraid of intrusting these things to the care of the seedsmen. JAMES GORDON, Jr., is I believe, one of the best, yet one cannot be sure that they will always continue to be faithful and honest. If MICHAEL COLLINSON will be kind enough to undertake the affair, no person is more proper. I will see him as soon as I can, and endeavour to prevail upon him. Should he decline it, and no other person seem more suitable, send thy boxes to JAMES FREEMAN, mercer, in Gracious Street; and any instructions thou thinks proper to me, and I will take care they shall be duly executed.

I am pleased that thy son WILLIAM is engaged in describing the Tortoises of your country. America seems to abound with this species of animal, more than any other country. As the inhabitants increase, these, as well as the native plants, will be thinned; and it is, therefore, of some consequence to begin their history as soon as possible.

I would not limit him, either in respect to time or expense. He may send me his drawings, and accounts of their history, as he finishes them; and I will pay his demands to his order.   *   *

I shall expect the *Colocasia*, when convenient to send it, and shall do my best to preserve it. I doubt not but my friend, B. FRANKLIN, has executed his commission. However, I hope to see him, shortly, and shall endeavour to inform myself of what is done, and acquaint thee with it.

The present gardener at Kew is, from general account, a very ingenious, sensible, honest man. It will be much in his power to determine the royal personages ; and I think it would not be improper to write to him, if any plants are sent. His name is AITON ; and if a line or two are sent to him, I will take care to convey it safely.

As I wish to make thee adequate satisfaction for the trouble thou hast taken, and may take on my account, I should be glad to know in what way I can most satisfactorily make thee compensation. Through the favour of Providence, and much careful labour, I want for nothing ; and therefore would desire that all due satisfaction may be given to those who are kind enough to do anything for me.

This, perhaps, will be delivered by Doctor RUSH, a young man who has employed his time with great diligence and success, in prosecuting his studies here ; who has led a blameless life, so far as I know ; and it seems but just that those who have endeavoured to deserve a good character, should have it when it may be of use to them.

My engagements in the duties of my station, may, perhaps, render me a very irregular correspondent ; but my inclination to show regard to every person who was the friend of my deceased friend, P. COLLINSON, will always lead me to be as diligent as I can.

I am thy obliged, respectful friend,

J. FOTHERGILL.

Direct for me, in Harpur Street, near Red Lion Square, London.

London, 13th 1st month, 1770.

DEAR FRIEND :—

I have now before me thy two kind letters of the 26th and 28th November last. I have received the box of plants, the cask of *Colocasia*, and the Bull-frogs alive. I likewise received a roll of drawings, directed to me, all safe and very acceptable.

The plants came in good condition. The roots of the *Colocasia* seemed but in a doubtful situation. However, they are planted, part at Kew,* and part in a little piece of water at Upton, my little residence, exactly agreeable to thy instructions.

     *   *   *   *

A place is not yet fixed upon for the Bull-frogs to be put in. In the mean time, however, they are kept in a shallow vessel of water, the bottom covered with moss, where they may either put their heads above or under water, as they like. We have now a severe frost; but when this goes off, they will be set at large, somewhere, and in safety. We have none of the kind in England. The King is acquainted with their arrival, also the *Colocasia*, and from whom they come.   *   *   *   *   *

Mention is made in thy letter of some drawings designed for the Duchess of Portland. I received only one roll, and that directed to me, consisting of drawings of the *Colocasia*, a new species of *Momordica*, Shells, &c., six in number. If any of them are designed for the Duchess, be pleased to inform me. If they are for me—which I hope—be kind enough to give me some intimation of their value, which I will pay to my kinsman.

I must still desire that thy son will favour me with drawings of the rest of your American Tortoises, with such remarks on them as occur to him. As the inhabitants increase, the species of this and some other animals, as well as vegetables, will, perhaps, be extinguished, or exist only in some still more distant parts. It would, therefore, be of great advantage to natural history, to have everything of a fugitive nature consigned to paper, with as much accuracy as possible; and in inquiring into the value of these drawings, I do not so much want to know at how low a price he can afford them, as what, in his own opinion, will be a proper compensation for his labour and his time. And whatever he attempts of the kind, let it be well finished; and I hope he will not find me niggardly.   *   *   *   *   *   *

I hope to send thee, in the spring, some little account of our late kind friend P. COLLINSON's life and services in respect to Botany. For several years past, I have left London about ten weeks in the summer, and get about one hundred and sixty miles

---

* In the *Hortus Kewensis* (*first edition*, 1789), this plant is said to have been "*introduced* 1787, by Sir JOSEPH BANKS, Bart." P. COLLINSON and Doctor FOTHERGILL had made repeated attempts, several years before that time, to obtain it, through the agency of JOHN BARTRAM and HUMPHRY MARSHALL; as demonstrated by their correspondence.

from it, in order to recruit my strength against winter, for the duties of my station. It was in one of these intervals that our friend was carried off, by a suppression of urine. Had I been present, I know not that anything more could have been done, to have saved him.

When I was informed of his decease,—partly to indulge my sorrow—partly to pay some tribute to his memory, I employed myself in drawing a short account of his character. A few copies will, I believe, be printed this spring, for the satisfaction of his friends ; and I will take care that a few be sent to thee.

I have not leisure to become a perfect Botanist. I love the vegetable creation. I love its rarities, and cultivate it as an amusement. Every new plant is an addition to my pleasure. I have most of the common produce of America, and they flourish with me, more than anywhere else.   *   *   *

Thy assured friend,

J. FOTHERGILL.

ESTEEMED FRIEND :—

Having an opportunity of sending thee the inclosed performance of my friend, JOHN ELLIS, by a young man who comes over as an apothecary to your hospital, I could not well avoid just sending thee two or three lines, though much straitened for time. *   *

Thy son will be kind enough to continue his drawings of any nondescripts he may meet with, either plants or animals ; and I shall endeavour to make him proper satisfaction.

I hope soon to send thee a short account of the life of our late worthy friend, P. COLLINSON ;—at least an essay towards his character. A few copies will be printed, to give amongst his friends ; and no one is more entitled to this epithet than thyself. I am, with much esteem,

Thy assured friend,

JOHN FOTHERGILL.

Harpur Street, 19th, 3, 1770.

[No date, probably 1772.]

ESTEEMED FRIEND :—

Constant and various engagements have long prevented me from writing to thee. For some years past I have retired from London to a considerable distance, for about two months, in order to recover strength sufficient to undergo the duties of my profession. Here I used to have a little time to correspond with my distant friends ; but last year I was wholly prevented.   *   *   *

The Frogs came safe, and lively. I transcribed thy account of them, and had it delivered to the King, with an intimation that they were in my hands, and should be sent whenever he would please to order. No order ever came to me.   *   *   *

I imagine they are quite forgot, and will never be called for ;* and having once made the offer, through a channel of some consequence, I shall make no farther overture.

*   *   * In a letter to my nephew, thou intimates that probably WILL. YOUNG may have endeavoured to raise some prejudice against thee. He has not. He durst not attempt it, as he knew my esteem for thee. He never spoke one word to thy disadvantage. My silence has been solely owing to incessant occupation. I have endeavoured to assist this poor man, and have aided him considerably ; but he will not succeed, nor can he be supported.

A few weeks ago I received a letter and some drawings, from thy son WILLIAM, in Carolina. For his sake, as well as thine, I should be glad to assist him. He draws neatly ; has a strong relish for Natural History ; and it is pity that such a genius should sink under distress. Is he sober and diligent ? This may be an uncommon question to ask a father of his son ; and yet I know thy integrity will not suffer thee to mislead me. I would not have it understood that I mean to support him. I would lend him, however, some little assistance, if he is worthy. He proposes to go to Florida. It is a country abounding with great variety of plants, and many of them unknown. To search for these, will be of use to science in general; but I am a little selfish. I wish to introduce into this country the more hardy American plants, such as will bear our winters without much shelter. However, I shall endeavour to assist his inclination for a tour through Florida ; and if he succeeds, shall, perhaps, wish him to see the back parts of Canada. Many curious flowering plants will doubtless be found about the lakes, that will grow anywhere.

* About those days, the premonitory symptoms of the American Revolution were making their appearance, and his Britannic Majesty had *American productions* to attend to, which were rather more interesting to him, at that time, than our bull-frogs.

We have totally lost, in this country, the *Tetragonotheca*. Will it be possible to get some seeds, or a few roots of it ? I believe nobody in America knows it, or where it is to be found, but thyself.

My garden is pretty large, well sheltered, and a good soil. The North American plants flourish with me exceedingly. I have most of the common plants usually sent over ; but have room for everything. I am fond of the Ferns. I have several from America, but not all. I do not want to have a specimen of every thing that grows, in my garden ; but plants that are remarkable for their figure, their fragrance, or their use, are exceedingly acceptable.

I must own that with this inclination to increase my collection of plants, I have very little time to spend amongst them. I see them now and then, transiently. But I look forwards, and that it is not impossible but I may live long enough to think it proper to decline all business. Then an amusement of this kind will have its use ; to lessen the tediousness of old age, and call me out to a little exercise, when subsiding vigour prompts to too much indulgence.

I hope thou will perceive from this, that my regard for thy deserts is undiminished, and that, for thy own sake, as well as my deceased friend, P. COLLINSON'S, I am thy assured friend,

JOHN FOTHERGILL.

DR. FOTHERGILL TO WILLIAM BARTRAM.

London, 22d Oct., 1772.

RESPECTED FRIEND :—

I received thy obliging letter, and the drawings that accompanied it. They are very neatly executed ; and I should be glad to receive the like of any new plant or animal that occurs to thee. If it was possible to be a little more exact in the parts of fructification, and where these are very diminutive, to have them drawn a little magnified, I should be pleased ; and at the same time if the plants, or seeds of such curious plants, could be collected and sent hither, it would be very acceptable.

I should have wrote by the person who brought thy letter and the drawings over, but he went away before I was apprised of it. I shall desire Dr. CHALMERS, of Charleston, to make thee a little present for the drawings ; and I should be glad to contribute to thy assistance, in collecting the plants of Florida, if thou would suggest what terms might be agreeable. That no time, however, may be lost, should this come to thy hands, at Charleston, I shall desire Dr. CHALMERS to confer with thee on this subject, and to render thee such assistance as may be immediately wanted.

The drawings I could wish to have pretty correct ; and shall be willing to make due acknowledgment for them.

As I imagine thou art well acquainted with the method of packing up plants and seeds, I shall say not much on this head. All bulbous roots are easily managed. Let them be taken up when the flower fades ; dry them a little in the shade, put them in a box, either wrapped up in papers, or in dry sand, and they will come very safe.   *   *   *   *   *

I am not so far a systematic botanist, as to wish to have in my garden all the grasses, or other less observable, humble plants, that nature produces. The useful, the beautiful, the singular, or the fragrant, are to us the most material. Yet despise not the meanest. Land, river, or sea shells, would also be acceptable ; or correct drawings of them, where the originals cannot easily be procured.

Mind thy studies in drawing. Thy hand is a good one ; and by attention and care may become excellent.

But in the midst of all these attentions, forget not the one thing needful. In studying nature, forget not its Author. Study to be grateful to that hand which has endowed thee with a capacity to distinguish thyself as an artist. Avoid useless or improper company. Be much alone, and learn to trust in the help and protection of Him who has formed us, and everything. Fear Him, and He will raise thee friends, and keep thy foot from sliding.

For thy father's sake, I wish thee all good ; and for thy own, a constant, reverent trust, and hope in that Power who is ever near to help those who confide in him.

I am, and wish to be,

Thy friend,

J. FOTHERGILL.

DOCTOR FOTHERGILL TO JOHN BARTRAM.

London, 1772.

MY ESTEEMED FRIEND :—

I received thy kind letter, and am pleased that my employing thy son affords both him and thyself some satisfaction.

He may, perhaps, in the space of two or three years—if his life is spared—get into a good livelihood, by sending boxes of plants and seeds to Europe, from those less frequented parts of America.

The money advanced on his account, viz., £17, I will pay JAMES FREEMAN for thy use. A correspondent of mine, at Charleston, has directions to accommodate him, as his occasions may require.

I have lately wrote to WILLIAM, pointing out what I would principally wish him to attend to ; and I hope he will meet with suitable assistance, in journeying through those provinces, which, at present, are almost an unknown country.   *   *   *

By the kindness of my friends, and some expense, I have got together a pretty large collection of valuable plants. The North Americans prosper with me, full as well as they do anywhere else. I have likewise got a fine young Tea tree from China.   *   *

Earnestly desiring for thee all kind of comfort and satisfaction, I remain

Thy assured friend,
JOHN FOTHERGILL.

London, 8th, 7th month, 1774.

ESTEEMED FRIEND :—

I received thy very acceptable letter of the 14th, 4th month last, and am pleased to find thy health so well preserved,—so well in the evening of life.

I had a letter the other day from Doctor CHALMERS, who mentions that he had a letter lately from WILLIAM, who was going towards East Florida, and well. I have received from him about one hundred dried specimens of plants, and some of them very curious ; a very few drawings, but neither a seed nor a plant.

I am sensible of the difficulty he is at in travelling through those inhospitable countries ; but I think he should have sent me some few things as he went along. I have paid the bills he drew upon me ; but must be greatly out of pocket, if he does not take some opportunity of doing what I expressly directed, which was, to send me seeds or roots of such plants, as either by their beauty, fragrance, or other properties, might claim attention. However, I shall hope he will find means of fulfilling my orders, better than he has done hitherto.

If thy son JOHN meets with anything new in his travels about the country, I should be glad if he would send me at least a part of his discoveries ; and I hope I may be able to content him for his trouble. I am obliged to him for the seeds of the Orange-coloured *Hibiscus.* I have a good many plants of the *Illicium.* I have planted these in the natural ground, and shall give them a little shelter in the winter. It has a most grateful fragrance, and will be a pleasing green-house plant.

Please let him know that I received the Turtle in good health ; and shall be much obliged to him if he will procure me a male and female Bull-frog. Mine are strayed away notwithstanding my best endeavours. If they are put up in a little box of wet moss, they will come safe ; at least, I received a little American Frog, the *Rana ocellata,* in a box of plants, filled up with moss. They should be sent in autumn.

I shall be much pleased to see the *Tetragonotheca.* There is not, I believe, a plant of it now in England.

We have got the true Green Tea. I have a plant in the natural ground near five feet high. Mine has been sheltered in the winter, but old JAMES GORDON left his exposed to all weathers, this last winter, and yet it thrives very well. We shall propagate it as fast as we can.

Do not imagine that all the people in this country are against America. We sympathize with you much. It may be our turn to suffer next. We hope, however, that the impending storm may blow over, and that you may be enabled to act your part properly.*

I am thy assured friend,
JOHN FOTHERGILL.

* The liberal and friendly sentiments of Doctor FOTHERGILL, in relation to the difficulties of the American Colonies with the mother country, are very remarkable, and worthy of commemoration. In addition to the feelings and views indicated in his letters to JOHN BARTRAM and HUMPHRY MARSHALL, there are preserved in Doctor LETTSOM's edition of his works, two *Addresses* to his countrymen,

JOHN BARTRAM TO J. F. GRONOVIUS.*

November the 30th, 1743.

RESPECTED FRIEND DOCTOR GRONOVIUS :—

I received thy kind letter, and LINNÆUS's *Characters*, with thy *Index Lapideæ*, by the hands of my friend PHINEAS BOND. I have got them neatly bound up together in one book ; since which, I have received the second part of the *Flora Virginica ;* all which I am very much obliged to thee for, and shall endeavour to send thee specimens of what I suppose may be acceptable. I have put in the box, a glass bottle with one of our red-bellied snakes *   *
[*Hiatus in MS.*]

J. F. GRONOVIUS TO JOHN BARTRAM.

DEAR SIR :—

In the month of Juny I was surprised to see such a variety of natural things, which you are pleased to send to me. I assure you I shall always endeavour to deserve your favour, and not keep your observations for my own, but make them public to the learned world. And, to be short, I shall give you an account how I proposed to go on. First, I propose to dispose all what you send me in their orders, vid., regnum lapideum, vegetabile and animale ; and secondly, in their classes, genera, and species. This being done, I endeavour to explain every particular, of which I give you the following scheme about the petrifications.

Transeundum nunc est ad tales lapides, qui simulacrum ani-

at home, which, for vigour of style, cogency of appeal, and the sturdy spirit of freedom which they breathe, will compare favourably with the patriotic manifestos issued by our revolutionary fathers.

* JOHN FREDERIC GRONOVIUS, a physician and botanist of considerable learning, was born in Holland, in 1690. He took his Doctor's Degree at Leyden, in 1715. He received from CLAYTON various specimens of Virginian plants, which he, with the assistance of LINNÆUS, then resident in Holland, arranged according to the Sexual System, and with proper specific characters, descriptions, and synonyms, published under the title of *Flora Virginica*, in 1739, in 8vo. In 1740, he published his *Index Suppellectilis Lapideæ*, or a scientific catalogue of his own collection of Minerals, drawn up under the inspection and with the assistance of LINNÆUS. In 1755, came out his *Flora Orientalis*, in 8vo., the materials of which were afforded by the very magnificent Herbarium of RAUWOLF, collected in his travels in the East, during the years 1573, 1574, and 1575. GRONOVIUS died in 1762, at the age of 72 years.

malis, vel ejus tectum et domicilium representant, quales PETRI-
FICATA *appellare consueverunt authores, quæque in veritatem dilu-
vianæ inundationes adducere non dubitarunt. Hæc vario sita
loco observavit vir egregius* [JOANNES BARTRAM]; *alia quippe in
superficie terræ, alia in profundo. Quæ enim in Australi* [?]
*Pensilvaniæ plaga, immensos Canadæ lacus respiciens, occurrebant,
in superficie terræ jacebant: imo in itinere, quo aliquot centum
milliaria absolvit, ea ubique sparsa reperit.* * * * * *
And in this way I propose to go on with every particular subject
you send me. In things now which are *extra sphæram meam*, I
address myselv to such gentlemans, which I know that have any
notion of them. You never can believe how our Virtuosos are
pleased to see the cells of the Wasp nests filled with Spiders, of
which they never have heard before. Professor MUSCHENBROEK
and LUHOTS cannot enough admire that mechanica. They hope
with me to give you a good account of it; only we wish you could
sent to us at an occasion one of the Humble Bees himself, and also
one long, blac Wasp num. 25 and 26. We have discovered, that
all the chrysalides of them, and those that are still in their silk
folliculus are still in life. So that you see by this way everything
will be welcome.

Pray, can you tell me how goes the Loadstone Rok, out of
which you split the Cotton Stone, num. 6? Doth she go from
east to west, or from south to north, or else way? You send to
me a shell with a sort of a Lapster in it. The shell is the *Cochlea
perlata Bonan. rar.*, class 3, *num.* 167. The animal in it is the
Heremite Krab of CATESBY, *Nat. Hist.*, vol. 2, tab. 33, fig. 2, the
Soldger of ROCHEFORT, p. 122. * * * But the paper wherein
it was involved, was inscribed with the name of Antiqua. I wish
to know if this is the Indian name. It will be very convenient
always to have the Indian names. As much as possible you
must endeavour of the *conchæ bivalves* to get both the valves.
You never can belive what a great rarity there is amongst the
muscles num. 1, and particular amongst the small ones, of which I
find severall different varietys. I belive upon strik enquiry, that
in your sea and rivers, are to be found all the species of *Conchæ*
and *Cochleæ*, which are to be found everywhere; for I see that

---

* For a translation of this passage, see Doctor COLDEN's letter to JOHN BAR-
TRAM, under date of May 9, 1746, page 331. The word "*Australi*" is evidently,
as Doctor COLDEN suggested, a mistake for *Boreali*.

under num. 2, amongst the Salt Water Shells, you send a *valva cava pectinis aurit.*, but the other ones are the most curious—to my knowledge only to be found at Curaçao, in the West Indies, and at Amboina in East India ; they are one of the valvæ of the *Ostrea perlata capite foraminoso* PETIV. *mus. n.* 823, and *Concha subrotunda, una valva perforata, cujus multiplices sunt varietates,* GUALT. *Ind. test. tab.* 97.   *   *   *   *   *

Your consideration upon the fragments of variety of pots, num. 4, is really some thing news. I don't find any mention about the earthen pots of the old Indians, before they were acquainted with the Europeans, in our Voyageurs, except SLOANE, Introd. p. 47 et 70 ; who, tabula 2, gives the figure of an *Urna,* found in Jamaica. So that your pot is a great antiquity, worth to be set in a public Musæum.

I admire so many things discovered by you in Pensilvania, which are the same in Germany. It brings me in mind a pro-blema of the botanist, that *Plantæ alpinæ ubique eædem ; plantæ ejusdem climatis fere eædem ;* and at present by your observation, we may conclude, *terram ejusdemque contenta sub eodem sæpe eadem :* for *num.* 7, the marble of your contrey is the *Stalactites calcis solidæ, Supell.* p. 15, No. 12.

*   *   *   *   *   *   *

You shall very much oblige the learned world with your commu-nications ; particular with your Yournal to the Five Nations. I am particularly desired by some learned gentlemen to ask you about the Loadstone, of which they wish to know what the longest and the thikkest piece was you remember to have seen ; and if you could spare, to have a little pieces of the same you send me, which is the most curious they ever have seen, to make experiments with it.

As soon I have an occasion to send to Mr. COLLINSON some-thing, I shall send to you the sheeds you want to compleat your *Characters,* besides another copy of the *Characters* for a pocket-book ; and another copy of my *Index supellectilis.* Pray, my service to Doctor PHINEAS BOND.

We hath here this winter, one of the Dutch ministers from Pensilvania, studiing in physick. I have seen him once in my house, but seeing that he was a man of no knowledges of all, I would not los my time with him.

Now, dear sir, I finish these, with many thanksgivings for so many curious things, which I hope, in short, to make public to the whole world, and do as PLINIUS says :—*ingenuum est profiteri per quem profeceris.*

Wishing you all health and prosperity,

I remain your most obedient servant.

J. F. GRONOVIUS.

Leyden, 25th of July, 1744.

JOHN BARTRAM TO GRONOVIUS.

December the 6th, 1745.

ESTEEMED FRIEND DOCTOR GRONOVIUS :—

I have received thy kind letters of July the 25th, 1744, and April the 14th, 1745, with thy observations on the Shells that I sent thee, and the skin of the Fish, with its fins curiously displayed on paper; all which was very acceptable. But as I did not receive a line from thee since I sent those curiosities to thee, about two years ago, until late this fall, so I could not procure any Fish, nor Insects for thee. But since I received thy letters, I have rode about the country to gather what I could for thee, and particularly to the Loadstone quarry, and bought a few Loadstones, two of which I send to thee for those two gentlemen who were so desirous of them ; with whom I should be glad to correspond by letters ; for I am ready to learn of any learned person that will be so kind as to instruct me in any branch of Natural History, which is my beloved amusement.

The Loadstone lieth in a vein of a particular kind of stone [Serpentine ?] that runs near east and west for sixty or seventy miles or more, appearing even with, or a little higher than its surface, at three, five, eight, or ten miles distance, and from ten to twenty yards broad, generally mixed with some veins of cotton [*Asbestos*].

The earth of each side is very black, and produceth a very odd, pretty kind of *Lychnis*, with leaves as narrow and short as our Red Cedar, of humble growth, perennial, and so early as to flower, sometimes, while the snow is on the ground [probably *Arenaria stricta*, Mx.] ; also, a very pretty *Alsine* [perhaps *Cerastium villosum*, Muhl., *C. oblongifolium*, Torr.]. Hardly anything else grows here. Our people call them *Barrens;* but if this black light mould be spread upon other kinds of soil, it will produce corn and grass, finely.   See more in the papers in which I have wrapped some of both the common rock and loadstone.

I have sent thee many curiosities in a box directed to thee; which I hope our worthy friend, PETER COLLINSON, will send to thee according to my direction,—if the French and Spaniards don't hinder him from the opportunity of obliging us.   Indeed, it is very discouraging to think that all my labour and charges, may very likely fall into such hands as will take no farther care of them, than to heave them overboard into the sea, as I suppose they did all that I sent last year, by the Queen of Hungaria.   If I could know that they fell into the hands of men of learning and curiosity, I should be more easy about them.   Though they are what is commonly called our enemies, yet, if they make proper use of what I have laboured for, let them enjoy it with the blessing of God.

I have sent a variety of the clay-cells, which the singing Wasps built last summer; but the wasps were gone, or dead, before thy instructions came to my hands.   I believe we have a great variety of these kinds.   I design, next summer (if my affairs go on pretty well), to make a fine collection of insects and fishes for thee.

I sent by the last ship, to Mr. COLLINSON, a Muskrat's skin, with its feet, tail, and part of its head, for thee to make particular observations thereof.

*   *   *   *   *   *   *

I have sent thy observations on the Shells, I sent thee, to our friend Dr. COLDEN; and thy letter to him, with the book for the Doctor at New York,—who died a few days before I received them.

Dr. COLDEN and I often send letters to one another.   He is a worthy gentleman, of pleasant and agreeable conversation, and great humanity.   He staid at my house one night, last year; and next day, I went with him to JAMES LOGAN'S, and from thence to Philadelphia.

Doctor MITCHELL lodged several nights at my house.   Last year, he came up to town for the advantage of better health.   He is an ingenious man: but his constitution is miserably broken, and if he don't remove soon from Virginia, he can't continue long in the land of the living.

Our friend, Dr. PHINEAS BOND, gives his service to thee.   He hath a great respect for thee.

I have lately been upon the branches of the Susquehanna, to the mountains, to fetch some roots of my great *Magnolia* [*M. acuminata*, L.]; and measured a common dry leaf fourteen inches long, and seven broad,—the trees very large and straight. I have not yet received those books thee was so kind as to send, for which I return my sincere love. I hope they are coming in the next ship from London.

* * * * * * *

I shall be much obliged to thee, if thee would please to write all thy further observations—which thee pleases to communicate to me—in English; which I can understand much better than *Latin*, which is troublesome to me to understand your sentiments. But now, dear sir, pray make use of every opportunity, that falls into thy hands, to write to me. A brisk and cheerful correspondence is very agreeable to thy sincere friend,

JOHN BARTRAM.

I have a copy of my Journal to *Onondaga*, twice,—which hath been taken; since which, I have not wrote it over again. Perhaps I may send it, next summer, again.

J. F. GRONOVIUS TO JOHN BARTRAM.

DEAR SIR :—

The 19 of May I hath the favour to get your letters, dated the 16 Novemb. and 6 December, 1745, with a good number of exceeding fine curiosities, which I partly, for short time and several occupations, have examined, and of which I send to you my observations, having the occasion that my friend, Dr. DUNDAS, is going to London. I wish you would examine if the Muskrat hath not four *mammœ*—two at the breast and two at the belly.

Professor MUSCHENBROEK is much obliged to you for the account you have given of the loadstone, and the situation of the rokke,— of which he at an occasion shall make use, and remember you as is decent.

I am sorry your voyage [journey to *Onondaga*] is fallen into the hands of the French; but I hope this present warre may be soon turned into peace; and by that occasion we may see another copy.

I am sorry you hath not received the books I hath send to you: wherefore I send to you another copy of the *Characters of* LINNÆUS; and an edition of the *Systema Naturæ* in octavo, which is very convenient for the pocket: besides, two copies of the New Chimney, translated into Dutch, of which you will be so kind to send one at an occasion to Dr. COLDEN, who hath been so kind to communicate that book, in English, to me. That invention hath found a great applause in this part of the world which is the reason that I could not hinder to let it be translated into Dutch, and no doubt soon into French. In the plate, you shall see a little alteration, what is occasioned by very skilfull people.

I send also a copy of my *Index Lapideæ;* but at present my collection is three times larger, so that I think for a new edition.

All things you send to me came very well over, except the two fishes, which were spoiled. I take, therefore, the liberty to communicate to you two prescriptions; of which one is a varnish that preserves the fishes, and any other thing, in a great perfection, viz.:

> R. Gumm. Copal. ℥iij.
> Mastiches,
> Sandarach. a ʒij.
> Spirit. vini rectificatiss. ℔ijss.
> M. lege artis.

The other is a powder, by which any creature, as quadrupeds and birds, are preserved and become very hard. I have several times made the experiment with a fowl, larger than a duck, putting him, with his excrementæ and all, into a box, which is well closed, and putting this dose of a powder all over it: when the creature became in few weeks very hard.

> R. Pulv. aloes, ℥iij.
> Myrrhæ, ℥ij.
> Sulphur,
> Alumin. a ʒj.—M. f. Pulvis.

I don't doubt it will do very well with the fishes, without taking the intestines out of them, except they may not be too thick [or large]; then the intestina must be carefull (by a gentle hole, made in the mids of the belly) taken out.

*   *   *   *   *   *   *

I hope you received my letter dated in April, 1745, by Mr. SCHOEMAKER, to whom I pray my service: likewise to Dr. COLDEN,

Dr. PHINEAS BOND, and JAMES LOGAN. I hope that he will remember me concerning the desperate affairs of our Synodus,
which are in the hands of Mr. PETERS, according to the last
account of it.

I am sorry to hear that Dr. MITCHELL is so ill. I hope he may
recover soon.

Yesterday night, I got a letter from Mr. COLLINSON, dated the
16 of May, in which he acquaint me that Dr. MITCHELL was taken
by the Tiger privateer, from St. Malo, Captain PALLIER, who took
from him all his learned observations; for which I am sorry.*

As you doth not mention a word of the caracter of a new genus
of plants, I suspect that you know nothing of it. You must know,
that with the assistance of LINNÆUS, and other friends, we discovered severall new genera, quite different from al these which
are known; and so there is made one *Bartramia,* and another
called *Coldenia.*

I can't say positively in what book they, with severall other new
characters, are printed; but I am sure that they will be found, or
in *Fauna Suecica,* or the *Acta Suecica;†* which books were in
April send from Stockholm by sea, so that they are expected here
every day : when I shall send to you that book, if there are send
duplicates of it. However, that you should know what plant it is,
I send to you the character.

BARTRAMIA.

Lappula benghalensis tetraspermos, ribesii folio, echinis orbiculatis
  ad foliorum ortum plurimis sessilibus.—*Pluk. Almag.* p. 206,
  tab. 41, fig. 5.

CAL. *Perianthium* quinquepartitum, laciniis linearibus, infra apicem
  acuminatis, deciduis.

COR. *Petala* quinque cuneiformia, unguibus longitudine calycis,
  limbo patente obtuso.

STAM. *Filamenta* decem capillaria, longitudine tubi corollæ.
  Antheræ subrotundæ.

PIST. *Germen* subrotundum. *Stylus* capillaceus, longitudine
  staminum. *Stigma* simplex.

---

* P. COLLINSON, through whom this letter was sent, adds in a note—" but Dr.
MITCHELL is arrived safe, with his wife, at London, and is much recovered."

† The genus probably first appeared in the *Flora Zeylanica,* p. 174, published
in 1747.

PERIC. nullum. *Fructus* globosus echinatus, dissiliens in
SEMINA quatuor aut quinque; hinc convexa, echinata spinis
hamatis, inde angulata.
Facies *Triumfettæ* et *Urenæ ;* sed diversissima planta.*

COLDENIA.

Teucrii facie bisnagarica tetracoccos rostrata, pilis scatens, foliis
profunde venosis. *Plukn. Alm.* p. 363, tab. 64, fig. 6.
CAL. *Perianthium* tetraphyllum, foliolis lanceolatis erectis.
COR. monopetala infundibuliformis, longitudine calycis; limbo
patulo obtuso equali quadrifido.
STAM. *Filamenta* quatuor, tubo corollæ inserta. *Antheræ* sub-
rotundæ.
PIST. *Germina* quatuor ovata. *Styli* totidem capillares, longitu-
dine staminum. *Stigmata* simplicia persistentia.
PERIC. nullum. *Fructus* ovatus scaber compressus, rostris quatuor.
SEM. quatuor acuminata, hinc convexa, scabra, inde angulata.
Facies *Neuradæ,* sed diversissima planta.

Pray, when you write to that learned gentleman, send to him a
copy of this character, and acquaint him that I, with great pleasure, perceived by your letter that my pakket is come to his hands;
but that I am extremely sorry that his things for me were taken
by the privateers.

Pray acquaint me in your next, how it goes with your learned
newly erected Society, and what improvements they have made.

This is all, dear sir, what I could perform since the 19 of May,
being now obliged by the departure of my dear friend, Doctor
DUNDAS, to finish these; wishing you and all friends health and
prosperity, wherewith I remain

Your most obedient servant,

JOHANNES FREDERICUS GRONOVIUS.

Leyden, 2 Juny, 1746.

* This plant, on which it was then proposed to establish the genus *Bartramia,*
was finally referred to *Triumfetta,* of *Plum.* and *Linn.* It is now the *Triumfetta
angulata, Lam. Dict. DC. Prodr.* 1, p. 507; *T. Bartramia, L.* (partly); *Willd. sp.
pl.* 2, p. 854; *Lappago Amboinica, Rumph. Amb.* 6, p. 59; *Bartramia, Lam. Ill.*
tab. 400, f. 2; *B. Lappago, Gaertn. Fruct.,* tab. 111.

The name was afterwards (1789) given, by HEDWIG, to a genus of humble
Mosses.

JOHN BARTRAM TO GRONOVIUS.

The 15th of 12th month, 1746.

DEAR FRIEND DOCTOR GRONOVIUS :—

I received thy kind letters of June the 2d, and September the 9th, 1746; also the second edition of LINNÆUS'S *Characters*, and thy *Index ;* all which impressions thee sent me before. But the *Systema Naturæ,* which is now received, I never had before. I have not travelled much abroad, this year, by reason of the wars and troubles, both in Europe and on our back inhabitants. The French Indians have been very troublesome, which hath made travelling very dangerous beyond our inhabitants, where I used to find many curiosities; and, indeed, these troublesome times are a great hindrance to any curious inquiries. While we may daily expect invasions, we have little heart or relish for speculations in Natural History. * * [*Cetera desunt.*]

J. F. GRONOVIUS TO JOHN BARTRAM.

DEAR FRIEND :—

It is more than four years that I have not heard from you, of which the last war was the cause. I let you know by these that I am printing a new edition of my *Index supellectilis lapideæ ;* wherein you shall find the names of all the minerals and fossils you ever had send to me, with an encomium and thanks of all the benefits you have bestowed upon me. As soon as this book is printed, I shall send a copy of it for you to Mr. COLLINSON, who is now my only correspondent in London, being our good friend Mr. CATESBY dead. You perceive how I expect to hear from you.

The bearer of these is Mr. ADOLF BENZEL, son to the Archbishop ERIC BENZEL, of Upsala, whom I recommend to you.

Wherewith, I remain

Your most obedient, humble servant,

JOHN FRED. GRONOVIUS.

Leyden, 2 July, 1750.

[The Editor is indebted for the following letter, to his friend Doctor GRAY, of Cambridge, who is in possession of the original.]

JOHN BARTRAM TO GRONOVIUS.

November 30, 1752.

DEAR FRIEND :—

I received thy kind letter of March the 24th, 1752, by Mr. SCHLATER, which pleased me· well. Pray, how doth the Water Mill prove? Doth it answer expectation? After what manner doth it work? I should be glad to know something of the nature of it.

I am in expectation of enjoying great satisfaction by thy next letter, and KALM'S Catalogue of Plants, which thee mentions thee designs to send me. I sent thee last spring, a box of fossils, and curious stones, with a letter; but have not yet received any answer.

I have not travelled much this year, it being a very bad seed year. I hope next may be better ; and I design to travel most of the season, if Providence affords me health and opportunity, when I hope to pick up some curiosities for thee of the fossil kind.

I have had several accounts from curious observers, of many fish which have been catched near the middle of the sea, in which there have been shell-fish, and sand reptiles, and several such like submarine fish, whose abode is on sandy shoals; which inclines me to query whether there may not be vast chains of mountains, of many hundreds of miles extent in the sea, as well as at land ; and whether the tops of these may not be large sand-banks, which may produce food for many kinds of fish (that never swim near the shore), which resort to these banks for their daily food, whose summits may be nearer the surface than most people may expect, and where they may suppose it to be unfathomable ; as there are islands already known, many of which are dispersed in most parts of the sea, at unequal distances, where ships take their course in sailing to the East and West Indies ; and it's very likely many more are yet undiscovered, by reason of the vast tract of sea where ships have not yet sailed, as may be observed by consulting the Sea Journals.

These islands being the tops of vast mountains, appearing above the surface, so I think it's very likely that hundreds of them may be placed as different in altitude as magnitude, or distance ; so, consequently, many of them may be in the reach of common sounding, not yet known, by reason that the navigators never sound but when they expect they are near some coast.   But if our cruising vessels (for merchant ships can't lose so much time, unless in a calm), were to sound every day far from shore, perhaps they might find fine banks, where many kinds of fish frequent for food, and might be improved for good fisheries, for the benefit of mankind.   *Query*, whether these vast chains of mountains, if there be such, may not be, in part, the cause of the currents in the sea, which our navigators complain so much of ; and is it not probable, that there may be various kinds of fish in the great vales, between these ridges, which never appeared, nor can live, near the surface of the water ?

Thy answer to these queries will be very acceptable to thy sincere friend and well-wisher,

JOHN BARTRAM.

P. S. Our worthy friend BENJAMIN FRANKLIN, desires thee to send him a Dutch translation of his new-invented stove, or fireplace ; and one book of his Electrical Experiments, if it be translated into Dutch.   He wants to make a present of them to a friend in York.   He is willing to satisfy thee for them, cost what they may.

Thine, as before,

J. B.

J. F. GRONOVIUS TO JOHN BARTRAM.

DEAR FRIEND :—

I received your letters, dated January and November, 1751, March and November, 1752 ; besides one of your son MOSES ; and lately, by my good friend, Mr. COLLINSON, yours of 6 of Novemb. 1753.

My own and public affairs, and an indifferent health, have hindered me to show my thankfulness to all my friends and benefactors, being in great fear to become totally paralytic ; but since I turn myself to a way of living, as our old patriarchs did, I am quite recovered, for I drink no wine, coffee or thé, but only small beer, and milk mixed with water.   My dinner consisted in gruttos

and greens boiled in water, without butter,   *   *   avoiding all
the delicate aromata which the East and West Indies send to us.
What a change it must make in my body, that was from his yought
customed at dinner and supper, to a bottle and a half wine, besides
the rest when I get a friend! However, I can tell to you, that I
left it all at once ; in three days the swelling of my feets and cruel
pains went off, and I my selv became not at all week, but contrary
I get a great strength, and sleep exceeding wel. So that I at
present am entirely at the service of my friends ; and now my
worthy friend, the Rev. Mr. SCHLATTER, returning to you, I take
the opportunity to send these to you.

I am obliged to you for the description of the gape near the
Blew Mountains, all filled with stones. Betwixt Utregt and the
Loo, a country place builded by King WILLIAM the III., is the
country all covered with sand-hills for about eighteen Dutch miles ;
but heer and there some low planes for a quarter of an hour,
which are all fild with stones, les and great, some larger than my
head, and most part flint stones. I believe realy all the country
under the sand there is covered with such stones. I have seen in
Flanders, when the King of France made a new rode about Brussels, that they removed some immense sand-hills, and found at last
the ground all filled with loose stones all roundish, and here and
there some petrifications of a yellowish colour, but not separated ;
but shells of differend kind and cochles joined to one another by
the same calcarea materia of which the stones consists, so as
RUMPHIUS represents in tab. 58, E.

I am infinitely obliged to you for the petrified shells, with the
belemnites and other stones. I was surprised to see these shells,
for as much as I know, they are originally from the coast of Sicily,
and that way, under the name of *Bucardia*, of which several other
species are to be found upon the Alpes in Switzerland, and upon
the Mounts of   in Italy ; but this particular species was never
met calcinated or petrified. It is pity it was broken. Question is,
how now, and when, these creatures are brought from Sicily to
your country. It must be agreed, that there must have been a
passage by water betwixt these two places ; but what time it was
so, no body can say. That all the petrifications should be attribute to the general deluge, is what I never shall agree ; but I
think, that with good reason we may derive them from the time of

the creation of the world, so that they should not be taken for *diluviana*, but *antediluviana*.

It is also probable that after the creation, there have been as well storms as in our time, when the sea overflowed several countrys. To these overflowings I attribute the strata, and per consequence, so many strata there are, so many overflowings there have been. We see that confirmed in this country; for when we dig three feet, we find a stratum all of shells, the same as we have at our sea-coast, under it a stratum of clay, and then again a stratum of shells. It is also confirmed, that before the sand-hills were thrown up by a great storm, this country was not habitable in winter time, by the overflowing of the sea, and that the few inhabitants of it were obliged to remove to *Batavodurum*, which is thirty-six miles from hence.

So farther, I suppose the sea had overflowen the land, and left there a stratum of shells; this was easily overspread by the flying sand, upon which the waters coming, or by the rain, or by any other way, and standing there make a sedimentum, out of which there becomes by time a marshy ground, being the matrix of the *Sphagnum* and likely sort of plants; and from which, in time, by the accession of other particulars, are produced the different sorts of clay and humus, and so by succession we get a fertile ground.

It is a great hardship to me, I must tell you, that the water-mill of Mr. GENETE is woll finished, but the experiment is not yet taken with it. Every one talks very indifferently of it, and the most part have no opinion of it.   *   *   *   *

That there are vast chains of mountains in the sea, where they are called islands, and banks, is not to be contradicted, and I believe several petrified subjects are the prove of it.   *   *

Yea, I believe that Majorca and Minorca are only the tops of mountains standing in a large province under sea, where many fishes find their food. We know by Mr. CLEGHORN's observations, that there is no places where more variety of fishes is, than at Minorca; and I have by reports of some of our sea officers the confirmation of it.

And now lastly to your letter dated the 6 of December, 1753, which I get by our good friend Mr. SLATTER, I hope you shall hear from him, that he hath been here with good success; at list I have contributed what is in my power. He hath a great patrone to Mr. THOMSON, the minister at Amsterdam, to whom I commu-

nicated Mr. PETERS' letters ; having Mr. THOMSON promised me
to give answers to them in my name. When you see Mr. PETERS,
tell him that.

I send you here a copy of the new-invented stove : but of a
Dutch translation of his experiments upon the electricite, I don't
know anything. But in few days I go to Amsterdam ; if I find
it there, I shall send it immediately to Mr. COLLINSON, by a friend
that goes in a few weeks to London. Pray my service to Mr.
FRANKLIN. I wish I could do to you and him any service. I
wish you good success with your book about trees. Wherewith
wishing to you all health and prosperity, I remain, dear friend,
your most obedient servant,

JOH. FRED. GRONOVIUS.

Leyden, 10 Juny, 1754.

JOHN BARTRAM TO JOHN MITCHELL.*

June the 3d, 1744.

DOCTOR MITCHELL :—

I have now before me thy kind letter of May the 5th, which
pleaseth me well. I should have been exceedingly pleased to have
been acquainted with thee when I travelled in your country, in the
year 1738, when I lodged in Fredericksburgh ; from whence I
travelled near sixty miles down Rappahannock, thence over Dragon Bridge to JOHN CLAYTON'S (where I was disappointed of seeing
him, he being gone towards the mountains), thence to Williamsburgh ; so up James River to Goochland, where I saw a pretty
little tree of the *Arbor vitæ*, on the west bank of the river. It
was about six inches diameter. Thence travelling to your Blue
Mountains, headed Rappahannock, fell upon the branches of
Shenandoah, a great branch of Potomac, kept the great vale,
between the North and South Mountains, till crossing Susque-

---

* JOHN MITCHELL, M.D., a botanist and physician, came from England to
Virginia, about the year 1700. He died in 1772. His residence was chiefly at
Urbana, a small town on the Rappahannock, about seventy-three miles from
Richmond. He appears to have been a man of observation, acuteness, and enterprise, as well as learning. Among his various publications, was a useful work on
the general principles of Botany, containing descriptions of a number of new
genera of plants, 4to., 1769. The worth and scientific labours of Dr. MITCHELL
will be effectually commemorated among Botanists, by the beautiful little American perennial which bears his name (*Mitchella repens*, L.).—BLAKE'S *Biog. Dict.*

hanna, took the nearest way I could, home. Since which time I have travelled many times over East and West Jersey, and up the North River to the great falls of the Mohawks' River, and twice climbed up the great Katskill Mountains (which is near three times as high as any other I ever climbed), where is a fine prospect over a great part of New England. These mountains produce the greatest variety of plants and trees, of any particular spot of ground I know of. The Balm of Gilead Fir grows here a hundred feet high, very straight ; so doth two or three kinds of the Newfoundland Spruce Firs, with several kinds of curious pines, and a fine species of the Paper Birch, whose bark yielding leaves [or laminæ] above three feet square, of fine paper for either writing, drawing, or printing,—and several other species of Birch ; Cherry trees five feet high, not of the bird, clustered kind ; Quicken Tree [*Sorbus*] fifteen feet high ; a fine species of *Viburnum*, with broad leaves, shaped like a heart ; several species of the *Aralias*, and *Araliastrums*, *Christophorianas*, Lady's Bowers, Herb Paris [*Trillium*], with many other very odd kinds of plants and shrubs ; and upon the same ridge with your South Blue Mountain, by Hudson's River's bank, grow large trees of the *Arbor vitæ*, and in the swamps, fine Larch Trees. This last sheds its leaves in autumn, though a fine resinous tree. Last July I went with our interpreter [CONRAD WEISER] to Onondaga, to make peace between your people and the Six Nations, on the account of the skirmish with your back inhabitants ; from whence I went down the river to the great Lake Frontenac [Ontario]. In this journey I observed many curious trees, shrubs, and plants, particularly a fine *Magnolia* [*M. acuminata, L.*], above sixty feet high, and three diameter, the cones three or four inches long, the leaves a foot long, and six inches broad, a little hairy, the winter bud covered with down, or short hairs, to defend it from the severity of the cold, in that rigorous climate. I sent a specimen of it to our friend PETER, last fall. He writes me, thee sent him specimens of the same species three years ago.   *   *   *

DR. JOHN MITCHELL TO JOHN BARTRAM.

London, June 2, 1747.

SIR :—

I have a long while waited an opportunity of writing something to you, that might be acceptable, and am glad of this opportunity of doing it. I am desired to get a parcel of seeds for the Duke of Argyle, and know of none whom I would sooner depend upon than you, to do it. He would have a large quantity, but fears the season may be too far advanced, before you receive this, to collect them, and so desires you would send as many as you can afford for five pounds. If they please, I doubt not but he will desire more— as well as my Lord Bute, who gave me this commission. They desire chiefly flowering trees and shrubs. Some of the new *Magnolia*, if you can get it; and particularly some of the White Cedar, which I told them you would be sure to send.

Mr. COLLINSON tells me he has sent for seven such parcels this year, already; so I doubt not but you may have some that are curious, collected. He [the Duke] has many of the common things already, and wants chiefly the Papaw Tree, or *Anona*, the two new *Chamærhododendrons*, Sugar Tree, Orange *Apocynum* [*Asclepias tuberosa*, L.], Scarlet *Spiræa*, *Euonymus scandens* [*Celastrus*], the large Ketmia, with flowers like Cotton, *Leonurus* [?], or Oswego Tea [evidently a mistake, *Leonurus* for *Monarda didyma*], the new Pines, which I think you said you had seen; he has all the common sorts.

I am glad to hear that your industry this way is like to be of some service to you. I hope it may be in my way to promote it, which you may depend upon. This is the only way I ever knew it of any service to anybody; for Botany is at a very low ebb in England, since the death of Lord PETRE. Dr. DILLENIUS is likewise dead. I should be glad to hear from you, and what new plants you find.

I have wrote a long letter to Mr. FRANKLIN, which I hope, he will receive, and desired a specimen of the water that turns iron to copper, and the earth, salts, &c., about it, which I would analyze; and should be glad of an account of its effects with you, and the way of operating with it there, to see if it would do the same here. I likewise desired some specimens (and a quantity of them), of the blue stones in your Yellow Springs, which pray tell him of, if mine to him should miscarry. I fancy it may be more in your way than his to procure them, by which you would highly oblige me.

Remember me particularly to him, and your good spouse, and Dr. BOND. I have nothing worth while to say to them, else should not fail to do it.

You may direct the box of seeds, &c., to the care of Mr. Col-
LINSON, with the others.

From your humble servant,
John Mitchell.

Sir :—

I have received several letters from you, since my last, for which
I return you thanks. The reason why I have been so long in
writing to you, is, that I have been in Scotland, and over most of
that country, with the Duke of Argyle, since my last to you; and
since my return here, have been so engaged in writing some other
things, which has disagreed so with the state of my health, that it
gives me pain even to sit down to take a pen in my hand, and very
often I am unable to do it, on account of a vertiginous disorder
which it has occasioned, and brings on; so that you must excuse
me from writing fully and particularly to you, till I can do it with
more safety.

The plants and seeds which you sent for the Duke of Argyle,
came safe to hand; and I have long ago paid Mr. COLLINSON for
them. I lately, likewise, got two or three seeds of the new *Magnolia* from him, which I carried to the Duke, but there is none of
them come up; and it is to be feared that we cannot expect any
from about eight or nine seeds which I had, as they are so apt to
miscarry, at the best.

*   *   *   *   *   *   *

I have been obliged to give over my botanical pursuits, for some
time, so that I have not anything to say to you on that head at present.
But I have often mentioned you to several great men, whom I have
had an opportunity of seeing here, who are very glad to hear of
industry and laudable endeavours, but are very backward in re-
warding them, at least, with anything that is real and substantial;
which is the most of what I can say on that head, although if it
lies in my power to recommend you to anything—or to be of any
service to you, in any shape, you may freely command, and depend
upon   Your very humble servant,

John Mitchell.

London, August 1, 1750.

DEAR SIR:—

I received yours, in which you complain that you had neither received any letter from me, nor any account of the seeds you sent me, which I am surprised at; I having wrote you a letter particularly for three boxes of seeds the last year, of which I have received only two.   *   *   *   *

*   *   * You must excuse me, if I do not write to you so often and fully as I would incline to do. I have had so much business of that kind upon my hands, since I came to England, that I have contracted a disorder by it, which makes me unable to pursue it any longer, or even to sit down to write a letter, especially that requires any thought, without being sensibly the worse for it. I hope, however, to be able, some time or other, to make amends for my omissions of this kind.

We have had two great losses, lately, in Planting and Botany, in England, which will hardly be repaired, I am afraid, and are rather greater than the loss they sustained by the death of Lord PETRE.

The Duke of Richmond, and the Prince of Wales, are suspected both to have lost their lives by it, by being out in their gardens, to see the work forwarded, in very bad weather. The Prince of Wales—whose death you will hear of by these ships—manifestly lost his life by this means. He contracted a cold, by standing in the wet to see some trees planted, (through a sort of obstinacy against any precautions of that kind, which it seems the whole family are blamed for,) which brought on a pleurisy, that he died of, lately.

If anything occurs worthy your notice, I shall consider of it, at more leisure, by next opportunity.

I am, sir, your most humble servant.

JOHN MITCHELL.

London, March 30th, 1751.

PETER KALM* TO JOHN BARTRAM.

Because I have an opportunity of writing to you, sir, I would

* PETER KALM, a celebrated naturalist, and pupil of LINNÆUS, was a native of Finland, born in the year 1715. Having imbibed a taste for the study of Natural History, he pursued his inclination with much zeal and industry. His reputation as a naturalist caused him to be appointed Professor at Abo; and in October,

have the honour to tell you, that I now have come here to Quebec. I do now send my servant-man from me to Philadelphia, to gather there seeds of all trees and herbs he can find, or which I have found there before.

I am obliged to stay here myself to the middle of September, to have several seeds, which not can be ripe before; and when I have gathered them, I think to retourn from hence, and will have the honour to see you in the beginning or middle of October.

I have found great many trees and plants, which I not have seen before; but you have in Pensylvania, too, great many trees and herbs, that do not grow here: Poplar, Sweet and Sour Gum, Laurel, Chesnut, Mulberry trees, Black Walnut, Sassafras, Magnolia, and great many others you can't find here. The Oaks of all sorts have taken leave, only some small shrubs of Black Oak do grow here by this town.

I have made great many observations in all parts of the Natural History. If you do see Mr. EVANS, pray remember my most humbly duty to him, and tell him that I hope to satisfy his curiosity in true maps of Canada: but the map of Canada he was

1747, he set out upon his travels, sailing from Gottenburg for America, where he arrived the ensuing year.[a] Having spent two or three years in travelling through Canada, New York, Pennsylvania, and the adjacent Provinces, he returned to his Professorship at Abo, in 1751. His discoveries in Botany materially enriched the *Species Plantarum* of his great master. Professor KALM's travels in America have been published in English, and are quite interesting; though he seems to have been remarkably credulous; and moreover, it is alleged, has taken to himself the credit of some discoveries which rightfully belonged to JOHN BARTRAM. He departed this life in the year 1779, aged 64. His name has become enduringly associated with a genus of our most elegant evergreen Shrubs.

---

[a] Mr. KALM came to America by way of England, whence he brought the following letter of introduction; for a copy of which, the editor is indebted to E. D. INGRAHAM, Esq.

"To BEN. FRANKLIN, Philadelphia.

"London, June 14, 1748.

"FRIEND FRANKLIN:

"The bearer, Mr. KALM, is an ingenious man, and comes over on purpose to improve himself in all rational inquiries. He is a Swede per nation; and is, as I am informed, employed by the Academy of Upsal to make observations on the pts of the world. I recommend him to thy favour and notice. By him I send the first volume of the Voyage to Discover Northwest Passage. I hope the pacquet, &c., sent under the care of HUNT and GREENLEAF is come safe to hand.

"I am thy sincere friend,

"P. COLLINSON."

so kind and write for me, had once (it was not far from it) thrown me in the other world. The reason was, that he has not put down a great river between Fort Ann and Crown Point, that runs in Woodcreek. My guides did not very well know the way, and we did go down this river, where such Indians did live that do kill all the English the see; but to our happiness we did by good time find that we were wrong, and returned.

Fifteen years ago, when the French King did send several of his learned men to Swedland to measure there a degree of latitude by the North Pol, our King in Swedland did let them have all thing the wanted gratis, or for nothing. In recompense thereof, the French King have given orders to his gouverneurs here in Canada, that I too shall have everything as victuals, lodgings, men to carry me to which place I will, &c., for nothing. It is not permitted to me to pay any thing, but the French King he pays that all.

You can, sir, inform my man in several thing where he can find some rare plants, pray do it. Show him all places, where you have seen some small Mulberry Trees, or Grapes, but especialement Mulberry Trees,—these I cannot have too many. I am persuaded it will be a pleasure for you to assist me. When I do returne from hence, then I can inform and satisfy your curiosity in great many thing in all parts of Natural History.—My respect, sir, to madam, your wife. My man he can in great many things, too, satisfy your curiosité.

I am, sir, your most humble servant,

PETER KALM.

Quebec, the 6th day of August, 1749.

JAMES GORDON* TO JOHN BARTRAM.

MR. BARTRAM :—

I return you my thanks for many curious seeds, which my good

* JAMES GORDON was an eminent nurseryman at Mile-End, near London, who introduced many new plants to the knowledge of the curious, or rather cultivated with great skill and success, such as were communicated to him from various quarters, by the collectors and naturalists of that day ; among whom were BAR-TRAM, COLLINSON, ELLIS, and many others. He was a frequent correspondent of LINNÆUS, and sent him several living plants, especially of North American origin. The famous *Loblolly Bay*, of our Southern States (which was named *Franklinia*, by MARSHALL), is referred to *Gordonia*, a genus which commemorates the name and botanical services of this gentleman.

friend, Mr. Peter Collinson, has given me through your means. If there is any seeds here, which you think worth your having, please let me know, and I'll endeavour to procure you some of them; and I am,

Sir, your obliged servant,

James Gordon.

London, Mile-End, March 3, 1750–1.

[On the back of the preceding, Peter Collinson wrote the subjoined paragraph:—]

" Our friend Gordon is a very modest man, and can't speak himself; but a few *Magnolia* cones, of the two or three sorts growing with you, will be acceptable to him."

JOHN BARTRAM TO THOM. FRANC. DALIBARD.*

[Not dated.]

To Monsieur Dalibard, a Paris:—

Our very worthy friend, Benjamin Franklin, Esq., whom I have the pleasure (as well as honour) to be intimately acquainted with, showed me a letter wherein thee mentioned a book thee designed to send me, which will be very acceptable, for I love Botany, and Natural History, exceedingly.

I shall be well pleased to correspond with one so curious, and shall make use of all opportunities to oblige; and as an introduction, I have sent a little parcel of seeds, and specimens, which I gathered. But as you are possessed of so large a part of North America, I suppose it will be difficult to send you any plant that you have not, although I believe we have several which you want; but the difficulty is, to know which they are. If I had a catalogue either of what you have, or what you want, I will endeavour to supply you, which I suppose must be carried on by the good offices of Benjamin Franklin here, or my first correspondent in London, the generous Mr. Peter Collinson, who is ready to oblige all men.

* Mons. Dalibard was a French botanist, who, in 1749, published a duodecimo volume, entitled *Floræ Parisiensis Prodromus*. His name is commemorated by the genus *Dalibarda*, L.

JOHN BARTRAM TO CHARLES LINNÆUS.*

[Not dated, 1752 or 3.]

RESPECTED AND WORTHY FRIEND:—

I received, about two months past, a letter from thee dated August the 10th, 1750.† I was exceedingly pleased to receive so kind a letter from one that so deservedly bears so superior a character for learning ; but was very much concerned that I could not have had it sooner than above two years after it was wrote; and much the same misfortune happened to several pamphlets thee sent to Dr. COLDEN and Mr. CLAYTON, which our worthy friend BENJAMIN FRANKLIN showed me last week, which he had just received, and intended to send according to direction, by the next post.

I travelled, in 1751, most part of the autumn, and found several new species of plants, and shrubs, which I should have sent to thee, if I had known they would have been acceptable.

We have four or five beautiful species of *Jacobæa* [*Lilium*], that you have not in Europe. One species grows in our marshes, another on flat stiff ground, another on cold shady banks, by the rivers, another on loose slaty soil on the great mountains; and most of these species are much valued by the Indians, and back inhabitants, for the cure of the same diseases that the ancients used their *Jacobæa* for, though not one of them knew the name of the plant.

I hope thee hath received the *Medicina Britannica.*‡ I hope to send thee some specimens next fall. We are all surprised that we have not one letter from PETER KALM.

[Also without date, perhaps 1753.]

To LINNÆUS :—

Respected friend,—As I wrote to thee last spring, and have yet received no answer, I have not much to say.

---

* No biographical notice of " *the immortal* SWEDE" is deemed requisite here, except perhaps, merely to say that he was born May 24th, 1707, and died January 11th, 1778, aged near seventy-one years.

† The letters *from* LINNÆUS *to* JOHN BARTRAM are all missing.

‡ An American edition of a work with that title, with *notes* and an *appendix* by JOHN BARTRAM, published at Philadelphia in the year 1751.

Pray, how doth our friend KALM go on with his history of our country plants ? He promised me to send me one, as soon as printed, and that he would do me justice in mentioning what plants or specimens I showed him; but I never can get a letter from him since he left my house. I should be very well pleased to see what he hath wrote of our plants.

I here send thee two specimens of a curious evergreen *Veratrum* [probably *Helonias bullata*, L.]. It grows in wet, swampy, shady, cold ground. The root is white and fibrous, from which proceeds sixteen, more or less, of longish narrow leaves, pointed at the extremity. The leaves of the second year lie on the ground, spread in rays round the summer's leaves, which stood more erect, yet bending towards the ground, and surrounding a central bud which is set in the fall, and if for flowering, is like a pointed cone whose base is near an inch diameter, which next spring shoots up a single stalk eighteen inches high, with short pointed leaves set without order round it, gradually diminishing in magnitude unto the spike of flowers, two or three inches long, the petals of a flesh-colour, the apices [*anthers*] bluish, and standing out longer than the petals, which makes a pretty appearance. See the imperfect specimen, as it flowered after transplanting.

JOHN BARTRAM TO JARED ELIOT.*

February the 12th, 1753.

RESPECTED FRIEND ELIOT :—

I have been long waiting for an answer to my letter which I sent last spring; but lately our good friend BENJAMIN told me our letters had miscarried. So now I venture to trouble thee with a few more of my rambling observations.   *   *   *

* JARED ELIOT, minister of Killingsworth, Connecticut, graduated at Yale College, 1706; ordained 1709 ; and died 1763, aged 78. He was a botanist, and a scientific and practical agriculturist. The White Mulberry tree was introduced by him into Connecticut. He discovered a process of extracting iron from black sand. He was the first physician of his day, in the Colony. Living on the main road from Boston to New York, he was visited by many gentlemen of distinction. Doctor FRANKLIN always called on him when journeying to his native town. For forty years he never omitted preaching on the Lord's day.—BLAKE's *Biog. Dict.* Of that worthy man, ST. JOHN DE CREVECŒUR, in his "*Lettres d'un Cultivateur Americain*," says, "Qui ne connoit de réputation le savant ELIOT, ce digne ecclésiastique, ce vertueux et utile citoyen ? Qui n'a pas lu ses ouvrages agricoles ?"

I have, in my travels abroad, but much more near home, observed
with concern, our approaching distress on the account of our want
of timber for fencing, and indeed many of our necessary uses. A
great part of the country that was first settled, hath not near timber enough on each tract for one set of new fence, nor one half of
the old good enough to keep a cow in the field, or a horse out.*
Ditching helps us very little; and a quick hedge less, by reason of
the horned cattle and sheep. The latter kill the Quickset, with
cropping the tender shoots; and the former, not only with brows-
ing, but when it is grown, they twist and break the bushes, and
tear down the bank with their horns, tho' never so well turfed with
grass. I have made great, deep ditches, and consequently, high
banks; if I made them steep, the frost and rain would moulder
and wash the bank down; if I made them wide and slanting, the
cattle would climb up and tread them down; if the ditch is narrow, they step over. About sixteen years past, I planted a hedge
of Red Cedars (one foot long), on a small bank, about two feet
asunder. They grew so well, that in three or four years I had a
fine hedge four feet high, two feet thick, and so close that a bird
could not fly through it. Then I thought I had been furnished
with the only material that was requisite for a strong, lasting,
beautiful fence, that had all the good properties that the others
wanted; as, first, it would grow well on all our different soils;
secondly, none of our cattle would crop them;† thirdly, * * *
[*Reliqua desunt.*]

March the 14th, 1756.
DEAR FRIEND ELIOT :—

I have, since I left thy house, been very much hurried in travelling, and sending my curiosities to Europe; after which, I
married my daughter to a worthy young man, whose house is in
sight of mine, and about half an hour's walk. Since which, our
friend BENJAMIN FRANKLIN hath been a great while in the back
parts of our country, building forts. Since his return home, he

---

* This apprehension was very prevalent among the old farmers of Pennsylvania,
until within a few years past; but the threatened evil was always exaggerated,
and since the working of the coal mines, the alarm has almost wholly subsided.

† Experience has shown that the Red Cedar (and probably every other *thorn-
less* plant) is unfitted to make an effective hedge, in this region. It is believed
that the *Cratægus Crus-Galli*, L., affords the best material for hedging, though
even *that* requires great care and skilful management, to insure a perfect hedge.

is so much engaged in public business, that we had no convenient opportunity of sending a letter until now; but I assure thee, I have not forgot thee, nor the agreeable hours I spent with thee.

I have often thought, that your salt marsh mud, may be so ordered as to be of extraordinary benefit to your country, and you have enough of it. Suppose you were to dig a large quantity of it, and haul it to shore, as you may easily do in the winter, when the ground is froze. Our ditchers choose to do it in winter; they are not so subject to catch cold. They have strong, tight boots. They dig ditches twelve or fourteen feet wide, and four feet deep, to drain our marshes; and we commonly dig pits eight feet deep, to mend them, or to haul the mud on our fast land to enrich it, which will last near twenty years. You should put a layer of mud, half a foot or more thick, then such a quantity of common mould, then a layer of mud, *stratum super stratum*, until your bed is four feet thick. Let it lie and ferment a year; then cut down to the bottom, and toss it all together into another bed, and let it remain half a year longer, or more, then spread it on your ground.

I have had an account from Sicily, that they manure their wheat ground there with salt, mixed after this manner with mould; but it is observed that the salt fetched from one place doth not agree with all sorts of the soil on the island, but they adapt the salts made in different parts to the different soils. Perhaps, if required, I may give thee a more particular account; but our travellers into the different parts of the world are very deficient in relating the true methods of agriculture, which the inhabitants practise in their respective countries. They think, if they relate their observations of the old ruins, the extravagant diversions of the people, their government, and superstition,—then, they think they have done much; although it is little more than what many of the former travellers have done long before them.

January the 24th, 1757.

WORTHY FRIEND ELIOT :—

I did not receive thy kind letter of March the 14th, until lately. Our friend BENJAMIN had put it in his drawer, and could not find it, when he looked for it.

I am sorry thee did not get my son's drawings. The rector got all of them. My son wrote thy name on those for thee; and the

hollow stick was filled with indigo seed. I am often recollecting
our conversation with pleasure.

I am apt to think, that if your salt marsh, that is drained, was
ploughed and planted with Indian corn for several years, it would
bring it into good order for corn or grass. That crude, saline
nature, should be exposed to dews, and rains, and sun.

I told thee, that I had been informed that the grindstones, and
millstones, were split with wooden pegs, drove in; but I did not
say that those rocks about thy house could be split after that
manner; but that I could split them, and had been used to split
rocks, to make steps, door-sills, and large window-cases all of
stone, and pig-troughs, and water-troughs. I have split rocks
seventeen feet long, and built four houses of hewn stone, split out
of the rock with my own hands. My method is, to bore the rock
about six inches deep, having drawn a line from one end to the
other, in which I bore holes about a foot asunder, more or less, according to the freeness of the rock; if it be three or four or five
feet thick, ten, twelve, or sixteen inches deep. The holes should
be an inch and a quarter diameter, if the rock be two feet thick;
but if it be five or six feet thick, the holes should be an inch and
three quarters diameter. There must be provided twice as many iron
wedges as holes; and one half of them must be made full as long
as the hole is deep, and made round at one end, just fit to drop into
the hole; the other half may be made a little longer, and thicker
one way, and blunt-pointed. All the holes must have their wedges
drove together, one after another, gently, that they may strain all
alike. You may hear by their ringing, when they strain well.
Then, with the sharp end of the sledge, strike hard on the rock,
in the line between every wedge, which will crack the rock; then
drive the wedges again. It generally opens in a few minutes after
the wedges are drove tight. Then, with an iron bar, or long
levers, raise them up, and lay the two pieces flat, and bore and
split them in what shape and dimensions you please. If the rock
is anything free, you may split them as true, almost, as sawn timber; and by this method you may split almost any rock, for you
may add what power you please, by boring the holes deeper and
closer together.   *   *   *   *   *

JOHN BARTRAM TO PHILIP MILLER.*

April the 20th, 1755.
WORTHY FRIEND PHILIP MILLER :—
I have received thy kind letter of February the 19th, 1755, which gave me much satisfaction; and some uneasiness, that so many years have elapsed wherein we might have reciprocally communicated our observations to each other : and although thee had incomparably the advantage over me, yet, notwithstanding, I love to peep into the abstruse operations of nature. Perhaps I might, by thy familiar instruction, have made some remarks that might have been satisfactory. But, for the time to come, I hope we may double our diligence, if the war with France do not obstruct our endeavours.

The Catalogue of Shrubs and Trees is very acceptable, or any other books in Natural History. I have thy first and second book of the Gardener's Dictionary,—one sent me by Lord PETRE, the other by Dr. DILLENIUS.

I design to take particular care to send those seeds thee mentioned, which I can procure; and if thee will please to send by the first opportunity, it may come to me soon enough to send, next

---

* PHILIP MILLER, a celebrated gardener and botanist, was born in Scotland, in 1694. His father had the superintendence of the Physic Garden at Chelsea, belonging to the Apothecaries' Company, and founded by Sir HANS SLOANE; to which appointment he himself succeeded in the year 1722. In this situation, he became distinguished by his practical knowledge of plants, and especially by his skill in their cultivation. In 1731, appeared the first edition of the " Gardener's Dictionary," in folio, the most celebrated work of its kind; which has been translated, copied, and abridged, at various times, and may be said to have laid the foundation of all the Horticultural taste and knowledge in Europe. LINNÆUS said of this Dictionary, " non erit Lexicon Hortulanorum, sed Botanicorum."

MILLER continued to attend to his duties, and his favourite pursuits, to an advanced age; but was obliged at length, by his infirmities, to resign[a] the charge of the garden. He died soon after, at Chelsea, December 18, 1771, in his seventy-eighth year.—REES's Cyclopæd.

---

[a] Mr. ELLIS, (who, however, had been engaged in a controversy with MILLER,) in a letter to Dr. GARDEN, dated January 2, 1771, says, " PHILIP MILLER, the Gardener of Chelsea, is turned out of his place for his impertinence to the Apothecaries' Company, his masters. They have got a much better one, FORSYTH, late Gardener to the Duke of Northumberland, who has an excellent character, and will revive the credit of the garden, which was losing its reputation, and everything curious was sent to Mr. AITON, the Princess of Wales' Gardener at Kew."

fall, any other curiosity thee pleases to mention: for time is so far spent, past our meridian, that the affair calls for diligence.

I design to collect specimens of our Pines, just when they are in flower, and the young cone just impregnated, which is to ripen, not this ensuing fall, but the next; when it immediately dischargeth its seed, before it is well dry; whereas other trees keep their cones shut for several years, containing perfect ripe seeds, and then discharge them. Pray, do all your European Pines set their cones on the same spring's shoot, and perfect them the succeeding year—or the second year's wood, as, by your draught, the Scotch Pine doth? Although the species of Pines, and Fir, may, many of them, be distinguished by their cones, in Europe, they are no certain distinguishing character in America, except Lord Weymouth's Pine.   *   *   *   *

*   *   * I am obliged to thee, for thy good advice, to contract my descriptions. I own, the leaves, acorns, and especially the cups, are very material in ascertaining the different species of our Oaks; yet the description of the bark, and form of growth, are useful helps, in our mature Oaks. I can often discover our different species of Oaks, one from another, by their form of growth, half or a whole mile distance; and I am sure he must be very sharp-sighted that can know them, at half that distance, by their leaves, acorns, and cups, all together.

I take thy offer very kindly, to assist me in understanding LINNÆUS's system, which I am acquainted with in some degree; having several books of his setting forth, which Dr. GRONOVIUS, my good friend, hath sent me; and Mons. DALIBARD sent me his Catalogue of Plants growing near Paris; and HILL hath nearly translated LINNÆUS's Characters. But I find many plants that do not answer to any of his Genera, and are really new.

I have an account that he hath published, lately, two books containing all our North American plants which KALM observed, when he was with us. I showed him many, that he said were new Genera, and that LINNÆUS must make many alterations, when he was by him more truly informed of their true characters, as I should soon see when they were printed. I long to see these books, —to see if they have done me justice, as KALM promised me. Dr. GRONOVIUS promised to send them to me, as soon as they came to his hand.

I shall be much obliged to thee for thy Figures of Plants, as soon as finished.   I love to see nature displayed, in all its branches.

I shall be glad to assist thee with any new plant, or shrub—either dead or alive—in substance, or a particular description; as thee pleases to inform me after what manner it will answer thy intention the best.

*   *   *   *   *

PHILIP MILLER TO JOHN BARTRAM.

DEAR MR. BARTRAM :—

I have been favoured with your three kind letters, and the two boxes of plants which you was so good as to send me; for which I return you my thanks.   To the first of your letters, I returned an answer in September last; but for fear it may miscarry, I beg leave to repeat the substance of that, here.   I am sorry so many years passed without our having had an intercourse by letters, as I am sensible how many observations I have lost, which must have fallen in your way to have made.   As I seek after truth, so I shall always be glad to receive any informations from my friends, even if they should contradict what I may have published, yet I shall never think it derogatory to my character to own my mistakes, and rectify them.   *   *   [*Hiatus in MS.*]   *   * I have not seen what Dr. LINNÆUS has published from KALM'S observations, which he has mentioned in his Species of Plants, where he has added many new names to them, and inserted some which may probably be new.

KALM has published two volumes of his observations, in the Swedish language; but as I do not understand it, so I have not been curious enough to send for the book, nor do I hear any good character of it.   *   *   *   *

I sent you four numbers of my Figures of Plants, some time since, by our friend Mr. COLLINSON; and should have now sent you the others which are published, had I not waited for some which will be better coloured; for the persons employed to have the care of this work, have not done me justice, so I have been obliged to take it out of their hands.   *   *   *   *

I have also sent you a few plants of some of our best sorts of Roses, which I wish may prove such as you have not already; for,

as I am unacquainted with what has been sent you from England,
so I am at a loss to guess what I should send; but this, I hope,
you will soon set me right about.   So I shall add no more, at present, but to assure you I am your sincere friend and servant,

PHILIP MILLER.

Chelsea, Feb. 2, 1756.

DEAR MR. BARTRAM:—

I have just now been favoured with your kind letter, dated the
ninth of December; and although I wrote a long letter to you a
few days past, yet I take this opportunity to acknowledge the
receipt of yours, especially as I made a mistake in my last, in the
name of the ship by which I have sent you some seeds, with a basket of Roses and Cedar cones.   This mistake was occasioned by my
waterman, who carried the things to the ship; but the enclosed
note will set that right.

I am glad you like my Figures.   I hope to send you some much
better done, having changed my engraver.

You mention that you want the Norway Maple.   Had I known
this sooner, you should have been supplied; for we have a large
tree in our garden, which produces plenty of seeds, and young
plants come up in all the borders near it.   The cuttings will also
grow, like willows.   If another ship departs from hence, soon, I
will send you plants of it.

As you desire to know my wants, that you may supply them, so
I must desire you will acquaint me with what things you want from
hence, that I may make you some returns; and although in my
other letter I pretty fully told what would be acceptable, yet have
I here sent you a list of some things taken out of the *Flora Virginica*, which book I suppose you have, so will soon know what I
mean by the names.   Some of these you was so good as to send
me, in the last box; but as they were in a bad condition, so I
can't tell, yet, which of them are alive, as they had no titles to
them.

I shall take every opportunity to write to you, and shall always
be glad to hear from you, being your obliged friend and servant,

PHILIP MILLER.

Chelsea, Feb. 18, 1756.

DEAR MR. BARTRAM :—

I received your letter dated the third of November last. I have the disagreeable account, that neither of my letters, wrote last summer, have come to your hands; for which I am extremely sorry, because there were some queries therein which I should have been glad to be informed about, especially at this time, when I am revising the Gardener's Dictionary. One was, to know the characters of the *Gale asplenii folio* [*Comptonia*], which you say is not of the same genus with the Candleberry bush. I find there are authors who have ranged it with the *Liquidambar;* but I doubt much of their being right; so I shall be much obliged to you, if you can send me a perfect specimen, that I may determine its proper genus. *   *   *   * Your observations on the male and female flowers on the same, and also on different trees, are fully confirmed by many repeated observations and experiments, as you will see in this edition of the Dictionary; however, I shall not omit mentioning yours with the others. *   *   *   *

Pray, to what size does the Balm of Gilead Fir grow, in your country, and what is the soil in which it lasts the longest? for there is but one place, in *England*, where the trees live more than ten or twelve years. *   *   *   *

Pray, let me hear from you, which will greatly oblige your sincere friend and servant,

PHILIP MILLER.

Chelsea, Feb. 15, 1757.

JOHN BARTRAM TO PHILIP MILLER.

June the 20th, 1757.

DEAR FRIEND PHILIP MILLER :—

I have received thy kind letter of February the 15th, 1757, with six good cones of the Cedar of Lebanon, as also a fine parcel of the numbers of the Gardener's Dictionary, and of the Figures adapted to them; for which favour I am much obliged to my worthy friend. *   *   *   *

I have now sent thee, as thee desired, some specimens of the *Gale asplenii folio.* It differs much from Gale Candleberry Myrtle, and from the *Liquidambar*, and is, I believe, a new genus.

The basket thee mentions, with the Norway Maple, had also

some Roses in it. I told my friend, Dr. Bond, if he would take care of them, he should have one half of them, if no others could show a better right to them. The Roses all died; but two or three of the Maples are alive, as the Doctor tells me, and one or two is enough for me, of a sort.　　*　　*　　*　　*

Any sort of foreign trees and shrubs, that will bear our frost, will be acceptable. I have sent thee some specimens, and seeds, in a paper parcel, directed for thee to the care of P. Collinson.

Pray, my good friend, write often to me, and let me know wherein I can particularly oblige.

PHILIP MILLER TO JOHN BARTRAM.

Dear Mr. Bartram:—

I received your letters, the first dated October the 13, and the other November the 12, as also the box of plants.　　*　　*　　*　The specimens you were so good as to send me by Captain Lyon, would have been a treasure, had they arrived safe; but his ship was taken by the French, so those are all lost: which is a great misfortune at this time, when they would have been of great service to me, in ascertaining the names of some plants which remain doubtful. For, though many of the plants of your country do begin to thrive here, in several gardens, yet they are not come to the state of flowering, or producing their fruit; for which reason, fair specimens of them are of more value here, than they would be if they could be obtained here: and as my *Hortus siccus* is now replete with near ten thousand specimens, so I am very solicitous to make it as complete as I can.

I am afraid the cutting of the great *Toxicodendron* is perished; for it lay at the bottom of the box, where there had been wet. I am very desirous to get all the species of this genus which I can, and am making observations on their flowers and fruit: for Doctor Linnæus has joined these to his genus of *Rhus*, with which all the species of *Toxicodendron*, which I have yet examined, will by no means agree; for these are either male and female in distinct plants, or have male flowers in separate parts from the fruit on the same plant, which, according to his own system, must remove them to a great distance from the *Rhus*. The species I have, at present, in our garden, are these, viz.:—*Toxicodendron triphyllum glabrum*,

—— *triphyllum folio sinuato pubescente,* —— *rectum foliis minoribus glabris,* and the —— *foliis alatis fructu rhomboide, Hort. Eltham.* If you can add to these, you will greatly oblige me. *

If our friend Mr. COLLINSON thinks this a good opportunity for me to send you the remaining numbers of my Figures of Plants, they shall come now; but if he judges otherwise, they shall be sent by the first opportunity.   *   *   *   * I have the plant which Doctor LINNÆUS has named *Bartramia,* just beginning to flower in our stove: so I propose to send you a specimen of it, when it is perfectly dry. The flowers are so small as not to be discerned, by my eyes, without a glass.

 * * * * * * *

The *Mountain Magnolia,* which you mention, we have not in our garden: so if you can spare me a plant of it, you will much oblige me.

I shall miss no opportunity of writing to you, and shall send you plants of any other sorts you desire from hence; and therefore wish you will send me a list of them, that I may have an opportunity of showing you the pleasure I shall have in supplying you: for, as you observe, we may not long have it in our power to oblige. But you complain of age too soon. I am now entering on my sixty-fourth year; and, bless God, I am still hearty and well. Though not so active as formerly, yet can go through fatigue; and so long as I have health, am contented with doing what is in my power.

I sincerely wish you health and happiness; and remain your sincere friend,

PHILIP MILLER.

January the 12, 1758.

JOHN BARTRAM TO PHILIP MILLER.

June the 16th, 1758.

WORTHY FRIEND MILLER :—

I have received two very kind letters from my dear friend this spring, one dated August the 26th, 1757, and the other, January the 12th, 1758. I received, last summer, thy Figures of Plants to the number XXIII, and with them, the Gardener's Dictionary, to number XXV ; and this spring, I have received number XXVI to number XLIII. Now, how the eight numbers miscarried, I know not. I have received every article our worthy friend PETER mentioned, in the letters I received from him; and I have always, ever since I corresponded with him, found him to be as faithful, careful, punctual and true a correspondent as I believe ever lived: so that if they had ever come to his hands, he would have given me some account of them.

*　　　　*　　　　*　　　　*

Strange it is, but very true, that many seeds of plants we take little care of, as not being of general use, will keep good in the ground for seven years or more, before they all come up, and perhaps the ground tilled every year, too; but the nutritious grains, pulse, and other esculents, that are adapted for our general support, generally come up the first year they are sown. Oh! the wisdom of Divine Providence! The more we search into it, the more wonderful we discover its powerful influence to be.

*　　　*　　　*　　　*　　　*　　　*

[The following notice of the pernicious and troublesome *weeds* in *Pennsylvania*, accompanies the rough draught of the above letter to P. MILLER, and seems to have been appended to it; though P. COLLINSON apparently refers to it, in his letter of July 20, 1759. *See page* 219. As it presents an interesting account of the weeds of *Eastern Pennsylvania*, ninety years since, I have concluded to insert it; and cannot but remark how truly the statement describes the *actual condition* of the farms in that region.]

*A brief account of those Plants that are most troublesome in our pastures and fields, in Pennsylvania; most of which were brought from Europe.**

The most mischievous of these is, first, the stinking yellow *Linaria*. It is the most hurtful plant to our pastures that can grow in our northern climate. Neither the spade, plough, nor hoe, can eradicate it, when it is spread in a pasture. Every little fibre that is left, will soon increase prodigiously; nay, some people have rolled great heaps of logs upon it, and burnt them to ashes, whereby the earth was burnt half a foot deep, yet it put up again, as fresh as ever, covering the ground so close as not to let any

* In the third volume of the Annals of the New York Lyceum, there is an interesting notice, by the late Rev. L. D. VON SCHWEINITZ, of the *plants of Europe which have become naturalized in the United States.*

grass grow amongst it ; and the cattle can't abide it. But it doth not injure corn so much as grass, because the plough cuts off the stalks, and it doth not grow so high, before harvest, as to choke the corn. It is now spread over great part of the inhabited parts of Pennsylvania. It was first introduced as a fine garden flower ; but never was a plant more heartily cursed by those that suffer by its encroachments.

The common English *Hypericum* [*H. perforatum*, L.] is a very pernicious weed. It spreads over whole fields, and spoils their pasturage, not only by choking the grass, but infecting our horses and sheep with scabbed noses and feet, especially those that have white hair on their face and legs. This is certain fact, as generally affirmed ;* but this is not so bad as the *Linaria*. The hoe and plough will destroy it.

Wild Chamomile, called *Mathen* [*Maruta Cotula ?* DC.], is another mischievous weed. It runs about and spreads much, choking not only the grass, but the wheat, more than the other two ; but hath not yet spread so generally as they. But this may be killed by planting Indian corn, or sowing buckwheat on the ground, for several years successively. I had it brought many times in dung ; but when I find it I burn it root and branch.

Leucanthemum is a very destructive weed, in meadow and pasture grounds, choking the grass and taking full possession of the ground, so that the fields will look as white as if covered with snow ; but the hoe and plough will destroy this weed.

The great English single-stalked *Mullein*, grows generally in most of our old fields, and with its broad spreading leaves, takes up some room, in our pastures ; but it is easily destroyed with the plough, or scythe, having only single tap roots.

Saponaria is more difficult to eradicate, as it runs deep, and spreads much under ground ; but it is not yet spread much in the country. With care we may keep it under.

The great double *Dandelion* is very troublesome in our meadow ground, and difficult to eradicate ; but the hoe and plough will destroy it.

Crow Garlick is greatly loved by the horses, cows, and sheep,

* This is the opinion which universally prevailed, half a century since, among the farmers of Eastern Pennsylvania ; but I am now led to suspect its accuracy, by the fact, that the *Hypericum* still abounds, and the disease has disappeared.— See " *Agricultural Botany.*"

and is very wholesome early pasture for them; yet our people generally hate it, because it makes the milk, butter, cheese, and indeed the flesh of those cattle that feed much upon it, taste so strong, that we can hardly eat of it; but for horses and young cattle, it doth very well. But our millers can't abide it amongst corn. It clogs up their mills so, that it is impossible to make good flour.

Docks are very troublesome in our mowing ground; and, without care, they spread much by seed. They stifle the grass by their luxuriant broad leaves.

The *Scotch Thistle* [*Cirsium horridulum?*] is a very troublesome weed, along our sea-coast. The people say, a Scotch minister brought with him a bed stuffed with thistledown, in which was contained some seed. The inhabitants, having plenty of feathers, soon turned out the down, and filled the bed with feathers. The seed coming up, filled that part of the country with Thistles.

The foregoing are most of the *English plants* that have escaped out of our gardens, and taken possession of our fields and meadows, very much to our detriment.

I now make a few observations on some of our *native plants*, that are very troublesome, in our fields and meadows, and are with difficulty eradicated.

We have four kinds of the *Rubus*, beside our common black Raspberry. The great upright Bramble grows near an inch in diameter, and eight feet high, in good ground, though commonly about two-thirds of that magnitude. This grows in our old fields and hedges, bears berries plentifully, and spreads much under ground, sending up abundance of shoots at uncertain distances.

Another kind is much like the former, but more weak and leaning, bears plentifully, and spreads as the other. Any piece of the root left in the ground, though a foot deep, will soon send up a shoot.

Another kind, we call the Running Briar [*Rubus Canadensis,* L., or Dewberry], and is the most troublesome kind. It roots very deep; and if we grub them up half a foot deep, they will shoot, from the remaining root in the grounds several branches, which will run on the surface two, three, or four yards in one summer, and dip into the ground, where they take firm root, from whence they will run, and take root as before; whereby they soon spread over much ground, and neither the plough nor mattock can easily destroy them. Mowing will kill them in a few years, if repeated three or four times a year. They bear a large black berry, and as good as the others, and is the first ripe, near the latter end of June.

The fourth sort grows about three or four feet high, upright, and one side of the leaves of a fine silver.* These grow in few places ; but where they take root they seem to spread and cover the ground.

The next native, that is troublesome in our old fields, is a late-flowering, perennial, white *Aster*, with a spreading top [*A. ericoides*, L ?], the flower much like your single daisy. These will spread all over a field so thick as to destroy all the grass, and most herbs, too, except your *Hypericum*, which only is a fit match for it ; both which no creature likes to eat. Ploughing destroys most of the old roots, but increaseth the young ones, from seed ; for the year after a crop of wheat is cut, a field will appear as white as snow, when the plant is in flower.

The lesser *Ambrosia* is a very troublesome weed, in plantations where it hath got ahead. It is an annual, and grows with corn, and after harvest it shoots above the stubble, growing three or four feet high, and so thick that one can hardly walk through it. It is very bitter, and if milk cows feed upon it (for want of enough of grass), their milk will taste very loathsome. It seldom grows to any head the next year, nor until the field is ploughed or sowed again.

We have another weed, called Cotton Groundsel [*Erechtites hieracifolia*, Raf.], which grows with us six or seven feet high, and the stalk at bottom, near as thick as my wrist, in our new cleared land after the first ploughing, in the spring, or in our marshes, the year after they are drained and cleared. It grows there all over, so close that there is no passing along without breaking it down, to walk or ride through it ; but in old fields, or meadows, there is not one stalk to be seen. Now, if we put the question, how comes this to grow so prodigiously on the new land ploughed ground, and perhaps not one root growing within several miles, the answer is very ready : *it is natural to new land and not to old.*† But our

---

* This perhaps refers to the *Rubus cuneifolius*, of PURSH's *Flora*, published more than half a century afterwards.

† This " very ready" answer, might, perhaps, be very satisfactory, if we knew precisely what was meant by a plant being "natural" to land ; but the naked

philosophers say, that every plant is produced from the seed of the same species; but how came the small seed of this plant there, in such quantities as to fill a field or meadow of one hundred acres as full of plants as they can stand?

One day when the sun shone bright, a little after its meridian, my BILLY was looking up at it, when he discovered an innumerable quantity of downy motes floating in the air, between him and the sun. He immediately called me out of my study, to see what they were. They rose higher and lower, as they were wafted to and fro in the air, some very high and progressive with a fine breeze, some lowered, and fell into my garden, where we observed every particular detachment of down, spread in four or five rays, with a seed of the *Groundsel* in its centre. How far these were carried by that breeze, can't be known; but I think they must have come near two miles, from a meadow, to reach my garden. As these are annual plants, they do but little harm in the country.

The *Phytolacca* is troublesome in our new cleared meadows, and new fields. It comes up from the seeds being carried all over the settled parts of the country, by the birds, which are fond of them; but these may be easily destroyed by grubbing them up. Sometimes a very severe winter kills many of them, as they are natives of the Southern Provinces. When I first travelled beyond the Blue Mountains, I saw not one; but now there is enough of them.

Our *Elder* is exceedingly troublesome in our meadows. The roots run under ground and spread much; and I do not know that mowing will ever kill it; and grubbing will kill little more than the mattock takes up, for if there is but a little bit of the root left in the ground, it will grow. I have had a root growing in my kitchen garden about thirty years. It was ploughed once every year, and generally grubbéd and hoed once, or mostly twice, every summer; yet, last summer, two stalks put up, and if there is an inch of root left in the ground, if it be two feet deep, it will put up again. In short, I believe there is not a shrub in the world, harder to eradicate than our Elder. I wish I had some of your Elder seed to sow. I hear it grows much larger than ours.

Those above-mentioned, are most of the troublesome weeds that frequent our meadows, pastures, and corn-fields; but in our

phrase leaves us, I think, about as wise as we were before. The phenomenon observed by "BILLY," as described in the next paragraph, seems to afford quite as intelligible a clue to the mystery, as the above *natural* theory.

kitchen gardens, we have many that are troublesome enough, such as the *Chickweed*, which was brought from England. There is no getting rid of it. It flowers and seeds most part of the year.

The *Henbit* is also another, that flowers and seeds most of the summer.

Shepherd's Purse is very plentiful in good ground ; but many people make a good boiled salad of it ; so is our wild *Purslane* very troublesome, though good when boiled. The small running *Mallow* is pestering enough ; and two or three kinds of *Veronica.* The *Malvinda* [*Sida ?*] is very bad ; and so is the *Mollugo.* One very tall species of the *Amaranth* is very troublesome, but some boil it, to eat; and a species of *Orach*, which we call Lamb's Quarter, is very tender when boiled. *Docks* and *Sorrel* are plague enough in our pastures, meadows, and gardens, the last of which is very hard to root out. These are most of the noxious weeds of our gardens, that make us have so much work to destroy them, every year, beside the grasses.

PHILIP MILLER TO JOHN BARTRAM.

SIR :—

I was yesterday favoured with your letter, dated June 16th, 1758, by which I am informed that part of the numbers of my Figures of Plants, which I sent you, have miscarried ; which gives me some concern, because they were duly sent as opportunities offered.   *   *   *   *   *

I sent to Mr. COLLINSON all the remaining numbers of my Figures of Plants, and also those of the Gardener's Dictionary, which have been printed since the last I sent you; which are directed for you, and Mr. COLLINSON promised me to forward them immediately to you ; so I hope you will receive them safely. In your next, pray inform me what numbers are wanting in each, that I may replace those which are lost.   *   *   *

In the clod of earth which you sent me, there came up one sort of *Cratœgus*, which flowered last spring, and has now ripe fruit upon it, which is small, round, and black ; but it came too late to be inserted in the *Dictionary*, so may be brought into a supplement.

There is no determining the difference between *Cratœgus*, *Mespilus*, and *Sorbus*, either by the number of their styles, or that of their seeds. The latter is very inconstant in all the pomiferous fruits. *Apples* and *Pears* have sometimes five, at others, six or seven seeds in each; so that to make that a character of the genus would be very absurd. Doctor LINNÆUS has joined so many genera together, as occasions confusion. The Apple and Pear are undoubtedly of different genera. They will not take upon each other, either by budding or grafting [?]; and it is well known, from experience, that all trees of the same genus will grow upon each other.

*   *   *   *   *   *

I want much to see a specimen of a female plant of the *Gale Asplenii folio* [*Comptonia*]. I have only yet seen the male with its catkins, for we have not any female plants here, so far as I can learn; and I am in great doubt about the character of it. If you have any of the female plants, and will be so good as to send me a plant or two, as also a dried specimen, you will much oblige me.

*   *   *   *   *   *

The method in which I was under a necessity of publishing the Gardener's Dictionary, has in some measure prevented my inserting several new plants, which have come to my hands after the initial letters of their titles were passed over. I shall be obliged to add an Appendix to it, in which I propose to take notice of as many plants as shall come to my knowledge: so that, whatever you are so good as to send to me, shall be gratefully therein mentioned.   I am your obedient humble servant,

PHILIP MILLER.

Chelsea, Aug. 28, 1758.

DEAR MR. BARTRAM:—

I was this day favoured with your letter, dated 28th of September last, by which I am informed you have not received any letter from me since that bearing date of the 30th of May last. I wrote to you the 16th of July, to acknowledge the receipt of the specimens which you was so good as to send me in Mr. COLLINSON'S box, and to return you my thanks for them: and as you was so kind as to offer me plants of those sorts which you had in your garden, so I most earnestly wish to have of them, as I believe there are some new genera amongst them. The plant with a long spike of white flowers, and grass leaves, appears to me to be an *Ornitho-*

galum [probably the *Helonias asphodeloides*, L.; *Xerophyllum*, of Mx.]; but the flowers are so much compressed as to render the distinguishing characters very doubtful.

*   *   *   *   *   *

The Yellow-root [*Hydrastis Canadensis*, L.] has flowered, and ripened seeds, in our garden, two years past, from some roots which were sent me from the inland parts of your country. It is a new genus. I have figured, and described it, by the title of *Warneria*.

The *Gale Asplenii folio* has produced male flowers in our garden, the last year; but as there was no appearance of female or hermaphrodite flowers, nor any rudiment of fruit, so I suppose it to be male and female in different plants. The two specimens you was so kind as to send me, were one male and the other female: so I shall be glad to be informed if they were taken from the same plant.*

*   *   *   *   *   *

Your Dwarf Cherry [*Cerasus pumila*, Mx.?] I believe is the same which I have figured. The stones came from Canada to Paris, and were sent me from thence. It produces great numbers of flowers along the branches, so makes a good appearance in the spring, and the fruit is. black, about the size of our small black cherries, here, but of a disagreeable flavour. The plant propagates so fast, by cuttings and layers, that it is now common in our gardens.   *   *   *   *

I am your friend and servant,
PHILIP MILLER.

Chelsea, Nov. 10, 1759.

JOHN BARTRAM TO DR. GARDEN.†

October the 12th, 1755.

RESPECTED FRIEND, DR. GARDEN :—

I received thy kind letter of May the 18th, 1755, which was

---

* The *Comptonia asplenifolia*, Ait., is now known to be a *Monoicous* plant.

† ALEXANDER GARDEN, M.D., F.R.S., a native of Scotland, and educated at Edinburgh, resided at Charleston, South Carolina, where he was extensively engaged in the practice of physic for near thirty years. He married there, on Christmas eve, 1755, as appears from one of his letters to Mr. ELLIS, with whom he maintained a frequent scientific and friendly intercourse, and by whom he was introduced to the correspondence of LINNÆUS. Botany, and some of the more

very acceptable, as will also be any of your country seeds of plants, or shrubs; some of which are hardy enough to endure our severe winters. Of the *Catalpa*, I have enough from Dr. WITT. Very few of those seeds thee sent me, came up; only the *Indica*, and the *Thea*, which I find to be a *Sida;* two or three plants of a smooth, oblong, thick, shining leaf, growing opposite. Pray, what is your *Palmetto royal?* How high doth it grow, before it bears fruit? which is very pretty tasted. I am apt to think I have three come up. The leaves are shining, something like parsley, and grow opposite.

I hope thee art fallen into good business: being so much confined in town, I shall be glad if it don't endanger thy health.

As to the sudden changes of heat and cold, in your climate, as well as ours, I suppose they are caused by our open exposition to both. As we are situated so near the open sea, and southern heats, so we are also exposed to the greatest extremity of the northern blasts, a little tempered by the intermediate heat in adequate degrees to the power and progress of the southern currents of air: for I can't find that there is, in all North America, any chains of mountains so high as to intercept the currents of the air

obscure departments of Zoology—especially Fishes and Reptiles—were his constant resources for amusement and health, amid the sometimes overwhelming duties of his profession, and the inconveniences of a delicate constitution. In Natural History he was, throughout, a zealous and classical *Linnæan*. No one welcomed the publications of the Swedish luminary, from time to time, with more enthusiasm, or was better able to appreciate them; for he had felt by experience the insufficiency of preceding systems of Botany, and had been, in consequence, near giving up the science in despair.

When the political disturbances of America came on, Dr. GARDEN took part with the British government; and, like many others, suffered a very considerable loss of property. He returned to Europe, about the end of the war, with his wife and two daughters, residing for some years in Cecil Street, in the Strand. A pulmonary consumption, confirmed by the effects of sea-sickness, terminated his life, April 15, 1791, in the sixty-second year of his age. His son conformed to the new American government, and remained in Carolina.

The cheerful, benevolent character of Dr. GARDEN is conspicuous in his letters. His person and manners were peculiarly pleasing; and he was a most welcome addition to the scientific circles in London, as long as his declining health would permit. In compliment to his botanical attainments and services, his friend, Mr. ELLIS, dedicated to his name that elegant and delightful shrub, the *Gardenia florida*, commonly called Cape Jessamine, of which so many other species have been since discovered, that it is now one of the most extensive, as it is certainly one of the most beautiful and fragrant genera in the whole vegetable kingdom.—SMITH's *Linnæan Correspondence.*

of the frigid zone, from the highest latitudes, all the way over land, as there is in Europe and Asia, which have also the great advantage of having the sea north of them, except about Nova Zembla.

As for rain, I suppose it to be collected from the sea, the rivers and lakes, vegetables and mountains. The sea affords materials abundantly for the formation of rain, as it is continually in agitation, especially near the shore, the waves dashing and breaking against it into steam, and rising in vapour. The rivers afford large quantities of vapour, both from their even surface, their agitated waves, and at their falls, as may be observed in a frosty morning in a thick fog. Plants and trees send up great quantities of vapour, from which, perhaps, most of dews are formed; and lastly, the mountains not only collect and condense the vapours, by their coldness and height, but also direct the course of the rains, in some situations ; as is evident on the coast of Coromandel in Asia, Mount Atlas in Africa, the Cordilleras in America, with many others, too tedious to name ; all which are, doubtless, very instrumental in furnishing the inland parts of the globe with the necessary liquid element.   *   *   *

March the 14th, 1756.

RESPECTED FRIEND DOCTOR GARDEN :—

I have just received thy very kind letter of February the 13th, 1756, but alas! very short. I am glad that the bulbous roots flourish with thee. I sent thee a fine variety of Tulip roots ; but they all came too late, though sent by the first opportunity.

I long to see thy Journal to and from Saluda. Pray, what is your Palmetto Royal ? Is the fruit wholesome to eat ? Is it a tree or shrub ? How soon doth it bear from seed ? I am glad thee art so well settled in business, and I hope art possessed of a sweet, dear, agreeable consort. This winter, I have married my daughter MARY to a very worthy, rich young man, who lives in sight, and about half an hour's walk distant from my house.

I am much obliged to thee for thy kindness for my son WIL-LIAM. He longs to be with thee ; but it is more for the sake of Botany, than Physic or Surgery, neither of which he seems to have any delight in. I have several books of both; but can't persuade him to read a page in either. Botany and drawing are his delight; but I am afraid won't get him a living. I have some thoughts of putting him to a merchant. I have wrote several times, last fall, to PETER COLLINSON about him, and expect an answer by the first ships.   *   *   *   *   *   *

I have often thought of proposing a scheme, which I am apt to believe would be of general benefit to most of our colonies, if put in practice ; and as a particular curious friend, I first acquaint thee with it, and perhaps I may mention it to my friend PETER COLLINSON.

It is, to bore the ground to great depths, in all the different soils in the several provinces, with an instrument fit for the purpose, about four inches diameter. The benefit which I shall propose from these trials, is to search for marls, or rich earths, to manure the surface of the poor ground withal. Secondly, to search for all kinds of medicinal earths, sulphurs, bitumens, coal, peat, salts, vitriols, marcasites, flints, as well as metals. Thirdly, to find the various kinds of springs, to know whether they are potable, or medicinal, or mechanical.

Now, to bring this into practice, suppose there was appointed, in every province, a curious, judicious, honest, careful man, as overseer ; that he should choose such men as understood boring in rocks and earth, and furnish them with proper instruments ; that he, or any whom he may depute under him, shall take particular care to write down, in a book for that purpose, the time and place, when and where, they began to bore, and the particular depth of every *stratum* they bore through, examining curiously the contents of the bit, every time the auger is drawn out, and the depth from whence it was drawn. Minute it down, so that they may know the exact depth, whether it be marl, chalk, coal, salt, or any other mineral ; or the springs of water, and how deep they are from the surface, so that every proprietor may know what riches are in his possession, and may guess what expense he must be at to come at the benefit of them. I am persuaded that most sandy, desert soil, hath under it a large bed of marl, or saline earth, which, if brought on the sandy surface, would make the surface fruitful ; and most countries, far from the sea, have vast beds of rock salt, at uncertain depths, which, if they were discovered, would be of great advantage to the inhabitants. Moreover, how exceeding useful and satisfactory will it be, to curious philosophical inquirers, to know the various terrestrial compositions that we

daily walk over. By this method, we may compose a curious sub-
terranean map.*   *   *   *   *

I want much to come to Carolina, to observe the curiosities toward the mountains ; but the mischievous Indians are so treache-
rous, that it is not safe trusting them, even in their greatest
pretence of friendship. They have destroyed all our back inhabitants. No travelling, now, to Doctor COLDEN's, nor to the back
parts of Pennsylvania, Maryland, nor Virginia.

Pray, how far do you commonly reckon it, from Charleston to
the Cherokee Mountains ? I should be glad to search them, if it
could be done safely ; but must wait till these troublesome times
are over.

You have growing with you a pretty sort of a red flower, the
root of which is a sovereign cure for the worms,† as I am informed.
Pray send it me ; I want it much.

Have you the right *Senna,* growing plentifully? Thee promised
me some seed.

I believe I can make most of your perennial plants live over our
winters, by covering them over with straw; but some of your
shrubs and trees will not. I suppose they are such that naturally
grow to the southward of you; and though they seem to grow and
seed with you, yet can't bear much more cold.

DOCTOR GARDEN TO JOHN BARTRAM.

October 25th, 1760.

MY DEAR FRIEND :—

I have received two very kind letters from you, since you left
this place, neither of which it has yet been in my power to answer.
Ever since I saw you, I have lived in a greater hurry than when I
had the pleasure of your agreeable company. Often since our
parting, have I reflected with concern, that I had then so little
time to enjoy you.

* This "scheme" of JOHN BARTRAM's—if original with him,—would indicate
that he had formed a pretty good notion of the nature and importance of a *Geological Survey and Map,* more than half a century before such undertakings were
attempted in our country, or even thought of by those whose province it was to
authorize them.

† No doubt the *Spigelia Marilandica,* L., commonly called " Carolina Pink."

I read with great satisfaction your account of the rarities of North Carolina.

I examined the tree in my garden, which I formerly took to be a Holly, like Mr. WRAGG'S; but I find it quite different, as is likewise that one in Governor GLEN'S garden, which is of the same kind as mine. It is a new genus, and a beautiful enough Evergreen.

My close confinement deprives me of that happiness which I would have, in searching our woods.

Your plants, in my garden, thrive surprisingly well, and they are now ready for your boxes; one or two are dead.

As I met lately with LEE on Botany, I bought two copies, one of which I have sent you, and beg you'll accept of it, from

Your sincere friend,

ALEXANDER GARDEN.

Inclosed you have a letter from Mrs. LOGAN, which has been with me some time, for want of an opportunity.

DEAR SIR :—

I received your kind letter, with your present of apples and plants, for both which please to accept of my thanks. The apples were extremely good, and have kept much beyond any that ever I had before. You made me very happy in the Newfoundland Spruce, Hemlock Fir, and *Kalmia*. I wanted these very much, and you gave me fine thriving plants. The others, viz., the Lavender, Sabina, and *Rhamnus*, with the Fraxinellas, are all growing beautifully, so that I expect to have great pleasure in them all the summer.

I hope you may have like pleasure in those that I now send you. I need not tell you to plant them out immediately, and in a shady moist place. The box is rather too full; but the reason is, my not choosing to remove the earth from the roots of the plants as they grow, so that earth taken up with them soon filled up the box.

Your four Umbrellas are all alive, and very thriving; so is the great *Magnolia*. The Atamasco Lilies are all alive; the Four-Leafed *Bignonia*, and the fine blue purple flower.

I could not find the Worm-grass root, so that I am afraid it is dead ; but I shall soon replace it to you with some others. The *Asarum*, and *Solanum triphyllum* [*Trillium*], are both in good health, and blooming. I sincerely wish they may arrive safe. I have watered them again, to-day ; and the Captain says, that he'll sail to-morrow. May God grant him a speedy and prosperous voyage, and thus give you a further opportunity of viewing and admiring the beauties of some more of his amazing and wonderful works. How eminently happy are these hours, which the humble and philosophic mind spends in investigating and contemplating the inconceivable beauties and mechanism of the works of nature, the true manifestations of that supremely wise and powerful Agent who daily upholds and blesses us.

May that fatherly Being continue to enlighten your mind, till that hour come, when the parting of this veil will lay before your eyes a new and more glorious field of contemplation, and still more unutterable sights of bliss.

Be assured that I offer, in great sincerity, my kind respects to all your family.

And am, dear friend, yours,
ALEXANDER GARDEN.

February 23d, 1761.

N. B. I should be much obliged to you for some Hyacinths, and some *Narcissus* with the largest *Nectariums*,—we call these *Horsenecks*.   *   *   *   *   *

MY WORTHY FRIEND :—

I received your obliging letter, informing me of the safe arrival of the plants. I rejoice with you, on your increasing collection of these curious productions of the allwise hand of our omnipotent Creator. May your soul be daily more filled with an humble admiration of his works, and your lips exercised in his praise. How glorious are those hours of contemplation and enjoyment, that the ravished soul passes through, when viewing the wonderful manifestations of his power, wisdom, and goodness. When this scene of things passes away, and the great and first Author of all leads us to fields of a more rich and fertile clime, there shall we proceed with fresh vigour, and enlarged faculties, to view him nearer, worship and adore more strongly, and live more willingly within the

pale of universal love. How great is our God! How wonderful
are his works, sought out of all them that take pleasure therein.

Your letters particularly give me pleasure. They always contain something new and entertaining, on some new-discovered work
of God.   *   *   *   *   *

I could not get *Beureria* [*Calycanthus*], when I sent the box;
and my own had died in the winter; but I'll try to get two or
three plants this year.   *   *   *   *

This will be delivered to you by a lady, whom I have the honour
to be acquainted with, and who has a very pretty taste for flowers,
and the culture of curious plants. She intends to pay you a visit,
while she stays at Philadelphia; and I take the liberty to beg
your civilities to her, not doubting but it will give you joy, to see a
lady coming so far, to view and admire your curiosities.

My wife offers, along with me, our best respects to your wife,
and all the rest of your good family.

Believe me to be yours,
ALEXANDER GARDEN.

June 17th, 1761.

JOHN BARTRAM TO DR. GARDEN.

March the 25th, 1762.

I received thy very kind letter of February the 15th, am glad
my remarks of the Ohio gave thee such satisfaction.   *   *

I have just received two very loving letters from New England,—
one from Doctor GALE—the other from Doctor ELIOT, a very
worthy Presbyterian minister [see page 372], one that spends his
time in pious exercise, and in promoting the general good of mankind. He found out the method, about three months past, to make
out of sea-sand excellent iron. One hundred weight of sand will
yield fifty of good iron. I think little coal will do it. It was
advertised in the York paper, a month past; and many curious
people thought it so very improbable, that they gave little or no
credit to it. He sent me a specimen of both the sand and iron.
I showed it, not only to our smiths, but to the owners of the fur-
naces and forges, and they allowed it to be very fine, and some
thought it would make choice steel. And now, dear friend, not to
keep thee too long upon the rack,—and as mutual friends should

always ease, and not torment—explain, and not perplex one another,—the sand out of which he makes his iron, is not the white crystalline sand; but a black, bright, fine mixed sand, in great beds, that will adhere to the magnet, as the filings of iron. But the grand query is, from whence it came, and how it got there.

My dear worthy friend, I am much affected every time that I often read thy pious reflections on the wonderful works of the Omnipotent and Omniscient Creator. The more we search and accurately examine his works in nature, the more wisdom we discover, whether we observe the mineral, vegetable, or animal kingdom. But, as I am chiefly employed with the vegetable, I shall enlarge more upon it.

What charming colours appear in the various tribes, in the regular succession of the vernal and autumnal flowers—these so nobly bold—those so delicately languid! What a glow is enkindled in some, what a gloss shines in others! With what a masterly skill is every one of the varying tints disposed! Here, they seem to be thrown on with an easy dash of security and freedom; there, they are adjusted by the nicest touches. The verdure of the empalement, or the shadings of the petals, impart new liveliness to the whole, whether they are blended or arranged. Some are intersected with elegant stripes, or studded with radiant spots; others affect to be genteelly powdered, or neatly fringed; others are plain in their aspect, and please with their naked simplicity. Some are arrayed in purple; some charm with the virgin's white; others are dashed with crimson; while others are robed in scarlet. Some glitter like silver lace; others shine as if embroidered with gold. Some rise with curious cups, or pendulous bells; some are disposed in spreading umbels; others crowd in spiked clusters; some are dispersed on spreading branches of lofty trees, on dangling catkins; others sit contented on the humble shrub; some seated on high on the twining vine, and wafted to and fro; others garnish the prostrate, creeping plant. All these have their particular excellencies; some for the beauty of their flowers; others their sweet scent; many the elegance of foliage, or the goodness of their fruit: some the nourishment that their roots afford us; others please the fancy with their regular growth: some are admired for their odd appearance, and many that offend the taste, smell, and sight, too, are of virtue in physic.

But when we nearly examine the various motions of plants and
flowers, in their evening contraction and morning expansion, they
seem to be operated upon by something superior to only heat and
cold, or shade and sunshine ;—such as the surprising tribes of the
Sensitive Plants, and the petals of many flowers shutting close up
in rainy weather, or in the evening, until the female part is fully
impregnated: and if we won't allow them real feeling, or what we
call sense, it must be some action next degree inferior to it, for
which we want a proper epithet, or the immediate finger of God,
to whom be all glory and praise.

*   *   *   *   *   *

I don't dwell so long in the vegetable kingdom, as though I
thought the wisdom and power of God were only manifest therein.
The contemplation of the mineral, and especially the animal, will
equally incline the pious heart to overflow with daily adorations
and praises to the Grand Giver and Supporter of universal life.
But what amazing distant glories are disclosed in a midnight scene!
Vast are the bodies which roll in the immense expanse! Orbs beyond orbs, without number, suns beyond suns, systems beyond
systems, with their proper inhabitants of the great Jehovah's
empire, how can we look at these without amazement, or contemplate the Divine Majesty that rules them, without the most humble
adoration? Esteeming ourselves, with all our wisdom, but as one
of the smallest atoms of dust praising the living God, the great
I AM.

DOCTOR GARDEN TO JOHN BARTRAM, AT ST. AUGUSTINE.

S. Carolina, February 12th, 1766.

MY DEAR OLD FRIEND :—

How do you do? It is so long since I had a line from you, and
then it was so short, containing no botanical news, that I scarcely
could believe it came from you.

Think that I am here, confined to the sandy streets of Charleston, where the ox, where the ass, and where men as stupid as
either, fill up the vacant space, while you range the green fields of
Florida, where the bountiful hand of Nature has spread every
beautiful and fair plant and flower, that can give food to animals,
or pleasure to the spectator.

Pray, out of the abundance of what you see, send me some curiosities, particularly seeds for my garden. But let these be confined wholly to what is new and curious. Some young plants, in a box, would be very acceptable.

My best wishes always attend you; and I am, dear sir,

Yours, &c.,

ALEX. GARDEN.

DOCTOR GARDEN TO JOHN BARTRAM, AT ST. AUGUSTINE.

[Not dated.]

MY DEAR FRIEND:—

It appears to me to be an age since I have had the pleasure of hearing from you. Pray, write me, and tell me what you are doing; for I know you can't be idle. Tell me what you are discovering; for I know your imagination and genius can't be still. How many wonders of creation do you daily see? Why won't you let me know a few?

Some time since, I had the inclosed from your wife, which I now send to you.

Your friend, Mr. LAMBOLL, informed me of this conveyance, and I am just to send him this letter. Remember me to your son: and I am, dear sir,

Yours, &c.,

ALEX. GARDEN.

I have your letter to your son, which I shall send by first opportunity; but at present, all communication is stopped.

JOHN BARTRAM TO MISS JANE COLDEN.*

January the 24th, 1757.

RESPECTED FRIEND JANE COLDEN:—

I received thine of October the 26th, 1756, and read it several times with agreeable satisfaction; indeed, I am very careful of it,

---

* Miss JANE COLDEN was the daughter of Doctor COLDEN, of New York. Some brief but interesting notices of this accomplished lady, may be found in the first volume of the *Linnœan Correspondence*, published by Sir J. E. SMITH; and also in the *Selections from the Correspondence of* CADWALLADER COLDEN, in the forty-fourth volume of SILLIMAN's *Journal*, by Professor A. GRAY.

and it keeps company with the choicest correspondence,—European letters.*

The Viney plant thee so well describes, I take to be the *Dioscorea* of HILL and GRONOVIUS ; though I never searched the characters of the flower so curiously as I find thee hath done ; but pray search them books, thee may presently find that article.

I should be extremely glad to see thee once at my house, and to show thee my garden. My BILLY is gone from me to learn to be a merchant, in Philadelphia, and I hope a choice good place, too (Captain CHILDS). I showed him thy letter, and he was so well pleased with it, that he presently made a packet of very fine drawings for thee, far beyond CATESBY'S, took them to town, and told me he would send them very soon. I was then in a poor state of health ; but am now well recovered. We very gratefully receive thy kind remembrance, and my two dear friends, thy father and mother. I want once more to climb the Katskills ; but I think it is not safe to venture these troublesome times.

I have had several kinds of the *Cochleata*, or Snail Trefoil, and *Trigonella*, or Fenugreek; but, being annual plants, they are gone off. The species of Persicary thee mentions, is what TOURNEFORT brought from the three churches, at the foot of Mount Ararat.

The *Amorpha* is a beautiful flower ; but whether won't your cold winters kill it ?

If the Rhubarb from London be the Siberian, I have it. I had the Perennial Flax, from Livonia. It growed four feet high, and I don't know but fifty stalks from a root ; but the flax was very rotten and coarse. The flowers were large and blue. It lived many years and then died.

JOHN BARTRAM.

JOHN BARTRAM TO B. FRANKLIN.†

July 29th, 1757.

DEAR BENJAMIN :—

I now take the freedom of thy usual benevolence, and favour of thy wife, to inclose this letter in hers ; hoping this way we may

---

* That letter, however, which would now be read with so much interest, is among the missing ;—as well as those from LINNÆUS, and many others.

† BENJAMIN FRANKLIN was born in the year 1706, and died on the 17th of April, 1790, aged eighty-four years and three months. No intelligent reader on either side of the Atlantic, will require to be informed of the history or career of Doctor FRANKLIN.

keep the chain of friendship bright. While thee art diverting thyself with the generous conversation of our worthy friends in Europe, and adding daily new acquisitions to thy former extensive stock of knowledge, by their free communications of their experimental improvements, thy poor, yet honest friend BARTRAM, is daily in mourning for the calamities of our provinces. Vast sums spent, and nothing done to the advantage of the King or country. How should I leap for joy, to see or hear that the British officers would prove by their *actions*, the zeal and duty to their prince and nation, they so much pretend in *words*.

I am not insensible of the burden thee art charged with; and perhaps thee may meet with some that are not so sincere as our dear PETER, who, Captain LYON told me, in a grateful zeal, was, he believed, one of the best men in London.

Pray, my dear friend, bestow a few lines upon thy old friend, such-like as those sent from Woodbridge. They have a magical power of dispelling melancholy fumes, and cheering up my spirits, they are so like thy facetious discourse, in thy southern chamber, when we used to be together.

We have had this summer abundance of thunder, which hath done much damage. Several houses have been much shattered. In one house, two young women were killed, one of which had a child in her lap two weeks old, which was found on the floor, and still liveth. All in the room were so stupified, that they can't give any account how they were hurt. One saith, he saw a ball of fire break into the room, and spread about. Several were singed, as with fire.

DOCTOR FRANKLIN TO JOHN BARTRAM.

London, January 9, 1769.

MY DEAR OLD FRIEND :—

I received your kind letter of November 5, and the box directed to the King is since come to hand. I have written a line to our late dear friend's son, (who must be best acquainted with the usual manner of transacting your affairs here,) to know whether he will take charge of the delivery of it; if not, to request he would inform me how, or to whom, it is to be sent for the King. I expect his answer in a day or two, and I shall when I see him, inquire how your pension is hereafter to be applied for and received ; though I suppose he has written to you before this time.

I hope your health continues—as mine does, hitherto ; but I wish you would now decline your long and dangerous peregrinations, in search of your plants, and remain safe and quiet at home, employing your leisure hours in a work that is much wanted, and which no one besides is so capable of performing—I mean the writing a Natural History of our country. I imagine it would prove profitable to you, and I am sure it would do you honour.

My respects and best wishes attend Mrs. BARTRAM, and your family.

With sincere esteem, I am, as ever,

Your affectionate friend,

B. FRANKLIN.

P. S. January 28. The box is delivered, according to Mr. MICHAEL COLLINSON'S directions, at Lord BUTE'S. Mr. COLLINSON takes it amiss that you did not write to him.

I have sent over some seed of Naked Oats, and some of Swiss Barley, six rows to an ear. If you would choose to try some of it, call on Mrs. FRANKLIN.

London, July 9, 1769.

DEAR FRIEND :—

It is with great pleasure, I understand, by your favour of April 10, that you continue to enjoy so good a share of health. I hope it will long continue ; and although it may not now be suitable for you to make such wide excursions as heretofore, you may yet be very useful to your country, and to mankind, if you sit down quietly at home, digest the knowledge you have acquired, compile and publish the many observations you have made, and point out the advantages that may be drawn from the whole, in public undertakings, or particular private practice.

It is true, many people are fond of accounts of old buildings, monuments, &c., but there is a number, who would be much better pleased with such accounts as you could afford them ; and for one I confess, that if I could find in any Italian travels, a receipt for making Parmesan cheese, it would give me more satisfaction than a transcript of any inscription from any old stone whatever.

I suppose Mr. MICHAEL COLLINSON, or Doctor FOTHERGILL, have written to you what may be necessary for your information, relating to your affairs here. I imagine there is no doubt but the King's bounty to you will be continued; and that it will be proper for you to continue sending, now and then, a few such curious seeds as you can procure, to keep up your claim.

And now I mention seeds, I wish you would send me a few of such as are least common, to the value of a guinea, which Mr. FOXCROFT will pay you for me. They are for a particular friend who is very curious.

If in anything I can serve you here, command freely,

Your affectionate friend,
B. FRANKLIN.

P. S. Pray, let me know whether you have had sent you any of the seeds of the Rhubarb, described in the inclosed prints. It is said to be of the true kind. If you have it not, I can procure some seed for you.

London, Jan. 11, 1770.

MY EVER DEAR FRIEND :—

I received your kind letter of Nov. 29, with the parcel of seeds, for which I am greatly obliged to you. I cannot make you adequate returns, in kind ; but I send you, however, some of the true Rhubarb seed, which you desire. I had it from Mr. INGLISH, who lately received a medal, of the Society of Arts, for propagating it. I send, also, some green dry Pease, highly esteemed here as the best for making pease soup ; and also some Chinese Garavances, with Father NAVARETTA'S account of the universal use of a cheese made of them, in China, which so excited my curiosity, that I caused inquiry to be made of Mr. FLINT, who lived many years there, in what manner the cheese was made ; and I send you his answer. I have since learnt, that some runnings of salt (I suppose runnet) is put into water when the meal is in it, to turn it to curds.

I think we have Garavances with us ; but I know not whether they are the same with these, which actually came from China, and are what the *Tau-fu* is made of. They are said to be of great increase.

I shall inquire of Mr. COLLINSON for your Journal.   I see that
of East Florida is printed with STORK'S Account.

My love to good Mrs. BARTRAM, and your children.   With sincere esteem, I am ever, my dear friend,

Yours affectionately,
B. FRANKLIN.

London, Feb. 10, 1773.

MY DEAR GOOD OLD FRIEND :—

I am glad to learn that the Turnip seed, and the Rhubarb, grow
with you, and that the Turnip is approved.

It may be depended on, that the Rhubarb is the genuine sort.
But, to have the root in perfection, it ought not to be taken out of
the ground in less than seven years.

Herewith, I send you a few seeds of what is called the Cabbage
Turnip.   They say that it will stand the frost of the severest
winter, and so make a fine early feed for cattle, in the spring,
when their other fodder may be scarce.   I send, also, some seed
of the Scotch Cabbage ; and some Peas that are much applauded,
here, but I forget for what purpose, and shall inquire, and let you
know, in my next.

I think there has been no good opportunity of sending your
Medal,* since I received it, till now.   It goes in a box, to my son
BACHE, with the seeds.   I wish you joy of it.

* This *Medal*, which is of gold, and weighs four hundred and eighty-seven
grains, was sent by a society, at Edinburgh, established in 1764, for the purpose
of importing seeds of useful trees and shrubs.

   The Medal is now in the possession of Mrs. JONES, a descendant of the distinguished botanist.

Notwithstanding the failure of your eyes, you write as distinctly as ever.

With great esteem and respect, I am, my dear friend,
Yours most affectionately,
B. FRANKLIN.

Paris, May 27, 1777.

MY DEAR OLD FRIEND :—

The communication between Britain and North America being cut off, the French botanists cannot, in that channel, be supplied as formerly with American seeds, &c. If you, or one of your sons, incline to continue that business, you may, I believe, send the same number of boxes here, that you used to send to England; because England will then send here, for what it wants in that way. Inclosed, is a list of the sorts wished for here. If you consign them to me, I will take care of the sale, and returns, for you. There will be no difficulty in the importation, as the matter is countenanced by the ministry, from whom I received the list.

My love to Mrs. BARTRAM, and your children. I am ever, my dear friend,
Yours most affectionately,
B. FRANKLIN.

JOHN CLAYTON* TO JOHN BARTRAM.

Gloucester, July 23d, 1760.

DEAR SIR :—

Having so fine an opportunity by my neighbour, Captain RICHARD BENTLEY, I have sent you inclosed some of the seeds

---

* JOHN CLAYTON, an eminent botanist of Virginia, was born at Fulham, in the county of Kent, in Great Britain. He came to Virginia with his father, in the year 1705, and was probably then in his twentieth year. His father was an eminent lawyer, and was appointed Attorney-General of Virginia.

Young CLAYTON was put in the office of PETER BEVERLY, who was Clerk or Prothonotary for Gloucester County, Virginia. He succeeded Mr. BEVERLY as clerk of that county, and filled the office fifty-one years. He died on the 15th of December, 1773, in his eighty-eighth year.

During the year preceding his decease, such was the vigour of his constitution, and such his zeal in botanical researches, that he made a botanical tour through Orange County; and it is believed that he had visited most of the settled parts of

you seemed desirous of having, when I had the pleasure of your agreeable company here. I hope you got safe and well home, and that you found your good wife and family all in perfect health.

As we were just beginning an acquaintance, the parting with you so soon made me very melancholy for some time; and I have since frequently wished that I could have prevailed with you, by some means or other, to have stayed with me much longer.

I quite forgot to show you my specimens of dried plants, of which I have a pretty large collection, also, a few other natural curiosities. Several plants, too, in my garden, which I wanted much to have your opinion of, were entirely forgot to be shown you. But I hope, if ever Providence orders it so that you should have a call into this province again, you will make me ample amends for this last transient visit.

If you have any of the seeds ready of the underwritten plants, the bearer will give 'em a safe conveyance to, dear friend, your most sincere friend and humble servant,

JOHN CLAYTON.

August 30, 1760.
DEAR SIR:—

Captain BENTLEY not setting out for Philadelphia so soon as he intended, gives me the further opportunity of writing to you; and, as he tells me, he believes he shall stay there till the latter end of September, and promises me to take particular care of anything you shall please to send by him, I think it is happened very luckily for me, especially as the season will be tolerably good for removing rooted plants; and he proposes coming from your city in a vessel down Delaware, and then in his own vessel down Chesapeake Bay, quite to within about three miles of my house. It will do much

Virginia. As a practical botanist, he was perhaps inferior to no botanist of his time. He left behind him two volumes of manuscript, nearly ready for the press, and a *Hortus siccus*, which were unfortunately destroyed by the torch of an incendiary. He is chiefly known to the learned, especially in Europe, by the *Flora Virginica*, published in 1739, at Leyden, by GRONOVIUS. It is to be regretted that succeeding botanists are in the habit of referring to that *Flora*, as the work of GRONOVIUS, though its great value is derived from the masterly descriptions communicated to the Leyden Professor by CLAYTON. In America, his name is familiar to every student of Botany, from the prevalence of the pretty little plant (*Claytonia Virginica*), dedicated to his memory.—*See* BARTON'S *Med. and Phys. Journ.*, vol. ii.

better than sending by the shallop to Colonel HUNTER'S, as was
concluded upon, when I had the pleasure of your company here.

I presume there will be no occasion to put you in mind of the
plant you were so kind to promise me; yet I can't forbear mentioning that the *Meadia*, *Arbor Vitæ*, and Northern Spruce Fir,
were to be among 'em. I shall be always very ready to retaliate
your favours, and am, dear sir, your sincere friend and most humble
servant,

JOHN CLAYTON.

DEAR FRIEND :—

I have sent you, inclosed, some seed of a new plant, which I
presume is a stranger in your northern part of the world. Indeed,
it grows here only in the southern parts of the colony. I have it
in my garden, but have quite forgot whether I showed it to you,
when I had the great favour of your company. If I did, I believe
I told you that it was to be called *Amsonia*, after a doctor, here;
but I think the name inscribed upon the inclosed more proper, as
it answers to the particular form of its seed.

I intend to send you some seed of our thorny Sensitive Plant,
[*Schrankia ?*] by the first opportunity that offers, after it is ripe ;
And remain, dear sir, your sincere friend
And most humble servant,
JOHN CLAYTON.

September 1st, 1760.

February the 23d, 1761.
DEAR FRIEND :—

I received your agreeable letter of the 16th of November last,
about a month ago, and am very much obliged to you for the seed
therein inclosed. It was a long time in coming, and had passed
through various hands, insomuch that the folds were quite worn
out ; and some person or other had taken out the paper with the
striped Stock July flower seed ; the loss of which I regret very
much, as it is so great a curiosity. I was a little doubtful of my
Pyrethrum seed ; but, as you guess, it was really the very best I
had. If, hereafter, I should happen to save any better, you may
depend upon participating with me in that, as well as in the others
you mention in the letter ; for, at present, I have not one grain of
the seed of *Stœchas*, nor of the *Tetragonotheca*, nor *Staphisagria*.

I am very glad to hear that you are perfectly well recovered of your troublesome cough and fever. I assure you, I was under a good deal of concern for your going away, with such a disorder upon you.

There was one paper of seed you were so kind to send me, inscribed *Dracocephalum*, which, by the appearance and smell of the dry calyces, I take to be the same plant which I have had several years in my garden. It is called three-leaved American *Moldavica*, with a strong scent of Balm of Gilead.

I have a species of *Aconite* [*A. uncinatum*, L. ?] in my garden, which grows about five feet high. I found it at our little South-west Mountains. The flowers are blue, and grow in the same manner as those on your large tall species, according to your description. In its natural place of growth, it blossoms in October; but in my garden it is about three weeks forwarder. You say you never found any real species of the true *Aconite*, except that tall one, near our South Mountains. Now I should be glad to know what you take our Stagger-weed to be.

The places you mention for our meeting at again are, my dear friend, such as I fear I shall never be able to travel to.

Captain BENTLEY, at his return, told me he was at your house, but could not see you, because, as some of your family informed him, you were gone a long journey in search of plants, &c., and could not be expected at home while he stayed.

When Mr. FRANKLIN was at Williamsburgh, he desired me—if I had occasion to write to you, or Doctor GARDEN, by the way of Philadelphia, to send the letters under a cover directed for him, in order to save paying postage; but now, as he is not in America, I don't know very well how to act, if I should have no other way of writing to you than by the post.

I have sent you, here inclosed, three papers of seeds, such as I judged would be most acceptable. They are all natives of Virginia.

This comes by a young gentleman, a friend and neighbour of mine, whose name is RICHARD BLACKNALL, who, I am confident, may be relied upon for his utmost care of a box of rooted plants— if you'll please to be so kind as to send it by him, to, dear friend, your most sincere and affectionate friend,

JOHN CLAYTON.

Pray, don't forget to put a root or two of Madder in the box.

DEAR WORTHY FRIEND :—

I have been in great expectation, a long tedious time, of having the satisfaction of receiving a letter from you; but alas! my wishes and expectation have hitherto been quite disappointed; and if it was not for my correspondence with Mr. COLLINSON, and now and then meeting with persons from Philadelphia, I should be totally in the dark as to your being still in the land of the living.

I have wrote to you several times, since I received your entertaining, agreeable letter; and the last I sent, was (I think) by one Mr. WM. ADCOCK, who, I am informed, lives in your city, and is in partnership with one Mr. JOHN PEYTON, an elderly man, and I have great reason to believe that that letter, with several sorts of seed inclosed, got safe to your hands.

I hear, by common fame, that you have made some excursions, in quest of vegetables, as far as the Lakes Michigan and Superior, and should be highly delighted with some few sketches, or an epitome of your travels and discoveries in the vegetable kingdon. I had much rather have it from you, than at second-hand from our friend COLLINSON, who is generally, upon such a topic, too concise.

I should, in particular, be very glad to know if you saw anything of the Canada Bonduc, or Nickar-tree [*Gymnocladus Canadensis*, Lam.], and if you brought any of the seed home with you. I should esteem it a great favour to be admitted to participate with you in that, or any other curious seed, where your stock is sufficient.

This comes by a gentleman of Philadelphia, Mr. WILLING, who, I understand, sets off from Colonel BYRD's the beginning of next month; and who, I dare say, will take particular care of any letter or parcel you shall please to send me, and forward it (in case he should not return soon to Virginia) by a safe, careful hand, to Colonel BYRD, whom I have the honour to be well acquainted with, and without vanity, esteem him one of my friends.

I wish you and all your family, health and prosperity; and am, dear sir, your sincere, affectionate friend,

And humble servant,

JOHN CLAYTON.

March 16, 1763.

February 25, 1764.

DEAR FRIEND :—

I received your agreeable letters of the 16th of June, and 3d of December last, about ten days ago, and am really concerned to hear that my last letter went to you by the post ; for I fully intended and directed it to go by the favour of Mr. WILLING, brother to Colonel BYRD'S lady, who was at that time setting off for Philadelphia ; but the person I intrusted it with, instead of sending it to Westover, (Colonel BYRD'S seat, upon James River,) put it into the post-office at Williamsburgh.

The reading the account of your travels, and the many curious and uncommon vegetables which you discovered in your long journey, gave me a vast deal of pleasure ; and at the same time excited in me a longing desire to partake of the seeds, or roots, of such of 'em as are not too great favourites with you to be parted with.

By your short description of the evergreen shrub, growing over Colonel CHISWELL'S lead mine, I conjecture it may perhaps be a species of the *Taxus* (Yew tree) ; for we have some of those trees, more shrubby than the European kinds, growing in the western parts of what you call Old Virginia.

Your new *Osteospermums*, *Silphiums*, and *Chrysanthemums*, must certainly be delightful plants. I heartily wish it was in my power to see 'em all, and your other curious plants and flowering shrubs ; at the same time, too, to have the conversation of my worthy friend in his garden.

I sow always my Stavesacre seed in the autumn, for if it is kept till spring, not one seed in a hundred will come up, and those that do, make poor stunted plants, and flower so late that the frost kills 'em, before the seed is perfected. I have not, at this time, any of the seed, nor of the red *Chelone ;* but will take care to save some of both this year, in order to be sent you by the first opportunity ; or by the post, under cover, as this goes, to Mr. FRANKLIN.

I should be very glad of a little seed of the Carolina *Tipitiwitchet*, or Sensitive Plant, with a few directions as to the time of planting, and the soil it most delights in, &c. I dare say, my friend Mr. FRANKLIN would be kind enough to frank a small parcel of seeds from you to him, who is your sincere and affectionate friend,

JOHN CLAYTON.

Dear worthy Friend :—

I received the favour of your letter by Mr. Fox, with some curious seeds inclosed, for which I am much obliged to you, and return you my hearty thanks.

I now send you the seed of the red flowered *Chelone* and the *Staphisagria*, which I saved this last year out of my garden, and hope they will prove acceptable.

We have had, hitherto, a very severe winter. The frost set in about the latter end of December, and has continued, with very few and short intermissions, and now and then very intense, and accompanied with abundance of snow to this day; and even now, there is no prospect of its breaking up.

I was taken with an intermitting fever, about the latter end of October, which reduced me so low, that I have been confined to my house almost ever since. All my hopes are, that I shall recover my usual good health in the spring.

My garden is entirely ruined with the cold piercing winds and frosts. All the flowers which were in the leaf, tender, as *Narcissus*, *Polyanthus*, *Ixia*, *Leucojum*, &c., are destroyed. I fear much that it has been severe with you.

I sincerely wish you health and happiness; and remain, dear friend, your affectionate friend, and most humble servant,

JOHN CLAYTON.

Feb. 6, 1765.

PETER TEMPLEMAN TO JOHN BARTRAM.

Sir :—

As the surest method of improving science, is by a generous intercourse of the learned in different countries, and a free communication of knowledge, the Society established at London for the encouragement of Arts, Manufactures, and Commerce, take this liberty of addressing themselves to you, to intreat the favour of an answer to the following inquiry:

Do any herbs, or species of grass, grow in your country, during the most inclement part of the year (which we consider to be the months of December, January, February, March, and April), so as to supply all sorts of cattle, at that time, with a vegetating food?

Induced by reason and analogy, we are inclined to think that the common Parent of all has not left the preservation of such animals solely to the care and industry of man, to furnish them at that season of the year with dry fodder only; but that proper herbs and vegetables are afforded them to support themselves, at least in some tolerable condition.

We know that nature has disseminated her bounties variously, through the habitable world, so that some species of fruits and herbs arise spontaneously in one country, and others in another; but that most of them are capable of being transplanted, and will thrive in the most distant regions.

It is the business of the philosopher and naturalist to explore these treasures of nature, and spread the knowledge and use of them for the benefit of mankind.

Such are the sentiments of the Society I have the honour to be secretary to, and they address themselves to you as animated with the same generous way of thinking.

All the plants, herbs, and grasses, which grow here, in England, both in winter and summer, are enumerated in RAY'S synopsis.

If there are any other species that flourish in the winter season with you, not cited by RAY, and proper for the food of cattle, in the above-mentioned months, the Society beg the favour of you to transmit an account of them, with the nature of the soil they grow in, and the culture they require: and intreat you to procure a sufficient quantity of the seeds of each kind, to try the experiment of their thriving here, in England, and to send, at the same time, a botanical description of them.

Your kindness in answering these requests will lay an indispensable obligation on the Society to requite the favour, whenever they shall have it in their power; and, with the greatest pleasure, they will embrace the opportunity.

I have the honour to subscribe myself, in the name of the Society,

Your most obedient humble servant,

PETER TEMPLEMAN,

Secretary.

Strand, London, September 16, 1760.

MARTHA LOGAN* TO JOHN BARTRAM.

SIR :—

I have, last week, received both your favours, with the seeds therein mentioned, for which am much obliged; and wish you had been so kind to let me know what we have that would have been most acceptable to you; but, as you did not, have sent, inclosed, the little bag, which contains some variety, but few of a kind (as you requested). The middle division is flowering shrubs, trees, and vines, which we esteem, and wish they may be new to you. I doubt not you have many things which I should be glad of.

*   *   *   *   *

I do again assure you of the truth of my assertion, relating to the striped Stock Gillyflowers. If the seed should produce you flowers of a plain red, I beg you'd not be discouraged, but make a second trial the next season; by which I am persuaded you will be convinced of the truth.

The seeds I sent you, by the name of Virgin Stock, was of the same little flower you so much admired in my garden, and hope they have succeeded with you; but have again sent a few more, for fear of any accidents; and am, with greatest sincerity, sir,

Your assured friend and humble servant,

MARTHA LOGAN.

Charleston, 20 December, 1760.

My best wishes attend your family.

SIR :—

I wrote you, some little time since, requesting your instructions in my flower garden, which I hope you will grant.

I make no doubt you have received the seeds I sent by Doctor GARDEN'S conveyance, and wish they may succeed to the uttermost of your desires; and if it is in my power to oblige you with any-

---

* MARTHA LOGAN, a great florist, was the daughter of ROBERT DANIEL, of South Carolina. In her fifteenth year she married GEORGE LOGAN; and died in 1779, aged seventy-seven. At the age of seventy, she wrote a treatise on gardening.—BLAKE'S *Biogr. Dictionary.*

thing in this province, only let me know, and you shall find no person more ready.

*   *   *   *   *

In the mean time, I remain, with true regard, sir, your assured friend and humble servant,

MARTHA LOGAN.

February 20, 1761.

WILLIAM BARTRAM, SEN., TO JOHN BARTRAM.

DEAR BROTHER :—

I hope you're all in good health, as we enjoy at present, thanks be to the Almighty. I have nothing strange to acquaint you with. I send my son, BILL, by Captain GULLEY. I expect he will incline to stay with you awhile, to go to school.

Dear brother, I make bold to trouble you for one favour more, which shall always be acknowledged; that is, that you and your sons, ISAAC and MOSES, will take into your care my son BILL; hoping and not doubting but you'll instruct and advise him for the best, to his advantage and credit. Cousin BILLY adviseth me to put my son BILL to school, in Philadelphia, for several reasons assigned; but I shall leave that to your judgment. If he stayeth in Philadelphia, I have wrote my cousins, ISAAC and MOSES, to let him live with them. If out of town, beg you'll let him live with you.

This notion has happened so suddenly, that I am unprovided to send but little with him; but, whatever charge and trouble you're at, on his account, shall be as soon as possible paid, with many thanks for your care and trouble.

From your brother, &c.

WILLIAM BARTRAM.

[Cape Fear, N. C.], Aug. 5th, 1761.

MARTHA LOGAN TO ANN BARTRAM.

October 18, 1761.

MADAM :—

I received your favour by Captain NORTH, and am much obliged for taking the trouble of answering mine, in Mr. BARTRAM's absence. I hope he is, by this, returned to his family, and well. Pray, give my respects to him, and tell him I should be very glad he would tell Mr. RATLIVE what the *Andromeda*, on the road he mentioned to me, is,—and I will most certainly get it, and send at a proper season. But I cannot find it out from Doctor GARDEN.

Mr. RATLIVE is my neighbour, and will inform me better than any letter can.

I herewith send some roots of the Indian or Worm Pink [*Spigelia*], as the seeds were all fallen, before I had yours about them.

In the same tub, are some slips of Mrs. BEE's little flower, lest the seeds should fail. The berries on the trees are not yet ripe enough; but, if I live, your spouse may certainly expect them, with the other things. I am, with great truth, your well-wisher and friend,

MARTHA LOGAN.

JOHN BARTRAM TO ARCHIBALD BARTRAM.

1761.

My friend, GEORGE BARTRAM, showed me two letters, and *two coats of arms*, that thee sent him, wherein thee desired me to write an account of our family;* but, as I was but young when

---

* The following sketch was obligingly furnished by EDWARD ARMSTRONG, Esq., of Philadelphia, a gentleman eminently distinguished for his attainments and skill in historical, genealogical, and heraldic lore:—

"It has not been in the power of the writer of this note, from the materials within his reach, to throw any light on the early history of the family of Mr. BARTRAM, beyond that to be obtained from the account preserved by Mr. BARTRAM himself, unless the arms found among his papers, and which correspond with those of the BARTRAMS of Scotland, should be accepted in proof that he was of Scottish origin.

"The names BARTRAM and BERTRAM are the same, as records abundantly prove; and it appears to be of Norman origin. Although there are instances of those who left England, went over to the Conqueror, and returned with him to partake the results of his achievements, it does not appear that this was the case with any BERTRAM; at all events, we cannot find the name in England, prior to the conquest. In NACE's[a] roll of the companions of the Conqueror, said to be the oldest list extant of the warriors who fought at Hastings, and which is now in the British Museum, but formerly belonged to Battle Abbey, we discover a ROBERT BERTRAM. In a list prepared by Fox, 'out of the ancient chronicles of England, touching the names of other Normans which seemed to remain alive after the

---

[a] Preface to 1st ELLIS's *Gen. Introd. to Domesday IX.*

my father and uncle died, so the best account I could have was from my grandmother, who lived some years after. She told me that my great grandfather's name was RICHARD BARTRAM. He lived in Derbyshire, and his father before him. RICHARD BARTRAM had one son, called JOHN, who married my grandmother, in Derby. They settled in the town of Ashburn, in the Peak, where they lived, and had three sons and one daughter. From thence they removed to Pennsylvania, before there was one house in Philadelphia. My grandfather, and his elder son, JOHN, died about sixty years past, and my uncle ISAAC a few years after, both bachelors. My father married, and had three sons and one daughter, who died a young woman. We three sons are, at present, all living. I am the eldest, and have six sons and three daughters alive. My brother JAMES is the next, hath had one son and two daughters, which are all dead. His eldest daughter left five daughters. My youngest brother, WILLIAM, liveth in North Carolina, hath one son and two daughters.

This is the best account I can give of our family. There was

battel, and to be advanced in the seigniories of this land,' there is to be seen the name of E. BERTRAM.ª But whether he is identical with WILLIAM DE BERTRAM, who is described in Domesdayᵇ as holding under the king as a tenant *in capite*, cannot perhaps now be decided.

"This WILLIAM, says KELHAM,ᶜ is supposed to have been the eldest son of RICHARD BERTRAM, by SIBIL, his wife, only daughter and heir of JOHN MITFORD, Lord of Mitford, in the county of Northumberland, from whom ROBERT MITFORD, the proprietor of the castle and manor of Mitford, was descended. He is also said to have been the founder of the Priory of Brinkburn, in Northumberland.

"In the reign of EDWARD I., 1296, the name of JOHN BERTRAM appears as a burgess in the submission of the Borough of Inverkeithyn,ᵈ a town about ten miles northwest of Edinburgh, and in the county of Fife. The name is afterwards to be found scattered at intervals through the Scotch and English records. It is also found in other counties than that of Northumberland; namely, in Kent, Sussex, Cumberland, &c. In the county of Kent, there was, in the year 1247, a RALPH BERTRAM,ᵉ Rector of Buckland."

"The *arms* of JOHN BARTRAM, as found among his papers, are as follows:—*Gu.* on an inescutcheon *or.* betwⁿ an orle of eight crosses pattée *ar.* a thistle-head ppr. *Crest* out of an antique crown *or.* a ram's head *ar.* Mottoes, '*J'avance*,' in one riband, '*Foy en Dieu*,' in another."

ª Second vol. of *New Eng. Genealog. and Antiquar. Reg.* 25, a recently established, but very valuable periodical.

ᵇ 1st ELLIS, 382; *Domesday*, 47.

ᶜ KELHAM's *Domesday*, 42; 1 DUGDALE's *Baron.* 543; 2 DUGDALE's *Monas. Anglican.* 153.

ᵈ 1st *Rotuli Scotiæ*, 159.   ᵉ 4 HUSTED's *Kent*, 52.

here, some years past, a Presbyterian minister, come from Scotland. He said that two brothers of our name came with WILLIAM the Conqueror, one of which settled in the north of England—of which, I suppose, my family came—and the other settled in Scotland, of which, I suppose, your family came, which corresponds with thy relation.

JOHN ST. CLAIR TO JOHN BARTRAM.

Belville, Nov. 4th, 1761.

MY DEAR SIR :—

I congratulate you on your safe arrival from Pittsburg, but at the same time I am vexed they should have let you go thither alone. This I must attribute to Captain OURRY'S not being at Bedford when you passed that way ; and I am afraid you met with nothing worth your while during your migration. That you found everything in good order at home, I am thoroughly persuaded of, from Mrs. BARTRAM'S great care. In this you have the advantage of me, that have no wife.

My greenhouse and stove are in a very flourishing state. I want you much to see them, and to consult you about many things; and before winter is over, I will come to pass a couple of days with you.

*   *   *   *   *   *

I give you many thanks for the valuable [*Pecan*] Hickory Nuts. I should have thanked you sooner for them, but I waited to see if I was to go on the expedition that is fitting out. Now I find that I am not to go ; but from my numerous acquaintances that are going to that climate, I may expect everything, in May, that grows in our islands ; so that if you want anything (be what it will) from these parts, let me know it. I have sent a venture of strong beer and the choice pieces of beef to my good friend Governor WORGE, at Senegal. He is to make me the return in African trees, shrubs, plants, and seeds. He is an excellent gardener, and I am sure will do me justice, as far as lies in his power.

If you will send anybody to this place, to bring a cow for Mrs. BARTRAM, she will oblige me in accepting of her. She is of the famous Rhode Island breed. *   *   *   *

I am, with great esteem, dear sir, your most obedient and most obliged humble servant,

JOHN ST. CLAIR.

GEORGE EDWARDS* TO WILLIAM BARTRAM, Jr.

Dear Sir :—

It being upwards of two years since I had the pleasure of a letter from you, I was willing to trouble you with a few lines, in order to be informed whether or not you have received a parcel, directed to you from me. It was the latter part of my works, called *Gleanings*, containing 100 coloured prints, with their descriptions in French and English. The book was very firmly bound and gilt. It was papered up, and delivered to our good friend, Mr. P. Collinson, in the month of January, *anno* 1760, in order to be sent with shop goods from him to Pennsylvania. It was directed to you, not only on the paper in which it was packed, but also withinside of the book; I think it was on the back of the title-page. I understood, by Mr. Collinson, that the ship in which it was sent arrived safe; but he could not tell me whether you had received the book or not. If you have not received it, it must have been secreted by some person who has no right to it. If you have seen or heard of a book answering the above description, it is certainly of right your property.

I should be very sorry to think it is not come to your hands. I shall be glad to hear of you and your father by the packet, or any other convenient means, the first opportunity; and if I find you have not received the book in question, I will, by such means as you shall direct, convey to you another copy of the same book in black prints; for if the first be miscarried, I cannot afford another neatly coloured, as the first was.

---

* George Edwards, the father of ornithologists, was born at Stratford, Essex. in the year 1693. He was brought up to trade; but the great powers of his genius began to be developed by the perusal of books on Natural History and antiquities, and at the expiration of his apprenticeship he travelled abroad, visited Holland, and, two years after, Norway. He corresponded much with Linnæus. The first of his learned and valuable labours appeared in the *History of Birds*, 4 vols. 4to., in the years 1743, 1747, 1750, and 1751; and in 1758, 1760, and 1764 three more 4to. volumes were added, called *Gleanings of Natural History*,—two most valuable works, containing engravings and descriptions of upwards of six hundred subjects in Natural History, never before delineated. This worthy man died 23d July, 1773, in the 81st year of his age.—Blake's *Biogr. Dict.*, and Rees's *Cyclop.*

These books contain all the small birds you were so good to send me two or three years ago.

Pray my kind respects to your father and all friends, and accept the same yourself, from

Your obliged friend and servant,
GEORGE EDWARDS.

College of Physicians, Warwick Lane,
London, November 15, 1761.

JOHN BARTRAM TO WILLIAM BARTRAM, Sr., AT CAPE FEAR, N. C.

December the 27th, 1761.

DEAR BROTHER :—

We have now very sharp weather: our navigation is quite stopped. I sent thee a box of Plum suckers and young seedlings of my English kinds, and wrote to thee, BILLY, Dr. GREEN, and the Governor, and delivered the letters into Captain SHARPLESS'S hands; but whether he is got out, I can't say. He set out from Philadelphia a little before the cold set in, and was to take some loading in at Cohanzey. Cousin BILLY is now at my house, where I am glad to see him; but he keeps very close to school. He tells me you have a root you call *Tanyers*, which I have often heard the Carolina people talk of.* I wish thee would put one or two in a box of plants for me.

We have had as healthy a fall as ever I knew, but now I am afraid of mortal sickness. Two of my neighbours are to be buried to-day, by two or three days' sickness.

I and most of my son BILLY's relations are concerned that he never writes how his trade affairs succeed. We are afraid he doth not make out so well as he expected. I should be glad he could gain credit, as ISAAC and MOSES have. They began with a little, and have unexpectedly dropped into fine business—fulfilled the proverb, *First creep, and then go.*

I have a great mind to drink, next fall, out of the springs at the head of Cape Fear River and Pedee, if God Almighty please to afford me an opportunity.

* *Tanyer* (called *Tallo* or *Tarro* by the New Zealanders, the *Arum esculentum*, Linn., or *Colocasia esculenta*, Schott.), is still cultivated occasionally in the gardens of Southern States, for the sake of the *cormus* or tuberous *rhizoma*, which is used at table as a substitute for the potato and yam.

Cousin BILLY desires to be remembered to thee and sister; so I conclude with much love to thee and sister, and remain your affectionate brother,

JOHN BARTRAM.

JOHN BARTRAM TO WILLIAM BARTRAM, JR., AT CAPE FEAR, N. C.

December the 27th, 1761.

MY DEAR SON:—

Cousin BILLY tells me that your Loblolly Bay, or *Alcea*, bears a very sweet blossom. I wish thee would look well out for some of its seed; perhaps it is not all shed, nor the water Tupelo. I want seed of everything we have not; and thee is a good judge of that. The Alcea and the Horse Sugar I want much. They are very difficult to transplant. I had them from Charleston, but they are gone off. Perhaps your northern one may do better. It is strange that the red sweet Bay, some of which grows naturally in Virginia, should not bear our frost; and yet the great *Magnolia*, that grows naturally on the south of Pedee, seems to bear our frost tolerably. What havoc our present frost will make with the rest, I can't yet say; but, however, I want to try all, to be enabled to judge which of your plants will bear our rigorous frost, and what will not.

Thee disappointed my expectation much, in not sending me any seeds by Captain SHARPLESS; and I know your seeds were, some or other, ripening from the day thee set thy foot on Carolina shore, until SHARPLESS'S departure, and such as were within a mile or two of thy common walks, or most of them within sight. And yet I have not received one single seed from my son, who glories so much in the knowledge of plants, and whom I have been at so much charge to instruct therein.

The fall is the best time to sow the native seeds. Spring may do; but many miss coming up that year.

I don't want thee to hinder thy own affairs to oblige me; but thee might easily gather a few seeds, when thee need not hinder half an hour's time to gather them, or turn twenty yards out of thy way to pluck them.

I remain thy loving father,

JOHN BARTRAM.

TO MOSES OR WILLIAM BARTRAM, AT CAPE FEAR, N. C.

November the 9th, 1762.

DEAR CHILDREN:—

I am now returned home in good health, in which I also found my family; God Almighty alone be praised.

I had the most prosperous journey that ever I was favoured with. Everything succeeded beyond my expectation; and my guardian angel seemed to direct my steps, to discover the greatest curiosities. The presence of God was with me; and my heart overflowed with praises and humble adoration to Him, both day and night, in my wakeful hours.

I met with MENDENHALL, a few miles after we parted, sixty miles from his house; so I set off directly to the Wateree, to SAMUEL WYLY'S, where I was recommended; but he was not at home, nor was expected for many days. He was gone a surveying; but it soon rained after I came, and he soon came home, and received me very friendly; and next day lent me his horse, to ride over the Congaree about seventy miles, to Georgia.

In this ride, I found a wonderful variety of rare plants and shrubs, particularly a glorious evergreen, about four or five feet high, and much branched, in very small twigs growing upright. The leaves are much like the Newfoundland Spruce, rather smaller, and grow around the twigs close, like it. The seed is very small, in little capsules, as big as mustard [*Cyrilla racemiflora*, L. ?]. Stayed at WYLY'S two whole days, to rest my horse; then set forward to the Moravian town, which is two hundred and fifty miles from Charleston; WYLY'S is one hundred and twenty; the ferry over the Congaree is one hundred and forty to Charleston. From the Moravian town it is thirty long miles to the settlements in the bottom, and a very bad road. The bottom is near twenty miles broad, and pretty good land. When I came to the last house, I inquired the way to the mountain, about ten miles off. They said there was four hunters just going over to the mine, and to Holston's River. This I took as a great Providential favour, indeed. * * * We headed the east branch of the Yadkin, in the mountain, and lodged on a little branch of the New River, at the distance of seven miles, or, as some said, fifteen, from the head of Dan; so that I believe Haw River doth not reach the South Mountain, but heads in the high hills on the south side of the bottom, which is near ten miles across.

These South or Alleghany Mountains, are really very high on Carolina side, and steep, full as high, if not higher, than our Blue Mountains; and still grow much higher against Georgia. There is much middling good land, and fine savannas, and plentiful streams, on these mountains; but it's so cold and wet, and the snow frequently two feet deep in winter (some say in October and November, but I believe not commonly then), that it must be uncomfortable living. It is commonly said, that it always snows or rains here. It rained the first day; but then it cleared up. We set out, after killing a deer and breakfasting on it; then rode a good pace till toward night. One of the hunters killed two deer, part of which we ate, and left the rest. Next morning we set out, and cleared the mountain about noon; thence had four or five miles to the mine. The afternoon was spent about the mine, and on the banks of New River, about ten yards over. Next morning, the overseer rode with me, crossed the river in a boat, and away to Fort Chesel [?], towards Holston's River; then to the Ferry, thirty miles, where it was three hundred yards broad. It was quite dark before we got to the house. The next day we travelled till dark, and went supperless to bed, on the ground, by the east branch of New River. Set out early, and by noon my guide parted with me, and I set forward alone; being obliged to my guide, and very thankful to Providence, being now on the branches of Staunton, and amongst the inhabitants.

Pray give my love to brother, sister, and cousins.

I was pleased with BILLY's temperance and patience, in his journey, and shall soon be daily expecting a packet of seeds, and a box of plants from you; which, with hearing of your welfare, will make glad the heart of your loving father,

JOHN BARTRAM.

JOHN BARTRAM TO WILLIAM BARTRAM, JR., AT CAPE FEAR, N. C.

May the 19th, 1765.

DEAR SON:—

I having now a fine opportunity, by my friend SMITH, send these few lines to let thee know we are all well at present, and have been all winter,—God Almighty be praised.

Lord GORDON was twice at my house last week. General BOU-QUET, the Governor, and many of the chief gentlemen came with him; and yesterday, I waited upon them at the General's. His Lordship is going to Quebec,—taking all the sea-ports in his way. He earnestly invited me to go with him in this journey, and he would bring me back again, all at his own expense. At the same time and place, the General—as several times before—offered to take me with him to Pensacola,—to find me a man to wait upon me, and an escort through the dangerous passes,—and it should not cost me a farthing. These are very generous offers. I should rather choose the last; but now can't comply with it.

I wait to hear further from Europe. We have expected two vessels, and the packet to York, for several weeks. My last letter was dated the 10th of February,—mentioning that Lord Bute and the Earl of Northumberland declared that it was necessary that the Floridas should be searched; and that I was the properest person to do it. How this affair will turn out, I can't yet say; but I have just wrote to PETER that I must have a companion.

My eyesight is so well returned, that I wrote this by candle-light, and without spectacles.

Pray remember my love to brother, sister, and cousins; which also receive thyself, from thy affectionate father,

JOHN BARTRAM.

June the 7th, 1765.

DEAR SON WILLIAM:—

Soon after Cousin SMITH set off for Cape Fear, I received a particular account that our King had appointed me his chief Botanist; and I am ordered to go directly to Florida,—and I have taken passage in a vessel bound to Augustine, and thence to Pensacola, with my good friend, General BOUQUET—for whose sake I go sooner than I intended. Perhaps the vessel may touch at Charleston. It's some question whether I shall not stay about Augustine, or Georgia, this summer, and perhaps winter in the Peninsula, or East Florida: but I can't yet tell which, till I speak with Governor GRANT, and the Superintendent of Indian Affairs, whom I must consult. I am daily waiting for further orders, and recommenda-

tions from court; but our friend PETER ordered me to take my
son, or a servant with me. And as thee wrote to me last winter,
and seemed so very desirous to go there, now thee hath a fair
opportunity; so pray let me know as soon as possible.

Our vessel is to sail in about two or three weeks; therefore, I
advise thee to sell off all thy goods at a public vendue, and give
thy accounts into the hands of an attorney there, properly proved,
who will recover thy debts better, and with a quicker despatch than
thee can thyself; and write directly to thy creditors, to let them
know how the affairs stand.

I believe thy best way to meet with me, will be about St. Augustine. I wish thee could send a letter to me there, as soon as
possible. I intend to hover about there, or Georgia, till near
winter.

Direct thy letters to the care of the Governors, at both places,
for me, which will be the likeliest places for me to meet with them
or thee. I suppose that vessels pass frequently between Charleston
and Georgia, or Augustine. Please to send them under cover to
Dr. GARDEN, or THOMAS LAMBOLL, who I shall write to send them
directly to Augustine, or Georgia. But pray let me know soon,
whether thee will come or not, that I may provide myself with
another companion. Perhaps next spring I may go to West
Florida; but can't say where yet. But, in the mean time, assure
thyself that I remain thy loving father,

JOHN BARTRAM.

Thy brother GEORGE [i. e. *brother-in-law*, GEORGE BARTRAM,
who married ANN BARTRAM, November 6th, 1764], or his brother,
who wants thee to come home and join in partnership with them,
desired me to write to thee.

JOHN BARTRAM TO MRS. BARTRAM.

Savannah, September 4th, 1765.

MY DEAR SPOUSE:—

This day we arrived at Savannah town, in Georgia, by ten
o'clock. This was reckoned a very hot day, here, with thunder
and showers, thermometer 86°. They have had here, as well as at
Charleston, the hottest summer and dryest, and wettest August,

that hath been for many years. Many great bridges are broken down, and we were forced to swim our horses over; but, God Almighty be praised, we are got safe into Georgia; and strange it is, that in all this dreadful season for thunder, and prodigious rain, we have not had occasion to put a great coat on, in both the Carolinas, nor rested one day, on the account of rain. But we can't expect to be favoured so, long; however, God's will be done.

We are now hearty, and have a good stomach. The people say, that if we can weather this month, we need not fear. We have been pestered, these two mornings and evenings, with very large mosquitos; but their bite is not near so venomous as the small sort at Charleston.

The land, in general, is pretty good most of the way from Charleston to this town, and the people very civil to us. We have just been with one of the Governor's council, Mr. HABERSHAM, to whom our worthy friend, Doctor WRANGEL, recommended me, to wait on the Governor; who received us with exceeding civility, offering to do me all the kindness that lay in his power; nay, that if any unforeseen accident should happen, if I wanted anything that he could help me to, he would immediately do it.

We design to set out, to-morrow, toward Augusta, one hundred and fifty miles up the river; where I have many great recommendations from the chiefs in Charleston: but, whether I shall set out from there, through part of the Creek Nation to Augustine, or come back again to this town, I can't say until I consult some very knowing gentlemen, at or near Augusta.

We are obliged to be at, or near, Augustine, by the first of October, or thereabouts; so that we have but about a month to travel five hundred miles in.

My dear love, my love is to all our children, and friends, as if particularly named, which I have not time nor room, at present, to do. It is by the Governor's favour, as well as information, that I met with this opportunity to deliver it to his care, in a letter to Mr. LAMBOLL.

Our son BILLY, I hope, if we have our health, will be of great service to me. He desires to be remembered to his mother, brothers, sisters, and friends.

September the 5th.—Thermometer 80°. Just ready to set out toward Augusta, when we have breakfasted. Perhaps the next letter may be dated from Augustine; but if we come back to this town, we shall be for writing here.

However, dear love, in the mean time, I remain thy affectionate husband,

JOHN BARTRAM,

In great haste.

This town is prettily situate on dry sandy ground, and generally good water. Great ships lie close, too, and safe harbour.

HENRY BOUQUET* TO JOHN BARTRAM.

Fort Pitt, 3d February, 1762.

DEAR SIR :—

The gentleman who will have the pleasure to deliver you this, is Lieutenant BREHM, an engineer sent by General AMHERST to our most remote posts, to the westward. He has been round Lake Erie, and through Lake Huron, and Lake Michigan.

I thought it might be agreeable to you to know what nature produces, in those wildernesses; and though the gentleman had observations of another kind to make, he may perhaps satisfy, in some respects, your curiosity, as you will certainly do his, by the large collection you have in your garden.

I should be much obliged to you, to send me, at your leisure, a catalogue of trees and plants, peculiar to this country, which are not natural to the soil of Europe; as I propose to send a collection to a friend, when we have more peaceable times.

I expected to have had the pleasure to see you, this spring; but I find I am to be confined here some time longer.

I am with great truth, dear sir,

Your obedient humble servant,

H. BOUQUET.

Fort Pitt, 15th July, 1762.

DEAR SIR :—

I received your letters of May the 3d, and June the 11th, which

---

* HENRY BOUQUET is believed to have been, at the date of this letter, a Colonel in the British Army; was evidently an intelligent, polite, and obliging gentleman, and ever ready to promote the interests of natural science. He appears subsequently to have attained to the rank of General, and to have died in the service, in Florida.

have given me great pleasure. I am much obliged to you for the curious list of North American Trees and Shrubs you sent me. I hope to understand it better, when I see the originals in your garden.

This war will not last for ever; and I hope we shall have some leisure, hereafter, to study the productions of nature, and bestow some time in cultivating plants, instead of destroying men.

I am glad of the success you have had, in the few plants you got, hereabout; and wish New River and Pedee may reward you for your trouble, if you undertake that journey, which, I fear, must be attended with great trouble and fatigue.

I got, a few days ago, a very great curiosity, from about six hundred miles down the Ohio;—an elephant's tooth, weighing six pounds and three quarters, and a large piece of one of the tusks; which puts it beyond doubt, that those animals have formerly existed on this continent.

I sent your letter to Mr. KENNY.

I am with great regard and friendship, dear sir, your most humble servant,

HENRY BOUQUET.

DR. H. SIBTHORP* TO JOHN BARTRAM.

SIR :—

As a correspondence, and communication of seeds and specimens, might be serviceable to both of us, I've the more particularly been desirous of cultivating such, and for that purpose have forwarded letters, by friend COLLINSON and others, to you heretofore, in hopes of an answer. * * * As no part of Europe has a larger collection than the SHERARDIAN and DU BOIS'S, many from CATESBY, HOUSTON, GRONOVIUS, CLAYTON, and others, are a further addition, with MORISON and BOBART'S collections. And the North American plants thrive well in our soil, being swampy, or low. Many from different parts, gardeners and others, send seed. Many boxes come through your friend COLLINSON'S hands, which

* At the close of this letter, the writer (in the original) gives his address as "Dr. SIBTHORP, *Professor of Botany at the Physic Garden, at Oxford.*" Although a genus of plants was dedicated to him for his services, it is alleged that he did much more for the science, by raising up a *son* (Dr. JOHN SIBTHORP) to cultivate it, than by any writings or investigations of his own.—*See* REES's *Cyclopædia.*

are often, by our custom officers and others, too much jumbled together, and, in regard to their quantity, oft best suitable to nurserymen, than those more curious.　Could you favour our garden with a small box of a few of each sort you may have gathered, fresh and good, and any seeds of perennial plants, the more ornamental the more preferable, any pains you take shall be most gratefully acknowledged and requited.　Nothing is more agreeable than the variety of Firs, Evergreens, or forest trees to us.　Some of the Spruce and Balm of Gilead we have.　The Weymouth Pine seed has miscarried, as well as the *Magnolias.* But nothing, indeed, can come amiss: and as I understand from your neighbour, Mr. FRANKLIN, who has done us the honour, to-day, of taking a degree, and now ranks Doctor of Civil Law, with us, you are about entering on a large excursion, I heartily wish you a safe return, and that you may meet with many curious plants.　And as he encourages me to write again, and promises more particularly to forward this, I flatter myself I may have the satisfaction of adopting your name in our public garden.　*　*

I shall add no further, at present, than my best wishes for your health, and a prosperous journey, and hopes of hearing from you by letter, directed, as below, to your faithful friend,

And very humble servant,

HUMPHREY SIBTHORP.

Oxford, April 30, 1762.

JOHN BARTRAM TO H. SIBTHORP.

[Not dated.　Autumn of 1762.]

WORTHY FRIEND :—

I have received thy kind letter of April the 30th, 1762, which is the second letter I ever received from thee; the first of which was left in town by the person that should have delivered it, long after it was dated.　I thought to have answered it, but no opportunity offering soon, I drove it off from time to time, till I was ashamed of it, and now beg pardon.　And now, if peaceable times come, I intend to double my diligence, for I am better stocked with materials than formerly, having now searched our North America from New England to near Georgia, and from the sea-coast to Lake Ontario, and many branches of the Ohio: so that now there are very few plants in all that space of ground but what I have observed,—nay, have most of them growing in my own garden.

I am just returned home from a very successful journey over the Congaree, near Georgia, and then up, across the country, to the Moravian Settlements, up to the head of the Yadkin, and over the South and Alleghany Mountains, to the New River, a great branch of the Ohio, on which I travelled four days, and toward Holston's River. In this journey I found many rare plants and shrubs, and gathered much seed,—part of which I send to thee. It is very good and ripe; and when I was upon the Wateree, I dug up many curious roots, of sorts which I could not gather seed from. These I planted in a box, to be sent one hundred and twenty miles to Charleston, to be sent to Philadelphia, which I have not yet received.

I was, several years ago, at Charleston and Cape Fear, and settled such correspondence there, that I have most of their Evergreens and Plants growing in my garden; and hope to have all that our climate will bear.

JOHN BARTRAM TO DR. SOLANDER.*

April 26th, 1763.

I received thy kind and agreeable letter of February the 10th,

---

* DANIEL CHARLES SOLANDER, LL.D., F.R.S., under librarian of the British Museum, was born in Nordland, Sweden, Feb. 28th, 1736; studied at Upsal, where he became a favourite pupil of LINNÆUS, and received the degree of M.D. He came to England in 1759, being consigned by his great preceptor, with peculiar earnestness, to the care of Mr. ELLIS. He was universally esteemed here for his polite and agreeable manners, as well as his great knowledge in most departments of Natural History. Being engaged by the illustrious BANKS, to accompany him in his voyage round the world, with Captain COOK, he was ever after the companion and friend of that distinguished patron of science, and was domesticated under his roof, as his secretary and librarian.

His life was suddenly terminated by apoplexy, on the 16th of May, 1782, at the age of 46. The dissipation of London society seems to have induced in him pernicious habits of indolence, and to have developed unfilial traits of character, rarely witnessed in a votary of " the amiable science." The evidences of this are furnished by the neglect of his epistolary correspondence with his great master, LINNÆUS; and still more strongly in the neglect experienced by his aged and doating mother; several of whose letters to her son, it is said, were found unopened after his death !—See SMITH's Linnæan Correspondence.

1762, and a number of curious pamphlets, which I wish had been in English, for Latin is too hard for me.

I was so hurried, last year, in travelling, that I had not time to answer thy letter to my desire, but desired our worthy friend PETER to return my respects, and show thee the specimens I collected in the Carolinas, and New Virginia, which I sent last fall.

I have a glorious sight of curious plants, from the Carolina and Alleghany Mountain seeds, coming up, which in time may furnish my friend with variety of specimens : and I have engaged to go with Colonel BOUQUET down the Ohio to the Mississippi, when peace is proclaimed, and he hath particular orders where to go, and what to do, of which he is in daily expectation : so that, at present, it is uncertain whether he will set out or return. But I shall not like to be at New Orleans, or Mobile, in the latter part of summer, when fevers are dangerous.

If I should perform this journey, and Providence grant me a safe return in health, I hope to make fine discoveries in this wilderness country. As the Colonel will take time to do his business well, so I shall have time to make full discovery of what comes in my way.

We have had a cold, constant winter, and late spring; but I have known it much colder.

    *   *   *   *   *

But most of the trees, or shrubs, that cast their leaves annually there [in South Carolina], will bear our frosts tolerably well. The *Bignonia foliis conjugatis* ran up the northeast corner of my house last summer, twenty feet high, the leaves and vines of which are now very green. But one at the southwest end is bare of leaves, though the vine is green. The Carolina Myrtles, several sorts, all growing near the coast, keep their leaves green all winter ; but, I think, shed them in the spring, when young leaves put forth. They cast them in the winter, with me, although I have one sort from Jersey, that keeps them on till summer.   *   *   *

The *Basteria*, or Sweet Wood [*Calycanthus floridus, L.*], was exposed to the severity of last winter ; yet I find not one bud hurt. But the *Bignonia*, or Yellow Jessamine [*Gelsemium nitidum*, Mx.], being an evergreen, is hurt, though under shelter. The *Melia*, that I left out, is wholly killed. The *Alcea* [*Gordonia?*] is killed, root and branch.

DR. SOLANDER TO JOHN BARTRAM.

SIR :—

Mr. HÆGGBLAD, that delivers this letter, is a Swedish clergy-man, that proposes to stay among you for some time. He is a lover of Natural Philosophy, and goes now into a country so well known to you, that nobody's friendship can be to more advantage to him than yours. I therefore will make myself so free, and beg the favour that you will give him advice how he best may employ the hours he can spend, in collecting plants, insects, and other curiosities.

How much I have been delighted in looking over the specimens you last sent to Mr. COLLINSON, I shall tell you in a letter that I intend to write next week. At the same time, our mutual friend, Mr. COLLINSON, likewise proposes to send you a letter.

Just now, at present, I am so hurried, that I have no more time than only to recommend the above-mentioned clergyman to your friendship, and to assure you that I always with great regard, remain,

Your most affectionate and sincere friend,

DANIEL C. SOLANDER.

London, July the 1st, 1763.

DR. JOHN HOPE* TO JOHN BARTRAM.

SIR :—

The great reputation which you have justly acquired, by many faithful and accurate observations, and that most extraordinary thirst of knowledge which has distinguished you, makes me ex-tremely desirous of your correspondence.

If you will be so kind as send me a few seeds of your new dis-covered plants, I shall on my part make a return of whatever is in my power, that I shall judge agreeable to you.

* JOHN HOPE was Professor of Botany at Edinburgh, and died in the year 1786. "This gentleman (says the Botanical Editor of REES's *Cyclopædia*, *Art. Hopea*,) richly deserves commemoration, as being one of the earliest lecturers on Vegetable Physiology, as well as an experienced practical botanist. Those who knew his personal merits, will readily accede to anything that may serve to embalm so worthy a name."

It will be agreeable to you to hear that Mr. SAMUEL BARD, son
of your friend Mr. BARD, of New York, is making most wonderful
progress in Botany, and has made a beautiful collection of near
four hundred Scots plants; by which he undoubtedly will gain the
annual premium.

I am, sir, with very great regard,
Your most obedient servant,
JOHN HOPE,
Professor of Medicine and Botany,
in University of Edinburgh.

Edinburgh, 4th November, 1763.

JOHN BARTRAM TO DR. JOHN HOPE.

October the 4th, 1764.

WORTHY FRIEND :—

I have received your proposals by the hands of our dear friend
BENJAMIN; and since, by a letter from the worthy, humane Dr.
BARD, of New York, in which he inserts a paragraph of a letter
from his son (whose person and activity I am not a stranger to),
wherein he writes to the same effect as thee wrote to BENJAMIN
FRANKLIN, signifying that you had laid a new botanic garden,
to be stored with exotics; that you were forming a laudable and
very necessary plan of storing your bare country with variety of
forest trees; that many gentlemen of rank and fortune had countenanced this scheme with an annual subscription, to enable a
botanist to make your desired collections; and that my answer
was desired, whether I would undertake to supply your demands,
which I consent to do, if your generosity is equal to them; for the
charges of collecting rare vegetables are in proportion to the distance from home, and hazards and dangers in collecting them.
I have, in thirty years' travels, acquired a perfect knowledge of
most, if not all of the vegetables between New England and
Georgia, and from the sea-coast to Lake Ontario and Erie.

Now what I have not yet discovered, is our new acquisitions in
the mountains of Georgia, in East and West Florida, up the Mississippi and the country of the Illinois, Lakes Michigan and Huron,
the upper lake. I suppose no great variety there.

All the plants north of 33 degrees will grow in the open ground at Edinburgh, and those in Georgia and East and West Florida with a protection from hard frost.

I have now sent, as a present, for thy curious amusement, one hundred specimens, some rare, with my remarks upon them, and to your new garden a parcel of curious seeds, near one hundred and fifty different species; and our friend, Mr. FRANKLIN, engaged me to send you a box of forest trees and shrubs, in which I am going to pack above one hundred different kinds, and send them in the next ship for London, which will sail in three weeks.

In the box of seeds I have put a capsula of the true *Colocasia* [*Nelumbium luteum*, Willd.], with some nuts, just gathered. Plant them in wet mire; they will not live anywhere else. The stalk and leaves grow five feet high, and often that depth in water.

DR. JOHN HOPE TO JOHN BARTRAM.

SIR:—

I was favoured with your letter of the 4th of October, and soon thereafter had the pleasure of receiving the small box of seeds and specimens of rare plants, which you was so good as to send me, and for which I heartily thank you, and shall be very glad of an opportunity of testifying my sense of your kindness.

The Society which was established here about a twelvemonth ago for importing foreign seeds, has it chiefly in view to import the seeds of useful trees, and in the second place ornamental shrubs.

As the members of this Society reside in very different and distant parts of Scotland, it is impracticable to attempt the importation of young trees or shrubs, and on this and other accounts have entirely laid aside all thoughts of importing them, confining themselves entirely to the importation of seeds.

*   *   *   *

As there is annually a ship or ships loaded with lintseed, which come from Pennsylvania to Leith, or some other port of Scotland, you will have an easy opportunity of sending such seeds as are ready at the departure of these ships.   *   *   *   If it is not inconvenient, we would be glad to have specimens of the wood of every tree of which you send us seeds; and you have an easy way of executing this, by making the tops, bottoms, sides, and divisions of the boxes of different wood, numbering each with references to the catalogue: the whole constituted in the same rough way packing boxes are usually made, beginning with all the woods of one genus, as the Pines, and then the Oaks, &c.   *   *

Although, from the tenor of this letter, trees and shrubs only are the general objects of the Society, yet some of us are desirous of having a few of new and curious plants, particularly those used in medicine or in dyeing. I should be particularly fond of having the seeds of the *Lobelia syphilitica.*

*   *   *   *   *   *   *

Wishing you much health and success, I am your most obedient servant,

JOHN HOPE.

Edinburgh, March 7, 1765.

SIR :—

You will recollect that some years ago, you sent to a Society at Edinburgh, a parcel of seeds, of crop 1765, amounting in all to £15, which seeds, by being sent to Ireland, instead of the port of London, according to directions, occasioned not only very great trouble and expense, but likewise the loss of the seeds; as, upon their being re-shipped and landed at Chester, they were there seized by the Custom-house officers, and, after a deal of work to obtain their release, sent by land to London; from whence they were again reshipped for Edinburgh; but so late, that they only came in time to be sown in the year 1767, and the greater part of them good for nothing, to the great disappointment of the members of the Society.

When I talked of this subject to my much esteemed friend, Mr. PETER COLLINSON, and informed him how discouraging this would be to the Society for importing foreign seeds, which had been lately established, and the funds of which at that time narrow, the excellent old man insisted that the Society and you should bear an equal loss, on this unlucky occasion. Accordingly, one half of the charge, viz., £7 : 10, was paid by the Society to Mr. COLLINSON on your behoof. And the managers of the Society, in order to make some amends to you for your loss, had intended to enlarge their commissions, annually; but you, discouraged, as it would seem by that loss, somehow declined answering their commissions to the full, which necessarily behooved to stop all further correspondence.

The funds of the Society being now fully sufficient to answer all demands, cannot be so properly applied as to make up to you the loss you sustained, on the above parcel of seeds. I shall therefore pay to any person you please to name, the above sum of £7 : 10.

The managers of this Society are very sensible of your great botanical merits, and would incline that the payment presently to be made to you, should in some degree convey with it the sense they have of your merit ; and therefore, would incline, instead of the £7 : 10 in specie, to send you a gold medal, or piece of silver plate, of at least equal value, with a suitable inscription thereupon.*

Be pleased, therefore, to inform me which will be most agreeable.

I heartily wish every good thing to you and to your family, and am, with much regard, sir,

Your most obedient, humble servant,

JOHN HOPE.

Edinburgh, 23d March, 1771.

THOMAS LAMBOLL TO JOHN BARTRAM.

South Carolina, Charleston, November 11th, 1763.

DEAR FRIEND BARTRAM :

Since my last of the 8th inst., per Captain MAYSON, he told me he should not sail before Saturday ; so I have got one other flour barrel filled for you with potatoes, mostly what are called Brimstone ; and another box with some young Loblolly Bays, one Senna bush, and the shrub you desired in earth.   *   *   *

Doctor GARDEN is in a very dangerous and critical state, with an abscess in his lungs ; and intends to leave this province soon, for his health.

I remain, with compliments,

Your real friend to serve,

THOMAS LAMBOLL.

South Carolina, Charleston, September 15th, 1764.

DEAR FRIEND BARTRAM :—

Your renewed favour of the 14th ult., with a box containing

---

* A *gold medal*, weighing one ounce and seven grains was subsequently sent.— See page 405.

Mrs. BARTRAM'S kind and acceptable present of *Angelica*, and some dried apples, came safe to hand the 5th inst.   On receipt whereof, I opened the box, and sent Mrs. GARDEN her parcel. What we had is excellent good, and well deserves mine, Mrs. LAMBOLL'S, and our family's thanks, which we hope you will both accept of.   I flattered myself (and therefore delayed writing until this day) I should have got the Umbrella Trees, to send by this opportunity; but the person I depended on does not yet appear and I would not miss writing.   Mrs. LAMBOLL, however, by way of return, has, in the mean time, filled your barrel with Pomegranates, China Oranges, and Sour Oranges, directed for you, on one of the heads.   *   *   *   *   *

Mr. DENNIS ROLLE, member of Parliament for Barnstaple, who arrived here some weeks ago, from London, has honoured me with a visit or two.   He purposes settling a little colony of his own, in Florida.

I conclude with my wife's and own compliments, to yourself and spouse.

Your sincere friend, to serve,

THOMAS LAMBOLL.

THOMAS LAMBOLL TO JOHN BARTRAM, JR.

Charleston, in South Carolina, August 31st, 1765.

SIR :—

On the 24th inst., I received your acceptable letter of the 4th— 13th inst., with the seeds there inclosed ; and the box of Lilies, from [query, for ?] Doctor GARDEN, in good condition ; and for which myself and wife are obliged and thankful, both to you and your good father.   He and your brother, Mr. WM. BARTRAM, left us, the 29th inst., in forenoon, to prosecute their intended journey by land, through this province and Georgia, to East Florida. Both of them were then in good health and spirits, proposing not to exceed the last of September, in their researches through the woods, on account of a Congress that is to be held at Augustine, the 1st of October.

Our *Stramonium* is not yet in blossom ; but you may be sure of some of the seeds of it, when ripe.

Mine and Mrs. LAMBOLL'S best compliments to your good
mother, and self, concludes me, sir,

Your most obedient, humble servant,

THOMAS LAMBOLL.

HENRY LAURENS* TO JOHN BARTRAM.

Charleston, S. C., 9th August, 1766.

SIR :—

I have had the pleasure of hearing, from some of our acquaintance here, that you were safely arrived in Philadelphia, but that
good news has been somewhat abated by Captain EASTWICK'S
account, that you were very sick, when he left that city. I hope
soon to know, from your own hand, that you are recovered, and as
well re-established as we poor brittle clay-shells can expect to be,
at threescore and ten.

Since you left Carolina, I have prosecuted my long-intended
voyage and journey through the southern parts of this country,
and Georgia, to East Florida ; and was near five weeks in the last-
mentioned province ; in which time I thrice visited the River St.
John, often landed upon each shore, exploring the swamps and
hummocks, pine barrens, and sand barrens, between the great lake
and the ocean ; and you may be sure I did not carelessly pass by
your son's habitation. I called upon him twice ; and as a confirmation of it, you will find inclosed in this, a letter from him, wrote
after my second visit.

Your knowledge of that country, together with the addition of
Mr. WILLIAM BARTRAM'S remarks upon his further experience,

* HENRY LAURENS, of South Carolina, was born in the year 1723. His manly
virtues, together with his services and sufferings during our Revolutionary
struggle, have rendered his name and memory dear to every American patriot.
Having presided in the Provincial Congress of Carolina, and succeeded JOHN
HANCOCK as President of the Continental Congress, and undergone a tedious and
cruel imprisonment in the Tower of London, he finally had the honour to be one
of the commissioners who negotiated the treaty of peace, which sanctioned our
national independence. He was, moreover, the father of the gallant Colonel
JOHN LAURENS, one of the last, and bravest, of the martyrs to American liberty;
and of MARTHA LAURENS RAMSAY, one of the most gifted, pious, and exemplary
ladies of the age in which she lived. HENRY LAURENS died at Charleston, in the
year 1792, aged 69.

renders it unnecessary, as it would be unedifying, for me to trouble you with my few general observations ; but I hope you will not think me quite impertinent, if I detain you to say a word or two touching the particular situation and circumstances of that poor young man ; and the less so, when you know that it is done partly at his request.

His situation on the river is the least agreeable of all the places that I have seen,—on a low sheet of sandy pine barren, verging on the swamp, which before his door is very narrow, in a bight or cove of the river, so shoal, and covered with umbrellas, that the common current is lost and the water almost stagnated, exceedingly foul, and absolutely stank, when stirred up by our oars, on both days of my landing there, though, at the same times, the river was said to be rather high, and the stream running down strong, beyond the cove. This, I should think, must make the place always unhealthy, as well as troublesome to come at, by water carriage, especially in dry seasons.

The swamp and adjoining marsh which I walked into, will, without doubt, produce good rice, when properly cleared and cultivated ; but both seem to be narrow, and will require more strength to put them in tolerable order, than Mr. BARTRAM is at present possessed of, to make any progress above daily bread, and that of a coarse kind, too.

There is some Cypress, which, if he had a little more strength, he might soon convert into shingles and ready money.

The Pine land (I am sorry to differ in opinion with you) is very ordinary ; indeed, I saw none good in the whole country ; but that piece of his may justly be ranked in an inferior class, even there.

At my first visit, your son showed me the growth of some peas, beans, corn, and yams, planted only four days before, in the sand on the swamp-edge, which then looked very flourishing ; but when I called three weeks after, although there had been much rain in the mean time, the progress was barely perceptible ; a remark that we both concurred in.

I found that he had, according to my advice, continued to clear the swamp, and in that time cut down part of an acre of trees ; but that sort of work goes on very heavily, for want of strong hands. He assured me that he had but two, among the six negroes that you gave him, that could handle an axe tolerably ;

and one of those two had been exceedingly insolent. I encouraged
and pressed him to put a little rice in the ground, even at that
late day (5th or 6th July); and he promised to do so the day
following.

The house, or rather hovel, that he lives in, is extremely confined, and not proof against the weather. He has not proper
assistance to make a better, and from its situation it is very hot,
the only disagreeably hot place that I found in East Florida: but
it should be remarked, that the weather had been uncommonly
temperate. His provision of grain, flesh, and spirits, is scanty,
even to penury, the latter article very much so. His own health
very imperfect. He had the fever, when I was first with him, and
looked very poorly the second visit. I am determined, by the next
conveyance, to send him a little rum, wine, sugar, tea, cheese,
biscuit, and other trifles, and charge the small amount to your
account; though I would most freely give him the whole, but for
fear that you should take it amiss.

Possibly, sir, your son, though a worthy, ingenious man, may not
have resolution, or not that sort of resolution, that is necessary to
encounter the difficulties incident to, and unavoidable in his present
state of life. You and I, probably, could surmount all those hardships without much chagrin. I very believe that I could. But, at
the same time, I protest that I should think it less grievous to dis-
inherit my own son, and turn him into the wide world, if he was of
a tender and delicate frame of body and intellects, as yours seems
to be, than to restrict him, in my favour, just in the state that
your son is reduced to. This is no doubt more than ever you
apprehended; and admitting that my account is in part erroneous,
(which I do not admit, meaning to speak nothing but truth,) yet
the general outlines of the foregoing description must affect and
grieve you. But it is by no means my design, or intention, to
compass any particular end by colouring too strongly. In fact,
according to my ideas, no colouring can do justice to the forlorn
state of poor BILLY BARTRAM. A gentle, mild young man, no
wife, no friend, no companion, no neighbour, no human inhabitant
within nine miles of him, the nearest by water, no boat to come at
them, and those only common soldiers seated upon a beggarly spot
of land, scant of the bare necessaries, and totally void of all the
comforts of life, except an inimitable degree of patience, for which

he deserves a thousand times better fate; an unpleasant, unhealthy situation; six negroes, rather plagues than aids to him, of whom one is so insolent as to threaten his life, one a useless expense, one a helpless child in arms;   *   *   *   *   distant thirty long miles from the metropolis, no money to pay the expense of a journey there upon the most important occasions, over a road always bad, and in wet weather wholly impassable, to which might be enumerated a great many smaller, and perhaps some imaginary evils, the natural offspring of so many substantial ones; these, I say, are discouragements enough to break the spirits of any modest young man; and more than any man should be exposed to, without his own free acceptance, unless his crimes had been so great as to merit a state of exile.

I had been informed, indeed, before my visit to Mr. W. B., that he had felt the pressure of his solitary and hopeless condition so heavily, as almost to drive him to despondency. He expressed an inclination to decamp from the place that I have endeavoured to describe; but was supported, by advice of a friend, to wait until he should see me, who was then daily expected in East Florida. He did not open his mind so fully to myself; but rather modestly appealed to me, upon his circumstances and situation, accompanying his complaints with the most dutiful and affectionate mention of his father, to whom he requested I would take some notice of them in my next letter: in answer to which, I gave him my sentiments very candidly, encouraging him at the same time to persevere until he should hear from you. I have presumed to say so much, in consequence of my promise to him upon that request, as well as from a natural and irresistible inclination to relieve every virtuous man in distress: and as the foregoing representation can have no evil effects, however it may be imperfect, or appear to be officious, I trust that I shall not suffer under your candid interpretation.

After this account of your son's circumstances, I might add a list of several necessary articles beside exchange of good negroes, in place of almost useless ones, that are wanting and will be wanted to mend them a little; but no doubt he has given some needful hints on that head, and if his modesty has restrained his pen, you will, if you pay any regard to what I have been so bold as to write upon so slight an acquaintance as ours, cheerfully and quickly give orders to supply him with such things as shall be necessary to

make his banishment less galling, and present him with some prospect of reaping the fruit of his labours.

Here I shall drop the subject; and, after presenting Mrs. LAU-
RENS'S and my own hearty good wishes, put an end to this long
letter, subscribing myself, sir,

Your most obedient servant,
HENRY LAURENS.

JOHN HILL* TO JOHN BARTRAM.

London, Dec. 6, 1766.

SIR :—

There is wanted here, on a very particular occasion, four
pounds of the root of *Lobelia syphilitica,* or the Blue Cardinal,
dry'd, to be used in medicine. My Lord Bute has given me permission to desire you to gather and send it over.

The same occasion wants, also, two ounces of the root of *Actæa
racemosa;* and eight ounces of *Collinsonia* root. If you will take
the trouble of adding these, it will also be very acceptable.

I believe the name of Doctor HILL is known to you, although
we never corresponded. I always have, and always shall espouse
your interest.

I am your faithful, humble servant,
JOHN HILL.

Please direct the roots to me, at my house in Arlington Street,
St. James's.

---

* Sir JOHN HILL, an indefatigable book-maker, and a person of much notoriety
in his day, was born in 1716. Possessed of some talents, great industry, and
infinite assurance, he made lofty pretensions to science, though the scientific of his
own time, and since, have ever regarded him as an empiric, both in Medicine and
Natural History. PETER ASCANIUS, in a letter to LINNÆUS, dated London, April 7,
1755, says, " Dr. HILL, the too famous naturalist of England, is in the lowest
possible condition. I do not think any mortal has ever written with more impu-
dence or more ignorance. His only excuse is, that he must write in order to
exist." Yet he obtained the patronage of the great—especially of the Earl of
Bute; and was such an assiduous courtier, that LINNÆUS, in allusion, it is said,
to his obsequious habits, named a plant *Hillia parasitica!* This remarkable man
died in November, 1775, aged fifty-nine years.

DOCTOR BENJAMIN GALE* TO JOHN BARTRAM.

Killingworth, 3d January, 1768.

DEAR SIR :—

I have not had the pleasure of a line from you for a long time; and had I not accidentally seen in one of the public papers, you was set out to visit Pensacola, or West Florida, I should have been inclined to think you either had lost all remembrance of me, or that you had taken your leave of this world, and called to have acted your part in some happier state of existence. But, by the favour of a visit from my good friend, Captain SMITH, I am informed you are still alive and well, and that you, not long before, was inquiring for an opportunity to write me.

I should be infinitely delighted to spend one evening with you (I mean a winter evening), to hear the journal of your travels into that southern part of America, and the just remarks you must have made, in your tour.

I want to know whether, in any of your travels, either in the Alleghany Mountains, or elsewhere, you have ever found any evident traces of the Deluge, or monuments of antiquity. If there ever was an universal Deluge, I cannot but think it must have left some evident traces of it, yet to be seen, in every part of the globe.

Have they any animals, serpents, or beasts of prey, in those southern Colonies, not common to us? Have you ever had such a description of the *Cortex Peruvianus*, as that you would know the tree from whence it is taken? I have heard much of the stones, made use of to extract the poison of vipers; are those stones natural, or factitious?

I wrote you some time since—whether ever you received it, or not, am not able to say—to request of you, whether ever you have met with the *Cicuta*, of Doctor STORK, or the Meadow Saffron. A description of the latter, I now inclose you. If but one half of the virtues, he ascribes to it, are in the plant, I should think it a

* BENJAMIN GALE graduated at Yale College, in 1733. He was an eminent physician and agriculturist; and was deeply concerned also in politics. He invented the drill plough; wrote a Dissertation on the Prophecies; and published a Treatise on Inoculation for the Small-pox. He died at Killingworth, the town in which he first settled, in 1790, aged seventy-five.—BLAKE's *Biogr. Dict.*

happy discovery, to find it in America.   If found in America, pray send me the seeds of both.

I want to know the botanical name of the American Blood-root [*Sanguinaria Canadensis*, L.].   Its virtues are great, and many; particularly, I look upon it a specific in the nervous headache, or sick-headache, as it is commonly called.

Inclosed I send you a news letter, in which is inserted the natural history of Black Grass [*Agrostis Indica*, L.?], at the request of our good friend Mr. COLLINSON.   Have you ever met with any grass similar to it, in any of the interior parts of this Continent? The conjecture I make, as to its origin, appears to me somewhat probable.   Perhaps your knowledge, in that matter, may determine the affair.

When your leisure will admit, and any opportunity presents, I should be pleased to receive a line from you.

My best regards to your son; and believe me, dear sir, that I am your most obedient and most humble servant,

BENJAMIN GALE.

My spouse [the daughter, it is believed, of JARED ELIOT] requests her regards may be presented to her father's friend.

C. M. WRANGEL TO JOHN BARTRAM.

Stockholm, in Sweden, July the 2d, 1769.

DEAR SIR AND BELOVED FRIEND:—

Whenever I think of America (which I do every day of my life), I think at the same time of you, and your house; and as ingratitude is what I detest, I cannot but bear you the warmest gratitude for all the civilities you were pleased to show me, while I had the pleasure to cultivate a friendship with you, at a nearer distance.

I always looked upon myself as one of your family, being happy enough to be counted so, by you and yours.

It grieved me, when I was in America, that your great merit had not, in my native land, received the marks of esteem, in the public, as it deserved; and therefore it gives me great satisfaction, when I now assure you, that you are well known here, from the throne to every one that regards learning; and the Society of Science, in Stockholm, which has from its first institution been

known for the greatest delicacy in choosing members of distinction
and note, has manifested their great regard for you by choosing
you a member, unanimously, at the proposal of Professor BERGIUS.*
I had the pleasure to be present, in the Society, that same day,
when you were proposed, and to deliver to the Society the drafts
of your son, and some other things, in your name; which were
received with much satisfaction.

Doctor LINNÆUS is so used to receive presents from all quarters,
that he hardly thinks of it; and therefore I took the liberty to
give what was intended for him, to the Society, as I expected that
they would show more gratitude; and I hope to have your approbation in it.

Your son's correspondence with Professor BERGIUS will no doubt
be of great use to him, and do him much honour.

I have not been like Professor KALM, in taking the honour to
myself of what belongs to others. I have given my dear friend,
Mr. JOHN BARTRAM, Jr., his due; and I hope he will not repent
of what he has done for Professor BERGIUS, who is a man, here
and abroad, of great repute; and at the same time very attentive
to anything that is done for him. He expects that his correspondent will send him some seeds.

You will, no doubt, be glad to hear that I have been received in
my native land in the best manner I could wish for. His Majesty,
the King, has shown me the greatest marks of clemency, and I
am now officiating, at his court, as first Chaplain, with great satisfaction, and have a prospect of being extremely well settled at

* The *Diploma*, or certificate of membership, sent by this Society to JOHN
BARTRAM, is in the following words:—

"ACADEMIA REGIA SCIENTIARUM STOCKHOLMENSIS solo, quo potest, modo indi-
care voluit, quanti faciat præclara in Scientias, præsertim Historiam Naturalem,
merita Viri celeberrimi, Domini JOHANNIS BARTRAM, Botanici Regii in America
Septentrionali ditionis Anglicanæ; ideoque hunc Dominum BARTRAM in suam
Societatem et inter Academiæ Membra recepit, die 26 Aprilis, Aº 1769. Eum
itaque, nomine Academiæ Rᵃᵉ Stockholmensis, hisce Litteris Socium saluto. In
rei actæ fidem, Sigillum Academiæ Majus subjungo.

                    "PETRUS WARGENTIN,
                    "Acad. R. Scient. Stockholmensis
                    "Secretarius perpet."

The *seal*, somewhat defaced and obscured by time, appears to have, for a de-
vice, a vertical star or sun, sending down its radiance upon the figure of a globe,
and other scientific emblems; surrounding which, is this inscription:—"*Kongl.
Svenska Wetenskaps Acad. Sigil.*"

home; and the poor state of my health, in which I have been for some time, hinders me from thinking of ever returning to America. Indeed, I should not be able to go through the hardships any more, which a faction of ungrateful hearers laid me under. Notwithstanding all this, my heart is always in America; and when I think of my friends there, it makes me wish to be amongst them.

I wish you and yours all the prosperity which this troublesome life will admit of; and beg to be kindly remembered to your dear spouse, and all the family, and am, with the greatest sincerity,

Dear sir, and beloved friend,

Your most humble and affectionate servant,

C. M. WRANGEL.

MICHAEL COLLINSON* TO JOHN BARTRAM.

DEAR SIR :—

Your favour of the 1st November is before me, inclosing the account between yourself and my dearest father, which I find to agree with the account current as per ledger; and which I have at last been lucky enough to discover.

I must beg you will let BILLY continue the account up to the time of my poor father's decease,—I mean as far as he is able, mentioning the number of boxes ordered, and sent; and if you are furnished with the names of the persons for whom they were designed, I shall be glad to have them.

I was, my dear sir, so entirely a stranger to my dear father's money affairs, that I positively assure you I was uncertain on which side the balance lay between you. Judge, then, of my amazement, when I discovered by you, and confirmed by the account, which has but just appeared, what an astonishing balance was against me; and in consequence of the idea I entertained, of something very inconsiderable subsisting betwixt you, I ventured, upon that supposition, long since to settle everything; and should have been highly obliged to have had earlier information how things stood, soon after the news of my dear father's demise reached Philadelphia; as very disagreeably, the book which alone could afford matter of information, was unaccountably mislaid at the time of my father's removal from Grace Church Street, and only very lately come to light.

* The only son of PETER COLLINSON, the old and faithful friend of JOHN BARTRAM.

I am projecting a little tour through France, part of Spain, and Italy ; but this will not be attended with the least postponement to finally balancing the above account,—as I shall take care your drafts on me shall be properly honoured ; so that you may draw how and when you please for it. When you draw, do it for near the whole, if you please, at once. It will be the most agreeable to me, to finish at once, if we can. If I go, it will be in a month's time ; and my absence will be about six or seven months.

You have, sir, of course, I conclude, heard from Dr. FOTHERGILL that I have let my premises at Mill Hill for two years, with a reserve, in the lease, that not a single plant—or the soil that contains them,—is upon any terms to be moved ; for, even yet there are still some very few fine plants remaining, of the rich collection which your bounty furnished us with,—the miserable remains of three most cruel robberies, which have torn the garden all to pieces, and left me only the wretched apprehension of finding fresh devastation on every little absence from home. This, with some other unimagined and disagreeable circumstances operating, rendered a residence at Mill Hill both uncomfortable and inconvenient, at present.

As no notice has been taken, to me, of the draft of the *Colocasia*, I conclude the Doctor will convey the same to the Duke of Portland, agreeably to your orders. Sir WM. BRETTON is acquainted with your pleasure respecting the King's bounty.

I should think some very singular kinds of fresh-water shells might be met with, on the shores of your vast interior lakes; and some of the land tribe, as well as river, I think must be a curiosity here, even in the best cabinets. I should be very glad to see a specimen or two of them.

I shall always find myself happy in hearing of the prosperity and health of a gentleman for whom my most valued parent felt the sincerest regard and friendship to his latest hour ; and I am sure it will be ever with the truest respect that I shall be, dear sir,

Your faithful and most obliged servant,

MICHAEL COLLINSON.

Manchester Buildings, March 1st, 1770.

Manchester Buildings, Jan. 9th, 1771.

MY DEAR SIR :—

It was with great pleasure, soon after my return home from the

Continent, that I received your agreeable favour of the 1st October last; and believe the account of boxes sent in 1767 and 8 to be right, though I have not been able to ascertain it, to a box, which is of little importance, as I have a most implicit confidence in your honour, and shall instantly direct the payment of the balance of the account, whenever you please to order it, to be paid to Mr. FREEMAN, or otherwise, which I shall not be sorry for, as it is a kind of weight upon me, especially as it is so very considerable, and unexpected by me. However, I have a principle of honour in my heart, which, if I know it, can never be capable of a shuffling or dishonest action. You may, therefore, my dear sir, be entirely satisfied, and make your demands whenever it suits you best.

In the course of my late tour, the objects that most struck me were the following: the forest of Fontainebleau, about thirty-five miles south of Paris, in which there is a most romantic range of rocks, not lying in strata, but roughly piled one upon another, and covered with silver bark Birch, and our common Juniper, growing ten and fifteen feet high; the wonders of Pont du Gard, a Roman work, being an astonishing aqueduct thrown across a deep valley, and joining two rocky mountains. This is situated near Nismes and Montpellier. Here, among the rocks, grew Myrtle; what we have by the name of the Lycian Cedar, *Arbutus ;* a fine species of Prickly Broom, and Wild Figs.   *   *   *   *   *

I was, my dear sir, delighted beyond measure, at perceiving the line which nature had drawn in the different latitudes, where one species and tribe of plants ceased, and another commenced.   *   *   * The lakes Garda, of Geneva, and Maggiore, are noble little Caspians here; but yet, how diminutive they appear in comparison with your Huron, Superior, &c., &c.! Upon a very lofty Tyrolese mountain, which with great labour I ascended, I found two species of *Rhododendron,* one in full bloom, and tinging the highest crags with the richest glow of colouring. Many other rare plants grew here, and upon Mount Cenis, the specimens of which, and account of, would have given infinite pleasure to my most dear parent, had Providence spared his life a little longer.

I make no doubt but you have seen the little pamphlet of some anecdotes of his life; for the principal part of which, I think myself highly obligated to my valued friend Dr. FOTHERGILL. If you have not, I have any number of copies at your service; and am, dearest sir, with true affection and esteem, your obliged and very faithful friend and servant, ˌ

MICHAEL COLLINSON.

Manchester Buildings, June 28th, 1771.

DEAR SIR :—

Both your favours of the 29th April, and 3d of May, are come to hand, for the last of which my best acknowledgments are due. I have accepted the bill for £200, and shall punctually discharge it when due. I have also inclosed the account between us according to the best lights I can obtain ; for the furnishing of which I am obliged to have recourse to the account you sent me in October last, of the boxes sent in 1767, and 1768, for my father's memorandums were so perplexed, that without yours and GORDON'S assistance I could have made nothing out. As I have a full confidence in your honour, I can implicitly rely on what you say is right ; and will to the best of my ability, faithfully on my side discharge the demand upon me, which being so very considerable, has, I confess, been a stroke upon me ; especially, being unacquainted with my dear father's concerns, and neither, for so considerable a time, hearing anything from yourself, nor being able to discover the account itself ; which was somehow mislaid at the time of my father's breaking up, in Grace Church Street. I really judged the balance, if anything, to be but very trifling.

The truth is, latterly my dear parent found those things a trouble to him, which was none a few years since, as he evinced on many occasions ; and which has occasioned me much confusion and trouble. His situation, too, in point of circumstances, was likewise mortifying. His business, at last, totally declined ; and you will, sir, I am sure, from the goodness and humanity of your own heart, and your long and unremitted friendship for him, be shocked when I tell you, that he solicited a small pension for an age near seventy-five—great part of which was employed in pursuits advantageous to his country—and was refused !

I am very certain that the King's bounty is regularly, and will always continue to be paid. My father received the half year to Lady Day, 1768, which was the last payment due in his lifetime ; and in the September following, the Deputy Privy Purse applied to me to know whether I would receive the six months then due, which I declined; and I have since introduced Mr. FREEMAN to Mr. MATTHIAS, and I heard Mr. MATTHIAS assure Mr. FREEMAN that it should be regularly paid, and that with as little trouble to Mr. FREEMAN as possible.

I think myself equally honoured and obliged by your favourable sentiments on my little remarks whilst abroad. I kept a daily journal of what struck me most during the whole expedition, for the advantage of my future memory and hours.

Your most sensible and pertinent remarks on your important quarter of the globe, I shall beg leave to consider some future opportunity; for neither my head nor paper will permit me to say more, but that I am, with high esteem and affection, dear sir,

Very faithfully yours,

MICHAEL COLLINSON.

Manchester Buildings, Aug. 16th, 1771.

DEAR SIR :—

I wrote you, a few weeks since, inclosing the account, as well as I could make it out, and also mentioning that I should duly discharge your draft upon me for £200 sterling, which I have since done; and shall be very glad to settle, as soon as may be, the remainder of an account concerning which I have such uncertain documents to direct me, and in which I have so much to trust to your honour.   *   *   *   *

I am highly delighted and obliged by your partial comment on my little remarks of Italy, &c. My notes, which I am recopying in order to serve for an occasional retrospect, and to assist my memory hereafter of past scenes, are indeed so multitudinous, that I am, on the revisal, surprised at my past labours, which were indeed daily, nay, frequently hourly repeated; as, on such occasions, the memory is too fallible to be depended much on, and I wished in particular to preserve the general idea of the country through which we passed, and the spontaneous productions of it.

Our route, my dear sir, comprehended a tract of about seven thousand miles, in which there was much to admire and observe.

＊   ＊   ＊   ＊   ＊

The Orange and Limon and Pomegranate gardens, the last of which is also indigenous everywhere, first made their appearance about Toulon and Nice, and afterwards in greater plenty between Rome and Naples, on the very beach of the Mediterranean Sea;

particularly near Mola de Gaeta and Terracina, perfuming the air, after sunset, with their excessive fragrance. On the quays, at Marseilles, we met with a very singular and most excellent species of China orange, brought from the Isles of Hieres, just by, the pulp of which is of the deepest crimson possible; and which we met with nowhere else. But, for magnificence of size, surely the limons of Naples exceed everything ; which the common people devour at a vast rate, sour as they are, and with as high a *goût* as ours here do the China orange. This operating with the salubrity of the sea and mountain air, I think, is a great means of preservation to this filthy generation, and secures them from the effects of their own excessive nastiness.

I am well assured that the Alps, and even Apennines, in point of elevation, much exceed any of the mountains of North America : though, at the same time, they fall greatly short of the tremendous region of the Andes, or Cordilleras ; and the lakes of Italy, though far surpassing any here, in this island, are yet but as the drop of the bucket, in comparison with your amazing inland oceans, Erie, Huron, &c., &c. The largest in Italy, are Lake Garda, and Lake Maggiore, the banks of which abound with the common eating Spanish Chestnut, and a few Italian and English Oak. That of Garda is about thirty-five miles long, and ten and fifteen broad, and abounds with tench and perch. Maggiore, near Milan, is near fifty miles in length, and about seven, four, and three broad.

I am, my dear sir, very respectfully, and very affectionately yours,

MICHAEL COLLINSON.

Manchester Buildings, March the 6th, 1772.

MY DEAR SIR :—

Your two most acceptable favours of the 12th of October, and 17th of December, came safe to hand ; and I wish you to believe, that no person whatever can receive greater satisfaction than I feel, from the very pleasing picture you have drawn, in the former, of the domestic felicity of your family ; which I hope will be as permanent as I am sure the cordiality of my wishes are truly sincere for its long, very long continuance.

CONDAMINE is a very instructing little book ; but I have never yet met with any work that is fully satisfactory, respecting the country of France and Italy, &c.   The traveller has generally exerted his abilities in deciphering some obsolete vestige of antiquity, or in describing the works of art, whilst the natural history of each kingdom is quite neglected.   He is wafted from city to city, and all the intermediate space, which I think a naturalist would wish to know something about, is, for what he says of it, a mere vacuum, or little better.

We were not, my dear sir, nearer to the grand Canal of Languedoc, to my great regret, than Montpellier, and which is but a short distance from it.   I very particularly wished to see it, as well for its own importance, as for the reason of botanizing in the hills of Narbonne, through which place we should of course have passed, and which are famous for most valuable productions in the vegetable world, and remarkably so for the *Orchis* tribe—my favourites—if we are to believe PARKINSON's Herbal.   Many very curious fossil shells are likewise picked up in the chalky hills of Narbonne.   There is, however, a most magnificent work lately finished, at Montpellier, and of miles in extent, being a noble aqueduct constructed of an elegant white stone, and designed to convey water from the mountains to a grand reservoir, for the service of the city; and I think I never tasted any water so deliciously pure and sweet.   It is built on the principle of the famous Roman one, at Nismes, not many miles distant, with this difference, only,—the former one consists of only two tiers, or rows of arches, whereas the Roman one has three.   My companions trembled for the imagined fervour of an Italian sun; and therefore were impatient to push away, before the heats commenced, so that Montpellier was our furthest point west in the whole journey.

Your account of the migration of the Bears, Rabbits, and Partridges, is really wonderful, but I believe in a manner local; as CADR. COLDEN, Esq., of New York, from whom I have just received a letter, takes no notice of any such circumstance, in those parts of the country.   Considering the destruction that is perpetually going on, I should not be surprised if the whole race of Bears should become extinct; and still more so with regard to the Beaver, there being an annual sale, here only, of between forty and fifty thousand of their skins; and I make no doubt, with CAMDEN, but that we formerly had the Beaver, among the unfrequented mountains and lakes in Wales, which, in the course of time, have been utterly destroyed.

You will please to draw for the balance, whenever it suits you; and the sooner, the more agreeable to, my dear sir, your most affectionate friend and servant,

MICHAEL COLLINSON.

Manchester Buildings, January 8th, 1773.

DEAR SIR :—

Your kind favour of the 11th of November last is now before me, the contents of which, however, equally surprise and concern me, in finding that neither of the two letters I troubled you with, of the 6th March and 14th June have come to hand, which I am indeed astonished at; as I delivered them both, myself, at the post-office, which conveyance I never found fail before, in any letter either, sir, to you or my friend CADR. COLDEN of New York: and till your present favour, I have not, my dear friend, heard a single tittle from you since the 17th December, 1771, to which I had long since replied.

This present scrawl shall be conveyed from the Pennsylvania Coffee-house, which may possibly be the surest mode of conveyance.

With regard to my letters, in point of consequence, they are less than nothing. On the contrary, yours, sir, are invaluable. Your sentiments are original, ingenious, and to the last degree pertinent, on the subjects on which they treat. They were held in a manner sacred by my dearest father; nor is their consequence sunk in the hands of his son, by whom they are considered as an inestimable treasure of American Natural History.

Though I never take any copies of my own insignificant epistles to my friends, yet I always memorandum the date of my letters to them, or the day they are consigned to the office; which makes me positive to the above, which have somehow strangely miscarried. *   *   *   Your ingenious idea respecting the former existence of certain kinds of animals, now extinct, I confess carries great weight with it, and yet, my dear sir, I cannot implicitly give my assent to it, in the whole. With regard to the Unicorn, I am rather divided in my judgment, even in respect to their present existence, in the interior region of Africa, of which, at this period, we are extremely ignorant. I have an old History of Abyssinia, that speaks positively to the fact; and there are other authorities on record, if they deserve credit, that support the same opinion.

I much fear the extirpation of that dreadful animal, the Rattle-snake, will be never accomplished, notwithstanding the perpetual war against the race. The continent of America is so vast, the retreats so many, and so secluded from human approach, that if it ever should take place, it must, I think, be many centuries first; for, please to remember, those reptiles are found as far south as the line itself, an immense tract; and how much farther, we know not. Pray, is the Rattlesnake found as far north as the Labrador coast? And if not, where is the line of termination drawn?

As to the poor Buffalo and Beaver, I believe their days are numbered; and sorry I am for the belief, especially with respect to the latter; which, from its extreme inoffensiveness and ingenuity deserves a better fate.

I shall follow this letter very shortly, by another, wishing to communicate something relative to a species of Snake, I observed in Italy, &c. &c. I have, therefore, only to add, that if wishes could have any effect, I would never cease wishing new, numberless, and happy years, to you and your worthy family, till I had not room enough left in my paper, to crowd in the useless name of,

Dearest sir,

Your truly affectionate friend,

MICHAEL COLLINSON.

Manchester Buildings, February 25th, 1773.

MY DEAR SIR :—

I troubled you with a letter dated the 8th ultimo, and I hope with better success than my two preceding letters met with.

Our winter, to this date, has been uncommonly mild, there having been nothing equal to it since 1750. One continued series of mild southwest winds having blown for four months past, with an intermission only of about a fortnight's moderate frost; so that, whilst vegetation has been surprisingly pushed forward, the rich and the great have been put to it, to fill their ice-houses. I am however, afraid there is a scouring yet in store for us; but, I hope not so intolerable a one as we experienced last May, when the severity of the northeast winds not only blasted all the bloom in our orchards, but our grass to such a degree as to double the price of hay.

Your American apples have been an admirable substitute, this season, some of our merchants having imported great quantities of them. They are, notwithstanding, too expensive for common eating, being sold for two pence, three pence, and even four pence an apple. But their flavour is much superior to anything we can pretend to, and I even think superior to the apples of Italy.

In Italy, I observed four species of the serpent kind; viz., our common Snake, Viper, Slow-worm, and a very singular species of snake, which I do not believe has been described by any one; the first three only being common to England. The first of this last kind, I met with at Rome, where a couple of Italians were showing tricks with it, having rendered it extremely familiar and tame. This was above six feet long.

I soon after met with another, near the celebrated cataract of Terni, which the guides despatched, in spite of my wishes to the contrary. I found, on examining the mouth, in which there were no fangs, and from its whole appearance, that it was but a simple snake. The colour—head, belly, and all, was of a plain shining ash colour, as glossy and free from scales as the slow-worm; but not partaking of its brittle quality.

Beside the common Toad, that is the same as ours, they have one of an enormous size, and frightfully deformed. These, the peasants destroy, whenever they meet them; and then suspend them by the leg to the next tree: in which situation I have contemplated many. They are all over of a dusky brown, with scarce any spots discernible; a broad, rough, furrowed head, and a mouth wide enough to ingulf a moderate-sized Toad. Upon the whole, it is the ugliest creature I ever beheld.

Beside our English Frog, they have also, in astonishing abundance, the Tree Frog, whose appearance is far from disagreeable. The males only are green and the females gray.   *   *   *
These gentry ascend the trees by millions, and serenade till the autumn, living upon the dews and insects. I have many times laboured to shake them from the saplings; but they stick so close, I was never able to accomplish it but once; and could only bring one home, which I presented to Dr. FOTHERGILL.

You could not, my dear friend, oblige me so much, as to send me a few specimens of your different kinds of Oysters, and River and Land Shells, of any sorts that may happen easily to come in your way, without hurrying yourself, or taking too much trouble. They might be packed in a box, and consigned with the Seeds to

GORDON, or Mr. FREEMAN, marked M. C.   The freight of which,
and other expenses, would be instantly paid by,

Dear sir,

Your truly affectionate servant,

MICHAEL COLLINSON.

Manchester Buildings, July 21st, 1773.

MY DEAR SIR :—

I am to thank you for your very obliging and instructive letter
of the 10th May last, and sit down to reply to it as well as I am
able; but, in the first place, beg you will never think of troubling
yourself to make any future apology, in regard to writing, &c.
Nothing can be more clear and comprehensive, notwithstanding the
increased imperfection of sight complained of; and which I shall be
most heartily rejoiced to hear proves only a temporary complaint;
and, I cannot help adding, that if the sincere and ardent wishes of
an individual can avail, there are many, very many happy years
yet to be added to a life, not more justly prized by its dearer and
nearer connexions, than it has, I am sure, proved an honour to
humanity, and the public at large.

The consideration you have been pleased to show to the communications of reciprocal friendship, for a series of years past, was
mutual between my dearest father and yourself.   He, also, preserved the letters of his old and beloved friend.   He considered
them, as they justly were, an invaluable mine of original American
knowledge; and I trust, at least, that the treasure will not sink in
its value, in the hands of his son.

The general remarks you make respecting the extirpation of the
native inhabitants of your vast forests are striking and curious,
and carry conviction along with them; and, indeed, I cannot help
thinking but that, in the period you mention, notwithstanding the
amazing recesses your prodigious continent affords, many of the
present species will become extinct, and perhaps the Indians
themselves; but of the humbler tribe, I feel most for the poor
ingenious Beaver, and read with indignation and concern the many,
many thousands of their furs imported from America annually,
advertised for sale in the papers.

I honour and admire the tenderness of your sentiments, even
with regard to that frequently fatal reptile, the Rattlesnake; and

the more so, as it is correspondent with my own feelings : for it is some years since, except in one or two instances only, that I have even deprived the minutest individual of life. I consider it as a heavenly spark, derived from the great Author and Fountain of life, which is to be held sacred, and which I have no right to injure or destroy.

The new species of Viper you mention, must have been a prodigious curiosity. What a dreadful creature ! Pity he could not have been preserved,—or at least his head,—to have contemplated the structure of his enormous fangs.   *   *   *

Though we have, every year, very considerable importation of the Italian viper, yet our apothecaries also employ their viper-catchers here, though, as our sun is less fervent, 'tis possible the virtue [!] of ours may not be equal to those from abroad. With respect to size and appearance they are the same, as I have had proof enough in my botanic rambles, having seen several of the former, both male and female, not only in the Campania of Rome, where they abound, but elsewhere.

One of our British viper-catchers—since dead—I knew well; and have seen him turn out of a bag into a room, fifty or sixty of them at once, all alive and vigorous. He informed me, that as soon as he seized a viper,—for which he was accoutred with a cleft stick, and an almost impenetrable pair of gloves,—with a steel instrument he immediately wrenched out the fangs, in which operation, in spite of all, he was now and then bit, and had many scars to show, but a little warm olive oil, with which he always went provided, rubbed into the wound, presently blunted the effects of the venom.

The proper distinction, my dear friend, between the male and female of this species is,—the *adder* is the male, the *viper* the female ; and very different they are. The adder is thicker, in proportion to its length, than the female, and is of an unvaried colour,—a dusky reddish-brown, with scarcely any perceptible marks on his back : on the contrary, the female, or viper, has a very singular, irregular, light-coloured list, something resembling, in its configuration, a chain of Death's heads, that runs quite down the back to the extremity of the tail ; and she is also, on the upper parts, of a brighter colour all over, and likewise more susceptible of danger, and livelier than the male. On the belly they are, both male and female, of a dun or darkish ash-colour.

Mr. BANKS' and Dr. SOLANDER's circumnavigation of the globe

is just published ; by which it appears that in the islands of the
South Seas, within the tropics, Nature has been as sparing of her
animal productions as of her vegetable. In the delightful isle of
Otaheite, in, I think, 19 degrees south latitude, the natives possessed no other quadrupeds than hogs and dogs, the latter of which
they preferred to the former. Fish, indeed, was the grand article,
their principal support, which abounded ; and, excepting the bread-
fruit, mentioned in Anson's Voyage, and the cocoa-nut, they had
little else to boast of. The adventurers, however, left them abundance of European pulse, stones of peaches, kernels of various
kinds, particularly Orange and Lemon, &c., &c., which promised to
enrich the island, as many of them sprouted with great luxuriance
before their departure.

I have now only just room to add, that it is with equal respect
and affection I remain, dear sir, your very gratefully obliged friend
and servant,

MICHAEL COLLINSON.

Manchester Buildings, March 5th, 1774.

MY DEAR FRIEND :—

Your most acceptable favour of the 8th of November last, came
safe to hand ; and I am to thank you for all your ingenious and
obliging communications, which never fail to make me a wiser man,
whilst at the same time they are the sources of much entertainment.

The few things you gave me the hopes of receiving, this [last ?]
autumn, I imagine you was disappointed in procuring : though
what I principally wished, was only a few perfect specimens of
your Oysters, to which, if a land or river shell, or so, had been
added, I should have been more than contented ; and have paid
freight, and any expense in procuring, that might have arisen.

With respect to Natural History, though I am at present, from
various wayward reasons, prevented from enjoying my beloved
amusement in botanical researches, yet I still flatter myself (perhaps vainly) with passing the autumn, or at least winter of my
days, in some sequestered situation, far removed from the tumult
and confusion of this metropolis, which are the utter aversion of
my soul.

In the mean while, I indulge in the contemplation of what my cabinets afford; many very curious materials of which, I am highly indebted to your bounty for.

We have had an exceeding tempestuous time, for a fortnight past, attended with violent rains; otherwise, the winter has been mild upon the whole, the severe weather seldom lasting above two or three days, and then changing with a southwest wind.

We have also had one of our spring cries already:—that of Primroses—which the lower class of people, at this season, usually plunder the woods of, a few miles from the city: for yet, my dear sir, there are a few woods left; though in my remembrance many fine ones have been grubbed up and turned into pasture, to supply the enormous increase of horses, which luxury and riches have found necessary for their use.

Things seem to be wearing a very serious face here, in regard to the Colonies. In respect to the business at Boston, concerning the Tea, *that* was certainly the act of a lawless rabble, and in that light only, I believe, the administration views it. Indeed, it is the general belief here, that much of the present disposition of the Colonies has originated from the incendiary arts of some interested people here, *not* American born; but who delight to inflame, and hope to find their account in fishing in troubled waters. The times are certainly eventful and distempered; and I should be very glad that something consistent could be adopted to heal the breach, agreeable to the wishes of America, and yet not derogatory to the honour of the mother country.

I remain, with great respect and regard, dear sir, your affectionate friend,

MICHAEL COLLINSON.

Manchester Buildings, September 22d, 1774.

MY DEAR FRIEND :—

Your very kind favour of the 7th June, is before me; and I am to thank you for its very obliging contents.

In regard to the critical situation of America, I sincerely join with you in sentiments; and I am sure I most sensibly feel for the distresses of the innocent part of its inhabitants. But, in certain situations, it is very difficult to separate the punishment of the guilty from the innocent.

As to the conduct of the Bostonians, it ought, I think, to excite the indignation of every honest mind. In all their late resolves and meetings, we hear of no proposal whatever to pay the East India Company, for the goods they robbed and plundered them of. But retribution they will be obliged to make, I firmly believe, some way or other; as they have now to deal with an administration firm and persevering.

If Lord Chatham's word is to be believed, "America was conquered in Germany." If so, we are not now to learn the price of blood and treasure we have paid on its account, and for its security and advantage. But the conduct of part of the Colonies, and their wishes for an illicit contraband trade, to the prejudice of the mother country, and their own separate emolument, is now pretty well understood here, and who are their principal abettors, on both sides the water. But enough, my dear sir, of this. It is a disagreeable subject, and we will, if you please, drop it.

When the lease of my habitation here expires, which will be in little more than a year, I shall, if I live, I hope, once more breathe the salubrious gale of the country, at my mansion at Mill Hill, which I am once more the proprietor of; and though no more than ten miles from the metropolis, commands distant and home views of several counties. I well remember my old friend, Mr. MOSES BARTRAM, being there. I hope he is well and alive. I have not heard a word of him for many years past.

The principal reasons of my leaving it at all, were the depredations committed in my garden, from whence all the fine plants, possible to remove, were carried off; and which were almost all derived from your bounty; to which may be added, my resolution of going into France and Italy, &c., on the loss of a most revered and beloved parent. But even now, the Blue Mountain *Magnolias* are still flourishing with amazing vigour, and are above (for there are two of them) thirty feet high, and flower prodigiously: but the seed-vessel is the most beautiful part of the plant, being, when ripe, of a rich deep crimson. But I have this from report; for I shall not have courage to look into the premises myself, till I go to reside for good, having a good tenant, for a year, who rents it ready furnished.

The more I see and reflect, the more I am satisfied in the justness of your remark; and think, I cannot too soon retire from "the extravagant, confused inventions of men."

I remain, dear sir, with great respect, most affectionately yours,

MICHAEL COLLINSON.

JAMES FREEMAN TO JOHN BARTRAM.

London, 7th mo., 13th, 1771.

ESTEEMED FRIEND:—

By return of Captain SPARKES, I now reply to thine 29th 4 mo., since which date thou will have received mine dated 16th 4 mo., by Captain OSBORNE; which I doubt not will fully satisfy thee that I have been neither unmindful of thy interest, nor the trust reposed in me. Since which I have received, as per statement annexed, from the King's Dispenser of the Privy Purse; which will no doubt be continued to thee in future, and be paid punctually to me, as it becomes due, on thy account.

*   *   *   *   *

Doctor FRANKLIN has not, but will, when he comes into the city, pay the charges for the box that thou sent him, as a present.

*   *   *   *   *

Uncle Doctor [FOTHERGILL] is well; but much hurried. I am afraid he has not time to write to thee, by this ship.

I am thy real and assured friend,

JAMES FREEMAN.

London, 2 mo., 16th, 1773.

ESTEEMED FRIEND:—

I received thine, and shall duly honour thy draught, and that of thy son. The seeds he sent this year, I am afraid will not all answer; there being much complaint, not so well put up, as last year. However, I hope to do my best.

Uncle Doctor is bravely, considering his hurry. By this time thou will have received a letter from him, which he told me he wrote some time back, wherein he mentions thy son, who was at Carolina.

I thought it would not be right to omit writing by thy countryman, Dr. PARKE, who has been our inmate during his stay in London; and by his good conduct gained the esteem of many friends here.

I am thy real friend,

JS. FREEMAN.

Thy salary is continued. After the next payment I shall transmit the account.

London, 12 mo., 20th, 1773.

ESTEEMED FRIEND :—

I received thine and thy son's letters.   *   *   *

It has been a great favour to be favoured with such a share of health and faculties to thy time of life ; and no doubt thou must expect the gradual decay of nature. But it's a happiness thou mayest enjoy, in having children grown up, and well disposed to render thee every filial comfort (for thy past care and attention during their tender years), which I hope will be continued to thee to the latest period.

Uncle desires his respects ; and that I would acquaint thee he wrote to Doctor CHALMERS, of Charleston, to supply thy son with some money, and he will draw on him, viz., Dr. FOTHERGILL, for the same : which may now make thee quite easy in that respect.

It will, to be sure, be the second month ere I can write again, when I hope to write to thy son. In the interim,

I remain thy friend,

Js. FREEMAN.

London, 12 mo., 18th, 1774.

ESTEEMED FRIEND :—

I received thine 29th, 9th mo. last, and was glad to find thee yet able to write; and the pleasure to look back to thy infancy, and on good grounds, I hope, to feel such comfortable reflection on the several parts of thy life,—now in advanced age,—must be unspeakably great; and I sincerely wish it may continue to thy conclusion.   *   *   *   *   *   *

I sincerely sympathize with the children of an ungrateful mother, in their present dilemma. Their *resolves* seem to be not hastily, but deliberately adopted, and some of them, I should hope, would be steadily abode by, even if the mother should repent her severity towards her children, and again restore to them their natural rights; those I mean are the abolition of the slave trade, and that of horse-racing, stage plays, &c., which, in the first case, would be full proof of their true idea of liberty ; and in the last, of their affection to their children, in preserving their morals from corruption, as far as in their power lies : for surely nothing

can tend more to corrupt the youth, than these dissipating
pleasures.

    *   *   *   *   * Thy obliged and sincere friend,

JS. FREEMAN.

London, 7 mo., 15th, 1775.

DEAR FRIEND :—

I think myself obliged to thee for thy kind intelligence, though
at the same time exceeding sorry, from humanity as well as interest,
that a civil war has taken place, and great effusion of blood
already been the consequence.

PENN is just come over, 'tis conjectured, with some kind of
offers from the Congress. If they are any ways concessory, so
that the grand point in question, the right of taxation, be settled
in your favour, we hope the King, whose benevolence has been
exhibited in many cases, and who, I am persuaded, feels deeply for
his subjects who fell lately near Boston, and thereby occasioned
great distress to many worthy families, would, if possible, sheath
the sword; to which, I have also heard, his servants are not
averse, but that some concession must first come from you. This
is the point of honour they stick on. Yet still, I think, in every
private society, if the first man among them commits an error,
which renders him obnoxious to his inferiors, when he becomes
convinced, if but in part, of his mistake, the acknowledgment and
concession to his inferiors ennobles him the more in their view.
Why not so in a monarch and his ministers ? That a speedy issue
to our troubles may be the result of your deliberations, and ours,
—both sides being open to conviction,—is the best wish of thy
affectionate

J. FREEMAN.

I think, when I wrote last, £296. 5s. 10d. was the balance in thy
favour; since which, having received £25 Lady Day last, the
balance is increased to £321. 5s. 10d.

Dr. F. is well, and desires his love.

DR. LIONEL CHALMERS* TO JOHN BARTRAM.

Charleston, 1st April, 1773.

DEAR SIR :—

I last night received your favour of the 13th ultimo, by your son WILLIAM, who is to dine with me this day, together with Dr. MORGAN, of your city, and some other friends.

According to our mutual good friend Dr. FOTHERGILL's desire, I shall immediately advance him ten guineas, to set him a going; and I doubt not but by his diligence and skill in Botany, as well as Zoology, he will pass his time agreeably to himself, as well as to the Doctor, who, beside the £50 sterling per annum, will pay him for his drawings. In the mean time, be assured, that whatever may be in my power, shall not be wanting to assist him in his progress.

I am much obliged to you for the promise you make me, of sending Bulbous Roots, when the season comes for taking them up. * * * * Our friend FOTHERGILL has often sent me varieties of flower-seeds, and plants: but the former never grew, and the latter were perished before they came to hand. My Carnations were all destroyed by a severe frost and snow we had about the 20th of February last, when they were shooting out strongly; so that a few seeds, or slips of them, will be welcome to, dear sir,

Your friend and servant,

LIONEL CHALMERS.

DR. LIONEL CHALMERS TO WILLIAM BARTRAM.

Charleston, 17th May, 1774.

SIR :—

Not having heard from you for many months, I feared the Creeks must have catched you, in some of your peregrinations. But your letter of — ultimo, which has just now come to hand, has relieved me from this apprehension.

---

* LIONEL CHALMERS, M.D., a physician of South Carolina, eminent for medical science. He first practiced in Christ Church, but soon removed to Charleston, where he continued till his death; which took place in 1777, at the age of sixty-two years.

I know not how to advise you, with regard to trusting yourself amongst the Creeks, who, from present appearances, seem still unsettled, with regard to their intentions towards us. Therefore, whichever way you direct your course, be sure to act with safety to yourself.

The enclosed letter from Dr. FOTHERGILL, I have had almost two months by me, not knowing how to forward it to you. He likewise sent me several reams of paper, in order to your collecting a *Hortus siccus;* and also two flat, tight, tin canisters, I take it, to preserve papers from wet.

Pray, likewise, preserve seeds from some of the most beautiful flowering plants, as well as of those which may be useful in Medicine, so far as their virtues may come to your knowledge, and give me a few of each sort.

Believing it might be satisfactory to your relations to be informed of your safety, I shall, to-day, inform your father thereof; and am your most humble servant,

LIONEL CHALMERS.

CAPTAIN FRASER TO [JOHN?] BARTRAM.*

Philadelphia, December 15th, 1777.

SIR :—

Unfortunately it has been impossible for me to prosecute the intention I set out from Britain with, of seeing your late respectable father, known to me by name and character only.

My next wish, on that disappointment, was to see yourself, and enjoy a few hours' conversation with you, such as curious men, and lovers of science have together. The sight of your garden, and its produce, would have pleased me much. I very soon, after my arrival here, waited on your brother MOSES, who very kindly would have assisted me, in making me as much acquainted with the plants of this country as he was able, and in putting me in the road of collecting seeds.

* This letter, written while the British troops were in possession of Philadelphia, was evidently designed for one of JOHN BARTRAM's sons: but, there being no superscription on the original, it is somewhat uncertain whether for JOHN, or WILLIAM. As, however, JOHN inherited the *Garden,* the letter was probably intended for him.

I am, in Britain, a pretty considerable improver in planting, on a small property I possess; and am very anxious to procure, and cultivate there, all your timber trees and large shrubs.

Your brother MOSES, I believe, gave you a note of mine, containing a requisition from you, of a list of all such as were produced in America, from the largest timber tree to the medium-sized 'shrubs, with their varieties, giving their classical names, of genera, species, and varieties, according to LINNÆUS; and those which you have, or know of, undescribed by him, to be titled by yourself: also their Provincial names.

I there desired you to mark with a (†) what of them would grow in open air, in Britain; and with a (*) those you could procure me now the seeds of.

You will much oblige me, in sending me by letter to your brother MOSES, an answer to this, and comply with the above request.

*   *   *   *   *   *

Any instruction for the preservation of them, in perfection, to England, would be useful.   *   *   *   *

If you come to Philadelphia, I beg to see you. Your brother MOSES will let me know, and I will call there.

It would be a very great satisfaction to me, on quitting this country, to be assured of a fixed correspondence with you, and a certainty of receiving, yearly, assortments of such seeds as I required. A compensation I would readily make, would you only prescribe the mode, and kind.

I am much at your service,

E. S. FRASER,

Captain Guards.

DR. MUHLENBERG* TO WILLIAM BARTRAM.

DEAR SIR :—

With the greatest pleasure imaginable, I received your kind letter, and the dried specimens of some plants new to me. Your

---

* HENRY MUHLENBERG, D.D., was born in New Providence, Montgomery County, Pennsylvania, November 17, 1753. He was educated in the common schools of Philadelphia, and, April 27, 1763, being near ten years of age, sent to Halle, with his two elder brothers, to finish his education in Literature and the Sciences, and to study Theology.

He returned in 1770; and in 1774, was appointed Assistant Pastor of the Lutheran Church, in Philadelphia. In 1780, he accepted a call from Lancaster;

brother could not be persuaded to remain any time amongst us; however, I have the promise of a visit some time in spring. I feel myself very happy in such friendly intercourse and botanical excursions, and shall do what lies in my power to make them agreeable to others. May I ever expect to see you at my house? I have EDWARDS, and CATESBY, JACQUIN, GÆRTNER *de Fructibus*, and several other valuable works; likewise WANGENHEIM on the Forest Trees of America, with figures, which I would wish to compare with you. My *Herbarium vivum* is pretty large, and would alone take a day to look attentively through. Do make it suit you; and, after letting me know a short time beforehand, that I may be certainly at home, stay with us, and make your home at my house.

I come to the answer of your instructive letter, and confess that I have made the same observation on LINNE'S *Species Plantarum*. The synonyma are very often misplaced; but, how could it be otherwise, in such a work? Americans, who see American plants in their native places, must compare them with good figures, and emend the species. *Helonias bullata*, I mean the plant I saw in your garden, with red [?] flowers, is no doubt described by MILLER under the name of *Veratrum Americanum;* which, in the latest edition of the *Systema Vegetabilium* is made a synonym to it. The figure, *Amœn.* III. t. 1, f. 1, is but indifferent. *Veratrum luteum*, MILLERI and GRONOVII, is figured better, III. t. 1, f. 2. I found it *floribus dioicis*, and *floribus polygamo-dioicis*,—some plants male, some male and hermaphrodite, on one stalk. THUNBERG describes a *Melanthium luteum*, and adds the synonym, *Veratrum luteum*, L. with yellow flowers. I would look upon that as a variety. In our parts, the *Veratrum luteum* (*Spica mascula circinata*) is called Devil's bit, the *Aletris farinosa*, Blazing Star [?]. In Maryland, I found a plant very much like the *Veratrum luteum*, with red flowers; but can't remember whether

in which situation, as pastor, he devoted himself assiduously and most faithfully to his duties, until the moment of his death, which occurred, by apoplexy, May 23, 1815, in the sixty-second year of his age.

He was a man of extensive science, and particularly eminent for his knowledge of Botany. He enjoyed a correspondence with many of the most distinguished cultivators of Natural Science; and was a member of several learned societies, at home and abroad. His letters are very frequently referred to, in WILLDENOW's edition of the *Species Plantarum*. His principal published works are, *Catalogus Plantarum*, and *Descriptio uberior Graminum*. His *Flora Lancastriensis* remains in manuscript.—See *Encyclop. Americana.*

it was the same with *Helonias bullata*. WALTER'S *Melanthium dioicum*, I take to be a good synonym of our *Veratrum luteum*.

The *Acnida cannabina*, in your marsh, pleased me a great deal, as I had never seen it before, and had looked anxiously for it.

Of all the dried specimens you sent, I have not seen any before, and as I only have the one specimen, I forbear to examine them closer, until I see them alive.

We have 2 *Cacalias;* but none is, by the smell, *suaveolens*. The one has very glaucous leaves; the other grows along the shores of the Pequea, and is more white. The first I take to be *atriplicifolia*.

The *Mespilus* and *Cratægus* should certainly be joined. Of the latter, I can't make out what is species, and variety. I think 5 species are really different, near Lancaster.

Vaccinium is likewise one of my *Adversaria*. I will give you the short description, to see how we can find the Linnæan names:

1. *Floribus racemosis bracteatis, foliis ellipticis subtus tomentosis, bacca purpurascente, caudice arboreo.* This is the largest sort, sometimes ten feet high; flowers May 1; grows in swamps; and I take it to be *corymbosum*.

2. *Racemis bracteatis, pedicellis bracteolatis, corollis campanulatis, foliis ellipticis subtus pallidis, bacca cœrulea.* This is our Blueberry; and I take it to be *frondosum* [*Gaylussacïa*, H. B. K.].

3. *Racemis bracteatis, pedicellis bracteolatis, corollis ovatis, foliis lanceolato-ovatis viscosis, bacca nigra.* This is the common black Whortleberry; and I take it for AITON'S *resinosum*, or CLAYTON 61.

4. *Pedunculis solitariis unifloris bracteatis, antheris corolla longioribus, foliis oblongis integerrimis, bacca globosa alba.* This is not eatable; and I take it to be, with some doubt, *stamineum*. It has many varieties. CLAYTON describes one much like it, which is classed under *frondosum*.

5. *Pedunculis solitariis unifloris bracteatis, foliis ellipticis et obovatis integris, bacca globosa atra.* This I never found in blossom. It is a low shrub.

The native *Salices*, likewise, prove very hard for me. I count seven or eight different species; but am not able to class them. However, as I have marked every sort, I hope by another year's full description to give a better account of 'em. A true Flora of a country is not the work of one man; but hands must be joined. And I prefer descriptions of a particular place, where the same plant can easily be found, and compared with former descriptions. How useful, in that respect, is a botanical garden! But even there, some plants alter so much, that you hardly know them in a wild state. *Quær.* Doth not *Podophyllum binatum* [*Jeffersonia*] alter the number of *stamina?* I wish I could get a few seeds of it, to observe it closer.

I mention some other genera, in which I could never satisfy myself, because some are badly described, some have too many species:—*Aster, Asclepias, Arabis, Amaranthus, Angelica (quær.* Could not the seed of the *lucida* be got anywhere?), *Chenopodium, Convallaria, Erigeron, Eupatorium, Galium, Hedysarum, Monarda, Orchis, Ophrys, Physalis, Polygonum, Smyrnium, Senecio, Solidago, Serratula, Thalictrum, Urtica,* besides *Juglans* and *Quercus,* are the hard genera. I intend to transcribe my descriptions for your perusal and criticism by and by, and hope you will assist me in clearing up some of the rubbish.

With great pleasure I observed a number of new plants, to me, in your garden. May I beg the favour of you to gather some specimens of such plants as seem worthy of observation to you? My father-in-law, PHILIP HALL, lives at Philadelphia; and whenever you please to let him know that you have any collected, he will send for them, and forward them to me. American plants I take the most delight in.

Have you the newest edition of the *Amœnitates Acad. Linn.*, in ten volumes, and of the *Systema Naturæ?* If not, I can spare them for your perusal, for some time. Your fine Catalogue of American Animals, in your travels, shows that you are a close observer.

Have you no particular Catalogue of Pennsylvanian Animals? The Fish, Serpents, and Testudines, have engaged my attention; but I am far back. I would like an *Index Faunæ Pennsylvanicæ.*

I see I can never leave off writing to a friend, whom I love and esteem, without forcing myself. Pray forgive the length of this letter; and believe me to be, with the warmest friendship,

Sir, your sincere friend and servant,

HENRY MUHLENBERG.

Lancaster, September 13th, 1792.

DEAR SIR :—

I was favoured with your kind letter, dated September 29th, this day ; and return you my warm thanks for the letter and the plants. No. 1, is an *Agrostis*, which I have never seen before, different from *Spica venti* by the *panicula purpurascente capillari*. No. 2, *Aster*, that grows with us on dry land (allied to a large *Aster* which grows on better land, and is, I think, *Novæ Angliæ*). No. 3. *Hibiscus coccineus*. 4. *Helianthus?* I never saw before ; the simple stigma of the disk flowers raises some doubt. 5. *Aster*, is different from ours. 6. I take to be a *Sonchus, calycibus et scapo? hispidis:* not here. I hope to see these plants in future travels, alive, and in greater number.

I agree with you in opinion, that the Blazing Star is neither a *Veratrum*, nor *Helonias*, nor *Melanthium*.* The plant is well known in Europe, and has been ranked with *Veratrum luteum*, as a variety. I find that a similar plant has been figured by EHRET, *per* TREW, t. 77, and MILLER, *Icon*. t. 272 ; but have seen neither of them.

A few seeds of the *Momordica ?* I herewith send. In my little *Index*, it is named *echinata ;* but the plant is one of my *Adversaria*. I likewise inclose a few seeds of a noble Grass, which will be a valuable acquisition to our country, if cultivated in meadows, the *Avena elatior*, L.

The *Amœnitates Acad*. I will send in numbers\to you ; and now begin with Vols. 7, 8, 9, which, perhaps, you have not seen. After you have read them, please give them to Mr. PHILIP HALL, whenever it suits you. The rest shall follow, after you have informed me which volumes you have perused already. I shall put some plants in Vol. 7, to have your opinion, as I am not able to name them after LINNE. If any are new to you, I will get seeds.

I would certainly be exceedingly pleased, if I could have your company at my house, and would do all to make your stay with us agreeable. If my health is spared, I shall be next year, the beginning of June, at Philadelphia, and then will be with you. Meanwhile, we can correspond together, and clear up our doubts. The *Plantæ palustres* of Schuylkill, in particular, I would like to see,

* Prof. A. GRAY, in his "*Manual*," adopts the generic name, *Chamælirium*, Willd.

and a number of Grasses, which I observed at a distance, at your noble river.

How does our friend Doctor BARTON do? He will find it a very difficult task to write a complete *Flora Pennsylvanica*, at this time; and I wish I could persuade him to take only his neighbourhood. Delaware, Schuylkill, the near parts of the Jerseys, will take a number of years to have all their plants well and satisfactorily described.

You will do me a great favour, if you continue to send me some specimens of dried plants, which you think curious, and rank me amongst the number of your sincere friends.

Remember me to your worthy brother, and believe me to be, with great esteem, sir, your most obedient and sincere friend,

HENRY MUHLENBERG.

Lancaster, October 8, 1792.

P. S. The post not going last week, I had an opportunity of opening the packet, and adding a wish, viz. I lately read an Appendix of your worthy father, in which several plants are named, which I can't make out by their description. You, no doubt, know them.

* * * No. 11, Blazing Star, LINNÆUS takes to be *Aletris farinosa*. You say it is what we hitherto named *Veratrum luteum*·

* * * No. 15, *Orchis*. I suppose the same we here name "Adam and Eve."

Any observations on this head will be extremely welcome. We ought, before all, to clear up what has been written already. In the same manner, illustrations of MARSHALL and WALTER will be necessary.

October 15th, 1792.

DEAR SIR:—

With inexpressible satisfaction I received and perused your kind letter, dated November 29, 1792; and now sit down to answer it.

The Oak, I sent, grows all along the banks of Conestoga, and is reckoned a valuable wood. I suppose it has been taken, by some botanists, as a variety of *Quercus Prinos;* but it differs from that, as likewise from the *Quercus alba palustris* MARSHALLII. MARSHALL, I think, has not described it. We call it "Yellow White Oak," "Water Chestnut Oak."

No. 4, looks like a *Hydrocharis*; but has three stamina, one differing in size and colour from the rest [*Heteranthera reniformis*, Ruiz and Pavon].   *   *   *   *

No. 24. *Asclepias tuberosa.* I agree with you in opinion, that *decumbens* and *tuberosa* are the same plant. I have found it *caule erecto et decumbente, foliis alternis et oppositis.*

*   *   *   *   *

No. 33, is a plant we call Adam and Eve. I think it is not described by Linnæus; and therefore named it, in my *Index, Ophrys hyemalis,* until better informed; because the leaves are green all winter.

I feel, with you, the many difficulties we are under, to come to a certainty, in respect of many plants; and it gives me some sort of satisfaction, that *your Plantæ adversariæ* are, or have been, *mine.* However, by assisting one another, we may do more. If I have cleared up a single doubt of yours, it shall be great satisfaction to me. By comparing notes we will go on cleverly.

As soon as I can get time, I will make out a copy of the *Index* I sent, 1790, to the Philosophical Society. It is printed in the 3d Volume of the Transactions; but will hardly be published soon. And then I will beg the favour of you, to inform me which plants don't grow with you, and which you don't find mentioned, though you know them to be Pennsylvanians. I would heartily wish to have a general index of such plants as have been already observed in Pennsylvania, or even in North America. Forster's Catalogue is very imperfect.

Sanguisorba Canadensis, and *Menyanthes trifoliata,* both grow with us. *Parnassia,* I have not seen alive; but the dried specimen was different from the European.

You complain that you are a stranger in the Cryptogamia class. I had the same complaint; but am getting acquainted with these humble and lovely inhabitants of the vegetable kingdom. They enliven my winter excursions, when all the rest of their companions are asleep; and they have this peculiar prerogative, that if you give them a little water, they will revive, even after a hundred years. In my first setting out, I thought them to be innumerable; but I find they can easily be counted. I know about half of them, and try to know the rest. If I could only get a sight of Dillenius's History of Mosses, with copperplates! Have you no friend that owns the noble work, and could be persuaded to let me have it, for a short time? You, my dear sir, should be a friend of this class, in particular; because your namesake, *Bartramia*, now lives amongst them. I love the little plant, now, twice as well, because it remembers me of such worthy friends. Before, it was *Bryum pomiforme*. How would you like it, if I would once send a party of these plants, with their proper names? Or, which would be better, will you clap every one of such you find in your neighbourhood in a little paper, and send them to me, after having them numbered? I will then faithfully tell all their names, as far as I know them. The hills and banks of your mild Schuylkill are full of them. Any time, from now till April, will give you a rich harvest.

The same proposal I make, in respect to Grasses. These are my particular favourites; and I have gathered from every quarter, and have a good collection of well-defined Grasses to compare them with. You would oblige me exceedingly, by gathering every species of them, for me.

In respect to trees, I am rather behindhand, for want of good eyes; and I confess, here, I have many *Adversariæ*. MARSHALL has given me some satisfaction; but his *Arbustum* wants some emendations. Any observation that way, where you think he is wrong, or where another name might have been given, would be pleasing to me. Both MARSHALLS, I am happy to say, are my friends. They have done away some of my doubts, but not all; *ex. gr.* What is *Andromeda plumata?* Does his description of the *Betulæ*, and the application of the Linnæan names, *nigra* et *lenta*, agree with your observations? How do his *Euonymi* differ? No. 2 or 1, is *atropurpureus*. Is *sempervirens, Americanus*, L.? *Fraxinus nigra* seems to me *excelsior*, L. however, a bad name for our species; *alba*, Marsh. *Americana*, L. *Laurus Benzoin*, Marsh. *æstivalis*, L.; but which is *geniculata?* *Lonicera Marilandica*—is this LINNÆI *Spigelia?* *Mespilus, Populus, Quercus, Juglans*, would allow many questions. *Rubus hispidus*—is it our Dewberry? *Salix, Viburnum, Vitis*, how many species? I propose to send you a number of observations I made on these heads, for your criticism; and anticipate the pleasure I shall have, when I, please God, can see you, next spring.

In respect to the *Regnum animale*, I have done but little, being closed up in a well-settled part of the country, where few animals, except the insects, can live. Besides, it seems much against my nature to kill an animal, ever so little,—only to examine it, and to know it. Therefore, my *Fauna Lancastriensis* is very small. *Birds*, I have observed only fifty, which I could find figured in EDWARDS. *Snakes*, very few. *Tortoises*, I think, eight different species, amongst them your *cœlata*, only less. Of these, I have gathered the shells, and would be exceeding glad to get some more. I have the Snapper, Land Turtle or *Carolina*, L., the striped (*picta*, GMELINI), dotted, musk, Terrapin, the running, or your *cœlata*—but a bad and too small exemplar; and miss one, which comes near to the Musk T., only that the under shell is wholly shut up. I observed it on the banks of your river. Of *Insects*, I have a middling collection; but can't class them, well.

Fish, we have but few, the Susquehanna being too far off. I only remember Pike, Catfish, Salmon Trout, Trout, Rock-fish, Sun-fish, Mullet, Sucker, Carp, Shad, Perch, Minnows, Eels, and, from the Susquehanna, Gar, and some straggling Herrings, and Sturgeons.

You have a noble seat, to observe fish and passage birds: and if ever your time would permit, I would be very happy to have, from your hands, a catalogue of the Delaware and Schuylkill fish. I have CATESBY; and if you could cite a figure, I would understand the name better.

However, it is time to drop the pen. You see I am very talkative, when I have to deal with a correspondent. Have patience with me, and retaliate.

Give my best respects to your brother; and believe me to be, with the greatest esteem,

Sir, your very sincere friend,

HENRY MUHLENBERG.

Lancaster, December 10th, 1792.

RICHARD ANTHONY SALISBURY* TO WILLIAM BARTRAM.

Chapel Allerton, near Leeds, Yorkshire, 7th July, 1793.

DEAR SIR:—

Though we have not the least personal knowledge of each other, I cannot miss an opportunity which now offers, of thanking you for

* The Botanical Editor of REES's *Cyclopædia*, under the Art. *Salisburia*, says that genus was so named "in honour of RICHARD ANTHONY SALISBURY, Esqr., F.R.S. and F.L.S., of whose acuteness and indefatigable zeal in the service of Botany, no testimony is necessary in this [the Linnæan] Society, nor in any place which his writings have reached."

the entertainment and assistance I have received, in the cultivation of plants (an employment to which I devote the greatest part of my time), from perusing your Travels through the Southern States. They have already enabled me to bring one plant, which never throve in the English collections, almost, I think, to as great a degree of perfection, as in the hot savannas of Florida; and that is the *Amaryllis Atamasco:* and it is to trouble you for a little information respecting this, and two or three more plants, that I now intrude this letter upon you.   *   *   *   *   *

*   *   *   I know not if you are acquainted with a beautiful *Fumaria*, which SOLANDER called *fungosa*, in his MSS. [now called *Adlumia cirrhosa*, Raf.]; and from which a *specifica differentia* of it has been inserted in the *Hortus Kewensis*, published a few years ago. But it came, I believe, from you to FOTHERGILL, and I am very anxious to know the place and soil it grows wild in. I have had it twelve feet high, in a large glass case, where I cultivate such plants as come from the more temperate parts of the globe.

In a catalogue, which is now printing, of the collection here, I have ventured to call a very beautiful little genus after your father, whose MSS. are in Sir JOSEPH BANKS'S Herbarium; and I wish it may meet with your approbation : the more so, as the genus which GÆRTNER has given him can hardly, I think, stand; and is never likely to be a plant cultivated by man. I wish I had a copy of this catalogue ready to send you, but I will take the first opportunity of offering it to you. In the meanwhile, I send the page which contains *Bartramia ;** and shall be much obliged to you for any information respecting the soil and time of flowering, in America, of these two plants.

Whenever you can spare time to reply to these inquiries (if, indeed, you ever favour me with any reply), your letter will reach me readily by the common mail; and I do not mind postage.

I remain, with great respect,

Your obliged servant,

RICHARD ANTHONY SALISBURY.

* This does not appear among the BARTRAM papers; nor has the editor met with any account of *this Bartramia*, in the books.

ALEXANDER WILSON* TO WILLIAM BARTRAM.

Union School, May 22d, 1804.

MY DEAR FRIEND :—

I truly sympathize, though not without a smile, at the undeserved treatment you have experienced from your busy colony. Recollection of the horrible fate of their fathers, smothered with sulphur; or, perhaps, a presentiment of what awaits themselves, might have urged them to this outrage; but had they known you, my dear friend, as well as I do, they would have distilled their honey into your lips, instead of poison, and circled around you, humming grateful acknowledgments to their benevolent benefactor, who spreads such a luxuriance of blossoms for their benefit.

Accept my thanks for the trouble I put you to yesterday.

Mrs. LEECH requests me to send Miss BARTRAM two birds; and thinks they would look best, drawn so that the pictures may hang their length horizontally.

I send a small scroll of drawing paper for Miss NANCY. She will oblige me by accepting it; and as soon as I get some letter paper, worthy your acceptance, which will be to-morrow, I shall be happy of the opportunity of supplying you.

There are some observations in your last which I would remark on; but am hurried at the present moment. Farewell.

Yours, sincerely,

ALEX. WILSON.

Philadelphia, November 16th, 1806.

MY DEAR FRIEND :—

Mr. JONES will hand you this, and receive any notes you may have had leisure to draw up, for the Cyclopædia. I shall be extremely happy to receive the additional matter, which you think necessary to add to your father's memoirs; and I think that if time would permit you to draw up a short account of the commencement and progress of botanical research, in this country, it would afford you an opportunity of doing justice to many worthy

---

* ALEXANDER WILSON, the father of *American Ornithology*, was born in Scotland, July 6, 1766; emigrated to the United States in 1794, and died in Philadelphia, August 23, 1813, aged forty-seven years. For a most interesting memoir of this amiable man, by GEORGE ORD, Esq., see HARRISON HALL'S edition of the American Ornithology, published in 1828.

characters, who might otherwise be forgotten, as well as the valuable services they had performed, for the advancement of this sublime science.

In doing this, I would suggest, that you be perfectly impartial, and relate your own discoveries, as you would those of a friend; bestowing due praise where justly merited. All this might be done concisely, and would be a valuable addition, introduced under the article BOTANY.

I send for your perusal the eighth volume of TILLOCH'S Philosophical Magazine: at page 149 of which you will find a long account of *Asclepias Syriaca;* which I request your opinion of, and any additional observations you may see proper. Please to return it any time this week, by a safe conveyance. Perhaps Mrs. HOLSTEIN may do this; and I shall call on her in market.

I am, my dear friend, yours, sincerely,

ALEX. WILSON.

THOMAS JEFFERSON TO WILLIAM BARTRAM.

Washington, November 23, 1808.

THOMAS JEFFERSON presents his compliments to his friend, Mr. W. BARTRAM, and his thanks for the seeds of the Silk Tree, which he was so kind as to send him. These he shall plant, in March, and cherish with care, at Monticello. The cares of the garden, and culture of curious plants, uniting either beauty or utility, will there form one of his principal amusements. He has been prevented, by an indisposition of some days, from having the pleasure of seeing Dr. SAY, except on his first visit. An esteem for his character, of very early date, as well as a respect for Mr. BARTRAM'S friendships, will insure to Dr. SAY the manifestation of every respect he can show him.

He salutes Mr. BARTRAM with friendship and respect.

F. ANDRE MICHAUX* TO WILLIAM BARTRAM.

Paris, March 12th, 1810.

DEAR SIR :—

I am sincerely obliged to our common friend, Mr. WILSON, to

* FRANÇOIS ANDRE MICHAUX, son of ANDRE MICHAUX, author of the *Flora Boreali Americana*, was born in 1770. He is the author of the splendid work on the Forest Trees of North America, published in 1817.

have give me, in his last letter, news of you and family. The marks of friendship that you have invariably bestow on my father and me, will be constantly present to my memory.

I have received, some weeks ago, the small envoice that I had ask to you, by my friend, Mr. DUBAC.

The seeds came in hand in good order. The only thing I cannot but observe, is, that really you put too much of each kind for the small sum of money that I have sent; consequently, I am under a double obligation toward your brother JOHN, and your nephews.

By this same occasion, I send somme Literary Journals for the Philosophical Society. In the same paquet, I include a small parcel of seeds of two sorts of Pine, *Pinus maritima*, et *P. Laricio*. This last is a very interesting species, growing in the mountains of Corsica. As it grow very well at Paris, I suppose he will support well your climate. You claim those seeds of Mr. J. VAUGHAN.

Since my return, not a day is passing away without working steady to my *American Sylva*. Drawers, engravers, type and copper printers, are busy about it; and the French edition, or at least the first number, is to appear by the first of May; and by the same time, I shall send over the engravings to be added to the American edition, in case Mr. S. BRADFORD will be disposed to republish. I am very anxious to know how he will meet in America; and in particular, your opinion respecting it. Also of Mr. HAMILTON, and Dr. MUHLENBERG.

Our great Emperor is about to marry. The only good that will do, at present, is to prevent a great effusion of blood, by preserving the life of many thousand; considering that event will afford a Continental peace, for some time.

With respect, and an unalterable attachment, I remain your most obedient friend.

F. ANDRE MICHAUX.

END OF THE BARTRAM CORRESPONDENCE.

REMINISCENCES

OF

HUMPHRY MARSHALL,

AND

HIS CORRESPONDENTS.

TO THE

Chester County Cabinet of Natural Science,

THESE REMINISCENCES

OF THE VENERABLE MAN,

WHOSE SCIENTIFIC LABOURS AND ATTAINMENTS REFLECT HONOUR UPON OUR COUNTY,

AND WHOSE NOBLE EXAMPLE

IT SHOULD BE OUR CEASELESS ENDEAVOUR TO EMULATE,

ARE RESPECTFULLY INSCRIBED BY

THE EDITOR.

CONTENTS.

*

482 CONTENTS.

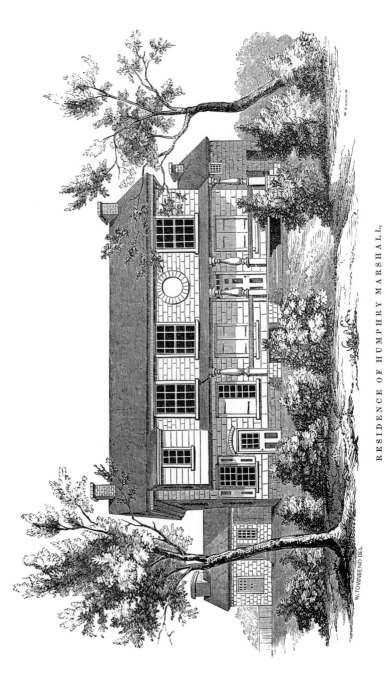

W. TOWNSEND DEL.

W. B. GIHON SC.

RESIDENCE OF HUMPHRY MARSHALL,

BUILT WITH HIS OWN HANDS, A.D. 1773.

BIOGRAPHICAL SKETCH

OF

HUMPHRY MARSHALL.

HUMPHRY MARSHALL was born in the township of West Bradford, County of Chester, and province of Pennsylvania,* on the
10th day of October, 1722. His father, ABRAHAM MARSHALL, was
a native of Gratton, in Derbyshire, England, born in the year 1669,
came to Pennsylvania about the year 1697, and settled near Darby,
where, on the 17th of January, 1702–3, he married MARY, the
daughter of JAMES HUNT, of Kingsessing, also an emigrant from
England, and one of the companions of WILLIAM PENN. Some
time after his marriage, viz., in the year 1707, ABRAHAM MARSHALL
removed to the forks of the Brandywine, near the western branch
of that stream, where he purchased large tracts of land, among the
Indians, and continued to reside until his death, which took place
December 17th, 1767, at the age of about ninety-eight years. His
wife died in the spring of 1769, aged eighty-seven years.† They

* It is curious to remark the state of *information*, among certain book-makers
on the other side of the Atlantic, respecting the *Author of the first indigenous treatise* upon American Plants. For instance, DE THEIS, in his *Glossaire de Botanique,*
published in 1810, mentions him as " H. Marshall, *Anglois,* dont on a eu, en 1778
[1785], l'Histoire naturelle des Arbres et Arbustes de l'Amerique septentrionale."
And in LOUDON's *Encyclopædia of Plants,* he is spoken of as " *Henry* Marshall, an
Englishman, author of *a sort* of history of the Trees and Shrubs of North America,
published in 1778" !

† The following note (in the handwriting of HUMPHRY MARSHALL, eighty years
since), is still preserved among the *Marshall Papers.*

" On the 4th of this instant [*March,* 1769], departed this life, in the eighty-
seventh year of her age, MARY MARSHALL. Born in Kent, in old England; arrived

were both interred in the Friends' burying-ground, at Bradford meeting-house, which meeting they had been mainly instrumental in establishing. Throughout their long lives, they had been truly useful and exemplary members of society, ABRAHAM, moreover, having been for many years an approved minister among Friends, as is attested by a Collection of Memorials, published by the Society in 1787. ABRAHAM and MARY MARSHALL had seven sons and two daughters. Of these nine children, HUMPHRY was the eighth. In those primitive times, the opportunities for school-learning, in Chester County, were scanty and limited. The children of the early settlers were, from necessity, kept at home and put to hard work, as soon as they had acquired sufficient muscular strength to be serviceable. HUMPHRY MARSHALL used often to state, that, he never went to school a day, after he was twelve years of age; and consequently, was instructed only in the rudiments of the plainest English education. Being constitutionally robust and active, he was employed in agricultural labours until he was old enough to be apprenticed to the business of a stone-mason. This trade he learned, and followed, for a few years, during the summer season, extending his engagements, occasionally, into the county and town of Lancaster, and also into the neighbouring province of

at Philadelphia, with her parents, about the year 1684, and settled at Kingsessing Township; was married on the 17th of the 1st month, 1702–3, to ABRAHAM MAR-SHALL, who was born in Derbyshire, and arrived in this country about the year 1697, as appears by letters from thence; and, soon after they were married, re-moved to the Forks of Brandywine, where they lived together in love until the 17th day of the 12th month, 1767, having been married sixty-four years and nine months; when he departed this life, by the generally-supposed account, in the 97th year of his age, but by JOHN GRATTAN's Journal, 103; having been a public minister amongst the people called Quakers, from the eighteenth year of his age. He was not more conspicuous for his zeal and indefatigable labour in the Gospel, than for rectitude of life, which, with a meek and humble deportment, adorned the doctrine he preached. The patience and Christian fortitude, manifested in his last tedious illness, evidenced his subjection to the will of God; and the serenity of spirit with which he met the messenger of death, being sensible of his approach-ing change, gives just ground to hope, that he now experiences the verity of that sacred truth, *Blessed are the dead who die in the Lord,—for henceforth they rest from their labours, and their works follow them.* Although they lived to such an advanced age, and departed quiet and easy, their children can truly say, that it hath been very afflicting to part with such good and pious exemplary parents. She was at-tended to her funeral, on the 6th of the 3d month, 1769, by a large number of her friends and relatives; at which time and place, being met by the corpse of PHEBE HADLEY, an ancient minister, and a number of friends attending thereon, the solemn time and occasion must be remembered for years to come, by some."

New Jersey. The winters were passed at the residence of his father.

That he was an excellent workman, is still evident from the walls of his residence, at Marshallton, which he built with his own hands, in the year 1773. In one corner of this dwelling, he contrived a small but convenient stove, or hot-house; and from the second story he projected a little observatory, in which to indulge his fondness for astronomical observations.

On the 16th of September, 1748, HUMPHRY MARSHALL was married to SARAH, daughter of JOSEPH PENNOCK, of West Marlborough, in Chester County. After his marriage, he took charge of his father's farm, near the west branch of the Brandywine. He seems, about this time, to have turned his attention, earnestly, to the acquisition of knowledge, evincing a decided partiality for Astronomy and Natural History. He procured books, and commenced the collection and culture of the more curious and interesting indigenous plants. A number of ornamental trees and shrubs, in the vicinity of the paternal mansion, still attest his predilection for the beauties of the vegetable kingdom.*

As an evidence of his devotion to literary and scientific pursuits, it may be mentioned, that his name is found, written with his own hand so early as 1753, in COLES's *Latin Dictionary*, QUINCY's *Medical Lexicon*, GERARD's *Herbal*, a *Treatise on Navigation*, and several other works of similar character, which he had procured about that period.

That he possessed the confidence of his fellow-citizens, is shown by the fact of his appointment of County Treasurer, in 1762, in which office he was continued until the year 1766, inclusive.

In 1764, it became expedient to enlarge the dwelling in which he resided with his parents. This addition was built of brick; and the entire work of digging and tempering the clay, making and burning the bricks, and building the walls, was performed by HUMPHRY himself. He also erected a green-house, adjoining the dwelling; which was, doubtless, the first conservatory of the kind ever seen, or thought of, in the county of Chester.

---

* It is altogether probable, that HUMPHRY MARSHALL's taste for Horticulture and Botany may have been awakened, and promoted, by a familiar intercourse with his cousin, JOHN BARTRAM, and by the attractions of that cousin's interesting *garden*. Enjoying such privileges, he would at once catch the spirit, and profit by the skill and experience, of his enthusiastic relative.

At his father's death, in 1767, HUMPHRY MARSHALL came into full possession of a large portion of the patrimonial estate, which he had previously held as a tenant, paying a moderate annual rent. He now erected a grist or merchant mill, and made other considerable improvements on the premises, and continued thereon until the year 1774; when he removed to his newly-erected dwelling, on a tract of land which he had purchased, near the Bradford Meeting-house, adjoining the site of the present village of *Marshallton*.

The *Botanic Garden*, at Marshallton, was planned and commenced in the year 1773, and soon became the recipient of the most interesting trees and shrubs of our country, together with many curious exotics; and also of a numerous collection of our native herbaceous plants. A large portion of these yet survive, although the garden, from neglect, has become a mere wilderness; while a number of our noble forest trees, such as Oaks, Pines, and Magnolias (especially the *Magnolia acuminata*), all planted by the hands of the venerable founder, have now attained to a majestic altitude.

For several years prior to the establishment of the Marshallton Garden, HUMPHRY had been much engaged in collecting native plants and seeds, and shipping them to Europe; but after that event, being aided by his nephew, Dr. MOSES MARSHALL, he greatly extended his operations, and directed his attention with enhanced zeal and energy to the business of exploring, and making known abroad, the vegetable treasures of these United States. The present generation of botanists have but an imperfect idea of the services rendered to the science, by the skill and laborious industry of those faithful pioneers; but the letters here given, will show that they contributed largely to the knowledge of American plants.*

Those active pursuits, however, did not interfere with the performance of his social duties, nor prevent him from attending to the business and interests of the religious Society, of which he was an exemplary and influential member. Neither did they

---

* Dr. FOTHERGILL, speaking of his own garden, in a letter to H. MARSHALL, dated 9th month, 1772, says, "It is acknowledged by the ablest botanists we have, that there is not a richer bit of ground, in curious American plants, in Great Britain; and for many of the most curious, I am obliged to thy diligence and care."

prevent his services, in a public capacity, from being occasionally put in requisition. The Legislature of Pennsylvania, in February, 1773, passed an act establishing a Loan Office, and appointed HUMPHRY MARSHALL, of Chester County, one of the trustees. These trustees were continued in office until December, 1777, when, owing to difficulties in the discharge of their duties—arising out of the Revolutionary conflict—they neglected or refused longer to serve, and were superseded.

In 1780, HUMPHRY began to prepare an account of the forest trees and shrubs of this country, which was completed and printed in the latter end of the year 1785, under the title of "ARBUSTUM AMERICANUM: THE AMERICAN GROVE, or an Alphabetical Catalogue of Forest Trees and Shrubs, natives of the American United States."

It formed a duodecimo volume of near two hundred pages; and is believed to be the first truly indigenous Botanical Essay published in this Western Hemisphere. The arrangement, being alphabetical, is rather inconvenient, and ill-suited to investigators who are unacquainted with the genera. But the descriptions are in accordance with the Linnæan system, and are, for the most part, faithful and satisfactory. The book is dedicated to the officers and members of the American Philosophical Society; and was, for that day, and under the circumstances, a useful and highly creditable performance. Like its respectable author, it was at least half a century in advance of the community in which it appeared; and consequently was neither understood nor appreciated at home. But among the scientific of the old world, it was received with marked approbation, and was promptly translated into the prevalent languages of continental Europe.

On the 29th of March, 1785, HUMPHRY MARSHALL was elected an honorary member of the Philadelphia Society for promoting Agriculture, "the Society inviting his assistance." And in February of the following year, he sent them an essay on the importance of botanical knowledge to the cultivators of the soil. That essay was never published; but it has been preserved in the archives of the Society, an interesting memento of the intelligence, forethought, and practical sagacity of the author. It will be found at the close of the present volume.*

* The editor has been highly gratified in finding his own humble efforts, in behalf of Agricultural Botany, thus preceded and sanctioned. As a Chester County

Men of science, in our own land, now began to be aware of the existence, and meritorious labours of the unpretending farmer and gardener of West Bradford; and we learn, from his Diploma (still carefully treasured by his relatives), that, on the 20th of January, 1786, " *The* AMERICAN PHILOSOPHICAL SOCIETY, *held at Philadelphia, for promoting useful knowledge, desirous of advancing the interest of the Society, by associating to themselves men of distinguished eminence, and of conferring marks of their esteem upon persons of literary merit,"* had " *elected Mr.* HUMPHRY MARSHALL, *of Chester County, a member of the said Philosophical Society,"* thereby " *Granting unto him all the rights of fellowship, with all the liberties and privileges thereunto belonging.*"*

On the 27th of July, 1786, HUMPHRY lost his first wife, who died at the age of nearly sixty-six years: and on the 10th of January, 1788, he again married. His second wife was MARGARET, daughter of THOMAS MINSHALL, of Middletown (then of Chester, now) Delaware County. He had no offspring by either marriage.

In SCHREBER's edition of the *Genera Plantarum,* published in 1791, a genus of plants, belonging to the natural family of *Compositæ,* or compound syngenesious flowers, was dedicated to HUMPHRY MARSHALL and his nephew; for which, it would seem, they were partly indebted to the kind interposition and friendly attention of Dr. MUHLENBERG, the correspondent of SCHREBER. Four species of the genus *Marshallia* are enumerated in TORREY and GRAY's *Flora,* all natives of our Southern States.

In the latter years of his life, HUMPHRY's vision was greatly impaired by cataract, for which the operation of couching was performed by Dr. WISTAR, in 1793, with but partial success. It was proposed to be repeated in the year 1800, and preparation made with that view, as may be gathered from some of Dr. WISTAR's letters; but it is the opinion of his relatives, of the present day, that a second operation was not performed. His sight, however, was never so entirely lost, but that he could discern the walks in his garden, examine his trees, and recognise the localities

man, he cannot but feel proud, that his venerable fellow-citizen so early perceived, and so forcibly urged, the importance of giving a scientific character to the profession of Agriculture.

* The certificate of membership was signed by B. FRANKLIN, *President;* JOHN EWING, WILLIAM WHITE, and SAMUEL VAUGHAN, *Vice-Presidents;* and attested by JAMES HUTCHINSON, R. PATTERSON, SAMUEL MAGAW, and JOHN FOULKE, *Secretaries.*

of his favourite plants. In tracing those walks with his friends, pointing out the botanical curiosities, and reciting their history, he took the greatest delight to the last.

But even while yielding to the infirmities of age, he continued to take a lively interest in whatever concerned the welfare and progressive improvement of society. Among the latest manifestations of his zeal, in that behalf, may be mentioned his co-operation with some active philanthropists in procuring the erection of a county alms-house, for the accommodation of the sick and infirm poor; and especially, the aid and counsel he afforded, in projecting and organizing that valuable institution for the education of youth, the *West-town Boarding School*, established by the Society of Friends, near the close of the eighteenth century.

His life having been protracted to a good old age, HUMPHRY MARSHALL finally sank under an attack of dysentery, on the 5th of November, 1801, aged seventy-nine years and twenty-five days. His second wife survived him nearly twenty-two years; having died August 6th, 1823, at the age of eighty-two. HUMPHRY, and both his wives, were interred in the same burial-ground with his parents, at the Bradford Meeting-house: but, as no stone, nor other sepulchral memorial, was tolerated by the Society to which he belonged, the precise spot where his remains repose, is already difficult to be ascertained, and will soon be wholly merged in doubt and uncertainty.*

In person, HUMPHRY MARSHALL was above the medium size, erect and robust, with features strong yet regular; his forehead square and ample. His eyes were dark gray; his hair dark, inclining to sandy; his mien rather grave and reserved, but his manners inspiring respect, confidence, and esteem. A son of one of his most intimate friends, in Philadelphia, writing to the editor, under date of November, 1847, says, "I well recollect that venerable man, in his visits to the house of my father; and although I was then a child, I was peculiarly struck with his *deep-toned* and *tremulous* voice: he was my ideal of a sage who had given his days and nights to meditation and study."

---

* The following passage, in reference to cemeteries, and memorials of the departed, is from the pen of that eminent and estimable lady, the late DEBORAH LOGAN:—"I know of nothing with respect to the polity of *Friends*, and the care of their institutions, that I think so exceptionable as their disregard of a decent attention to the places of interment belonging to their Society."

The following extracts, from the Preface of PURSH'S North American *Flora*, tend to illustrate his character, as a lover and cultivator of the Science of Plants :—

"My first object, after my arrival in America [in 1799], was to form an acquaintance with all those interested in the study of Botany.   *   *   *   *   "I next visited the old established gardens of Mr. MARSHALL, author of a small *Treatise on the Forest Trees of North America*. This gentleman, though then far advanced in age, and deprived of his eyesight, conducted me personally through his collection of interesting trees and shrubs, pointing out many which were then new to me, which strongly proved his attachment and application to the science in former years, when his vigour of mind and eyesight were in full power."

The tenor of the correspondence with HUMPHRY MARSHALL will indicate the subjects on which his mind was habitually engaged; and will show that he was a man of an active, persevering disposition, taking a lively interest in all the concerns of civilized life, more especially those connected with the advancement of society, the security of human rights, and the highest state of intellectual refinement.

In conclusion, the editor is gratified in being able to state, that the *Town Council of the Borough of West Chester* have recently manifested a becoming sense of what was due to the character and memory of HUMPHRY MARSHALL, by adopting the following preamble and resolution :—

" Whereas it has been deemed expedient and proper to improve the public Square, on which the upper reservoir connected with the Water-works of the borough is situated, by laying out the same in suitable walks, and introducing various ornamental trees and shrubbery :   And whereas it will be convenient and necessary to designate the said Square by some appropriate name :   And whereas the late HUMPHRY MARSHALL of Chester County was one of the earliest and most distinguished horticulturists and botanists of our country, having established the second botanic garden in this republic ; and also prepared and published the first treatise on the forest trees and shrubs of the United States, and diffused a taste for botanical science which entitles his memory to the lasting respect of his countrymen :

" *Therefore resolved, by the Burgesses and Assistant Burgesses of the Borough of West Chester, in Council assembled,* That the public Square, aforesaid, shall for ever hereafter be designated and known by the name of 'THE MARSHALL SQUARE,' in commemoration of the exemplary character, and scientific labours, of our distinguished fellow-citizen, the late HUMPHRY MARSHALL, of West Bradford Township, Chester County."

Passed, March 13, 1848.

Frien.d. Osborne   Chester County 9 : 5 : th : of y 10 : mo 1772

    I have sent
here with to thee the Box of Insects for
Dr Fotherguill I have Incloped the they to thee
according to the Dr Directions that thou might
open the Box at the Custom house if the officers
inspect on it I desire that thou may take good
Care of it & put it in as Dry a plaice in the
vessell as posible for Moisture will Damage
the Insects much perhaps in some Corner of y
Cabbon or steerage I shewny sent a letter I hope
thou'l be Carefull & not forget them

        From Thy real Wellwisher

                Humphry Marfhall

To
Capt Peter Osborne

CORRESPONDENCE.

London, 2d 3mo. 1767.

Respected Friend :—

I received thy kind letter, as well as the box of seeds, and the duplicate it contained. I think myself much indebted to thee, and shall endeavour, as occasions may offer, to show that I am not insensible of thy kindness, nor ungrateful.

I knew not whether anything would be more acceptable to a botanist, than Miller's *Gardener's Dictionary*, which I hope thou will receive with this; and if thou art possessed of one before, dispose of it, and accept the produce as an acknowledgment for thy kindness.

As it may suit thy other concerns, I should be glad if thou would proceed to collect the seeds of other American shrubs and plants, as they fall in thy way; and if thou meets with any curious plant or shrub, transplant it at a proper time into thy garden, let it grow there a year or two; it may then be taken up in autumn, its roots wrapped in a little moss, and laid in a coarse box, just made close enough to keep out mice, but not to exclude the air.

If thou knows of any plant possessed of particular virtues, and that is known by experience to be useful in the cure of diseases, this I should be glad to have in particular, both the parts used, and seeds of the same.

I accept thy offers to collect for me the curious animals of your country, very readily; and, as I may, shall readily make such acknowledgments as may be agreeable : and in doing this, I shall take it kind, if thou will just point out in what manner I can render thee most service.

Except the Rattlesnake, I have scarce any of your reptiles, and but few insects. Whatever of this kind occurs, may therefore be laid aside for me. The reptiles may be put together in a little common spirit: and the insects stuck through with a pin, and fixed on the inside of a box made of some soft wood. Small birds may be gutted and dried, filling them with tow and tobacco dust; larger may be opened and gutted; then filled with salt and pepper.

Whilst, however, I am putting thee upon these services, I must desire thee not to give into these searches so much as either to lessen thy attention to the duties of thy station here, or thy regard to the more essential ones of another life. I endeavour to keep all these things in their proper place; and by no means permit them to interfere with more important considerations. They are lawful, but may not be to all expedient; and whilst I am gratifying an inclination the most innocent, I would take care not to hurt another. I shall be pleased with thy correspondence, and, if occasion offers, shall gladly promote thy interest here, as well as contribute to it myself; but still, remember these pursuits are not the main business of life, but may be allowable relaxations.

My brother SAMUEL remembers thy family, and speaks of them with esteem.

Follow the example of wise men; seek their company, and then thou will become such thyself, and an example to others. Farewell.

JOHN FOTHERGILL.

London, 18th 5mo. 1767.

ESTEEMED FRIEND:—

Thou will see by the inclosed, that it was wrote a considerable time ago, to acknowledge the favour of thy collection of seeds. I was at that time prevented from sending it, and the more discouraged, as I could not get MILLER's *Gardener's Dictionary*, which is still out of print. I have sent, however, an abridgment of this work, not long since published, which I hope will prove acceptable; though this is not intended as a compensation for thy trouble, but merely as an acknowledgment.

If thou will continue thy farther care in collecting American seeds, and inform me in what manner I can, with most advantage to thyself, compensate thy care and labour, it will be an additional satisfaction to

Thy friend,
J. FOTHERGILL.

London, 29th 10mo. 1768.

RESPECTED FRIEND :—

I am greatly obliged to thee for several parcels of curious seeds, birds, and insects. I should have acknowledged thy last valuable cargoes sooner, but have been searching, in vain, for thy last letter, having somehow or other mislaid it ; and with it, the list of books thou mentioned as being acceptable to thee.

I have sent by our friend, JOHN HUNT, who is returning to Pennsylvania, a small pocket-glass for viewing flowers, and ten guineas in consideration of thy time and trouble, in collecting these things for me. If THOMAS FISHER has not yet sent thee a set of ANTHONY PURVER'S Translation,* upon showing him this note, I doubt not but he will deliver thee one, and may place it to my account.

As it may fall in thy way, I should be glad thou would continue thy care in collecting for me such seeds and plants as I have not hitherto received from thee ; and I think it would be worth while to sow a part of all the seeds thou gathers, in thy own garden, or some little convenient spot provided for the purpose. There are many curious seeds that lose the property of vegetation by a sea-voyage. The plants thus raised by seed at home, might be removed from the bed they were sown on, the second autumn, or spring following, into boxes of earth, and sent to us in the spring, so as to arrive here in the third or fourth month, and would then succeed very well.

I doubt not but many of our gardeners would be glad to purchase such boxes, containing assortments of new and curious plants, at a considerable price, and sufficient to pay for the care and pains in raising them.

There is a curious water plant, the *Colocasia*, that grows in some deep waters in the Jerseys, perhaps in your province likewise. It has a beautiful red flower, broad leaves, and a singular seed-vessel, formed like a cup cut off and covered with holes containing large round seeds.† It is well known to thee, I doubt not. We have

---

* This refers to a translation of the *Bible*, then recently published under the auspices of Dr. FOTHERGILL. The "set," mentioned in the letter, was duly received, and is still carefully preserved in the MARSHALL family.

† The "*Colocasia*," here spoken of, is the *Nelumbium luteum*, of WILLDENOW, a magnificent aquatic, sometimes called "Water Chinquapin," in the vernacular.

had the seeds sent over in great perfection ; they germinate, and then die. I wish the roots could be sent over, wrapt in moss and then put into a box. I imagine they would come safe; or else put into a tub, and the tub filled up with the mud they grow in. I should be glad thou would endeavour to send some both ways; and the ripe seeds likewise, put into a wide-mouthed bottle filled with mud, and covered over with leather. Of all the seeds sent over, there are scarce any so perishable as acorns. These should be planted at home, in autumn ; they would come up next spring, and the spring following they might be transplanted into boxes, and sent home. By this means, we might have all your variety of Oaks with great facility. All seeds should be sown in a place where they are defended from a hot noonday sun, otherwise the young plants are soon scorched up and die.

I should be glad thou would again mention the books thou was desirous of having, and I shall take care to send them, as I think it may make thee proper satisfaction.

There is a kind of *Dogwood*, whose calyx is its greatest beauty ;* it chiefly grows in Virginia,—whether with you I know not. I want a few plants of it; and, indeed, it would be always agreeable to receive young well-rooted plants of any kind. If they are taken up with a little earth, and a good root, early in the spring, and the earth tied close about them with strong paper and packthread; or if they are put into boxes with moss only about their roots, and sent away in the spring, they would come very safe. The boxes should not be nailed so close but a little air may get in. Would it be impossible to send one of those pretty little *Owls*, alive ? I wish I could see one. Most of the captains in the trade, I believe, would endeavour to take care of it, and a *Mocking-bird*, if they

It was found, at an early day, in the river Delaware, below Philadelphia, and subsequently in various places throughout the Southern and Western States. Dr. FOTHERGILL probably considered it as being identical with the *N. speciosum*, Willd., or "*Sacred Bean*," of Egypt, India, and China (to which, in fact, it is very nearly allied), which is mentioned in PLINY's Natural History (*fide* DE CAND.) by the name of *Colocasia*. The Oriental plant has, for the most part, a rose-coloured or "red-flower," as Dr. F. says; but the flower of the American species is usually pale *yellow*. The eagerness and persevering efforts of the Doctor to possess the splendid rarity, are abundantly manifested in the following letters of that estimable man.

* This is the *Cornus florida*, L., a shrub or small tree, common throughout the United States, of which the large white four-leaved *involucre*, (or "calyx," as Dr. F. terms it,) is so conspicuous in our woodlands, about the middle of May.

could easily be had : but it is the best to keep these things alive with you, if possible, all winter, and send them in the spring. In autumn, the ships have often long passages, bad weather on our coast, and the seamen have neither time nor inclination to attend to anything but their business. In the spring they have often better weather, and the birds come to advantage.

Whatever may be sent to me, if it is directed either to DANIEL MILDRED, or to D. BARCLAY *and sons*, will always be taken care of. Give me a line, at the same time, with the particular marks.

Letters may be directed for me, in Harpur Street, near Red Lion Square, London.

I am thy obliged friend,
JOHN FOTHERGILL.

ESTEEMED FRIEND :—

Before this time I hope thou hast received a pretty long letter by our friend JOHN HUNT, to whose care I also committed ten guineas, and a small glass for viewing the flowers of plants.

I have just received thy last collection of seeds, and the box of plants that accompanied it; both were very acceptable, and the plants came in as good condition as possible.

By this opportunity I have sent two glasses of the value thou desires; and if these are not satisfactory, either in size or shape, please to dispose of them, and give me proper dimensions, and I will take care that they shall be sent. In respect to the seeds and plants to be sent in future, please to keep this general order in view, viz. :—To send me any new plant that occurs to thee, that thou hast not sent to me before ; and of the more curious flowering plants or shrubs, I shall always be glad to receive duplicates of the plants, when occasion offers. The *Magnolias, Kalmias, Rhodo-dendrons,* &c., are always acceptable.

I have very few of the American *Martagons,* and should be glad of any varieties that occur. The roots may be taken up and planted in a box of earth, as soon as they have flowered ; some of the seeds may likewise be scattered in the same earth. By these means we have a double chance of raising them ; and this may be successfully practised in many other particulars.

You have a very numerous tribe of plants under the character of *Lychnoideas,* and very great ornaments in their season. It would be worth while to collect as many of these as possible; plant them not far asunder; observe their diversity, and send the most curious. These, next to the Martagons, I should be glad to have. Raise them from seed, at home, and send the plants in boxes of earth, two or three of the different kinds.

The seeds of Pines, and acorns of all sorts, may be promiscuously thrown amongst them. We take care of all the earth we receive plants in, spread it carefully in a border, and oft receive some curiosity which perhaps our correspondents did not know was contained in their present. I think I mentioned the *Colocasia*, in my last,—a water plant with a large pleasing flower, a very broad leaf, and a most singular seed-vessel. It grows in some parts of the Jerseys. Send us some seeds in a pot of mud, just covered with bladder or leather, to keep it a little moist. And some of the large tuberous roots, likewise, some wrapped round with moss and put in a box without anything else, some put in a cask near full of mud, and a few gimlet-holes made in the upper part to admit of a little air. I would not desire thee to travel far in search of anything curious. Observe carefully what lies within the reach of thy usual business; and I shall endeavour to satisfy thee for thy pains herein.

If the seedling plants, intended for me, were planted in boxes early in autumn to take a little root, and sent by the latest ships hither, with the seeds, or else shipped early in the spring, so as to arrive here in the third or fourth month, they would come very seasonably. But please to remember to raise a few of all the curious plants whose seeds occur to thee, and send here, and some of the seeds likewise, together with any account thou can collect of their real virtues and uses.

I believe JOHN BARTRAM'S son had directions from me, through our late friend, P. COLLINSON, to make me a collection of *drawings*, together with an account of all your *land Tortoises*. If, therefore, anything upon this subject occurs to thee, or thou meets with any new kind, please to send them to him.

It is very admirable that you abound with many plants, many animals, altogether unknown in other parts of the globe, not dissimilar in temperature. *Golden rods, Asters, Lychnoideas, Sunflowers,* you have more than all the world besides. *Tortoises,* I think, likewise, and some other animals, are peculiarly abundant with you.

I shall think of the books thou desires, when I can meet with them.

I am thy obliged friend,

JOHN FOTHERGILL.

London, 25th 1st mo. 1769.

London, 15th 3d mo. 1770.

ESTEEMED FRIEND:—

Though I intended thee a long letter, yet I am, through unavoidable engagements, obliged to send thee only two or three lines.

I received the seeds, plants, and cask with the *Colocasia*, in very good order. Nothing ever, I believe, came over in better condition than the plants. I hope some of the roots of the *Colocasia* will live; but they were, some of them, quite rotten by the moisture. It will be a better way, I see, to send them over in moss, than in mud: and please to send me a root or two in this manner, next autumn.

Dr. FRANKLIN will send all the instruments thou requests, for which I shall pay him, cheerfully. Some of the books thou desires are, at present, out of print; but I shall get and send the rest as soon as I can.

I have sent, under Captain FALCONER'S care, an empty box, locked, and the key secured to one of the handles. It is designed to secure any *Insects* that may fall in thy way. The drawers are lined with cork; and it will be easy to fix either Moths, Flies, or Beetles upon them, so as to come with safety. A great variety of Beetles must be found under the bark of all your old decayed trees.

Continue to send me such new seeds or plants as occur to thee. *Ferns* and *Polypodiums*, of many kinds, are yet to be found among you; many water plants, likewise, which, wrapt in wet moss, would come to us safe.

A friend of mine has lately published a tract, describing in what manner plants may be best conveyed to us, together with a description of your *Dionœa*. Perhaps it may afford thee some little assistance in sending thy plants over.

I doubt not but you have many curious *herbaceous* plants yet unnoticed: struck with the greater objects of shrubs and trees, these humbler ones have been overlooked. Get a complete collection of these into some corner of thy garden, and send us a few roots, as thou art able to propagate them. There are few trees in your parts, and not many shrubs, which we have not in our gardens. We have many herbaceous plants, likewise; but I dare say, a very small number of those that are natives of your parts of America. Look carefully after some *Ferns* for me; as also *bulbous* plants, as they flower early, for the most part: and all sweet-scented or showy flowers, or such as are of known efficacy in the cure of some diseases.

Thy account of the long-lived *Tortoise* is very agreeable; and I am much obliged to thy correspondent, BARTRAM, for some curious drawings. He has a very good hand; and I shall be glad to receive from him all his works, and satisfy him for his trouble, when he informs me how much I am indebted to him.

Perhaps thou will be surprised, when I tell thee one of my principal inducements to make these collections. It is, that when I grow old, and am unfit for the duties of a most active life, I may have some little amusement in store to fill up those hours, when bodily infirmity may require some external consolations.* I hope, however, not to forget that there are others, much more adequate to the desires of our better part; that part which, when separated from the body, may be enabled to see in a moment all that we seek for here with much solicitude and industry, and yet see it but in part.

Farewell, I hope thou will hear from me again, in summer.

J. FOTHERGILL.

London, 11th 2d mo., 1771.

ESTEEMED FRIEND :—

I have now before me thy two kind letters, one of the 25th 5 mo., the other, the 19th 11 mo., 1770. The former contains some

---

* The following passage, from the writings of that eminent botanist, Sir JAMES EDWARD SMITH, is admirably in harmony with the views and sentiments of Doctor F., as indicated in the text. "How delightful and how consolatory is it, among the disappointments and anxieties of life, to observe science, like virtue, retaining its relish to the last; smoothing the bed of age and infirmity, preserving the mind young and vigorous, alive to all its enjoyments, amid the wreck of its frail cottage; while, in communicating its own ardour and its own light to others, it tastes the happiness of a good father, who feels himself living over again in his children."

pertinent accounts of the medicinal effects of some of your native simples, for which I am much obliged to thee. It is quite proper to record all useful observations relative to your indigenous simples. It requires a long time, and much experience, to know the use of any one medicine. We are apt sometimes to ascribe effects to wrong causes : and if a disorder wears off, after the use of any medicine, it is usual to place the recovery to the account of the medicine.

The *Sassafras Bark*, I think, is a good medicine in various complaints ; and especially in all such as seem to arise from a thin, sharp, scorbutic humour, especially in cold constitutions, or aged people. From its sensible qualities it seems likely to expel wind, correct sharpness of the blood, and, if given properly, to increase urine and sweat. Attend to its effects, and give a strong infusion of it, in such of the complaints as may seem to proceed from these causes.

We are so well pleased with our *Ipecacuanha*, it operates so certainly, so gently, that we shall scarcely be soon prevailed on to admit of any substitute. I wish, however, your Ipecac. may be attended to. Gather it when the leaves are decaying : wash it clean, dry it in the shade, and powder it fine. In case of sickness, where a vomit is required, give ten grains ; wait half an hour, give a second dose, and try by such means how small a quantity will answer the purpose.

I should be exceedingly glad to hear that you had any indigenous medicine, or simple, that would operate pretty freely, and certainly, by urine. We want such a remedy much. We can promote all the natural discharges, with some degree of certainty, but this. We can vomit, purge, sweat, to what degree we please ; but we have no certain diuretic. This is much wanted in the cure of dropsies, and other complaints. Listen carefully after such a remedy. And now to thy second letter.

Captain OSBORNE has been arrived some time ; but has been hindered from delivering his goods, by a severe frost, and the want of hands, from pressing. The *plants* and *seeds* are, however, at length delivered, and sent down to my garden, but I have not yet seen in what condition. We have still a hard frost, and much snow, so that I must keep them as they are, till the weather breaks. In the Catalogue, I see a great number of curious things ; and we shall take all the care we can to raise them, and revive the plants.

The box with *Insects*, by Captain SPARKS, came very safe, and the insects in tolerable condition, for the most part. Some of them had suffered, by being put up in the box before they were quite dry, and from insects that had got amongst them. I have returned the box for another cargo, if any variety occur; and likewise for duplicates of as many of those that were first sent to me, as may be easily procured, for most of them were damaged. Your *Cedar* is too hard and gummy. It exudes a kind of liquor that spoils insects. Your softest *Fir* would do much better. But my box is preferable to anything. Let the boxes be taken out and well dried, before any insects are put in. Let the insects likewise be well dried, and a bit of camphire and powdered pepper be tied in a rag, and fixed in each partition.

As I have now got most of the common American plants in plenty, I would not give thee the trouble of sending more seeds or plants, of the kinds I have received from thee, except such as I may hereafter desire to make up for my defects. Any new kinds, either plants or seeds, will be very acceptable.

WILLIAM YOUNG sends his plants over very safely, by wrapping them up in moss, and packing them pretty close in a box. They come thus very safe, and we lose very few of them. He ties the moss in a ball about the roots, with a piece of packthread or matting, or hemp strings, and puts them so close as to prevent them from shaking about in the box. It is surprising how well they keep in this manner. I have recommended the following method to my friends, likewise, of sending over *seeds* in a vegetating condition:—Make a box of any width and length, but not very deep; six or seven inches may be sufficient. Cover the bottom with moss (*Sphagnum*), not quite dry. On this lay acorns, or any large kinds of seeds. Cover these with moss, and upon that another layer of large seeds, in patches; that is, half a dozen, or half a score together, according to their plenty. Cover these with moss, and strew on the top, in patches likewise, any small scarce seeds. These, sent off in autumn, will be committed to proper earth early in the spring, here, and will probably supply us with many plants that we should otherwise procure with difficulty.

I wish we may be successful with the *Colocasia*. We will do all we can, and I shall acquaint thee with the success.

The *Alder* is a fine one; the seeds are taken care of, but try to propagate it both by seeds, layers, and cuttings; and let us have a few plants.

I hope to write to thee again, by Captain OSBORNE. In the mean time, accept my grateful acknowledgments, and think me to be thy obliged friend,

J. FOTHERGILL.

P. S. The *Mocking-Bird* unfortunately perished in the passage. The box for Insects will come by Captain OSBORNE.

London, 23d 4th mo., 1771.

ESTEEMED FRIEND :—

I acquainted thee, in a letter by Captain SPARKS, that I had received all thy cargo safe and in good order. We have had a winter exceedingly unfavourable to Botany. Not less than four successive frosts, with intervening thaws of a few days' continuance, so that many hardy things have suffered much. I had luckily ordered all the. plants I received from America, the beginning of winter, to be planted, and then covered quite over with dry fern. This has preserved them from the severe weather; and I have reason to think I shall not lose a plant.

Our winter was not vigorous ; but the spring has been so, and I believe no one remembers the like. We have not the least verdure in the fields; no green on the hedges; not a leaf on any tree, the Gooseberrys excepted; and these are not fully expanded. I think we are almost *six weeks* later than I have seen. Not a Pear tree yet in bloom.

These serve to accompany my empty box for Insects, and a little box of roots of the Alpine Strawberry. If these do not arrive in a growing condition, I will send thee seeds, and some plants, early in the autumn. Let the beds they are planted on be dug up, every two years, or they will degenerate, and plant fresh ones. They continue good, two successive years; the third, they grow small and lose their flavour.

In the insect box I have put up a little tract, tending to show in what manner *plants* may be best conveyed to Europe, and *insects* collected. There is, likewise, a small Botanical Dictionary, and an introduction to a translation of some of LINNÆUS'S works, which I thought would not be wholly useless to thee, or unacceptable.

If thou wants any further helps, that I can give thee, let me know, and I shall supply them as far as I can.

I am not yet in possession of a living root of your great Water Lily, or *Colocasia*. I could wish to have a large one taken up in autumn, well wrapped up in moss, and sent as early as may be convenient, or else soon in the spring.

I think I pointed out a method of sending over seeds in a state of vegetation, by putting them on moist moss. All sorts of acorns may be brought over this way, in a vegetating state, as well as other seeds.

I am now in possession of the common North American plants; but there are new discoveries made every day. Early spring flowers of any kind, or plants or shrubs that are either useful or curious in their appearance, will be acceptable; and I shall not value the things I receive merely by their quantity, but their worth, when viewed in the light I have described. A curious *Fern* is as acceptable to me as the most showy plant.

If the box for insects is returned, please to deliver the key to the Captain, that he may have it to open the box at the Custom House; otherwise it will be broke open, and the insects by this means demolished.

I am economist enough to save the covers of my letters, instead of throwing them into the fire. I give them to my gardener to wrap his seeds in; some of them I have thrust into the empty box, for the like purpose.

If I should omit sending thee the future translations of LINNÆUS's work, put me in mind of it.

I am thy assured friend,

J. FOTHERGILL.

Near Middlewich, in Cheshire, 9th mo. 1772.

ESTEEMED FRIEND, H. MARSHALL :—

Though I write this at a great distance from London, I have not left that city, or its neighbourhood. For about ten weeks, every summer, my sister and myself retire to this distance, in order to enjoy a little quiet, and recess from the constant hurry we are kept in during our residence in town. For, between the business of my profession, attention to some services in the Society, and various other engagements, I am kept in as constant a state of full engagement as I know how to undergo. It is from this place, commonly, that I endeavour to borrow a little time for my correspondence. But the last year, I was even deprived of this opportunity, by the necessity I was put under of defending myself against an adversary of the worst sort, a man of much cunning, and very little principle. From this I am in part released, though not entirely; for though a court of justice set aside an award most partial and unjust, even from the very evidence he himself brought to prevent its being set aside; yet his rancour is such, that in anything he can possibly disquiet me, I know he will endeavour to do it. This affair claimed a good deal of the time that I could have wished to dispose of in a more agreeable manner;—to have recruited my worn out strength; and to have acknowledged the kindnesses I had received from my correspondents, thyself in particular.

But such was my embarrassment, both during my stay here, and the crowd of business that oppressed me at my return to London, that it was not in my power to write a single letter to any friend in America, except one or two on business of extreme urgency.

I have given thee this full account of my situation, in order to inform thee of the occasion of my silence, and which I think thou will acknowledge is not of the least moment. Another distressing circumstance, likewise, during the winter and the spring, kept my mind exceedingly engaged; and that was my deceased brother Samuel's indisposition. He lived near two hundred miles from me, so that it was not in my power to attend him personally. My sister was much with him; and I saw him before his conclusion. But the necessity of frequently corresponding with his physicians, and my own anxiety about him, joined to all the other occupations I was engaged in, indeed, kept my head and hands and heart as fully engaged as I know how to express. He was removed just as our yearly meeting was over; and I came down hither to feel more fully than I could before, how much of my comfort in this life was taken away from me. A brother—a friend—a counsellor—an example—a cause of much reputation to his family and the church, all in one valuable life. But we know not what is best; only, that we endeavour to profit by such dispensations, and to sit looser and looser to every enjoyment here. By the favour of Providence, this I hope will be my future engagement, and to look at the end of all things.

Thy exceedingly valuable box of plants came very safe, and I

hope we did not lose the least particle of a root: for we save all
the earth, and even the moss, from America, throw it upon some
vacant border, and cover it with a little earth, that even if a few
casual seeds should be in it, we may save them.

Our spring was late and unfriendly to plants, so that many were
but just showing themselves above ground when I came away
(about two months ago); but my gardener writes to me, that they
are in a very prosperous condition, and some never seen in England before. Under a north wall, I have a good border, made up
of that kind of rich black turf-like soil, mixed with some sand, in
which I find most part of the American plants thrive best. It has
a few hours of the morning and evening sun, and is quite sheltered
from mid-day heats. They are well supplied with water during
summer; and the little shrubs, and herbaceous plants, have a good
warm covering of dry fern, thrown over them when the frosts set
in. This is gradually removed, when the spring advances, so that,
by never being frozen in the ground while the plants are young
and tender, I never lose any that come to me with any degree of
life in them; and it is acknowledged by the ablest botanists we
have, that there is not a richer bit of ground, in curious American
plants, in Great Britain: and for many of the most curious, I am
obliged to thy diligence and care. My garden is well sheltered;
the soil is good, and I endeavour to mend it as occasion requires.
I have an Umbrella Tree, above twenty feet high, that flowers with
me abundantly, every spring. The small *Magnolia*, likewise,
flowers with me finely. I have a little wilderness, which, when I
bought the premises, was full of old Yew trees, Laurels, and weeds.
I had it cleared, well dug, and took up many trees, but left others
standing for shelter. Among these I have planted *Kalmias*, *Azaleas*, all the *Magnolias*, and most other hardy American shrubs.
It is not quite eight years since I made a beginning; so that my
plants must be considered but as young ones. They are, however,
extremely flourishing. The great *Magnolia* has not yet flowered
with me, but grows exceedingly fast. I shelter his top in the
winter; he gains from half a yard to two feet in height, every
summer, and will ere long, I doubt not, repay my care with his
beauty and fragrance.

Amongst the rest of the plants, which thou had sent me, was
the *Claytonia*, of which there is not, I believe, another plant in
England: a new species of *Serapion*; and a most curious *Adian-*

tum. Other things will show themselves, I doubt not, to both our satisfaction.

It has given me much concern, that I could not, before this time, give thee the satisfaction of knowing that thy endeavours to serve me have been so effectual and pleasing.

I did not intend that the boxes, in which the seeds were to be conveyed should be divided into small partitions. It will be sufficient, if the several acorns of the same kind, and seeds, likewise are laid upon the mosses in little patches, asunder from each other, and that the moss should be nearly quite dry. The acorns succeeded extremely well; we scarcely lost a single one, and a fine collection of Oaks I have.

I just received thy last letter, the 8th of 5th mo., 1772, together with the box of snakes, &c., as I was leaving London; which was very acceptable. And thou will plainly see by this, that I have no intention of dropping my correspondence with thee. On the contrary, I shall endeavour, as well as I can, to acknowledge the labour and time thou employs so successfully in adding to my collection.

In about two weeks, we shall leave this place, and return to our habitation in the city. If the ships are not all sailed for your port, I propose to send some books by them, which I hope may prove acceptable. And in the mean time, I shall be glad thou may now and then be picking up one little addition or another, to the stock of plants thou hast already furnished me with.

The *Tetragonotheca*, a native of your Province, but known chiefly, I believe, to JOHN BARTRAM, is no longer in England. I write to him by this opportunity, to request a root or two, if he can procure them, or a few seeds. If they fall in thy way, please to add them to the rest. I had a plant of the great American *Nymphœa* [*Nelumbium*], from W. YOUNG. It put out leaves, and the appearance of a flower; but did not flourish. I should be glad of another root, if it could be easily obtained. It will come safe in a little box by itself, wrapped up in wet moss. I will put it into another piece of water. From the seeds I expect nothing: I have tried them in all the manners I could, set in mud, and kept in the open air, in the green-house, the stove, but in vain; and I believe no person has been much more successful, or if a plant has been raised, it has not prospered.

I know not whether J. BARTRAM or any of his family continue

to send over boxes of seeds as usual. He collected them with much care, and they mostly gave satisfaction. W. YOUNG has been very diligent, but has glutted the market with many common things; as the *Tulip trees*, *Robinias*, and the like. But, contrary to my opinion, he put them into the hands of a person who, to make the most of them, bought up, I am told, all the old American seeds that were in the hands of the seedsmen here, and mixed them with a few of W. YOUNG'S, to increase the quantity. Being old and effete, they did not come up; and have thereby injured his reputation. I am sorry for him; have endeavoured to help him; but he is not discreet.

The Insects should be put into the box as dry as may be; and the box itself should also be well dried, either in the sun, or before a good fire. They are apt to be mouldy for want of this little caution, and soon perish.

Having proceeded thus far, I shall conclude this before I leave the country; and add what may be farther necessary, when I come to London. In the mean time, I think myself thy much-obliged friend,

JOHN FOTHERGILL.

London, 6th 2d mo., 1773.

ESTEEMED FRIEND :—

I received thy box of *Insects* very safe, and in very good order. Many of them are nondescripts; and the rest in excellent order, a few excepted, which had suffered before they were put into the box.

Let it be well dried in the sun or before a fire, before any others are put into it; and deliver the key to the captain, as before, which saves a great deal of trouble.

*   *   *   *   *   *   *

I must desire thee still to proceed in thy vegetable researches, as it falls in thy way. *Bulbous roots* of all kinds are easily conveyed. The *Orchis's*, likewise, may be easily sent. Let them be taken up when the flower fades, with a large clod of earth about them; pick this off carefully, that none of the roots may be broke, and dry them a little in the shade; wrap them in papers, keep them from vermin, and put them up with the other plants, or in a little dry box by themselves. I had an *Orchis* sent me from Philadelphia, in a letter, which is very prosperous. Don't forget the *Fern* tribe. This is a very pleasing part of the creation.

*   *   *   I have sent the second part of LINNÆUS, and shall not omit the rest, as they are published. I have also sent a few numbers (all that are yet published), of a very useful work for young botanists, now carrying on here. There are three plates to each plant, and one sheet of description. The coloured plates make the price high; and the whole, when finished, will come to upwards of 15 guineas. These will not be half the money; and in respect to use, are as valuable as the whole. I shall continue to send them to thee, as they come out, which is very slowly.

A set of WILLIAM PENN'S select works, some smaller series, and the Insect Apparatus, will make up my present cargo. I consider myself much in thy debt; and shall procure thee anything here thou chooses to have, to the value of ten guineas, or make thee a remittance of that sum, if thou chooses it, which may entitle me to thy future regard, in these respects: for the labourer is worthy of his hire.

The insects were, divers of them, singularly beautiful, the moth tribe especially. We have not yet succeeded with the *Colocasia.* I think the water about this city does not suit it; but try to get us some good roots. I think by the help of such a bended fork as is used by farmers to drag the dung out of their carts, tied to the end of a long pole, would fetch up a good root; and I am persuaded it would come as safe in a box of wet moss, as by any means whatsoever. The best time would be to take it up late in autumn, and send it home by the spring ships. I see by the Chinese drawings, that it grows in shallow ponds very freely, as well as in their deep waters.

We have got the true *Tea Plant,* at length, in England. We are endeavouring to propagate it, and hope we shall succeed, not so as to raise it as a commodity, but merely, in this country, as a curious article. It would thrive in Virginia and Maryland extremely well. I propose to send thee a pretty good account of it, wrote by an acquaintance of mine.

I think the account of the deluge contains as many things untrue as true. I have it not by me; but if I meet with it, I will endeavour not to forget it.

This little cargo I expect will be delivered by Dr. PARKE, whose

conduct has gained him esteem, and whose future usefulness to
community, I trust, will gain him deserved reputation.

I am thy obliged friend,

JOHN FOTHERGILL.

London, 28th 6 mo., 1774.

ESTEEMED FRIEND :—

I received thy last favour, and am obliged to thee for thy kind
intention of looking out for a few more plants for me.

I hope the glasses came safe, and were agreeable to thy orders.
I intended them as a compensation for thy endeavours to serve me,
and shall readily do what further thou may think needful, as an
equivalent. I have sent two more numbers of MILLER's botanical
work; and a treatise on *Coffee*, with an excellent coloured plate.
Nothing more of LINNÆUS's is yet translated; when it is, I shall
not fail to send it.

I shall hope to receive, by the autumn ships, some little addition
to my garden, as it may occasionally fall in thy way. I have most
of your usual plants; but there are divers still unnoticed. I hope I
have a plant of your large *Nymphæa*; but, for all that, I should
be exceedingly glad to have another. If seeds are sent, be kind
enough to crack the shells of some of them before they are put into
the mud they should be sent in. I find the shells are so hard, that
they will not give way to the embryo plant without this aid, at
least in this country.

Look carefully after your *Ferns*. You have a great variety. I
have more American Ferns·than most of my acquaintance; but I
know you must have more, and various *Polypodies*, likewise. I am
reckoned to have the best collection of North American Plants of
any private person in the neighbourhood. I am obliged to thee
for many of them; and shall readily make what acknowledgment
thou thinks proper, if I do not do it quite to thy satisfaction.

When I sent the glasses away, I had not time to write a line to
anybody. As I am just retiring from this place, for a few weeks,
I may possibly get time to look over thy letters again, and get
leisure to acknowledge them more at large. Tell me wherein I
can make thee any suitable compensation, and I shall do it very
cheerfully :—

Being thy assured friend,

JOHN FOTHERGILL.

23d, 8 mo., 1775.

ESTEEMED FRIEND :—

I am much obliged to thee for several very kind letters, and a box of plants, amongst which are some *new Ferns*, and a few other rare plants. For these, and many others, I am still in thy debt, but, at present, without any opportunity of repaying thee.

I sent the last numbers of the plates that are published; and am not quite sure if I did not send one twice over. If I did, only let me know it; it needs not be returned. I hope it will be finished the next spring; and I shall send it as I may have opportunity.

At present, I cannot expect anything, as all intercourse between America and Britain will be cut off, and I am afraid for a long time. Be attentive, however, to increase thy collection at home, by putting every rare plant thou meets with in a little garden, and as much like their natural situation, as to shade, dryness or moisture, as possible. For instance, most of the Ferns like shade and moisture; these may be planted on some north border, where the sun shines but little except in the morning; and so of the rest.

A little mattock and a spade are the best instruments for taking up plants. With the first, make a little trench round the plant, at some distance, then raise up a large ball with the spade ; the earth may then be gently pared away, so as not to hurt the roots, and in this manner it may be safely conveyed any whither, and in any season. I write this from *Cheshire*, one hundred and sixty miles from London, to which place I retire for a couple of months every year. Nearer London, I should have no quiet. My garden is about five miles from London, warm and sheltered, rather moist than dry ; and I have the satisfaction of seeing all North American plants prosper amazingly. There are few gardens in the neighbourhood of London, *Kew* excepted, that can show either so large or so healthy a collection.

I have there, likewise, a fine young *Tea tree*. It is now, my gardener writes me word, seven feet and a half high, extending its branches in proportion. It flowered the last year, in autumn, and will do so this. It is in the natural ground, but sheltered in winter by a glass, and covered at night with a mat. It is the finest Tea-tree in Europe. We are endeavouring to increase it, both by cuttings and layers.

Many of thy plants are there in good perfection. The poor *Turtle* came to us alive, and continued some months. We suspected he had got some hurt on board the ship, as he looked uncommonly heavy about the eyes, and did not care for stirring. He had water enough, and land at his choice, and also the shelter of a warm hovel. I am not, however, the less obliged to thee for thy kind attention.

When once the communication is opened, let me know how I can, most satisfactorily to thyself, discharge the debt I have contracted, and I will do it speedily. I have forborne taking any notice, till now, of the public distress that now afflicts America, and must soon, in some shape, come home to ourselves. I do not think that our superiors will at all listen to any terms, but such as must be disagreeable to America. I therefore expect that much mischief will be done, that a large army will be sent over, and that orders will be given to wage war in every part of America.

I have no other foundation for this opinion, than from what appears to be the general tendency of the preparations, and the infatuation of the times.

It seems not unlikely but we may be rendered a severe scourge to each other. It will be happy for those who know where to seek for a quiet habitation, both internally and externally.

This I wish most sincerely for all my friends, myself, and everybody. What little lay within my reach to do, I have endeavoured to do it honestly; but it's all in vain. Providence may see meet, by this dreadful work, to bring us back to ourselves, and rouse us to better considerations. Many lives will be lost, many fine fabrics demolished, the labour of ages ruined; and all this chiefly at the instigation of some proud discontented people, who have been in office in America: and I am sorry to join with them the generality of the Scotch, many of whom being high in authority here, and seeing the * * * *† rather set against you, urge on these violent councils; in the first place, to gain favour with * * *, and in the next, to wreak their revenge on the English, by setting them to work to destroy one another.

Whilst the packets continue to sail, it will not be very difficult, now and then, to send little parcels of curious seeds in a letter to thy assured friend.

† The *King*, is obviously the word intended to fill the blanks, prudently left in this letter. The same prudential motive, no doubt, induced Dr. F. to omit putting his name to this, his *last* epistle to our countryman.

P.S. I omitted to mention, in the inclosed, that the two little *owls*, by Captain FALCONER, came very safe and healthy. We put them into an open and proper cage, secure enough from vermin of any large kind,—as rats, weasels, and the like : but one morning, the larger was found killed, and its brains picked out. We attributed this to its mate ; but if so, it was not for want, for they had always plenty of victuals.

The *instruments* are all sent by Dr. FRANKLIN ; and I shall call to pay for them in a few days. If a bill is not inclosed with them, I think it not improper for thy own satisfaction to know that they cost £14. 16*s.* 6*d.* Captain FALCONER is very careful of everything sent under his care for me ; and as we are at a considerable distance from one another, I do not sometimes see him, to make proper acknowledgments. As thou mentions J. HUNT's name, it puts me in mind to ask whether thou received the ten guineas I sent by him. Farewell.

DOCTOR FRANKLIN TO HUMPHRY MARSHALL.

London, July 9th, 1769.

SIR :—

I received your obliging favour of April 13th, with specimens of the several *colours* suitable for painting, which you have found in different parts of our country. It gives me great pleasure to see them ; and I have shown them to many persons of distinction, together with your letter, which is allowed to contain a great many sensible and shrewd observations.

There is at present an appearance as if the great ones were about to change their conduct towards us : I believe they begin to be a little sensible of their error.

It is perhaps too much to expect that they will become thoroughly wise at once ; but a little time, with a prudent, steady conduct on our side, will, I hope, set all right. I shall be obliged by a continuance of your correspondence, being, very respectfully, sir,

Your most obedient, humble servant,

B. FRANKLIN.*

---

* Those letters of Dr. FRANKLIN, which were not sent by a private conveyance, were forwarded post-free, and are endorsed by him at the lower left-hand corner, with the words " *B. Free Franklin.*"

London, March 18th, 1770.

Sir :—

I was duly favoured with yours of October 30th, and glad to hear that some of the colours, on experience, were found useful. I showed the specimens you sent me to an ingenious, skilful French chemist, who has the direction of the Royal Porcelaine Manufacture, at *Sevres*, near Paris, and he assured me that one of those white earths would make a good ingredient in that kind of ware.

Our people in Philadelphia have done well in keeping, as you say they do, steady to their agreements for non-importation. The duties on paper, glass, and colours, are now repealed; and if our merchants continue their resolutions another year, there is good reason to believe all the rest will follow. Should any of the merchants give way, and import, which I trust they will not, I hope the country people will have the good sense and spirit not to buy; and then the others will soon be weary of importing.

Certainly we are under small obligation to the merchants here, who grow rich by our folly, and yet moved in this affair but slowly; and under none to the manufacturers, who refused to move at all.

The nation are all besotted with the fancy that we cannot possibly do without them, and must of course comply at last. But, if we encourage necessary manufactures among ourselves, and refrain buying the superfluities of other countries, a few years will make a surprising change in our favour, in the plenty of real money that must flow in among us, and the rising value of our estates.

Immediately on the receipt of your letter, I ordered a reflecting *telescope* for you, which was made accordingly. Dr. Fothergill has since desired me to add a *microscope* and *thermometer*, and will pay for the whole. They will go with Captain Falconer.

I thank you for the *seeds*, with which I have obliged some curious friends.

I am, sir, your most obedient servant,

B. Franklin.

London, April 22d, 1771.

SIR :—

I duly received your favours of the 4th of October, and the 17th of November. It gave me pleasure to hear, that tho' the merchants had departed from their agreement of non-importation, the spirit of industry and frugality was likely to continue among the people.

I am obliged to you for your concern on my account. The *letters*, you mention, gave great offence here; but that was not attended with the immediate ill consequences to my interest, that seem to have been hoped for by those that sent copies of them hither.

If our country people would well consider, that all they save in refusing to purchase foreign gewgaws, and in making their own apparel, being apply'd to the improvement of their plantations, would render those more profitable, as yielding a greater produce, I should hope they would persist resolutely in their present commendable industry and frugality. And there is still a farther consideration. The Colonies that produce provisions grow very fast; but of the countries that take off those provisions, some do not increase at all, as the European nations, and others, as the West India colonies, not in the same proportion. So that, though the demand at present may be sufficient, it cannot long continue so. Every manufacturer encouraged in our country, makes part of a market for provisions within ourselves, and saves so much money to the country, as must otherwise be exported to pay for the manufactures he supplies. Here, in England, it is well known and understood, that wherever a manufacture is established, which employs a number of hands, it raises the value of lands in the neighbouring country all around it, partly by the greater demand near at hand for the produce of the land, and partly from the plenty of money drawn, by the manufacturers, to that part of the country. It seems, therefore, the interest of all our farmers, and owners of land, to encourage our young manufactures, in preference to foreign ones imported among us from distant countries.

I am much obliged by your kind present of curious *seeds*. They were welcome gifts to some of my friends. I send you, herewith, some of the new *Barley* lately introduced into this country, and now highly spoken of. I wish it may be found of use with us.

I was the more pleased to see, in your letter, the improvement of our *paper*, having had a principal share in establishing that manufacture among us, many years ago, by the encouragement I gave it.

If in anything I can serve you here, it will be a pleasure to
Your obliged friend and humble servant,
B. FRANKLIN.

London, March 20th, 1772.
SIR :—

I received your obliging letter of Nov. 27th. It was forwarded to me from Bristol, by Mr. COWPER, who mentioned on the back of it, that the box should be forwarded, also, as soon as it came on shore. Not receiving it in some time, I wrote to him about it, and had for answer, that it had been sent three weeks since, and I should find it, on inquiry, at Gerrard's Hall, Basing Lane. I have inquired there, and they know nothing of it; so, I fear it is lost, which I am the more concerned at, as your *Observations* were in it, which I am now deprived of. I shall, however, make some farther inquiry, and write to you more fully per next opportunity. In the mean time, it is both Dr. FOTHERGILL'S advice and mine, that you never send anything, for London, by way of Bristol, that conveyance being subject to such accidents, but always directly hither.

I am, sir, your obliged friend and humble servant,
B. FRANKLIN.

London, Feb. 14th, 1773.
SIR :—

A considerable time after its arrival, I received the box of *seeds* you were so good as to send me, the beginning of last year, with your *Observations on the Spots of the Sun.** The seeds I distributed among some of my friends who are curious: please to accept my thankful acknowledgments for them. The *Observations* I communicated to our astronomers of the Royal Society, who are much pleased with them, and hand them about from one to another, so that I have had little opportunity of examining them myself, they not being yet returned to me.

Here are various opinions about the solar spots. Some think

* For a portion of these "Observations," see the Transactions of the Royal Society, at London, vol. lxiv. p. 194.

them vast *clouds* of smoke and soot, arising from the consuming
fuel on the surface, which clouds at length take fire again on their
edges, consuming and daily diminishing till they totally disap-
pear. Others think them spots of the surface, in which the fire
has been extinguished, and which by degrees are rekindled. It is,
however, remarkable, that tho' large spots are seen gradually to
become small ones, no one has observed a small spot gradually to
become a large one ; at least, I do not remember to have met with
such an observation. If this be so, it would seem that they are
suddenly formed of the full size. And perhaps if there were more
such constant and diligent observers as you, some might happen to
be observing at the instant such a spot was formed, when the appearances might give some ground of conjecture by what means
they were formed.

The professor of astronomy at Glasgow, Dr. WILSON, has a new
hypothesis. It is this : that the sun is a globe of solid matter, all
combustible perhaps, but whose surface only is actually on fire to
a certain depth, and all below that depth unkindled; like a log of
wood whose surface, to half an inch deep, may be a burning coal,
while all within remains wood. Then he supposes, that by some
explosion, similar to our earthquakes, the burning part may be
blown away from a particular district, leaving bare the unkindled
part below, which then appears a spot, and only lessens as the
fluid burning matter by degrees flows in upon it on all sides, and
at length covers or rekindles it. He founds this opinion on certain
appearances of the edges of the spots, as they turn under the sun's
disk, or emerge again on the other side ; for, if they are such
hollows in the sun's face, as he supposes, and the bright border
round the edges be the fluid burning matter flowing down the banks
into the hollow, it will follow, that while a spot is in the middle of
the sun's disk, the eye, looking directly upon the whole, may discern that border all round ; but when the hollow is moved round to
near the edge of the disk, then, though the eye, which now views
it aslant, can see full the farthest bank, yet that which is nearest
is hidden and not to be distinguished. And when the same spot
comes to emerge again on the other side of the sun, the bank which
before was visible is now concealed, and that concealed which before
was visible, gradually changing, however, till the spot reaches the
middle of the disk, when the bank all round may be seen as before.
Perhaps your telescope may be scarce strong enough to observe
this. If it is, I wish to know whether you find the same appear-

ances. When your *Observations* are returned to me, and I have considered them, I shall lodge them among the papers of the society and let you know their sentiments.

As to procuring you a correspondence with some ingenious gentleman here, who is curious, which you desire, I find many who like to have a few seeds given them, but do not desire large quantities; most considerable gardens being now supply'd, like Doctor FOTHERGILL'S, with what they choose to have; and there being nurserymen now here, who furnish what particulars are wanted, without the trouble of a foreign correspondence and the vexations at the custom-house. You will therefore oblige me by letting me know if in any other way I can be serviceable to you.

With great respect and esteem, I am, sir, your most obedient humble servant,

B. FRANKLIN.

London, June 26th, 1774.

DEAR SIR:—

I received and am obliged by your favour of May 14, in which you express so fully your just sentiments of the present disputes between the two countries, as to give me great satisfaction. Here is at present, great inquiry after news from America, our friends wishing to hear of our steadiness, and our enemies fearing it; for if these their violent measures do not succeed, they must quit their places to men of more moderation and wisdom. And we have reason to hope they will not succeed in making us submit to be taxed from hence; for if they once get that settled, they will fix our fetters for ever, making us pay the charge of the iron; that is, we must maintain the soldiers necessary to compel the payment of those taxed, and a train of placemen and pensioners besides, to harass and oppress us. Nothing will, as you observe, restore harmony, but the good old way of requisition from the crown, and voluntary grants from the people.

Your remarks on the spots in the sun were well received by the Royal Society, and are taken notice of in the Transactions.

I do not enlarge, as I hope soon to have the pleasure of conversing with you; being, with much esteem,

Dear sir,

Your most obedient humble servant,

B. FRANKLIN.

London, March 13th, 1775.

SIR :—

I duly received your favour of Nov. the 26th, but having mislaid it, I postponed answering it till I should find it, not recollecting perfectly what were the books you wrote for. I now send the Nautical Almanack for the current year ; that for 1776 is not yet published. The *Philosophical Transactions*, if you mean a complete set, will cost near £30. Therefore, not knowing fully your mind, I have not bought them.

The controversy will soon end in our favour, notwithstanding the present measures, if America is steady in the non-consumption agreement. All the hopes and dependence of the ministry are in dividing us, by working upon our fears and hopes. If we are faithful to each other, our adversaries are ruined.

I am, with much esteem, sir,
Your most obedient humble servant.

Philadelphia, May 23d, 1775.

DEAR SIR :—

I received your favour of the 13th inst. I think, with you, that the non-importation and non-exportation, well adhered to, will end the controversy in our favour. But, as Britain has begun to use force, it seems absolutely necessary that we should be prepared to repel force by force, which I think, united, we are well able to do.

It is a true old saying, that *make yourselves sheep and the wolves will eat you:* to which I may add another, *God helps them that help themselves.*

With much esteem, I am, sir,
Your most obedient humble servant.*

* In the hurry of writing these last two letters (one immediately before leaving London, and the other soon after his arrival in Philadelphia), Doctor F. omitted to put his name to them. But there is no mistaking the well-known chirography of the originals, and every reader will recognise the familiar maxims of "Poor Richard."

HUMPHRY MARSHALL TO DR. FRANKLIN.

West Bradford, 5th of the 12th mo., 1785.

RESPECTED FRIEND :—

I congratulate thee on thy appointment to the station of President of the State of Pennsylvania ;* and hope thou will be of considerable service, in that public office, by thy deliberate and wise counsels. And if the multiplicity of the business concerning the government of the state should admit of any spare hours, I had it in contemplation to mention to thee for thy approbation, or sentiments thereon, a proposal that I had made, last winter, to my cousin, WM. BARTRAM, and nephew, Dr. MOSES MARSHALL, of taking a tour, mostly through the western parts of our United States, in order to make observations, &c., upon the natural productions of those regions; with a variety of which, hitherto unnoticed, or but imperfectly described, we have reason to believe they abound; which, on consideration, they at that time seemed willing to undertake, and I conceive would be so still, provided they should meet with proper encouragement and support for such a journey ; which they judge would be attended with considerable expense, for the transportation of their collections, &c., and for their subsistence during a period of fifteen or eighteen months, or more, which would at least be necessary for the completion of the numerous observations, and objects they would have to make remarks on, and collect. Should such proposals be properly encouraged, I apprehend they would engage to set out early in the spring, and throughout their journey make diligent search and strict observation upon everything within the province of a naturalist; but more especially upon Botany, for the exercise of which there appears, in such a journey, a most extensive field ; for, from accounts of our western territories, they are said to abound with varieties of strange trees, shrubs, and plants, no doubt applicable

* Doctor FRANKLIN received this appointment, immediately after his return from France, where he had been residing for several years, as Minister Plenipotentiary of the United States. This prompt and earnest appeal, in behalf of the interests of *Natural Science*, at so early a period in the history of this Republic, while it demonstrates the forecast and expanded views of HUMPHRY MARSHALL, does equal honour to the venerable statesman and philosopher to whom it is addressed, by the implied confidence in his liberality and public spirit.

to many valuable purposes in arts or manufactures, and to be replete with various species of earths, stones, salts, inflammables, minerals, and metals (the many uses of obtaining a knowledge of which is sufficiently obvious); remarks, experiments, &c., upon every of which they propose making; as also to make collections, and preserve specimens, of everything that may enrich useful science, or amuse the curious naturalist; to the conducement of which, they would willingly receive and observe any reasonable instructions that might facilitate their discoveries, or direct their researches.

I have taken the freedom to mention these proposals to thee, knowing that thou was always ready and willing to promote any useful knowledge and science, for the use of mankind; and if, on consideration of the premises, thou should approve thereof, thou may communicate them to the members of the Philosophical Society, or any other set of gentlemen, that would be willing or likely to encourage such an undertaking. Perhaps Congress, or some of the members, might promote their going out with the surveyors, when they lay out the several new states.

I conclude, with being fearful of trespassing on thy patience, by adding, that I have ordered my nephew, the Doctor, to present thee with one of my Catalogues of the Forest Trees of our Thirteen United States; which I hope thou'll accept of, for thy perusal. Hoping to be excused for errors, imperfections, &c.

I am thy obliged friend,

And the public's well-wisher,

HUMPHRY MARSHALL.

DR. THOMAS PARKE* TO H. MARSHALL.

Philadelphia, May 4th, 1771.

ESTEEMED FRIEND :—

As I intend to embark for London, in about three weeks' time, I

---

* THOMAS PARKE was born in East Caln Township, Chester County, Pennsylvania, on the 6th of August, 1749. Having a desire to engage in the study of medicine, he went to Philadelphia, at the age of sixteen years, to acquire a preliminary education, and there became the pupil of ROBERT PROUD, the historian. In 1767, he began his medical studies under Dr. CADWALADER EVANS, of Philadelphia, and took the degree of Bachelor of Medicine at the College and Academy, in the same city, on the 5th of June, 1770. In the year 1771, he crossed the Atlantic, to avail himself of the advantages of medical instruction in Great Britain

thought thee might probably have something to send, or communicate by letters, &c., to Drs. FRANKLIN or FOTHERGILL, or
some other of thy correspondents there.

If thee thinks me a convenient opportunity, I shall take a great
pleasure in serving thee, in anything that lays in my power.

I remain thy affectionate friend,

THOMAS PARKE.

London, July 5th, 1772.

ESTEEMED FRIEND :—

I received thy agreeable favour during my abode in Edinburgh.
I should long ere this have done myself the pleasure of answering
it, had not the difficulty of getting a letter conveyed to thee from
Scotland, together with my being much engaged in my studies,
prevented it. I am particularly obliged to thee for thy kind notice
and good wishes. I shall always esteem myself happy if, by ren-

He first visited London, where he enjoyed the friendship and kind offices of the
justly distinguished Dr. JOHN FOTHERGILL. He next proceeded to the school at
Edinburgh, then in the zenith of its strength, where he attended the lectures of
CULLEN, BLACK, and MONRO.

Returning to London, he attended the clinical practice of Guy's and St. Thomas's Hospitals, and finally set his foot on his native shore, in the year 1773.

On the 13th of April, 1775, he was married to RACHEL, eldest daughter of JAMES
PEMBERTON, and immediately established himself in the practice of physic, at No.
20, South Fourth Street, Philadelphia, where he remained upwards of forty years,
well known as a skilful, kind, and attentive physician. In 1816, he removed to
Locust Street, where he resided during the remainder of his life.

He lost his wife, to whom he was most affectionately devoted, in the year 1786;
and never again married. He was a member of the principal scientific, literary,
and benevolent institutions of the city. In January, 1774, he was chosen a
member of the American Philosophical Society. In April, 1776, he became a
contributor to the Pennsylvania Hospital; and in May, 1777, was unanimously
appointed one of the physicians of that institution, a station which he held, unin-
terruptedly, for more than forty-five years. In May, 1778, he was elected a
Director of the Philadelphia Library Company; in which situation he was continued until his death, a period of nearly fifty-seven years. In 1787, the College
of Physicians was established; of which he was one, and remained a member
until his death. At the decease of Dr. ADAM KUHN, he succeeded that gentleman,
as President of the College, in July, 1818.

Doctor PARKE died on the 9th of January, 1835, in the eighty-sixth year of his
age; being at that time the oldest physician in Philadelphia. He was not only
an excellent physician, but also a public-spirited citizen, and an excellent man,
at all times the intimate, the constant, and highly-valued friend of HUMPHRY
MARSHALL.

dering thee any services, I can merit a continuance of thy friendship.

I have taken some pains to oblige thee, in endeavouring to recommend thee to some seedsmen, &c., in England; but fear I have had but poor success, as yet. I shall, however, continue to make inquiry, and if any should choose to employ thee, I shall immediately acquaint thee.

In coming up to London, from Scotland, I came through Derbyshire, in part to endeavour to gain some intelligence of thy father's age, as I remember to hear thee say that thee would be glad to have it exactly ascertained. I made inquiry of some of the oldest people in the neighbourhood of *Gratton* (which was the place I understood he once lived), but none of them could inform me any more than one MARSHALL was born there, but was gone long since.* But there are very few now living at the place, that can

---

* The following extracts from two letters (on one sheet of paper), found among the MARSHALL papers, will throw some light on this subject :—

JOHN MARSHALL, OF GRATTON, TO H. MARSHALL.

COUSIN HUMPHRY :—

I not hearing of your family, of a great number of years, expected I should never have heard of you more; nor had not now, but by Mr. STORRS' inquiry after your father's age, and whether any of his family or relations was living. I, JOHN MARSHALL, am all the nephew your father hath living, and live in a hamlet called Gratton, in the parish of Youlgreave, and in the county of Derbyshire: that is, I live in the same hamlet where my uncle ABRAM was born, and all his brothers. His brothers' names were HUMPHRY, SAMUEL, and JOHN MARSHALL. My father, HUMPHRY, died when he was about sixty years of age,   *   *   * was a stone-cutter, or what we call a mason, and I learned the same trade with my father, and still follow it. I am now in the sixty-eighth year of my age, and have eight children now living, five sons and three daughters.

*   *   *   * Dear cousin, if these lines come safe to you, which I hope they will, I beg you will be so kind, as soon as you conveniently can, as to send me a few lines of the number and welfare of your family: for you see, by my age, that my glass runs apace, and I must expect soon to be called hence; but should be glad, if God permit, to hear from you before I die. May the blessing of God attend you, and all your family, and all your undertakings.

This from your loving cousin,

JOHN MARSHALL.

Gratton, August 14th, 1771.

JOSEPH STORRS TO H. MARSHALL.

Chesterfield, 8th month, 28th, 1771.
FRIEND MARSHALL :—

Thy letter to my father came duly to hand; agreeably whereto, I have made

be called very old, otherwise I might probably have gained a more satisfactory account.

I am happy in being able to inform thee, that I have received many very kind marks of respect from the several gentlemen to whom I was recommended, particularly from Drs. FOTHERGILL and FRANKLIN; which renders an absence from my relations and friends much more agreeable than it otherwise possibly could be. Yet, although I am favoured with the friendship of so many kind and agreeable friends, and situated in a country cultivated to the highest degree, which is really beautiful both from nature and art, America, in my opinion, has something more agreeable. If it is not adorned with the grandeur of England, it is blessed with peace, which many here are strangers to.

Before this comes to hand, thee will probably hear of our friend SAMUEL FOTHERGILL being deceased. He departed the 15th of last month, after a long and tedious illness, of a complicated disease. Thou art too well acquainted with his character, not to be sensible of the great loss his removal will be to the Society.

The curiosity which Captain FALCONER brought from thee for Doctor FOTHERGILL, is seized by the custom-house officers. Whether they will give it up again, is yet a matter of doubt; but I am rather inclined to think they will, as the snake, if entire and alive, would do no harm to the nation: and certainly the skin cannot.

The trading part of the city of London is, and has been for two or three weeks, in great confusion, owing to the failure of several

some inquiry about thy father's age, and thy relations, as follows:—HUMPHRY MARSHALL, the eldest brother of ABRAM, was born and registered at Youlgreave, in the year 1667. ABRAM was the next son, and two years younger, according to thy cousin JOHN's account, but is not to be found in the register. As they were often without a parson, the register was neglected. His sister Sarah married one WILSON, and hath one daughter living, called SARAH. I don't hear of any more of the relations, except JOHN, the writer of the annexed letter, who lives very reputably, and I believe is a sober, religious man (of the Church of England). His children have all done well. *   *   *   *   *   *

One of HUMPHRY's brothers died a *Friend*, at Aldwark, and was buried at Monyash, in this county. Others were most convinced, but not so as to be joined to Friends. This is what intelligence I have procured, and hope will be satisfactory.

Gratton and Youlgreave are about thirteen miles from this place.   *   *   *

I remain thy friend,

JOSEPH STORRS.

of the greatest houses in London, whose connexions being very extensive, have affected trade in general; and occasioned numbers to stop payment all over the nation. Many, experienced in business, say there has not been such a stroke these forty years.

I intended to have given thee some account of my tour through England and Scotland, but find my time and room insufficient; must therefore omit it at present.

Being in haste, I conclude with best wishes for thyself and wife, thy real friend, &c.,

THOMAS PARKE.

P. S. Please to give my respects to Dr. MORRIS as soon as opportunity serves.

Philadelphia, 10th November, 1779.

RESPECTED FRIEND :—

I received thy favour of the 8th instant, requesting my advice in the case of thy nephew, MOSES MARSHALL'S, attending the Medical Lectures this winter. In answer to which I may briefly say, it will undoubtedly tend greatly to improve his medical knowledge, to spend the winter here, as thee mentions; particularly those on Anatomy and Chemistry, with the practice of the Pennsylvania Hospital, of which I can more particularly inform him, on his coming to town. The expense will be considerable. On inquiry, I find the price of each ticket will be £150, current money;* and except in the capacity of an assistant apothecary in the hospital, I know of no place he could be profitably employed: and of this I am not quite certain. Any advice I can give him, he may depend on having cheerfully conferred at all times. *   *   *

We have no late accounts from Dr. FOTHERGILL; though we have reason to believe he is still alive.†

In haste, I remain thy friend,

THOS. PARKE.

* To understand the seeming exorbitance of the price here mentioned, it is only necessary to recollect, that the paper currency of that period, called " continental money," was exceedingly depreciated.

† Dr. FOTHERGILL died, December 26, 1780 : that is, upwards of thirteen months after the date of this letter.

Philadelphia, 5th September, 1782.

The bearer, WILLIAM HAMILTON, Esq., intending to pass through part of Chester County, is desirous of being introduced to my friend MARSHALL'S acquaintance. His knowledge of Botany and Natural History—his taste for cultivating the many curious productions of America, united to his very amiable character—will, I am confident, gain him a welcome reception at *Bradford*.

Any civilities and marks of friendship he may receive, shall be esteemed as obligations conferred on thine, &c.,

THOMAS PARKE.

Philadelphia, 14th March, 1785.

RESPECTED FRIEND :—

I should have answered thy two letters much sooner, had I not waited to gain some intelligence from the Philosophical Society, on the subject of thy nephew's intended *tour to Kentuck*,—which I mentioned to one of the secretaries ; but am sorry to inform thee I can obtain no encouragement for the undertaking. Few among us seem devoted to investigate the beauties of Natural History ; and the expense will fall heavy on individuals, unless the community contribute sufficient to encourage the journey.

Our Legislature are busily engaged in revising the *Funding Bill*, for paying the interest on all public debts. 'Tis not yet finally determined whether it will pass in the form published for consideration ; but it is generally believed a law nearly similar will be enacted this session,—which will saddle the public with heavy taxes for many years, to pay only the interest due on the enormous debt assumed by this state.

The law for building a new *court-house*, &c., in *Chester County*, is (I am informed) likely to be suspended ; which will be throwing away another sum of money,—as I suppose the building already erected will be useless for other purposes, and must have cost a large sum of money.* I remain, with respect and esteem, thy assured friend,

THOMAS PARKE.

* The *court-house* here referred to, was the one erected near the " Turk's Head" —now the *Borough of West Chester*—preparatory to making that place the seat of justice for the ancient county of Chester. That court-house (a wretched spe-

Philadelphia, 27th April, 1785.

RESPECTED FRIEND :—

In answer to thine of yesterday, I now inform thee I received, by the Harmony, Capt. WILLETT, (who arrived a few days ago,) two small parcels ; one from R. BARCLAY, and the other from W. HAMILTON—which the bearer undertakes to deliver to thee. * * *

W. HAMILTON has sent a number of curious flowering shrubs and fruit trees, to be transplanted at his seat on the Schuylkill ; and his gardener informs me, the most of them are healthy, and appear likely to live.

I have lately received a letter from my friend, ROBERT BARCLAY, dated in December last, wherein he requests I would apply to thee to send him a collection of *seeds* of such *herbaceous plants* as were in thy list of the year 1783. He adds, if they could be sent in March, by some safe conveyance, he should be glad to have them forwarded ; but, as his letter did not reach me in time, I expect it will not do to forward them before next fall. However, I leave it to thy better judgment,—and request thee to collect the seeds, and send them when thee thinks the season will be most favourable.

With esteem and respect, I remain thy friend,

THOMAS PARKE.

Philadelphia, 18th June, 1786.

RESPECTED FRIEND :—

A young gentleman being about to sail for London, from whence he intends to go to Edinburgh to finish his medical education, is desirous of taking a box of seeds of the *most curious* flowering shrubs, &c., to present to the Professor of Botany in that University. If they can be procured and sent to Philadelphia by the 22d or 23d inst., they will be in time to reach him before he embarks. He is willing to pay £3 for the collection, and expects to have a sample of the most curious, particularly of the *Franklinia*.

cimen of architecture) was built amidst much strife and contention,—and was finally completed in the year 1786. Sixty years afterwards, it was superseded by an edifice worthy of the county, and creditable to the taste and spirit of an intelligent and prosperous people.

As the vessel is expected to sail the 23d, they must be here by that time; otherwise he cannot receive them.

I am, with respect and esteem, thy friend,

T. Parke.

Philadelphia, 4th September, 1786.

Respected Friend :—

In answer to thine of yesterday, just received, I may inform thee thy friend Samuel Vaughan has determined to return to England. His family are already gone; and he proposes embarking some time this fall, or winter. Though some oddities shade his character, I think he possesses many qualities that might render him a useful member of society in this country.

Our friend Hamilton lately returned from Europe in good health, and much pleased with his tour. I am glad to hear thy nephew is endeavouring to oblige Sir J. Banks. I hope he will succeed. Having no intelligence to add,

I remain, in haste, thy friend,

Thomas Parke.

Philadelphia, 10th October, 1788.

Respected Friend :—

By the Pigou, Captain Sutton, I received several parcels from my friends Barclay and Lettsom; among them, some are intended for thee, which only wait a convenient opportunity to be forwarded. I intended to have sent thee a copy of Walter's *Flora Caroliniana*; but find one is already thy property, by direction of Doctor Lettsom.

Philada., 28th Oct. '88. No opportunity presenting, I could not sooner forward the above. Thy books are now sent by E. Sugar, who brought me thy nephew's favour, with a box for Sir J. Banks, which shall be forwarded by the Pigou, as requested; and as the ship is not expected to sail before the 10th of November, an opportunity is afforded to send anything in answer to Doctor Lettsom's letter.

Being in haste, I must conclude.

With respect, thy assured friend,

T. Parke.

Philadelphia, 18th May, 1789.
RESPECTED FRIEND :—

In answer to thy letter of the 16th instant, I have to inform thee no letters came in the London ships for thee, that I can find.

*   *   *   *   *   *

R. BARCLAY writes me that he is much pleased with the plants received, which, with W. BARTRAM'S drawing of the *Franklinia*, arrived in good order. The botanists in England will not, however, allow it to be properly named.* BARCLAY says he shall want some plants from thee in the fall; and wishes to know whether the *Cranberry plant* cannot be sent to England, to be propagated. In his next letter, he promises to say more on this subject; of which I shall acquaint thee.   *   *   *   *   *

In haste, I am, with esteem, thy friend,

T. PARKE.

Philadelphia, 20th April, 1790.
RESPECTED FRIEND :—

In compliance with thy request, I apply'd to J. B. for the plants thee mentioned. I could not procure the whole number ordered, but, as a great favour, obtained some of each sort, with a few of some he calls a *new species*, as per his account inclosed.

*   *   *   *   *

Did thee not promise some seeds for Lord SUFFIELD ? If a few could be sent him, I think he would be pleased; and as the plants cannot go till the fall, it would manifest an attention to his orders.

Doctor FRANKLIN died a few days since, and is to be buried to-morrow.

I remain, with respect and esteem, thy friend,

T. P.

Philadelphia, 29th April, 1795.
RESPECTED FRIEND :—

Sir JOHN MENZIES wishes to improve his grounds, in Scotland, by mixing such of the American *forest trees* with the native Pines

---

* The *Franklinia* of MARSHALL has been referred to the genus *Gordonia*, of ELLIS, which had the priority; and therefore, according to the canons, must be retained.

of Great Britain, as are likely to agree with the soil and climate; and desires a collection of such trees as can be got in Pennsylvania, or rather, that an assortment of seeds may be sent him by the first opportunity. He also wishes a small assortment of apples, pears, and peaches, of the best grafted or inoculated kinds, in trees of two or three years old, put up in such manner as will most probably secure them for a passage to England.

I shall be obliged to thee, if thee will inform me whether thee can furnish him with the aforesaid articles, and at what time they should be forwarded.   *   *   *   *

I remain, with esteem, thy friend,

THOMAS PARKE.

DR. PARKE TO HUMPHRY AND MOSES MARSHALL.

Philadelphia, 19th October, 1796.

RESPECTED FRIENDS :—

I have received a letter from ROBERT BARCLAY, which contains the following paragraph:—

" Pray desire H. and M. MARSHALL to send me a box of plants for my friend T. KITT, of Norwich, who is well versed in plants, and will be pleased with a nice collection, mixed as usual with herbaceous; remembering to add several *Kalmias, Azaleas,* &c., and everything new or curious."

I expect the ships for London will sail the beginning, or by the middle, of next month, by which time I shall be glad to have the plants, agreeably to my friend ROBERT BARCLAY'S request.

I am, with respect and esteem, your friend,

THOMAS PARKE.

MARY NORRIS* TO H. MARSHALL.

Philada., 12th mo. 23d, 1778.

RESPECTED FRIEND :—

I was glad to find by thy letter that you were favoured with health. We enjoy the same blessing at present.   *   *   *   *   I don't find there is any certain account where the

---

* This excellent lady was the only daughter of JOSEPH and MARY PARKER, of Chester, on the river Delaware ; and, at the date of these letters, was the widow of CHARLES NORRIS, of Philadelphia.

troops, that were said to have embarked, are gone. Everything we hear seems uncertain. As to news, in this place, there seems to be little stirring. If thee has seen the late newspapers, thee must have observed that some of our great people have been vindicating and giving an account of their conduct.* I live so out of the world, I know very little but what is in the public papers.

My cousin DICKINSONS left me this day week. My daughter is gone to Kent with them. When the roads and weather permit, I think thee might spend a few days with thy friends in town.†

*   *   *   *   *

I am thy obliged and affectionate friend,

MARY NORRIS.

Philadelphia, February 3d, 1779.

ESTEEMED FRIEND :—

I am very glad to find that you are favoured with health. We are bravely, and have been so through the winter. My daughter is down in Kent, with Cousin DICKINSONS.   *   *   *

We have had accounts, for some time past, of the English being in Georgia; and now it seems to be confirmed, as it is published in the newspapers that they are in possession of the sea-coast of that

---

* The reference here is, probably, to some controversial publications, which appeared about that time, between SILAS DEANE and the LEES (viz., ARTHUR, RICHARD H., and FRANCIS LIGHTFOOT LEE); in which both parties appealed to the public in vindication of their conduct, as public servants.

† In those days of unaffected hospitality, it was the custom with country people, when they went to "town," to stop without ceremony at the houses of their city friends. The residence of Mrs. NORRIS was usually the city home of HUMPHRY MARSHALL, when he visited Philadelphia. It was also a favourite resort of polished society, whether residents or strangers.

On one occasion, when a French gentleman of distinction was among the visiters, HUMPHRY MARSHALL, in all his old-fashioned plainness and simplicity, arrived. Mrs. NORRIS's daughter DEBORAH (afterwards the accomplished wife of Dr. GEORGE LOGAN) gracefully received her venerable friend from the country, and, with the address of a well-bred lady, introduced him to the distinguished stranger, although not without some slight misgivings, from the apparent want of congruity in the parties thus brought together. She was much gratified, however, to observe that they soon became closely engaged in conversation; and, after they separated, the French gentleman, with an air of lively interest, inquired, "Miss NORRIS, *have you many such men as this Mr.* MARSHALL *among you?*"

state. We have no public account of their being in Carolina, though some think they are, by this time.

Thee will observe, in yesterday's paper, that they have taken a French Island, St. Lucie. General WASHINGTON left Philadelphia yesterday, to go to the army. It was reported, that a party of British troops had landed at Elizabethtown.

We hear many reports, some with, others without foundation. As to what thee says you have heard, of some going away privately, I believe there is nothing in that.

I wish this unhappy affair was settled. If an end is not put to it soon, I don't know how we shall live. For my part I never experienced so many difficulties before. You, who live in the country don't know, nor cannot have an idea of, the expense of living in town now, every necessary is at such an excessive price. The prospect before us looks very dark; to me, never more so than now.

*   *   *   *

I hope, as the spring comes on, I shall have the pleasure of seeing some of you in town. My sons and girls send their love to you.

I am, with kind respects, thy obliged and sincere friend,

MARY NORRIS.

I don't know the date of the prophecy; but believe it was in Charles the First's time.

MARY NORRIS TO H. MARSHALL.

*   *   *   *   *

We now have winter in good earnest; but, with good fires, are pretty comfortable. I hear no public news of any kind, except that on the 22d of this month, General WASHINGTON resigned his commission to Congress; and at the same time made a most pathetic and eloquent speech, which was answered by the President.

The Council of Censors sit; but I don't hear anything of their proceedings.   *   *   *   *   *

I am thy obliged friend,

MARY NORRIS.

Philada., Dec. 30th, 1783.

Philadelphia, Feb. 28th, 1784.

MY RESPECTED FRIEND :—

*   *   *   *   *

I have had the pleasure to receive letters from my son ISAAC, dated Dec. 1st and 9th, from Liege. He had enjoyed very good health, was pleased with the country, and in the spring intended for Paris. I hope it will not be long before thee pays thy Philadelphia friends a visit. Has thee heard of the Balloons, by which they take journeys in the air? It is said they are making one in Philadelphia.   *   *   *   *   *

I am thy obliged friend,
MARY NORRIS.

MY RESPECTED FRIEND :—

Captain WILLIAMS is arrived from Leghorn, and has brought a box and a letter for thee, from the Abbé FONTANA. The letter is at my house; but as I suppose thee must come down for the box, and as I am not certain how safely, or how soon, the letter might come to thy hand, I thought it best to keep it, and to give thee this notice. We are all very well. My kind love is to thee, thy wife, and ALICE.

I am thy obliged friend,
MARY NORRIS.
Philadelphia, June 29th, 1784.

MY RESPECTED FRIEND :—

*   *   *   *   The town is at this time greatly entertained with a course of lectures on the Philosophy of Chemistry and Natural History, by Doctor MOYES. He is a most extraordinary man. He had the misfortune to lose his eyesight, at eighteen months old. By all account of him, he is a worthy, agreeable, sensible, and good man. People of every description, men and women, flock to the lectures. They are held at the University, three evenings in a week.   *   *   *

*   *   * My son and daughter LOGAN are in town. They are come, like the rest of the world, to the lectures.

 *   *   * Please to present my love and respects to
thy wife; and accept it from thy obliged friend,

MARY NORRIS.

Philadelphia, February 23d, 1785.

Philadelphia, December 30th, 1785.

MY RESPECTED FRIEND :—

 *   *   * I have heard from my son JOSEPH, so
lately as the 15th of October.   He had returned from Ireland,
where he had spent the summer, five weeks of the time in the
north, among the linen manufactories.   He was in London when
he wrote, and was preparing for his journey to Paris.   He proposes to spend the winter in France, in order to attain the language, previous to his going to Holland and Germany.   He intends
to return home, the next summer or fall.   *   *   *

 *   *   * Doctor LOGAN has been with me all the
time the Assembly sat.   They have now broke up.   He, DEBBY,
and their child, are well.   The Doctor attended very constantly,
all the time they sat.   He seemed to give up every private concern to serve his country to the best of his knowledge.   Whether
they are in a way to do anything advantageous to their country,
time must show.

We have nothing new or important stirring, that I hear of.
Times are allowed to be very bad; and I believe all feel the difficulty of the times, one way or other.

I lately heard that our friend, JOHN PEMBERTON, was going on
a visit to the Orkney Islands.   I believe no *Friends* have ever
visited them.

Farewell, my good friend.   May thee, and thy good companion,
if it pleases Providence to restore her health, experience every
blessing, is the sincere wish of

Thy obliged and affectionate friend,

MARY NORRIS.

DOCTOR BOND TO H. MARSHALL.

August 7th, 1779.

SIR :—

Knowing you to be a lover of useful knowledge and acquisitions,
I take this opportunity, by your unfortunate neighbour, to let you

know Mons. GERARD, the French minister, is a gentleman of the same turn.

His knowledge as a naturalist and politician is great; his humanity and love of mankind is greater. To support their happiness and natural enjoyments is his unbounded wish. It is in his power—it is his wish, to improve the useful productions of this new world. He wants our curiosities and novelties : we want his valuable collections from all other parts of the world. This is, therefore, to request you would come forth with me, to make an offer of mutual good offices; and to furnish me with a list of such seeds, vegetables, plants, trees, &c., as this country wants, and what we could give him. If you come to town in a week or ten days, pray let me see you.

I am yours, respectfully,

THOMAS BOND.

November 3d, 1779.

DEAR SIR :—

I received your botanic collection for our friend Mr. GERARD, which I am certain, from the list, will be a very agreeable present to a man who will not only prize them duly, but will show a grateful acknowledgment for them. They shall be sent to him in your name, with great care, by the first opportunity.

I was sorry to hear of your indisposition, and hope to have the pleasure of seeing you better, soon.

I am yours, most respectfully,

THOMAS BOND.

October 18th, 1780.

DEAR SIR :—

I received yours of the 4th instant, and am disappointed in my expectations of hearing from Mr. GERARD, which, I apprehend, arises totally from his hurry of business on his arrival, and the opportunities of writing to America being rare. I cannot hear of his having wrote to a single person, and begin to suspect his constant attention to the affairs of the *Cabinet* will prevent our hearing from him often, until the return of peace affords him more leisure to attend to lesser matters: for which reason, I think it best not to make any more collections than those that are easily come at, until we are certain of proper returns.

I am your respectful, humble servant,

T. BOND.

October 26, 1780.

DEAR SIR :—

Since my last, no intelligence from Mr. GERARD : but Mr. MAR-BOIS, has apply'd to me in behalf of the Marshal NOAILLES, and the Royal Garden at Paris, to enter into a commerce of exchange of such trees, plants, &c., as would be a mutual advantage and improvement, in the natural productions of Europe and America. They do not desire botanical curiosities ; but such things only as would enrich France,—such as *Pines, Oaks, Hickories, Poplars, Persimmons, Magnolias*, &c., and wish to have a parcel of the *nuts* sent as soon as possible—for planting next spring.

The proposal is public-spirited, and worth our notice,—and if it will not be too much trouble to you, I should be glad to accept it. I will do all I can : but I think it would be best to carry on the correspondence ourselves,—to write to these gentlemen and know what they require, and to inform them what we want. I also think it would be best to send the box you have prepared to them. A line from you on this occasion would much oblige

Your respectful, humble serv't,

TH. BOND.

Philadelphia, Nov. 20, 1780.

DEAR SIR :—

Your two letters and botanic collection came safe to hand ; but not being at home, I missed a wished-for opportunity of writing to you, and sending the list of seeds which our new correspondents desire to have sent them. It has been in my possession some time, from not seeing any person going directly to your neighbourhood. I think it would be best for you to come up yourself, and hear what proposals the Minister of France and Mr. MARBOIS have further to make ; the catalogue being very large, and will give you much trouble to collect.

I perceive by your last letter, 'tis your inclination to send this box to our former friend, Mr. GERARD, on the generous plan of reciprocal correspondency. This I highly approve, and shall ship it this week ; and make no doubt he will make a very useful exchange for us and the public.

I am yours most respectfully,

Th. Bond.

December 2, 1780.

Dear Sir :

I received last night your letter and box, which I shall inform the Chevalier of, and know his pleasure about it. The collection, though small, is valuable and curious. I wish to keep up a correspondency in Europe, on a small scale, and solely with a view of furnishing each country, reciprocally, with such things as may be useful. This I hope you will enable me to do. As the other is a very large affair, and will cost you much trouble, you ought to be well paid for it. I had not time to translate the direction, about the manner of preserving the seeds : you must, therefore—when you have perused it, send it again ; or rather bring it—and I will introduce you to the Minister. The ships are not yet sailed for France.

I am yours, most respectfully,

Th. Bond.

March 16, 1781.

My kind Friend :—

This covers a letter from Mr. Marbois. I have received a very friendly letter from Mr. Gerard. He desires me to present you with his kind respects and sincere attachment, and desires we would continue our correspondency. He sent us two boxes of curious seeds by Captain Smith, who was drove into Boston, and says he has sent them forward by a safe conveyance. They are long in coming. Another may be expected every day. Mr. Wharton tells me, the King of France examined every article of our collection, and was extremely pleased with it. This is a very respectful and may be a very useful correspondency. Let us support it with the patriotic spirit it deserves. I have a prospect of adding to it greatly, via Pittsburg.

Believe me to be, with great regard,

Your humble servant,

Th. Bond.

July 12th, 1781.

DEAR SIR :—

There lately arrived here, after a series of misfortunes, a young Swede gentleman, by name of GUSTAVUS FREDERIC HILLMAN, a regular bred physician, a good naturalist and botanist, and was bred under LINNÆUS. He appears to me to be a man worthy and learned, and may be of great use in this country, in many respects. I think he might be of service to your neighbours, as a physician, and to you, in your botanic collections. As you have a large house and small family, if it was not inconvenient to you to let him have lodgings with you, for a short time, I am persuaded you would be much pleased with his acquaintance; and it would be a great gratification to a very distressed, but worthy character. If he has not a favourable answer from you soon, he will be obliged to re-embark for Europe.

WASHINGTON is actually advancing towards New York.

I am your very respectful friend,

TH. BOND.

Philadelphia, Aug. 24th, 1781.

DEAR SIR :—

I find a letter I wrote you, some time since, concerning Mr. HILLMAN, was not come to hand. He is since engaged in the Pennsylvania Hospital.

The *Opium* you sent, is pure and of good quality; I hope you will take care of the seed. Several of the botanic plants GERARD sent, have grown, but the greater part failed. There is one very fine plant of the *Jalap*. The *Gentian* did not grow. The garden seeds mostly grew; some of them are an acquisition. I wrote to Mr. MARTIN, about the seeds you mentioned, but have not received an answer.

There is not the least prospect of peace. A very large fleet will be here, that is, on the coast, in a few days. I believe CORNWALLIS in Virginia, will be their object; 'tis too late for New York. We expect the grand French Cavalry here, in a few days, on their way to the southward.

I think it will be best to make another collection for our friend

GERARD. I will write to him for more *seeds*, to be put up more carefully.

I am sorry for your good wife's affliction, and wish it was in my power to mitigate it.

I am, dear sir,

Yours, most respectfully,

TH. BOND.

DR. LETTSOM* TO H. MARSHALL.

[Not dated.†]

ESTEEMED FRIEND :—

I received thy letters dated the 19th and 29th of October, and November 10th, with some shrubs, and afterwards various seeds.

I think full half the shrubs are now in a thriving state, and many of the seeds are above ground. For these last I am still indebted to thee five guineas.

I spoke to ANN FOTHERGILL respecting thy services to the Doctor, her brother ; but she does not think that he considered himself, at his death, indebted to thee, and that she had not heard him mention anything respecting MILLER's *Plates*, which alone sell for twenty guineas.‡ But, willing to do credit to her brother's

---

* "JOHN COAKLEY LETTSOM, a physician, was born on a small island, called Little Vandyke, near Tortola, in 1744. His father was a planter, and his mother was descended from a respectable Irish family. They were of the Society of Quakers ; and young LETTSOM, being sent to England, was placed under the care of SAMUEL FOTHERGILL, a celebrated preacher of that sect, who sent him to an Academy at Warrington. On arriving at a proper age, he was bound apprentice to an apothecary of Settle, in Yorkshire ; after which, he became a pupil of. St. Thomas's Hospital. The death of his elder brother induced him to visit his native island, to look after his property ; but, finding that it chiefly consisted of *slaves*, he emancipated them all, and settled at Tortola. His stay there was not long ; and, on his return to Europe, he took his doctor's degree at Leyden. He then fixed his residence in London ; where, by the friendship of Dr. FOTHERGILL, and his connexion with the Quakers, he obtained a most extensive practice. Doctor LETTSOM, however, quitted the Society, some years before his death, which happened November 1, 1815. He was a zealous philanthropist, and a member of most of the Literary and Scientific Societies in Europe and America. His works are numerous and well known."—BLAKE's *Biog. Dict.*

† This letter is *without date ;* but, from the contents, was evidently written soon after the death of Dr. FOTHERGILL, who died December 26, 1780.

‡ Whatever may have been the fact, with respect to *indebtedness*, there can be no doubt, from the tenor of Dr. FOTHERGILL's letters, that he intended to furnish

memory, she referred the matter to my decision, and I mentioned a gratuity of twelve guineas, which she is willing to pay on thy draft. Add, therefore, my five guineas to it, which will then make seventeen guineas; for which thou may draw, thus addressed to me, which I will pay.

"Fourteen days after sight pay to * * * seventeen guineas, on account of the Executors of Doctor FOTHERGILL, deceased, and thyself."

(To be signed, and dated, and directed to Dr. LETTSOM.)

On the other side I have sent thee some books, &c., which I hope will arrive safe, and meet with thy free acceptance.

From thy friend,
J. C. LETTSOM.

When occasion offers, I hope our correspondence may not cease, particularly if additional objects of Natural History should occur.

Sambrook House, Basinghall Street,
London, Feb. 28, 1784.

RESPECTED FRIEND :—

Thy very obliging letter, with the present of the *seeds*, came safe, for which I return many thanks.

I have wrote to Dr. PARKE by this opportunity, and desired him in my name, to make some compensation for thy trouble for the same, and for such as thou choose to send me by the subsequent opportunities.

I have not yet introduced many exotics into my grounds. I have a few *Magnolias, Kalmias,* and *Evergreen Oaks;* but, as I have devoted a large space of ground for American shrubs and trees, duplicates will not be disagreeable to me. *Seeds* I shall take the best care of; but shrubs, and trees growing, fruit-trees, and any others, will be full as acceptable as seeds, where they can be sent: but both shall receive a hospitable reception at my villa of *Grove Hill.*

HUMPHRY MARSHALL with a complete copy of MILLER's valuable *Gardener's Dictionary.* But it appears, evidently, from Dr. F.'s *last* letter, written in August, 1775, that when their correspondence was finally interrupted by the American Revolution, H. MARSHALL was warranted in reckoning on a balance due him. The words of Dr. F. are—"When once the communication is opened, let me know how I can, most satisfactorily to thyself, *discharge the debt I have contracted,* and I will do it speedily." The communication was not again open during the life of Dr. FOTHERGILL.

The major part of Dr. FOTHERGILL'S hot and green house plants I purchased; but I had no Americans,—which were in general in his ground; and this leaves me more open to receive duplicates. I should wish to have some little information respecting soil and growth, though ever so short.

I collect, likewise, fossils, ores, earths, minerals, animals, particularly I have a copious museum of stuffed birds, and some quadrupeds. I have the American Bull-frog, Virginian Nightingale, and Mocking Bird.

I collect, also, small specimens of wood, dried plants, and other departments of Natural History.

When convenient, shall be glad to hear from thee; and am thy friend,

JOHN COAKLEY LETTSOM.

HUMPHRY MARSHALL TO DR. LETTSOM.

West Bradford, 4th of 10th mo., 1785.

ESTEEMED FRIEND :—

*   *   *   *   *   *   *   *   *   *

I must acknowledge myself much obliged to thee, for getting my thermometer repaired, and sending me the several books thou hast. But, instead of LINNÆUS'S *Genera Plantarum*, translated into English by COLIN MILNE, thou hast sent the Lichfield publication, which I had sent me before by my friend BARCLAY.   *   *   *

I hope still to continue our correspondence; and have therefore sent thee, by this opportunity, two of our Land Turtles, alive—a male and a female, I think. The one that I take to be the female, hath a piece broke out of the shell, near the head, and looks as if she might be very old—perhaps fifty or sixty years.

It may not be unpleasant to thee, perhaps, to be informed how we come to the knowledge of this little animal's longevity, in America. Out of curiosity, several of the inhabitants have been in the practice, when they have found this little harmless creature creeping about their meadows, or fields, eating strawberries or mushrooms, in the summer season,—they have, with their knives, cut the first two letters of their names, and the date of the year, on the under shell, where it will remain to be seen for a great number of years. I remember to be sent for, by one of my neighbours, to see one that he had set the first two letters of his name on, and dated

in the year 1724, which was about ten years ago; and the name
and date were then very plain to be seen, which had been, at
that time, dated above fifty years: and the old man told me that
the turtle looked no older, he thought, at that time, than when he
dated it. It was likewise remarkable by being a little scorched on
the back, by fire, at the time he marked it. And he said he saw it
almost every year, in the meadow, when mowing the grass; by
which it appears they are no great travellers.

I hope they came over alive; for I believe they will live a considerable time without food. I conceive they lie shut up close, all
winter, and hide under the leaves, by the side of old logs, or fences,
as I never remember to have seen one creeping about, during that
season.

I have likewise sent a small box, with a curious stone that seems
to show us the very formation and growth of crystals; and some
old, defaced, Indian axes—not being able to procure one that was
complete. However, these will show the form; and by what means
they must deaden the timber, and get bark to build their wigwams.
By twisting a withe of Hickory round the stone, they make a helve,
and so cut and bruised the bark round the trees. The box is filled
up with some other articles, as per catalogue inclosed, being a few
seeds, nuts, &c., not dried much,—which, if they don't mould, will
come over in perfection; and if they do, they may vegetate, perhaps, better than if dried.

I shall be pleased with a continuance of our correspondence, if
life and health permit.

HUMPHRY MARSHALL.

DR. LETTSOM TO H. MARSHALL.

London, July 14th, 1787.

ESTEEMED FRIEND:—

It somehow happened that a packet for Dr. PARKE, one for Dr.
FRANKLIN, and one for thyself, miscarried together: but I cannot
explain the incident further than that they were delivered by me.

I have sent thee a few books; but whether I shall be able to
include LINNÆUS, I am not certain, as it is a work not always to
be had. I hope, however, to do it by the next vessel. I think
myself, nevertheless, not out of thy debt, even when LINNÆUS is
received, or, at the most, I shall have no demand upon thee: for I
am not disposed to be illiberal; and at the same time, either living
plants especially, and a box of seeds, or whatever else occurs to

thee, will be acceptable; and will be acknowledged either in a pecuniary way, or in any other more agreeable form.

As it is a pleasing circumstance to hear of our old acquaintance, I have the pleasure to announce the good health of one of the *tortoises* thou some time ago sent to me: one died by too long confinement in my green-house, when I knew less of their economy. I wish I had a companion, or even a pair, as companions to my survivor, who has grown considerably, and is very lively.

My garden is about two acres; at present pretty well filled with plants: but I have paled off an *Arbustum* round two of my fields, which measures nearly a mile, and this is filling pretty fast; there is, however, room to introduce some hundreds of shrubs and plants.

In this city, the Royal Society has admitted *Natural History* into their Transactions. A Society, however, purely of Natural History, is instituted in London, and will, I think, flourish.* I am a member, though a very unworthy one, as I rarely attend.

Such a Society, established in *Philadelphia*, might be very important. A man of Dr. PARKE's influence, with very few others to begin it, would excite emulation in your citizens, and give vigour and permanency to such an institution.† Should that not be effected, any communication to me should be laid before our Society.

Let me hear from thee, when occasion offers, and believe me thy friend,

J. C. LETTSOM.

DR. MOSES MARSHALL‡ TO DR. LETTSOM.

Bradford, Chester County, May 7th, 1788.

ESTEEMED FRIEND :—

In November last, was forwarded to the care of CHARLES EDDY,

---

* The allusion here is, doubtless, to the "*Linnæan Society*," established in the year 1788, and incorporated in 1802; of which the estimable and accomplished botanist, Sir JAMES EDWARD SMITH was the principal founder, and, during his life, the President.

† Such an institution, after some abortive efforts, was successfully established in Philadelphia, just thirty years afterwards, to wit, in the year 1817, by the name of "The Academy of Natural Sciences;" which has signally flourished under the auspices of its munificent patrons, and, by the labours of its learned members, has acquired a distinguished rank in the scientific world.

‡ MOSES MARSHALL, son of JAMES MARSHALL (the younger brother of HUM-PHRY), was born in West Bradford, Chester County, on the 30th of November,

merchant, London, a box of seeds for thee. The plants and tortoises, designed to be sent, through some impeding circumstances, were neglected.

At this time, I have sent a small box containing three tortoises, perhaps one male and two females, which I hope may arrive safe : to favour which, I have placed grass sods at bottom of the box. There are, also, a few potatoes and grains of corn, a few pieces of apple, and mushrooms put therein. This I mention, as it may lead to discover whether they subsist without nourishment during the voyage or not. Mushrooms and strawberries are substances of which they are known with certainty to feed upon. At this time I am not altogether prepared : by another opportunity I may probably transmit thee some considerable observations relative to their natural history.

In a corner of the box, are a few small plants, which I believe are yet undescribed, viz., a species of *Sedum ;* a species of *Portulaca,* the root perennial, the stem short, thickly set with cylindrical succulent leaves standing somewhat erect ; from the centre shoots forth a very slender, naked, reddish stem, four or five times the length of the leaves, branching at top, and supporting reddish flowers, which expand about noon, and continue open about three hours.* Also a species of *Veronica,* and a small *Evergreen* from

1758. He received a tolerable education, both English and classical, and studied Medicine with Doctor Nicholas Way, in Wilmington, Delaware, from 1776 till 1779. He had an extraordinary opportunity of being initiated into Surgery, in attending the soldiers who were wounded in the battle of Brandywine, September 11th, 1777. After practising Medicine a short time, he seems to have become an inmate in the family of his uncle Humphry, devoting his time and services, exclusively, as an aid to his uncle, in the business of collecting and shipping plants and seeds to Europe. He made several long exploring journeys, in that pursuit, through the wilds of the West and Southwest. He was a good practical botanist, well acquainted with most of our indigenous plants, and rendered valuable assistance to his uncle, in preparing the *Arbustum Americanum.* On the 6th of April, 1796, Governor Mifflin appointed him a Justice of the Peace ; in which office he did excellent service, as a peace-maker, in the community around him. In all his acts he was a remarkably cautious, upright, conscientious man. The editor had the happiness to know him well, and passed many pleasant, instructive hours with him, investigating the plants in the Marshallton Botanic Garden. Dr. Marshall discontinued the business of sending plants and seeds to Europe, soon after his uncle's death, and the garden, in consequence, has ever since been almost wholly neglected. Dr. M. died on the 1st of October, 1813, aged fifty-four years and ten months.

* This is a good description, as far as it goes, of the little *Talinum teretifolium,* Ph. ; written long before the plant was generally known to the botanists, or pub-

the mountains, the characters of which I have attempted drawing, though from the dissection of but a single flower :—

Cal., three-leaved, the leaflets very small, coloured, one above and two beneath.

Corol., sub-papilionaceous, the *standard* wanting ; the *wings* inverse-egg'd, spreading, free ; the *keel* subcylindrical, oblong, divided at the apex by the nectarium, the segments emarginate.

Nectarium, an inflated body, at the end and between the divisions of the keel, including and covering the parts of fructification, rising at the fore-part, and bearing a fringed tuft.

Stam., six, slender, somewhat clubbed, joined to the keel near the middle, and about half the length of it ; *antheræ* roundish.

Germen, inverse-egg'd, compressed ; *style* the length of the keel, clubbed and rising at the apex ; the *stigma* thickish, truncated and torn or two-lipped.

Seed-vessel, a capsule, inverse-hearted, compressed, two-celled and two-valved.

Seeds, two, solitary or one in each cell, begirt with a three-parted covering.*

To this plant, should it prove to be a new genus, I had some time since designed the appellation of *Lettsomia*, with this provision, that it might not be unpleasing to thee, and that, in the interim, I should not be able to discover a plant more exalted, conspicuous, and worthy.

I have, indeed, had a design highly favourable to discoveries in view,—a journey to the Mississippi, westward ; but have not yet been at leisure to prosecute it. I have, therefore, at present, but this humble offering to make.

The autumn will be more favourable for sending of plants, &c.,

lished in the books. It grows abundantly on the Serpentine rock, in the vicinity of Marshallton, HUMPHRY MARSHALL's former residence, where Doctor M. pointed it out to the editor, several years prior to the publication of PURSH's *Flora.*

* This plant proved to be a *Polygala ;* and the species, from which the description is taken, was doubtless the pretty little *P. paucifolia*, of WILLDENOW.

Among the MARSHALL Papers, there is one, without date, but apparently of this period, or earlier, on which is a sketch of the genus *Xanthorhiza ;* and also an excellent description (with a rough drawing) of the *Floerkea proserpinacoïdes*, of Willd. From diffidence, or want of opportunity to publish, many of the discoveries, and much of the credit, really due to BARTRAM, MARSHALL, and MUHLENBERG, have been ascribed to, or appropriated by, European botanists.

at which time we shall endeavour to find something to furnish thy garden, or cabinet. In the mean time, I should wish thee to send LINNÆUS'S *Genera* and *Supplementum Plantarum*, the latest and best edition. Also, a surgeon's pouch, or case of pocket instruments.

I am, with respect, thy friend,

MOSES MARSHALL,

Residing with, and writing by direction of, my uncle, HUMPHRY MARSHALL.

DR. LETTSOM TO HUMPHRY MARSHALL.

London, August 10th, 1788.

ESTEEMED FRIEND:—

I have the pleasure to tell thee that the three turtles arrived safe, and continue in good health in my garden. The plants accompanying seem dead.

The plant described by thee, and designed to honour my name, is a species of *Polygala*, and is, I believe, a new one [*P. paucifolia*, Willd.].

Perhaps thou may send me some plants, at the fall of the leaf; and it is necessary that I should compensate thee; and therefore, I give thee the liberty of drawing upon me for ten pounds sterling.

I wish a healthy plant of *Ginseng* could be sent with the plants.

I write now in haste; but a letter from thee will always be acceptable to

Thy friend,

J. C. LETTSOM.

HUMPHRY MARSHALL TO DR. LETTSOM.

Nov. 4th, 1788.

ESTEEMED FRIEND:—

Thine, dated 10th of August, with several books, came safe to hand.

With this, I send a small box of plants — the list of contents inclosed—which I hope will not prove unacceptable; though there is little of novelty in the collection to recommend it, except the *Azalea*, which I believe is yet rare.

I had discovered my error, with regard to the small plant sent thee last year,* and might sooner have done it, had I been careful. However, it has gone but to thyself, except lately, by the name of *Polygala*, to Sir JOSEPH BANKS.

The *Plumed Andromeda*, of BARTRAM, is the *Cyrilla*. The *Franklinia*, I believe, is a species of *Gordonia*.

I am much pleased with WALTER'S *Flora*, which appears to be well executed. Every addition to botanical knowledge will always prove acceptable.

DR. LETTSOM TO H. MARSHALL.

London, Feb. 2, 1789.

ESTEEMED FRIEND :—

I write now to acknowledge the receipt of thy letter of November last, and to add that yesterday the box was safely landed ; and, on a cursory inspection, the plants contained seem healthy.

At the expense of much labour and money, I have brought some fine bog earth on my premises which your countrymen thrive best in ; and I hope soon to possess an ample collection of them.

I am obliged to thee for thy intention of increasing my Americans, as opportunity may offer. FRASER, to whom a few of us in London subscribed an annual sum, has not answered our expectations. His *catalogue*, enclosed, are the seeds and plants of his own property. His subscribers, at least I—had very few indeed.

I would observe that the plants sent by thee, in the Pigou, whose numbers are fastened with *wire*, answered effectually to distinguish the shrubs, and this plan should be continued.

I am thy friend,
J. C. LETTSOM.

I shall pay thy draft, when I receive it.

JOHN JACKSON† TO H. MARSHALL.

ESTEEMED FRIEND, HUMPHRY MARSHALL :—

I herewith send thy brush by the bearer, CALEB HARLAN, being the first opportunity. Mind not the cost until I see thee. I have

---

* The proposed *Lettsomia*, which proved to be a *Polygala*. About seven years afterwards, a Peruvian shrub was dedicated to Dr. LETTSOM, by the Spanish botanists, RUIZ and PAVON.

† JOHN JACKSON, of Londongrove Township, Chester County, was one of the very

this request to make, if thou pleases; to save me some seed of the *Geranium*, when ripe: also if thou couldst procure me a set or two of *Rosemary*, I should accept it as a favour, having lost mine the hard winter, and not got any since. Perhaps some slips set in the ground in season, would take root, and be safely moved towards fall.

I hope the public peace will add fresh life and vigour to every useful science that may tend to adorn and enrich our country: the propagation of plants being one, and much my delight. I take every help that I receive this way as a kindness.

From thy friend,

JOHN JACKSON.

Londongrove, the 30th 3d mo., 1789.

DOCTOR LOGAN* TO H. MARSHALL.

" SIR :—

" We wish to be informed if we can be supplied with any of the natural productions of America, either by barter for the productions of Italy, or at a moderate price.

few contemporaries of HUMPHRY MARSHALL, who sympathized cordially with his pursuits. He commenced a garden soon after that at Marshallton was established, and made a valuable collection of rare and ornamental plants; which is still preserved in good condition by his son, WILLIAM JACKSON, ESQ. JOHN JACKSON, was a very successful cultivator of curious plants, a respectable botanist, and one of the most gentle and amiable of men. He died in 1822, at an advanced age.

* GEORGE LOGAN, M.D., son of WILLIAM, and grandson of JAMES LOGAN, the distinguished friend and secretary of WILLIAM PENN, was born at Stenton, near Philadelphia, September 9, 1753. He was sent to England for his education when very young, and, on his return, served an apprenticeship with a merchant of Philadelphia. He had early a great desire to study medicine, which he undertook after he had attained to the years of manhood. After spending three years at the medical school of Edinburgh, he travelled through France, Italy, Germany, and Holland, and returned to his own country in 1779.

He applied himself for some years to agriculture, and also served in the Legislature. In June, 1798, he embarked for Europe, for the purpose of preventing a war between America and France. For this step he was violently denounced by hostile political partisans;[a] but he persevered, and succeeded in his intentions.

[a] Dr. LOGAN was not only " denounced by hostile political partisans," for his benevolent efforts on the occasion, but there was, also, an Act of Congress placed in our statute book, which is palpably aimed at such interference, and which, it is too probable, originated in the resentful feelings of the administration and its supporters, towards the estimable citizen who planned and consummated that philanthropic movement. The act referred to, was passed January 30, 1799, and prescribes a " Fine of 5000 dollars, and imprisonment, for citizens holding corre-

" Quadrupeds, birds, insects, worms or serpents, the last, of which may be preserved in spirit of wine ; minerals, seeds, and plants,— particularly that plant called *Dionœa muscipula,* which is found in low marshy places in South Carolina. For such articles we shall be willing to pay the customary price, or return the value of them in such plants as we are in possession of ; a catalogue of which we now send you.

" If any gentlemen of the Philosophical Society of Philadelphia are willing to enter on such a friendly intercourse with the Royal Museum of the Grand Duke, they will please address their letters to *Monsieur L'Abbé* FONTANA, *à Florence.*"

RESPECTED FRIEND :—

The above is a translation of a letter from the Abbé FONTANA. I have taken the earliest opportunity of sending it to you, in which I have been in some degree influenced by the necessity of informing you, that Mr. WILLIAMS will sail by the 15th of next month. You will be the best judge what plants, or other natural productions, may with safety be sent by the present opportunity.

I wish you to write to the Abbé. Give him such information as

He was a Senator from Pennsylvania, in the Congress of the United States, from 1801 to March 1807. In 1810, he visited England—as formerly France—with the same philanthropic desire of preserving peace between the two countries. Here, though he failed in effecting the good which he had so much at heart, yet his reception by men of the highest respectability of both parties was highly flattering. He was exceedingly grieved at the war which followed. His health gradually declined for some years, and he died April 9, 1821.

Mr. DUPONCEAU said of him : " And art thou too gone ? friend of man ! friend of peace ! friend of science ! Thou whose persuasive accents could still the angry passions of the rulers of men, and dispose their minds to listen to the voice of reason and justice."

He was an active member of the Agricultural and Philosophical Societies ; and published experiments on gypsum and on the rotation of crops.—*Encycl. Americana.*

spondence with foreign governments or their agents, in order to influence their conduct in relation to the United States," &c. It is remarkable that the dead letter of this obnoxious statute was raked up, in the U. S. Senate, nearly half a century afterwards, by one of the " Democracy" *par excellence,* with a view to apply its penalties to the worthy gentleman who humanely persisted in nego-tiating a peace with unhappy, prostrate Mexico—even after his mission had been revoked by the administration which sent him, but which dared not reject the treaty thus concluded !

you may think proper, and testify your desire of doing anything in your power to serve that grand Institution.

If agreeable, I will inclose your letter in one I shall write to the Abbé. You must not be concerned on account of your writing in English. I think this gentleman has been in England, and is sufficiently acquainted with the language to understand it, though not to write it with correctness.

Any little collection you may send to my care, shall be forwarded.

I am your assured friend,

GEORGE LOGAN.

Philadelphia, August 26th, 1783.

THE ABBE FONTANA* TO H. MARSHALL.

Pisa, in Tuscany, 16th January, 1784.

SIR :—

It is with a great pleasure that I have received through Captain HUMPHR. WILLIAMS, the favour of your letters, and the two boxes of American plants, which you was so good to forward to us; which came almost all alive, and hope they will thrive well in our country. Captain WILLIAMS may inform you by what accident I am not in Florence now; and consequently it is not in my power to send you anything, except few seeds that I shall endeavour to get from the garden of the University, reserving to me self the pleasur to send you something more by the first occasion. However, I must confess to you the greatest gratitude and obligation,

---

* FELIX FONTANA, an eminent Italian philosopher and naturalist, was born at Pomarolo, in the Italian Tyrol, in 1730. Having completed his studies at the Universities of Padua and Bologna, he went to Rome, and thence to Florence. The Grand Duke, FRANCIS (afterwards Emperor), appointed him Professor of Natural Philosophy in the University of Pisa. The Grand Duke LEOPOLD (afterwards Emperor LEOPOLD II.), invited him to Florence, but permitted him to retain his office at Pisa, and employed him in forming the Cabinet of the Natural Sciences, which is yet one of the ornaments of the Florentine capital.

FONTANA is the author of several works on scientific subjects, one of the best known of which is a Treatise on Poisons. His writings show him to have been an ingenious and indefatigable observer.

The political principles which he avowed during the events of 1799, in Tuscany, involved him in some difficulties. He died in 1805; and was buried in the Church of Santa Croce, by the side of GALILEO and VIVIANI.—*See Encyclopædia Americana.*

both by the pleasure you have made to us, as well as by that I have had in stiling myself, with the greatest respect and consideration,

Sir, your most humble and obedient servant,

FELIX FONTANA.

DR. M. MARSHALL TO H. MARSHALL.

Bedford, June 27th, 1784.

DEAR UNCLE:—

After many tedious delays, we have reached this place, all in good health, but tired with travelling so slow. We have been with the wagons all the way from Carlisle.

These four days past, we have been amongst the Pine Mountains, where we have seen plenty of the Cucumber Trees, Rhododendrons, and Mountain Raspberry [*Rubus odoratus*, L.]: and yesterday, about Juniata, we found broad, willow-leaved Oak [*Quercus imbricaria*, Mx. ?], and red-berried Elder.

In coming along, I have seen many strange plants; but may be chiefly varieties of what we have already. However, I shall gather what seed I can, of any such, or bring the plants.

As for shells, minerals, &c., we have seen none yet. I believe we shall leave the wagons now, and go on to Pittsburg, about three days' journey from here; where we may, perhaps, have a greater chance of finding something new.

Thy affectionate nephew,

M. MARSHALL.

JOSEPH CRUKSHANK* TO H. MARSHALL.

Philadelphia, 4th mo. 28th, 1785.

RESPECTED FRIEND:—

I have made a calculation of the expense of printing thy book, and suppose it will, including the paper, cost £70 or £80. The price of binding, or sewing in a pamphlet, will depend on the manner thou hast them done. I allowed to do a thousand copies; and will stand about 1s. 6d. apiece, in sheets.

---

* JOSEPH CRUKSHANK, a respectable printer and bookseller, in Philadelphia, was the publisher of the *Arbustum Americanum*.

S. Vaughan has not called since I wrote thee last; nor have I gone to him.

If thou should desire to have Proposals printed, should be glad thou wouldst write them and send me a copy, and we shall endeavour to get them done to thy mind.

From thy friend,
Jos. Crukshank.

Philadelphia, 2d month, 7th, 1786.

Esteemed Friend :—

I received thine of the 3d, and delivered the enclosed, and one of thy books, bound, to Samuel Vaughan, Esq. The Society for Promoting Agriculture are to meet this evening,—when he proposes to present the book, and the paper enclosed in thy letter to him.   *   *   *   *

I have forwarded twelve of "The Grove" to James Gibbons; and have had accounts from Trenton and New York: but there is not one subscriber in either place. They sell but slow: I think we have not sold a dozen, beside those to the subscribers.

I send one, bound, herewith.

From thy friend,
Jos. Crukshank.

Thy letter, and the book for the Philosophical Society, were delivered, some time ago, to Samuel Magaw.

Philadelphia, 9th mo., 4th, 1786.

Respected Friend :—

In answer to thine, I have to inform thee that our friend Vaughan's family sailed for Liverpool three or four weeks ago. He is to remain some time here, himself, having some business to settle; but have not heard, for certain, how long he will be detained.

No vessel has arrived from London, except a small schooner, that brought but few letters.   *   *   *   *

I have lately had an account from New York. The books don't sell there, except two copies, and the sale appears to be over here.*

From thy friend,
Jos. Crukshank.

---

* Humphry had the *privilege*, if not the satisfaction, of attempting to instruct his contemporaries pretty nearly at *his own expense!*

SAMUEL VAUGHAN* TO H. MARSHALL.

Philadelphia, 30th April, 1785.

SIR :—

The day after your departure, I laid your *Botanical Catalogue* before the Society for Promoting Agriculture, and on Friday, before the Philosophical Society. They each were sensible of the merit and utility of the work, and wished it might be published; but the present state of their finances did not authorize them to undertake the publication.

I then left the manuscript with Mr. CRUKSHANK, desiring him to let me know the expense of furnishing *one thousand*, completely printed and sewed in pamphlets; and though I called upon him several times, it was but this day that I received his answer, that by computation they would come to £70 or £80. After some time he agreed to undertake it for £70, including an alphabetical index of the names in English, which will be absolutely necessary, and which I am now making out.

As this work will give much original botanical information of the New World, be of public utility, also reputable and serviceable to you, by collecting for the curious, I am very anxious for its immediate publication; therefore, would venture, in behalf of my friends here and in Europe, to subscribe for fifty or sixty copies, and also use my interest for procuring other subscriptions; but sorry to find, on inquiry, that a work of this kind is not likely (on this Continent) to meet with the encouragement it deserves. I, however, wish to see you, as soon as you can make it convenient, in order to devise means for expediting my wishes.

* SAMUEL VAUGHAN, an English gentleman who resided some years in the city of Philadelphia, and, at the date of these letters, was one of the Vice Presidents of the American Philosophical Society. He is said to have been a man of some eccentricity of character, but withal possessing much intelligence and enlightened public spirit.[a] He was the father of the late JOHN VAUGHAN, so long the librarian of the Philosophical Society, and so well known, in Philadelphia, for his active participation in many literary and charitable institutions, as well as for his kind and ever-ready attention to all visiters and strangers, whose position or necessities gave them a claim upon his hospitality or benevolence.

[a] See Dr. PARKE's letter of September 4, 1786, p. 530.

Inclosed you have Mr. BOARDLEY'S summary of Courses of Crops in Maryland, &c., as also an Address from the Philadelphia Society for Promoting Agriculture, of which you have been chosen an honorary member; the certificate of which I should have inclosed, but that the secretary is not to be found.

I am, sir, your assured friend and servant,

SAM. VAUGHAN.

Philadelphia, 14th May, 1785.

SIR :—

Conformable to your letter of 5th inst., I sent an advertisement to the papers,* and hope it will have the desired effect; but if not, as I think it calculated to promote botanical knowledge, hitherto but little attended to in the New World, it shall not want the neces-

---

* In the "Pennsylvania Mercury and Universal Advertiser," published by DANIEL HUMPHREYS, in Dock Street, May 13, 1785, is the following advertisement, no doubt the one here referred to :

TO THE PUBLIC.

Few countries are richer in botanical productions than America; but in no country has less attention been paid to collecting an account of them. Natives and foreigners have frequently had occasion to lament the want of some work, which might serve as a register of past discoveries, and lead to future ones. It cannot be compiled at once, or by one man; but it is the duty of every one to contribute what he can towards it.

Influenced by this motive, and at the request of many respectable persons, proposals are made for printing by subscription,

AN AMERICAN BOTANY,

Or an Alphabetical Catalogue and Botanical Description of the Forest Trees, Shrubs, &c., natives of the United States, arranged according to the Linnæan System, with the English names also annexed, and an account of the appearance, manner of growth, &c., of the different species and varieties, with some hints of their use in medicine, manufactures, dyes, and domestic economy, with proper indexes. The whole compiled from actual observation by HUMPHRY MARSHALL.

It will be printed in 8vo., and put into the press as soon as a sufficient number of copies are subscribed for to pay the expense of printing; the author having no view of private emolument.

Price to subscribers 3s. 9d. Money to be paid on subscribing. Subscriptions taken by Messrs. HALL and SELLERS, CRUKSHANK, BRADFORD, and HUMPHREYS.

Philadelphia, May 11th, 1785.

sary assistance to carry it on. But this keep to yourself, as it might, if known, injure the subscription.

I can by no means approve of its being published in *England*, as I wish *America* to have the whole merit; and it will be sooner accomplished.

Mr. CRUKSHANK'S character, as well as his candour, deserves a preference; but as his was an old type, and to satisfy myself as to the price (which I found to be reasonable, on inquiry), I was recommended to a Mr. CIST, who also bears a good character, has had a liberal education, studied Botany, and has a new clean type, who asks £72; but I doubt not, if asked, would do it on the same terms with Mr. CRUKSHANK. CLAYPOOLE and DONALDSON have offered to do it for less, but, as CIST has a neat type, and qualified as well as promised to correct the press, I apprehend it will be done more correct by him than any other person, more especially as you are at such a distance.*

I am now planting trees and shrubs in the State House Square; and as I wish to collect there a specimen of every sort in America that will grow in this state, I wish to have your advice and assistance as soon as convenient.

> I am, with great regard,
> Dear sir, your assured friend,
> SAM. VAUGHAN.

Philadelphia, 28th May, 1785.

DEAR SIR:—

As it is my wish to plant in the State House Square, specimens of every tree and shrub that grows in the several states on this continent, that will thrive here, I have enclosed a sketch of such as I have been able to procure since the 7th of last month, with a list of such others as have occurred to me hitherto: but, as I am unacquainted with the vast variety remaining, and that you have turned your thoughts in that line, I have to request, and shall be much obliged to you for a list of such as occur to you, with directions in what state, or place, they are to be had; that I may lay out to procure them, to plant in the fall.

I am very solicitous for the early publication of your *Catalogue;*

---

* The work, however, was printed at the close of that same year (1785), by JOSEPH CRUKSHANK, in Market Street, between Second and Third Streets.

therefore wish you may expedite the correction as soon as possible : when I shall get Mr. CIST to revise and to publish it, as soon as possible.

I am, with great regard,

Dear sir, your assured friend,

SAM. VAUGHAN.

Philadelphia, 22d May, 1786.

DEAR SIR :—

Doctor SAM. WILLIAMS, Hol. Prof. of Cambridge College, Massachusetts, wishes to ascertain the *climate*, in different parts of America, by meteorological observations which are customary ; and to mark the times when several of the fruits of the field vegetate, and animals first begin to appear, &c., with an inclosed plan : to add to the materials of American knowledge.

As the design deserves encouragement, I have taken the liberty to inclose one, requesting the favour, if you or any of your friends find time, to note these appearances ; and, should opportunity offer, to inclose the result to the Doctor ; otherwise to me, which will much oblige,

Dear sir, your assured friend,

SAM. VAUGHAN.

TIMOTHY PICKERING* TO H. MARSHALL.

Philadelphia, February 15th, 1786.

SIR :—

Mr. VAUGHAN handed to the Philadelphia Society of Agriculture, your *Observations on the propriety of applying Botanical knowledge to Agriculture, feeding cattle,* &c. The paper was read last evening before the Society, who are much obliged by the communication. They believe such application would be of very extensive utility ; and would be very happy to receive a plan for

---

* The character and career of TIMOTHY PICKERING, as a soldier, statesman, and patriot, it is presumed, is too familiarly known, to every American, at least, to require a detailed notice here. He was born in Salem, Massachusetts, July 17th, 1745 ; graduated at Harvard College in 1763 ; served in various capacities, civil and military, throughout the revolutionary contest ; was subsequently at the head of every Executive Department of the General Government, under President WASHINGTON ; and for years after that, a senator and representative in Congress, &c. He was, also, a devoted friend to the interests and pursuits of Agriculture. His death took place January 29th, 1829, in the eighty-fourth year of his age.

reducing the idea to practice. A calculation of the expense of the undertaking would be very necessary to accompany it. If your leisure will permit you to digest such a plan, the Society will be highly obliged by your doing it.

I am, sir, respectfully,

Your most obedient servant,

TIM. PICKERING.

Philadelphia, December 18th, 1792.

SIR :—

The Philadelphia Society for Promoting Agriculture, on a review of the communications which they have from time to time received from the active friends of rural affairs, with pleasure acknowledge the obligation for those with which they were favoured by you.

These communications have generally been published in the newspapers. But, to render them more permanently useful, a committee is now appointed, who, after a careful examination of the whole, are to select such as they shall judge most useful, to be published in a volume.

A like selection will be made from other communications which shall be received until the work shall be sent to the press.

The Society proposing in future to make and publish similar selections, as materials shall be furnished, request the continuance of your aid in advancing the interests of Agriculture; and that you will forward, by post or otherwise, such information on the subject as your inquiries and observation enable you to collect.

In behalf, and by order of the Society,

I am, sir,

Your most obedient servant,

TIMOTHY PICKERING,

Secretary.

SIR JOSEPH BANKS* TO HUMPHRY MARSHALL.

London, Soho Square, April 5th, 1786.

SIR :—

I wish to try some experiments upon curing the root of *Ginseng*,

---

* Sir JOSEPH BANKS, sprung from a family of Swedish origin, was born in 1743, at Revesby Abbey in Leicestershire, and educated at Eton and Oxford. His love of travelling, and of Natural History, prompted him to explore foreign countries;

which, if they succeed, may become of importance both to your country and mine.

I shall, therefore, be obliged to you, if you can procure me one or two hundred weight of fresh roots, gathered after the seed is ripe, and, if possible, after the stalk is dried up.

They should be picked for the largest and fairest, and the bud, if there is any on their crown, carefully preserved; should be packed as soon as possible, after they are dug up, in damp moss (the white, found on the swamps, is the best), and headed up in a cask; in which manner they will come safe, if stowed in a cool place, and sent as speedily as convenient.

I shall be glad to pay the amount of their cost, to whomever you may appoint; being, sir,

Your most obedient servant,
Jos. Banks.

Please to direct them to Sir Jos. Banks, President of the Royal Society, Soho Square; and give me a line of advice.

HUMPHRY MARSHALL TO SIR JOSEPH BANKS.

West Bradford, Chester County, Pennsylvania,
the 14th of the 11th mo., 1786.

Respected Friend :—

I received thy favour, dated April the 5th, 1786, in which thou seems desirous of trying an experiment upon the curing the root of *Ginseng ;* for which purpose thou desires that I would procure thee one or two hundred weight of the fresh root, gathered after the seed is ripe; and pack it up in damp moss, headed up in a cask, and sent as speedily as convenient; and thou'll pay the cost to such persons as I should appoint to receive it; which requisition I have endeavoured to comply with, but have not been able to pro-

---

and, accordingly, in 1763, he made a voyage to Labrador and Newfoundland; in 1768, accompanied the great navigator, Cook; and, in 1772, visited Iceland, and the Western Isles of Scotland.

On his return, the University of Oxford conferred on him the degree of Doctor of Laws. In 1778, he obtained the Order of the Bath, and the Presidency of the Royal Society. This situation he held until his death, which occurred on the 19th of June, 1820.

He wrote some papers in the Philosophical Transactions, and a tract on the rust in wheat. His collection of books on Natural History was the most complete in Europe.—*See Encycl. Americana,* and Blake's *Biographical Dictionary.*

cure for thee more than about one hundred weight of the fresh root, and that at a considerable expense; having to employ a young man, a nephew of mine, that lives with me, to travel about two hundred miles to the westward, through a dismal mountainous part of our country, as the Ginseng is either dug up for sale, or rooted up by the hogs so much, that it begins to grow scarce in the inhabited parts, especially where the people are any ways thick settled; and seems likely to be entirely demolished, amongst the inhabitants in a few years.

He was likewise obliged to hire a person, at a dollar a day, to assist him in digging said Ginseng, both of them being obliged to encamp in the mountains, strike up a fire and lie by it all night, in the morning take their hoes and knapsacks on their backs, and climb up the sides of the mountains, and dig till towards evening, and then bring what they had dug to their camp, and cook their morsel and eat it. It took him about twenty days, in going and coming home again, digging the roots, and packing up, &c., the expense of carriage being considerable. Therefore, it being procured and carefully put up according to thy direction, I hope that it may arrive safe; and if so, I expect thou'll be willing to pay a reasonable compensation, which would be, at least, an English crown a pound, I should apprehend. But, if thou thinks that too much, be pleased to pay what thou thinks would be a compensation, adequate to the trouble and cost the young doctor hath been at; and I hope, if thou, or any of the members of the Royal Society, should see cause to employ him, or me, in future, that we would endeavour to serve you as reasonable as any other persons; and as my nephew is well versed in the knowledge of Botany, and would gladly be employed in researches in that line, or to explore our western regions in search of minerals, fossils, or inflammables, and objects of Natural History, &c., provided he could meet with proper encouragement, I, therefore, make free to mention something of the kind to thee, that if the Royal Society should have a mind to employ any person, on this side the water, for such purposes, he would be willing to serve them.

I have sent thee one of my pamphlets, entitled the *American Grove*, and expect thou'll present it to the Royal Society, in my name, if thou thinks it worth their notice and acceptance; as also one for thyself, which I hope will be accepted.

From thy real friend and well-wisher,

HUMPHRY MARSHALL.

P.S. If the *Ginseng* is to plant, as I expect it is, it should be planted in a shady situation, and in a rich black mould, or soil: as I have experienced it will not bear our summer heat, without being shaded,—especially in the middle of the day.

But your country not being so hot, perhaps it may bear the heat of the sun with you. However, I should advise a shady situation for it, and rich ground. And if any more should be wanted, perhaps it might be procured some small matter reasonabler than this sent, my nephew having found, in his route, where it grows pretty plenty.

SIR JOSEPH BANKS TO H. MARSHALL.

Soho Square, May 6, 1789.

SIR :—

Your box of plants was received safe, and to all appearance in good order.

I have no doubt that, as the spring advances, we shall find in it several plants which will enrich our botanical knowledge. The sum of two guineas, the price your letter fixed upon them, was readily paid to Mr. CHARLES EDDY, on your account.

The *Franklinia* is, as you conjecture, a species of *Gordonia*. A drawing of that plant, sent here by Mr. BARTRAM to Mr. BARCLAY, has been compared with specimens; so that no doubt now can remain on that subject.

Mr. AITON* has desired me to request from you a similar box of plants, by the next fall, for his Majesty's garden, where those of the last box are already planted; and has given me the underwritten list of plants more particularly wanted there :

Ascyrum villosum.	*Kuhnia eupatorioides.*
A—— hypericoides.	*Hedysarum*, all the species.
Polygala, all the species.	*Helonias*, ditto.
Portulaca.	*Aster,* ⎫
Viola, all the species.	*Solidago,* ⎬ any curious species.
Anemone thalictroides.	*Eupatorium,* ⎭
Martagon Lilies,	Grasses, ⎫ more particularly.
Epigaea repens.	Ferns, ⎭

---

* WILLIAM AITON was " Gardener to His Majesty," and author of the " *Hortus Kewensis*, or a Catalogue of the Plants cultivated in the Royal Botanic Garden at Kew," an interesting and useful work at that period; being published the same year in which this letter is dated. A *second edition* was published in 1810–13, under the supervision of that "*facilè Princeps Botanicorum*," ROBERT BROWN.

These, sir, packed and directed in the same manner, with as
many of these particular plants as you happen to meet with, will be
very acceptable here.

I beg the favour of you to advise me of the ship by which they are
sent, and I shall with great pleasure pay the amount.

I am, sir, your most humble servant,

JOS. BANKS.

London, Soho Square, April 3, 1790.

SIR :—

The plants sent by you, this year, arrived safe and in good condition, except that some of the pieces of the root of *Violas*, &c.,
were so small, that I fear we shall not be able to preserve them.   I
should be glad if larger pieces could be sent in future, even though
a higher price was charged.

Your bill was—as your bills always will be—honoured immediately.

Enclosed is a list for this year : the plants of which I should wish
to receive in the autumn, about the same time as the last came
here, as that is the best season for sending.   The list is forwarded
early, as some of the plants may be to be sought for, in the course
of the summer.

I am, sir, your most humble servant,

JOS. BANKS.

DR. MOSES MARSHALL TO SIR JOS. BANKS.

Philada., October 30th, 1790.

SIR JOS. BANKS :—

Your order of April last, addressed to my uncle, was duly received;
and in compliance therewith I send a box of plants,—list of contents, &c., inclosed.   *   *   *   *   *

In May last, I sat out upon a botanic tour, by way of Juniata to
Pittsburg, thence southward, up the Monongahela, upon Green
Briar River, over New River to Holston, Nolichucky, &c.   Then
crossing the high and great chain of mountains, came upon the
head waters of Santee, in South Carolina ; thence by Ninety-six to
Augusta, and to Savannah town, and continuing southwest to the
river Alatamaha, in Georgia.   I here found the *Franklinia*, or
Gordonia sessilis, better called : i. e. *floribus sessilibus*.

I then returned to Charleston—making a route of about 1600 miles; and thence by water to Philadelphia In this route, by reason of the unfavourable season of the year, I was unable to procure scarce anything but specimens. Of these, a few perhaps are new; but several are spoiled with dampness, &c. I designed forwarding the most curious; but through hurry left them at home; that is, thirty miles west of Philadelphia, from whence I now write. However, they shall be forwarded by another opportunity.

Notwithstanding the great fatigue, the danger, and expense in travelling, I have in contemplation a second, and yet more extensive route.

Meantime, with perfect respect,

I remain your humble servant,

MOSES MARSHALL.

SIR JOS. BANKS TO H. MARSHALL.

Soho Square, March 2d, 1791.

SIR :—

Your box has been duly received and your bill honoured. Everything is in good condition, and everybody here satisfied.

I wish you to charge, in future, three guineas, and put plants in proportion, as you shall think just and right. I say this, because I find you fair and honest, such a one as I can put confidence in. I hope you will always find similar treatment from me.

I shall be very glad of specimens, when you collect them, especially of new or very rare plants, with such names as you choose, written upon them; as they will serve as interpreters between us; and I will allow in cash for them what will satisfy you, if you will, as in the case of the living plants, charge them in your bill; only I must request you to keep the two charges separate, that I may know what the living and the dried plants cost, respectively.

The enclosed *leaf* grows here, from one of your plants; but as it does not flower, we have no means of discovering what it is. I shall thank you, if you can spare a specimen of it with the *flower*, to enclose it to me in a letter; or, at least, let me know what name it is known by.

Your humble servant,

JOS. BANKS.

DR. M. MARSHALL TO SIR JOS. BANKS.

Philadelphia, Nov. 10th, 1791.

SIR JOSEPH BANKS:—

Your letter of 2d March last came duly to hand.   In compliance with the order thereto annexed, I have now shipped, per Pigou, Capt. LOXLEY, a box of plants, being as nearly conformable to order, as could at this time be executed.   *   *   *

My attention has been diverted considerably, this summer, from botanical pursuits.   I have, therefore, no specimens collected, having observed nothing new, except the small one inclosed.

The *leaf* you enclosed, desiring a specimen, is, I believe, a species of *Ophrys*, say *hyemalis*.   I could not procure a flowering stem.

Astragalus Caroliniensis I am not possessed of.   The *Podophyllum diphyllum* [*Jeffersonia*] grows in great plenty, about two hundred and fifty miles to the westward, and not nigher, I believe.

I remain, with respect, &c.,

M. M.

If there are any particular objects you wish to be furnished with, or region of America you wish to be explored, I shall probably be at leisure one other summer.

SIR JOSEPH BANKS TO HUMPHRY MARSHALL.

Soho Square, Aug. 28th, 1793.

SIR :—

The Baron ITZENPLITZ, who writes to you with this letter, is a particular friend of mine, and has opened a correspondence with you at my desire.   You will find him a man of probity in his dealings, on whom you may fully depend, a paymaster in whatever he may order from you; and I should think it probable, if you oblige him, that he may have it in his power to recommend you to much business in *Germany*.

Your humble servant,

JOS. BANKS.

MARY DICKINSON TO H. MARSHALL.

RESPECTED FRIEND HUMPHRY MARSHALL :—

A relation of mine in England, who is wife to DAVID BARCLAY, has requested me to send her some seeds of the most curious natural productions of America. I thought I would take the freedom to ask thy assistance, knowing how very curious thee is in this way. If thee can oblige me, I shall esteem it a particular favour.

We are agreeably settled in Wilmington; and it will give us pleasure to see thee here.

I am, with respect, thy friend,

MARY DICKINSON.

June 12th, 1786.

JOHN DICKINSON* TO H. MARSHALL.

MY ESTEEMED FRIEND :—

Dr. DANIEL BANCROFT having a demand, from Europe, for some samples in Natural History, described in thy book, wishes thy acquaintance.

* JOHN DICKINSON, an eminent political writer, statesman, and patriot, was born in Maryland, in December, 1732, and educated in Delaware, to which province his parents removed soon after his birth. He read law in Philadelphia, and resided three years in the Temple, London. After his return to America, he practised law with success in Philadelphia. He was a member of the Pennsylvania Assembly in 1764; and of the general Congress held at New York, in 1765. The attempts of the mother country upon the liberties of the Colonies, early awakened his attention. In 1767, he began the publication of his celebrated *Farmer's Letters*, which had a great influence in enlightening the American people on the subject of their rights, and preparing them for resistance.

He was a member of the first Revolutionary Congress in 1774, and also in subsequent years. While in Congress, he prepared a number of petitions, addresses, and resolutions, all among the ablest state papers of the time. As an orator, he had few superiors in that body. He penned the famous Declaration of the United Colonies of North America (July 6, 1775); but he opposed the Declaration of Independence, believing that compromise was still practicable, and that his countrymen were not yet ripe for a complete separation from Great Britain. This rendered him for a time so unpopular, that he withdrew from the public councils, and did not recover his seat in Congress until about two years afterwards. He then returned, earnest in the cause of Independence. His zeal was shown in the ardent Address of Congress to the several States, of May, 1779, which he wrote and reported. He was afterwards President of the State of Pennsylvania, from

I therefore beg leave thus to introduce him ; being well assured it will give thee pleasure to pay attention to a gentleman engaged in such pursuits, as well as to serve our native land, by rendering the products, with which it is so eminently blessed, more known in other parts of the world ; an office that perhaps may communicate benefits to distant regions, and generations yet unborn.

I am thy sincere friend,
JOHN DICKINSON.

Wilmington, October 29th, 1791.

MY DEAR FRIEND :—

ARCHIBALD HAMILTON ROWAN,* for whom I have a particular esteem, has been requested by his excellent wife, from whom he is so unhappily banished, to send her a collection of American seeds ; and it will afford me a great deal of pleasure, if I can assist him in making it.

I understand that the seeds intended are those of flowers and shrubs, but chiefly the latter, with some few seeds of trees.

If thou or the Doctor will be so kind as to give directions for my being supplied with a collection to the amount of ten or fifteen dollars, it will be regarded as a great favour by

Thy sincere friend,
JOHN DICKINSON.

Wilmington, November 1st, 1796.

The collection will be the more valuable, if the properest names are given, and the seasons for planting mentioned.

November, 1782, to October, 1785. In the year 1786, he retired to private life, at Wilmington, Delaware, where he died, February 14, 1808.

His retirement was spent in literary studies, in charitable offices, and the exercise of an elegant hospitality. His *political writings* were collected and published, under his immediate supervision, in two neat octavo volumes, in the year 1801.

* The editor, when a youth, had the honour of a slight personal acquaintance with that distinguished " Exile of Erin," whose graceful salutations to all he knew, as he walked the streets of Wilmington, with his favourite dogs, are doubtless freshly remembered by the surviving residents of that period. He was one of the finest specimens of an *Irish gentleman* that ever visited these United States. An amusing and highly characteristic anecdote of Mr. ROWAN, is related in Sir JONAH BARRINGTON'S *Sketches*.

My dear Friend :—

I have only a few moments to remind thee of my very earnest request, to have seeds, &c., to the amount of sixteen or twenty dollars, supplied to me this year, for a present to the wife of an unfortunate foreigner [A. H. Rowan].

Thy attention, and thy worthy nephew's, will particularly, very particularly, oblige

Thy affectionate friend,
John Dickinson.

Wilmington, July 31st, 1797.

DR. WISTAR* TO H. AND M. MARSHALL.

Respected Friends :—

With this I send a Treatise on the effects of *Foxglove*, which I mentioned to friend H. M. when he was last in town. Dr. M. will be pleased to find that he is in possession of a plant of such efficacy, and perhaps will cultivate a greater quantity of it. As the book is in great demand, I wish he would return it by the first opportunity that offers, after he has read it.

If you have any of the plant to spare, I will be much obliged to

---

* Caspar Wistar, M.D., a skilful physician, and learned professor in the University of Pennsylvania, was born in 1760. His father was a German, of the Society of Friends, and settled in New Jersey. In 1783, he went to England in order to complete his medical education. His father's death put him in the possession of a large fortune; but he was not induced to relax his exertions for usefulness and eminence. He returned to Philadelphia in 1787, and was immediately appointed Professor of Chemistry and Physiology in the College of that city. He also commenced the practice of Medicine, and was chosen one of the attending Physicians to the Dispensary and Hospital. In 1808, he succeeded to the Professorship of Anatomy [having been an *adjunct* of Dr. Shippen, and doing the chief duties of the chair, for a number of years prior to that appointment]. Such were his talents, and his popular manners, that the Medical School of Philadelphia was much indebted to his influence for the high reputation it has acquired. Dr. Wistar was confessedly one of the first physicians of his time, in this country; and he was well known by his correspondence with learned men in Europe, as a gentleman of extensive erudition. He was a member of several of the most distinguished literary and scientific societies. On the 6th of January, 1815, he was elected President of the American Philosophical Society, in place of Thomas Jefferson, resigned; which office he held until his death. His chief work is a System of Anatomy, in two volumes. He died on the 22d of January, 1818. In the same year, a genus of plants was dedicated to his memory, by Mr. Nuttall.

you for a few leaves of it, and also a few seeds, with the book, when it is returned.

I cannot omit mentioning, that a patient in the Edinburgh Infirmary, who took the medicine *as directed by Dr. Withering*, vomited to death. This determined me to avoid the medicine; but dropsies are so often fatal, that we must try everything.

I am, with great respect,

Your assured friend,

CASPAR WISTAR, JR.

October 21st, 1787.

[In the year 1792, the *American Philosophical Society* (of which HUMPHRY MARSHALL was a member) appointed a committee, consisting of THOMAS JEFFERSON, BENJAMIN SMITH BARTON, JAMES HUTCHINSON, and CASPAR WISTAR, "for the purpose of collecting and communicating to the Society materials for forming the Natural History of the Insect called the *Hessian Fly*, as also information of the best means of preventing or destroying the Insect, and whatever else relative to the same may be interesting to Agriculture." That committee prepared a circular, containing a number of *queries* relative to the insect, and its habits; and a copy was sent to H. MARSHALL, accompanied by the following note, from Dr. WISTAR.]

RESPECTED FRIEND:—

I trust the importance of the subject will be a sufficient apology for the trouble I am about to give thee.

The Society was induced to undertake the inquiry respecting the *Hessian Fly*, by the hope of ascertaining some method of avoiding its ravages, as well as by a wish to establish the fact, that it is not carried with the grains; an apprehension of which has been injurious to the sale of our wheat in Europe.

Any observations thee may have made, or can collect, will be gratefully received by the committee, and will particularly oblige

Thy respectful friend,

CASPAR WISTAR, JR.

May 27th, 1792.

P. S. Has Dr. MARSHALL any inclination to explore the country west of the Mississippi? If so, I shall be very glad to see him when he comes to town.

DR. WISTAR TO DR. M. MARSHALL.

RESPECTED FRIEND :—

By a conversation with thy uncle, I find that thee is already acquainted with the wishes of some gentlemen here, to have our continent explored in a western direction. My reason for writing, at present, is to inform thee of the present state of the business.

Mr. JEFFERSON and several other gentlemen are much interested, and think they can procure a subscription sufficient to insure one thousand guineas, as a compensation to any one who undertakes the journey, and can bring satisfactory proofs of having passed across to the South Sea.

They wish the journey to be prosecuted up the Missouri, as the easiest, and perhaps most interesting track. A Spanish gentleman who is now here, and lives near the mouth of the Missouri, says that a caravan of traders go off every year up the Missouri, and penetrate fifteen hundred miles up it, to the Mahaw Indians, who are very friendly indeed. These traders go off from the Mississippi about the first of August, so that any one who thinks of it this year, ought to lose no time.

If thee has any inclination, I think it would be very proper to come to town immediately, and converse with Mr. JEFFERSON, who seems principally interested.

I am confident that no small matter will stop them, if thee is disposed to engage in the business. At any rate, I shall be very glad to hear from thee as soon as possible,

And am, with respect for thy uncle and self,

Thy assured friend,

CASPAR WISTAR, JR.

June 20th, 1792.

DR. WISTAR TO HUMPHRY MARSHALL.

RESPECTED FRIEND :—

I am apprehensive that it will not be in my power, on account of my inoculated patients, to see thee before the middle of May; and hope to be able to specify the time precisely, when I see thy wife at the Spring Meeting.

I believe it will be most proper to continue in the use of that diet, which experience has shown to be most convenient to thy constitution, until a week previous to the operation, when a vegetable and milk diet will be most proper. No medicine will be necessary, on account of the intended operation, until a few days previous to it.

When thy wife returns from the Spring Meeting, I will send by her every additional direction; and, in the mean time, am, with great regard,

Thy assured friend,
C. WISTAR, JR.

Philadelphia, April 11th, 1800.

RESPECTED FRIEND :—

Thy letter of the 13th inst. came at a very convenient season, as I have been anxious, for some days, to find an opportunity of writing to thee. I hope to be able to be at thy house in the course of a week from this time; but do not fix a day, as the calls upon me are so very various and uncertain; and probably I may be prevented by them from setting off at the time I have fixed upon. *   *   *   * [After some directions, concerning a proper regimen, &c., preparatory to the operation of couching, Dr. W. proceeds]: I have only to add a request, that no strangers may be invited to attend the operation, as they may interrupt that composure which is necessary, both in the patient and operator, in business of this kind. I expect Dr. MARSHALL'S assistance; and that is all that will be useful.

These particulars would have been stated to thy wife; but she went from this town before I expected. No time, however, has been lost, as it would not have been in my power to fix the time before this period.

With sincere wishes for thy restoration,
I am thy assured friend,
C. WISTAR, JR.

Philadelphia, May 16th, 1800.

REV. SAMUEL KRAMSH TO H. MARSHALL.

Nazareth, July 2d, 1788.

DEAR SIR :—

I take the liberty, though not personally acquainted, but highly esteemed by your excellent botanical work styled *Arbustum Ame-*

ricanum, or American Grove, to trouble you with a few lines.
But before I continue further, I must first acquaint you a little of
my person and place.

I am a German by birth; and, therefore, you will excuse my
faults in expressing in a strange language, which, for all, is very
agreeable to me in learning. I came to this country in the year
1783, at the latter end of it. I belong to that Society which is
called the United Brethren, or, as they call them here, the Mora-
vians.

First I lived at Bethlehem, Northampton County; but at the
latter end of the year 1786 I moved to Nazareth, eight miles from
thence, and eight miles distant from the Blue Mountains. I do
not know whether you know our Society or places, or not; but
that is no matter.

As I loved the study of Natural History, and especially Botany,
from my childhood, I was very happy, also, in that respect, when
my call brought me to North America. The first year, I searched,
with great care, the country about Bethlehem, to examine new
plants I never saw before. The two following years, time would
not allow in following my inclination so as I would. I inquired
very often if nobody ever undertook to write a botanical work for
this country, a *Flora Americana,* or the like; but I could not learn
of any. But how glad was I, when I first saw your excellent book
advertised. My colleagues in that science, viz., Rev. Mr. HUBNER,
the Rev. JACOB VAN VLECK, and Dr. KAMPMAN, each of us, we
procured us with it.

I got new feal [qu. field?] in Botany, when I came to Nazareth,
in searching the country round about. Natural History, and especially Botany, was one of the sciences I should teach here in our
boarding-school, or academy; and my young scholars were exceeding glad to see a book in that science also from their native country: and perhaps it is the first place where it is used as a school-
book.

But, dear sir, though I am not a native of these states, but a
warm friend to them, and because it is my ardent wish that also
Natural History, as other sciences, should become more extensive
and flourishing, I beg your pardon that I remember here your
promise, given at the introduction to the *American Grove.* "The
author would have been happy, could he have given also a descriptive catalogue of our native herbaceous plants. At present,

circumstances oblige him to confine himself to forest trees and shrubs; however, he has such a work in contemplation should this meet with the encouragement of the public."

I know that such a work is most impossible for one alone without assistance, and I know, on the other hand, that such a work cannot be done in the space of one or two years; but that it requires much diligence and time. But, for my part, I should be glad to see you as the undertaker or author of such a work, because you, by your first, was laying the foundation, and nobody else should build upon. Therefore I think it would be necessary to consider once about the plan, that it may become as useful as possible to the public. I would flatter myself, if you would be incited, through these lines, to consider the matter once more. Perhaps you could hear some or other thought, if you would put once something about this point in a public paper, Columbian Magazine, or American Museum; and perhaps by that channel your learned friends in the United States could lend their accounts, hints, or notes, for public use to you.

Would you do me the favour to inform me where one could get Dr. KALM's Journeys through N. America, and CLAYTON's *Flora Virginica*, it would be greatly obliging to me.

I beg once more, dear sir! excuse my liberty, and especially my stammering English: for I would do it myself, and not with assistance of others. It would be a great honour to me, to favour me with an answer. If there is no other opportunity at hand, please forward it to Philadelphia, either to the Rev. Mr. MEDER, or GODFREY HAGA, Merchant, Race Street, or to Mr. BARSTOW, Merchant, Second Street.

I have the honour to be,
Dear sir,
Your humble servant,
SAMUEL KRAMSH.

Salem, State of North Carolina,
July 25th, 1789.

DEAR SIR:—

You will have wondered that I did not sent you any lines in answer of your obliging letter, dated Sept. the 25th; but give me leave to tell you the reason, and excuse me in neglecting the opportunity of your correspondence such a long time.

About the latter end of October, I got a call to Salem, in North Carolina, where I am at present. On my travelling through Bethlehem, I received your agreeable letter. Time was too short to answer directly; and here the opportunities were very scarce, in the beginning.

I pity you extraordinary that you met with so little encouragement for a description of the herbaceous plants, occasioned by the dull sale of the American Grove. I always think some hints, either in the Columbian Magazine, or the American Museum, should encourage this study.

The spirit of home-made manufactories is now happily spread abroad. We begin to look upon everything what might be useful for it. We should now also know what treasures we possess in the United States, concerning vegetables. Proposals should be made in that respect, to get a complete catalogue; and afterwards, we should learn and discover all the use of them.

I botanized hereabouts, as much as time would permit it, and found a great variety of plants between here and my former place; though much more difficulties concerning the heat, and especially the insects called *Tiks*. As soon as time is over for that purpose, I shall sent you the catalogue of all my plants, which I have found here and in Pennsylvania. Meanwhile, I shall be much obliged if you would favour me with an answer. The letter may be directed, To the Rev. SAMUEL KRAMSH, (or as you please,) Salem, Surry County, North Carolina; to the care either of THOMAS and DRINKER, Merchants, or THOMAS BARTOW, Merchant, or GODFREY HAGA, Merchant, all in Philadelphia.

Your affectionate friend and servant,
SAMUEL KRAMSH.

Salem, in North Carolina,
the 20th of February, 1790.

DEAR SIR :—

Your favour of the 30th of October I received by way of Charleston, on the 15th of January, 1790, and was much obliged for it.

I pity it extraordinary that I was not able to serve you with the least produce of our country; for soon after, when I wrote to you my last letter, in the month of August, I got a dangerous lingering

fever, for several months successively, so that I was obliged to keep in my room and bed, instead of my darling study.   *   *
*   *   This situation of my weak health and constitution makes me consider whether I shall stay in this climate, or not. The change of the weather is sometimes extraordinary, viz., my thermometer (FAHRENHEIT'S) was lately twelve degrees above 0; and in a few days after, it was 72°. But to return to Botany, and to your letter. When I wrote my last letter to you, I imagined to make a good harvest in the fall, concerning seeds, fruits, and the like; but by my sickness, I lost not only that treasure, but also most all the plants which are to be found in that late season. This was indeed a great loss. As more necessary business occupied the little time I was able to do anything, it was not in my power to bring the list of plants in order, and to copy it for you. For that reason you will have patience.

I cannot say that it is a very fine country here, or that the land is very good; at least, not where I live.

The scarlet blowing *Azalea*, I shall hardly find living sixty miles distant from the big mountains. For the *Physik nut* I will inquire.

I hope I shall be able to enclose my list in the next letter. I remain

Your affectionate friend and servant,

SAMUEL KRAMSH.

REV. HENRY MUHLENBERG TO H. MARSHALL.

DEAR SIR :—

I would have answered your kind letter, and have returned my thanks sooner for the shrubs and roots you were pleased to send to me, if I had not waited, though in vain, for an opportunity of sending the *Viburnum Opulus* you wanted. I have been all about, and can find none that are small enough. However, I shall try again, in spring, at some other places, where I formerly have seen some.

I have made different excursions this year, after I had the pleasure of seeing you here; and have added greatly to my Flora. If I am not mistaken, I found a great number of your *Spiræa hypericifolia* at the Susquehanna. It blossoms the latter end of July, with a fine yellow flower; but I doubt whether it should not be called *Hypericum Kalmianum* or *prolificum*, as the capsule is very different from *Spiræa*. When the exemplar you sent to me blossoms, I will be better able to judge.

Your *Arbustum* has been translated and reprinted in Germany. I have wrote for several exemplars and expect them this year.

As I know that your nephew has studied physic, I make bold to send him the late edition of Linnæi *Materia Medica*, and hope the present will be not unacceptable. I have a great many botanical writings, and shall be happy if I can serve you or him in botanical researches, through a loan of them. Pray remember my best respects to him; and tell him how gladly I would embrace an opportunity of a correspondence, which certainly would be an advantage to our botanical studies.

You were pleased to mention to me, that you had an edition of Walter's *Flora Caroliniensis*. If you could spare that work for a few weeks, and send it to Lancaster for my perusal, I should think myself greatly indebted to you. It should be returned with expedition and undamaged.

If the Lord spares my health, I shall pass by your house, the latter end of May, on my way to Philadelphia; and then hope to see you, your nephew, and your garden. Against that time, I expect to receive a great many of fresh seeds from Germany, of which you shall have whatever may be pleasing.

God preserve you in good health. Believe me to be with great regard, sir,

Your sincere friend and servant,
Henry Muhlenberg.

Lancaster, January 18, 1790.

REV. H. MUHLENBERG TO DR. M. MARSHALL.

Dear Sir :—

I beg leave to inform you, that the new edition of the *Genera* Linnæi is safely arrived. The first volume arrived some time ago; the second very lately. The first is only bound in paper. I am happy to see that the editor, my friend D. Schreber, has done what I required from him. He has given your name to a hitherto undescribed plant, that belongs to the *Syngenesia*, *Polygamia æqualis*, which he names *Marshallia*.

The price of both volumes is 24s. 4d. If you still incline to have them, pray let me know where to send them.

I intend, please God, to be down your way this day a fortnight, on a journey to Philadelphia; and hope then to see you, and spend a few hours or more with you.

If you could spare me a plant of what your uncle calls *Sedum verticillatum*, I would be very glad to have it in my garden. It is a fine little plant.

Give my best respects to Mr. HUMPHRY MARSHALL, and believe me to be with great esteem,

Sir, your humble servant,
HENRY MUHLENBERG.

Lancaster, April 9, 1792.

WILLIAM HAMILTON* TO H. MARSHALL.

The Woodlands, November 22d, 1790.

DEAR SIR:—

I herewith return, with many thanks, the draft you were so obliging as to send me. I fully intended myself the pleasure of delivering it, myself, at Bradford; but was detained so much longer at Lancaster than I expected, that the moment I finished my business there, I was fain to hurry home with all possible expedition. I came through from Strasburg to the Woodlands in one day.

I was truly sorry that I did not see you when you were last at Philadelphia. I hope, the next time you come down, you will give me a call. If I can tempt you no other way, I promise to show you many plants that you have never yet seen, *some of them curious.*

I am, dear sir, with truth,
Your real friend and humble servant,
W. HAMILTON.

---

* WILLIAM HAMILTON, Esq., was long and well known to the lovers of Nature, for his public-spirited exertions in introducing and cultivating rare and beautiful plants, at his elegant residence, called " *The Woodlands*," on the right bank of the Schuylkill, near Philadelphia. During a tour in Europe, he collected many curious exotics, which he brought home with him: among others, the once favourite tree— the " Lombardy Poplar" (*Populus dilatata*, Ait.) was introduced by him, in the year 1784.

Mr. HAMILTON died in the beginning of June, 1813. Since his death the " *Woodlands*" have been appropriated to the sacred purpose of a *cemetery;* and, certainly, it would be difficult to find a more beautiful place for a " city of the dead."

The Woodlands, 23d November, 1796.

Dear Sir :—

I am much obliged to you for the seeds you were so good as to send me, of the *Pavia*, and of the *Podophyllum*, or *Jeffersonia*.

When you were last here it was so late, and you were of course so much hurried, as to prevent your deriving any satisfaction in viewing my exotics. I hope when you come next to Philadelphia, that you will allot one whole day, at least, for the *Woodlands*. It will not only give me real pleasure to have your company, but I am persuaded it will afford some amusement to yourself.

Your nephew did me the favour of calling, the other day; but he, too, was in a hurry, and had little opportunity of satisfying his curiosity. I flatter myself, however, that during his short stay he saw enough to induce him to repeat his visit. The sooner this happens, the more agreeable it will be to me.

When I was at your house, a year ago, I observed several matters in the gardening way, different from any in my possession. Being desirous to make my collection as general as possible, I beg to know if you have, by layers, or any other mode, sufficiently increased any of the following kinds so as to be able, with convenience, to spare a plant of each of them, viz. :—*Ledum palustre*, *Carolina Rhamnus*, *Azalea coccinea*, *Mimosa Intsia*, and *Laurus Borbonia*. Any of them would be agreeable to me; as also would be a plant, or seeds of *Hippophaë Canadensis*, *Aralia hispida*, *Spiræa nova* from the western country; *Tussilago Petasites*, *Polymnia tetragonotheca*, *Hydrophyllum Canadense*, *H. Virginicum*, *Polygala Senega*, *P. biflora*, *Napæa scabra dioica*, *Talinum*, a nondescript *Sedum* from the west, somewhat like the *Telephium*, two kinds of a genus supposed, by Dr. Marshall, to be between *Uvularia* and *Convallaria* [probably the *Streptopus*, of Michaux, which the Marshalls proposed to call *Bartonia*], and *Rubia Tinctorum*. I should also be obliged to you for a few seeds of your *Calycanthus*, *Spigelia Marilandica*, *Tormentil* from Italy, and two of your *Oaks* with ovate entire leaves.

*　　*　　*　　*　　*　　*　　*

With respects to Mrs. Marshall, and your nephew, I remain, sir,

Your friend and humble servant,

W. Hamilton.

The Woodlands, May 3d, 1799.

DEAR SIR :—

Having been unwell and confined with the gout, for several weeks past, I have not until this time been able to comply with my promise of sending you a *Tea Tree.*

I now take the opportunity of forwarding you, by the stage, a very healthy one, as well as several of other kinds, which I believe are not already in your collection ; together with a small parcel of seeds : the whole of which will, I flatter myself, prove acceptable to you.

Should anything else, in my possession, occur to you as a desirable addition to the variety in your garden, I beg you will inform me. You may be assured, whatever it is, if I have two of the kind, you will be welcome to one. Sensible as I am of your kindness and friendship to me, on all occasions, you have a right, and may freely command every service in my power.

Doctor PARKE informs me you were lately in Philadelphia. Had it been convenient to you to call at the *Woodlands,* I should have had great pleasure in seeing you. I have not heard of Dr. MARSHALL's having been in this neighbourhood since I was last at *Bradford.* From the pressing invitation I gave him, I am willing to hope that, in case of his coming to town, he will not forget to give me a call. I beg you will present him with my best respects, and request of him to give me a line of information, as to the *Menziesia ferruginea,* particularly of its *vulgar name,* if it has one, where it grows, if he knows the name of any person in its neighbourhood, who is acquainted with it, so as to direct or show it to any one who may go to look after it.

I intend, next month, to go to Lancaster ; and if convenient to me, when there, to spare my GEORGE, I have thoughts of sending him to Redstone, for the *Menziesia,* and *Podophyllum diphyllum.* If Dr. MARSHALL knows of any curious and uncommon plants, growing in the neighbourhood with those I have mentioned, I will be obliged to him to give me any intelligence by which he may suppose they can be found : or, if he knows any person or persons at Redstone, or Fort Pitt, who are curious in plants, of whom any questions on the subject may be asked, he cannot do me a greater service than by giving me their names and place of abode.

I do not know how your garden may have fared during this truly long and severe winter, which has occasioned the loss of several valuable ones in mine; amongst which are the Wise Briar [probably *Schrankia uncinata*, Willd.; *Mimosa Intsia*, Walt.] and *Hibiscus speciosus*, which I got from you. The plants, also, of *Podophyllum diphyllum*, which I raised last year, from seeds I received from your kindness, have, I fear, been all destroyed. They have not shown themselves above ground this spring. A tree, too (the only one I had of *Juglans Pacane*, or Illinois Hickory), which I raised twenty-five years ago from seed, is entirely killed.

In case you have seeds of the kinds named in the list hereto adjoined, I will thank you exceedingly for a few. Any of them which you have not, at present, I beg you will oblige me with them in the ensuing fall. I am very desirous to know if your *Iva*, or Hog's Fennel, from Carolina, produces seeds. In that case, I must entreat you for a few of them.

You will permit me, also, to remind you of your promise to spare me a plant or two of the *White Persimmon*, one of *Azalea coccinea*, and of the sour *Calycanthus*. If convenient to let me have a plant or two of your *Stuartia Malachodendron*, and of *Magnolia acuminata*, you will do me a great favour.

Anything left for me at the toll-gate, on the middle ferry wharf to the care of Mr. TRUEMAN, who constantly attends there, will reach me the same day that it arrives there.

I beg you will be so good as to present my respects to Mrs. MARSHALL; and am,

With best wishes for your health and happiness,

Dear sir,

Your real friend and servant,

W. HAMILTON.

I am very desirous to compare a flower of your *Stuartia* with J. BARTRAM'S; and will be obliged to you for a good specimen.

DR. M. MARSHALL TO GRIMWOOD, HUDSON, AND BARRIT.

GENTLEMEN :—

Yours of the 18th June, I duly received; and in compliance therewith, have herewith sent, per ship George Barclay, Captain

COLLETT, one box plants, and one small box of seeds, the bill of lading and list of contents inclosed.

You will find that several things are wanting; which, in part, may be attributed to the great sickness and mortality in Philadelphia, by the yellow, West India fever; which, in August, September, and October, carried off above four thousand inhabitants. This rendered it doubtful, whether there would be any shipping for London this season. We, therefore, in this time of suspense, became careless in procuring some things, especially those at a distance, till too late; as the *Juniperus* and *Rhododendron* seeds. The *Sarracenia purpurea*, *Helonias asphodeloides*, and *Cypripedium acaule*, natives of New Jersey, at sixty miles distance, the route through Philadelphia, were not procured from the above cause; though these I still designed to get: yet, the day on which I had purposed setting out on that errand, there fell a snow eighteen inches in depth. Thus, you see, though the intention to serve you was good, yet it has been in part diverted and defeated, by intervening casualties.

The *Magnolia auriculata* cannot be had, I believe, without going to the place of its native growth; which is (at least, what I have seen,) in South Carolina, about two hundred miles from the sea-coast. I have but one plant; and BARTRAM two or three, which he does not incline to part with. There are some, that M. MICHAUX, a French botanist, procured, and sent from Charleston, a few years since. But he has since been in Canada, and I believe is now in Kentucky.

Of the *Magnolia grandiflora*, I have two fine plants, too large to send abroad. I am in nearly the same situation with respect to *Stuartia* and *Fothergilla*. There is none to be had nearer than Carolina; where also grows the *Sarracenia flava*.

With respect to *new* things, when I consider that a KALM and a CLAYTON have been here, I have little hopes of making discoveries; yet I find there are many little plants that escaped their view. In a circuitous route of about seven hundred miles, which I took this summer, I have observed several small herbaceous, and two shrubby plants, which I believe are new. One of the shrubs is, perhaps, a *Spiræa:* the other, the Oily Nut [*Pyrularia*, Mx., *Hamiltonia oleifera*, Muhl.], of which I formerly sent a specimen to Sir JOSEPH BANKS. It grows to the height of six or eight feet; the flowers

are small, and make little appearance; but the fruit is perfectly
oily.   *   *   *   *

As I have discovered this to grow at the distance of only two
hundred and fifty miles, if those I now have should not shoot, in
the spring, I intend setting out for a new supply. Thus you may
see to what fatigue, expense, and misfortune, we are subjected, who
undertake to supply Europeans with curiosities; and judge how
small our recompense.   *   *   *   *

I remain, &c.,
M. MARSHALL.

December 11th, 1793.

In a folio volume of Manuscript Records, in the Library of the
Philadelphia Society for Promoting Agriculture, the following
communication is preserved :—

MR. HUMPHRY MARSHALL'S OBSERVATIONS ON BOTANY
AS APPLICABLE TO RURAL ECONOMICS.

Read in the Society, February 14th, 1786.

OBSERVATIONS, TENDING TO SHOW THE UTILITY OF BOTANICAL KNOWLEDGE IN RELATION TO AGRICULTURE, AND THE FEEDING OF CATTLE, ETC.

THE SCIENCE OF BOTANY certainly holds its most dignified
station when subservient to Medicine; but its utility does not
terminate in this alone, though it has too long been considered as
having no other connexion. This, notwithstanding, is but a partial,
nay, even an injurious idea of it; for nothing has more retarded its
usefulness, than this contracted notion. It has a relation in a
variety of ways, to many other arts and sciences, among which may
be mentioned the arts of painting and dyeing: but of all others,
Agriculture certainly claims the strictest relation, some of its most
important branches being greatly dependent upon it; and others,
from a happy application of it, being perhaps capable of future
emolument.

But however great the real dignity and importance of this art,
yet it must be allowed that it has not been cultivated sufficiently

on scientific principles, nor advanced in equal proportion with other branches of knowledge.

It is not many years since Dr. HOME observed, that VIRGIL and COLUMELLA, old as they are, remained almost the only writers worth consulting on this subject.

Many others have appeared since, which roused a laudable spirit throughout Great Britain, for the improvement of arts and sciences, under the protection of their public institutions; and every branch of agriculture seems to be studied as it deserves (by them both in Britain, and on the continent of Europe), and is attended with that success which commonly results from the right application of knowledge to the purposes of human life.

The Swedes have made great progress in the improvement of this branch of economics. In France, DU HAMEL has rendered himself conspicuous by his writings on this subject; and in various parts of Europe, societies have been formed with a professed view for this purpose. It may be mentioned with peculiar pleasure, that of Padua, over which Dr. ARDUIN presides; who, by the munificence of the Venetian State, has a garden for the cultivation of such vegetables as they wish to subject to experiments in agriculture, dyeing, and other arts: a noble institution, and worthy of imitation (by us Americans).

Amidst that almost infinite variety of vegetables with which the beneficent hand of Nature has replenished our earth, those which go under the general name of *Grasses* form the principal food of our cattle. Next to these, among the natural classes of plants, none are more acceptable than the *Diadelphous* or *Leguminous Herbs*. Of this class is the *Clover*, the *Saint-foin* (or Cock's head), and the *Lucerne*, or Medic fodder, much used in France.

Beside these, our horses, horned cattle, sheep, &c., will all in their turn, eat with equal pleasure, and some with more avidity, a great variety of other vegetables. Numerous instances occur, where one species of animals will feed greedily upon those herbs which others refuse to touch, and will almost famish rather than eat them.

Some plants are highly noxious, and even poisonous, to certain kinds of animals; while they are eaten by others without the least subsequent ill effect: to instance, the *Cicuta virosa*, or long-leaved Water Hemlock, 'tis said, is fatal to cows, when through scarcity of food they are obliged to eat it: yet sheep and horses feed upon

it with impunity.   Facts of this kind must, in some measure, have
been obvious to the most incurious of mankind, even in the earliest
ages.   The first race of shepherds had daily instances among their
flocks (I make no doubt), of the selection and refusal of particular
herbs ; and subsequent observations must have multiplied and confirmed them.   But they were still only known in the general ; and
no experiments had been instituted to ascertain *the precise species*
thus eaten or rejected.

Facts are at this time undeniable.   It is well known, that *Flags,
Hound's-tongue, Henbane, Mullein, Nightshade, Hemlock*, several
Docks, Arsesmart, Agrimony, several of the *Crow-foots, Marsh
Marygold, Horehound, Fig-wort*, many *Thistles, Ferns*, and other
plants, are commonly neglected by our cattle, and stand untouched,
even in pastures where it might be expected that necessity should
have constrained them to have eaten anything that was green,
almost.   These are but few out of many instances.   There are
more than might be imagined ; and it is desirable, in consequence
of these observations, that a course of experiments should be instituted to elucidate this instinct, in that part, especially, of the
brute creation, which is so immediately subservient to mankind.

The utility of such experiments must be evident ; as they must
necessarily lay the foundation of farther improvements in the economy of cattle.   The intelligent husbandman would, by this means,
have it in his power to rid his pastures of noxious and useless plants,
and give room for the salubrious ones.

In this view of the affair, it will be seen that physicians are not
the only persons who may study Botany to advantage.   Many
others would find, not only a fund of pleasure, from this study, but
numberless other advantages, resulting from the knowledge of the
plants of their own country.   In the instance before us, science has
opened the way : and surely it is not too much to say, that it evidently points to greater improvements, in one of the most important branches of agriculture,—as it relates to economy of cattle.
More than this ought not to be expected from its aid.   It is to the
intelligent grazier, and the gentleman well versed in the knowledge
of indigenous plants, fraught with careful observation, and practised
in the economy of cattle, that the rest must be owing.   Nothing
but the want of this knowledge, in such gentlemen as reside in the
country chiefly, can deprive us of the benefit which might otherwise accrue from reducing it into practice.

The eradicating from pastures, poisonous and useless weeds, would be but one—although indeed no mean one—among many other advantages.   Further than this, the husbandman would be better enabled to suit his several sorts of cattle to the different pastures in his possession, more to their benefit, and consequently his own.   Even in marshy grounds, where it is a difficult undertaking to mend the soil, the growth of many plants might be encouraged, and the seeds of others sown, which are highly acceptable to different kinds of cattle.   By degrees, too, we should undoubtedly be led to the cultivation of other vegetables beside clover and timothy, as fodder, which perhaps might be done to advantage in soils and situations where these would not thrive.   Our hay would in consequence be much improved : for although cattle will eat those herbs among hay, which they will reject while green and growing, yet it does not follow, that all are, in their dried state, equally nutritive and wholesome.

The benefits, in fine, which would arise from a diligent and general pursuit of these hints, would undoubtedly be various and extensive; and many more, in all probability, in course of years, than can at present be thought of.

FINIS.